MW01017120

The Writer's Craft

The Writer's Craft

SENIOR AUTHOR

SHERIDAN BLAU

University of California at Santa Barbara

CONSULTING AUTHOR

PETER ELBOW

University of Massachusetts at Amherst

SPECIAL CONTRIBUTING AUTHOR

DON KILLGALLON

Baltimore County Public Schools

SENIOR CONSULTANTS

Arthur Applebee

State University of New York at Albany

Judith Langer

State University of New York at Albany

McDougal Littell

A HOUGHTON MIFFLIN COMPANY

Evanston, Illinois • Boston • Dallas

SENIOR AUTHOR

Sheridan Blau, Senior Lecturer in English and Education and former Director of Composition, University of California at Santa Barbara; Director, South Coast Writing Project; Director, Literature Institute for Teachers

The Senior Author, in collaboration with the Consulting Author, helped establish the theoretical framework of the program and the pedagogical design of the Workshop prototypes. In addition, he guided the development of the spiral of writing assignments, served as author of the Literary Workshops, and directed the Contributing Authors in the completion of Guided Assignments.

CONSULTING AUTHOR

Peter Elbow, Professor of English, University of Massachusetts at Amherst; Fellow, Bard Center for Writing and Thinking

The Consulting Author, in collaboration with the Senior Author, helped establish the theoretical framework for the series and the pedagogical design of the Writer's Workshops. He also provided material for use in the Writing Handbooks and reviewed selected units for consistency with current research and the philosophy of the series.

SENIOR CONSULTANTS

These consultants reviewed lesson prototypes to ensure consistency with current research. In addition, they reviewed and provided editorial advice on the completed Writer's Workshops.

Arthur N. Applebee, Professor of Education, State University of New York at Albany; Director, Center for the Learning and Teaching of Literature; Senior Fellow, Center for Writing and Literacy

Judith A. Langer, Professor of Education, State University of New York at Albany; Co-director, Center for the Learning and Teaching of Literature; Senior Fellow, Center for Writing and Literacy

SPECIAL CONTRIBUTING AUTHOR

Don Killgallon, English Chairman, Educational Consultant, Baltimore County Public Schools. Mr. Killgallon conceptualized, designed, and wrote all of the features on sentence composing.

ACADEMIC CONSULTANTS

In collaboration with the Consulting Author and Senior Author, the Academic Consultants helped shape the design of the Workshops. They also reviewed selected Workshops and mini-lessons to ensure appropriateness for the writing classroom.

Linda Lewis, Writing Specialist, Fort Worth Independent School District

John Parker, Professor of English, Vancouver Community College

CONTRIBUTING AUTHORS

C. Beth Burch, Visiting Assistant Professor in English Education, Purdue University, Indiana, formerly English Teacher with Lafayette High School

Sandra Robertson, English Teacher, Santa Barbara Junior High School in California; Fellow and teacher-consultant of the South Coast Writing Project and the Literature Institute for Teachers, both at the University of California, Santa Barbara

Linda Smoucha, formerly English Teacher, Mother Theodore Guerin High School, River Grove, IL

Carol Toomer Boysen, English Teacher, Williams School, Oxnard, California; Fellow and teacher-consultant of the South Coast Writing Project and the Literature Institute for Teachers

Richard Barth-Johnson, English Teacher, Scattergood Friends School, West Branch, Iowa; National Writing Project Fellow

Robert and Marilyn Shepherd, education consultants and writers, Rockport, MA

John Phreaner, formerly Chairman of the English Department at San Marcos High School, Santa Barbara; Co-director of the South Coast Writing Project and the Literature Institute for Teachers

Wayne Swanson, Educational Materials Specialist, Chicago, IL

Joan Worley, Assistant Professor of English and Director of the Writing Center at the University of Alaska, Fairbanks; National Writing Project Fellow

Cherryl Armstrong, Assistant Professor of English at California State University, Sacramento; National Writing Project Fellow

Valerie Hobbs, Co-director of the Program in Intensive English, University of California, Santa Barbara; Fellow of the South Coast Writing Project and the Literature Institute for Teachers

STUDENT CONTRIBUTORS

Patrick Curley, Des Plaines, IL; Tony Figliolini, Watertown, MA; Elena Gallegos, Houston, TX; Debbie Henderson, DeSoto, TX; April Hicks, Jackson, MS; Beth McCarron, Seattle, WA; Sarah Olson, Cedar Rapids, IA; Michelle Ray, DeSoto, TX; Josh Smith, Birmingham, AL.

TEACHER REVIEWERS

Dr. Joanne Bergman, English Teacher, Countryside High School, Clearwater, FL

Regina Dalicandro, English Department Chairperson, Mather High School, Chicago, IL

Becky Ebner, Trainer for the New Jersey Writing Project in Texas; English Teacher, Clark High School, San Antonio, TX

Sister Sheila Holly, S.S.J., M.A., English Department Chairperson, Saint Maria Goretti High School, Philadelphia, PA

Dr. William J. Hunter, Assistant Principal, English Department, John Jay High School, Brooklyn, NY

Rene Bufo Miles, English Teacher, Academic Magnet Program at Burke High School, Charleston, SC

Margaret N. Miller, Language Arts Consultant (6-12); Library Coordinator (K-12), Birdville I.S.D., Fort Worth, TX

Janet Rodriguez, English Teacher, Clayton Valley High School, Concord, CA

Mark Rougeux, English and Journalism Teacher; Newspaper Advisor, Glenville High School, Cleveland, OH

Bennie Malroy Sheppard, English Teacher, High School for Law Enforcement and Criminal Justice, Houston, TX

Sue Wilson, English Department Chairperson, Wade Hampton High School, Greenville, SC

Beverly Zimmerman, English Department Chairperson, English High School, Jamaica Plain, MA

Printed in the United States of America.

ISBN 0-395-86382-1

1 2 3 4 5 6 7 8 9 10 — DCI — 01 00 99 98 97

Contents Overview

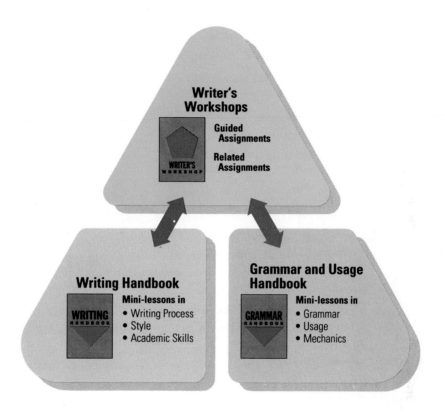

Writer's Workshops

Guided Assignments

Related Assignments

WRITER'S WORKSHOP

Writing Handbook

Mini-lessons in
- Writing Process
- Style
- Academic Skills

WRITING HANDBOOK

Grammar and Usage Handbook

Mini-lessons in
- Grammar
- Usage
- Mechanics

GRAMMAR HANDBOOK

Y ou are an individual. You think and act in ways that are uniquely your own. This book recognizes that individuality. On every page you will be encouraged to discover techniques best suited to your own personal writing style. Just as important, you will learn to think your way through every writing task.

In each of the Writer's Workshops, you will experiment with ideas and approaches as you are guided through a complete piece of writing. Cross-references to the Handbooks will allow you to find additional help when you need it. Then, as you write, you will discover what you think about yourself—and about the world around you.

Table of Contents

For more in-depth treatment of each stage of the writing process, see the Writing Handbook, pages 333–428.

Writer's Workshops

1 WRITER'S WORKSHOP 1

Personal and Expressive Writing

Observation and Description

Narrative and Literary Writing

Informative Exposition: Classification

Informative Exposition: Analysis

Informative Exposition: Synthesis

Persuasion

Writing About Literature

Reports

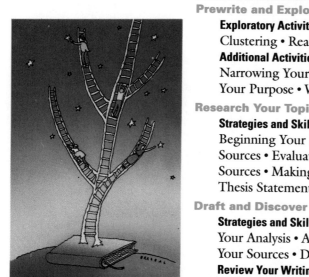

Writing for Assessment

Writing Handbook Mini-lessons

W·R·I·T·I·N·G   P·R·O·C·E·S·S

Prewriting

Drafting

Revising and Publishing

STYLE

Grammar and Usage Handbook Mini-lessons

Before You Begin

THINKING ABOUT WRITING

Why do people write? Writing down your thoughts is more time-consuming than simply reflecting on them, but it offers unique opportunities for insight, for invention, and for action.

Writing for Insight

> I write to find out what I'm thinking about.
>
> **Edward Albee, dramatist**

The playwright Edward Albee knew something that you may never have realized—that writing is thinking on paper.

It is, therefore, a valuable learning tool. You can write to record events or facts—tracking your progress toward a goal, for example. You can also write to explore things that puzzle you, seeking relationships that you sense but have not yet proved. You can also write purely for pleasure, experimenting with sounds, words, and their effects. In all these instances, you are writing to gain insight and make meaning.

Tracking Your Development Recording your thoughts as well as saving completed pieces of your work can help you evaluate and apply the insights you gain from writing. You can use journals, learning logs, and writing portfolios to clarify and experiment with your ideas and writing techniques, and to discover how your interests and writing style change over time. One student found that her writing portfolio even helped her to choose a career.

> When I looked back at the topics I'd written about during my junior and senior years, I saw that almost all of them dealt either with animals or with medicine. That's when I started thinking about veterinary school.
>
> **Elena Gallegos, veterinary student**
> **Houston, Texas**

Discovering Your Voice One of the most important insights you can gain from writing is knowledge of yourself. As you write, you begin to recognize and develop your writing voice, identifying what makes it—and you—unique. You begin to notice what sounds like you and what doesn't. The strength of any writing lies in the writer's ability to remain true to his or her own voice. The more you learn about your writing voice, the stronger and more confident your writing will become.

Writing for Invention

In addition to providing insight into the way things are, writing enables you to imagine the way things might be and to create a world that never existed.

> What I like best about writing is that there are no limits to what I can do or say.
>
> **Patrick Curley, student**
> **Des Plaines, Illinois**

Like Patrick, many students find the inventive aspects of writing to be the most rewarding. Freed from the restrictions of space, time, and even logic, writers can let their imaginations run wild. Interestingly, however, many of these wild imaginings, which seem radical when they are first written, turn out to be remarkably prophetic. For example, within your own lifetime, you have probably seen the seemingly preposterous ideas of science-fiction writers, such as people walking in space and talking computers, routinely become reality.

Not only are there no limits to what you can do or say in writing, there are no limits to how you do or say it. You can write a story, a play, a poem, a letter, a journal entry, an eyewitness report, an interior monologue, a song, or even invent your own form. For example, the book *archie and mehitabel* by Don Marquis was allegedly written by a cockroach who tapped out poems at night on a typewriter, key by key. Because he could press only one key at a time, the book contains no capital letters, colons, or quotation or question marks. In the musical play *Cats,* the feline characters interact in an elaborate junkyard. A page in Laurence Sterne's novel *Tristram Shandy* is entirely blank. These are just a few examples: invention in writing is limited only by your imagination.

Scene from Sir Andrew Lloyd Webber's play *Cats*

Writing for Action

Besides being a means for gaining insight, writing is also a tool for making things happen. Writing clear directions for friends who are coming to your house for a party may not guarantee that your party will be a success, but it can at least ensure that your guests will find your house. Writing to the manufacturer of your new electronic keyboard to complain of a defect can get you a replacement for the defective model. Writing to the editor of a newspaper, alerting the community to a problem, can persuade others to join you in suggesting changes. In all these cases, you are writing for action, writing to make things happen.

Writing with Power Writers have power. Your life is shaped by people who have been able to organize ideas and put them into words, from the framers of the United States Constitution to the writers of the advertisements for your favorite cereal. Your writing, too, can shape your world. A letter you write to a school administrator may determine whether you are allowed to take a class you especially want. A campaign speech you write may determine whether you are elected to the student government. The more effective your writing, the more power you can have over your own life.

▼

Writing isn't magic. But then, magic isn't magic either. Magicians know their craft, and writers must also know their craft.
Donald Murray, writer and educator

Writing Within a Community Learning to write effectively isn't easy. Although writing is a natural process, you must hone your skills through both individual practice and working with others, just as you would if you were learning to play tennis or sing. As you establish and refine your writing process, you become part of a community of writers working alone and together. Your first community is your classroom, with your teacher as co-writer and coach, and your fellow students as peer planners and readers.

You also begin to take your place within a larger community of writers: in your school, where you may write for the newspaper, the yearbook, or a school literary magazine; in your town, where you may write a letter to the editor of the newspaper or contribute a letter of opinion to be read as part of a local TV news editorial. In each instance, you will be using writing to address both your own needs and the needs of the community in which, and for which, you write.

In a community of writers, though you often write alone, you may have opportunities to participate in collaborative writing as well. For example, you may collaborate with other interested students on writing a statement of purpose for a new school club. When you write collaboratively, you are enriched by hearing many points of view and by receiving much helpful support. These benefits are so valuable that, in the business and academic worlds, much writing is produced, at least in part, by committees or teams. This textbook, in fact, was written by many people working both individually and collaboratively. The skills you learn in this book will enable you to become a fully contributing member of the community of writers in your school, your community, and beyond.

According to author and educator Roger Garrison, "The way to learn to write is by writing. Not by reading about writing; not by talking about writing; but by writing, writing, writing." This book allows you to do just that. It gives you numerous and varied opportunities to write and ways to learn from what you do.

The book is divided into three sections: **Writer's Workshops** and two handbooks—a **Writing Handbook** and a **Grammar and Usage Handbook.** You will begin writing immediately, following specific guidelines in the Workshops. The workshops direct you to specific Handbooks for additional help as you write, and you can consult them as needed. The diagram at the right shows how this process works, and the explanations that follow describe each section of the book in more detail.

Writer's Workshops Each Writer's Workshop focuses on a specific kind of writing or writing strategy. You will learn each skill by practicing it in any or all of three different settings—a guided assignment and two related assignments.

Guided Assignments The guided assignments do precisely that—guide you through the creation of a specific piece of writing. If you have any questions that are not answered in the guided assignment, or if you need more help, explanation, or practice, you can turn to the handbooks at the back of the book. At each step in your writing process, you are encouraged to explore alternate approaches and to discover a way of writing that works for you.

Related Assignments Each guided assignment is accompanied by two related writing applications that can be done instead of or in addition to the main assignment. The related assignments enable you to build on and extend the skills presented in the guided assignments, providing minimal guidance and the chance to take complete charge of your own writing process. Like the guided assignments, however, the related assignments also refer you to specific handbook sections for additional help.

• **Additional Writing Opportunities** Not all the writing you do results in a polished, publishable piece, and at regular intervals throughout the book you will find opportunities to do short writings for fun and practice. The **Sketchbooks** give you a chance just to play with your ideas without worrying about presenting them in finished form. The **Sentence Composing** features enable you to improve your own writing technique and style by analyzing and imitating various types of sentences written by professional writers.

Handbooks Writing must be learned, and since no one is perfect, often relearned as well. This book includes two handbooks that you can use no matter what you already know about writing, what you need to find out, or what you once knew but have forgotten. The **Writing Handbook** provides information about the writing process, style, and academic skills; and the **Grammar and Usage Handbook** covers grammar, usage, and mechanics.

The guided and related assignments include thorough cross-references to appropriate handbook sections, and you can consult these, or any other sections, at any point in your writing process. You can use the handbooks for anything from a quick review of the correct use of commas to extensive practice in writing introductions and conclusions.

Making the Book Work for You There is no right or wrong way to use this book. You will probably find yourself using it differently for different assignments, since your skills in one area differ from your skills in another. You will probably also use it differently from your classmates, since no two writers are the same.

For example, a student who has had much experience writing science lab reports and understands the forms and techniques used in drawing conclusions would probably need little of the help provided in that guided assignment. At the teacher's discretion, that student might do one of the related assignments in the exposition workshop instead of the guided assignment.

The same student, however, may need a great deal of practice in writing a literary review and would want to follow that guided assignment closely and work through all the exercises in several handbook sections.

You bring to this book a unique set of experiences, knowledge, interests, skills, and learning styles. Here you will find all the help you need in learning to write, and all the flexibility you need in helping yourself to learn.

Discovering Your Writing Process

To communicate, whales sing, bees dance, and monkeys chatter. Human beings, however, are the only creatures who can communicate with one another using written symbols.

Even if you have never written anything before, you would still bring to this book many of the essential skills you need for writing. Writing is just an extension of the familiar processes of thinking and speaking, yet it also offers new strategies for understanding, creating, and communicating ideas.

THE STAGES OF THE WRITING PROCESS

If everyone is thinking alike, then somebody isn't thinking.
General George Patton

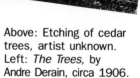

Above: Etching of cedar trees, artist unknown.
Left: *The Trees,* by Andre Derain, circa 1906.

Just as there is no right way to think, there is no right way to write. Not only is every writer different, but individual writers often vary their process for each writing task. The right process is the one that works for you.

Like most writers, however, you will probably go through four basic stages at some point as you write:

- **prewriting** "breaking the ice" by exploring ideas and collecting materials. During this stage, you begin to consider the writing variables—your general purpose and specific personal goals, your audience, and the form of your writing.
- **drafting and discovery** getting your ideas on paper to discover how they fit together and where they lead. At this stage you may be able to clarify your writing variables.
- **revising and proofreading** shaping your material to make sure it reads well and accomplishes your goals. To do this, you will evaluate the content and structure of your writing, perhaps also asking for responses from your peers. You will also proofread it for mechanical errors.
- **publishing and presenting** sharing your writing. You are encouraged to share your writing at every stage of the process, and in a variety of forms.

These stages of the writing process are not separate steps that you must complete sequentially. For example, sometimes you might not do any prewriting. Other times, you might write a draft that needs little or no revising. On the other hand, you might continue revising your work even after it is published. As the diagram shown below illustrates, the writing process is not static; it is truly a process—a flexible, dynamic approach to writing that you will personalize and make your own.

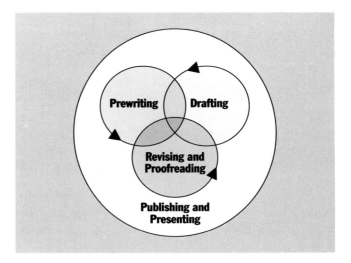

To get a feel for how the writing process can work, follow the process of one student, Dana, as she worked through an assignment for her World Civilizations class. The students had been given a chance to explore their personal interests and extend their knowledge by researching and writing about an aspect of Chinese, Japanese, or Korean culture.

Prewriting

Dana had only a general knowledge of the Far East, so she wanted to explore ideas before she began writing. She realized that at some point during her writing process she would have to decide on a topic and determine her general purpose and specific, personal goals. She would also eventually have to identify her audience, choose a form for her writing, and gather and develop her information. She kept these points in mind as she proceeded. As you follow Dana's process, think about ways to adapt her methods to fit your own personal style.

Choosing a Topic   Since Dana had little personal knowledge of the Far East and liked working with other people, she decided to pool her ideas with those of her classmates in her search for a writing topic. In a brainstorming session, the students came up with topics such as the following: Chinese calligraphy, martial arts, Kabuki theater, Japanese tea ceremony, and Korean cooking. Dana was intrigued by the name *martial arts,* which sounded like a contradiction in terms to her. She decided to pursue her curiosity by focusing on the martial arts.

Dana first consulted a reference book and made a list of the most popular martial arts: *judo, karate, kung fu, tai chi ch'uan, tae kwon do,* and *aikido.* She didn't know much about any of these, but thinking about why people might practice martial arts, Dana remembered a film her class had seen about daily life in China. She had been impressed by a scene in the movie showing Chinese men, women, and children of all ages performing graceful tai chi exercises in the early morning in front of their factories, schools, and offices. Dana decided to find out more about tai chi and the people who practice it. To focus her research, she developed the following list of questions.

- How can the slow, graceful movements in tai chi be a part of a martial art?
- What is the history of tai chi?
- Why is tai chi so popular in the Far East?
- How and when was tai chi introduced into the United States?
- What is its status in this country?
- What are the mental and physical benefits of tai chi?

Establishing a Purpose   You can write for a variety of purposes, for example, **to express yourself, to analyze, to inform, to entertain, to persuade,** or to achieve a combination of these. For example, if you were going to write a report comparing and contrasting two forms of martial arts, your primary purpose would be to inform. In writing an article about karate as self-defense, you might have two purposes: to inform readers about karate and to persuade them to become involved in it themselves.

In addition to identifying an overall purpose for your work, you must at some point in your writing process determine the more specific goals you want to accomplish. These specific goals include those you want to accomplish for yourself as a writer, and those you hope your writing will accomplish for your readers. For example, a goal in writing about martial arts might be to show how mastering a martial art can increase self-confidence. Early in the writing process, many writers discover their purpose and develop their personal goals by asking themselves the following questions:

- What do I want to accomplish in my writing?
- How do I want my audience to respond to it?
- What can I learn from the process?

Because Dana had only started exploring her topic, she did not feel ready to state the specific goals of her writing or what she felt she could learn from the process. She did have some ideas, however, about her general purpose and how she wanted her audience to respond to her writing.

The scene in the film our class saw showed how beautiful and graceful tai chi is. I'd like to help my audience appreciate that beauty and to tell them about what tai chi is and why people practice it.

Identifying Your Audience To determine what information to include and how to present your material, you will need to identify your audience. Writing is, after all, a form of communication. If you don't know who you want to reach, you can't be sure you will get your message across. Sometimes your audience is chosen for you, as in a classroom assignment, but often you can choose whom to share your writing with or even whether to share it at all.

In general, identifying your audience will help you to communicate your ideas clearly. Asking yourself questions such as the following will help you understand your readers and meet their needs while achieving your goals:

- What do my readers already know about my subject? What do they need to know?
- What aspects of my subject will my readers find most interesting?
- What approach and language will be most effective?

Dana's assignment was for her World Civilizations class, but her teacher had asked the students to find a way to share their writing with the community as well. Dana remembered that the local library was sponsoring a World Neighbors program that would include lectures and displays. She made a note to find out the specific requirements but assumed for the time being that the audience for the program would include people of all ages and interests.

Choosing a Form The **form** is the type of writing in which you express your ideas. For example, you could choose to write a poem, a play, a letter, an article, a journal account, or a speech. Like your purpose for writing, your form may not be clear before you begin writing. However, it may emerge as you consider your topic, goals, and audience, as Dana's did.

Because my audience will be a varied group of people from the community and I want each of them to experience what tai chi is all about, I think a speech would be the best way to present my information. That way I can answer their questions and personalize the presentation as I go. I can also demonstrate some of the moves or maybe invite an expert to do that. The audience could even participate in a tai chi mini-lesson. That will also give me a chance to do tai chi myself and should be a lot of fun for everyone.

Gathering and Developing Information   Dana knew she needed to gather more information before beginning to write her speech. Since she was becoming very caught up in her topic, Dana decided to use this growing personal interest to help her develop her ideas. She started from what she already knew, writing down what she remembered from the movie she had seen. However, she really wanted to see tai chi in action for herself, so she found out that there was a tai chi class held at a local community center and made an appointment to observe it. As she watched, she jotted down her impressions.

ONE STUDENT'S PROCESS

The teacher leads exercises. Students, various ages, move in slow motion. Good balance and flexibility. Only sound is deep, relaxed breathing. Mood peaceful.

After watching the class, Dana interviewed the instructor. She asked questions she had developed earlier in her writing process as well as others that arose during her observation.

ONE STUDENT'S PROCESS

Question: What is tai chi?
Answer: Tai chi is an ancient Chinese system of meditation, physical coordination, and self-defense.

Question: Why do people of all ages practice it?
Answer: Unlike "hard" martial arts such as karate, which require speed, strength, and muscular power, tai chi is a "soft" art. It stresses concentration, relaxation, flexibility, and fluid motion, qualities that anyone can develop.

Question: How do the slow, graceful movements serve as a martial art?
Answer: Tai chi develops physical and mental awareness. Those qualities can help a person avoid a fight, or, if necessary, predict what an opponent is about to do and respond appropriately and quickly.

Question: What have you gained personally from doing tai chi?
Answer: Physically, I've become less tense and more graceful. I've also developed and can maintain a feeling of peace and well-being.

Drafting and Discovery

Drafting is often the most exciting part of the writing process. It is the time when you put it all together, making meaning from your ideas and the information you have gathered and so making them your own. Drafting is the discovery stage in the writing process—the time to get your thoughts on paper, allow new ideas to emerge, and experiment with ways of expressing them. During the drafting stage, you may find that you want to backtrack—to change your purpose, to try a new form, or even to switch topics. Because of these possibilities, don't worry yet about making mistakes in grammar, usage, and mechanics. You will have time to deal with those issues once you know what you want to say and how to say it.

Dana had no trouble getting her ideas on paper until she tried to describe some tai chi exercises. The notes she had taken while visiting the class described general impressions rather than specific movements, and the explanations she had found in books were not completely clear to her. Dana, therefore, decided to visit the class again and take more notes as the students performed their exercises. She also asked if she could participate to get a personal, physical knowledge of the movements.

Because Dana made new discoveries about her topic as she drafted, she simultaneously reworked and reshaped her writing. You, too, should feel free to revise your writing as much or as little as you like during the drafting stage of your writing process. Sometimes your first draft will need very little revision. At other times you may need to complete several drafts to identify problems and find a solution that works. Whatever drafting method you use, however, ask yourself the following questions:

Ideas
- Where is my writing taking me?

- Am I developing my original idea, concentrating on one aspect of it, or going off in a different direction?

- Where should I go from here?

- What additional information might my readers need?

Organization
- How are my main ideas and supporting details related?

- Are they presented in terms of time, space, importance, cause and effect, or similarities and differences?

- Does my presentation of the ideas make the relationships clear?

Peer Response

Although writing is largely a solitary activity, your classmates can help at any stage of the writing process by reading your writing and responding to both your ideas and the way you present them. For example, Dana had worked with her peers to explore writing ideas. Other readers can provide new perspectives on your writing and can help you find and clarify new ideas and identify problems. Each reader brings a unique point of view to a piece of writing and can help you see your work more objectively.

After Dana had finished the first draft of her speech, she set it aside for a few days. When she reread it, she knew it wasn't quite right. She decided to read her speech to several peers and have them react to it, considering the following questions:

- What parts did you like best? Least?
- What message do you think I am trying to get across? How would you summarize it?
- Why do you think I chose to write about this topic?
- What did you want to know more about? What parts did not seem necessary?
- Did the beginning work for you? Did the ending?
- Did you have any trouble following my ideas?

Here are some of the responses that Dana's peers gave after reading a paragraph from her first draft.

I like this beginning.

I'd like to know more about the specific exercises.

Are you talking about tai chi as self-defense or as exercise?

I'm not sure how dance is related to your topic.

I don't understand what you mean by "reaction time."

I like this. It's clear and to the point.

Martial arts—it sounds like a contradiction in terms. If you have ever watched people practicing tai chi, however, you would know that strength can be beautiful. Tai chi is a method of self-defense. But many people are more interested in the health benefits. Some tai chi exercises involve stretching. These increase a person's grace and flexibility. For this reason, dancers often study tai chi. In fact, when watching people perform tai chi exercises, I was sometimes reminded of ballet dancers. Other tai chi exercises improve your balance and reaction time. These can help an athlete perform better. The most important benefit of tai chi, however, is the feeling of health and well-being that comes from moving slowly and breathing deeply.

Revising and Proofreading

Now that Dana had evaluated her own work and asked several peer readers for their opinions, she was ready to revise her speech.

Like Dana, you should set aside your first draft for a few hours—or even a day or two, if you have time. Your most important task in revision is to review your personal goals for your paper and assess whether or not you have achieved them. Make sure you have communicated your ideas clearly and completely, saying exactly what you wanted to say.

Consider your peer readers' comments carefully, but remember that you do not have to use all, or even any, of their suggestions. Before incorporating a change, decide whether it will help you fulfill your purpose and improve your writing. If you do decide to make a change, determine which of the following three major types of revision it involves:

• Rethinking content
• Reworking structure
• Refining mechanics and usage

Content   Often, drafting leads you to new information, perspectives, or approaches, as Dana discovered. You or your peer readers also may find problems with the basic message of your writing. Then you can simply loop back to the beginning of the writing process. You may be able to rework your initial draft, or you might want to discard it and start over. When rethinking the content of your writing, ask yourself questions about the focus of your paper and the clarity of each idea you present. The "Checklist for Rethinking Content" on page 417 lists specific points to consider in evaluating your basic message.

Structure   When you are basically satisfied with your content, but realize from rereading and your peers' responses that you haven't communicated it effectively, you need to revise the structure of your writing. First, examine the overall organization of your paper. Check to see that you have included all the important information and taken out unrelated facts and opinions. Also make sure that your writing flows smoothly and logically. See the "Checklist of Reworking Structure" on page 418 for specific questions that will help you assess the structure of your writing and reshape it as necessary.

Mechanics   When you are satisfied with your content and structure, you can refine and polish your draft by **proofreading** or **copy editing,** your writing. In this final revision, you will need to read your draft closely to discover errors in punctuation, capitalization, spelling, grammar, and usage. To refine your paper thoroughly, use the "Checklist for Refining Mechanics" and the standard revising and proofreading marks on page 419. Dana used several of these marks in making the final revision of her first draft. Notice that she incorporated most, but not all, of the suggestions made by her peer readers. She also corrected some defects she found in the structure and mechanics of her paragraph.

Martial arts—it sounds like a contradiction in terms. If you have ever watched people practicing tai chi, however, you would know that strength can be beautiful. Tai chi is a method of self-defense. But *Although* many people are more interested in the health bene- fits. Some tai chi exercises involve stretching. These *in a gentle, continuous motion.* increase a person's grace and flexibility. For this rea- son, dancers often study tai chi. ~~In fact, when~~ ~~watching people perform tai chi exercises, I was~~ ~~sometimes reminded of ballet dancers.~~ Other tai chi exercises improve ~~your~~ balance and reaction time. *a person's* These can help an athlete ~~perfom~~ better. The most im- *perform* portant benefit of tai chi, however, is the feeling of health and well-being that comes from moving slowly *peace* and breathing deeply.

There are 108 patterns of movements, or forms, in tai chi.

Publishing and Presenting

Sharing your finished work is usually the last stage of the writ- ing process. Of course, you might choose not to share your writing, or you might share it and then revise it again. Though your audience usually consists of teachers and classmates, you can find additional ways to share your writing with others, as Dana did.

- **Readers' circles** Form a reader's circle with three or more other writers in your class. Read your writing to the group and discuss the thoughts and feelings it evokes.

- **Writing exchange groups** As a class, share your writing with another class at your school or a class at a different school.
- **Collected works** Publish a small book of student writing of a particular type or regarding a particular subject.
- **Print media** Submit your writing to your local or school newspaper or to a commercial magazine.
- **Performances** Transform a story or poem into a script and produce it for the class or school assembly.
- **Videos or multimedia presentations** Create a video or multi-media presentation of your work, using music, slides, pantomime, or dance to illustrate or accompany a reading of your work.
- **Portfolios** Keep your writing in a file and reread it in a month or two. Then choose the best pieces and mount them in a portfolio of samples of your writing.

EXTENDING YOUR WRITING PROCESS

Writing is truly a process: what you learn through the activity and how you develop as a writer are as important as the final product. To benefit fully from this process, after you have completed a piece of writing, think about and evaluate the experience. Asking questions such as the following can help you focus your thinking.

- What did I gain by writing about this topic?
- Which aspects of this process were easiest for me? Which were most difficult?
- What part of the writing process is getting easier for me?
- What problems did I encounter as I wrote? What solutions did I find?
- How can I improve my writing process?
- How does the style of this piece compare with that of the other pieces in my portfolio?
- What features of my peers' or professional writers' work would I like to try to achieve myself?
- How can I apply the skills I have learned?

Record your answers to these questions and attach them to your finished piece of writing. As you continue writing, and you discover the writing process that works best for you, these notes will allow you to track your progress and to continue to grow as a writer.

Sketchbook

Writers, like artists, need to sketch out their ideas before turning them into finished pieces. Use the words and images on the Sketchbook pages that appear throughout the book to try out writing ideas and have fun with them. You might find that your sketches give you ideas you will want to polish later, but for now, just see where your thoughts take you.

The People Teens Confide In

Males		**Females**	
Male friends	27%	Female friends	38%
Mother	24%	Mother	27%
Female friend	10%	Boyfriend	13%
Girlfriend	9%	Sister	8%
Nobody	8%	Brother	5%
Father	7%	Nobody	3%
Other categories	15%	Other categories	6%

Source: *Who's Who Among High School Students* survey

Whom do you confide in?

Additional Sketches

Describe the feeling or emotion you understand best.

What song has a special meaning for you? Explain why the song is important to you.

Personal and Expressive Writing

Guided Assignment
MEMOIR

Related Assignment
COLLEGE APPLICATION

Related Assignment
SONG LYRIC

Look back. Look forward. Look at the moment. Add it all up. *You* are the sum—the total of all your memories, feelings, and hopes for the future. Writers draw on this sum total of experience to express themselves. In the workshop that follows, you will examine ways of transforming your personal experience into a memoir, a college application, and a song lyric. In the memoir, you will explore an experience that has special meaning for you. In the college application, you will examine ways of presenting yourself in the best light. In the song lyric, you will draw on personal experience to express ideas that could come only from you.

FROM THE TOWN DUMP

BY WALLACE STEGNER

Everyone has had experiences that were especially meaningful, moments of special beauty, drama, or excitement. Such experiences are the material of memoirs. Writers take them, explore the meanings they attach to them, and create personal writing that tells as much about them as about the experience.

In his memoir "The Town Dump," American novelist Wallace Stegner looks back on incidents from his childhood years in a Canadian frontier town. As you read, look for the details he uses to evoke the meaning the dump has for him.

The town dump of Whitemud, Saskatchewan, could only have been a few years old when I knew it, for the village was born in 1913 and I left there in 1919. But I remember the dump better than I remember most things in that town, better than I remember most of the people. I spent more time with it, for one thing; it has more poetry and excitement in it than people did. . . .

If the history of our town was not exactly written, it was at least hinted, in the dump. I think I had a pretty sound notion even at eight or nine of how significant was that first institution of our forming Canadian civilization. For rummaging through its foul purlieus I had several times been surprised and shocked to find relics of my own life tossed out there to rot or blow away.

The volumes of Shakespeare belonged to a set that my father had bought before I was born. It had been carried through successive moves from town to town in the Dakotas, and from Dakota to Seattle, and from Seattle to Bellingham, and Bellingham to Redmond, and from Redmond back to Iowa, and from there to Saskatchewan. Then, stained in a stranger's house fire, these volumes had suffered from a house-cleaning impulse and been thrown away for me to stumble upon in the dump. One of the Cratchet girls had borrowed them, a hatchet-faced, thin, eager, transplanted Cockney girl with a frenzy, almost a hysteria, for reading. And yet somehow, through her hands, they found the dump, to become a symbol of how much was lost, how much thrown aside, how much carelessly or of necessity given up, in the making of a new country. We had so few books that I was familiar with them, all, had handled them, looked at their pictures, perhaps even read them. . . . Finding those three thrown away was a little like finding my own name on a gravestone.

And yet not the blow that something else was, something that impressed me even more with the dump's close reflection of the town's intimate life. The colt whose picked skeleton lay out there was mine. He had been incurably crippled when dogs chased our mare, Daisy, the morning after she foaled. I had labored for months to make him well; had fed him by hand, curried him, exercised him, adjusted the iron braces that I had talked my father into having made. And I had not known that he would have to be destroyed. One weekend I turned him over to the foreman of one of the ranches, presumably so that he could be cared for. A few days later I found his skinned body, with the braces still on his crippled front legs, lying on the dump.

Not even that, I think, cured me of going there. . . .

The dump was our poetry and our history. We took it home with us by the wagonload, bringing back into town the things the town had used and thrown away. Some little part of what we gathered, mainly bottles, we managed to bring back to usefulness, but most of our gleanings we left lying around barn or attic or cellar until in some renewed fury of spring cleanup our families carted them off to the dump again, to be rescued and briefly treasured by some other boy with schemes for making them useful. Occasionally something we really valued with a passion was snatched from us in horror and returned at once. That happened to the mounted head of a white mountain goat, somebody's trophy from old times and the far Rocky Mountains, that I brought home one day in transports of delight. My mother took one look and discovered that his beard was full of moths.

I remember that goat; I regret him yet. Poetry is seldom useful, but always memorable. I think I learned more from the town dump than I learned from school: more about people, more about how life is lived, not elsewhere but here, not in other times but now. If I were a sociologist anxious to study in detail the life of any community, I would go very early to its refuse piles. For a community may be as well judged by what it throws away—what it has to throw away and what it chooses to—as by any other evidence. For whole civilizations we have sometimes no more of the poetry and little more of the history than this.

Think AND Respond

In this memoir, Wallace Stegner recalls the "poetry and excitement" of a town dump. How does he make the special qualities of the dump clear to the reader? What details does he use to make his descriptions vivid? What memories do you have that you could explore in a memoir?

INVITATION
—TO—
Write

Wallace Stegner told of the rich meaning he found in an unlikely place. Now it's your turn to write a memoir that explores the meaning of an experience or event in your own life.

A memoir allows the writer to be both a storyteller and an interpreter. As the writer of a memoir, you will tell about an experience that has special meaning for you. The experience may be one in which you were personally involved or one to which you were a witness. You will interpret the experience through reflection; that is, you will look inside yourself to see how you feel about the experience and explore the meanings you attach to it. The excitement of the memoir is found in this search for meaning. What you discover may be as much a surprise to you as to the reader.

PREWRITE AND EXPLORE

1. Explore your experiences. You are a wealth of experiences and feelings. To dig into the richness of your experiences and find a single event to explore for its meaning, you may want to try one or more of the following activities.

Exploratory Activities

- **Journal** Look back through your journal and find an entry that tells of something you did or observed that had an impact on you. Don't overlook what may seem to be small, ordinary events. They may have a great deal of meaning for you.
- **I wish I had done that** Think back to times you witnessed someone else doing something you wish you had done, or when you had a chance to do something but did not. List the thoughts you have about each recollection.

HANDBOOKS
FOR HELP & PRACTICE

Personal Techniques, pp. 339–342
Writing Techniques, pp. 344–346

- **I remember when** In a small group, take turns telling a story from your experience. Begin with "I remember when . . ." and continue around the group as many times as possible. Have each person speculate about why the story stayed in his or her memory. Members of the group may question other members to bring out more details.
- **Photo share** Bring in a photo of a person, place, or event. Share your remembrances about the subject of the photo. Use your partners as questioners to bring out as much information as possible and to allow you to remember more and more.
- **Reading literature** Think about memoirs and personal essays you have read, such as Wallace Stegner's remembrance of the town dump. You also might consider Richard Rodriguez's *Hunger of Memory* or James Baldwin's *Notes of a Native Son.* Do they bring to mind any personal experiences you could write about?

How can I identify experiences that are important to me?

Daydreams of Magritte 2, by Pete Turner

2. Freewrite about some of your experiences. Now you should have a variety of ideas. Take some time to freewrite on several of them to see which one you might like to pursue. Ellen found one idea in a photo of her next-door neighbor. Here are her initial thoughts on this idea. Throughout this assignment, you will follow Ellen's process with this idea and her memoir.

ONE STUDENT'S PROCESS

This is a picture of my friend Audrey. She may not look like much to you, but I see her as beautiful. She is my next-door neighbor. To meet her, you wouldn't think much of her maybe. She wouldn't smile and if she said anything it would probably be in a grouchy tone. She is filled with complaints. She complains about how my parents park their cars in front of her house, about noise, about why people get upset when she sleeps late in the morning, about the mail, about the cost of things, about having to go out of her house. She complains about just about everything.

Now it gets hard to explain why we are friends considering she is so grouchy, but she and I share many of the same beliefs and she doesn't talk to me like I'm a child who doesn't know anything just because I'm a teen-ager. We both like to read and gossip, and we appreciate each other's way to have fun—I go to parties and she hangs plastic lemons on a dead tree in her backyard. She's special.

3. Select a writing idea. Focus on one of your ideas. If you are still searching, look in your journal, at the Sketchbook writing you did on page 20, or in "Apply Your Skills" on page 34.

4. Explore your idea. Look back at any freewriting you've done on the idea or freewrite about a new idea. Then explore the meaning of the experience by asking yourself, "So what?" When you've written an answer, pause for a while and then say to yourself "and so . . ." Then write some more and repeat the prompt.

5. List your goals. Listing your goals may help to direct your attention as you write. Ellen listed these goals.

ONE STUDENT'S PROCESS

—to tell how much I liked Audrey and to show why
—to tell why she was such a special friend and how she made me feel special too
—to show how we are both weird
—to show why she was important in my life

Sometimes your goals become clearer as you begin to write.

6. Examine your audience. When you write a memoir, you are writing largely for yourself and for others who are genuinely interested in what you think and feel. You are also probably writing about an experience you feel that others can relate to. By reading your memoir, your readers will learn about you, but they will also learn about themselves. To make your readers respond to your memoir, you will need to be honest with them and to speak to them in a voice that is conversational and intimate rather than academic and formal.

 Writer's Choice Do you want your memoir to be humorous or serious? The choice will depend largely on your subject. A humorous memoir can have a serious meaning beneath the humor.

DRAFT AND DISCOVER

1. Begin your draft. The exploratory nature of the memoir makes the first draft a search for meaning. The discoveries you make may take you by surprise if you are willing to allow the ideas and writing to come about without worrying whether there are better ways to say what you want. Feel free to change what you've written as you go along in order to make your memoir express most accurately what you want it to say. The following strategies can help focus your thinking as you write your draft.

HANDBOOKS
FOR HELP & PRACTICE

Envisioning
Structure,
p. 361
Introducing/
Concluding
Narratives,
pp. 386–390
Types of
Elaboration,
pp. 397–400
Dialogue in
Nonfiction,
pp. 464–465

PROBLEM

S O L V I N G

**How can I best
communicate this
experience?**

Strategies

- **Description** Using vivid details to describe people, places, and events can make your memoir more real for the reader. Notice how Wallace Stegner used description to show that the objects found in the dump were more than junk.
- **Narration** You can make the ideas in your memoir come alive by describing any events that are part of your experience in the order in which they happened or by recreating a series of related incidents.
- **Dialogue** Recreating actual conversations can add interest to your memoir and help make your experience more immediate for readers.

2. Explore approaches as you draft. Many memoirs tell stories and relate events in chronological order. Others, like Wallace Stegner's, recall a series of events that support an overall impression.

Ellen began her draft about her neighbor Audrey by introducing and describing her and explaining how they became friends. Then she narrated an incident—something special that Audrey did—that she found particularly memorable. She concluded her draft by explaining why her friendship with Audrey was so important to her. The following is the beginning of Ellen's unrevised draft.

ONE STUDENT'S PROCESS

My neighbor Audrey was about sixty-five, and she always sat at her kitchen window reading *The New Yorker* magazine. Whenever I came home from school, she was there. I could have chosen to ignore her because she seemed so grouchy. She complained about my stereo being too loud, about my parents parking in front of her house, about the mail, and about the high cost of everything. She would lean out the window and shake her glasses at people when they were bothering her. But instead of ignoring her, I decided to make friends with her.

3. Review your draft. Set your completed draft aside for a while. Then reread it and share it with your peer readers, using questions such as the following to focus your thinking.

Ideally, set your draft aside for one or two days before you review it.

R E V I E W   Y O U R   W R I T I N G

Questions for Yourself

- Have I explored what makes my experience significant?

- Have I managed to convey what this experience really meant to me?

- Have I captured how I really felt about my experience?

- Did I include only those ideas, descriptions, or events that are clearly related to my experience?

- Will my readers understand what happened? Have I left out any critical information?

Questions for Your Peer Readers

- In your own words, what do you think I'm saying in my memoir?

- What is the most interesting part of the memoir to you?

- Is there anything you would like to know more about?

- Have I provided any unnecessary information?

- What do you think I discovered from this experience? Why do you think it was important to me?

- Do you feel I could have been more truthful?

Writer's Choice While you were writing, did you think of any other experiences that would make good memoirs? You can write another first draft using one of these ideas and then decide which to revise.

R E V I S E   Y O U R   W R I T I N G

1. Evaluate your responses. Review your own responses to your memoir and those of other readers. As you think about which suggestions you want to follow, also keep in mind that an effective memoir generally displays certain basic characteristics.

HANDBOOKS
FOR HELP & PRACTICE

Unity/Coherence, pp. 401–414
Evoking Peer Responses, pp. 423–425
Incorporating Peer Responses, p. 425

Standards for Evaluation

An effective memoir . . .

- describes an experience or series of experiences clearly and shows why they were significant to the writer.
- elaborates on the meaning of the experience(s).
- uses description and dialogue as appropriate.
- includes a well-developed introduction, body, and conclusion.
- uses a logical and effective pattern of organization.
- uses transitional words and phrases to show relationships among ideas.

2. Problem-solve. Decide what changes you want to make and then rework your draft.

Ellen made these changes in response to comments from one peer reader.

COMPUTER
TIP

Most word-processing programs allow you to move blocks of type. Use this function when you want to move whole sentences or even paragraphs.

ONE STUDENT'S PROCESS

I like the story about the lemons—it's the best part.

Nice details!

I'm confused. Why is this incident important to you?

I will always remember her "lemon" tree. One day,
she called out, "Ellen, I've been doing some gardening. Come see." ¶
when she spotted me coming home from school, she ac-

tually left her kitchen window perch, which was quite

unusual, and made me walk into her backyard. In the
But this day it was sprightly and colorful.
middle of the yard stood a dead mulberry tree, and she
bright yellow
had put plastic lemons on all its branches. She laughed

and giggled like a little girl when she showed me the

tree. She even tried to kick up her feet. She was so
she never took the lemons down. They
proud of her eccentric behavior that could be seen from
other back
several yards around the neighborhood.

It became our little joke on the neighbors and helped cement our friendship.

3. Proofread your work. After you rework your draft and prepare a clean copy of your memoir, your final step is proofreading for mistakes in grammar, usage, and mechanics. These mistakes could distract your reader and take away from the power of your ideas.

Grammar
— TIP —

Did you describe how your experience *affected* you? Remember that *affect* is a verb meaning either "to influence" or "to pretend." *Effect* as a verb means "to accomplish" or "to produce as a result."

LINKING
GRAMMAR AND WRITING
Pronouns and Antecedents

An antecedent is the noun or pronoun to which a pronoun refers. Writers use many pronouns as they refer to different people, places, and things in memoirs. Often problems occur when pronouns are used without clear antecedents. Reword a sentence when you need to clarify to whom or what a pronoun refers.

UNCLEAR: Chris told Amos that he needed a wrench. (Who needs a wrench—Chris or Amos?)

CLEAR: Chris asked Amos to give him a wrench.

See Grammar Handbook 35, pages 725–727, for additional help with this problem.

PUBLISH AND PRESENT

- **Make a book of memoirs.** Collect the memoirs the class has written and bind them together. Individual students can check out the book from the classroom library. Next year's students may want to look through it as well.
- **Read your memoir aloud.** Form a readers' group with two or three other writers. Read your memoirs to one another and discuss your reactions to them.
- **Submit your memoir for publication.** Send your memoir to a local newspaper, journal, or magazine. You may also research state or national writing contests and choose an appropriate contest for submitting your memoir.
- **Share the memoir with people familiar with the subject.** Would friends enjoy having their memories jogged? Would the person you wrote about enjoy seeing how important he or she was to you?

HANDBOOKS
FOR HELP & PRACTICE

Speech Preparation/ Delivery, pp. 515–517
Sharing and Publishing, pp. 427–428

Audrey

Ellen Hayashi

I can't remember exactly why I first tried to make friends with Audrey, our next-door neighbor. I guess it was because I was new in the neighborhood and didn't know anyone yet.

Audrey was kind of eccentric—a sixty-five-year-old woman always sitting at her kitchen window reading *The New Yorker* or complaining about something that was going on. She would complain about the way my parents parked their cars in front of her house, or noise, or the mail, or the high cost of everything. She always wore a faded, baggy muumuu and when she had a complaint against someone in particular she would take off her glasses, lean way out the window, and shake those glasses toward the people who were bothering her. She almost never left her house.

I could have ignored her. After all, once she aimed one of her complaints at me.

"Stop playing that stereo so loud," she had called to me soon after we moved in. "It's driving me crazy. Bang, bang, bang. It's not even music!" My parents had told me the same thing, so I turned the stereo down—for a while.

So why did I want Audrey for a friend? Maybe I saw a challenge and decided I would win her over. Here's what I did. Every day after school when I saw her at the window I would wave. At first she just kind of mumbled a grouchy hello when I did that. Then, after a few days, I boldly began to walk across the lawn and go to the window to talk to her. I would tell her something that happened in class that day or talk about the weather.

I guess our friendship really got going because she was smart and liked to hear about what was going on even though she hated to leave her house. For a person who stayed at home, she knew a lot about what was happening by reading so much and watching TV. She liked to talk about the books I was reading, and we both just loved to gossip. Sometimes, though, she made me uncomfortable by complaining about too many things and I would want to leave. Still, the next day I would be back because she seemed to have a special kind of understanding—as if she could remember back to when she was a teen-ager and knew just what I was going through.

I will always remember her "lemon" tree. One day, when she spotted me coming home from school, she called out, "Ellen, I've been doing some gardening. Come see."

She actually left her kitchen window perch, which was quite unusual, and made me walk into her backyard. In the middle of the yard stood a dead mulberry tree. But this day it looked sprightly and colorful. She had put bright yellow plastic lemons on all its branches. She laughed and giggled like a little girl when she showed me the tree. She even tried to kick up her feet.

She was so proud of her eccentric behavior that she never took the lemons down. They could be seen from several other backyards around the neighborhood. It became our little joke on the neighbors and helped to cement our friendship.

My relationship with Audrey wasn't a typical friendship. I couldn't demand things of her. I had to have patience and listen. She, in turn, listened to me, treated me as an equal. There were so many differences—age, outlook, experiences. I was never going to change her. She never tried to change me. But we found our common ground in human concerns and we shared conversations that will last a lifetime.

Uses dialogue to move the narrative along

Explains the significance of the friendship by telling an insightful anecdote

Includes a well-developed conclusion

LEARNING FROM YOUR WRITING PROCESS

WRITER TO WRITER

One writes out of one thing only—one's own experience. Everything depends on how relentlessly one forces from this experience the last drop, sweet or bitter, it can possibly give.

James Baldwin, novelist, playwright, and essayist

FOR YOUR PORTFOLIO

1. Reflect on your writing. Now that you have completed your memoir and have read several others, think about the process you followed. Ask yourself the questions below and record your answers in your writing log, or attach the page you record your answers on to your memoir.

- What advice about finding a topic and developing a draft would you give someone who was just starting to write a memoir?
- What was easiest about writing your memoir? What was hardest?
- As you wrote, did you discover anything about your topic or yourself that you didn't realize you knew? If you did, what was it that you discovered?
- Of all the memoirs you read, including the one by Wallace Stegner, the one you wrote, and those of your classmates, which did you like the most? What made it an especially effective piece of writing?

2. Apply your skills. Try one or more of the following activities.

- **Cross-curricular**   Recall a time when you learned or experienced something startling or extraordinary in math or science. Describe the experience and explore why it had a strong impact on you.
- **Literature**   Think back to a favorite novel, story, or poem. Write a memoir from the point of view of one of the characters.
- **Related assignments**   Follow the suggestions on pages 38–46 to write a college application essay and a song lyric.

34   Workshop 1

On the Lightside

IN CASE OF FIRE, BREAK GLASS

When I plead, as I often do, for greater precision in our use of words, perhaps it is because I am so prone to confusion. I remember as a little boy reading the signs on some highways and bridges: **HEAVY TRAFFIC NOT PERMITTED.**

It puzzled me for a long time how the individual motorist was going to decide whether the traffic was too heavy for him to continue on the road or over the bridge. It was a year or more before I realized that the sign meant: **HEAVY VEHICLES NOT PERMITTED.**

And I may have been more stupid than most, but when I heard in fourth grade that a special class was being formed for "backward readers," I silently wondered how many of my classmates possessed that marvelous gift of being able to read backward.

A friend recently told me of an incident in a veterans' hospital. The physician in charge of the mental ward had a sign on his door: **DOCTOR'S OFFICE. PLEASE KNOCK.** He was driven to distraction by an obedient patient who carefully knocked every time he passed the door.

Even idiomatic phrases are not without their danger to the growing mind. James Thurber confesses, in one of his delightful books of reminiscences, that whenever his mother would say at dinner, "Dad is tied up at the office," he had a mental picture of the old man struggling to free himself from the bonds that were lashing him to his chair.

Another of my own childhood perplexities was the sign: **IN CASE OF FIRE, BREAK GLASS.** I couldn't figure out how breaking the glass was going to help put out the fire, and it's a good thing I was never called upon to turn in an alarm.

I am not suggesting that everything should be spelled out in a-b-c fashion, thus reducing us all to the condition of children or savages. But words should be *accurate* and *explicit;* except for poetry, they should say no more and no less than they actually mean.

As Mark Twain remarked, "The difference between the right word and the almost right word is the difference between lightning and the lightning bug." **Sydney J. Harris**

35

College Application

Does the idea of writing an essay about yourself for a college application make you feel uneasy or self-conscious? Many high-school students feel exactly the same way. Writing about yourself can be difficult, especially when the stakes are high. However, a personal essay can also be an opportunity, a chance to speak for yourself and to distinguish yourself as a unique and desirable college candidate.

The following essay was written in response to a prompt that asked the applicant to tell about a significant experience that changed his or her life. Notice how Seana Gamel uses anecdotes from her past to create a positive and engaging self-portrait.

I USED TO LIVE FOR GLORY.
NOW I LIVE FOR LIFE.

For at least the first thirteen years of my life I had the will to win, but that was all I had. I believed it was necessary for me to attain recognition for my academic endeavors. I had to read the most pages every week. I had to do my multiplication tables the fastest. I had to be the best in my class. Fourth grade introduced me to the city spelling bee. I remember spending late nights begging my father to quiz me just one more time. I wanted to make absolutely sure I knew every single word on the list. I felt that I had to win in order to live up to my own personal standards. Determination and diligence helped me to win the spelling bee two years in a row. Sixth grade, though, brought defeat, disappointment, and depression, and the word C-O-M-B-U-S-T-I-B-L-E became my enemy for life.

Fourth grade also introduced me to the world of music in the form of my first violin. True music would not be mine for at least a few years, though. Instead, I was again driven by a yearning to be the best. I was the first in my class to memorize "Twinkle, Twinkle Little Star," and the first to learn to read music. From then on I simply hammered out the notes in the effort to retain first chair in the city honor orchestra. I was interested more in playing notes than in thinking about making music. Grasping victory, then losing it, soon became the traumatic story of my life. I remember blinking back tears for days after I had to relinquish my glorious first chair to another player.

During the summer after seventh grade, though, my life began a turnaround, for which I am still grateful. That wonderful summer I attended my first music camp and made a marvelous discovery. It was there that I finally saw music in a special new light. I was suddenly surrounded by nearly one hundred people who absolutely loved to play music. Watching them play was a completely new experience, for when I watched them I would actually sense their emotions. I could feel their music beating in my heart. I wanted to play like they did. I wanted to play music, and that is what I spent two weeks learning to do. I returned to Boise that summer with a new outlook. I believe that it was then that I finally realized I had been silently killing myself trying to be the best at everything. I finally realized that not only was I missing out on the beautiful enjoyment of music, I wasn't enjoying life.

To play music as music, and to live life as life has been an accomplishment difficult to master. Because of it, though, today I am able to enjoy a peaceful life, always learning and deriving joy from every experience.

Seana Gamel

Think AND Respond

In her college-application essay, Seana Gamel created an appealing self-portrait. What main point was she making about herself? Why might a college admissions committee consider this a positive attitude? If you were writing an essay about yourself, what aspects of your life and personality would you want to emphasize?

INVITATION
— TO —
Write

Seana Gamel used a series of well-developed anecdotes to portray herself as a reflective person, capable of change. Now write your own application essay, one that would encourage the college of your choice to accept you as an undergraduate.

Most colleges require high-school applicants to submit a personal essay as part of the application process. Like all personal essays, this one focuses on "self," describing the applicant's interests, accomplishments, goals for the future, and sometimes, as in Seana Gamel's essay, includes some statements about the applicant's philosophy on life and learning.

PREPARING AN APPLICATION ESSAY

HANDBOOKS

FOR HELP & PRACTICE

Collaborative Planning,
pp. 370–373

Introducing/ Concluding Narratives,
pp. 386–390

Developing Writing Voice,
pp. 445–446

Applying for College,
pp. 523–524

1. Answer all of the questions on the application. Draft an answer to every question on the application before you begin your essay. Avoid using the personal essay to repeat any information you have included elsewhere on the application. For example, if you list your work with a local environmental-protection organization as one of your extracurricular activities, do not simply repeat the fact again in your essay. You may, however, use your essay to expand on something you have mentioned, describe it in detail, or reflect on what you have learned from it.

2. Write about what you know best. If you are completing this workshop as a practice essay, use the prompt that Seana Gamel responded to. If you are responding to directions on a real application and there is a choice of essay topics, choose the one about which you can write most honestly and believably. You might try freewriting about a few of the topics to determine which one you are most comfortable with. Also, do not try to convince the admissions committee that you are an authority on a subject you know little about. Colleges are not looking for accomplished specialists in their incoming first-year students; rather, they want students who have sought opportunities to explore and grow and who can write intelligently and engagingly about what they have learned from these experiences.

3. Explore appropriate prewriting techniques to help you gather ideas. If you are planning to write about personal achievement, for example, you may want to create a time line about your life, listing important events, turning points, and accomplishments in your past and then imagining and adding the successes you would like to achieve in the future. If you are writing about an influential person, idea, or event, you might use a cluster diagram to examine the reasons your subject is important to you. Consider exploring ideas for your essay in conversation with friends and family members. Often they can remind you of some strength or skill you might write about in your essay. As you gather ideas, from time to time look at the essay topic to which you are responding to be sure you are addressing the issues the college wants articulated.

 Writer's Choice You may want to generate ideas for answers to more than one essay topic, or explore different treatments of the same subject, before you decide which one to develop in essay form.

4. Consider your audience. You can learn about the college to which you are applying from its catalog and other publications, from your guidance counselor, from resources such as Fiske's *Selective Guide to Colleges,* and from students attending the college. Use what you learn to shape your essay. Highlight the attributes and talents you have that the college seems to value. Whether you present yourself as a hardworking school newspaper reporter to a college with a strong journalism program or as a multisport intramural player to a university seeking well-rounded students, be sure the details in your essay support your claims.

DRAFTING YOUR ESSAY

1. Create a strong beginning. Read the first two sentences of Seana Gamel's essay. With these dramatic statements, she not only piques her reader's curiosity but also states the theme of her essay.

Consider the form your essay is going to take, and then experiment with different ways to begin it. You want the opening paragraph to be engaging and informative without sounding cloying or contrived.

2. Use specific details to engage your readers. As you write, choose distinctive details to develop your subject and convey the desired image of yourself. Notice how lively details in Gamel's essay, such as the misspelled word that became her "enemy for life" and her "blinking back tears for days," create a vital, believable portrait of a unique individual.

3. Use narrative and dramatic techniques. Bring readers directly into the scene you are describing. Let them see the people, hear the dialogue and feel what you felt. If you are describing a change in your life or an important realization you had, your essay will have a natural dramatic structure. Notice how Gamel uses the first part of her essay to show what she was like as a child, then shares the experience that caused her to change and finally explains the conclusion she drew from her experience.

4. Conclude with a forceful summary of your main point. Seana Gamel asserts that, although changing was difficult, she has derived great benefits from her effort and suggests that this attitude makes her an excellent candidate for college life. Consider suggesting your suitability as a college candidate in a similar way. Just be sure that the details you include support the conclusion that you have stated or that you have asked the admissions committee to draw.

1. Put your essay aside before evaluating it. When you read it again, imagine you are a tired admissions officer with hundreds of applications stacked on your desk. Is this essay original and lively enough to catch your attention? Does it make you want to meet the writer? Is the essay thoughtful and carefully written? Does it begin strongly and move energetically to a conclusion? Has the writer responded to the directions in the application?

2. Ask friends, family, or teachers to react to what you have written. Choose readers who have not helped you with your essay and ask them to be honest. Is what you say engaging and distinctive? Have you omitted any significant details or examples? Ask your readers to discuss point by point what your essay says directly about you and what it suggests. Consider their responses as well as your own evaluation in revising your work.

3. Edit your essay meticulously. An admissions board will not be impressed by someone who did not take the time to polish an application essay. After you have revised your essay for content and style, check for errors in usage, punctuation, mechanics, and grammar. In addition to using a dictionary, thesaurus, and writing handbook, you may want to consult a friend, teacher, or parent with a good grasp of language for a final review.

4. Type a neat final copy. Do this yourself, following the directions in the application. Proofread the final draft at least twice. Retype the essay if you discover errors.

- **Submit your personal essay.** When you send your application to the college of your choice, use this essay as part of it.
- **Create a drama.** Ask four or five of your classmates to pretend they are members of a college admissions committee. Have them read portions of the personal essays that have been submitted (their own or someone else's). Create a dialogue by imagining what the members of the committee might say about each applicant's essay and whether he or she would be considered for admission to the college.

Song Lyric

Have you ever heard a song that seemed to speak directly to you? Sometimes the words of a song are so expressive and personal you almost feel as if the songwriter has looked inside your soul. At other times, song lyrics may express your feelings or describe a personal experience so well that you find yourself wishing you had written them.

Like the earliest poems, lyrics are accompanied by music and are meant to be sung. Like poems, too, most song lyrics have a regular pattern of rhythm and rhyme. As you read this song, notice how musician and song writer Tracy Chapman's lyrics express her feelings and share something she has learned.

ALL THAT YOU HAVE IS YOUR SOUL
Tracy Chapman

My mama told me
'Cause she say she learned the hard way
Say she want to spare the children
She say don't give or sell your soul away
'Cause all that you have is your soul.

Don't be tempted by the shiny apple
Don't you eat of a bitter fruit
Hunger only for a taste of justice
Hunger only for a world of truth
'Cause all that you have is your soul.

I was a pretty young girl once
I had dreams I had high hopes
I married a man he stole my heart away
He gave his love but what a high
    price I paid
And all that you have is your soul . . .

I thought that I could find a way
To beat the system
To make a deal and have no debts to pay
I'd take it all take it all I'd run away
Me for myself first class and first rate
But all that you have is your soul

Here I am waiting for a better day
A second chance
A little luck to come my way
A hope to dream a hope that I can sleep again
And wake in the world with a clear
    conscience and clean hands
'Cause all that you have is your soul

All that you have
All that you have
All that you have
Is your soul

Think AND Respond

"All That You Have Is Your Soul" is a song based on Tracy Chapman's personal experience. It is also a powerful warning from one young person to others. What experiences does Tracy Chapman describe in this song? How does she develop the theme, or message, of her song? What distinctive song characteristics, such as rhyme or use of refrain, do her lyrics have? Perhaps you have experiences or realizations you would like to share with others in the form of a song. What would you say in your lyrics?

INVITATION TO Write

Tracy Chapman's song tells the story of a young woman's gradual realization of the importance of integrity. Write a song lyric of your own about something—a feeling, a principle, an experience—important to you.

A song is a particularly creative way of expressing ideas and feelings that are important to you. Like poems, song lyrics are especially effective for communicating deeply felt experiences or values. Perhaps this is because the form of the song or poem defines the choices a writer may make and produces a dynamic, creative tension with words. In addition, the music that accompanies the lyrics can underscore the emotions being expressed.

FINDING A SONG TO SING

HANDBOOKS
FOR HELP & PRACTICE

Personal Techniques,
pp. 339–342
Unity,
pp. 401–403
Types of Language,
pp. 450–451
Figurative Language/ Sound Devices,
pp. 453–457
Speech Delivery,
pp. 515–517

1. Select a meaningful idea or experience. Think about personal experiences, feelings, and ideas that you could describe in a song. You might decide to write a song about a social issue that concerns you. Perhaps, like Tracy Chapman, you may want to share something you have learned about life.

2. Evoke your experience. After you have selected a subject, imagine and recall it as fully as possible. Use all your five senses and explore your emotions as you think about the idea or experience you will describe in your song. Freewrite about your subject as a way of exploring it. Highlight the words and phrases that express strong emotion or reveal important attitudes or ideas.

3. Develop your message, or theme. You may want to make a cluster diagram or do more freewriting to explore what your central idea, image, or experience really means to you. Begin the diagram with a word or phrase that describes your subject, and then write down words that come to mind. Once you have explored the range of your ideas, identify the message you want to convey.

Writer's Choice Will your theme be an underlying message that is merely suggested by the details in your lyrics or one that is stated outright, perhaps in the title or the refrain of your song?

WRITING YOUR SONG LYRIC

1. Develop a stanza format. Begin drafting the first stanza of your lyric. As you arrange the words and phrases that will express your theme, experiment with and arrive at a format you can follow as you develop the following stanzas of your song. How many lines will your stanza have? Will every line be about the same length? What type of rhyme scheme, if any, will you use? As you draft, keep your theme firmly in mind. Choose words, phrases, and images that help you to express that theme.

2. Draft subsequent stanzas. Use the format you developed for your first stanza to draft the remaining stanzas of your lyric. You may want to think of each stanza as a paragraph that develops a single idea, as in the Tracy Chapman lyric. Or you may choose to have the content of one stanza flow into the next stanza.

3. Consider adding a refrain. A refrain, the repetition of a line or lines in a regular pattern throughout a poem or lyric, is a time-honored poetic device for repeating important ideas, feelings, or images. Most songs include a refrain. It may be a single line repeated at the end of a stanza, as in Tracy Chapman's song, or it may be a separate stanza repeated several times throughout a song. Think about whether and how a refrain might help you communicate the theme of your lyric.

4. Use comparisons to crystallize your ideas. Create symbols, metaphors, personification, or other types of figurative language to bring abstract ideas to life. Notice how in the second stanza of her song Tracy Chapman uses a metaphor, "a taste of justice," to make the mother's advice tangible and understandable. Experiment with figurative language that will give your ideas the same qualities.

5. Play with sound, rhythm, and repetition. Try reading your lyric aloud as you refine the format. You may want to use alliteration, or the repetition of the initial consonant sounds of words within a line, to add texture to the sound of your lyrics. You may want to try repeating certain phrases. As you experiment, pay attention to the repetition. Does it underscore your ideas, suggest an appealing playfulness, or add a striking rhythm? Be sure the repetitions or other sound effects are consistent with the message of your lyrics.

REVIEWING YOUR WRITING

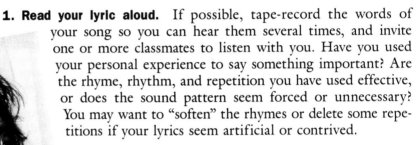

John Lennon, member of the Beatles, who later wrote and produced several solo albums

1. Read your lyric aloud. If possible, tape-record the words of your song so you can hear them several times, and invite one or more classmates to listen with you. Have you used your personal experience to say something important? Are the rhyme, rhythm, and repetition you have used effective, or does the sound pattern seem forced or unnecessary? You may want to "soften" the rhymes or delete some repetitions if your lyrics seem artificial or contrived.

2. Evaluate the form of your song. Do the stanzas express individual ideas? If not, is the flow of ideas from one stanza to the next clear? Do the lines break in reasonable ways? If you used a refrain, does it become more meaningful or powerful each time it appears? Do the grammar, punctuation, and capitalization you have used help to convey your message?

3. Rewrite your lyrics. Revise your lyrics, incorporating your own and your classmates' suggestions into a final draft. Proofread the draft carefully.

4. If possible, add music. You may want to write your own music or ask a musically talented friend or teacher to collaborate with you on your song. Be sure that the music you add is consistent with the mood and message of your lyrics.

PUBLISHING AND PRESENTING

Imagine, one of Lennon's most successful albums

- **Sing your song.** If you have put your song to music, perform it for a group or ask a friend to do so. If you do not yet have music, read it aloud to an audience just as you would read a poem.
- **Send your song lyric to a music publisher.** Books such as *Song Writer's Market* list music publishers and give suggestions for submitting song lyrics.

Sentence

Analyzing Sentences

By analyzing and imitating sentences by professional writers, you will learn to use different structures to achieve variety and richness in your own writing. The first two Sentence Composing lessons introduce you to general techniques for sentence elaboration: analyzing, unscrambling, imitating, combining, and expanding sentences. In the remaining lessons, you will practice specific methods for elaborating on clauses and sentences.

Notice the differences in structure in each of the three sentences below, describing pilots on an aircraft carrier.

MODELS

1. As streaks of light appeared in the east, pilots came on deck.
2. Bundled like animals awakened from hibernation, they waddled purposefully to their jets.
3. The last to climb aboard was Cag, stocky and round like a snowball.

James A. Michener, _The Bridges at Toko-Ri_

To analyze these sentences, break them into parts. Notice how each part relates to the parts that come before and after it.

1. As streaks of light appeared / in the east, / pilots came on deck.
2. Bundled like animals / awakened from hibernation, / they waddled purposefully to their jets.
3. The last to climb aboard / was Cag, / stocky and round / like a snowball.

A. Identifying Imitations   Break the sentences below each model into parts similar to those shown above. Then identify the sentence that has the same structure as the model.

Model: As streaks of light appeared in the east, pilots came on deck.

1. a. The car missed and backfired, a jolt that got his attention.
   b. While their parents lounged at poolside, kids splashed in the ocean.

Model: Bundled like animals awakened from hibernation, they waddled purposefully to their jets.

2. a. Filled with chocolate imported from Belgium, it rested alluringly on the dessert tray.
   b. From the wire shelf under his chair, Sam grabbed an armful of books, getting up.

Model: The last to climb aboard was Cag, stocky and round like a snowball.

3. a. When she heard her name on the loudspeaker, she slouched back down on the bench.
   b. The first to come home was Gram, hearty and warm as fresh-baked bread.

B. Unscrambling Sentences The sentence parts below are similar in structure to the parts of the models they follow. Unscramble each group of sentence parts. Then write them in an order that matches the order of their model. Punctuate as the models are punctuated.

Example	As streaks of light appeared in the east, pilots came on deck. a. with her key b. after the doctor on call arrived c. students poured into the health center
Unscrambled Sentence	After the doctor on call arrived with her key, students poured into the health center.

Model: As streaks of light appeared in the east, pilots came on deck.

1. a. carriages clattered down the lane
   b. while buses with tourists traveled
   c. on the highway

2. a. toward the fence
   b. one blade caught on a rock
   c. when the lawnmower turned

Model: Bundled like animals awakened from hibernation, they waddled purposefully to their jets.

3. a. it shone beautifully in the sunshine
   b. gleaming like a tabletop
   c. polished with wax

4. a. filled with cookies and milk
   b. satisfied as little kids
   c. they returned gladly to their chores

Model: The last to climb aboard was Cag, stocky and round like a snowball.

5. a. efficient and sleek as silver bullets
   b. were the computers
   c. the first to start up

6. a. was the mouse
   b. quick and elusive as lightning
   c. the hardest to catch

C. Imitating Sentences Write a sentence that imitates the structure of each model sentence below. Major parts of each model are separated by slash marks (/). Punctuate your sentences as the models are punctuated.

1. There, / above the cloud now, / reappears the rocket, / only a very bright star, / diminishing every second.
   Anne Morrow Lindbergh, "The Bird Perched for Flight"

2. Long before the sun / struck the face of Lookout Mountain, / curls of smoke rose / from the earth houses at its feet. **Mari Sandoz, "The Birdman"**

3. They wanted to hurl themselves / over the fence, / into the street, / and shake the truth out of his collar. **Gwendolyn Brooks, "Home"**

4. He fell back, / exhausted, / his ankle pounding.
   Ralph Ellison, "Flying Home"

5. The snow was fine, / falling gently, / not yet making an impression on the pavement. **Truman Capote, "Miriam"**

Application Write a paragraph describing a scene involving many people (for example, a group of busy workers and customers in a fast-food restaurant). In your paragraph, include sentences that imitate two or more of the model sentences in this lesson. Notice how these sentences add variety to your writing.

Grammar Refresher Some model sentences in this lesson are simple (containing only one clause); others are complex (containing a main clause and one or more subordinate clauses). For more on simple and complex sentences, see Handbook 32, pages 629–635.

Sketchbook

Photographer Dorothea Lange traveled throughout rural America in the 1930's, documenting the plight of poor people during the Depression. Lange made these notes about the photograph below of a migrant farm worker, taken at a camp in California:

Migrant mother and children, 1938.
Photograph by Dorthea Lange

Camped at the edge of a pea field where the crop had failed in a freeze. The tires had just been sold from the car to buy food. She was thirty-two years old with seven children.

What stories do you see in people around you?

Additional Sketches

Imagine that you are the first reporter on the scene of a major news story—either a recent event or an incident from history. Describe what you see.

Write a dialogue between yourself and someone you admire but have never met. It could be someone famous or unknown, living or dead.

Observation and Description

Guided Assignment
THE INTERVIEW PROFILE

Related Assignment
EYEWITNESS REPORT

Related Assignment
ORAL HISTORY

You head for the airport to pick up an uncle you have never met. How will you recognize him? How will he recognize you? You and your uncle will need to call on your observation and description skills to give each other an accurate picture of yourselves.

As a writer, you can use these same skills to make your vision of people, places, things, and events come alive. In the next three assignments, you will have the opportunity to hone your own observation and description skills by writing a profile of another person, an eyewitness report, and an oral history.

Interview Profile

"Artist"

FROM *THE NEW YORKER*

Pick up any magazine, and the chances are good that many of the articles will be profiles of interesting people. A profile draws a word picture of a person, providing the reader with a close-up introduction. Reading a profile is like having a short, but intense, encounter with the person who is its subject.

As you read this profile from *The New Yorker,* notice how the writer uses description, details, and dialogue to relate a distinct impression of an unusual artist.

The first question that people ask Hani Shihada, a Jordanian-American artist who draws copies of Michelangelo and Raphael in pastels on the pavement, is "What is it that you do?" The other afternoon, for instance, while Mr. Shihada was in the middle of his latest major work—a pavement triptych . . . a young woman . . . came up, said she was an art director, looked at his work, and then asked him what it was he did. "Are you an artist?" she said.

Without looking up (he was carefully laying down a striated pattern of dark blues, violets, and whites . . .), Mr. Shihada said yes, he was an artist. The young woman asked, "Well, what *kind* of an artist are you?" Mr. Shihada explained that he was the kind of artist who draws copies of Michelangelo in pastels on the pavement of Manhattan. "Oh," she said, and then—perhaps thinking that she was being got at in some subtle way, but still determined to be *appreciative*—she asked him if he had a rep [representative], or something, who might be able to show her some of his work.

"New York is a very strange place," Mr. Shihada said after she left. "If I am copying Michelangelo and Raphael on the pavement, it must be in order to draw attention to my own work, someplace else. I try to tell people, I do this in order to be doing it."

Mr. Shihada, who was born in Jerusalem and grew up in Jordan, began his career as a sidewalk artist in Perugia. "In Italy, this kind of art is a very old tradition," he said. "It was first done centuries ago by unfortunate people, without legs. They drew Madonnas of Raphael on the pavement, and they became known as *madonnari*. Now it is a profession, a métier. I tried first in Perugia—a Madonna of Raphael, very badly drawn. People encouraged me, however. Then I met an American girl, we were married, and I told her that I would continue my profession in New York. I drew my first work here in 1985—a Delphic Sibyl in Washington Square. I did well, and I have kept on. An Israeli artist named Dani showed me how to make my own pastels—that is my only expense. I have worked south as far as the World Trade Center, where I did a scene from the Creation, and north as far as the Bronx—two saints. Mostly, though, I do Sibyls and Prophets, Sibyls and Prophets, all over the West Side."

Mr. Shihada works from April to October every year. It takes him about five days to complete a major figure group. He uses black pastel to lay out the outlines of his figures, in a free, dancing hand, and then slowly fills in each area with stripes of pastel and smooths them together with his hand or a small piece of plastic foam so that the highlights merge fluidly into the surrounding colors. As he works, he glances at a collection of extreme-close-up black-and-white photographs of the Sistine Chapel from a book published in 1948. "It's good—the only useful book," Mr. Shihada says. "You can see the brushwork, the modelling." (Much of what looks like freehand, Expressionist inflection in his Sibyls and Prophets is in fact a faithful rendering of the outsize detail in the book.)

Since Mr. Shihada works from black-and-white photographs, he has to choose colors himself; he visited the Sistine Chapel once, eleven years ago, but he cannot remember all the colors in the frescoes. Generally, he chooses bright colors; the background of the figure blowing the Trumpet of Doom in the Broadway piece, for instance, is mixed orange and yellow. When Mr. Shihada began in New York, he received a certain amount of gentle, condescending advice from amateur art critics—they would suggest that his coloring was too bright. Then the Sistine Ceiling was cleaned. "I was not surprised," he says calmly. "Only timid, frightened men use dark colors. Michelangelo was not a timid and frightened man." Mr. Shihada is particularly proud of the deep look his pastels take on after a rainfall. His colors are not water soluble. "What happens when it rains?" is the second question everyone asks him.

Mr. Shihada makes a living from contributions that passersby throw in the tray where he keeps his pastels. His one regret is that he cannot often see his children—a boy and a girl. (He is divorced from his first wife.) They live upstate, and he draws every day, usually from 3 P.M. to 2 A.M. When his children visit, he takes them to museums, and he buys them toys. "The turtles. Ten dollars apiece: Raphael, Michelangelo . . ."

A man in an Italian-silk suit walks up and looks very carefully at Mr. Shihada's picture. He nods—a man who knows his Michelangelo. "What do you do? You're an artist?" he asks. Mr. Shihada nods. "Well, listen," the man says. "I have interests in some restaurants around here. They might not look bad with some decoration." Then, bending down and leaning over Mr. Shihada's shoulder, his shoes planted amid the heroic figures and only a couple of feet from the four beautiful Muses, the man says, "Not to put *pressure* on you, or anything, but you just might find it in your interest to let me have a look at some of your work."

Think AND Respond

The author of the profile of Hani Shihada uses words to paint a portrait of the man. What did you learn about Hani Shihada as an artist? What did you learn about his personality? Why does the author include quotations from people other than Hani Shihada in the profile? Think about an interesting person you know who could be the subject of an interview profile.

INVITATION TO Write

The profile you have just read gives a distinct impression of an uncommon artist. Now write a profile, based on observation and interviews, about a person you know or would like to know. Use the following suggestions for guidelines as you write.

A profile can let you get to know its subject personally and up close. It will probably tell you something about the person's accomplishments, opinions, and beliefs, but it can also probe the subject's background, formative experiences, family, habits, and lifestyle. Many profiles tell about people who are public figures because they are rich and famous, but profiles can be equally successful when they shed light on the personalities and experiences of everyday people from all walks of life.

A good profile satisfies our curiosity about what people are really like and the ways they differ from or resemble us. This type of writing has applications in a variety of academic and vocational fields, including literature, social studies, journalism, police work, psychology, and medicine.

PREWRITE AND EXPLORE

1. Become familiar with profiles. Profiles based on personal observation and interviews are one of the most popular types of articles in magazines and in newspaper feature sections. To familiarize yourself with different approaches to writing profiles, read profiles in a variety of publications and also look at character sketches in your literature book.

2. Look for people to profile. Think of the people you encounter every day. Who intrigues you? Who do you think has an interesting story to tell? Whom would you like to know more about? You may wish to try one or more of these activities to help you find subjects for your profile.

HANDBOOKS
FOR HELP & PRACTICE

**Personal Techniques,
pp. 339–342**
**Sources of Information,
pp. 512–513**
**Listening Skills,
pp. 541–542**

Exploratory Activities

- **Whom do you know?** Think about friends, family members, neighbors, and other acquaintances. Make a list of people who might have an interesting story to tell.
- **Whom do you want to know?** Whom do you admire? Who has an interesting or unusual job or profession? Freewrite about the people in your school or community you would like to know.
- **What are your interests?** Is there a subject, a career, or a hobby that you're particularly interested in or one you'd like to learn more about? One way to learn is to get to know the people involved. Make a list of activities; list possible people to profile from each activity.
- **Who are your classmates?** You are surrounded by interesting characters and personalities. Select a few classmates and freewrite some descriptions and questions you have about the people you choose.
- **Which literary characters do you remember?** Think about compelling characters out of the pages of literature—such as the members of the Snopes family in "Barn Burning" by William Faulkner. Do they remind you of anyone you might use as a character for your profile?

Veterinarian treating a turtle in the Metro Zoo, Miami, Florida.

3. Select a subject. Freewrite about some of the ideas you generated through doing the Exploratory Activities to see if you can identify one you would like to pursue. You also may wish to check the writing you did for the Sketchbook on page 50 or the "Apply Your Skills" section on page 67 for ideas. As an additional option, the whole class might want to produce a collection of profiles that includes every class member.

4. Gather background information. To write an effective profile, you need to know as much about your subject as possible. Look for anything that has been written about your subject or that your subject has written. Also learn about your subject's area of expertise so that you can ask informed questions.

5. Interview others. Talking to people who know your subject can give you insights that will make both your writing and your interview with your subject richer.

6. Interview your subject. When you contact your subject, clearly state your purpose and ask to set up an interview. Then when you conduct the interview, keep these points in mind.

- **Come prepared with a list of good questions.** Ask probing questions that will invite revealing answers—answers that will show what your subject is really like.

- **Show a genuine interest in your subject's answers.** If *you* are genuinely interested, you will be aware of opportunities for follow-up questions—questions that you cannot prepare in advance but that will occur to you in the course of a lively interview. Notice the opportunity for more information that was lost in the following exchange when the interviewer stayed strictly to the prepared list of questions and did not follow up on the answers:

  > **Interviewer:** "Tell me about your family."
  > **Subject:** "I come from a family of nine children."
  > **Interviewer:** "Do you have any hobbies?"

  A student who was genuinely interested in the subject would surely want to find out what it was like to live in a family with so many children and how the subject felt about growing up in such a large family.

- **Do not interrupt.** Give your subject time to respond to your questions. Often a little silence on your part can do more to encourage your subject to disclose additional information than any new questions you might ask.

- **Capture actual speech.** When taking notes, try to capture some of the flavor of your subject's speech. You don't need to write down everything that is said, just a few characteristic phrases or quotable sentences.

 Writer's Choice You can rely on your written notes, or you can take along a tape recorder to capture nuances of meaning. If you plan to tape the interview, be sure to request permission first.

One student, Sheri, for years had been curious about her father's experiences as a soldier during the Vietnam War. She decided to write a profile about him, focusing on how the war affected him. You will follow the evolving of Sheri's essay in the rest of this workshop. Notice the questions that Sheri wrote down in preparation for interviewing her father.

PROBLEM SOLVING

How can I prepare questions that might serve as a springboard to deeper insights?

1. When and why did you join the service?
2. Knowing what you know now, would you do it again?
3. What were your responsibilities in the service?
4. How did your anticipation of war compare with the reality?
5. How accurate is Hollywood's portrayal of war?
6. How long were you in Vietnam?
7. What kinds of dangers did you face?
8. How did you feel when it was time to come home?
9. Did you have trouble readjusting to civilian life?
10. What did you learn from the experience?

7. Gather details. Throughout your research, and especially during your interview with your subject, keep your eye out for interesting details. Note your subject's characteristic way of dressing, moving, or gesturing. Look for telling details in your subject's possessions and surroundings, such as a favorite photograph, or distinctive or unusual furnishings. Also look for anecdotes, key phrases, and comments that seem to characterize your subject.

8. Identify your purpose and goals. Your overall purpose is to present a portrait of the person you are profiling, but you may have goals that are more personal. For example, you may want to learn more about someone you find fascinating, or draw attention to someone you think is noteworthy.

9. Identify your audience. Before you begin drafting your profile, consider who your readers will be. If you are writing for classmates about a classmate, you may be able to assume your audience will understand informal phrases and references commonly used by members of your class. However, if you are writing for a broader audience, or if you are writing about someone who uses specialized terms, be sure to use more formal language and explain all unfamiliar references.

Writing
——TIP——

Share your notes and any other information with a small group of writers. See what angle *others* see emerging.

D RAFT AND DISCOVER

1. Look for a dominant impression or angle. As you begin drafting, keep in mind that effective profiles tend to offer a particular angle of vision on their subjects. They present a dominant impression of their subject, usually by emphasizing one aspect of the subject's personality or lifestyle, or else they focus on some special dimension of a subject's life. For example, the profile of Hani Shihada from *The New Yorker* focused on his commitment to his art. You might emphasize your subject's occupation or interest—athlete, aspiring actor, future teacher, pet lover, music enthusiast, computer wizard—ideas, opinions, or personal history.

HANDBOOKS
FOR HELP & PRACTICE

Point of View, pp. 458–463

Dialogue in Nonfiction, pp. 464–465

Character, pp. 468–470

Your angle on your subject will serve you in much the same way as a thesis does: it will help to bind together the varied details and anecdotes of your profile into a coherent essay.

2. Organize your draft. Profiles can be organized in many ways. Often, profiles are presented as narratives that tell the story of the interview, like the *The New Yorker* profile of Hani Shihada. Others are a series of sketches, showing the subject in a variety of characteristic activities. Some are organized by presenting the subject's views on a series of topics.

 Writer's Choice Do you want to present your profile as a first-person narrative, with you as a participant, or do you want to present it from a more objective third-person point of view?

PROBLEM

S O L V I N G

**Which strategies
can I use
to present a
strong profile?**

3. Elaborate on ideas. You may find one or more of the following strategies for writing helpful in focusing your thinking as you present your impressions of your subject.

Strategies

- **Description** Use description rich in details and figurative language to bring your subject to life on the page. If your subject's surroundings are relevant to understanding him or her, also describe them using concrete, sensory language.
- **Comparison and contrast** Compare your subject to someone else, or use analogies and metaphors to highlight aspects of his or her personality. Be sure to develop your comparison adequately by including specific details and examples.
- **Dialogue** Use dialogue to reveal your character's personality and distinctive way of talking. Notice how the profile from *The New Yorker* uses dialogue to present both Hani Shihada's views and the reactions of others to his work.

Notice that to give her readers a more complete picture of her father, Sheri began her draft with a description of how he looked and acted as they began the interview. To strengthen the picture, she used a simile to describe his actions.

COMPUTER
—TIP—

**Before revising,
copy your draft
into a new docu-
ment; in case you
later change your
mind about some
of the revisions,
you will still have
your original copy.**

ONE STUDENT'S PROCESS

As my dad folded his large frame into the big recliner directly across from me, I could tell he was getting nervous. Crossing and uncrossing his legs several times, he couldn't seem to find a comfortable position—although this was his favorite chair. His fingers tapped on the chair arms like a drummer trying to pick up the rhythm of an unfamiliar piece.

4. Take a break. After completing your draft, set it aside. Then review it and ask your peer readers to respond to it.

REVIEW YOUR WRITING

Questions for Yourself

- Does the personality of my subject come through in my writing?
- Do I accurately present my subject's thoughts?
- Have I presented a vivid description of my subject and his or her surroundings?
- Have I found a strong angle, or is my profile a collection of random pieces of information?

Questions for Your Peer Readers

- What is the dominant impression you have of my subject?
- Is there anything in my essay that is unclear or irrelevant?
- Which sentences or passages in my essay stand out for you as particularly vivid or memorable?
- What do I tell about in my essay that you would like to know more about? less about?

Writing **TIP**

Have your subject read your draft to correct any factual errors or to elaborate on unclear or insufficient information.

REVISE YOUR WRITING

1. Evaluate your responses. Consider how you want to rewrite your essay. Remember that you are free to use or to ignore the advice and observations of your readers. Also keep in mind these guidelines, which are often used to evaluate profiles.

Standards for Evaluation

An effective profile . . .

- presents a dominant impression of the subject.
- uses facts, anecdotes, and description to draw a vivid picture of the subject.
- clearly and accurately presents the thoughts of the subject.
- employs a consistent tone and point of view.
- uses a logical and effective organizational pattern.
- uses transitional words and phrases to show relationships among ideas.

HANDBOOKS
FOR HELP & PRACTICE

Incorporating Peer Responses, p. 425

2. Problem-solve. Decide what changes you want to make and then rework your draft. Sheri made these changes to a portion of her draft in response to some comments she received.

ONE STUDENT'S PROCESS

He started our conversation slowly, not revealing too much. My dad He joined the service in 1963. because He figured that he'd be drafted eventually, so this way he might be able to get a meaningful job instead of being an infantryman. (Infantrymen do most of the fighting.) "Now that he looks back, he I can't think I guess he probably wouldn't have been drafted. I think I could have applied for an occupational deferment." Given the choice to do it again, however, he would have done exactly the same thing. "What was my option? To run from my duty and from my responsibility? I couldn't do that."

"I was twenty-two when I join ed, single, and a graduate of Purdue University. In 1965 I got married and was stationed in Georgia. My base was in a very beautiful part of the state. I've never been back there since, and I'm not sure it would seem quite as beautiful to me now. Six months later, I was teaching some young troops, eighteen- and nineteen-year-olds, how to throw grenades."

3. Proofread your work. Prepare a clean copy of your essay, incorporating all the revisions you have decided to make. Then reread your revised essay, keeping your eyes open for errors in the punctuation of quotations.

Grammar
—**TIP**—
Switch papers with a peer reader and read each other's quotations aloud, checking for the correct use of quotation marks.

LINKING
GRAMMAR AND WRITING
Punctuating Lengthy Dialogue

When the exact words of the speaker extend beyond one paragraph, omit the quotation marks at the end of the first paragraph. Then begin the next paragraph with quotation marks and also place quotation marks after the speaker's final words. Notice how quotations marks are used in the following example:

In response to my question, Dr. Johnson said, "People should be aware that they need to take care of their animals' teeth. This means, for example, that owners should brush their dogs' teeth. Let me explain a little further.

"Because veterinary medicine has become more sophisticated, pets are living longer. If an animal's teeth are not taken care of, the teeth will decay before the animal reaches an advanced age and the animal will lose its teeth, in much the same way that people can lose theirs."

See Grammar Handbook 40 for additional help with this problem.

PUBLISH AND PRESENT

- **Submit your profile to a newspaper or magazine.** Contact the feature section of your school or community newspaper or a magazine.
- **Post your profile on the classroom bulletin board.** Place a photograph of your subject alongside it.
- **Do a videotape profile.** If appropriate, capture your subject working, as the written piece from *The New Yorker* does.
- **Collect all the profiles written by class members.** Bind them into a single anthology.
- **Save your work in your writing portfolio.**

HANDBOOKS
FOR HELP & PRACTICE
Speech Preparation/ Delivery, pp. 515–517
Sharing and Publishing, pp. 427–428

War

Sheri Preo

Uses vivid description and a simile to show what subject is like today and to establish a dominant impression of a man deeply affected by war

As my dad folded his large frame into the big recliner directly across from me, I could tell he was getting nervous. Crossing and uncrossing his legs several times, he couldn't seem to find a comfortable position—although this was his favorite chair. His fingers tapped on the chair arms like a drummer trying to pick up the rhythm of an unfamiliar piece. In his eyes I saw something other than nervousness—a combination of anxiety, fear, and perhaps even excitement. It was obvious that the memories he was about to recount were still very much alive and that the Vietnam War had had a profound influence on his life.

Presents the interview as a narrative story

He started our conversation slowly, not revealing too much. My dad joined the service in 1963 because he figured that he'd be drafted eventually, so this way he might be able to get a meaningful job instead of being an infantryman. (Infantrymen do most of the fighting.) "Now that I look back, I don't think I would have been drafted. I think I could have applied for an occupational deferment."

Given the chance to do it again, however, he would have done exactly the same thing. "What was my option? To run from my duty and from my responsibility? I couldn't do that.

Uses quotations to present the thoughts and feelings of the subject

"I was twenty-two when I joined, single, and a graduate of Purdue University. In 1965, I got married and was stationed in Georgia. Six months later I was teaching some young troops, eighteen- and nineteen-year-olds, how to throw grenades."

His orders for Vietnam soon came through. He was given thirty days before he had to report to Ton Son Nuit Airbase in Vietnam. Some of his friends chipped in for a trip to Florida for him and his wife before he was to go to Vietnam. They wanted to make sure he carried some happy memories with him to Vietnam in case he never came back. "It was really like that—that final," he told me.

He flew to Vietnam from Oakland, California, along with about two hundred other soldiers. "I wasn't prepared for war at all, except for being vaccinated. In fact, I'd say I was excited about going. I was filled with heroic images from old war movies and was eager for action."

He was a military policeman in Saigon, in charge of traffic control and security of the city. He was given the order to shoot on sight if <u>anyone</u> was out past curfew, and he did.

"The recent movies about the war are fairly accurate," my dad asserted. "Now I can see them without getting upset, but it's taken me a long time to get to this point. One thing wrong with the movies, though, is that they portray too much action; they show men fighting constantly. In reality, we would fight for about two hours and then have plenty of downtime. The combination of boredom and fear of the next attack kept me on edge and made me question what I was really doing there."

During my dad's off-hours, he would go to the VAA (Vietnamese American Association) across town to teach English to the Vietnamese. This was a chance for him to get to know the people better and to make a little

Has a clear focus—the mid-1960's and war experiences of the subject.

Details show the realities of war.

money. He also spent some of his free time at movies, which would come around a couple of times each week.

My dad can still vividly remember when he found out he was going home. He had been counting down the days for the past year because he had known his ETS (estimated time of separation) from the moment he hit country, or got to Vietnam. On his last day, he had to report to deportation depot, a place where he was given shots and his papers were processed. Soldiers waited at the depot for planes to take them to the military airport in California. My dad ended up waiting four or five days before space was available on a plane.

Facts explain the danger of the situation and agitation of the subject

As it turned out, these last few days were the days that he was in gravest danger. Agitated, my dad began relating the story. "On my first night there, the depot was attacked. It was a perfect target for the enemy because of all of the Americans who were there. The barracks next door to mine went under fire. Four men died. I was scared and angry. It seemed so unfair that we had made it this far, and now some of us still would not make it home. I would have done anything to get on a plane," he said.

Sums up the subject's reactions to his experience

When he finally did board the plane and the engine started, he experienced a feeling he's never had since. Shifting in his seat and finally smiling, my dad said, "I can't remember more adrenaline flowing or more excitement. And when we landed in California, my buddies and I ran down the steps of the plane and kissed the ground. I can't describe how wonderful it was to be home at last!"

WRITER TO WRITER

Writing a profile is an invitation to seek out interesting people, learn from their experiences, and at least for a short time, become a part of their lives.

Wayne Swanson, journalist and editor

1. Reflect on your writing. Write an introductory letter to your profile essay evaluating its effectiveness. Tell what you were trying to accomplish in it and discuss how well you think you accomplished your goals. What advice would you now give yourself if you were about to write another profile essay? Attach your introductory letter to your essay when you submit it to your teacher or when you place it in your portfolio.

2. Apply your skills. Use your skill to try one or more of the following activities.

- **Cross-curricular** Interview a teacher from a department other than English. Focus on what makes his or her area of expertise so fascinating to him or her. Provide that teacher with a copy of your finished profile. Then submit the profile for publication in the school newspaper.
- **Literature** Imagine that you were able to interview a literary character who has made an impression on you, such as the narrator in "The Open Boat" or Nicholas Nickleby in Dickens's novel. In your profile, focus on what the character has to say about his or her life.
- **General** Interview an out-of-town friend or relative by telephone. Prepare your list of questions in advance and take notes on the answers, just as you would in a face-to-face interview. You could also mail your list of questions and ask the subject to respond by writing a letter or recording a cassette tape. Your profile should include quotes taken directly from the letter or transcribed from the tape.
- **Related assignments** Use the suggestions on pages 70–78 to write an eyewitness report and create an oral history.

FOR YOUR **PORTFOLIO**

Nicholas Nickleby, a novel by Charles Dickens, concerns a young man who must overcome tremendous hardships in Victorian England.

Eyewitness Report

FROM

"THESE PEOPLE HAVE NO FEAR"

BETTE BAO LORD

Every day, you are an eyewitness to events happening around you. They may be small, seemingly inconsequential moments, but they could turn out to have a lasting significance.

Bette Bao Lord was an eyewitness to history one day in 1989. She was in Beijing, China, when the Chinese Democracy Movement took to the streets. The demonstrations were ultimately crushed in a bloody massacre, but Lord filed this eyewitness report during the heady time when it appeared the Democracy Movement would bring sweeping change to China. As you read, notice how she captures the excitement of the moment.

It is dark. A cameraman, a veteran of world events, returns from shooting in the Square of Heavenly Peace with tears brimming in his eyes. Applause had greeted him every step of the way. Nowadays prying foreign devils are no longer suspect.

I sit inside the Shangri-la Hotel surrounded by telephones, but they seldom ring. Can everyone be out? My television is never off, but on American channels there are no new images, only the recooking of old rice. On Chinese channels, the redishing of Li Peng's speech to staid party loyalists.

Too jittery to stay put, I stroll outside. There is a full moon, a gentle breeze and crowds of hundreds at each intersection. *One, two, three, ho!* Middle-school students are pushing huge concrete cylinders to form barriers in strategic places on the road. Everywhere neighbors chat. At their feet, enough bottled water to last the vigil. I pass a row of blind men and women who have walked miles to be there. "When the convoys come, we'll lie across the road. We must. Didn't that grand prime minister of ours extend us a personal invitation?"

A car approaches and is quickly surrounded by people drawn to it like iron shavings to a magnet. I climb atop a trash container to see above the sea of black-haired citizens. There is no pushing or shoving, only persuasive talk. The car backs up to choruses of hallelujahs and wild clapping. My spirits soar as I step down from my perch. Nowadays Chinese hearts are one.

I read homemade signs. "Kind people, protect the students." I hear the debunking of the old, the extolling of the young. I sense a new self-confidence and a new self-respect that are infectious.

A peasant drives past hauling the rusty remains of an abandoned bus to be off-loaded closer to the square. How the cheers must swell him with pride.

A van filled with plain-clothed soldiers blasts forth, only to be halted by concrete and completely enveloped by people 20 deep. Over a portable bullhorn, a student calls for discipline and calm. The vehicle is courteously pushed back two blocks and allowed to return whence it came.

These people have no fear. They think the People's Liberation Army will never hurt them. Maybe not, but what of the riot police with their shields, helmets and billy clubs? I escape my imagination by retreating to this typewriter. . . .

INVITATION
TO
Write

Bette Bao Lord crafted a compelling eyewitness account of the demonstrations for democracy in China in 1989. Now write your own eyewitness report about an event that has personal or historical significance.

An eyewitness report, like an interview, requires careful and accurate observation and recording. In fact, because an eyewitness reporter has the advantage of being at the scene of the action, readers expect the writer to provide those special, specific details that make an event come to life: the particulars of how one burning building set an entire block ablaze; the feelings and thoughts of the protestors at a demonstration; the sights, sounds, and smells of the county fair on opening day. A good eyewitness report captures a special moment in time and reveals all of its aspects for the readers.

DEVELOPING AN EYEWITNESS REPORT

HANDBOOKS
FOR HELP & PRACTICE

Observing,
p. 340
Chronological Order,
pp. 363–364
Quotations,
pp. 381, 398–399
Using Words
Precisely,
pp. 434–439
Dialogue in
Nonfiction,
pp. 464–465

1. Practice the art of observation. Wherever you may be during the day—in a classroom, on the street, at home—become aware of what is going on around you. Use your five senses to focus your observations. What do you hear, see, touch, taste, and smell? In the excerpt, for example, Lord notes both the full moon and the gentle breeze and then goes on to include the shouts of the middle-school children "One, two, three, ho!" as they push barriers in place. These are the kinds of details needed to make a scene come alive for a reader.

2. Find an event to witness and report on. For the next week or two, carry a small notebook with you wherever you go. Use it to record the particular events you witness that might make interesting eyewitness reports. Keep in mind that eyewitness reports are written not just about events of great significance, such as revolutions. An account of a brief, intimate moment between a father and his young child at a park can be just as compelling as the story of a dramatic police chase through downtown streets at high noon. You might spend an afternoon observing the workings of a small claims court, take in an appearance by a national politician, or attend a concert or a sporting event. Local newspapers often include listings of upcoming events you may want to attend. Wherever you go, look and listen for special moments you'd like to share with readers.

 Writer's Choice Do you wish to write your eyewitness account in the present tense in order to accomplish a sense of immediacy?

The Chinese gambled they could force their leaders to reform. Two weeks before the Tiananmen Square Revolt, they crafted a "Spirit of Liberty" from Styrofoam and plaster.

3. Take careful and complete notes. Start out by writing down the *who? what? where? when?* and *why?* of the situation you are recording. Then jot down the sensory details that accompany the situation. Don't trust your memory—write down everything you observe, even those details that seem minor or insignificant. Later you can select the most appropriate details for your eyewitness account.

4. Enhance your report with direct quotes. On-the-spot interviews or reporting the reactions of others can add authenticity and human interest to your report and will enhance your reader's sense of "being there." Think about the impact that the words of the blind people had on you as you read the excerpt. "When the convoys come, we will lie across the road. We must. . . . " The people's words give you a sense of the atmosphere far more eloquently than the author's description could have.

Writing ——**TIP**——
You may find it helpful to tape-record some parts of the event, such as speeches and on-the-spot interviews.

5. Take photographs. If you have access to a camera, one or two photographs taken at the scene will add to your memories of the event. Don't rely on photographs, however, to take the place of your notes.

DRAFTING YOUR EYEWITNESS REPORT

1. Begin with some attention-grabbing aspect of the event. Remember that a good eyewitness report gives the reader a sense of having been there. So, as you begin drafting, forget for a moment about the specifics of the event and recall the dominant mood or the central significance. The excerpt, for example, begins with a reference to a cameraman "with tears brimming in his eyes" who has been met with cheers and applause and who is no longer thought of as one of the "prying foreign devils." Such an incident illustrates the spirit of change that Lord wishes to convey in her account.

2. Draft your report logically. Most eyewitness accounts are organized chronologically. This type of organization provides the account with a strong narrative flow, enables the readers to follow the action easily, and enhances the readers' identification with the event. In some accounts, such as the excerpt about the Chinese demonstrations, the writer may choose to include spatial organization, reporting on actions one by one similar to the way a camera would record them. This too, enhances the reader's sense of participation. However you organize your account, keep in mind the dominant feeling, mood, or tone you want to impart as you draft.

3. Include all important details of the event. As you draft, refer often to the notes you made. Be sure you include all of the significant details that will make your account memorable to your readers. Weave these details into the fabric of your account so they occur naturally.

4. Use precise verbs and sensory language. Your purpose is to relate what you experienced in vivid enough detail so that your audience can imagine the event clearly and personally. So choose words and images that will fire your readers' imaginations. For example, in the excerpt, the writer's comparison of people drawn to the approaching car like "iron shavings to a magnet" give a graphic sense of the spontaneous movement of the crowds in the square.

Writing
TIP

If you were unable to write down someone's exact words, you can paraphrase his or her remarks. Remember not to use quotation marks when you paraphrase.

1. Reread your draft. Does your account accurately reflect what you observed? Have you made the importance of the event clear? Have you included all of the important facts of the event? Have you reported the views of the other participants, if appropriate?

2. Have a classmate read your draft. Ask whether you have communicated the mood or overall point you intended. Do your language and your choice of quotations bring the scene to life for your peer reader? Ask whether you need to clarify anything so that your audience will feel as if they witnessed the event.

3. Revise your report. Incorporate your own ideas and your classmate's suggestions. Check to see that you have correctly identified the people you interviewed and quoted them accurately. Proofread and correct any spelling, punctuation, usage, and grammar errors.

PUBLISHING AND PRESENTING

- **Publish your eyewitness report.** Present your eyewitness report to your school or community paper as a feature story. Include any photographs you may have taken.
- **Make your report part of the yearbook.** If your report relates to a school event, submit it to your class yearbook committee. Again, include any photographs you have taken.

In the Garden No. 201, by Jennifer Bartlett, 1983

Oral History

Anna Tutt

AS TOLD TO

LYNN BUTLER

Have you ever listened to an older person—a grandparent, or an uncle or neighbor, perhaps—tell stories about how things were in "the good old days" and wished that you could tape-record his or her words? Fortunately, many such *oral histories* have been recorded. In fact, oral history is an ancient form of literature that flourished even among people who had no written language, much less tape recorders.

The selection on these pages is from a collection of oral histories based on interviews conducted by some students in Georgia. Notice how student Lynn Butler has allowed Anna Tutt to tell her story in her own characteristic language.

We lived on a large farm in Columbia County, Georgia, when I was small. My father was a tenant farmer and we lived in a house there on the land.

We children had chores to do. One of them was getting the cows to and from the pasture— that was fun! We'd have a row of cows going down the road toward the pasture, and sometimes they'd get on the other side of the creek that ran through the pasture when it had been raining, and the water would get up and they couldn't get back across until the water subsided.

We used to go to school through pine thickets and broom sage, because it was a bit of a ways there. If we had fried rabbit in our lunch pail, we'd sit so everybody could see it. That was a big treat. But if we had peas and cornbread or something like that, we'd always turn our backs and sit on a log to eat it, because that wasn't very special.

School was fun then, really. We'd sit on benches and there was a big old stove in the center of the room to keep us warm. It took me the longest time to learn my ABC's. I could say them by heart but I didn't know what they looked like. And I used to read by the pictures. If I saw a picture of a bird or a kite in the primer, I'd just say "bird" or "kite" when the teacher asked me. I couldn't spell either. If they told me to spell cake, I'd spell it k-a-k-e and get it wrong.

We could look out the windows at school and see men digging ditches for waterlines and our teacher said, "You see those men out there? It takes ten or fifteen men two or three weeks to dig that ditch now, but one day they'll have a machine that will dig it in so many minutes with one man operating the machine."

We said, "Oh, he doesn't know what he's talking about." We couldn't see it back then, but it's here now. Everything's push-button.

Think AND Respond

Based on details revealed in this oral history, describe Anna Tutt and the kind of childhood she had. Did her childhood seem happy or difficult? Why do you think Lynn Butler chose the details she did to use in the history? What is she trying to communicate to her readers about Anna Tutt's life? Are there questions you would have asked Anna Tutt? Do you know someone with an interesting history whom you might interview?

INVITATION TO Write

Anna Tutt's oral history describes her childhood as the daughter of a tenant farmer in Georgia. Now interview someone who has an interesting life or a good story to tell, and then write up the interview as an oral history.

An oral history, like an interview, begins with the interviewer's questions. However, the interviewer usually has a less prominent role in a transcribed oral history. Rather than presenting a great deal of explanation, writers of oral histories simply allow their subjects to "tell" their own stories, in their own words.

Oral histories can bring to life the history of a particular group of people, a particular period, or a special place. However, the people who are interviewed needn't be well-known or important. Tutt's oral history, for example, is simply a personal account of growing up poor on a tenant farm in early-twentieth-century Georgia. The person simply has to be someone who can share the details of a place, time, or way of life that others may not know about.

CONDUCTING THE INTERVIEW

HANDBOOKS
FOR HELP & PRACTICE

Questioning,
pp. 392–394
Interviewing,
p. 396
Focusing on a Topic,
pp. 349–352
Listening Skills,
pp. 541–542

1. Choose someone to interview. Think of someone who has something interesting to share with an audience. Have an idea of what you want to learn from him or her. Then telephone or write to your subject, and set a date, time, and place for the interview.

2. Prepare open-ended questions. Because you want your subject to talk at length, avoid questions that require only a yes or no answer. For instance, the interviewer in *Foxfire* probably asked Tutt, "What was your life like as a child?" This open-ended question prompted a flood of reminiscences. Also allow your subject to introduce topics of personal interest.

3. Take notes as you listen. You may tape-record the interview, but you might also jot down important points or follow-up questions as you think of them.

4. Ask follow-up questions. The ideal time to clarify confusing points and get more information is while the person has warmed to the topic and is remembering details and recounting memories that he or she might not have thought of in years.

SHAPING YOUR INTERVIEW

1. Choose a focus. Listen to the tape to decide which details in the narrative you want to stress. In Tutt's oral history, the focus was memories of childhood on the farm and in school.

2. Select a structure. Once you have selected a focus for your oral history, decide how to present this focus most effectively. You can structure your oral history as a running narrative, like the Anna Tutt history, or as an interview. The narrative approach suits histories that focus on chronological recollections. The question-and-answer approach suits histories that focus on various topics with no respect for chronology.

3. Transcribe the tape. You will find it easier to edit material later if you transcribe your subject's words on numbered index cards. Also, as in any interview, you must quote your subject's words exactly. Remember that the subject's choice of words often reveals something of the flavor of his or her personality.

 Writer's Choice If your subject speaks a dialect do you wish to use apostrophes and irregular spellings to convey appropriate sounds?

4. Edit the transcript. As you edit the transcript, keep the focus of your oral history in mind. You need not include everything the person you interviewed said, but do try to transcribe enough to make your subject come alive for the reader. If you omit a portion of the transcript, be sure to use ellipses correctly. Three dots (. . .) mark words left out of the middle of a statement. Four dots, a period plus an ellipsis, indicate an omission at the end of a sentence. If you must add material to the transcript to clarify a confusion, place the additional information in brackets [ ].

Although it is not necessary to put your subject's words in quotation marks since the entire piece is meant to reflect his or her words, you should use quotation marks to indicate the exact words of any speaker other than the subject of the oral history. Note that in Anna Tutt's history, the teacher's words about the ditchdiggers are in quotations.

5. Draft an introduction.   Include any necessary background information, such as the setting, the name and age of the person you interviewed, and perhaps the focus of the oral history.

REVIEWING YOUR WRITING

1. Evaluate reader responses.   Show the oral history to a friend. Ask whether it is a coherent narrative or interview. Then show it to the person you taped. Ask the following questions: Did I quote you accurately? Does the oral history capture your personality and the texture of your life? Is there anything you would like to add, change, or delete?

2. Revise your draft.   Make any changes you think are necessary based on your readers' responses. Pay special attention to the suggestions made by your subject to make sure you've presented him or her fairly and accurately. As you make changes, however, do not lose sight of the central focus of the oral history. It is up to you to both capture the personality of your subject and produce a coherent piece of writing.

PUBLISHING AND PRESENTING

- **Promote an oral history night.**   Ask your local library or historical society to sponsor an oral history night featuring the people interviewed by you and your classmates. Create a bulletin board for the occasion that displays your oral histories and photographs of your subject.
- **Compile an anthology of oral histories.**   Collect the oral histories written by your class. If you have access to a desktop publishing system, you can design and print a collection of oral histories and distribute the anthology to friends and classmates. You may want to include photographs of your subjects in this anthology.

Sentence

Elaborating on Sentences

Through the use of descriptive phrases and clauses, experienced writers create rich, detailed sentences. In this lesson you will begin learning to write such sentences. You will practice the basic skills of identifying sentence foundations and elaborating on them.

Contrast the two sets of sentences below. The first consists of only the main clause of each sentence, the part containing the subject and verb. The second set uses phrases and clauses to elaborate on the information in each main clause. Notice in the second set the increased information, sophistication, and style.

Foundations

1. Generally, ships sailed in long convoys.
2. She moved slowly toward him.

Original Sentences

1. Generally, ships sailed in long convoys, merchant ship after merchant ship, like trains of vessels on the water strung out almost as far as the eye could see.
   Edward Rome Snow, "The Light at South Point"
2. She moved slowly toward him, cautiously, as she might toward a wounded animal.
   John Steinbeck, *East of Eden*

A. Combining Sentences Each sentence foundation is followed by two other sentences. These sentences contain bracketed phrases or clauses that can be combined with the foundation. Decide where each elaboration fits best in the foundation. Then combine each group to form one elaborated sentence. After you finish, compare your sentences with the originals on page 327.

Example

1. The old man was sleeping again.
   Ernest Hemingway, *The Old Man and the Sea*
   a. The old man was [up the road].
   b. The old man was [in his shack].

Combined   Up the road, in his shack, the old man was sleeping again.

1. She looked up every few minutes.   **Conrad Richter, "Early Marriage"**
   a. She was [sitting in the shadow of the wagon].
   b. She was [facing the direction in which he had gone].

2. The snake vibrated his rattles.   **Frank Bonham, *Chief***
   a. The snake was [tightly coiled].
   b. The vibration was [in a prolonged hiss].

3. On weekends his Rolls-Royce became an omnibus.
                                        F. Scott Fitzgerald, *The Great Gatsby*
   a. It was [bearing parties to and from the city between nine in the
      morning and long past midnight].
   b. It did this [while his station wagon scampered like a brisk yellow bug
      to meet all trains].

4. She just stood there a long time, trying to figure me out, the way mothers
   are always doing.   **Toni Cade Bambara, "My Delicate Heart Condition"**
   a. She was [looking at me].
   b. [But] mothers [should know better].

B. Imitating Sentences Each model sentence below is divided into a
foundation (underlined) and elaborations. Write a sentence that imitates the
structure of each model. Divide each of your sentences into a foundation
and elaborations, and be sure these parts match the model parts in
structure.

> ***Example***   He was absolutely motionless, / his young face
>   tense and shining, / his eyes devouring the
>   mountain / as a lover's might devour the face
>   of his beloved.   **James Ramsey Ullman, *Top Man***

> ***Student Sentence***   Grandpa was sound asleep, / his long body re-
>   laxed and still, / his snores shaking the house
>   / as a sleeping bull's would jar barnyard
>   serenity.

1. She had been sitting in the shade of the earthen bank of the tank, / moving
   her bare feet in the cool water, / watching the ripples in the hot south
   wind.   **Conrad Richter, "Early Marriage"**

2. For there, / following a few steps behind, / came Charley, / proudly
   carrying a brown paper bag full of sweet potato pie.
                                        Eugenia Collier, "Sweet Potato Pie"

3. Blinded by the glare of the headlights / and confused by the incessant groaning of the horns, <u>the apparition stood swaying for a moment</u> before he perceived the man in the duster. **F. Scott Fitzgerald, *The Great Gatsby***

4. As darkness settled finally, / <u>the shine of the light</u> / lifting from the sea in the south, / <u>changed to full gold.</u> **Stephen Crane, "The Open Boat"**

C. Expanding Sentences In the following sentences, foundations are underlined. Expand each foundation by adding elaboration beginning with the bracketed words. Write out your elaborated sentences. Then compare them with the originals on page 327.

> **Example**   [Bleeding. . .], <u>he had never been closer to death</u>. **J.D. Salinger, "The Laughing Man"**

> **Student Sentence**   Bleeding from the deep gash in his forehead, he had never been closer to death.

1. [Arriving. . .], <u>the boy leaned against the barbed wire fence</u>.
   John Steinbeck, *The Red Pony*

2. [Slowly and. . .], <u>he ate all of the wedge-shaped strips of fish</u>.
   Ernest Hemingway, *The Old Man and the Sea*

3. With one cat in her lap and another [licking. . .], <u>Loma sat drinking coffee</u> and [reading. . .] **Olive Ann Burns, *Cold Sassy Tree***

4. <u>Atticus switched on the ceiling light in the livingroom and found us there</u>, [frozen. . .]. **Harper Lee, *To Kill a Mockingbird***

5. <u>Aunt Pearl got busy quieting them down</u>, [feeding. . .], [helping. . .].
   Robert Lipsyte, *The Contender*

Application From something you have written recently, select five sentences to improve through elaboration. Find the foundation of each sentence. Then, using sentence parts similar to those in this lesson, make at least one addition to each sentence. If possible, insert your additions at the beginnings of some sentences, and in the middle or at the end of others. Notice how elaboration increases detail and adds style to your sentences.

Grammar Refresher To find the foundation (main or independent clause) of a sentence, you must be able to identify the subject and predicate. For information on identifying subject and predicate, see Handbook 31. For more on independent clauses, see Handbook 32.

Sketchbook

Garrison Keillor, a writer and radio personality, invented an imaginary town, Lake Wobegon, Minnesota, "where all the women are strong, the men are good-looking, and all the children are above average." Every week on his radio program, *A Prairie Home Companion,* Keillor told stories that sprang from common, everyday observation about his town. One of his stories started like this:

It has been a quiet week in Lake Wobegon. It was cloudy and rainy and pretty chilly, and in a town that's plain to begin with, when it gets wet and cold you lose most of the charm you didn't have in the first place. Some storytellers would take one look at a little town on a cold wet fall day and tell you about a family on a vacation trip through the Midwest who wonder why this town seems so deserted and get out of their car and there on Maple Street, coming at them with a pitchfork, is a gigantic man with no eyes and chunks of his face falling off and big clods of brown dirt stuck to his bib overalls, but I am a storyteller who, for better or worse, is bound by the facts, so I simply observe that nobody was out walking because it was raining, a steady discouraging rain. But there were strange cars driving through.

Tell a story about your own town or neighborhood. Begin with, "It has been a quiet week in . . . ."

Additional Sketches

Have you ever been so mad that you "made a scene"? What was your experience like?

Try writing about a dream. The dream could be one you have had, or one you'd like to have. After all, you are the creator of your own dreams.

Narrative and Literary Writing

Guided Assignment
THE SHORT STORY

Related Assignment
DRAMATIC SCENE

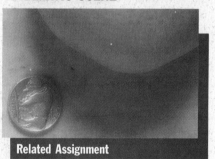

Related Assignment
NARRATIVE POEM

*O**nce upon a time, in a faraway land, there lived a beautiful girl and her handsome brother. Although they were poor, they were happy, for their needs were simple. But one day . . .*

You could easily fill in the rest of the plot yourself, drawing on childhood memories of how such a story usually unfolds. Long before there were writers, people gathered together and told stories. Today, this ancient love for storytelling finds many outlets, from short stories found in magazines to stories told in movies, television dramas, and music videos. In the next three assignments, you will use your imagination to create a short story, a dramatic scene for a play, and a narrative poem.

A Delicate Balance

JOSÉ ARMAS

Everyday life is made up of simple routines that we often take for granted. But what happens when one of these routines is changed? José Armas deals with this question in his short story "A Delicate Balance."

As you read, notice the conflict that results from a minor, well-intentioned change in the everyday routine of a small community. Watch for how the interaction of the characters reveals this conflict and how it is ultimately resolved.

Romero Estrada had his home near the Golden Heights Centro where he spent a lot of time. He would get up almost every morning and clean and shave, and then after breakfast he would get his broom and go up and down the block sweeping the sidewalks for everyone. He would sweep in front of the Tortillería América, the Tres Milpas Bar, Barelas' Barbershop, the used furniture store owned by Goldstein, the corner grocery store, and Model Cities office, and the print shop. In the afternoons, he would come back and sit in the barbershop and just watch the people go by.

Sometimes, when there was no business, Barelas would let him sit in the barber chair, and Romero would love it. He would do this just about every day except Sundays and Mondays when Barelas' was closed. Over time, people got to expect Romero to do his little task of sweeping the sidewalks. When he was feeling real good, he would sweep in front of the houses on the block also.

Romero took great care to sweep cleanly, between the cracks and even between the sides of the buildings. Everything went into the gutter. The work took him the whole morning if he did it the way he wanted.

Romero was considered a little crazy by most people, but they pretty much tolerated him. . . .

Romero received some kind of financial support, but it wasn't much. He was not given any credit by anyone because he would always forget to pay his bills. He didn't do it on purpose; he just never remembered. The businessmen preferred just to do things for him and give him things when they wanted. Barelas would trim his hair when things were slow; Tortillería América would give him *menudo* with fresh tortillas; the grocery store would give him overripe fruit and broken boxes of food that no one would buy.

When Barelas' oldest son, Seferino, graduated from high school, he went to work in his shop. Seferino took notice of Romero and came to feel sorry for him. One day, Romero was in the shop and Seferino decided to act.

"*Mira, Romero. Yo te doy 50 centavos cada vez que me barras la acera.* Fifty cents for every day you do the sidewalk for us. *¿Qué te parece?*"[1]

Ten Brooklyn Storefronts (detail)

Romero thought about it carefully. "*Hecho.* Done," he exclaimed. He started for home right away to get his broom.

"What did you do that for, *m'ijo?*"[2] asked Barelas.

"It don't seem right, Dad. The man works, and no one pays him for his work. Everyone should get paid for what they do."

"He don't need no pay. He has everything he needs."

"It's not the same, Dad. How would you like to do what he does and be treated the same way?"

"I'm not Romero. You don't know about these things, *m'ijo.* Romero would be unhappy if his routine was upset. Right now, everyone likes him and takes care of him. He sweeps the sidewalks because he wants something to do. Not because he wants some money."

"I'll pay him out of my money; don't worry about it."

"The money is not the point. The point is that money will not help Romero. Don't you understand that?"

"Look, Dad. Just put yourself in his place. Would you do it? Would you cut hair for nothing?"

Barelas knew his son was putting something over on him, but he didn't know how to answer. It made

sense the way Seferino explained it, but it didn't seem right. On the other hand, Seferino had gone and finished high school. He must know something. Barelas didn't know many kids who had finished high school, much less gone to college. And his son was going to college in the fall. Barelas himself had never even gone to school. Maybe his son had something there; yet on the other hand. . . . Barelas had known Romero a long time. . . . Despite his uncertainty on the matter, Barelas decided to drop the issue and not say anything else about it.

Just then, Romero came back and started to sweep in front of Barelas' shop again, pushing what little dirt was left into the curb. He swept up the gutter, put the trash in a box and threw it in a garbage can.

Ten Brooklyn Storefronts (detail)

[1] What do you think?
[2] my son

85

Seferino watched with pride as Romero went about his job, and when Romero was finished Seferino went outside and told him he had done a good job and gave him his fifty cents.

Manolo was coming into the shop to get his hair cut as Seferino was giving Romero his wages. He noticed Romero with his broom.

"What's going on?" he asked. Barelas shrugged his shoulders. "What's with Romero? Is he sick or something?"

"No, he's not sick," explained Seferino, who now was inside. He told Manolo the story.

"We're going to make Romero a businessman. Do you realize how much money he would make if people just paid him fifty cents a day, if everyone paid him just fifty cents? He does do a job, you know."

"Well, it makes sense," said Manolo.

"Maybe I'll ask people to do that," said Seferino. "That way the guy could make a decent wage. Do you want to help, Manolo? You can go with me to ask people to pay him."

"Well," said Manolo, "I'm not too good at asking people for money."

This did not stop Seferino. He contacted all the businesses in the neighborhood, but no one else wanted to contribute. Still, that didn't discourage Seferino either. He went on giving Romero fifty cents a day.

A couple of weeks later, Seferino heard that Romero had gotten credit at the grocery store. "See, Dad, what did I tell you? Things are getting better for him already. And look, it's only been a couple of weeks."

But, for the next week, Romero did not show up to sweep any sidewalks. He was around, but he didn't do any work for anybody. He walked around Golden Heights Centro in his best gray work pants and his slouch hat, trying his best to look important and walking right past the barbershop.

The following week, he came and asked to talk with Seferino in private. They went into the back, where Barelas could not hear, and Romero informed Seferino that he wanted a raise.

"What! What do you mean a raise? You haven't worked for a week. You've only been doing this a couple of weeks, and now you want a raise?" Seferino was clearly angry, but Romero was calm and persistent. He pointed out that he had been sweeping the sidewalks for a long time—even before Seferino finished school.

"I deserve a raise," he insisted.

Seferino stared at Romero coldly. It was clearly a standoff in a labor-management confrontation.

Seferino said, "Look, maybe we should forget the whole thing. I was just trying to help you out, and now look at what you do."

Romero held his ground. "I helped you out, too. No one told me to do it, and I did it anyway. I helped you many years."

"Well, let's forget about the whole thing then," said Seferino.

"I quit then," said Romero.

"Quit!" exclaimed Seferino, laughing at the absurdity of the whole thing.

"Quit! I quit!" said Romero as he stormed out the front of the shop, passing Barelas who was cutting Pedrito's hair.

Seferino walked into the shop, shaking his head and laughing.

"Can you imagine that old guy?" he said. Barelas, for his part, did not seem too amused. He felt he could have predicted something like this would happen.

The next day, Romero was back sweeping the sidewalks again, but, when he came to the barbershop, he walked completely around it and then continued sweeping the rest of the sidewalks. After about a week of doing this everyday, he began sweeping the sidewalk all the way up to Barelas' and then pushing the trash to the sidewalk in front of the barbershop.

He had also stopped coming to the shop altogether. When he and Barelas met in the street, they would still greet each other. And Barelas would never bring up the fact that Romero kept pushing the trash in front of the shop. Things went on like that for a long time, until fall came and Seferino went off to college and stopped helping his father in the shop.

It was then that Romero began sweeping *all* the sidewalk again. He was happier then, and he even whistled and sang at his job.

Ten Brooklyn Storefronts, by Martin Wong, 1985.
Courtesy SmithKline Beecham

Think AND Respond

What is the conflict that must be resolved in "A Delicate Balance"? How does the author reveal, develop, and resolve that conflict? What impression does the story give you of Romero and of Seferino? Think about your own life. What experiences could you write about in a short story?

INVITATION
—TO—
Write

José Armas created a compelling story from a small change in a man's simple life. Now use your imagination and experiences to create a short story.

There are as many ways to tell a story as there are people to tell them. Most stories, however, share several basic elements, including **characters, setting,** and **plot,** and they revolve around a central **conflict,** or struggle. This conflict takes place within a character or between the character and some external force, such as another character, a natural phenomenon, an idea, or a social or political institution.

There are also as many reasons to tell a story as there are storytellers. Stories often are intended to entertain, but they also can be a means to explore ideas and emotions, to make a point, or even to inform readers about a topic that is important to the writer. As a short-story writer, you are free to go in whatever direction your story takes you.

▶REWRITE AND EXPLORE

HANDBOOKS
FOR HELP & PRACTICE

Writing Techniques,
pp. 344–346
Collaborative
Planning,
pp. 370–373
Point of View,
pp. 458–463
Character/Setting,
pp. 468–472

1. Look for ideas. The "seeds" for stories are all around you—in your daily activities, in the daily news, and in your private thoughts. Use one or more of the following activities to help you explore some possibilities.

Exploratory Activities

- **Daydreams** When your thoughts wander off, where do they take you? Recall some of your daydreams and free-write about them.
- **News stories** As you read the newspaper or watch the news on television, look for stories that interest

you. Share with your classmates news clips, photographs, quotations, or situations that might be sparks
for stories.

- **Experiences** Make a list of memorable events from
  your own life. Then choose several and quickly jot
  down what really happened or what might have happened if one aspect of the incident were changed.
- **What if?** Set your imagination free by asking youself
  "What if?" questions. Consider, as José Armas did, what
  significant consequences might result if a minor change
  were made in a routine or activity. Use "What if" questions to think about the improbable. For example,
  following the lead of Ray Bradbury in "A Sound of
  Thunder," you might ask yourself, "What if it were possible to go on time travel safaris to the past or future?"
- **Reading literature** What types of short stories do you
  like to read? For example, are you drawn to Ursula Le
  Guin's science fiction, Flannery O'Connor's sense of the
  grotesque, or F. Scott Fitzgerald's rich use of language?
  Freewrite about the writing you like and about stories
  you might write using those same qualities.

2. Choose an idea. Look over the ideas you have generated and
choose one you find particularly promising. If you are having trouble finding an idea, you might also look to your journal, your writing for the Sketchbook on page 82, and the suggestions in the
"Apply Your Skills" section on page 101.

Then, with a small group of classmates, share your freewriting and
talk about how your stories might take shape. What are your fellow
students' expectations about what might happen in your story?

3. Explore the elements of your story. You can begin your exploration with any of the key elements of a story: character, setting,
plot, or conflict. To focus your thinking, you may wish to freewrite
about each of the following elements or use charts or clusters to
gather details for developing your story.

- **Character** Who is your main character? Jot down all the
  details you can think of to describe aspects of this
  person—physical appearance, personality traits, attitudes,
  beliefs, and perhaps even a brief personal history.
- **Setting** Where does your story take place? Think about
  both the time period and the physical setting. Is yours a

**How can I decide
what to include
in my story?**

The Short Story   **89**

**You may wish to
map your plot on
a sheet of paper,
using some sort
of diagram to
show conflict, ex-
pansion, and
resolution.**

contemporary story, or does it take place in another time? What role does the physical setting play in the story? For example, do the shadows of an overhanging cliff provide a haven for the characters or loom ominously over them?

- **Plot**   What happens in your story? In many stories the beginning presents a problem or conflict. The middle expands on the problem, perhaps showing some attempts at a resolution. The end resolves the conflict or solves the problem. You may want to vary the form, or you may simply wait to see where your story leads you as you write.

- **Conflict**   What conflict must be resolved? In "A Delicate Balance," the conflict between the characters illustrates what can happen when the values of a small community are challenged by those of a different world. You may wish to experiment by freewriting about a turning point that changes the course of your character's life, or sketch out a showdown in which your character confronts a problem.

   Writer's Choice   Will the conflict in your story take place within a character or between your characters and an external force?

4. Create a mood.   Now consider the general emotional quality, or atmosphere, you want to create as a backdrop to your story. Will your story be suspenseful? dramatic? funny? scary? Experiment with descriptions of your character or setting to see how you can convey the mood you've chosen.

5. Choose a point of view.   A story can be told from the first-person point of view, using pronouns such as *I* or *we,* by a narrator who is also an active participant in the story. It can also be told from the third-person point of view, using such pronouns as *he, she,* or *they,* by a narrator who stands outside the story and reports on the actions of the characters. A third-person narrator can be omniscient, aware of what is going on in the characters' minds as well as their actions. The narrator of "A Delicate Balance" is aware of the characters' thoughts and feelings, but sometimes lets their actions express what is going on inside them. This is especially true in the case of Romero, whose state of mind is often revealed by the way he sweeps the sidewalks.

6. Identify your purpose, goals, and audience. When writing a short story, your purpose is usually to entertain. Think about your goals for your story. For example, do you want your audience to appreciate your main character or to know how sad someone's life can be? One of Armas's goals might have been to make readers think about the disruption that can occur in the relationship of the individual to the community when even a small shift in values is introduced. Also think about your audience. Are you writing for children, for your peers, or for a general audience? Knowing who your audience is can give direction to your work and help you make appropriate language choices.

To begin the writing process, some writers go over experiences in their minds, thinking about the best way to present or change them, before they put anything on paper. In this workshop, you will follow the process of one student writer, Robin, as she used her writing to help her think about and deal with a painful experience. She began by freewriting about how her experience might become a story.

ONE STUDENT'S PROCESS

My grandmother died only a year ago. We were so close, it was really hard on me. When she was sick, I wouldn't believe she could die. I even denied there was anything wrong with her—to myself and to others—so I wouldn't have to think about losing her. I think this would be a good idea for a story—this denial, but I get upset when I think about Grandma dying. So I won't use a character like me and I'll put it in a different setting—maybe in the country, with a boy and his grandfather. What if the grandfather lived on a farm and the boy spent summers with him, learning about the woods and fishing and things like that? The main conflict would be the boy's struggle inside himself to accept that his grandfather is dying. I probably should have another character at least—the boy's mother?—so I can show him denying what is happening.

Writer's Choice What tone do you want to use? Do you want to convey an attitude of compassion, anger, sarcasm, horror, wonder, or some other emotion?

D RAFT AND DISCOVER

HANDBOOKS

FOR HELP & PRACTICE

**Shaping Writing,
pp. 361–369
Introducing/
Concluding
Narratives,
pp. 386–390
Figurative Language,
pp. 453–457
Dialogue in Fiction,
pp. 465–466**

Writing
——TIP——

To create believable dialogue, have a friend role-play one character while you play another. Ad lib, and use a tape recorder to record your words to each other.

1. Begin your draft. You can start writing with any part of your story—with the conclusion, with the incident that introduces the central conflict, with the first incident that happens, or with some background description. Just see where your writing takes you. You can rearrange the sections later.

2. Elaborate on ideas. To develop your story, consider using some of these strategies.

Strategies

- **Dialogue** Having characters speak in their own words is an effective way to reveal what characters are really like. Think about how your characters would talk. Would they use formal or informal language? Slang? Dialect? Dialogue can also create a sense of place. In "A Delicate Balance," dialogue in Spanish reminds the reader that the setting is an ethnic neighborhood that has its own culture and set of values.
- **Description** Description is valuable for setting a scene—for giving the reader the feeling of being present in the action of the story. Try to show, not tell, what is happening in your story by choosing details that are revealing. For example, a torn button on a coat might reveal that there has been a struggle, or a gate with peeling paint might reveal that a character is too ill to take care of household duties.
- **Figurative language** Think about metaphors, similes, and other figures of speech that you can use to describe individual characters or scenes. You might frame your story as an extended metaphor to make a point about an issue or idea that is important to you.
- **Suspense** To create suspense include dialogue, description, or narration that raises questions in the reader's mind.

The Hedge Maze at Longleat House in England is the world's largest three dimensional maze. What kind of story could take place there?

3. Organize your story. Some writers begin with the first incident and then tell about each event in chronological order. Others begin in the middle, describing some attention-grabbing incident. Later in the story, using a technique called flashback, they go back and fill in the events that led up to the opening incident.

Remember that whatever else your story does, it should show the development and eventual resolution of a conflict. You may want to think of the development and resolution as the backbone that holds the rest of the story together.

Robin needed to figure out how to organize the events in her draft so that they would lead to the central conflict. After jotting down some notes, she decided to start writing to see what would develop.

How can I best present the events in my story?

ONE STUDENT'S PROCESS

What events should I include?

—Scene to introduce conflict:
   Boy denying his grandfather is dying
   Should be making denial to someone—
   Mother and grandmother? Where? At breakfast?

"Why does everybody have to treat him as if he were

going to die!" said Matthew, pushing away from the ta-

ble and throwing a biscuit down.

The Short Story   **93**

4. Take a break. Lay aside your story for a time. Then reread it and ask your peer readers to respond to it.

COMPUTER
—TIP—

Once you have saved your first draft, try shifting paragraphs around so that the story starts with an exciting event. Then you can use a flashback to explain what previously happened.

R E V I E W   Y O U R   W R I T I N G

Questions for Yourself

• Does my story have a central conflict that is introduced, that develops, and that is resolved?

• What would happen if I changed the point of view?

• Does my story create a single mood or impression?

• What details can I add to make my characters more realistic? Do my characters have distinct voices?

Questions for Your Peer Readers

• Do my characters seem real? What seemed natural and convincing in their dialogue? What didn't?

• Can you vividly picture the time and place in your mind? How does the setting make you feel?

• How do your feelings change as the story progresses? What can I do to involve you more fully in the story?

R E V I S E   Y O U R   W R I T I N G

HANDBOOKS
FOR HELP & PRACTICE

Unity/Coherence,
pp. 401–414
Refining Voice
and Style,
pp. 444–448
Types of Language,
pp. 450–452

1. Evaluate your responses. Then, based on these responses, re-work your draft. The following are some standards for evaluation that you might keep in mind as you revise.

Standards for Evaluation

An effective short story . . .

- uses the elements of character, setting, and plot to create a convincing world of its own.
- develops and resolves a central conflict.
- uses description, dialogue, figurative language, and other techniques as appropriate to enhance the story.
- tells a clearly organized story.
- uses language appropriate for its intended audience.

2. Problem-solve. Revise your draft, making changes based on your review and the comments made by your peer readers. Notice how Robin revised one part of her draft in response to some comments.

ONE STUDENT'S PROCESS

"Why does everybody have to treat him ~~as if he were~~ *like   he's*

going to die!" said Matthew, pushing away from the ta-

ble and throwing a biscuit down so hard that it
slopped gravy
splashed ~~stuff~~ out of his plate and onto the *Granny's* tablecloth—
hand-embroidered   she   "comp'ny."
the one that ~~Grandmother~~ put out for ~~company.~~

"Matthew!" cried ~~matthew's~~ mother. "Look what you've

done!"
"Aw, don't worry about that now,"   Granny, distracted.
"It's okay. Don't worry about it," said ~~Grandmother.~~
"I'm sorry," said Matthew, his voice showing that he wasn't sorry at all.
Matthew said he was sorry, but his voice indicated
"But if you keep up like that, talking death and dying all the time, you're going to
he really wasn't. He felt that if everyone kept talking
kill him. God knows the things he's overheard."
about death and dying, his grandfather would die. He

was afraid his grandfather would overhear.

Your beginning sure got my attention!

Can you use more specific descriptions to help me visualize the setting and character's actions?

This dialogue doesn't sound real.

Could you <u>show</u> Matthew's words instead of <u>telling</u> what he said?

3. Proofread your work. Once you finish your revisions, make a final copy and proofread it carefully for errors in grammar, usage, and mechanics.

LINKING
GRAMMAR AND WRITING
Punctuating Dialogue

You can add interest to dialogue by varying the position of speaker's tags. They can go before, after, or in the middle of the speaker's words. Notice how punctuation and capitalization are used with speaker's tags in different positions.

TAG AT BEGINNING: Dan asked, "Would you like to go to a movie?"

TAG IN MIDDLE: "Well," replied Robin, "that depends on what's playing."

TAG AT END: "There's a Tom Cruise movie at the Biograph," Dan answered.

See Grammar Handbook 40, pages 824–826, for additional help with this problem.

PUBLISH AND PRESENT

FOR HELP & PRACTICE

**Sharing Writing,
pp. 427–428**

PROBLEM

S O L V I N G

**What is the
best form of
publishing for
my short story?**

• **Publish your story in a literary magazine.**   If your school doesn't have one, consider starting one or creating one just for you and your classmates.

• **Form a readers' group with friends and classmates.**   Read your stories to one another, focusing on their strengths.

• **Publish your story in a magazine.**   Many professional magazines publish fiction by young people. Check such reference works as *Writer's Market* at your library for guidelines and requirements for story submissions.

• **Adapt your story for the stage.**   Create a dramatic version of your story. With several classmates, present it as reader's theater or a play.

• **Begin a "cassette portfolio" of your work.**   Tape your short story as you read it aloud. As you write more short stories and poems, add them to your cassette portfolio.

The Mentor

Robin Lamb

"Why does everybody have to treat him like he's going to die!" said Matthew, pushing away from the table and throwing a biscuit down so hard that it slopped gravy out of his plate and onto Granny's tablecloth—the hand-embroidered one that she put on for "comp'ny."

"Matthew!" cried Matt's mother. "Look what you've done!"

"Aw, don't worry 'bout that now," said Granny, distracted.

"I'm sorry," said Matthew, his voice showing that he wasn't sorry at all. "But if you two keep up like that, talking death and dying all the time, you're going to kill him. God knows the things he's overheard." And with that Matthew grabbed his cap and ran from the breakfast table.

He was still shaking when he reached Tobias Grider's hog lot, which adjoined his grandparents' property. He crossed through the barbed-wire fence carefully, thinking how Grandpa had taught him to pass a rifle through such a fence, to lean it butt down against one of the posts, to walk down the fence row "a piece," and then to separate the wires and climb through.

Matt and his grandfather had hunted together often. They had combed the woods for rabbits, squirrels, blackberries, and sassafras. They'd fished for bluegill, bass, perch, and crappie. They'd gone "dry land fishin'," as Grandpa put it, searching out those prodigious morel

Active beginning with dialogue and details that show rather than tell

Each character speaks in his or her distinct voice.

Conflict is revealed.

Omniscient third-person point of view shows what the character is thinking as well as doing.

Setting is important to understand relationship of characters.

The Short Story   **97**

mushrooms that appear, as if spontaneously, in the dark, leafy humus after summer rains. Grandpa knew the ways of mushrooms. And of owls, fish, foxes and even the moon. He knew about secret places in the earth, about caverns and springs. He knew a lot. <u>More than I'll ever know, Matt thought.</u>

For most of his seventeen years, Matt had been coming to see his grandfather from July through September. Summer after summer, the two had plumbed the hills and hollers together, the old man teaching without having to resort to words, the boy learning how to see and hear and smell and taste and feel as though he, himself, were a creature of the woods. Now, in mid-October, Matt had suddenly been called back from school. <u>And for what reason? No reason. None.</u>

Matt chased Tobias Grider's hogs, knowing that old Toby would bellow like a calving cow if he saw him. Matthew didn't care. He chased the hogs some more. Tiring of that, he climbed through the fence on the opposite side of the lot. Then he struck off across an open pasture, up a steep hill, and into a stand of trees—oaks, maples, scrawny "iron woods," and a lone persimmon. The trees blazed feverishly—red and yellow and orange. Plunging into the coolness under this fervid pavilion, Matthew made his way down the opposite side of the hill to a small pond that Toby and his grandfather kept stocked with bait fish—minnows and chubs.

A late-summer growth of algae and lily pads choked the leeward side of the pond. Grasshoppers and crickets roared in the weeds. A bullfrog croaked, "Knee deep.

Plot: refusal of character to accept inevitable

Descriptive details enhance reader's understanding of character and setting.

Knee deep. Come in." That was Grandpa's joke. <u>Grandpa had been sick before. TB. It came and it went, and then it came and went again. All they had to do was shut up talking about his dying and let him get well.</u> Matt gathered some stones for skimming, but when he hurled them into the pond, it was all at once. He sat down on the bank and cried.

Coming back over the hill, he paused and looked long at his grandparents' house. Mother, Granny, and Aunt Lucy were bunched up together on the front porch, Mother on a cane-bottomed chair, Granny and Aunt Lucy on the porch swing with a bowl of snap beans between them. They were stringing and breaking up the beans for supper. When Matt opened the gate, he noticed it needed paint. "He wants to see you," Mother said.

Grandpa was sitting up in bed, wearing his overalls instead of his pajamas—a good sign, for he hadn't been out of his pajamas, except for baths, for weeks. "Come over here, boy," he said, mustering his forces. "I want to talk to you." Matthew sat down on the stool beside the bed.

"You remember when you and your mother came down and you asked me straight out if I was dying?"

The boy nodded.

"I lied to you then. It was one of those lies people tell when they don't expect to be believed and it's easier to pretend. You know what I mean, don't you."

The boy knew.

"I don't want there to be any lying between us. Not now. So I told your mother I'd talk to you." The grand-

Conflict is developing.

Organization is chronological.

Dialogue *shows* the scene between grandfather and grandson.

Climax

father looked at Matt. Then he seemed to look off into the distance. "I want you to think about an old tree that's been struck down by lightning or disease or just plain tiredness. It lies there for a long time, and it rots. And a million tiny bundles of life—insects, funguses, molds, plants of all kinds—feed on it. Maybe some fox or bird builds a nest in the trunk. Life goes on, and death makes it possible, makes it what it is."

Matthew wanted to say something but couldn't. Grandpa took his hand, ministering.

"The way I figure it, when an old person dies, a young person learns that death is real. And that knowledge makes the child into a man or a woman who understands how precious life is, who lives fully and completely without compromises.

"You're going to be like that, boy. That's what I leave to you. That's what you do for me. Now go out and let me rest."

Resolution of conflict

Matthew's mother went into town to buy groceries, though there really wasn't anything the family needed. Not long after, Aunt Lucy went to check on Grandpa and came running to get Granny. It seemed like hours later when Granny and Lucy came from the bedroom—two old ladies, propping each other up. Matt couldn't look at them. He rose from the sofa and went out to the front porch, the screen door slamming behind him. He bit down hard, remembering.

Figurative language shows death and life moving on.

A declining sun cast spears through the browning leaves of a sycamore on the front lawn. Geese honked across the sky, heading south.

WRITER TO WRITER

Ends always give me trouble. Characters run away with you, and so won't fit on to what is coming.

E. M. Forster, English short-story writer and novelist

1. Reflect on your writing. Take some time to think about your experiences as a writer of a short story to make some notes about the process in your journal. Ask yourself questions such as the following to focus your thinking.

- What aspects of short-story writing intrigue you most? Which are easy for you? Which do you need to develop?
- Has writing a short story caused you to view short stories and their authors differently? Have your feelings toward José Armas's "A Delicate Balance" changed since you first read it? How do your experiences affect your response to Robin Lamb's "The Mentor?"
- Did writing this story give you ideas for other stories? Would any of the notes or thinking that you did in preparation for this story be useful for another story?

2. Apply your skills. Use your skills to try your hand at some of these writing activities.

- **Cross-curricular** Writers often create fictionalized versions of historical events. Choose a character or event from history and explore the possibility of writing a story about this subject.
- **Literature** Choose a poem about a person or an event such as Edwin Arlington Robinson's "Richard Cory." Then write a short story based on the poem.
- **General** People sometimes use stories to emphasize points when they are making speeches. Think of a speech that you've heard lately. Then create a story that the speaker might have used to emphasize one of his or her points.
- **Related assignments** Using the suggestions on pages 104–112, create a dramatic scene or compose a narrative poem.

FOR YOUR
PORTFOLIO

Dramatic Scene

Related
ASSIGNMENT

FROM

THE MOONCUSSER'S DAUGHTER

by Joan Aiken

Thornton Wilder, a famous American playwright, once called the theater "the perpetual present tense." This definition conveys the excitement and immediacy of drama. When you are sitting in the darkness of a theater, you enter into the lives of the characters as they are living them. For the moment, you share their triumphs and their frustrations at the conflicts they face.

As you read the following scene by Joan Aiken, notice the hints in the dialogue about a suspicious secret buried in the characters' past. What else do you learn about this strange threesome?

Scene One. *[Inside Sabertooth Lighthouse] RUTH BILKANCHOR, who is blind and wears dark glasses, sits knitting and rocking in rocking chair. She is thin, gentle, in her fifties, white hair plainly arranged, perhaps in a bun. FRED'S ghost, dressed as a sailor but all in white . . . is sitting on the windowsill. . . . Elevator doors open to admit SAUL BILKANCHOR, who is about the same age as RUTH, with long white hair, whiskers, and beard.*

SAUL   *[pacing about]* I'm accursed! I'm the outcast of mankind. *[He has taken off seaboots and is in socks with large holes; every now and then he trips.]* I'm a haunted man, I tell you.

RUTH   *[knitting away]* Yes, you do tell me—often. . . .

SAUL   For twenty years a curse has lain on me.

RUTH   Nineteen this March. . . .

SAUL   Oh, why did I follow the dreadful trade? Why did I do it?

RUTH   Well, dear, for ten years you used to say you did it for kicks. Then, for the last nine, you've been saying you did it because society owed you more than a lighthouse-keeper's salary [plus] free fishing and electricity.

SAUL   Free electricity! Pah! I live in a darkness of my own making, haunted by the thought of a brother's unforgiving ghost.

RUTH   *[patiently]* Look, Saul, for the umpteenth time, Fred *has* forgiven you. He forgave you right after it happened, nineteen years ago. Didn't you, Fred?

FRED   *[moving forward]* That's right. Never one to bear a grudge, I wasn't. Anyhow—easy berth being a ghost. No worries. Go wherever you like. Except I mostly like to stay here. Better than all that running I used to have to do. . . .

102

RUTH   See? He's forgiven you. He says so.

SAUL   *[who can't see or hear FRED]* Haunted, haunted, I tell you by my past crimes—*[tripped by his flapping sock, he falls heavily]*. . . Ruth! I wish you'd mend my socks.

RUTH   *[calmly]* Dear, I've told you over and over that mending socks is a thing you just can't do when you're blind. . . . Now if you'd allow little Sympathy to come home, I daresay she'd do a bit of mending for you.

SAUL   Never!

RUTH   Helpful little thing she used to be.

SAUL   My daughter must never return to this accursed spot. . . .

[Door opens; a voice shouts Postman! and a letter is tossed through.]

RUTH   *[joyfully]* Oh, it'll be a letter from Sympathy! . . . Do read it aloud. . . .

SAUL   "Dear Mum. I hope you are well. Why do you never write to me anymore? . . . I have finished at ballet school and got my diploma, and I'm fed up with being away from home, so I'm coming back for a bit and shall arrive on Tuesday. . . ."

RUTH   Tuesday! But that's *today!* Oh, I am pleased! . . .

SAUL   Well, that settles it. She's not coming here. If I see her coming it's her own responsibility.—I shall warn her off just as I would anybody else. *[He takes gun— a large bell-mouthed blunderbuss—from rack and goes upstairs.]*

RUTH   Oh, dear. Has he taken the gun, Fred?

FRED   Yes.

RUTH   That's going to be awkward. What shall we do?

FRED   I dunno.

Think AND Respond

What character in this scene is experiencing the most anguish? Does the anguish seem to be justified? Why or why not? How does the writer use details and dialogue to reveal what this character is like and the problems he or she is facing? What conflict remains looming at the end of the scene? Can you imagine a conflict or problem that would make a good subject for a dramatic scene?

INVITATION TO Write

In *Mooncusser's Daughter,* the playwright creates a story using only dialogue and stage directions. Now write your own dramatic scene, based on a piece of fiction or an incident of your own creation.

Like novels and short stories, plays tell a story about characters facing conflict. Playwriting is unique, however, in that all information about the characters and their problems must be conveyed through dialogue or in stage directions. The term **dialogue** refers to the spoken words of the characters. **Stage directions** include information about the setting of the play; the gestures, body movements, and tone of voice of the actors; and other details about the physical production of the play, such as lighting, costumes, and props. Together, these two elements advance plot, develop characters, and provide an entertaining hour or two for an audience.

PLANNING YOUR DRAMATIC SCENE

HANDBOOKS

FOR HELP & PRACTICE

Envisioning Structure, p. 361

Choosing Different Voices, pp. 446–448

Dialogue in Drama, pp. 466–467

Character, pp. 468–470

1. Consider your purpose and audience. Who will read or watch your scene? Are you writing a play for children or for adults? What kind of action or story line is most likely to appeal to them?

2. Choose or create an incident that involves conflict. Consider dramatizing a conflict from a short story or a historic or current event. Works of fiction, history texts, periodicals, film, television, news headlines, and even popular songs can be sources of ideas.

If you prefer to invent your own incident, begin with a conflict or character that interests you and offers dramatic potential. To find original ideas for dramatic conflicts, think about your own experiences or those of people you know. List these conflicts and the elements that make them compelling, entertaining, or moving.

3. Establish your characters. Just as you would do for a short story, fully develop the key characters for your play. Consider their role in the plot, their relationship to one another, and any important functions they must perform (providing background information, or serving as a foil or confidante to the hero, for example). Try writing brief character sketches that describe both the internal and external characteristics.

4. Plan your script. Sketch out the series of actions and events in your dramatic scene. You may wish to arrange them in sequence, like this:

Opening Situation	Problem(s)	1st Event
Saul, Ruth, and Fred confined in lighthouse	Saul is haunted by Fred, under a curse, and determined to keep Sympathy away.	Saul gets a gun to drive off Sympathy.

DRAFTING YOUR SCENE

1. Set the scene. In the opening stage directions, make it clear who your characters are and where they are gathered. In *Mooncusser's Daughter,* for example, you are told immediately that the scene takes place "Inside Sabertooth Lighthouse." In your scene, describe the actual stage scenery, or **set,** as much as you think necessary to set up the situation and introduce your characters to your audience.

2. Let your characters provide any necessary background. If the audience needs background to understand the scene, use dialogue to present information. Notice, for example, the lines in the scene from *Mooncusser's Daughter* that tell you that Sympathy has been to ballet school, that Saul has forbidden her to come home, and that Saul did something terrible to Fred twenty years ago.

3. Use dialogue and stage direction effectively. Both can be used to develop characters and advance your story. Let your audience get to know your characters through their words and actions. For example, you learned about Saul's distress in the stage directions where he is described as pacing and tripping; his tendency to overdramatize is shown when he says of himself, "I'm accursed! I'm the outcast of mankind. . . . For twenty years, a curse has lain on me."

4. A play must appeal to both the eyes and the ears. Keep the dialogue lively, natural, and interesting. Build in action and movement where possible. Finally, create an interesting set and useful props with which your actors can interact.

5. Use accurate stage directions. Describe on-stage movement using the terms shown in this diagram:

Upstage

Up Right   Up Left

Stage Right   **Center Stage**   **Stage Left**

Down Right   **Downstage**   Down Left

Audience

REVIEWING YOUR WRITING

1. Evaluate your opening and development. Do your opening stage directions and dialogue establish the setting and introduce the characters? Is the conflict made clear early in the scene? Does the scene progress quickly to a development of the conflict?

2. Examine dialogue and stage directions. Do the dialogue and stage directions present everything the audience will need to understand and appreciate your scene? Will they evoke the right response?

3. Ask a classmate to read your dramatic scene. Then ask your reader: Do you understand clearly what happens? Do you feel that you know the characters? Does the dialogue sound like real conversation? Were you concerned about the outcome of the conflict?

PUBLISHING AND PRESENTING

- **Acting as director, plan a dramatization of your scene.** Have classmates audition for the various parts and for the roles of stage designer, props manager, and costumer.
- **Videotape your scene.**

On the Lightside

WARMEDY

In addition to filling the airwaves with entertainment, television is filling the dictionary with new words. As the TV networks think up new forms of entertainment, they also think up new

words to describe their creations. The television industry seems especially to thrive on creating new word blends as a form of shorthand to describe their entertainment offerings.

Situation comedies have been shortened to *sitcoms;* made-for-TV movies that combine aspects of documentary and drama are now *docudramas;* and *simulcasts* are broadcast simultaneously on TV and radio.

One of the most recent inventions is the *warmedy.* Take an idea for a comedy, build the show around warmhearted, traditional family values, and what you come up with is a warmedy. As *Newsweek* reported:

NBC, along with both its rivals, would have us believe that prime-time entertainment is in the throes of a massive revival of the kind of warm family comedies (or *warmedies,* as the industry now calls them) that cast a cozy glow over our memories of television's youth.

Warmedy cannot be found in the dictionary, but given time, it may earn the broad-based acceptance that will land it there alongside the other traditional and television-generated forms of entertainment.

Narrative Poem

OR-NGES

by gary soto

Long ago people gathered around fires and spun stories to entertain one another, to pass on information, and to preserve their history. Some of these stories took the form of songs or poems, which were easier for listeners to remember.

Today, people continue to tell stories through poems. The following poem tells about a boy's first walk with a girl. As you read, imagine the same story written in prose form. Which elements would remain the same? What would change? Which version do you think would be more effective?

The first time I walked
With a girl, I was twelve.
Cold, and weighted down
With two oranges in my jacket.
December. Frost cracking
Beneath my steps, my breath
Before me, then gone,
As I walked toward
Her house, the one whose
Porchlight burned yellow
Night and day, in any weather.
A dog barked at me, until
She came out pulling
At her gloves, face bright
With rouge. I smiled,
Touched her shoulder, and led
Her down the street, across
A used car lot and a line
Of newly planted trees,
Until we were breathing
Before a drugstore. We
Entered, the tiny bell
Bringing a saleslady
Down a narrow aisle of goods.
I turned to the candies
Tiered like bleachers,
And asked what she wanted—
Light in her eyes, a smile
Starting at the corners
Of her mouth. I fingered
A nickel in my pocket,
And when she lifted a chocolate
That cost a dime,
I didn't say anything.

I took the nickel from
My pocket, then an orange,
And set them quietly on
The counter. When I looked up,
The lady's eyes met mine,
And held them, knowing
Very well what it was all
About.
       Outside,
A few cars hissing past,
Fog hanging like old
Coats between the trees.
I took my girl's hand
In mine for two blocks,
Then released it to let
Her unwrap the chocolate.
I peeled my orange
That was so bright against
The gray of December
That, from some distance,
Someone might have thought
I was making a fire in my hands.

Think and Respond

In a few words, sum up what actually happens in this poem. Why do you think the poet wrote about this incident? What techniques does the poet use to help you visualize the events? What event have you witnessed or been part of that might be the basis for a similar story poem?

INVITATION
TO
Write

The poem "Oranges" recreates a memory that the speaker treasured. Now write a poem of your own that tells a story, either a real one from your experience or one from your imagination.

The elements of good storytelling are the same in poetry as in prose. Character and a sequence of events, or plot, are two major elements, and setting may also play an important role. In a poem, however, the story is usually told in a more concise form and conveys some message, mood, or theme that the poet feels is important. Also, poetic elements such as rhyme, rhythm, imagery, symbolism, and figurative language may be used to emphasize meaning or to evoke a more powerful response in the reader.

PLANNING A STORY POEM

HANDBOOKS
FOR HELP & PRACTICE

Personal Techniques, pp. 339–342
Figurative Language/ Sound Devices, pp. 453–457
Character/Setting, pp. 468–472
Speech Delivery, pp. 515–518

1. Look for inspiration. Sometimes, it seems, there are dozens of good ideas to choose from: inspirations appear out of nowhere, like fireflies at night. More often, however, you have to make an effort to find just one workable idea. Use the same exploratory techniques to find an idea that you would use if you were writing a short story. Perhaps a recent news item, a family anecdote, or a personal experience will inspire you, just as a personal experience may have inspired "Oranges."

2. Think about your purpose or message. To be effective, your story must have some significance, both for you and for your reader. Consider *why* this particular incident seems important to you. Then ask yourself what meaning it could have for your readers.

Writer's Choice You may decide to address your narrative poem to a general audience or to a specific group such as classmates, grandparents, or other family members.

▶RAFTING A POEM

1. Begin writing. As soon as you get an idea, begin to explore it on paper or on the computer screen. For now, don't worry about the poetry. Just try to sketch out your story line, as well as phrases or images that you associate with each event. For example, Gary Soto recalled the images of "frost cracking/Beneath my steps" and "candies/tiered like bleachers."

2. Consider the speaker and point of view. Who will tell the story in your poem? Will it be your main character, or someone who merely observed the events? Also think about what kind of language your speaker would use, as well as the mood and tone you want to convey.

Writing
━ TIP ━
Try making word associations to spark ideas. Visualize a character or a place, and let your mind make connections from that starting point.

3. Experiment with the form of your poem. For example, to create a very contemporary feel, you may want to try out unorthodox capitalization or punctuation. Will you break your poem into stanzas? Note that "Oranges" uses no rhyme, specific rhythm, or punctuation, but is written in free verse, a modern verse form. Will you use a definite meter or rhyme scheme? Also play with other poetic elements. Could sound devices such as alliteration or assonance be used to help create a mood? Would figurative language help enhance an image?

Robin Williams in *Dead Poets Society,* a movie about a teacher whose personal enthusiasm for poetry inspires his class

REVIEWING YOUR WRITING

1. Read your poem aloud to yourself. Does it tell the story in an interesting way? Does the form of the poem enhance the meaning?

2. Ask others to read your poem. Have several questions prepared for your readers. Questions might include: "Does the story hold together or are there parts that are missing or don't seem to belong? Which words or phrases are most effective? Which poetic devices particularly pleased you?"

3. Rework your poem. Keep experimenting with different images and phrasing. Choose those that best communicate your vision of the poem.

PUBLISHING AND PRESENTING

- **Set your poem to music.** Sing it, or speak it to musical accompaniment. Invite classmates to listen and comment.
- **Enter your poem (or song) in a writing contest.** Go to the library and look in *The Writer's Digest* and other magazines for information on writing contests.
- **Organize a round-robin reading of classmates' poems.** Limit the readings to five or six, but suggest a series of such readings if other students are interested.

Sentence

Inverting and Compounding Subjects and Verbs

Sentences with just one main (independent) clause are called "simple" sentences, yet even these sentences can be rich and varied in style. In this lesson you will learn how to add depth and sophistication to simple sentences by inverting or compounding subjects and verbs.

In the model below, notice how the usual subject-verb word order has been reversed (inverted) to emphasize the word *pool*.

MODEL

       V   S

Twenty feet below him was a pool, ringed, crystal clear, and motionless as glass.   **James V. Marshall, *Walkabout***

A. Identifying and Writing Imitations In each set below, identify the sentence that has the same structure as its model. (Hint: begin by noting the order of subject and verb.) Next, write a sentence of your own that imitates the structure of each model.

1. Tethered to the rear of the wagon stood her saddle mare, Fancy, with pricked-up ears.   **Conrad Richter, "Early Marriage"**
   a. Riding in the front of the roller coaster was our little sister, Karen, with a self-satisfied grin.
   b. Around the curve of the track Arthur came flying, gripping the baton as if his hand were welded to it.

2. There, lying to one side of an immense bed, lay grandpa.   **Katherine Mansfield, "The Voyage"**
   a. Overhead, like a haze of pulsing light, the icy stars shone.
   b. Inside, stretching at the barre in the deserted room, stood the ballerina.

3. On a tarnished gilt easel before the fireplace stood a crayon portrait of Miss Emily's father.   **William Faulkner, "A Rose for Emily"**
   a. From the shiny new car in the fast lane came the heavy stench of diesel exhaust.
   b. On the scuffled linoleum floor of the classroom the papers lay scattered in all directions.

4. Below him spread the river, ice-locked between the hills.

Elliott Merrick, "Without Words"

   a. Beside Marty ran a dog, mud-spattered to its shoulders.

   b. Before us the lake stretched, weed-choked near the shore.

Compound subjects and compound verbs add detail to simple sentences. Notice the intensity and rhythm created by the compound elements.

MODELS

COMPOUND SUBJECTS

     S   S   V

1. Uncle John and the preacher were curled in the middle of the truck, resting on their elbows and staring out the back triangle.　**John Steinbeck, *The Grapes of Wrath***

COMPOUND VERBS

     S V   V

2. It ran wildly in circles, biting at its tail, spun in a

                    V

frenzy, and died.

Ray Bradbury, "There Will Come Soft Rains"

Punctuation Note: Two subjects or verbs are joined by a conjunction or, rarely, by a comma; if there are three or more subjects or verbs, follow the rules for serial commas.

B. Combining Sentences　In each set below, the first sentence is the foundation. Combine it with the appropriate parts of the others to make a new sentence with compound subjects or compound verbs.

1. a. Mrs. Breedlove slipped noisily out of bed.
   b. She put a sweater on over her nightgown (which was an old dress).
   c. Mrs. Breedlove walked toward the kitchen.

Toni Morrison, The Bluest Eye

2. a. There were white houses and red brick ones.
   b. There were tall elms blowing in the wind.
   c. There were tall maples and horse chestnuts.

Ray Bradbury, "Mars Is Heaven!"

3. a. Gerard, his elbows spread wide on the arms of his chair, stretched his legs further under the table.
   b. Gerard also looked at the fire.

Elizabeth Bowen, "Foothold"

4. a. I went into the First Building.
   b. I walked up the stairs where Finny had fallen.
   c. I joined my 11:10 class, which was in mathematics.

John Knowles, _A Separate Peace_

C. Imitating Sentences Imitate the structure and punctuation of each model below, using your own content. Like the models, each of your imitations should contain a compound subject or a compound verb.

1. His little dark eyes, deepset under a round forehead, and his mouth, surrounded with wrinkles, made him look attentive and studious.

Albert Camus, "The Guest"

2. Plays, dances, concerts, bazaars, suppers, parties followed on one another in staggering succession. **Mary Elizabeth Vroman, "See How They Run"**

3. He jerked the tiller free from the rudder and beat and chopped with it, holding it in both hands and driving it down again and again.

Ernest Hemingway, _The Old Man and the Sea_

4. He picked up a sharp blade of stone, scraped at the wound, sawed at the proud flesh, and then squeezed the green juice out in big drops.

John Steinbeck, "Flight"

5. Mrs. Jones stopped, jerked him around in front of her, put a half nelson about his neck, and continued to drag him up the street.

Langston Hughes, "Thank You, M'am"

Application Write a paragraph that describes a complex scene (such as a parade or a crowded arena). Begin with a sentence in which subject and verb are inverted. In several other sentences, use compound subjects and verbs; notice the rhythm and drama they add.

Grammar Refresher For more about inverted subject and verb (predicate), see Handbook 34, page 692. For more about compound subjects and verbs, see Handbook 31, page 579.

Sketchbook

Mirror

I am silver and exact. I have no preconceptions.
Whatever I see I swallow immediately
Just as it is, unmisted by love or dislike.
I am not cruel, only truthful—
The eye of a little god, four-cornered.
Most of the time I meditate on the opposite wall.
It is pink, with speckles. I have looked at it so long
I think it is a part of my heart. But it flickers.
Faces and darkness separate us over and over.

Now I am a lake. A woman bends over me,
Searching my reaches for what she really is.
Then she turns to those liars, the candles or the moon.
I see her back, and reflect it faithfully.
She rewards me with tears and an agitation of hands.
I am important to her. She comes and goes.
Each morning it is her face that replaces the darkness.
In me she has drowned a young girl, and in me an old woman
Rises toward her day after day, like a terrible fish.

Sylvia Plath

©Rollie McKenna

Imagine you are an object. Write a poem or paragraph from the point of view of that object, explaining what you are.

Additional Sketches

Define a place. Try to capture the heart of what it is.
Make a list of the "top ten" in any one field.

Informative Exposition: Classification

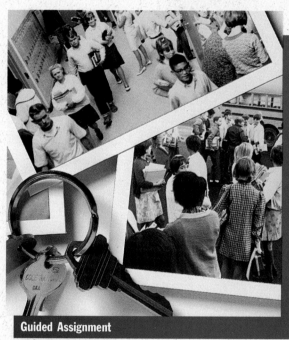

Guided Assignment
CLASSIFICATION

Related Assignment
COMPARISON AND CONTRAST

Related Assignment
ORGANIZATIONAL CHART

Classification plays a vital part in every field of human activity. Zoologists classify animals by their species; doctors classify burns by their degree of severity; social scientists classify nations by their form of government; football coaches classify players by their field positions; grocers classify food products into categories so that consumers can easily locate them on the shelves. Writers use classification as well, to organize their material and give structure to their writing. In this workshop, you will explore strategies for classifying subjects and for comparing, contrasting, and organizing their individual characteristics and qualities.

Classification

from
A Former Good Guy And His Friends

JOSEPH EPSTEIN

Look around at your classmates. What traits do they have in common? What sets some apart from others? In other words, how would you classify your classmates?

In the following essay, Joseph Epstein classifies himself and his fellow students at Nicholas Senn High School into a number of different categories. As you read, notice the categories he identifies and how he examines the category in which he classifies himself.

I recently saw a copy of the high-school newspaper that appeared the week of my class's graduation and found myself a bit miffed to discover that I was not voted Most Popular or Best Liked or Most Friendly or Best Personality or any of the other categories that speak to the ideal, vivid in the days of my youth, of being a Good Guy. It may seem immodest of me to talk about myself in this way, and normally I should refrain from doing so, but the plain fact is that I worked sedulously[1] at being thought not merely a Good Guy but an extraordinarily Good Guy and felt that I had greatly succeeded. Whence this interest on my part in being such a devilishly Good Guy, you may ask. I suppose it came about as a matter of elimination. Since I was neither a first-rate athlete, nor a notably successful Lothario, nor even a half-serious student, all that was left on the buffet of roles for me to choose from was Good Guy or thug, and since I hadn't the wardrobe for thug I went for Good Guy—and I went for it in a big way. Almost anyone who attended Nicholas Senn High School in Chicago when

I did will, I feel confident, tell you, "Sure, I remember Epstein. He was a Good Guy."

What a Good Guy is turns out not to be so simple a question. If Aristotle had gone to Nicholas Senn High School—a notion it gives me much delight to contemplate—he would doubtless have been able to posit[2] no fewer than eleven kinds of Good Guy and compose an ample disquisition[3] on the nature of Good Guy, or Good-Guyness. Perhaps a disquisition is required, for there is apparently some disagreement about what constitutes a Good Guy. Not long ago, for example, when I remarked to a friend from my high-school days that I thought I used to be a fine specimen of the type known as Good Guy, he replied that he thought I had not quite made it. I was very popular, he allowed, but I wasn't bland enough. The pure Good Guy, he argued, should be very bland.

Your true Good Guy should never give offense, or even hint at the potentiality for giving offense, and I, who was locally famous for an above-average sharpness of tongue, was considered verbally too dangerous to qualify as a pure Good Guy. Very well. I can accept that. Let me, then, revise my earlier statement: Almost anyone who attended Nicholas Senn High School when I did will, I feel confident, tell you, "Sure, I remember Epstein. He was a Good Guy—only don't cross him." . . .

[1]*sedulously*—diligently; persistently

[2]*posit*—to set down as fact; to postulate to be true

[3]*disquisition*—a formal discussion of some subject

119

INVITATION
TO
Write

Joseph Epstein used classification to present an ironic
view of himself and his fellow students. Write an essay,
report, or review that uses classification to accomplish
your goal.

Classification is the process of grouping or organizing subjects or
classes or categories. It is a means of examining characteristics, features, and elements, as well as of comparing and contrasting similarities and differences, or advantages and disadvantages. You can
classify a subject by identifying the larger class to which it belongs
and then examining how it fits the qualities of that class, or by
studying the parts of a broad subject and then exploring the parts
and their relationship to one another.

Classification can play a role in many types of writing, such as reviews, consumer reports, surveys, essays, and lab reports. Often,
however, classification may provide only a framework for examining
the subject, while other strategies are used to elaborate on and explore connections among ideas.

PREWRITE AND EXPLORE

HANDBOOKS
FOR HELP & PRACTICE

**Analyzing the
Writing Community,
pp. 335–338**

**Analysis Frames,
p. 356**

**Category Charts,
p. 357**

**Reference Works,
pp. 507–512**

1. Look for ideas. Although almost any subject may be classified,
you can probably do your best writing about a familiar subject that
interests you or a new one that you would like to explore. Try any
of the following activities to help you uncover possible topics.

Exploratory Activities

• **Categorizing** Joseph Epstein categorized the members
of his student body. Alone or with a classmate, think of
large groups of people or things that you could classify.
Then list the categories you might use to examine each
group.

- **Gleaning** As you read articles that interest you in magazines and newspapers, look for current events and technological and scientific breakthroughs that lend themselves to classification. Jot down interesting topics.
- **Surveying** Brainstorm alone or in a small group to think of topics for surveys you could conduct, such as music, movies, or products that many of your classmates use. For each idea you jot down, list categories of information you would need to ask about to make your survey complete and informative.
- **Comparing** Here are two proverbs that classify people:

"There are two kinds of people in one's life—people whom one keeps waiting, and the people for whom one waits."

S. N. Behrman

"The well-fed does not understand the lean."

Irish proverb

Freewrite for five minutes on either of these topics, or think of other proverbs you know that classify people.

- **Reading literature** Think of authors you have studied, such as Mark Twain, Alice Walker, or James Thurber. How would you classify their works? Does each writer fit in more than one class? What other writers have you read who might fit into the same classes?

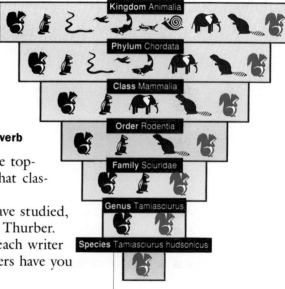

2. Review your ideas. Look over the subjects and categories you have listed. Which ideas would you like to explore further? Which might lead you to new ways of looking at things? Freewrite for about ten minutes on the ideas that most intrigue you. Then select one of them as a subject to explore through classification. You may also wish to consult your journal, look back at the writing you did in the Sketchbook on page 116, or check the "Apply Your Skills" section on page 129 for possible topics.

3. Classify your subject. Classification can help you explore your topic and organize your approach to it. If you have chosen a broad subject, you can classify it by examining its component parts. For example, to write about personal computers, you might examine such features of the category "computers" as memory capacity, disk drives, and operating system.

PROBLEM SOLVING

How can I identify the distinctive features or characteristics of my subject?

If you have chosen a narrow subject, you can identify a larger class to which it belongs and then examine the characteristics that make it part of that class. Keep in mind that you may be able to classify your subject in more than one way. For example, oranges might be classified as a type of fruit, but also as a type of healthy snack, or as a source of vitamin C. Each way of classifying the subject suggests a different set of traits to be examined.

One or more charts can help you analyze and classify your subject. Nina, who is considering a career in transportation engineering, decided to write about some topic in the broad area of rail transportation. The following chart shows how she used classification to analyze her subject. Throughout this assignment, follow Nina's process as she writes her essay about transportation.

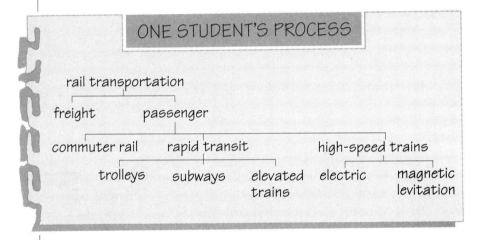

ONE STUDENT'S PROCESS

rail transportation

freight   passenger

commuter rail   rapid transit   high-speed trains

trolleys   subways   elevated   electric   magnetic
                           trains   levitation

Nina decided to write about high-speed trains, so she concentrated on examining the qualities of these trains and how they compared to those of other types of trains.

4. Determine your purpose. Ask yourself what you plan to accomplish with your writing. Do you want to inform, persuade, entertain, or express your opinion? Consider your personal goals too. What subject or question may you clarify in your own mind by writing this piece?

5. Suit your topic to your audience. How much do your readers know about your topic? What will interest them the most? Answering these questions can help you decide what type of information to present and how much detail to include.

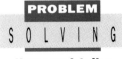

PROBLEM
S O L V I N G

How can I tailor my topic to my audience?

6. Choose a format. What form will your writing take? Do you want to write a consumer report about a product or a lab report? Do you want to write a review or an essay? Choose whatever form suits your topic and audience.

7. Gather information. In considering what type of information to gather, let your purpose, your intended audience, and your way of classifying your topic guide your choices. If you are analyzing a broad subject, you will need to gather details that explain the qualities of each component feature or characteristic. If you have chosen a narrow subject, you need to find specific details and examples that show how your subject fits its larger class or what makes it unique within its class.

For example, Joseph Epstein identified the qualities of "Good Guy" to show that he was a member of that larger class, and then explained how his sharp tongue made him unique within the class.

 Writer's Choice Do you want to examine the categories that comprise your subject, or do you need to identify the category to which your subject belongs and then examine how it compares to other items in its class?

DRAFT AND DISCOVER

1. Begin drafting. Some writers prefer to write a loosely structured draft from rough prewriting notes. Others choose a highly structured draft, in which they carefully follow a detailed writing plan, changing little of the content or organization. Use whichever approach works best for you.

2. Think about the organization of your draft. Although your subject matter will largely determine the structure of your paper, classificatory writing generally follows one of two patterns.

- If you are tackling a broad subject, you can divide it into its component parts, identify and describe each part, and discuss the relationship of that part to all the other parts.
- If you are focusing on a narrow subject, as Joseph Epstein did, you can define the larger class to which it belongs, identify other examples of the class, discuss the characteristics of the class and how your subject fits in, and point out the characteristics that set your subject apart from all other members of its class.

HANDBOOKS

FOR HELP & PRACTICE

Types of Elaboration, pp. 397–400

Unity/Coherence, pp. 401–414

Using Words Precisely, pp. 434–439

PROBLEM
S O L V I N G

How can I
elaborate on my
ideas as I write?

3. Elaborate on ideas. Remember that classification is generally a framework for analysis. To develop your writing, you will probably need to use other strategies, such as the ones below.

Strategies

- **Description** Use concrete descriptive details to identify the qualities and characteristics of your subject. Point out subtle differences between your subject and other items in the same larger class.
- **Comparison and contrast** Examine the likenesses and differences or advantages and disadvantages among various items in a given category, or among different categories of items.

Nina identified two categories of high-speed trains to cover in her report and began her draft by comparing these trains to conventional trains. Here is a portion of her draft.

ONE STUDENT'S PROCESS

There are two types of high-speed trains, electric and magnetic-levitation trains. They already speed passengers to their destinations in Japan and Europe.

Electric trains known as "bullet" trains are powered by electric locomotives that receive electricity from an overhead wire system. They have several advantages over conventional diesel-electric trains. They put out less pollution than trains operating on diesel oil, and they seem to be a lot safer. They can also travel at speeds faster than 125 mph. They have operated in Japan since 1964. The French, too, have a high-speed electric train. It is called train à grande vitesse, or TGV. One of these trains has reached a record speed of 299.5 mph.

As you can see, the bullet trains have many advantages. Even so, the other type of high-speed train, the maglev, may be the train of the future.

4. Take a break. When you have finished your draft, set your writing aside. Later, reread your work or ask a peer to review it. The following questions can help you focus on crucial issues.

COMPUTER
TIP

Remember to save your writing on disk every ten or fifteen minutes so that your work will not be lost if your computer loses power.

R E V I E W   Y O U R   W R I T I N G

Questions for Yourself

- Does my writing have a clear focus?

- Would my readers be interested in what I have to say? If not, how can I make my writing more interesting?

- Have I clearly identified the category or categories that characterize my subject?

- Have I used details, examples, and comparisons to explore each category?

- Is my organization clear? Does it suit my purpose, or would a different type of organization work better?

- Did my purpose change as I was writing? Does my draft accomplish my current purpose in this piece of writing?

Questions for Your Peer Readers

- What is the subject being classified? How is it classified?

- Can you name the categories or parts used to classify the subject? Are they appropriate?

- Are my ideas fully developed? Which parts need further development?

- Are there enough sensory descriptions, specific details, and examples or illustrations to make my writing interesting?

- Should any information be left out?

- Have I used any unfamiliar terms that need to be defined?

REVISE   YOUR   WRITING

1. Evaluate your responses. Think about the responses you have received from your readers, and reflect on your own responses as you revise your writing. Also keep in mind that good classification has the following characteristics.

HANDBOOKS

FOR HELP & PRACTICE

Art of Revision, pp. 416–421

Evoking Peer Responses, pp. 423–425

Grammar
——**TIP**——

If you are using a piece of slang or jargon in your writing, enclose it in quotation marks the first time it appears to show that it derives from a certain group or context and is not yet formally accepted usage.

Effective classification . . .

- clearly identifies the subject to be classified and the features or categories to be examined.
- fully examines each feature or category, using appropriate comparisons and contrasts, specific details, and clear description.
- uses a logical and effective organizational pattern, and uses transitional words and phrases to show relationships among ideas.
- demonstrates a clear sense of audience through the use of appropriate language and apt choice of details.

2. Problem-solve. Decide which responses you wish to use and rework your draft. Nina made these changes to strengthen her examination of bullet trains.

ONE STUDENT'S PROCESS

Sounds a bit choppy—combine sentences maybe.

Intriguing information! But could you explain how the maglev works?

How do they compare to other trains?

Despite the advantages of
~~As you can see,~~ the bullet trains have many advan- ~~tages. Even so,~~ the other type of high-speed train, the "maglev," may be the train of the future. magnetic levitation or maglev is the term used to describe a train that floats, or levitates, on the air, just inches above a steel guide rail. Two countries, Japan and West Germany, have already developed maglevs that have reached speeds of up to 300 mph on test tracks. Like electric-bullet trains, maglevs are less polluting than conventional diesel-electric trains, and they could be virtually soundless as they whisper by.

An extremely powerful magnetic field supports the train as it rides an electromagnetic wave that propels it forward.

3. Proofread your work. Proofreading is the final step in the revision process. Read your work carefully and correct any errors you find in grammar, usage, punctuation, capitalization, and spelling. Consult a dictionary to check the spelling of unfamiliar words. Use proofreading marks to indicate any changes on your paper. Then make a clean final copy of your work.

GRAMMAR AND WRITING
Using Transitions

Using effective transitions can help you examine relationships among the qualities or characteristics of your subject. Transitions such as *similarly, equally,* and *likewise* can draw attention to similarities; transitions such as *yet, nevertheless, despite,* and *in contrast* point out differences.

Transition showing comparison
In addition to speed, these electric trains provide other advantages over conventional diesel-electric trains.

Transition showing contrast
Despite the advantages of the bullet trains, the other type of high-speed train, the "maglev," may be the train of the future.

See Handbook 10, pages 404–408, for additional help with this problem.

PUBLISH AND PRESENT

- **Deliver an oral presentation of your work.** Use your writing as the basis for a lecture to your classmates. Illustrate your talk with appropriate charts, drawings, photographs, or slides.
- **Display your writing on your classroom bulletin board.** You and your classmates might group together similar types of writing, such as all surveys, all reports, or all essays.
- **Make a booklet or magazine of your writing.** You may choose to focus on either a single subject or various subjects. Lay out the writing in columns. Use photos and illustrations.
- **Save your work in your writing portfolio.** Reread it at a later time. Your own insights may surprise you.

HANDBOOKS
FOR HELP & PRACTICE

Speech Delivery,
pp. 515–517
Sharing and
Publishing,
pp. 427–428

Classification **127**

High-Speed Trains: The Future Is Now

Nina McMahon

Imagine gliding along the countryside at a speed of more than 300 miles per hour inside a sleek, modern railroad car. That dream is already a reality in other countries, and one day the technology for high-speed rail transportation may come to the United States.

Presents the classification and then breaks the general subject into two categories

High-speed trains of two types, electric and magnetic levitation, already speed passengers to their destinations in Japan and Europe. They provide an efficient alternative to auto, plane, and conventional rail transportation for trips of between 100 and 500 miles.

Uses concrete details to identify the features of the category

Electric trains known as "bullet" trains are powered by electric locomotives that receive electricity from an overhead wire system. These trains, which travel at speeds greater than 125 mph, have operated in Japan since 1964. The French, too, have a high-speed electric train, the *train à grande vitesse* or TGV. The TGV *Atlantique* has reached a record speed of 299.5 mph, and it regularly cruises at a more conservative speed of 186 mph.

Uses comparison and contrast to examine the category fully

In addition to speed, these electric trains provide other advantages over conventional diesel-electric trains. They are less noisy and do not pollute the air with smoke, as do slower trains operating on diesel oil.

Makes a smooth transition to an examination of the second main category

Despite the advantages of the bullet trains, the other type of high-speed train, the "maglev," may be the train of the future. Magnetic levitation, or maglev, is the term used to describe a train that floats, or levitates, on the air just inches above a steel guiderail. An extremely powerful magnetic field supports the train as it rides an electromagnetic wave that propels it forward. Two countries, Japan and West Germany, have already developed maglevs that have reached speeds of up to 300 mph on test tracks. Like electric-bullet trains, maglevs are less polluting than conventional diesel-electric trains, and they could be virtually soundless as they whisper by.

Uses comparison to show similarities between the two categories

Maglevs are still in the testing stage, but during the 1990's they could begin whooshing between cities in Japan, Europe, and the United States. Along with the bullet trains, they represent important transportation alternatives to our overcrowded roads and airways.

Eudora Welty, American novelist and storywriter

WRITER TO WRITER

In writing, as in life, the connections of all sorts of relationships and kinds lie in wait of discovery, and give out their signals to the Geiger counter of the charged imagination, once it is drawn into the right field.

Eudora Welty, novelist

FOR YOUR
PORTFOLIO

1. Reflect on your writing. Look back over the process you have engaged in from the time you first began this assignment to the time you finished your classification paper. In a brief informal report, which you might attach to your paper or record in your journal, consider the following questions:

- How did I come up with a topic for my classification paper?
- What activities helped me to find my subject?
- Where did I find information to use in developing the body of my paper? What other sources of information might I have used?
- What did I learn about my subject in the course of writing my paper?
- How would I change my paper now, if I had the time and interest?

2. Apply your skills. Try one or more of the following activities.

- **Cross-curricular** Write a "consumer report" on a product or service or institution (colleges, summer camps, record stores, school clubs), classifying and evaluating the options.
- **Literature** Review the stories and novels you have studied during this academic year and write a short report classifying the heroes you have encountered in these works. See if you can draw any conclusions about what sorts of heroes are likely to appear in literary works assigned in high school.
- **Related assignments** Follow the suggestions on pages 132–139 for writing a comparison/contrast piece and completing an organizational chart.

Related ASSIGNMENT

Comparison and Contrast

FROM

The Sea Around Us

Rachel Carson

The sea transforms climate.
And how completely it does so is strikingly
seen in the differences between the
Arctic and the Antarctic.

H ow does one college differ from another? Which set of headphones should you buy? How has your hometown changed in the last two years? When you analyze questions like these involving similarities and differences, you are using comparison and contrast techniques.

In *The Sea Around Us*, Rachel Carson explains the important and varied ways that the sea affects climate by contrasting two geographical regions—the Arctic and the Antarctic. As you read the excerpt, think about the characteristics of these two places and about how the contrasts between them demonstrate the sea's influence.

The Arctic is a sea almost closed in by land; the Antarctic is a continent surrounded by ocean. The ice-covered Antarctic is in the grip of high winds that blow outward from the land. They ward off any warming influence that might otherwise come to the continent from the sea. So the Antarctic is a bitterly cold land. Here and there over the snow is the red dust of very small and simple plant cells. Mosses hide from the wind in the valleys and crevices. But of the higher plants only a few skimpy stands of grasses have managed to find a foothold. There are no land mammals. The animals of the Antarctic continent are birds, a wingless mosquito, a few flies, and a microscopic mite.

Think AND Respond

What details about the Antarctic and the Arctic did Rachel Carson contrast in her descriptions of the two regions? In what ways did these contrasts help her illustrate the sea's effect on climate? How could you use a comparison or a contrast to explain an unfamiliar idea, to clarify a point, or to make a decision or choice?

Contrast with this the summers of the Arctic! Its flat, treeless plains are bright with many-colored flowers. Everywhere except on the Greenland icecap and some Arctic islands, summer is warm enough for plants to grow. They pack a year's growth into the short, warm, Arctic summer. The limit of plant life toward the poles is set not by latitude, but by the sea. For the influence of the warm Atlantic is borne far up into the Arctic, making it in climate as well as geography a world apart from the Antarctic.

INVITATION
—TO—
Write

Rachel Carson contrasted two geographic regions to show how the sea affects climate. Now write your own comparison or contrast essay in which you explore the relationship between two persons, places, or things.

We compare and contrast often in daily life—choosing between courses at school, deciding whether or not to take a part-time job, or explaining, in a social studies paper, the strengths and weaknesses of the two armies in the Civil War. When you make such comparisons and contrasts, you are classifying two objects, effects, or experiences in terms of their likenesses or differences. Such classification can help you form a judgment about the relative value of the two things, draw conclusions about the relationship between the two subjects, as well as understand a difficult problem or clarify a new idea.

PREPARING TO COMPARE AND CONTRAST

HANDBOOKS
FOR HELP & PRACTICE

Comparison/Contrast Charts,
p. 357
Comparison/Contrast Order,
pp. 366–367
Specific Examples,
p. 398
Using Comparisons Correctly,
pp. 745–747

1. Give yourself a purpose. You might choose to inform a classmate—or yourself—about an unfamiliar subject by comparing and contrasting it with a familiar one. You might also illustrate a process or a natural force by comparing and contrasting its effects upon two objects, as Rachel Carson does by examining the influences of the sea on the Arctic and Antarctic in her essay. You might also persuade a friend to choose one course of action over another by comparing and contrasting the results or consequences of the two actions.

Writer's Choice Do you want your comparison-and-contrast essay to focus on a topic from history, for example, rather than on something from your personal experience?

2. Decide exactly what you will compare or contrast. Often, showing both the similarities and differences between two subjects can help you make your point. For example, if your goal is to explain how attitude affects personal achievement, you could compare and contrast two periods in your life—one in which you enjoyed success and satisfaction and one in which you experienced failure or disappointment. You would then look at what factors were constant in both periods and what varied or differed.

3. Chart points of comparison and contrast. Charting will help you organize the information you will cover in your essay. For example, a chart analyzing your personal achievement may contain vertical columns labeled *This Year* and *Last Year* and horizontal ones labeled *Achievements* and *Missed Opportunities*. You might note details about variations in your attitude at the bottom of each year's column.

DRAFTING A COMPARISON-AND-CONTRAST ESSAY

1. Choose an organizational pattern. You can choose one of two basic patterns for organizing comparisons and contrasts. Using the subject-by-subject approach (as Carson does), you would discuss your achievement and attitude this year, then proceed to last year. Or you could organize according to features—for example, academic performance in the two years, then friendships, family, personal interests, and so on.

2. Draft your comparison/contrast. Begin writing at whatever seems the natural starting place—either with the details of the comparison/contrast itself or with the main idea (for example, attitude affects achievement). Keep your purpose and audience in mind.

3. Give specific examples and details. Provide the most specific and interesting information possible. Of course you will need to make occasional general statements, but be sure to support them with vivid examples and details. Rachel Carson, for instance, supports the statement "the Antarctic is a bitterly cold land" with details like "mosses hide from the wind in the valleys and crevices."

4. Write a conclusion. When you feel that you have thoroughly compared and contrasted your subjects, write a brief summarizing paragraph that restates your main idea or draws a conclusion about the comparison.

R EVIEWING YOUR WRITING

1. Be sure your organization and purpose are clear. Have you maintained a consistent organization—either the subject-by-subject or the feature-by-feature format? Does your essay achieve your general purpose and your personal goal?

2. Ask another person to review your essay. Have your reader point out any confusing passages, unsupported statements, or unnecessary information. Determine whether the point you were trying to make or the conclusion you drew was clear to your reader. Revise on the basis of this feedback.

P UBLISHING AND PRESENTING

- **Submit your essay to a school publication.** Accompany it with appropriate photographs or charts.
- **Create a book.** If you and several classmates wrote on similar topics, such as making a consumer-oriented decision or how to clean up the environment, compile them in a book.
- **Present your comparison/contrast orally.** If possible, share your essay with your classmates in an oral presentation. You might wish to prepare a chart (based, perhaps, on your prewriting notes) that summarizes the main points of your comparison/contrast.

Collection of Whitney Museum of American Art. Purchase, with funds from the Howard and Jean Lipman Foundation, Inc. 70.1572

Lucas Samaras. *Chair Transformation Number 10A*. (1969–70). Wood, formica and wool.

On the Lightside

WORD BLENDS

After Alice stepped into a new world in Lewis Carroll's *Through the Looking Glass,* she had a conversation with a famous language expert—Humpty Dumpty. "You seem very clever at explaining words, sir," said Alice. "Would you kindly tell me the meaning of the poem called 'Jabberwocky'?"

One by one, Mr. Dumpty explained the strange words in that nonsense poem. *Slithy,* for example, is a combination of *lithe* and *slimy. Mimsy* combines *miserable* and *flimsy.* "You see, it's like a portmanteau —there are two meanings packed up into one word," he said. A portmanteau is a large suitcase with two compartments. Humpty Dumpty's analogy has provided a common term for word blends—portmanteau words.

Blends have been a part of the language for centuries. Early examples include *glimmer,* a combination of *gleam* and *shimmer,* from the 1400's, and *clash* (*clap* plus *crash*) from the 1500's. Some of the blends Lewis Carroll contributed to English include *squawk* (*squeak* plus *squall*) and *chortle* (*chuckle* plus *snort*). More recent blends are *brunch* (*breakfast* and *lunch*), *smog* (*smoke* and *fog*), and *motel* (*motor* and *hotel*).

Just as more information can be packed into sentences by combining them, more information can be packed into words by creating blends. As Humpty Dumpty noted, however, "When I make a word do a lot of work like that, I always pay it extra."

Organizational Chart

Have you ever been grateful for a chart that clarified a complicated subject for you? A chart can display the different aspects of a complex topic clearly and economically.

Consider exercise routines, for example. Each offers individual benefits and each requires different equipment. The chart on this page enables you to see at a glance how each exercise stacks up in a number of different categories. As you look over the chart, notice how its format enables you to make quick comparisons among the different types of exercises.

		BENEFITS	LIMITATIONS	CALORIES BURNED PER HALF HOUR
RUNNING (5.2 mph)		Expands capacity of heart, lungs, and blood vessels; relaxation; strengthens bones	Strengthens lower body only	Approximately 275
SWIMMING (crawl strokes)		Exercises upper and lower body; strengthens heart; improves flexibility and strength	Does not qualify as a weight-bearing exercise	260
AEROBIC DANCING		Good aerobic exercise; promotes flexibility	Does not build muscle strength	210
BICYCLING (10 mph)		Good aerobic exercise; exercises lower body, especially quadriceps	Does not build upper-body strength	200
WALKING (4 mph)		Tones up calf, hamstring, and buttocks muscles; raises heart rate	Does not build upper-body strength	165
RESISTANCE TRAINING		Promotes joint flexibility; speeds up reflexes; builds muscles	Not a sustained aerobic workout	120

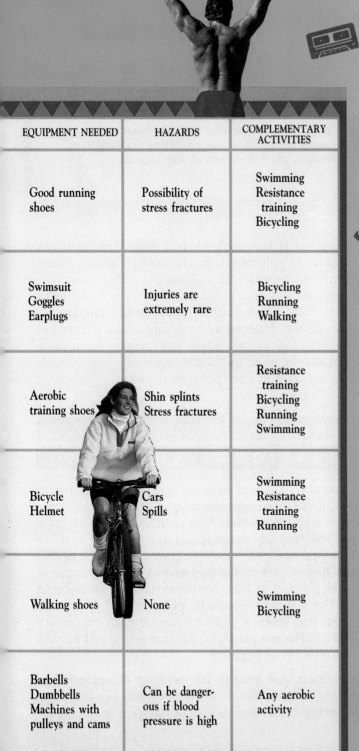

EQUIPMENT NEEDED	HAZARDS	COMPLEMENTARY ACTIVITIES
Good running shoes	Possibility of stress fractures	Swimming Resistance training Bicycling
Swimsuit Goggles Earplugs	Injuries are extremely rare	Bicycling Running Walking
Aerobic training shoes	Shin splints Stress fractures	Resistance training Bicycling Running Swimming
Bicycle Helmet	Cars Spills	Swimming Resistance training Running
Walking shoes	None	Swimming Bicycling
Barbells Dumbbells Machines with pulleys and cams	Can be dangerous if blood pressure is high	Any aerobic activity

AN EXERCISE TO FIT YOUR EVERY NEED

Your own recipe for keeping fit can be as individual as you'd like to make it. Most people need to alternate between at least two routines because each offers complementary advantages. Walking and swimming make a good pair, for example, because walking primarily exercises the lower body while swimming tones upper-body muscles as well. The exercises on this chart are listed in descending order of efficiency at burning calories.

Think AND Respond

Notice the information the author of the chart included about each exercise. Would you have added different information if you had been making the same chart? How did the form of the chart enable you to make comparisons among the different exercises more easily than if the information had been in paragraph form? How might an organizational chart help you to organize and illustrate a body of information that would be useful to you?

INVITATION
— TO —
Write

This organizational chart classifies six exercise programs according to six different categories. Use the following guideline to create an organizational chart that graphically displays information about a subject of your choice.

Organizational charts are classifying tools that show how items can be grouped, compared, or contrasted. As the example shows, charts demonstrate information graphically, or visually, rather than narratively. Charts show as well as tell and can reveal many different aspects of a subject. For example, a chart could show changes over time or could illustrate the structure of an organization. Charts can facilitate your research and writing when you prepare a paper or speech. A chart can also be quite useful for organizing and presenting the complex information in an expository report.

PREPARING AN
ORGANIZATIONAL CHART

HANDBOOKS
FOR HELP & PRACTICE

Limiting/Expanding
Topics,
pp. 351–352
Graphic Organizers,
pp. 353–360
Evoking Peer
Responses,
pp. 423–424
Reference Works,
pp. 507–512
Speech Preparation/
Delivery,
pp. 515–518

1. Choose your subject. Do you have a science or social studies assignment that requires you to organize a large amount of information? Would any of this information be easier to present in chart form? Perhaps you are currently deciding which colleges to apply to for admission. A comparison chart could help make the choices easier to see. You may be considering the purchase of an expensive item but don't know which brand to buy. An organizational chart could help you compare the different brands by price, quality, and other features. You might also make a chart to complete an expository essay for English class. The sample chart, for example, could be part of a report on various exercise regimens.

2. Analyze your subject and choose its defining characteristics. As you examine your subject, list its main categories in your planning notes. (The author of the sample chart organized it around six exercise routines.) Then think of common characteristics that could apply to each major heading. The author selected six characteristics that could be applied to nearly any form of exercise. Finally, look for specific details that will develop each of these subheads.

3. Develop information for your chart. Researching your subject might involve consulting reference books or magazines, conducting a public-opinion poll, interviewing subjects, or drawing on your own knowledge or experience. List your main heads and subheads, and search out specific details to develop each head. Double-check the accuracy of your research by consulting additional sources.

4. Organize your information. In what order will you present the information you've developed? Note that the exercises in the sample chart are listed in descending order of efficiency at burning calories. Your subject will determine how you organize your material— whether in chronological order, from largest to smallest, by price, or in some other way.

5. Choose a chart format that best conveys the information you want to share. In order to choose the proper format, consider the goal of your chart. The simple column format of the sample facilitates comparing and contrasting the different exercise routines. A cluster, or spider chart stresses relationships among the parts of a subject. This type of chart is especially helpful for breaking down several topics into their subsidiary parts. A timeline, often containing dates and events, can illustrate fluctuations of a subject over time. This might be useful in presenting scientific or historical data. A tree chart shows the connections among parts that stem from one main trunk. Such a chart might be used to illustrate family relationships.

CREATING YOUR CHART

1. Sketch your chart. Using your notes, sketch your chart and insert the information you've gathered. Notice that wording in the sample chart is very concise. Wordiness can make a chart difficult to interpret. Label columns and categories clearly and concisely.

2. Consider using graphic devices to make your chart more interesting. As your chart takes shape, think about how you could convey your information most compellingly. You might use color, symbols, designs, or other illustrations. For example, genealogical charts are often designed to look like trees.

Writing
—TIP—
Eliminate articles, adjectives, and adverbs to keep your entries short. You don't need to write complete sentences on a chart.

3. Add additional explanatory text. Give your chart an engaging title. If your chart employs graphic symbols, be sure to include a key that explains them. You may also need to write a short introduction that provides background and a context for the information on your chart. The sample chart's introduction, for example, explains that no one workout can meet all a person's needs. This introduction also alerts the reader to the category "complementary exercises," which shows how the various exercise regimens can be combined.

REVIEWING YOUR WRITING

1. Examine your chart and explanatory text. Are your chart's subject and purpose immediately clear? Does the chart make a strong visual impact? Is your format an appropriate one for the information you've chosen to present? Check to see that your explanatory material, labels, and key make your subject clear and your chart easy to interpret. Does each element of your chart help you to achieve your original goal—for example, showing relationships, comparing and contrasting, or showing change over time?

2. Ask a classmate to critique your chart. Does your chart present data in a way that a viewer can easily understand? Prepare some questions that your chart should answer and see if a friend can answer them solely from the information on your chart. Ask your friend for suggestions for graphic devices that would make your chart more interesting.

3. Prepare your final copy. An organizational chart is a visual aid. If you plan to feature your chart in an oral presentation, consider what materials you'll need to make your final copy legible from a distance. Your final copy should be neat, clear, and ready for public presentation. Proofread your chart and neatly correct any errors.

COMPUTER TIP

Some word-processing programs offer special style sheets for composing charts and graphs. If you are using a word-processing program, check to see what type of graphic assistance it may provide.

PUBLISHING AND PRESENTING

- **Use your chart as the basis for an oral report on your subject.**
- **Exhibit your chart.** Place it on a classroom bulletin board along with an explanatory text.
- **Make a transparency.** Then you can display your chart on an overhead projector.

Sentence

Elaborating on Simple Sentences

Good writers enrich the content of simple sentences by adding several kinds of phrases to the subject or the predicate. They vary their sentence structure by inserting the phrases in different parts of their sentences. In this lesson you will learn to apply their techniques to your own sentences.

In the models, the foundations (main clauses) are underlined. Notice that phrases can be added both before and after the foundations. Notice, also, how the phrases add detail and clarity.

MODELS

  S   V

1. <u>Alfred peeked at their faces</u>, black and sweating in the semicircle around him.   **Robert Lipsyte, *The Contender***

                                        S   V

2. Standing in an aisle in the library, <u>he can feel the eyes on him</u>.   **Judith Guest, *Ordinary People***

A. Unscrambling and Imitating Sentences In each set, unscramble the parts to form a sentence the structure of which matches that of the model. Then, using your own content, write a second sentence that imitates the structure of each model.

1. Inside the closed double lip of his jaws, <u>all of his eight rows of teeth were slanted inwards</u>.   **Ernest Hemingway, *The Old Man and the Sea***
   a. many of the auditioning actors were shifting nervously
   b. on the unadorned stage
   c. of the ancient theatre

2. <u>They followed him around the entire day</u>, pawing at him, talking to him, laughing at his jokes, and trying to hold his hand.
                                         Pat Conroy, *The Water is Wide*

   a. yelling at them
   b. stretching toward them
   c. and trying to approach the stage
   d. the audience applauded the group wildly
   e. vying for their attention

3. <u>The companions followed the shady woodroad</u>, the cow taking slow steps, and the child very fast ones. **Sarah Orne Jewett, "A White Heron"**
   a. but the rabbit an even faster one
   b. the dog keeping a fast pace
   c. the pair crossed the broad pasture

4. At five o'clock, in the starlight, <u>he was out on the river shore with a candle lantern made of a baking powder can</u>, examining tracks.
   Elliott Merrick, "Without Words"
   a. beating the heat
   b. at Barton Springs, outside Austin
   c. Tom floated on the clear water in his inner tube patched with red vinyl tape

Descriptive phrases can also be placed between subject and verb, a placement called the S-V split position.

MODEL

      s
<u>A succession of loud and shrill screams</u>, bursting suddenly
                                v
from the throat of the chained form, <u>seemed to thrust me violently back</u>.

Edgar Allan Poe, "The Cask of Amontillado"

B. Expanding Sentences Expand each sentence by adding a phrase between the subject and verb. Begin your elaboration with the bracketed words. Compare your finished sentences with the originals on page 327.

1. <u>Her big brown eyes</u>, [like. . .], <u>were warmer, softer</u>.
   Mary Lavin, "One Summer"

2. <u>The ashes</u>, [so. . .], <u>smelled raw, rain-wet</u>.
   Jessamyn West, "The Child's Day"

3. For a minute or more, <u>the hand</u>, [with. . .], <u>protruded out of the floor</u>.
   Arthur Conan Doyle, "The Red-Headed League"

4. Down below, in the garden beds, <u>the red and yellow tulips</u>, [heavy. . .], <u>seemed to lean upon the dusk</u>. **Katherine Mansfield, "Bliss"**

C. Imitating Sentences Imitate the structure and punctuation of each sentence below, using your own content.

1. Every day, a few minutes after two o'clock in the afternoon, the limited express between two cities passed this spot.
   Thomas Wolfe, "The Far and Near"

2. One night, unable to stand the heat anymore, he burst into the street at one A.M., a shadow of himself.   **Bernard Malamud, "A Summer's Reading"**

3. There was a slow, pleasant movement in the air, scarcely a wind, promising a cool, lovely day.   **F. Scott Fitzgerald, *The Great Gatsby***

4. Across a narrow little office sat a young black man in work clothes, his wife beside him holding their little girl in her lap.
   Jack Finney, "Of Missing Persons"

Application The phrases below could fit in various places within simple sentences. For each phrase, write a simple sentence foundation. Underline your foundation. Then add the phrase where it fits best (before or after the foundation, or between subject and verb). Use each position at least once.

Example	a. covered with grease and dirt

Student Sentences

(before foundation)   Covered with grease and dirt, <u>Jackson emerged from under the car</u>.

(after foundation)   <u>Lee's watercolor lay in the gutter</u>, covered with grease and dirt.

(between subject and verb)   <u>The cleanup workers</u>, covered with grease and dirt, <u>desperately battled the oil spill</u>.

1. with twenty volunteering
2. around the middle of June
3. hanging upside down
4. faster than an Olympic runner
5. to prove their school's worth
6. unlike the typical junior
7. from the top of the skyscraper
8. far beyond her expectations
9. bent almost double with effort
10. after a very difficult test

Grammar Refresher For more about kinds of phrases, see Handbook 32, pages 599–611. For help with writing simple sentence foundations, see Handbook 31, pages 578–579.

Sketchbook

The year was 1977, and disco dancing was the rage. But it turned out to be just a passing fad. Look around you. What things are people doing now that will have a lasting impact? Which do you think will turn out to be mere fads?

Additional Sketches

Write about a phase in your life, such as your "rebellious phase," your "goody-goody phase," or your "nerd phase."

Describe an invention that would change the world.

Informative Exposition: Analysis

Guided Assignment
EXAMINING CHANGES

Related Assignment
SCIENCE FICTION

Related Assignment
PICTORIAL ESSAY

"You can never step into the same river twice," said an ancient philosopher. He meant that everything in the universe is constantly changing, even things that seem to be permanent.

Recording change is one of the major reasons that writing was invented. Historians narrate the rise and fall of civilizations. Diarists keep track of the changes that fill their lives. Business documents note changing amounts of money, goods, and services. Writing is group memory. In this workshop, you'll explore three especially change-oriented types of writing: essays that examine change over time, science fiction, and the pictorial essay.

145

Examining Changes

FARTHER OFF FROM HEAVEN
by William Humphrey

Sometimes you probably find yourself thinking about the way things used to be—how school used to be, what the house or town you used to live in was like, what *you* were like. It's natural to want to understand how things change—and why.

In this excerpt, William Humphrey returns to his hometown, Clarksville, Texas, after being away for thirty years, to find it much changed from the way he remembered it. As you read, notice how Humphrey shows you the changes and tries to understand them himself.

The nearer I got to Clarksville the farther from it I seemed to be. This was not where I was spawned. Strange places had usurped the names of towns I used to know. It was like what the British during World War II, fearing an invasion, had done, setting real but wrong place-names and roadsigns around the countryside so that the enemy in, say, Kent would find himself in villages belonging to Lancashire.

Gone were the spreading cottonfields I remembered, though this was the season when they should

have been beginning to whiten. The few patches that remained were small and sparse, like the patches of snow lingering on in sunless spots in New England in March and April. The prairie grass that had been there before the fields were broken for cotton had reclaimed them. The woods were gone—even Sulpher Bottom, that wilderness into which my father had gone in pursuit of the fugitive gunman: grazing land now, nearly all of it. For in a move that reverses Texas history, a move totally opposite to what I knew in my childhood, one which all but turns the world upside down, which makes the sun set in the East, Red River County has ceased to be Old South and become Far West. I who for years had had to set my Northern friends straight by pointing out that I was a Southerner, not a Westerner, and that I had never seen a cowboy or for that matter a beefcow any more than they had, found myself now in that Texas of legend and the popular image which when I was a child had seemed more romantic to me than to a boy of New England precisely because it was closer to me than to him and yet still worlds away. Gone from the square were the bib overalls of my childhood when the farmers came to town on Saturday. Ranchers now, they came in high-heeled boots and rolled-brim hats, a costume that would have provoked as much surprise, and even more derision, there, in my time, as it would on Manhattan's Madison Avenue.

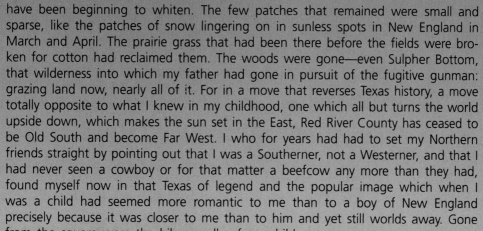

Think AND Respond

How does Clarksville appear to Humphrey now? How did Clarksville appear in his memory? What specific differences does he note in this excerpt between the Clarksville of memory and the Clarksville of actuality? Can you think of a place you know that has changed significantly?

**INVITATION
—TO—
*Write***

William Humphrey wrote about the changes he found when he returned to his hometown. Now write your own essay, report, or review that analyzes how a subject changes or has changed over time. Use the suggestions that follow for guidance as you write.

Exploring changes over time is a common type of writing. A social scientist might show how a mining community in West Virginia changes from generation to generation. Literary critics explore how characters change over the course of a novel or how a writer's style changes from book to book. Scientists write down their findings at specific intervals during an experiment. When you ask how and why changes occur, you analyze causes and effects and make comparisons. You acquire perspective on ideas, emotions, beliefs, and physical phenomena. You become a more sophisticated thinker.

ᑭREWRITE AND EXPLORE

HANDBOOKS
FOR HELP & PRACTICE

Sharing Techniques,
pp. 346–347
Collaborative
Planning,
pp. 370–373
Comparison/Contrast
Charts,
p. 357

1. Explore changes. You and the world around you are ever-changing. Here are suggestions for finding changes to write about.

Exploratory Activities

- **Snapshots** Imagine looking at snapshots of your life taken at regular intervals. What were you, your family, or friends doing ten years ago, or five years ago, or last year? Make some notes about what these snapshots reveal. Then look beyond the pictures. What has changed? Why?

- **Brainstorming** Try approaching the topic from another direction by brainstorming with your peer group about the causes of change: sickness, financial trouble, crossing a life milestone (graduating from high school or college or getting married, for instance), travel, education, the influence of other people. See if you can think of specific examples of how each of these phenomena can cause change.

- **Current events** Watch the evening news or read a daily paper and make a list of five subjects that interest you. With your peer group, discuss how these subjects have changed over time. Consider local, national, and international issues.
- **Technology** Think and take notes about how technology has made changes in the way we live. How have computers changed schools? How has play changed since you were a child? How has technology changed music and sports?
- **Reading literature** Consider striking characters you have read about and the changes they have experienced. You might examine a character from Bret Harte's "The Outcasts of Poker Flat," John Updike's "Separating," Kate Chopin's "Story of an Hour," or Stephen Crane's "The Open Boat."

PROBLEM

S O L V I N G

How can I find changes that are important to me?

The chameleon changes colors to survive.

Writer's Choice Do you feel more comfortable writing about changes in your own life and that of your family and friends or about changes in the outside world?

2. Select a topic and freewrite. Make a list of five or six promising topics. Narrow it down to one or two choices that feel most interesting to you. Freewrite for ten minutes on the topic from which you are likely to learn the most. What change can you study that will reveal the most to you about yourself, somebody else, a literary work, or a subject?

COMPUTER TIP

To aid in freewriting, turn down the screen light so that you can't see what you're writing.

PROBLEM
S O L V I N G

How can I begin
to analyze the
change I am
writing about?

3. Use collaborative planning. Meet with a partner and discuss your plans for producing an essay on changes over time. Give particular attention to the following questions:

- **Your topic and goals** Why did you choose your particular topic and what do you hope to achieve in your essay?
- **Your audience** Who are your readers and what do you want them to think or feel as a result of reading your essay? What do you have to do to make sure your readers understand you? How much background information do they need? How much knowledge do they already share with you?
- **Your sources of information** What resources might you use: your memory, interviews, reading, the library, direct observation?
- **Your method or form** What form of writing will best serve your purposes? Will it be an essay, a review, a report, a character sketch? Select the form that meets your needs.

4. Explore your topic. Making a chart is one way to discover both patterns of change and reasons for change. List different qualities your subject had at different time periods, or identify key qualities of your subject and list how those qualities changed over time.

Using the "Snapshots" activity, Tim took a verbal snapshot of the time he spent the Fourth of July in Germany as an exchange student. Then he made a chart exploring his feelings about the holiday—and about being an American—at different times. Throughout this assignment, you will follow Tim's process in writing his essay.

ONE STUDENT'S PROCESS

Before Germany	one Canadian parent, never celebrated the Fourth, not very patriotic
In Germany	for Germans, our 213th birthday nothing special (newspaper); for us, school holiday, picnic, flag on castle, picture-taking with flag
After Germany	Fourth and being American are special, pride glad for what we have, don't take education opportunities for granted

1. Begin drafting. As you write, remember that your goal is to analyze and explore changes that occur over time. Therefore, you need to show your reader *how* and *why* changes occur rather than merely present a chronology or list of changes. You may find one or more of these strategies helpful to you as you draft.

Strategies

- **Description** Create a vivid picture of your subject at each stage of change. Notice the details William Humphrey used to describe his hometown at two different stages.
- **Compare and contrast** Note the key characteristics of your subject, and examine how each one changed over time. Humphrey found striking contrasts in both the land and the people of his hometown after thirty years.
- **Cause and effect** Show how an action caused a change or series of changes, or examine the effects of change over a period of time.

2. Organize your draft. The way you organize your material will vary depending upon the types of changes you are examining. You may wish to tell a narrative. Arranging events in the order in which they occurred helps your readers see gradations of change. This technique can also be used to explain a "chain" of causes and effects, with each occurring in turn.

A second method is to concentrate on comparing and contrasting. Use either the block method of comparison, in which you describe all the qualities of your subject at one time period and then show how they changed, or the point-by-point method, in which you examine each quality in turn and show how it changed over time.

3. Elaborate on ideas. Keep in mind that change is relative and that you must illustrate the degree of change. What seems like a major or important change to you may go unnoticed by someone else. Use specific facts and details to show or illustrate the amount of change.

On the next page you will see what details Tim included to show how much the difference between America and Germany impressed him.

HANDBOOKS
FOR HELP & PRACTICE

Comparison/Contrast
Order,
pp. 366–367
Cause-Effect Order,
pp. 367–368
Facts/Statistics,
p. 397

Writing
—**TIP**—

Writers often combine organizing techniques.

American teenagers have a much greater range of educational options open to them than Germans do. After the fourth grade, students are separated into three different schools, according to their scores on a test. The three kinds of schools lead to trades or to industry, to more clerical careers, and to university education. Some people, therefore, are forced to decide on a career goal as children, as early as fourth grade. And following their eighteenth birthdays, all males must serve fifteen months with the armed forces.

Writing
—TIP—

The stage of "doing nothing," or letting go, can be a time when your writing can communicate back to you.

4. Take a break. Once your draft has "cooled," begin the process of reviewing it. Try reading it aloud once or twice to hear gaps in your thought or other problems. Then ask one or more peer reviewers to read it for you.

REVIEW YOUR WRITING

Questions for Yourself

• Have I specifically *shown* the changes?

• Do I explain *how* and *why* the changes occurred?

• Is my essay organized so that my reader can clearly see and understand the changes?

• Are there clear connections between causes and effects? Are points of comparison and contrast presented clearly?

Questions for Your Peer Readers

• Write down the changes that occurred over time—without looking back at the paper.

• Are my explanations for the changes thorough enough? Do you understand what occurred, how it occurred, and why it occurred?

• Can you think of a more appropriate way to present and organize my information?

Writer's Choice As you write, you may choose to focus more on *how* your subject changed, or on *why* it changed.

REVISE YOUR WRITING

1. Evaluate your responses. What responses do you want to incorporate when you revise your draft? Keep in mind these traits of effective writing that examines changes over time:

Standards for Evaluation

Good writing about changes over time . . .

- clearly presents the changes that occur and uses specific details to elaborate on their significance.
- uses comparison and contrast if appropriate to describe changes.
- shows a clear relationship between causes and effects of change.
- uses a logical and effective organizational pattern.
- uses appropriate language and details for the audience.

2. Problem-solve. Decide which responses you want to use, and rework your draft. Tim made changes as shown on the next page.

HANDBOOKS
FOR HELP & PRACTICE

Art of Revision, pp. 416–421

One of the most important events in recent history was the demolition of the Berlin Wall, uniting East and West Berlin for the first time since 1961.

Your example is good, but can you show even more?

It might be good to state clearly what the change was and how it happened.

^ perhaps America's proudest day,

I am not a very patriotic person the fourth of July

hasn't meant much to me. My parents always took me

to fireworks displays, but we never did much else that

Before last summer   no

made the fourth special to me. I guess I had never real-

¶ Then

ized many deep feelings about America. Last summer

my attitude toward America   For eight weeks of the

something happened that changed all that.

summer I lived in Germany.

I don't shiver when I see the American flag or hear the national anthem. My parents—one is Canadian—have never served in the armed forces or anything like that, so they have raised me as just an average person with no obviously deep feelings for America.

3. Proofread your work. Make a clean copy of your paper and correct any errors in spelling, grammar, usage or punctuation. When examining changes over time, pay particular attention to paragraphing, especially to signal new ideas during discussions of cause and effect or comparison and contrast.

Adverb Clauses

Adverb clauses, which begin with words such as *before, when, after, while, and as,* are often used to show time relationships in writing about changes over time. An adverb clause can appear at the beginning, at the end, or in the middle of a sentence. Notice how each adverb clause below is punctuated.

Adverb clause at beginning of sentence:
After the family moved, Max found it harder to adjust in school.

Adverb clause at end of sentence
Max found it harder to adjust in school *after the family moved.*

Adverb clause in middle of sentence:
Max, *after the family moved,* found it harder to adjust in school.

For more help, see Grammar Handbook 32, "Phrases and Clauses," page 623.

Grammar
—**TIP**—

Varying the positions of adverb clauses is one way to lend variety to your sentences.

PUBLISH AND PRESENT

- **Meet with other writers in your class or peer group.** Share your papers aloud. Collect papers on similar topics and reproduce them as a casebook or anthology. Choose one or more group members to serve as editors. Include an introduction, written by the editors, that provides an overview of attitudes and approaches—to change and to writing about change—that are reflected in the collection.
- **Submit your analysis of changes over time.** Try a local publication or the school newspaper. You could submit your writing as an article or as a letter to the editor.
- **Gather essays for your school's yearbook or newspaper.** In a feature called "Looking Back," focus on changes over time in yourself and your classmates.
- **Share essays with a social studies class.** Present four or five essays that analyze how social or governmental institutions changed over time.
- **Save your work in a writing portfolio.**

HANDBOOKS
FOR HELP & PRACTICE

**Graphic Aids,
p. 399
Sharing Writing,
pp. 427–428**

A Change in My Point of View

Tim Harms

"I am an American." That sentence has been written and spoken proudly many times over the past two hundred years. Rarely has it been used to illustrate its broad sense of citizenship; instead it has been used to relate a person to the many symbols of America—democracy, diversity, hard work, power, and freedom. In most contexts, "I am an American" is used to relate a person to some of these symbols of which he or she is proud.

Introduces the change that will be examined

I am not a very patriotic person. I don't shiver when I see the American flag or hear the national anthem. My parents—one is Canadian—have never served in the armed forces or anything like that, so they have raised me as just an average person with no obviously deep feelings for America. The Fourth of July, perhaps America's proudest day, hasn't meant much to me either. My parents always took me to fireworks displays, but we never did much else that made the Fourth special to me. Before last summer, I had no deep feelings toward America.

Then last summer my attitude toward America changed. For eight weeks of the summer I lived in Germany. Unless you've been out of the U.S., it's very hard to imagine a democratic, industrialized nation so different from America. For example, Germany has a multiparty system of government instead of a two-party system. In the workplace, Germans still must first be apprenticed before they can become masters and open their own businesses. The school system is also different. After the fourth grade, students are separated into three different kinds of schools, according to their scores on a test. One kind of school leads to apprenticeship in a trade or industry. Another leads to a more

clerical career. The third leads to university or to a higher-level position in business or government. Some, therefore, are forced to decide on a career goal as early as fourth grade. In addition, all males eighteen or over must serve fifteen months with the armed forces. These differences helped me gain a new appreciation for American life, but it was the Fourth of July in Germany that really made me realize how intensely American I am.

Compares conditions to explain the causes of the change

The morning newspaper had a small article in the back reporting the 213th birthday of the United States. To my host family, and other Germans, the day was nothing special. But the group of American students I was with took the day off from school and toured a small castle. Our host families came later to picnic with us on the castle lawn. Our tour ended on top of one of the towers, and as we looked down to the lawn where we had our picnic, we saw that an American flag had been set up. I don't think there was one of us who didn't take a picture of the American flag from the tower. Later, we American students continued celebrating by getting together and chatting. We reminisced about our American hometowns and talked about how lucky we were to be Americans. We felt good about ourselves and what we had at home. Maybe we were even a little homesick then. It was by far the best Fourth of July I've ever had, and it happened in a foreign country, where I was able to realize what a truly special day it is and where I became especially aware of the advantages of being an American.

Uses narration to present the change clearly

Uses an effective organizational pattern

I had been an American who took life in America for granted—my education, my opportunities, even what I could buy. Experiencing a different type of life in Germany, I realized that it is something special to be an American. I too can now proudly say, "I am an American."

Concludes by showing the effect of changes

WRITER TO WRITER

As people evolve and do new things, their language will evolve too. They will find ways to describe the new things and their changed perspective will give them new ways of talking.

Robert MacNeil, journalist

FOR YOUR
PORTFOLIO ▶

1. Reflect on your writing. Write a journal entry in which you analyze how you changed as a thinker and writer during the process of preparing this assignment. Write about your attitude as you began the assignment, your thoughts while you were working on the paper (what was difficult, what helped you most), and your insights on the value of the assignment. Did you sharpen your skills of evaluation and analysis? Did you become a keener observer? A more critical thinker? Share your insight with your peer group or with your whole class in a discussion.

2. Apply your skills. Here are some ways to apply what you have learned in this assignment.

- **Cross-curricular** Pick your favorite subject and analyze how its teaching has changed over the generations. Interview teachers as part of research.
- **General** Choose a relative or friend and write a "changes over time" biographical piece as a special birthday or anniversary gift. Interview the subject of the biography as well as people who know him or her.
- **The arts** Write a report analyzing how styles have changed during this century in an art form that appeals to you, such as painting, music, drama, poetry, or fiction.
- **Current events** Choose a major, continuing news topic such as a domestic or international crisis, an evolving social order, or a political campaign or upheaval. Research and write a paper on how the situation has developed over a period of weeks, months or years.
- **Other applications** Follow the suggestions on pages 163–170 to create a science-fiction story and a pictorial essay.

On the Lightside

THE WARS OF THE WORDS

This section from a book called Have a Word on Me *refers to a series of wars involving the parts of speech that took place many years ago. The writer claims that he found this account in an old manuscript that had been lost for years in a dusty desk drawer.*

A royal incident in the year 1213 precipitated the Wars of the Words. King John was in the Nominative case then, with many Subjects to do him honor. One of these Subjects—Matilda, the daughter of Robert Fitzwalter the Valiant, Lord of the Manor of Diss in the County of Norfolk—discovered that she had also become the King's Object; and she Objected.

There ensued a wrangle among the Nouns. Could a Subject also be an Object? And how could one tell which was which? Some hearty old Nouns declared themselves loyal Subjects, and proud of it; others admitted they were Objects. They said any Subject that acted upon them would do so at his own risk. Words led to blows, blows to a pitched battle, and the battle to a carnage among Nouns more bloody than our own Civil War.

Records of the first Wars of the Words are fragmentary, partly because it was difficult to separate who was fighting whom from whom was fighting who.

In the opening war, sometimes the Subjects were ahead and sometimes the Objects. When the Objects triumphed, they became the Subjects, and the Subjects became the Objects. But this simply meant that they exchanged armor and went on fighting. To make the scoring still more difficult, a Subject that became an Object remained, or became, the Subject of its Subject.

The outcome was the Dark Ages. Armies degenerated into marauding bands. Father turned on son, and brother on brother. Split personalities were the norm. No one is sure how many centuries this chaos lasted. We do know, however, that finally an ancient Noun—his name has long been forgotten—climbed to the top of a barrel in the marketplace of Diss and cried in a quavering voice, "This madness must cease. Whether Subjects or Objects, we are all Nouns together. We are the lords of creation—the First of the Parts of Speech. Who else can turn from Subject to Object and back again at will?"

From then on the Nouns were so busy and happy switching back from Subject to Object and back again that they had no time or stomach left for fighting.

Willard R. Espy

Science Fiction

Related ASSIGNMENT

from

EARTHMEN BEARING GIFTS

by
FREDRIC BROWN

Have you ever sat outside, gazing at the stars and wondering what it would be like to travel among them? Speculation about what may happen in the future, such as the discovery of extraterrestrial intelligence, forms the basis for a type of writing known as science fiction.

Science-fiction stories, like the excerpt on these pages, often use a fantasy about the future in order to comment on human behavior in present-day civilization. As you read the excerpt, think about what the author is suggesting about people today.

Mars was holding out, waiting for Earth to come. What was left of Mars, that is; this one small city of about nine hundred beings. The civilization of Mars was older than that of Earth, but it was a dying one. This was what remained of it: one city, nine hundred people. They were waiting for Earth to make contact, for a selfish reason and for an unselfish one.

Martian civilization had developed in a quite different direction from that of Earth. It had developed no important knowledge of the physical sciences, no technology. But it had developed social sciences to the point where there had not been a single crime, let alone a war, on Mars for fifty thousand years. And it had developed fully the parapsychological sciences of the mind, which Earth was just beginning to discover.

Mars could teach Earth much. How to avoid crime and war to begin with. Beyond those simple things lay telepathy, telekinesis, empathy . . .

And Earth would, Mars hoped, teach them something even more valuable to Mars: how, by science and technology—which it was too late for Mars to develop now, even if they had the type of minds which would enable them to develop these things—to restore and rehabilitate a dying planet, so that an otherwise dying race might live and multiply again.

Each planet would gain greatly, and neither would lose.

And tonight was the night when Earth would make its first sighting shot. Its next shot, a rocket containing Earthmen, or at least an Earthman, would be at the next opposition, two Earth years, or roughly four Martian years, hence. The Martians knew this, because their teams of telepaths were able to catch at least some of the thoughts of Earthmen, enough to know their plans. Unfortunately, at that distance, the connection was one-way. Mars could not ask Earth to hurry its program. Or tell Earth scientists the facts about Mars' composition and atmosphere which would have made this preliminary shot unnecessary.

Tonight Ry, the leader (as nearly as the Martian word can be translated), and Khee, his administrative assistant and closest friend, sat and meditated together until the time was near. Then they drank a toast to the future—in a beverage based on menthol, which had the same effect on Martians as alcohol on Earthmen—and climbed to the roof of the building in which they had been sitting. They watched toward the north, where the rocket should land. The stars shone brilliantly and unwinkingly through the atmosphere.

In Observatory No. 1 on Earth's moon, Rog Everett, his eye at the eyepiece of the spotter scope, said triumphantly, "Thar she blew, Willie. And now, as soon as the films are developed, we'll know the score on that old planet Mars." He straightened up—there'd be no more to see now—and he and Willie Sanger shook hands solemnly. It was an historical occasion.

"Hope it didn't kill anybody. Any Martians, that is. Rog, did it hit dead center in Syrtis Major?"

"Near as matters. I'd say it was maybe a thousand miles off, to the south. And that's damn close on a fifty-million-mile shot. Willie, do you really think there are any Martians?"

Willie thought for a second and then said, "No."
He was right.

INVITATION
—TO—
Write

Fredric Brown's science-fiction story sets up an ill-fated "meeting" between Earthpeople and Martians in an imaginary future. Create your own science-fiction story in which you present your vision of a possible future.

Unlike most fiction writers, science-fiction writers place their stories in a fantasized future. There they create a chronicle of events and changes they think may occur over time. Some authors accentuate the "science" of science fiction. Fredric Brown's story, for example, is full of seemingly realistic detail. Other authors emphasize the "fiction," creating fantastic alien characters in bizarre landscapes. Good science-fiction authors all base their stories on fact and logic, however, paying careful attention to the human conflicts that drive any story. As you get ready to create your own science-fiction piece, decide whether you would like to concentrate on science or fiction, but don't neglect the element of human conflict that will bring your story to life.

PLANNING YOUR STORY

1. Brainstorm with your classmates about what the future may be like. Consider future advances in such categories as homes, transportation, family units, technology, the workplace, politics, agriculture, recreation, and medicine. With each category as a heading, make a chart listing your class's ideas.

 Writer's Choice You may prefer to describe the future as less advanced than the present or past. Many science-fiction stories show the world after a final, devastating nuclear war, for example.

2. Choose an aspect of the future for your focus. Fredric Brown's story deals with interplanetary communication. You may choose to focus on other possible advances, such as eradication of disease. What might be the results of such an advance?

HANDBOOKS
FOR HELP & PRACTICE

Point of View,
pp. 458–463
Character/Setting,
pp. 468–472
Problem-Solving,
pp. 487–489
Reference Works,
pp. 507–512

3. Do research to create a believable background. Whether you are planning to write about robots, computers, space travel, or medical miracles, you should do some research in current books or articles to get realistic details. You might also want to read some other science-fiction pieces to see how different writers make their future scenarios seem believable. Arthur C. Clarke, Isaac Asimov, Ursula K. LeGuin, Robert Heinlein, and Anne McCaffrey are excellent science-fiction authors to explore.

4. Set a goal for your story. You may be most interested in telling a story, as Fredric Brown does, or you may want to concentrate on describing an exotic setting or painting memorable characters. If your main goal is to tell a story, consider what the point of the story will be. For example, one goal of the excerpt is to point out the shortsightedness of people who think technology alone holds all the answers. Whatever your goal is, keep it clearly in mind as you begin to write.

D RAFTING YOUR STORY

Writing
—TIP—

At the beginning of your story, be sure to locate your reader in time and space and to introduce your main characters.

1. Establish your setting. You could choose to set your story, or part of it, on another planet. If you set your story on Earth, you might show the environment of the future through human eyes or take the point of view of an extraterrestrial being.

2. Determine your point of view. Brown tells his story in the third person because he wants the reader to have information that neither the Earthmen nor the Martians alone could have. This approach gives an author the ability to stand above the characters and see everything that happens, but it sacrifices the intimacy of a first-person account. On the other hand, a first-person account can provide a novel point of view, such as that of an alien being, but it cannot go beyond what the speaker could realistically be expected to know.

3. Create credible characters. Notice how Fredric Brown, by carefully selecting details, shows rather than tells you about his characters. The Martians never say a word—they communicate telepathically—but they are enough like humans to make you sympathetic to their fate. You may want to create more fantastic characters, but don't lose sight of the basic human conflicts that are the basis of a good story.

4. Draft your story. Don't attempt to produce a finished product on your first draft. Remembering your goal, simply write down you main ideas and let your characters carry the plot through to the end.

5. Give your story a title. Fredric Brown's title highlights the irony of his story. Not only were the Earthpeople not bearing gifts, they extinguished a civilization that could have given them valuable knowledge. Make sure your title encourages others to read your story and gives them something to think about afterwards.

REVIEWING YOUR WRITING

1. Reread your story. Did you establish a believable imaginary setting early in the story? Did you keep a consistent point of view? Are the scientific aspects of your story a logical outgrowth of something that exists now? Did you work out the particular problem your story introduced?

2. Pay attention to the small details. Recheck the facts and details you used to lend credibility to your story. If you gave imaginary names to your characters and locations, make sure they are easy to read and pronounce.

3. Ask a friend to read your story. Pay attention to your classmate's suggestions about descriptions, dialogue, and plot. Ask if you have achieved the goal you set out to accomplish. Did you portray the future in a convincing way? Did your story make sense to your friend?

4. Rewrite your story. Incorporate the best of your friend's suggestions and your own revisions to improve your story. You may need to make several drafts of your story before you are satisfied.

PUBLISHING AND PRESENTING

- **Tell your story on audiotape.** Use appropriate music and sound effects in the background.
- **Enter your story in a science-fiction writing contest.**
- **Send your story to a science-fiction magazine.**
- **Prepare an anthology of class stories.** Include drawings or illustrations.

Pictorial Essay

"A Mountain Blows Its Top"

Journalists, artists, and advertisers all recognize the power of a picture or image to convey an idea. They also know that while a single picture can convey a wealth of detail, a series of pictures may tell a much more elaborate story.

Look, for example, at these pictures of Mount St. Helens before, during, and after the eruption of May 18, 1980. The written captions help explain the devastation wreaked by the volcano, but you can appreciate something of the sequence of events through the pictures alone. As you look at the images and read the captions, note the dramatic history conveyed by the careful combination of pictures and words.

It all begin at 8:32 A.M. An earthquake registering 5.0 on the Richter scale fractured the mountain's north slope. Volcanic gases and steam poured out, flattening forests up to 17 miles away. As magma—sticky, molten rock—rose from the depths of the volcano, water evaporated to steam and propelled 400 million tons of exploded rock dust into the air. Volcanic ash seethed down the mountain and buried the once-beautiful valley. More than 40,000 acres of fir trees went down as easily as matchsticks. Boiling mud buried bridges and devastated logging camps like this one near Spirit Lake.

Think AND Respond

Mount St. Helens towered majestically over neighboring peaks in southwestern Washington, a source of beauty and recreation in every season. When the volcanic mountain exploded with the force of five hundred atomic bombs in May, 1980, it spewed ash over much of eastern Washington, northern Idaho, and western Montana. How do the pictures and captions combine to convey the cataclysm and the resulting devastation?

INVITATION
── TO ──
Write

Various photographers captured the eruption of Mount St. Helens in pictures that tell a dramatic story. Create a pictorial essay to narrate a story of your own choice.

A pictorial essay combines photographs or pictures with words to convey a particular sequence of events. As you experiment with this type of essay, you probably will not choose to document a change as violent or sudden as the catastrophic eruption that destroyed a mountain. In fact, don't worry about trying to duplicate the intense drama of the example. Pictures showing changes that occur much more quietly or slowly can be equally compelling.

PLANNING YOUR PICTORIAL ESSAY

HANDBOOKS
FOR HELP & PRACTICE

Chronological Order, pp. 363–364
Cause-Effect Order, pp. 367–368
Support for Writing Plan, pp. 371–373
Vantage Point, pp. 462–463

1. Choose the story you want to tell. Look for one that describes a sequence, shows a cause-and-effect relationship, or explores a "before and after" situation, as the Mount St. Helens piece does. You may, for example, want to show the changes that take place as a person ages, a family grows, or a neighborhood develops. The construction or demolition of a building, the effects of an oil spill, or the results of a beautification project make good subjects for a pictorial essay. Pick a subject that means something important to you and try to convey that meaning to others.

2. Find pictures that tell your story. If you have access to a camera, take plenty of pictures so that you can select the best ones. Depending on your subject, you might use photographs from a family album. If you are documenting a news story, such as the Mount St. Helens disaster, you may be able to find photographs in magazines. Avoid, though, those that already appear in essay form. They leave you no room for your own interpretation.

3. Experiment with various layouts. Try to arrange your pictures so that your viewers will be able to "read" your story and follow the sequence of events. People usually expect the story to flow from left to right or from top to bottom. Notice how the pictures in the excerpt are arranged.

4. Make notes for your captions and title. Your captions and title should help achieve your particular goal for this piece. Your goal may be to teach something, to tell an emotional story, or to make a particular point. Think about what you want to say about each picture and about the group of pictures as a whole.

Writer's Choice You may choose to write an introduction for the entire piece, instead of creating a separate caption for each picture.

Writing
━TIP━
Look for newspaper photos on microfiche at your library and print out the ones you want.

CREATING YOUR PICTORIAL ESSAY

1. Make your final picture selection. Choose the best pictures you can find to achieve your goal. Try to summarize what each picture or group of pictures contributes with one sentence. Eliminate superfluous pictures that don't add anything of importance to your essay.

2. Determine your layout. Don't fill your space completely or overwhelm your viewers with too many pictures or too much prose. Devise a layout that will capture your viewers' attention and tell the story clearly and powerfully.

3. Write your captions. Captions should do more than merely label each picture. They should provide information that is not available from the picture alone. Keep them short, but make sure they add new information to your story.

4. Choose a title. Your title should reflect your goal for this piece, as well as engage your viewers' interest. "Mount St. Helens" would have been too vague for the model essay, and "Some Views of Mount St. Helens Before, During, and After the Eruption" would have been too long and dull.

◢ REVIEWING YOUR WRITING

1. Check your captions and title. Make sure you have included everything you need to make your story clear and complete. Proofread your work for spelling, punctuation, and grammar. Correct any errors you find.

COMPUTER TIP

Experiment with type size as well as boldface and italic type to create eye-pleasing captions.

2. Share your pictorial essay. Have a classmate first look at your pictorial essay without the captions. Do the pictures alone tell the story? Are they arranged in a way that makes the sequence of events clear? Then ask if the captions add details that make the story more full and interesting. You may also ask your classmate to read the caption copy independently and tell you what kinds of pictures the copy suggests.

3. Make your final copy. Incorporate any suggestions on layout and text. Attach your pictures to a strong backing that will enhance their appearance. Retype or rewrite your captions so that they fit your pictures precisely.

◢ PUBLISHING AND PRESENTING

- **Present your essays in class.** Ask your teacher to display the class's work on an opaque projector.
- **Publish your work in a newspaper.** If your photographs are original, submit your pictorial essay to a school or local newspaper. Find out first if the paper accepts only black and white prints, or if they need your original negatives.
- **Create a pictorial essay exhibit.** Get permission to display your exhibit in designated hallways or in the school library.

Sentence

Varying Sentence Types

An experienced writer can craft sentences in an almost endless number of ways. In this lesson you will learn how professionals create four main sentence types by using independent clauses and subordinate clauses. Here and in later lessons, you will learn to vary sentences by using these two kinds of clauses in many combinations.

The four sentences below, all based on one original sentence by Willa Cather, illustrate the four main sentence types. Slashes mark divisions between clauses. Notice the different levels and kinds of detail that each sentence type allows.

MODELS

SIMPLE SENTENCE (one independent clause)

1. All the actors and singers of any importance stayed there.

COMPOUND SENTENCE (two or more independent clauses)

2. All the actors and singers of any importance stayed there, / and / a number of the big manufacturers of the place lived there in winter.

COMPLEX SENTENCE (one independent clause, one or more subordinate clauses)

3. All the actors and singers of any importance stayed there / when they were in the city.

COMPOUND-COMPLEX SENTENCE (two or more independent clauses, one or more subordinate clauses)

4. All the actors and singers of any importance stayed there / when they were in the city / and a number of the big manufacturers of the place lived there in winter.   **Willa Cather, "Paul's Case"**

A. Unscrambling Sentences The model sentences are of all four types. First, locate the clause(s) in each model. Then unscramble the parts in each set to form a sentence that matches its model.

1. I had a farm in Africa, at the foot of the Ngong Hills. (simple sentence)
   Isak Dinesen, *Out of Africa*
   a. he kicked the ball (independent clause)
   b. near the front of the end zone (phrase)
   c. to Taylor (phrase)

2. Kino stepped with dignity out of the house, and Juana followed him.
   (compound sentence) **John Steinbeck,** *The Pearl*
   a. through the halls (phrase)
   b. but nobody heard it (independent clause)
   c. the bell rang as usual (independent clause)

3. Johnny was standing outside the Naurus' concrete-and-aluminum bungalow,
   taking a last look at the sky before turning in, when he became aware of a
   new sound above the thunder of the waves. (complex sentence)
   Arthur C. Clark, *Dolphin Island*
   a. when he became conscious of a familiar voice across from him in the
      dessert line (subordinate clause)
   b. surveying the assorted feast of salads, entrees, and vegetables before
      selecting any (phrase)
   c. Greg was standing at the sumptuous all-you-can-eat buffet
      (independent clause)

4. When I looked once more for Gatsby, he had vanished, and I was alone
   again in the unquiet darkness. (compound-complex sentence)
   F. Scott Fitzgerald, *The Great Gatsby*
   a. but mist was heavy still in the uplands (independent clause)
   b. the sun appeared (independent clause)
   c. after the rain blew away from the valley (subordinate clause)

B. Imitating Sentences Imitate each model, using your own content.

1. His hair was dead and thin, almost feathery on top of his head.
   Harper Lee, *To Kill a Mockingbird*

2. Holding firmly to the trunk, I took a step toward him and then my knees
   bent, and I jounced the limb. **John Knowles,** *A Separate Peace*

3. Most of the helmets were too big and came down almost over the ears of
   the men who wore them. **Ernest Hemingway,** *A Farewell to Arms*

4. They landed at Kennedy, and he took a shuttle bus to his connecting flight,
   which wasn't due to leave till evening. **Ann Tyler,** *The Accidental Tourist*

5. He set the cup down and was sitting there, staring at it, when Meo came in.
   Hal Borland, *When the Legends Die*

6. After my mother died, my father, a traveling man, sent me to live with his cousins, Verena and Dolly Talbo, two unmarried ladies who were sisters.
   Truman Capote, "The Grass Harp"

7. When he returned, the pause of the twilight had ceased, and the tune of the streets had changed.
   Willa Cather, "Paul's Case"

8. It was the years of straining at loads too heavy for them which had lifted their upper lips to bare their teeth in a seeming snarl, and this labor had set deep wrinkles in the flesh about their eyes and their mouths.
   Pearl S. Buck, *The Good Earth*

Application Below are first sentences of favorite stories. Imitate one, and use your imitation to start the first paragraph of a narrative. Your narrative may be about a real event or an imaginary one. Notice how the elaboration of the sentence adds detail and richness to your opening.

SIMPLE SENTENCE

1. At daybreak Billy Buck emerged from the bunkhouse and stood for a moment on the porch, looking up at the sky.
   John Steinbeck, *The Red Pony*

COMPOUND SENTENCE

2. In the town there were two mutes, and they were always together.
   Carson McCullers, *The Heart Is a Lonely Hunter*

COMPLEX SENTENCE

3. Ever since I was a young child, people have stared at me.
   Robert Russell, *To Catch an Angel*

COMPOUND-COMPLEX SENTENCE

4. When you are getting on in years (but not ill, of course), you get very sleepy at times, and the hours seem to pass like lazy cattle moving across a landscape.
   James Hilton, *Goodbye, Mr. Chips*

Grammar Refresher For more on simple, compound, complex, and compound–complex sentences, see Handbook 32, pages 629–635.

Sketchbook

If the world were a village of 1,000 people:

700 people would be illiterate

600 people would live in shantytowns

500 people would be hungry

60 people would possess half the income of the entire population

🚶 = 10 people
(Individuals can fall into more than one category.)

What do these figures tell you about life in a global village?

Additional Sketches

What could other people learn about you by studying your possessions?

Have you ever jumped to a conclusion that turned out to be totally wrong? Tell about the experience.

Informative Exposition: Synthesis

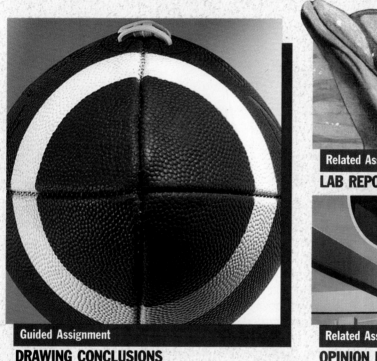

Guided Assignment
DRAWING CONCLUSIONS

Related Assignment
LAB REPORT

Related Assignment
OPINION POLL

Imagine a collage made of painted canvas with various objects glued onto it—old photos, news clippings, sunglasses, hairpins, lipstick tubes, and the like. Arranged on the canvas, these items take on a new meaning. Such a work of art is a **synthesis**—a bringing together of varied elements to form a new whole.

People often use synthesis in writing, and in this workshop you will learn how to do it in your own work. You'll learn how to collect information about a subject, analyze this information, and draw a reasonable conclusion. You'll also apply your ability to draw conclusions as you write a lab report and a report on an opinion poll.

175

Drawing Conclusions

A detective on a case, a scientist in a laboratory, and a researcher in the midst of a study are all likely to call on the same skills to go about their work. They will gather information, examine it to find relationships among ideas, and then try to draw conclusions.

Two psychology researchers, Tom Gilovich and Mark Frank, decided to study whether wearing black uniforms made football and hockey teams "meaner." The following excerpt from a magazine article explains how they went about their research. As you read, notice the facts they gathered and the experiments they conducted. Then consider the conclusions they reached.

The best measure of meanness, Gilovich and Frank decided, is the number of

penalty minutes or yards assessed. . . . So Gilovich and Frank looked into the histories of the NFL and NHL and tallied up the

DARK

penalties that were meted out between 1970 and 1986. "As predicted," the authors wrote in their study, "teams with black uniforms in the NFL are uncommonly aggressive. In all but one of the last 17 years, [the five black-clad teams] were penalized more yards than one would expect. . . ." In hockey the findings were similar. . . .

Two possible explanations are that the aggressive acts of black-uniformed teams caused them to be penalized, or that the *perception* of aggression had the whistles blowing. Penalties come from referees, and referees can be biased. As Gilovich and Frank put it, "They may view any given action as more malevolent if it is performed by a player in a black uniform." . . .

by sarah boxer One of the experiments that Gilovich and Frank devised to test the hunch that referees are biased against players wearing black involved two separate videos of two football plays. The action was staged as identically as possible in both tapes, but in one version the defensive team wore white, in the other it wore black. Twenty college and high school referees watched the "black" version of the video, and 20 watched the "white" version. Then, the referees were asked how likely they would be to penalize the defensive teams, and "their impression of the teams' 'dirtiness.' "

Sure enough, "the referees were more inclined to penalize the defensive team if they saw the black version . . . than if they saw the white version." The researchers concluded: "Teams that wear black uniforms receive harsher treatment from the referees."

That prejudice, of course, doesn't mean that players wearing black uniforms play

either black or white jerseys and split into two teams. Each team, while wearing white or black uniforms, had to decide as a group what game it would play.

The two teams never did actually play, because by then the researchers already had the data they were after. The study found that the two groups were indistinguishable in their appetites for aggressive games before they put on the uniforms, but that there was a huge difference afterward. The team with the black shirts *wanted* to play more violent games. "If the wearing of a black uniform can have such

more aggressively, any more than a highway trooper's bias against red cars means that red cars speed more. But real aggression is a tricky thing to test. It's hard to put a black shirt on someone and then figure out if he has become meaner. Nonetheless, this, in effect, is what the researchers tried to do.

To cover up their real intentions, Gilovich and Frank told the subjects of another experiment that they were participating in a study on "the psychology of competition" and that they could choose which events they would compete in by picking five activities from a list of 12. The choice of games ranged from patently aggressive activities—such as dart-gun duels—to basically nonaggressive games such as shooting baskets. Once the subjects had made their choices, they were each given

an effect in the laboratory," Gilovich and Frank reasoned, "there is every reason to believe that it would have even stronger effects on the playing field (or rink)."

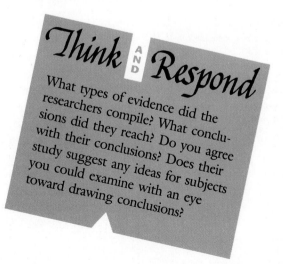

Think AND *Respond*

What types of evidence did the researchers compile? What conclusions did they reach? Do you agree with their conclusions? Does their study suggest any ideas for subjects you could examine with an eye toward drawing conclusions?

INVITATION
—TO—
Write

You have read about the conclusions drawn by two re-searchers from the evidence they gathered. Now gather your own evidence and draw your own conclusions about a subject that interests you.

The ability to draw conclusions is central to both thinking and writing. It allows you to see beyond the facts and then present what you have learned in a clear, easily understood manner. It also helps you lead others to a conclusion through your writing.

Drawing conclusions is an important tool in research, problem-solving, and decision-making. You use this skill in examining science and social-science issues, and in interpreting polls, surveys, and other collections of evidence.

PREWRITE AND EXPLORE

HANDBOOKS
FOR HELP & PRACTICE

General Techniques,
pp. 342–344

Inductive Reasoning,
p. 359

Collaborative
Planning,
pp. 370–373

Problem Solving,
pp. 487–490

1. Look for ideas. The opportunities to examine information and draw conclusions are limited only by your imagination. Try some of the following activities to look for ideas worth exploring.

Exploratory Activities

- **Opinion polls** Look at the people around you. What are their interests? their concerns? their hopes? their fears? their habits? Any of these questions might be developed into an opinion poll and then turned into a report that draws conclusions about people today.

- **Browsing and questioning** Look through some recent newspapers and news magazines for a controversial issue that deeply interests you. Then make a list of questions related to this issue. Include both questions of fact and questions of opinion. Freewrite your responses, probing for the significance of the issue to you.

- **Browsing and interpreting** Look in news magazines, newspapers, and almanacs (such as the annual report *The State of the World* by the Worldwatch Institute) for charts, tables, or graphs containing interesting statistics on social trends, habits, population growth, and so on. Freewrite in your journal about the topics and graphics that particularly interest you, and see what conclusions you might draw from them.

- **Brainstorming and collaboration** If you are interested in science or history, find a partner who shares your interest. Do some brainstorming together to come up with possible subjects for papers. For historical topics, think about the conclusions that can be drawn from events. Ask, "How can the lessons of these events help to shape our future?" For scientific topics, think about great conclusions that scientists in the past have reached. Consider exploring how the facts led them to these conclusions.

- **Reading literature** What do literary and artistic works reveal about the values or attitudes of the author, period, or culture? Think about such works as *Civil Disobedience* by Henry David Thoreau, "The Jilting of Granny Weatherall" by Katherine Anne Porter, or *Our Town* by Thornton Wilder. Reflect on the evidence in the texts that might allow you to draw conclusions.

2. Select a topic. Look back over the ideas you came up with during the exploratory activities. Choose the one that you think is most interesting or promising. You may wish to discuss this choice with some peers before making up your mind. They may see aspects of the topic that you do not. You may also wish to consult your journal, the writing you did for the Sketchbook on page 174, or "Apply Your Skills" on page 188 for ideas. Freewrite for ten minutes on what you know about your selected topic.

3. Gather information. There are many ways you can gather the information that is available on your topic. For example, you may explore your topic through personal observation and recollection, by conducting surveys, by interviewing peers or experts, and by doing research in the library. Look at your subject from as many viewpoints as possible and keep an eye out for conflicting information or interpretations.

Writing
—**TIP**—
Don't underestimate how much you already know about your subject. As part of your fact-gathering, do some freewriting about the subject or conduct a knowledge inventory.

4. Ask questions. Probe the meaning of the information you gather by asking questions and freewriting your responses. Consider such questions as these:

- What caused this to happen?
- Why is this true?
- What relationships do I see among the facts?
- What might happen as a result of this situation?
- What does it mean?

One student, Hector, was intrigued by the study of the effect of black uniforms on professional athletes. He decided to see if the results applied to high-school athletes. Here are the notes he wrote to answer the question, "What does it mean?"

Writing
━ **TIP** ━

Discussing a subject with others often helps you think your way through to a conclusion.

ONE STUDENT'S PROCESS

What does it mean? The findings of the researchers sound good on paper, but I don't know that I totally believe them. When I asked Coach Duchon, he didn't agree either. He made the point that "school spirit" really does mean something to high-school athletes, so school colors have meaning, no matter what colors they are. I need to talk to some of the players I know. I think there's more to it than just the color of a jersey, especially for high-school players.

5. Look for connections. Explore relationships, patterns, and inconsistencies in the information you gather. When you find inconsistencies, look for ways to explain them. When you find a relationship, ask yourself, "How extensive is it? Can it be stated as a general conclusion? If so, what conclusion can I draw?"

6. State your tentative conclusion. From your research so far, can you make a judgment, state an opinion, make a suggestion, or propose a solution? Freewrite about your conclusion. Keep in mind that your conclusion may not be completely clear to you until you are farther along in your writing. Consider evidence that contradicts your conclusion. What alternative conclusions might you investigate?

7. Try collaborative planning. Working with a partner, discuss your plans for writing your essay, paying special attention to the following questions.

- What goals do you want to achieve with your essay? Do you want to recommend an action, inform your readers on some subject, or prove a point? How will you achieve your goals?
- Who are your readers and what background information or explanations of basic concepts will they need?

DRAFT AND DISCOVER

1. Begin your draft. Don't try to write a perfect draft the first time around. However, you may want to pause a bit before you actually begin writing to think about your overall plan for the piece. Here are some possibilities for organization.

- **Facts followed by conclusion** Present the facts in an order that makes sense for your particular topic—perhaps in chronological order or in separate categories. Then end with the conclusion.
- **Conclusion followed by supporting facts** Begin with your conclusion. Then present the facts that back it up. Again, present the facts in an order that makes sense for your particular topic.
- **Initial question or situation, followed by examination of facts, followed by conclusion** This is basically a variation on the first method of organization. The only difference is that the whole piece is being framed as an answer to the question or situation presented in the introduction. Keep in mind that you may draw more than one conclusion from your research, as Sarah Boxer's article shows.

 Writer's Choice Do you have enough facts to support your conclusion, or do you need to do more research? Have you studied a wide enough variety of sources to anticipate and meet objections to your conclusion?

2. Elaborate on ideas. The following are some strategies that might help you examine your topic and explain your conclusion.

Strategies

- **Description** Use description to analyze key features of your subject or to present a clear picture of it.

HANDBOOKS
FOR HELP & PRACTICE

Introductions/ Conclusions, pp. 378–385
Facts/Statistics, p. 397
Persuasive Writing, pp. 490–493
Judging Evidence, pp. 546–548

PROBLEM SOLVING

What is the most effective way to present my information?

- **Narration** You might tell a narrative story about how you conducted the research that led you to your conclusion. If your conclusion is based on past events, on the other hand, you may wish to present the facts as they occurred, in the form of a narrative.
- **Persuasion** Perhaps your conclusion is that a certain policy should be adopted or that a certain action should be taken. If so, you may wish to combine the expository treatment of the facts of your piece with a persuasive treatment of your conclusion, including language meant to move your reader to think or act in a particular way.

Hector decided to begin his draft with a question that described Gilovich and Frank's study in terms of his own school.

ONE STUDENT'S PROCESS

Would the Old Green and White of Northside High win more games if they changed their uniform colors to black and blue? That intriguing possibility is presented in the findings of one psychological study. However, other people believe athletes, especially high-school athletes, may be colorblind.

3. Support your conclusion. You need to guard against drawing a conclusion based on too little evidence. Make sure you present sufficient facts to make your conclusion reasonable. As you write, keep using appropriate terms, such as *some, many, sometimes, often,* *usually,* and *among those studied,* to limit your conclusion and avoid overgeneralization and circular reasoning. (See "Avoiding Unsupported Opinions" and "Avoiding Circular Reasoning" on pages 429–430.

 Writer's Choice How do you want to state your conclusion? Do you want to make a judgment? state an opinion? end with a call to action?

4. Take a break. After your first or second draft, put your paper away for a while. Then when you come back to it, you can look at it with a fresh eye. You may also want to share it with a peer. Ask yourself and your peer reader the following questions.

R E V I E W   Y O U R   W R I T I N G

Questions for Yourself

- Have I presented sufficient evidence to support my conclusion?

- If my conclusion is an opinion, have I supplied enough facts to convince others to make it their own?

- Is my conclusion too broad? In other words, is it an overgeneralization?

- Did I explain or reconcile any conflicting evidence?

- Is there anything in my paper that should be clarified with additional details, descriptions, definitions, or background information?

- Does my introduction grab the reader's interest?

Questions for Your Peer Reader

- Can you restate my conclusion in your own words?

- Does my conclusion seem reasonable, given the facts I've presented?

- Have I overlooked any important facts that might help me support my conclusion or cause me to change it?

- What parts of the paper are most memorable? least memorable? most clear? least clear?

HANDBOOKS
FOR HELP & PRACTICE

**Art of Revision,
pp. 416–421
Incorporating Peer
Responses,
p. 425**

1. Evaluate your responses. Think about your own responses and those of your peers. Also keep in mind these guidelines.

Standards for Evaluation

Effective writing that draws conclusions . . .

- presents a sound conclusion based on sufficient evidence.
- explains all evidence and qualifies or limits its observations as necessary.
- draws on reliable sources and avoids generalizations.
- uses appropriate language and details for the audience.
- includes a well-developed introduction, body, and conclusion.

2. Problem-solve. Based on your analysis of the responses to your draft, rework it. Here are the changes Hector made to the concluding paragraphs of his draft.

ONE STUDENT'S PROCESS

Good point! Can you add specific details?

What factors? Adding details might strengthen your conclusion.

Coach Duchon reminded me about the weakest team
~~pointed out that~~

in the Conference. It is the only one to wear black—

The psychologists make some interesting points

about how athletes react to the color black however,

athletes and coaches contend that colors do not actually
interviewed for this article

determine behavior. Other factors are more important
, such as pride, team and school identity, and individual ability,

than any individual color.
uniform

A check of past football standings confirmed that the black-clad Jefferson High
Raiders have not had a winning season in five years.

3. Proofread your work. After your final revision, make a clean copy and correct any errors in grammar, usage, and mechanics.

GRAMMAR AND WRITING

Combining Sentences to Show Cause and Effect

The cause-effect relationship between two sentences can be highlighted by combining them into one, using subordinating conjunctions such as *before, after,* and *because,* or conjunctive adverbs such as *accordingly, finally,* and *therefore.* Notice how each is punctuated.

PROBLEM: Videos combine elements of music, theater, and dance. They are very popular.

REVISED: Videos are extremely popular because they combine elements of music, theater, and dance. (subordinating conjunction)

or

Videos combine elements of music, theater, and dance; therefore, they are extremely popular. (conjunctive adverb)

See Handbook 30, pages 572–573, for additional help with subordinating conjunctions and conjunctive adverbs.

Grammar
—TIP—

A conjunctive adverb is preceded by a semicolon and followed by a comma.

PUBLISH AND PRESENT

- **Give an oral report.** Share your paper with your classmates by presenting information from it aloud. However, instead of reading your paper word for word, use it as notes and speak extemporaneously. Use the blackboard, show slides, or bring in photographs to add an interesting visual dimension to your presentation.
- **Submit your work to the school newspaper if appropriate.** For example, if your topic is of particular interest to high-school students—say, a report on the relationship between television-watching and studying—the editor of the paper may be interested in publishing it.
- **Submit your work in another class.** If your paper is about a topic in math, science, history, art, or some other subject taught at your school, you may wish to share it with a teacher of that subject.
- **Save your work in your writing portfolio.**

HANDBOOKS
FOR HELP & PRACTICE

Sharing Writing,
pp. 427–428
Speech Delivery,
pp. 515–518

Do Bad Guys Wear Black?

Hector Alvarez

Includes a
well-developed
introduction

Would the old Green and White of Northside High win more games if they changed their uniform colors to black and blue? That intriguing possibility is presented in the findings of one psychological study. However, other people believe athletes, especially high-school athletes, may be colorblind.

Two psychologists conducted a study that led them to conclude that athletes who wear black uniforms are "meaner" than other athletes. The psychologists studied records of the National Football League and the National Hockey League, and they conducted their own experiments in order to reach their conclusion. Their findings indicated that in football and hockey, sports that rely on rough play, teams that want to win more might consider switching to black uniforms.

Yet players and coaches at Northside questioned the results. "It's a joke," said quarterback Jon Astroth. "I don't care if I'm wearing polka dots, it's not going to

Includes details
appropriate for
the audience

change the way I play." Several players pointed out that all teams wear different colors for home and away games, so teams with black jerseys wear them only half the time. "Does that make players mean only half the time?" asked linebacker Keith Coiley.

Coach Duchon also discounted the results. "We teach our athletes pride and school spirit. These things really mean something to the student athlete." He said that his players want to win for their school and their team, so the school colors are more important than any other color. Coach Duchon also pointed out that the weakest team in the conference is the only one to wear black. A check of past football standings confirmed that the black-clad Jefferson High Raiders have not had a winning season in five years.

The psychologists make some interesting points about how athletes react to the color black. However, athletes and coaches interviewed for this article contend that colors do not actually determine behavior. Other factors, such as pride, team and school identity, and individual ability, are more important than uniform color.

Draws on reliable sources

Presents and explains evidence

Qualifies its observations as necessary

Includes a well-developed conclusion

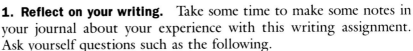

WRITER TO WRITER

The discipline of the writer is to learn to be still and listen to what his subject has to tell him.

Rachel Carson, naturalist and essayist

1. Reflect on your writing. Take some time to make some notes in your journal about your experience with this writing assignment. Ask yourself questions such as the following.

- How did you reach your conclusions? Was the process easy or difficult? Do you still believe your conclusion? If not, why not?
- In what ways was your essay different from or similar to Sarah Boxer's article and the piece by Hector Alvarez?
- How would you write your essay differently if you had to do it again? What changes would you make?

2. Apply your skills. Here are some examples of other writing activities that would use the skills you have learned in this lesson.

- **Cross-curricular** Do a sociological study for your social studies class. Choose a place, such as a park, a busy intersection, or public building, and observe the people and activities you see there. Write a report drawing conclusions about what you see.
- **Literature** Read some of the court documents from the Salem witch trials, and also read Arthur Miller's play *The Crucible*. Write a critical essay on Miller's play in which you discuss the theme of what happens to freedom when people feel frightened.
- **General** Conduct a product analysis to decide on a major purchase you or your family might make. This may entail comparing two or more choices (of automobiles, for example). Write a note to the other members of your family about your conclusion and the facts that back it up.
- **Related assignments** Follow the suggestions on pages 192–201 to write a lab report and an opinion poll.

On the Lightside

ENGLISH INTO ENGLISH

The following excerpt bridges the gap between the spoken word and its unspoken meaning.

Translation from the Teacher

"Oh, I wouldn't worry about that. At this stage, it's the social adjustment that counts."

The child cannot read, write or count beyond nine, but has stopped throwing modeling clay into the sand box.

"He shows a real ability in plastic conception."

He can make a snake out of clay.

"To be perfectly truthful, he does seem to have developed late in large-muscle control."

He falls on his head frequently.

"He's rather slow in group integration and reacts negatively to aggressive stimulus."

He cries easily.

Translation from the Parents

"We'll see."

The parent has no intention of taking the children to the movies (circus, beach) or of buying them a dog (a cat, a bicycle, a canary, . . . a hamster, a Ford Thunderbird).

"When I was a boy. . . ."

Father is going to tell big lies about the hardships of pioneer life before the advent of cellophane and the ball-point pen.

"Before I show you this report card. I'd like to ask you to remember how cute I looked in my baby pictures."

"I should say not."
Father is being firm.
"They're only children once."
Mother is unfirming Father. . . .

Translation from the Teenager

"Nobody understands me."

Nobody is prepared to grant her reasonable request to wear her father's shirt, her mother's diamond earrings, her brother's sneakers, and a sequin-covered derby hat on a three-day cooperative excursion on motorcycles to Las Vegas. All the other girls are doing it.

"You hate me. You just don't care whether I have a good time."

You have given her permission to go to Las Vegas as above. You think it would be nice if she used both hands to steer the motorcycle.

"I don't care what Grandmother made you do. Times have changed."

Of course you couldn't have had a blond streak bleached in your hair. It would have attracted dinosaurs.

Robert Paul Smith

Lab Report

Calls in the Night

From *Dolphins*, by Jacques-Yves Cousteau

Have you ever wondered about the way animals communicate with one another? Oceanographer Jacques Cousteau suspected that dolphins might have a language of their own, so he set out to investigate his suspicion. Read his report of the test he performed and the conclusions he drew. Notice his clear, step-by-step account of both the procedures he followed and the thinking that led to his conclusions.

During our expedition in the Mediterranean, we attempted to learn at least whether a captive animal could carry on a conversation with the school [of dolphins] to which he belonged. We therefore captured a female dolphin and placed her in the floating tank. [The ship] *Calypso* then moved away, leaving the dolphin alone in the tank. We remained at a distance of six and a half kilometers (about four miles) from the dolphin, but we were in constant contact with the tank by radar and radio.

In the middle of the night, the isolated dolphin began to make sounds. These were not ultrasonic noises. They were perfectly audible to us; and Albin Dziedzic and other experts in animal acoustics described their reception as perfect.

We were surprised by the persistence of the sounds made by our captive dolphin. And we thought that we sensed in her "voice" a certain note of emotion, of pathetic appeal. Her cries intensified and resembled those of a wounded animal. Was it a distress signal?

The female's cries were of such a wide range that our tapes of them represent truly an embarrassment of riches. Every indication is that the dolphin was calling in the night to the school from which she had been separated. If so, her efforts were not in vain. The school came, and other cries resounded in the dark water. But, as we have often observed on such occasions, as soon as the school understood that there was nothing it could do for its captured member, it fell silent and swam away.

It should be kept in mind that the school of dolphins, even though it did nothing, nonetheless came to see what had happened. Therefore, there must have been a moment during which information was exchanged between the dolphin in her tank and the dolphins in the open water. But does this imply the existence of a language, in the sense in which linguists accept that term?

"No," says [an associate,] Professor Busnel. The dolphin's sounds were merely relational acoustical signals. They were indeed signals, but not language. They were composed of elements which cannot be broken down; and those elements cannot be assembled according to the rules proper to language, that is, into combinations forming words and phrases. For language does not consist essentially in signals, however numerous, but in the ability to put these symbols together according to a system which engenders a more or less unlimited number of combinations. This is what is known as "syntax." But when two dolphins communicate, they make use of a single signal, or of successive unrelated signals. This is what specialists call a "pseudolanguage," or a "protolanguage," or a "zero-syntax language."

It is not impossible that, someday, dolphins may arrive at a true language. For the present, however, we have no proof either that dolphins speak, or that they are capable of speaking.

Think AND Respond

Explain the experiment the Cousteau crew set up to test the hypothesis that dolphins might have a language. What were the results of the test, and to what conclusions did the results lead? Why do you think Cousteau included a lengthy definition of language in his report? Think of ideas and questions you have about science and technology that could be tested with experiments.

INVITATION
═══ TO ═══
Write

Cousteau's report tells, step by step, how his team tested a hypothesis. Then the report explains how they reached a conclusion based on the test results. Test out a question or hypothesis of your own; then write a report of the procedure you used and the conclusions you reached.

When you write a science report or a lab report, you use two skills: those of explaining a process and drawing conclusions. Starting with a question and a hunch about the subject under consideration, you carry out an experiment to prove or disprove your supposition, or hypothesis. During the experiment, you carefully observe and record what happens. Then you draw conclusions based on your observations. Finally, you write up your report, explaining what you did, how you did it, what the results were, and what you think they mean. Reports like these are not relegated just to scientific journals. They often appear in newspapers and magazines and form the basis for television shows about science and technology.

PLANNING AND PERFORMING YOUR EXPERIMENT

HANDBOOKS
FOR HELP & PRACTICE

**Envisioning
Structure,**
p. 361
Unity/Coherence,
pp. 401–414
**Using Words
Precisely,**
pp. 434–439
**Formal/Informal
English,**
p. 449
Problem Solving,
pp. 487–489

1. Select a suitable subject. If you are taking any science courses this term, such as biology, earth science, or chemistry, you might choose an experiment from your textbook or lab manual. You might also choose a subject from your own experience. For example, do laundry detergents that promise to remove different types of stains really live up to their claims? You could experiment to find out.

2. Design and perform your experiment. Design an experiment that will test your supposition, or follow the steps outlined in your science books. If you're designing your own experiment, explain it to a friend or a teacher and ask him or her to evaluate it. When you perform your experiment, be sure to take all necessary safety precautions.

3. Take careful notes. As you set up and perform your experiment, take detailed notes. Record facts, figures, and observations. Recall that Cousteau carefully noted the distance the *Calypso* kept from the dolphin tank, the sound range of the dolphin's cries, and the actions of the dolphin school.

Writer's Choice Notes for a scientific experiment may be recorded in sentences or they may be recorded on a line graph or a chart. Choose the note-taking method that is most appropriate for your experiment.

Left: Scientists examining ocean life within one square meter. Below: Divers study a large grouper.

4. Review your findings and reach a conclusion. Discuss the results of your experiment with friends. Draw a conclusion based on the evidence you have gathered, and sum up your conclusion in a sentence or two. If any of your findings appear puzzling or contradictory, you may want to repeat your experiment.

DRAFTING YOUR REPORT

1. Choose a format. Some situations or assignments may require you to present your material formally, complete with a title page and bibliography. Check with your instructor to determine the specific requirements. Most reports, however, will include the sections described in the following steps.

2. State your hypothesis and describe your experiment. In an introductory paragraph like Cousteau's, present your hypothesis, supposition, or question. You may want to formulate a single sentence that tells the reader exactly what you are investigating. In the next paragraph, describe how your experiment was set up, listing any materials you used.

3. Describe what occurred. Recount, step by step, what happened during the experiment and what you observed at each step. You may want to begin a new paragraph for each significant development, as Cousteau did, or you may want to use one paragraph for each step or segment of time that elapsed. Be sure to include specific facts, details, and data.

4. End with the conclusion(s) you have drawn. As Cousteau does in the excerpt, use the last part of your report to explain what your conclusions are and how you arrived at them. Refer to the facts and data you provided in the body of your report that support your conclusion. End your report with a summary statement like Cousteau's final sentence.

REVIEWING YOUR REPORT

1. Examine your logic. Check your reasoning, and be sure the connections between your ideas are clear to the reader.

2. Check your transitions. In the body of your report, where you recount your experiment, be sure you have used transitions like *first, next, at this point,* and *afterward* to keep your reader oriented to the progress of your experiment. In the concluding sections of your report, be sure you have used transitions like *based on the fact that* and *for these reasons* so that the reader can follow your line of thinking. Note, for example, Cousteau's use of *therefore* in paragraphs 1 and 5, and *that is* and *for* in paragraph 6, to point out the steps in his logic.

3. Ask for feedback. Seek out people who did not work with you during the experiment, perhaps friends or teachers with an interest or background in the area you investigated. Ask if they could re-create your experiment on the basis of the information in your report. If not, you may need to include more specific facts and data from your notes.

© 1985, Washington Post Writers Group. Reprinted with permission

PUBLISHING AND PRESENTING

- **Present your report to classmates.** Read at least the report's beginning and conclusion aloud. Then summarize your experiment, demonstrating, if possible, the techniques you used to gather data, or perhaps showing classmates the apparatus you used to conduct the experiment.
- **Turn your experiment and report into a science-fair project.** Create visuals such as charts, photos, or graphics to accompany your report. Follow the guidelines for your school or county science-fair entries.
- **Send your report to your school or local newspaper.** If your experiment deals with matters that directly affect your school or community, such as recycling methods or the use or overuse of harmful pesticides, a local publication might be interested in publishing it.

Lab or
Science Report

195

Opinion Poll

Public opinion polls are becoming increasingly common in the United States. The public's interest in, and opinion of, everything from current fashion to international politics is monitored by organizations that use sophisticated formulas to devise questions, select respondents, and evaluate results.

In this report on an opinion poll conducted for *FORTUNE* magazine, 1,000 Americans were asked to express views on "personal hopes for the future." As you examine the poll, think about how the statistical information enabled the editors of *FORTUNE* to draw conclusions about the level of optimism in the United States.

THE U.S. MOOD:

EVER OPTIMISTIC

by Louis Kraar

That most American of character traits—optimism—is as strong in this era of fierce global competition as it was when the nation was triumphing over the worst economic depression in modern times. When *FORTUNE* published a poll of public attitudes in 1939, the mood of the country was "sweeping confidence that for the individual the present is better than the past, that the future will be better than the present." An [unusually] gallant faith in tomorrow emerges from a national survey of 1,000 Americans conducted this year for *FORTUNE* by Clark & Bartolomeo, Inc. The poll posed the same questions that *FORTUNE* asked the general public in 1939, and in many instances the results are startlingly similar. Remarkably, the nation's buoyant attitude toward the future has endured—even strengthened—after five decades of national and international tumult. . . .

HIGHER PERSONAL HOPES FOR
THE FUTURE

You have a good chance for personal advancement in the years ahead.

1939	1990
56%	64%

You have a better opportunity to succeed than your parents had.

1939	1990
61%	79%

Your children's opportunities to succeed will be greater than your own.

1939	1990
61%	66%

The American dream of upward mobility is more widespread than ever. Almost two out of three Americans believe they have a good chance for advancement in the years ahead. Today 79 percent feel they are more likely to succeed than their parents, up from 61 percent in the *FORTUNE* poll of 1939. And 66 percent now believe that the next generation's opportunities will be even better than theirs, compared with 61 percent in 1939. . . .

Ah, youth! People from 18 to 25 of all races and from all parts of the country turn out to be the most optimistic. Some 91 percent of them now believe they are likely to get ahead. In 1939 the young were also overwhelmingly the most hopeful age group: 74 percent expected brighter personal futures.

Think AND Respond

Look at the three statements to which the *FORTUNE* pollsters asked people to respond. Based on the responses, the pollsters concluded that people in the United States are at least as optimistic today as they were in 1939, and in some cases, more so. Is their conclusion justified? Can you think of a controversial or highly interesting topic you would like to investigate by conducting a public opinion poll?

INVITATION
TO
Write

The *FORTUNE* pollsters used three statements to determine how Americans' optimism today compares with their optimism in the past. Conduct your own opinion poll and explain your findings in a brief essay.

Public opinion polls are carefully crafted instruments for gathering information and drawing conclusions about people's attitudes and interests. The questions asked in a public opinion poll are meant to be as neutral as possible so that the respondents' answers won't be affected by their emotions. The respondents are chosen scientifically to ensure a good representative cross-section of whichever part of the population the pollsters want to question. Finally, the conclusions drawn from the poll are expressed as objectively as possible so as not to misrepresent the significance of the data.

▶ PLANNING AN OPINION POLL

HANDBOOKS
FOR HELP & PRACTICE

Questioning,
pp. 392–394
Interviewing,
p. 396
Peer Response,
pp. 422–426
Using Words
Precisely,
pp. 434–437
Listening Skills,
pp. 541–542

1. Choose a compelling or controversial topic. Brainstorm with friends to develop a list of topics you might use as the basis for a public opinion poll. A national or international issue, an upcoming vote on a constitutional amendment, or a topic affecting your school may provide you with an interesting subject for your poll. Choose a topic about which your respondents are likely to have a clear and strong opinion.

2. Focus your topic. Think carefully about your topic, considering all of its aspects, and zero in on one or two aspects you wish to investigate. In the *Fortune* poll, for example, the pollsters were not interested in Americans' definition of "optimism" or in their optimism about the possibility of avoiding war. Rather, the pollsters chose to focus on Americans' opinions about their own chances for "personal advancement." To help you focus your topic, think about the specific goal of your poll. What *exactly* do you want to know?

3. Identify an appropriate target audience. Your choice of respondents is crucial to the validity and usefulness of your data and any conclusions you draw. For example, suppose your goal is to determine how people feel about a proposal to raise the driving age to eighteen. In order to get a balanced response, you will probably need to target three groups of respondents: men and women under eighteen who already drive; men and women from eighteen to twenty-five who drive, and men and women of your parents' and grandparents' generation.

4. Draft questions or statements about your topic. Decide whether you want your respondents to answer questions or respond to statements. In either case, write statements or questions that can be responded to with a simple "agree/disagree," "yes/no," or "true/false." Another useful format asks respondents to rate their responses on a scale of 1 to 5, with 1 meaning "strongly agree" and 5 meaning "strongly disagree." Such a format allows people to express degrees of agreement or disagreement and provides the pollster with more specific data.

Write questions or statements that are as clear and unambiguous as possible. Your questions should not contain loaded language or words with strong positive or negative connotations. Write "Should the driving age be raised to eighteen?" Don't write "Should sixteen- and seventeen-year-olds be *denied* the *privilege* of driving until they are eighteen?" The second question uses language that will likely affect the way people respond.

5. Consider a procedure for your poll. Will you administer your poll orally, face-to-face with each respondent? Will you conduct a telephone poll? Should you mail your poll to prospective respondents? As you think about the procedure you will use, think also about these important considerations. If your poll asks personal or possibly embarrassing questions, you may not get an honest answer from a person you're talking to face-to-face. It might be better to conduct your poll over the phone or by mail. Some people, however, consider telephone polls a nuisance and will refuse to answer or will just hang up. If you decide on a telephone poll, try to pick a convenient time to call. Mail polls may also be ignored. If a mail poll is your choice, make it as easy as possible for your respondents to answer. Write simple, clear instructions. Keep the number of questions down to three or four. Provide a self-addressed, stamped envelope for the return of the poll.

6. Give your poll a brief test run. Choose several individuals who represent a small sample of those you will poll formally and administer the poll to them exactly as you plan to administer it to your target audience. Monitor whether these respondents find any aspect of the poll confusing, vague, or biased; whether their answers are easily tallied and analyzed; and whether the poll elicits the kind of information that satisfies your original goal. Revise your polling questionnaire or procedure as necessary.

CONDUCTING A POLL

1. Administer your poll as consistently as possible. It is important to make the conditions under which people respond as consistent as possible. For example, make sure that respondents are not rushed or disturbed by noise or other people. If you're conducting your poll by phone, call the respondents at about the same time—for example, between 7 and 8 P.M.

COMPUTER TIP

You may wish to use an appropriate software program to prepare forms for your poll and tally sheets.

2. Tally and analyze responses, and draw conclusions. When polling is complete, tally responses to individual items and determine the percentages of the total group of respondents these numbers represent. You might wish to develop a chart or graph as a visual aid so you can easily see the implications of the results you've gathered.

As you analyze the responses to each item, think about what conclusions you can draw. You should be able to draw at least one specific conclusion from each survey item and some general conclusions from the poll as a whole. Write each conclusion clearly in sentence form, and under each sentence list the statistics that support it. If you decide to apply your conclusions to a wider audience than the one you polled, take into account the demographic profile of your respondents—that is, their age, race, sex, and so on. Your conclusions can be applied only to individuals with a similar profile.

Be careful not to oversimplify or overgeneralize while drawing conclusions from your data. For instance, in analyzing the *Fortune* poll's first item, it would be overgeneralizing to conclude that Americans today are *more confident* than Americans in 1939. The editors of *Fortune* drew the accurate conclusion that "the American dream of upward mobility is *more widespread*" than it was in 1939.

3. Write a prose essay that summarizes your data and conclusions. Begin with any general conclusions about the survey as a whole. Then explain conclusions drawn from individual poll items.

Support your conclusions with references to the hard data from your poll. Notice that the essay in *Fortune* includes presentation of statistics, such as "today 79 percent feel they are more likely to succeed than their parents," as well as evaluations, interpretations, and conclusions such as "the results are startlingly similar," and "the nation's buoyant attitude toward the future has endured—even strengthened. . . ."

For your readers' information, include a brief description of the range of people you surveyed, the procedure you used, and the date(s) that polling occurred. Also, you will probably wish to illustrate your findings on a chart or graph, so that your reader can see at a glance the results of your poll.

REVIEWING YOUR FINDINGS

1. Check the accuracy of your mathematical calculations. Although this double-checking will take some time, it could save you from making an embarrassing mistake by basing a conclusion on faulty data.

2. Check the logic of your conclusions. Review each conclusion you have drawn to ensure that it follows logically from the facts you have gathered and tallied. Do you have statistics to back up each conclusion?

3. Review your written essay. Review your summary for accuracy, clarity, and strong written expression. You may wish to review it with a friend to help you spot passages that might need more explanation. Proofread your summary carefully and correct any errors in grammar, usage, mechanics, and spelling.

Editorial cartoon by Mike Jenkins, Courtesy Springfield (VA) Journal

PUBLISHING AND PRESENTING

- **Submit your poll results to a school or community newspaper.**
- **Present your findings in an oral presentation to the class.**

Writing
TIP

In your introduction, give your readers a preview of the conclusion or ask a thought-provoking question to catch their interest.

On the Lightside

SIMPLIFIED SPELLING

In 1867 Joseph Medill, publisher of the *Chicago Tribune,* wrote these words about the importance of spelling:

Lerning tu spel and red the Inglish langwaj iz the grat elementary task ov the pupol.

Medill was not a candidate for a remedial spelling class. Instead, he was advocating a simplified spelling system in a booklet he published entitled "An Easy Method of Spelling the English Language." Medill even tried out a few of the improved spellings in his newspaper, but to his disappointment the idea did not catch on.

Fifty years later, however, the idea was tried once again. Medill's grandson, Colonel Robert R. McCormick, was now the publisher of the *Tribune,* and by his decree eighty new words started appearing in the newspaper. They included *foto, grafic, thoro, thru, clew, biografy, frate,* and *fantom.* McCormick reasoned that a new word like *frate* sounded the same as the original *freight,* yet it was easier to spell. In addition, it had fewer letters, so it took up less space on the printed page and made the job of headline writers easier.

McCormick's experiment continued until 1955, when the *Tribune* finally gave in to the many critics of the simplified spelling system. It was particularly unpopular with teachers, who were not amused when their students would try to justify their misspellings by pointing to the *Tribune.*

foto

hite

clew

Sentence

Elaborating on Compound Sentences

Compound sentences are themselves a means of elaboration. By connecting two or more independent clauses that are closely related in meaning, you can more effectively express the relationship. In this lesson you will learn the two ways to connect independent clauses and to elaborate on the clauses by adding descriptive phrases. Notice that independent clauses can be connected with either (1) a comma and a conjunction or (2) a semicolon.

MODELS

1. My tongue was swollen and sore from drinking
   scalding-hot tea, AND the tip of my nose ached from
   frostbite.   **Richard E. Byrd, *Alone***

2. Quickly, frantically, he tried to slide back the hood
   with his left hand, BUT he had not the strength.
                           Roald Dahl, "Beware of the Dog"

3. Against the east the piling mountains were misty with
   light; their tops melted into the sky.
                               John Steinbeck, "Flight"

A. Combining Sentences Each set contains at least two independent clauses. Decide whether they should be connected by using ,*and* (to show a continuation of the same thought), by using ,*but* (to show a contrast), or by using a semicolon (;) (to show very close relationship). Then combine them. Compare your sentences to the originals on page 328.

1. a. Dvoira, the dark-uddered cow, was out in the field behind the hut.
   b. Yakov went out to her.   **Bernard Malamud, *The Fixer***

2. a. The sun was gone behind the westward mountain now.
   b. Still it glowed brilliantly on the oaks and on the grassy flat.
                                              John Steinbeck, "Flight"

3. a. The past and the future are cut off.
   b. Only the present remains.   **Anne Morrow Lindbergh, *Gift from the Sea***

4. a. Wanting to make some kind of a noise in the silence, she coughed.
   b. The small sound moved dustily into the darkness of the house.
   Shirley Jackson, "The Little House"

B. Imitating Sentences The models below include phrases that elaborate on the information in one or both independent clauses. Imitate each model, including descriptive phrases of the same structure, and in the same places, as those in the model. Descriptive phrases are bracketed.

> ***Example***   He stirred a little [on the bench]; he leaned
>   forward [with his elbows on his knees],
>   [looking at his strong hands].

> ***Student Imitation***   Jackson stepped down from the mound; he
>   walked slowly with a grin on his face,
>   kicking up the red dust.

1. He pulled a string [dangling from the ceiling], and a dozen naked bulbs flooded the room [with pools of yellow light].
   Robert Lipsyte, *The Contender*

2. Her collars and cuffs were white organdy, [trimmed with lace], and [at her neckline] she had pinned a purple spray of cloth violets, [containing a sachet].   **Flannery O'Connor, "A Good Man Is Hard to Find"**

3. All the lights were going on [in West Egg now]; the electric trains, [men-carrying], were plunging home [through the rain] [from New York].
   F. Scott Fitzgerald, *The Great Gatsby*

4. I turned to "Annabel Lee," and we walked up and down the garden rows, [the cool dirt between our toes], [reciting the beautifully sad lines].
   Maya Angelou, *I Know Why the Caged Bird Sings*

5. The bride, [in her bridelike traveling dress], [surrounded by her maids], stood between her parents, [each of them holding her by a hand], and their three faces were calm, grave, and much alike.
   Katherine Anne Porter, *Ship of Fools*

C. Expanding Sentences Some compound sentences have more than two independent clauses. Expand each sentence by elaborating on the independent clauses with phrases like those used in the last activity. After you finish, compare your sentences with the originals, page 328.

1. Her hands trembled . . . , and her eyes had a feverish look, and her hair swirled. . . . **William Faulkner, "Dry September"**

2. His hands relaxed; the fork fell . . . ; his head lowered. **Hamlin Garland, "Under the Lion's Paw"**

3. The lights dazzled his eyes, and then a truck crashed . . . , and a baseball bat blasted. . . . **Robert Lipsyte, *The Contender***

4. The morning . . . was clear and sunny, . . . ; the flowers were blossoming . . . , and the grass was richly green. **Shirley Jackson, "The Lottery"**

5. His eyes were entranced, and he could sense . . . ; he could feel. . . . **John Steinbeck, *The Pearl***

Application The passage below begins a paragraph about a boy's first day as a grape-picker. Write a narrative paragraph about the first time you did something. Imitate the structure of the paragraph, using at least one compound sentence. Notice the rhythm that compound sentences lend to your writing.

> Around nine o'clock the temperature had risen to almost one hundred degrees. I was completely soaked in sweat and my mouth felt as if it had been chewing on a handkerchief. I walked over to the end of the row, picked up the jug of water we had brought, and began drinking. "Don't drink too much; you'll get sick," Roberto shouted.
> **Francisco Jiménez, "The Circuit"**

Grammar Refresher Connecting independent clauses incorrectly can result in comma splices or run-on sentences. To learn to avoid these errors, see Handbook 31, pages 592–594.

Sketchbook

Fran Lebowitz is a writer known for her facetious humor, often delivered in a deadpan manner. Here are some of her "Tips For Teens":

- *Should your political opinions be at extreme variance with those of your parents, keep in mind that while it is indeed your constitutional right to express these sentiments verbally, it is unseemly to do so with your mouth full—particularly when it is full of the oppressor's standing rib roast.*
- *Think before you speak. Read before you think. This will give you something to think about that you didn't make up yourself—a wise move at any age, but most especially at seventeen, when you are in the greatest danger of coming to annoying conclusions.*
- *Remember that as a teenager you are at the last stage in your life when you will be happy to hear that the phone is for you.*
- *Stand firm in your refusal to remain conscious during algebra. In real life, I assure you, there is no such thing as algebra.*

Now it's your turn. Write some "Tips for the Older Generation."

Additional Sketches

Do you think there are two sides to every issue? Why or why not?

Think about the last time you tried to convince someone to do something. What happened?

Persuasion

Guided Assignment
PERSUASIVE ESSAY

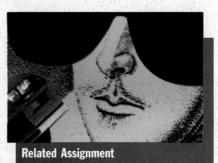

Related Assignment
SATIRE

Related Assignment
AD COPY

You probably use persuasion every day. It could be something as simple as convincing a friend to go to the movie you want to see or as challenging as convincing strangers to sign a petition. You may employ gentle coaxing, or you may make pointed demands. Persuasion is part argument and part enticement. It can be built on both logic and emotion. In the guided assignment that follows, you will study ways to marshal facts and opinions to support a position. In the related assignments, you will see how appeals to the emotions can provide the persuasive spark in writing satire and advertising copy.

Persuasive Essay

"WE HOLD THE ROCK"

Alcatraz Proclamation to the Great White Father and His People

The goal of persuasion is to change the feelings, attitudes, and actions of others. Writers use a variety of techniques to accomplish that goal, as you can see in the following excerpt.

In the fall of 1969, several dozen American Indians, led by Richard Oakes, a Mohawk, and Grace Thorpe, a Sac and Fox, invaded the abandoned prison on Alcatraz Island in San Francisco Bay and claimed it in the name of all American Indians. As you read their Alcatraz Proclamation, notice the factual and emotional arguments they use to present their position persuasively.

Fellow citizens, we are asking you to join with us in our attempt to better the lives of all Indian people.

We are on Alcatraz Island to make known to the world that we have a right to use our land for our own benefit.

We, the native Americans, reclaim the land known as Alcatraz Island in the name of all American Indians. . . .

We will give to the inhabitants of this island a portion of the land for their own to be held in trust . . . by the Bureau of Caucasian Affairs . . . in perpetuity—for as long as the sun shall rise and the rivers go down to the sea. We will further guide the inhabitants in the proper way of living. We will offer them our religion, our education, our lifeways in order to help them achieve our level of civilization and thus raise them and all their white brothers up from their savage and unhappy state. We offer this treaty in good faith and wish to be fair and honorable in our dealings with all white men.

We feel that this so-called Alcatraz Island is more than suitable for an Indian reservation in that:

1. It is isolated from modern facilities, and without adequate means of transportation.

2. It has no fresh running water.

3. It has inadequate sanitation facilities.

4. There are no oil or mineral rights.

5. There is no industry, and so unemployment is very great.

6. There are no health-care facilities.

7. The soil is rocky and non-productive, and the land does not support game.

8. There are no educational facilities.

9. The population has always exceeded the land base.

10. The population has always been held prisoners and kept dependent upon others.

Further, it would be fitting and symbolic that ships from all over the world, entering the Golden Gate, would first see Indian land, and thus be reminded of the true history of this nation. This tiny island would be a symbol of the great lands once ruled by free and noble Indians.

What use will we make of this land?

We plan to develop on this island several Indian institutions:

1. A Center for Native American Studies will be developed which will educate them [our people] to the skills and knowledge relevant to improve the lives and spirits of all Indian peoples. . . .

2. An American Indian Spiritual Center, which will practice our ancient tribal religious . . . ceremonies. . . .

3. An Indian Center of Ecology, which will train and support our young people in scientific research and practice to restore our lands and waters to their pure and natural state. . . .

4. A Great Indian Training School will be developed to teach our young people how to make a living in the world, improve our standard of living, and to end hunger and unemployment among all our people. This training school will include a center for Indian arts and crafts, and an Indian restaurant serving native foods, which will restore Indian culinary arts. . . .

Some of the present buildings will be taken over to develop an American Indian Museum which will depict our native food and other cultural contributions we have given to the world. Another part of the museum will present some of the things the white man has given to the Indians in return for the land and life he took: disease, alcohol, poverty, and cultural decimation (as symbolized by old tin cans, barbed wire, rubber tires, plastic containers, etc.). Part of the museum will remain a dungeon to symbolize both those Indian captives who were incarcerated for challenging white authority and those who were imprisoned on reservations. The museum will show the noble and tragic events of Indian history, including the broken treaties, the documentary of the Trail of Tears, the Massacre of Wounded Knee, as well as the victory over Yellow-Hair Custer and his army.

In the name of all Indians, therefore, we reclaim this island for our Indian nations, for all these reasons. We feel this claim is just and proper, and that this land should rightfully be granted to us
for as long as the rivers run
and the sun shall shine.
We hold the Rock!

Think AND Respond

What were the writers trying to accomplish with their proclamation? What techniques do they use to support their position? How do they present their argument? What issues that you feel strongly about does their proclamation bring to mind?

INVITATION
—TO—
Write

The Alcatraz Proclamation uses persuasive techniques to make its point. Now write your own persuasive essay designed to convince the reader to agree with your point of view on your chosen issue. Use the suggestions that follow as guidelines for writing your persuasive paper.

Persuasive writing is not simply a matter of stating a fact or personal preference. It involves examining an issue with distinctly opposing sides that people can evaluate and debate. Writers use persuasion for many reasons. They may want to present an opinion, a belief, or an argument, or they may want to take a stand, issue a demand, or appeal for support. Persuasive writing takes many forms, such as editorials, essays, proposals, petitions, and advertisements.

▶ P REWRITE AND EXPLORE

HANDBOOKS
FOR HELP & PRACTICE

Sharing Techniques,
pp. 346–347
Tree Diagrams,
p. 354
Pro-and-Con Charts,
pp. 355–356
Persuasive Writing,
pp. 490–493
Sources of Information,
pp. 512–513

1. Look for ideas. The Alcatraz Proclamation presents a position on an issue important to many Americans. What issues are important to you? The following suggestions may help you find one you would like to explore.

Exploratory Activities

- **Brainstorming** Get together with three or four classmates and brainstorm about controversial issues—for example, social problems that cry out for solutions, political issues that generate debate, or rules, laws, and customs that seem unfair or outdated.
- **Proclamations** The Alcatraz Proclamation declares the position of a group of American Indians. What would you like to proclaim? Freewrite your position.
- **Current events** As you read news magazines such as *Time* or *Newsweek,* look for articles about controversial issues that interest you.

- **Sentence completion** Write one or more endings for each of these sentences.
  It angers me that _____ .
  It angers/saddens me that students must _____ .
  It's so strange that most people think _____ .
  One thing we've got to do is _____ .
- **Reading literature** Henry David Thoreau said, "Cultivate poverty like a garden herb, like sage. Do not trouble yourself much to get new things, whether clothes or friends." Freewrite your response to his opinion or to the opinion of another author or poet you have read recently.

2. Test topics. Draw a ladder on a sheet of paper. On the rungs of the ladder, list the topics you have thought of, putting the one that interests you most on the top rung. Then freewrite on each topic to test your interest. Does the topic on the top rung still interest you the most? If you still have difficulty finding a suitable topic for a persuasive essay, try one of these strategies: see if you can find an idea in your journal; turn to page 223 and study the suggestions under "Apply Your Skills"; check the writing you did for the Sketchbook on page 206.

 Writer's Choice Do you want to tackle an acknowledged controversy, or do you want to persuade your readers to rethink an issue most people take for granted?

3. Share your ideas. Once you have narrowed down your choices to one or two promising topics, share them with a group of classmates. Listen for ideas in response to your topics, and also listen for ideas on other topics you might wish to pursue instead.

4. Choose a topic. Freewrite for ten minutes on the topic you find most promising to see if you want to continue working with it. Don't hesitate to explore the arguments against your position as well as those in favor of it. You will need to consider both sides as you write.

After one of her neighbors suffered serious injuries in a car accident, one student, Gina, became interested in the issue of whether motorists should be required to wear seat belts. Following are some of her initial thoughts. Throughout this workshop, you will follow Gina's process in writing her persuasive essay.

It angers me that so many of my friends just laugh off things like seat-belt laws. They say it's nobody's business whether they wear them or not. They make me feel like some goody-goody when I tell them to put one on. But I know what can happen to people. I saw how my neighbor's life was ruined. And it's <u>not</u> just a personal decision. The cost of medical bills and the loss of someone's abilities hurts us all. I know that sometimes government regulations go over-board, but I don't think this is one of those times.

Writing
—TIP—

If more than one topic is equally appealing to you, freewrite on both and see which case seems stronger.

5. Clarify your position. Look over your freewriting and think more critically about your position. You may wish to use a tree diagram to explore your position. First, on the trunk, write a simple statement of your position. Then, for the branches, list as many reasons as you can to support the statement. Finally, for the roots, examine your statements and see if you can list the basic assumptions that support your position.

Here is how Gina organized her responses.

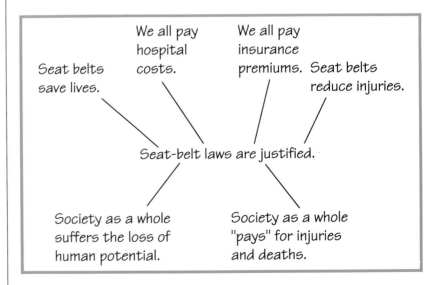

Seat belts save lives.

We all pay hospital costs.

We all pay insurance premiums.

Seat belts reduce injuries.

Seat-belt laws are justified.

Society as a whole suffers the loss of human potential.

Society as a whole "pays" for injuries and deaths.

6. Examine the opposing viewpoint. You need to understand the other side so that you can prepare effective counterarguments. You may wish to construct a tree diagram of the other side's position. By understanding the other viewpoint, you can anticipate opposing arguments and respond to them. You may also wish to work with another writer to brainstorm reasons to support and oppose both viewpoints.

7. Identify your goals. Ask yourself why the issue is personally important to you. Also consider what effect you want to have on your readers. Do you want them to think differently, act differently, write a letter, join a protest, volunteer time?

8. Identify your audience. Keep in mind that to be effective, persuasive writing must respond to the needs of its audience. Consider these questions.

- How much does my audience already know about my writing topic?
- How big a stake does the audience have in the topic? Will I have to overcome apathy?
- How fervently will the audience agree or disagree with my position at first? Can I find an initial point of agreement?
- What does the audience need to know in order to do what I ask?

PROBLEM
S O L V I N G

How can I get through to my audience?

9. Gather information. Gather information to support your position and counter opposing arguments by reading books, magazine articles, newspaper reports, and editorials and by interviewing people who are knowledgeable about the issue. Look for facts and statistics, examples, anecdotes, observations, and expert testimony.

DRAFT AND DISCOVER

FOR HELP & PRACTICE

**Introductions/
Conclusions,
pp. 378–385
Facts/Statistics,
p. 397
Language of
Persuasion,
pp. 544–545**

1. Begin drafting. Your prewriting activities have provided you with the information and ideas you will need to get started. As you write, keep in mind these suggestions for organizing your essay.

- **Introduce the issue.** Make the issue compelling to readers; show them why they should care about it. Sometimes writers do this dramatically, with a narrative, or a scene that illustrates their point.
- **State your position and support it.** Give a clear and direct statement of your position. If possible, use a point of common agreement to get readers involved and on your side from the first. Then present the evidence you have gathered to support your position.
- **Address opposing arguments.** State the opposing position and the evidence you have gathered to counter opposing arguments.
- **Write an appropriate conclusion.** If your aim is simply to change your readers' thinking on an issue, your conclusion should summarize your position and include a final appeal to accept the validity of that position. If you want your audience to take a specific action, you should say so clearly and forcefully. Be sure to give your readers the information they need to take the recommended action.

2. Elaborate on ideas. When you write persuasively, you may need to use a variety of strategies, such as the ones that follow.

Strategies

- **Comparison and contrast** Use this strategy to examine the pros and cons of a position, the similarities and differences in points of view, or the advantages and disadvantages of courses of action.
- **Cause and effect** If you are suggesting or attacking a particular plan or course of action, one way to help your reader understand your position is to explore its causes and effects as you see them.

3. Use persuasive language effectively. Although you should base your argument on well-supported facts, emotional appeals are often an important part of persuasive writing. You can draw attention to your position by using words with strong connotations. For example, a person who does something dangerous could be called both *courageous* and *foolhardy*. *Courageous* has a positive connotation, while *foolhardy* has a negative connotation.

Phrases and sentences can also draw emotional responses. For example, the Alcatraz Proclamation supports its position by noting the island would be "a symbol of the great lands once ruled by free and noble Indians." Notice also how the proclamation uses satire to draw attention to the ways Indians have been mistreated.

Gina decided to use an emotional appeal to open her essay.

PROBLEM
S O L V I N G

How can I draw attention to my argument?

ONE STUDENT'S PROCESS

On a warm June evening nearly a year ago, my neighbor got into his sports car and drove off for his girlfriend's house. But on the way he had an accident. When she saw him later, he was barely clinging to life after sustaining a head injury. His doctors say he has permanent brain damage and is unlikely to be able to return to work, or even to live independently. If he had been wearing a safety belt, his injuries would have been much less severe.

Writing
——**TIP**——

Do you know any anecdotes you could use to give your essay more emotional appeal?

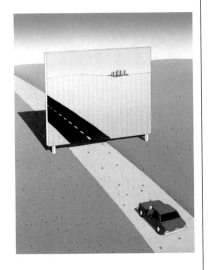

4. Avoid misleading language. Presenting your viewpoint in the strongest possible light is one thing. Using language to deliberately mislead is quite a different matter. For example, you should make every effort to avoid using judgmental words like "Everyone educated person knows" when discussing issues about which reasonable people often disagree. You should also try to avoid vague or undefined terms, confusion of fact and opinion, and bias. For more information about misleading language, see "Understanding the Language of Persuasion" on pages 544–545 in Writer's Handbook 29.

 Writer's Choice Do you want to use emotional appeals to draw attention to your argument, or rely on objectively presenting the facts of your position?

5. Take a break. Once you have completed your draft, set it aside for a while. Then review it and share it with a peer reader or readers.

R E V I E W   Y O U R   W R I T I N G

Questions for Yourself
- Have I clearly stated my position on the issue?
- Have I presented ample evidence to support my position?
- Have I noted opposing viewpoints and presented effective counterarguments?
- Have I written an appropriate conclusion?
- If I want the reader to take a specific action, have I provided the information necessary to do so?

Questions for Your Peer Readers
- What is my position on the issue?
- Have I provided enough background information about the issue? If not, what do you need more information about?
- What arguments did you find convincing?
- Have I addressed opposing viewpoints effectively?
- Can you think of other points to support or oppose my position?

REVISE YOUR WRITING

1. Evaluate your responses. Think about your responses and decide what changes you want to make. Also consider these characteristics of effective persuasive writing.

Standards for Evaluation

Effective persuasive writing . . .

- opens with a compelling introduction that clearly states the problem or issue and the writer's position.
- supports the writer's position with strong evidence.
- acknowledges opposing views and presents effective counterarguments.
- includes a conclusion that sums up the writer's position or provides a call to action.
- uses appropriate language and details for the audience.

2. Problem-solve. Rework your draft, incorporating revisions. Gina made the following changes to a paragraph from her draft.

HANDBOOKS

FOR HELP & PRACTICE

**Unity/Coherence,
pp. 401–414
Using Source
Materials,
pp. 495–501**

ONE STUDENT'S PROCESS

Opponents of safety-belt laws say that they *(e)* infringe *such laws*

on an individuals' freedom of choice. They feel that the

goverment *(n)* has no right to impose its Will on people *in a situation that only affects the individual who makes the choice.*

further, they say, it is not the role of goverment *(n)* to pro-

tect people from themselves and the consequences of the

choices they make. These arguments are so foolish they *However, as the evidence cited above demonstrates,*

hardly deserve a response. Its obvious that an individ-

ual's dicision *(e)* not to wear a safety belt can effect *(a)* society

at large. *Public funds sometimes have to be used in paying for the care of motorists who sustain serious injuries in traffic accidents—injuries that are likely to be much more severe if the victim is not wearing a safety belt.*

What does "they" in the first sentence refer to?

I think you're oversimplifying the opponents' position.

Your position could be stronger if you used facts, not opinion, to respond.

Print out a proofing copy on the printer's "draft" setting, one you can mark up before you print a final copy in the printer's best format.

3. Check your essay for balance.   Make sure that you have made the strongest possible case for your own viewpoint. At the same time, check to make sure that you have not been unfair to opposing viewpoints by using loaded language.

4. Proofread your work.   Make a clean copy that incorporates all your changes. Then look for errors in grammar, usage, spelling, and mechanics. Correct these errors so that readers will not be distracted by them.

LINKING
GRAMMAR AND WRITING
The Correct Use of *Hopefully*

The adverb *hopefully* means "in a hopeful manner." *Hopefully* is often used, however, when the writer or speaker means "I hope" or "It is to be hoped that." While this usage has become common, it is still considered nonstandard.

PROBLEM: Hopefully, Dr. Frankenstein will comply with the monster's request.

REVISED: I hope that Dr. Frankenstein will comply with the monster's request.

▶ PUBLISH AND PRESENT

• **Create a Speakers' Corner.**   Hyde Park in London is famous for its Speakers' Corner, where soapbox orators stand on wooden boxes and give speeches dealing with controversial issues of the day. Create a Speakers' Corner in your classroom, where students can get up on a "soapbox" and read their essays. The rest of the class can respond to the arguments and counterarguments that each speaker presents.

• **Submit your essay.**   Try a local newspaper or a national magazine that publishes student writing.

• **Present your essay orally to one of your other classes.**   Add models, charts or graphs, illustrations, video materials, or music.

• **Publish the essay as a flier or brochure.**   Distribute copies of it to your intended audience.

• **Save your essay in your writing portfolio.**

Buckle Up!

Gina Calabrese

On a warm June evening nearly a year ago, a twenty-one-year-old neighbor got into his sports car and set off for his girlfriend's house. He never arrived. When she saw him later that evening, he was in the intensive care unit of the local hospital, barely clinging to life after sustaining a severe head injury in a collision with another car. His doctors say that he has permanent brain damage and is unlikely ever to be able to return to work, or even to live independently. The doctors also say that if he had been wearing a safety belt, his injuries would have been much less severe.

Our state is not one of those that have a law requiring motorists to wear safety belts. I strongly believe that the state legislature should pass such a law as soon as possible.

Statistics show that safety belts are used on a regular basis by less that 20 percent of American motorists. It is estimated that the universal use of safety belts could save as many as 16,000 lives per year and could substantially reduce the number of moderate to critical injuries. According to the National Highway Traffic Safety Administration (NHTSA), the likelihood of serious or fatal injuries is reduced by between 40 and 55 percent when safety belts are used. In addition, NHTSA surveys have found that safety-belt use is substantially higher in areas that have laws mandating the use of such belts.

The universal use of safety belts would not only save lives and reduce injuries, but would also save society a great deal of money. Traffic accidents cost an estimated $8.5 billion per year. Universal safety-belt use could reduce this amount substantially by lowering the cost of medical benefits paid on behalf of accident victims as well as reducing the amount of time injured motorists are absent from work. In addition, universal safety-belt

Compelling introduction defines the issue and states the writer's position

Supports the writer's position with strong evidence

Persuasive Essay   **221**

use would result in a general reduction in motor-vehicle insurance premiums, since insurance companies would pay out less money in medical claims.

Opponents of safety-belt laws say that such laws infringe on an individual's freedom of choice. They feel that the government has no right to impose its will on people in a situation that affects only the individual who makes the choice. Further, they say it is not the role of government to protect people from themselves and the consequences of the choices they make. However, as the evidence cited above demonstrates, an individual's decision not to wear a safety belt can affect society at large. Public funds sometimes have to be used in paying for the care of motorists who sustain serious injuries in traffic accidents—injuries that are likely to be much more severe if the victim is not wearing a safety belt. If everyone would "buckle up," there would be a general reduction in motor-vehicle insurance premiums.

In addition, society suffers the loss of human productivity and potential as the result of motorists who do not wear safety belts. The case of my disabled neighbor illustrates how society pays when people refuse to wear seat belts. My neighbor's hospital bills have been so high that his medical benefits soon will be exhausted. Since he is unable to care for himself and his family cannot afford to pay for private nursing care, he soon will be placed in a state-supported nursing home.

The evidence showing that safety belts reduce traffic fatalities and the severity of injuries is clear and convincing. It is also clear that safety-belt use is substantially higher in states with laws mandating their use. Society's interest in reducing traffic-related deaths and injuries far outweighs the individual's right to freedom of choice in this matter. I strongly urge you to write to your state legislators to voice your support for passage of a law mandating the use of safety belts. You can obtain the names and addresses of your legislators by calling your local library or town hall.

WRITER TO WRITER

By persuading others, we convince ourselves.

Junius, pseudonym for the unidentified author of a series of letters to a London newspaper in the 1770's

1. Reflect on your writing. Now that you have completed your persuasive essay and read two others, you may wish to reflect on the process of writing involved. One way to do it is to ask yourself questions like those below. Record any useful thoughts or ideas in your journal or attach them to your finished paper.

- What parts of this paper or stages in writing it did I find most difficult? How did I overcome those difficulties?
- How has my opinion on my topic been changed by writing this paper? Do I now appreciate the other side more or less?
- What weaknesses do I now see in my argument that I didn't see or tried to hide when I wrote my paper? How could I revise my paper to overcome or acknowledge those weaknesses?
- In what other ways would I revise my paper if I had time to do it and felt like doing it?

2. Apply your skills. Use your persuasive writing skills to complete one or more of the following activities.

- **Literature** Identify a literary work you believe should or should not be taught in your school. Write an essay supporting your position.
- **History** Write a position paper supporting or opposing a policy or action you have studied in history or social studies. For example, you might oppose or support the colonization of America by England, the hunting of buffalo, the development of the atomic bomb, the Crusades, or any other action by governments or historical figures. You can write as a person living in any time period and take any side on the issue you choose.
- **Related assignments** Follow the suggestions on pages 226–234 to write a satire and ad copy.

Satire

These Foolish Things
by Michael Kinsley
Remind Me of Diet Coke

Did you ever read a piece of writing or see a picture that seemed to take its subject seriously but actually poked fun at it? *Satire* is a style of writing or visual expression that uses humor or exaggeration to criticize some human weakness or practice.

This excerpt from a satirical essay pokes fun at "paid product placements"—the subtle use of a product within a movie as a type of advertising. As you read the essay, try to figure out exactly who or what is being satirized.

Walt Disney Co. [is] soliciting paid product placements in a new film, "Mr. Destiny." Companies such as Campbell Soup Co., Nabisco Brands and Kraft General Foods Group are believed to have been contacted. . . . The cost structure, as outlined in letters to marketers, is $20,000 for a visual, $40,000 for a brand name mention with the visual and $60,000 for an actor to use the product.
   —Advertising Age

Dear Sirs and Madams:

We represent the playwright, producer and screenwriter William Shakespeare in the offering of prestigious product placements in his works. We feel, and Bill agrees, that an authentic Shakespeare play offers an unrivaled opportunity to showcase your product.

Billy is currently working on a docudrama about the life of King Richard III. . . .

Early in the play, Richard hires two thugs to murder his brother, the Duke of Clarence. In the scene as written, the murderers declare their intention to stab Clarence and then "throw him in the malmsey-butt in the next room," malmsey being a local beverage.

For $20,000, Bill is prepared to rewrite that line to read: "throw him in the super-jumbo cup of Diet Coke in the next room." For $40,000, Bill will move the scene to the next room and show the Duke actually being drowned in a large Diet Coke (logo prominently displayed). For $60,000, the murderers will also drink the Diet Coke and comment on its thirst-quenching qualities after their heavy labors.

Another Shakespeare production, still in the planning stage, involves the rise and fall of a Scottish king and offers a variety of rich product-placement opportunities. Three elderly sisters will be cooking onstage throughout the play, sometimes even reciting recipes. A single product reference—"Eye of newt, toe of frog, one-quarter cup ReaLemon reconstituted lemon juice"—will be $20,000. An entire couplet will be priced at $40,000. For $60,000, the sisters will say, "Heck, let's just dump this mess and call Domino's.". . .

A related opportunity involves the female lead, who is obsessed with personal hygiene. An entire scene is devoted to her washing her hands. Bill wants $20,000 for each soap product displayed on her vanity. For $40,000, after moaning "Out, damned spot," she will turn to the audience, smile brightly, and say, "And out it came, thanks to pure Ivory soap!" For $60,000, an attendant will comment that her hands are "not only clean, but soft as well, your Majesty.". . .

Think AND Respond

What do you think the author is trying to convey about the effects of advertising on art? Who is being criticized more—the advertiser or the artist? Why do you think the author uses Shakespeare as his example?

225

INVITATION
— TO —
Write

By imagining the results of having paid advertisements in Shakespeare's plays, the author of this excerpt pokes fun at the practice of advertising commercial products in movies. Using words or pictures, satirize a subject of your own choice.

Satire is a form of persuasive writing in which authors use exaggeration or humor to show readers that something in society should be changed. For example, instead of openly criticizing the use of advertisements in the movies, the author of the excerpt exaggerates the silliness of the idea by applying it to Shakespeare's plays. By using this kind of writing, you can expose truths in a striking and persuasive way that demands attention and influences opinion. Satire provides writers with creative opportunities and furnishes readers with the unexpected and welcome bonus of laughter.

PLANNING YOUR SATIRE

HANDBOOKS
FOR HELP & PRACTICE

Brainstorming,
p. 347

Types of Language,
pp. 450–451

Figurative Language,
pp. 453–455

Language of
Persuasion,
pp. 544–548

Speech Delivery,
pp. 515–516

1. Choose a subject to satirize. With a small group, brainstorm possible subjects for satire. Look for a subject about which you have strong feelings but that you could treat in a humorous way. The writer of the Shakespeare excerpt found his subject in a short item from *Advertising Age*. Try newspapers and magazines for other good ideas. You might consider satirizing a recurrent or timely political issue, a commonly recommended health tip, a school rule, or a habit that seems silly to you. You could also satirize a subject that is a personal pet peeve, such as people wearing animal furs or smoking in nonsmoking areas.

2. Select a form for your satire. Not all satire is written. Movies, television shows, and live comedy revues feature satirical skits and songs that poke fun at issues and personalities. Political cartoons are still another form of satire. Decide if you will write, draw, sing, or act out your satirical piece.

3. Set a goal that will determine the tone for your satire. Do you want to show people how ridiculous a certain rule is? Would you like to poke gentle fun at a local or national figure? Do you want to expose an example of hypocrisy that makes you angry? Satire can range from mild humor to savage sarcasm. Adapt the tone of your satire to suit your particular goal.

4. Choose a method of creating your satire. Will you simply exaggerate the flaws of your subject? For example, an incompetent politician could be satirized by "reporting" a blunder-filled speech. You could also choose to write a supposedly objective "analysis" that highlights the problems of a situation. You could also create a humorous analogy to the situation, as in the Shakespeare piece.

WRITING YOUR SATIRE

1. Introduce your subject. The author of the excerpt begins by citing the passage that stimulated him to write his satire. You may prefer to introduce your subject within the body of your satire, but make sure your purpose is clear from the beginning.

2. Don't give away your main idea. The author of the excerpt never actually tells you that he thinks ads in movies are a misuse of popular entertainment. Indeed, as "Billy" Shakespeare's agent he pretends to think such ads are a wonderful idea.

3. Use exaggeration to make your point. Putting product endorsements into the classic masterpieces of Shakespeare seems much worse than simply showing a product in a popular movie. These exaggerated examples forcefully drive home the author's opinion that such advertisements are exploiting the artist and the unsuspecting audience.

 Writer's Choice You may prefer to use understatement, especially if you are poking fun at something excessively ornate or expensive: a watch that costs "only" $5,000, for example.

4. Make sure your conclusion sums up your main idea. Let your examples build toward a strong climax of high exaggeration or outlandish humor. Save your best example for last. If it's funny to think of Macbeth's witches using a substitute ingredient, it's absolutely ridiculous to think of Lady Macbeth successfully washing her hands.

Writing
TIP

Use your imagination and sense of play to create colorful and amusing examples.

1. Reread your satire. Have you included examples that expose the humor or absurdity of your situation? Is your tone appropriate to your subject? Have you saved the most ridiculous example or consequence for last? Do you think your writing will help correct the situation you are satirizing?

2. Choose a title. Your title can be funny, but it shouldn't reveal everything you are going to say. Try to come up with a title that will make people want to read your satire. Did the title of the excerpt on page 224 stimulate your curiosity and give you a laugh?

3. Find a trial audience. Share your satire with others. Can your classmates tell right away what your subject is and that your work is satiric? Ask for suggestions about sharpening your piece. Can your friends give you more humorous examples or ideas?

H. Clay Bennett/Courtesy St. Petersburg Times

To test the effectiveness of your satire, ask your audience if they gained a new understanding of the situation from reading your work.

As you judge the reactions of your trial audience, keep in mind the fact that while humor can effectively be used to criticize, persuade, or make a serious statement, it should leave the reader smiling but unoffended.

PUBLISHING AND PRESENTING

- **Make a speech.** Use your essay as a lecture or adapt it as a comedy skit. Deliver it to classmates and friends. Remember that it will seem even funnier if you remain very serious while your audience is laughing.
- **Create a comedy magazine.** Feature written and cartoon satires of your classmates.
- **Become a journalist.** If your satire is newsworthy, send it to your local newspaper as a letter to the editor or as a guest editorial.

On the Lightside

WORD BORROWINGS

The influence of Spanish on the English language is all around us. It is carried by the breeze (from

"Matthews ... we're getting another one of those strange 'aw blah es span yol' sounds."

brisa, "northeasterly wind"), and it sits with us on the *patio* as we enjoy our *barbeque* (from a West Indian word picked up by Spanish explorers).

American English has borrowed, and continues to borrow, more words from Spanish than from any other language. The process began when sixteenth-century Spanish explorers, such as Coronado, Cortes, Ponce de León, Pizarro, and de Soto, encountered for the first time many of the plants, animals, people, and landforms of the New World and gave their discoveries Spanish names or names adapted from Native American ones. In time these words became accepted into English. *Potato* is a Spanish adaptation of a West Indian word. *Coyote, avocado,* and *tomato* are adaptations of Aztec words. *Alligator* comes from the Spanish *el lagarto,* "the lizard"; *mosquito* is Spanish for "little fly." *Tornado* comes form *tronada,* "thunderstorm," and *tornar,* "to turn and twist." The names of six states and more than two thousand cities and towns in the United States come from Spanish.

Our nation's large Spanish-speaking population and our interaction with the Spanish-speaking countries of Central and South America guarantee that Spanish will continue to enrich the English language.

Ad Copy

Related ASSIGNMENT

Suppose you're an executive for a major advertising agency. A new client with a product or service for sale comes to you and wants your staff to create an advertising campaign. What kind of ads will you recommend?

Examine the images and language in this advertisement. Try to notice the effect of the words, the images, and the ad as a whole. What direct messages and hidden persuaders are at work? Do these messages make you want to be one of the people who purchase the product?

JUNLE

The newest design in a road racing shoe—the beast. It's tough, it's durable, it's as lightweight as it gets. Cat's patented, new, extended-claw® midsole, assures you the impact protection and lasting comfort you need. Five exciting colors and looks.

This cat's a real beast.

TAKE A WALK ON THE WILD SIDE

CAT SHOES

Think AND Respond

How does this advertisement make you feel? Has it persuaded (or failed to persuade) you of something? What images and words seemed most powerful or persuasive? How could you persuade someone to purchase or believe something using only a few carefully chosen words and images?

INVITATION
—TO—
Write

This advertisement implies that you'll be a wild, exciting person if you purchase Cat shoes. Create your own advertisement that persuades a certain audience to purchase, believe, or do something.

Advertising is a form of persuasion: you create an ad for the purpose of convincing people to believe or do something. You achieve this goal by considering what a certain group of people want and then using specific words and images to appeal to that group's desires and feelings. Interestingly, the best ads are those that do not seem to be trying to persuade at all.

PLANNING YOUR ADVERTISEMENT

HANDBOOKS
FOR HELP & PRACTICE

Focusing a Topic,
pp. 349–352
Constructing
Writing,
pp. 362–369
Collaborative
Planning,
pp. 370–373
Using Words
Precisely,
pp. 434–437
Persuasive Appeals,
pp. 544–548

1. Decide what you will advertise. You can create an ad for a product or service you use or know well or for a product or service you've invented. Or perhaps you are more interested in people and ideas. You can create an ad urging voters to support a particular candidate or encouraging them to support a public program such as recycling or drug education.

2. Identify your audience. What kinds of people will naturally be interested in your product, service, or idea? For example, a middle-aged business executive might not be interested in buying disposable athletic shoes, but teenagers or athletes might. Make notes about your target audience. Consider its specific needs, interests, and buying power.

3. Examine different media. Television, radio, and printed media (magazines and newspapers) each offer certain advantages. TV ads offer lively, eye-catching blends of action-images and sounds. Radio ads use no visual images, but they can take advantage of the listener's imagination. The print media probably have the longest "life"—your ad's words and images remain before the audience for as long as people care to examine them. When choosing your medium, however, consider which kind your audience is most likely to use or be affected by.

4. Consider various advertising techniques. You probably know some advertising tricks already. Which one is most appropriate for your ad? For example, a testimonial (an expert's endorsement of a product or idea) can be very persuasive for medicines or specialized equipment. The bandwagon technique (join the crowd) or its high-class counterpart, snob appeal, might be useful for a product designed to lend status or popularity to the user. Techniques that utilize patriotic symbols or images of home and family might also help you achieve your purpose. Finally, don't forget slogans and jingles, catchy phrases that remain in the memory.

CREATING THE ADVERTISEMENT

1. Create a structure for your ad. Most ads are based on a few successful formulas. Consider one popular narrative format:

> A person has a problem or need that a product or service can solve.
> A friend shows the person how the product solves the problem.
> The person decides to buy the product as "the perfect solution."

Study a number of ads until you find a format that suits your product.

2. Keep the ad short, simple, and direct. Ads work best when a few carefully chosen phrases communicate the message. Present the product, state its benefits or appeals, and tell people how they can buy the product or act on the belief. Even ads that tell a story should somehow contain or imply this information.

3. Use strong images to help communicate your message. The power of imagery is important to consider. Notice how the images in the ad on pages 230–231 suggest feelings of strength, power, and unlimited excitement.

4. Use your sense of humor. Many good ads entertain as they persuade. Copy that provides a laugh is more apt to be remembered than is straightforward fact.

Writing
—TIP—

Avoid advertising "overkill." That is, don't say too much: Make people feel they are drawing their own conclusions.

1. Show your ad to a potential buyer. Does it quickly catch the person's interest? Does he or she grasp the message immediately? Is the ad persuasive? Does the person feel inclined to follow the ad's advice?

2. Be sure the words and images work together. Does the ad say too much or too little? Have you told the audience how to obtain the product or act on the belief?

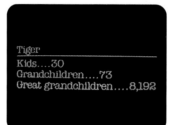

Tiger
Kids....30
Grandchildren....73
Great grandchildren....8,192

Tiger
Great, great
grandchildren....67,108,864

Real pets, real problems.

MSPCA
Massachusetts Society for the Prevention of Cruelty to Animals

- **Create a finished script of your ad.** Polish the wording and the performance time. Make a final layout if your ad is designed for print media.
- **Record your ad.** Make a cassette recording, or if equipment is available, a video recording of your ad. Have your classmates take part in the script. You may wish to use background music and act as director.
- **Display your ad.** Post your print-media ad on the bulletin board or submit it to the school newspaper. If you have access to a photocopy machine, make copies and distribute them to your friends.

Sentence

Elaborating on Complex Sentences

Writing complex sentences allows you to elaborate on ideas by adding less important information in a subordinate clause (or clauses) to the main information in the independent clause (or clauses). As with other sentence types, you can also elaborate on complex sentences by adding phrases.

Subordinate clauses begin with subordinating conjunctions such as *as, before, when,* and *since,* or with relative pronouns such as *who, whose, which,* and *that.* Note how these words show connections between ideas or events.

MODELS

          S   V   S   V

1. BEFORE he could dish up the food, <u>she was snoring gently</u>.
   Flannery O'Connor, "The Life You Save May Be Your Own"

                                    S   V

2. One evening in the fall, <u>George ran out of his house</u>

                            S   V

   <u>to the library</u>, WHERE he hadn't been in years.
   Bernard Malamud, "A Summer's Reading"

                              S   V

3. At a dance one night <u>she sat all evening in a motor-</u>

                                  S   V

   <u>boat with a local beau</u>, WHILE the New Yorker searched
   for her frantically.   **F. Scott Fitzgerald, "Winter Dreams"**

                  S   V

4. <u>That Frome farm was always 'bout as bare's a milkpan</u>

                  S   V

   WHEN the cat's been around.
   Edith Wharton, *Ethan Frome*

A. Unscrambling Sentences Unscramble the parts in each set to create a complex sentence. Many contain compound verbs. Some may be put together in more than one way. If your version makes sense, it is acceptable.

1. a. where buzzards were roosting
   b. there was a dead tree
   c. at the fork of the road

Ellen Glasgow, "Jordan's End"

2. a. WHO was sitting up against the pillows, knitting
   b. by the bedside of the old lady
   c. Christine herself was seated

Gaston Leroux, *The Phantom of the Opera*

3. a. she found a paper bag in the pantry drawer
   b. and carried the bag to the garbage pail by the back steps
   c. WHERE the bags had always been kept
   d. and scraped the rotten tomato from the window sill

Shirley Jackson, "The Little House"

4. a. to make himself appear big and significant in her eyes
   b. once on a summer night
   c. WHEN he was eighteen and in her presence had given way to an impulse to boast
   d. he had walked with her on a country road

Sherwood Anderson, "Sophistication"

B. Combining Sentences Combine each pair of sentences to make a complex sentence. First, decide which sentence(s) in each set should be subordinate. Then use the words in parentheses to connect subordinate clauses to main clauses. (You may have to drop some words from a sentence.) Finally, write an imitation of each complex sentence.

Punctuation Note: Use commas to set off introductory subordinate clauses and subordinate clauses in other positions that add essential information to a sentence.

1. Alfred quietly slipped out the back door and waited. Henry left. (UNTIL)

Robert Lipsyte, *The Contender*

2. Then they fled, houseless and foodless, down the valley. Their village, shredded and tossed and trampled, melted behind them. (AS)

Rudyard Kipling, *The Jungle Book*

3. In the town, in little offices, sat the men. The men bought pearls from the fishers. (WHO)

John Steinbeck, *The Pearl*

236 Sentence Composing

4. Mr. Delehanty went to the door. Mrs. Delehanty stood in the back of the room by the fireplace, unwilling to take one step toward meeting her visitors. (WHILE)   **Jessamyn West, "Then He Goes Free"**

5. About fifteen miles below Monterey, on the wild coast, the Torres family had their farm, a few sloping acres above a cliff. The cliff dropped to the brown reefs and the hissing white waters of the ocean. (THAT)
John Steinbeck, "Flight"

C. Expanding Sentences   The complex sentences in this lesson use phrases and subordinate clauses to add information to each independent clause. Expand each sentence by adding phrases or clauses that begin with the bracketed words. Compare your sentences with the originals on page 328.

1. [In. . .], Henry Crowfoot turned over and wearily punched the pillow, [which. . .].   **Frank Bonham, *Chief***

2. I used to have a cat, [an. . .], [who. . .].
Annie Dillard, *Pilgrim at Tinker Creek*

3. Upon the half decayed veranda of a small frame house [that. . .], a fat little old man walked nervously up and down.
Sherwood Anderson, *Winesburg, Ohio*

4. If our father was of royal blood [and. . .], our father was certainly the only person in the world [who. . .].
James Baldwin, *Tell Me How Long the Train's Been Gone*

Application   The passage below describes two friends watching a passenger train approach and speculating about the people inside it. Elaborate on the second, third, and fourth sentences. Then continue the paragraph, describing what you think the people on the train would be like. When you are done, look on page 329 to see how the author completed the paragraph.

> Eventually we'd hear a rumble on the tracks and then see a searching eye of light bearing down on us. Quickly we'd leap to our feet and get as close to the tracks as we dared, plugging our ears as. . . . As we stood there, we could see. . . . If. . . , we might catch a glimpse of. . . .   **Susan Allen Toth, *Blooming***

Grammar Refresher   For more on subordinating conjunctions, see Handbook 32, pages 620–627. For more on relative pronouns, see Handbook 30, page 561.

Sketchbook

SYLVIA

What sequel would you like to write?

Additional Sketches

Have you ever felt that an author, actor, or artist was speaking directly to you in his or her work? Tell about the experience.

How do you decide which books to read, movies to see, or records to buy?

Writing About Literature

Guided Assignment
CRITICAL ANALYSIS

Related Assignment
PERSONAL RESPONSE

Related Assignment
PARODY

Whenever you read a literary work or experience any other type of work of art, you have a chance to respond to it. No one can tell you what your response ought to be. It is whatever you happen to think, feel, or wonder as you experience the work. You engage in a process that includes reflecting, interpreting, and analyzing. Taken together, these are the thinking skills that are employed by literary, art, movie, and television critics, and by anyone who has a critical reaction to his or her experiences. In this workshop, you will explore your critical responses. You will also learn how to create parodies and write critical reviews of other works of art.

Critical Analysis

FROM

HARRISON BERGERON

by Kurt Vonnegut, Jr.

Writing about
a work of literature can
help you clarify and ac-
count for your response
to the work. In the pro-
cess you can arrive at
a better understanding
of it and of yourself as
a reader.

The short story
"Harrison Bergeron" by
Kurt Vonnegut, Jr., is a
satire, a form of litera-
ture that ridicules fool-
ish ideas or customs,
partly in the hope that
people might correct
their ways. As you
read the following
excerpt, think about
what the author is
ridiculing and how you
react to his satire.

The year was 2081, and everybody was finally equal.
They weren't only equal before God and the law, they
were equal every which way. Nobody was smarter than
anybody else; nobody was better looking than anybody
else; nobody was stronger or quicker than anybody
else. All this equality was due to the 211th, 212th,
and 213th Amendments to the Constitution, and
to the unceasing vigilance of agents of the United
States Handicapper General.

Some things about living still weren't quite right, though. April, for
instance, still drove people crazy by not being springtime. And it was in that
clammy month that H-G men took George and Hazel Bergeron's fourteen-year-
old son, Harrison, away.

It was tragic, all right, but George and Hazel couldn't think about it very
hard. Hazel had a perfectly average intelligence, which meant she couldn't
think about anything except in short bursts. And George, while his intelligence
was way above normal, had a little mental handicap radio in his ear—he was
required by law to wear it at all times. It was tuned to a government transmitter, and every twenty seconds or so, the transmitter would send out some sharp
noise to keep people like George from taking unfair advantage of their brains.

George and Hazel were watching television. There were tears on Hazel's
cheeks, but she'd forgotten for the moment what they were about, as the
ballerinas came to the end of a dance.

A buzzer sounded in George's head. His thoughts fled in panic, like bandits
from a burglar alarm.

"That was a real pretty dance, that dance they just did," said Hazel.

"Huh?" said George.

"That dance—it was nice," said Hazel.

"Yup," said George. He tried to think a little about the ballerinas. They
weren't really very good—no better than anybody else would have been,

anyway. They were burdened with sashweights and bags of birdshot, and their faces were masked, so that no one, seeing a free and graceful gesture or a pretty face, would feel like something the cat dragged in. George was toying with the vague notion that maybe dancers shouldn't be handicapped. But he didn't get very far with it before another noise in his ear radio scattered his thoughts.

George winced. So did two out of the eight ballerinas.

Hazel saw him wince. Having no mental handicap herself, she had to ask George what the latest sound had been.

"Sounded like somebody hitting a milk bottle with a ballpeen hammer," said George.

"I'd think it would be real interesting, hearing all the different sounds," said Hazel, a little envious. "The things they think up."

"Um," said George.

"Only, if I was Handicapper General, you know what I would do?" said Hazel. Hazel, as a matter of fact, bore a strong resemblance to the Handicapper General, a woman name Diana Moon Glampers. "If I was Diana Moon Glampers," said Hazel, "I'd have chimes on Sunday—just chimes. Kind of in honor of religion."

"I could think, if it was just chimes," said George.

"Well—maybe make 'em real loud," said Hazel, "I think I'd make a good Handicapper General."

"Good as anybody else," said George.

"Who knows better'n I do what normal is?" said Hazel.

"Right," said George. He began to think glimmeringly about his abnormal son who was now in jail, about Harrison, but a twenty-one gun salute in his head stopped that.

"Boy!" said Hazel, "that was a doozy, wasn't it?"

It was such a doozy that George was white and trembling, and tears stood on the rims of his red eyes. Two of the eight ballerinas had collapsed to the studio floor, were holding their temples.

"All of a sudden you look so tired," said Hazel. "Why don't you stretch out on the sofa, so's you can rest your handicap bag on the pillows, honeybunch." She was referring to the forty-seven pounds of birdshot in a canvas bag, which was padlocked around George's neck. "Go on and rest the bag for a little while," she said. "I don't care if you're not equal to me for a while."

George weighed the bag with his hands. "I don't mind it," he said. "I don't notice it any more. It's just a part of me."

"You've been so tired lately—kind of wore out," said Hazel. "If there was just some way we could make a little hole in the bottom of the bag, and just take out a few of them lead balls. Just a few."

"Two years in prison and two thousand dollars fine for every ball I took out," said George. "I don't call that a bargain."

"If you could just take a few out when you came home from work," said Hazel. "I mean—you don't compete with anybody around here. You just set around."

"If I tried to get away with it," said George, "then other people'd get away with it—and pretty soon we'd be right back to the dark ages again, with everybody competing against everybody else. You wouldn't like that, would you?"

"I'd hate it," said Hazel.

"There you are," said George. "the minute people start cheating on laws, what do you think happens to society?"

If Hazel hadn't been able to come up with an answer to this question, George couldn't have supplied one. A siren was going off in his head. . . .

Think AND Respond

What makes this story a satire? Why do you think Vonnegut chose to use satire instead of addressing the situation directly? What is your reaction to the "equality" Vonnegut describes? Do you see any elements of the society he describes in today's society?

INVITATION
—TO—
Write

Kurt Vonnegut, Jr., presents a picture of the future that is open to analysis and interpretation. Choose a literary work and write your critical analysis of some aspect of it. Use the following suggestions as guidelines as you write your critical analysis.

Most literary essays grow out of responses that readers experience while reading and reflecting on a text. Some essays explore and solve problems that troubled a reader; others explain insights that a reader has come to in the course of thinking about a text. Yet all literary essays enable the reader to understand a literary work better and to share that understanding with other readers in a literary community. The skills you employ in responding to a work of literature are like those with which you examine any work of art. You also employ these skills of critical analysis as you respond to most real human dramas, such as family conflicts or political events.

PREWRITE AND EXPLORE

HANDBOOKS
FOR HELP & PRACTICE

**Writing Techniques,
pp. 344–346**

**Thesis Statements,
p. 381**

**Point of View,
pp. 458–463**

**Character/Setting,
pp. 468–472**

**Reading Strategies,
pp. 494–495**

1. Choose a piece of literature to explore. What have you read recently that you found challenging, or rewarding, or troubling, or even upsetting? You may wish to explore your reactions to "Harrison Bergeron" or to a piece you are studying. Also consider these works: short stories "A Worn Path" by Eudora Welty and "Teenage Wasteland" by Anne Tyler, or poems "The Waking" by Theodore Roethke and "The Ball Poem" by John Berryman. If you are not satisfied with your topic, consider the ideas you experimented with in the Sketchbook on page 238, check the "Apply Your Skills" section on page 255, or refer to your journal.

Writer's Choice Do you want to reconsider a work you are already very familiar with or explore one that is relatively new to you?

2. Keep a reading log. In a section of your journal or a separate notebook, record your questions, critical responses, and interpretations as you read and reread the text you have chosen. The following activities can help you reflect on your reading.

PROBLEM SOLVING

How can I sort out my feelings about the texts I read?

- **Note taking** Write down the phrases and sentences that stand out most for you in the text. After each entry, respond to the words you quoted and discuss why you responded as you did. What does your response tell you about the text? What does it tell you about yourself?

- **Freewriting** Take ten minutes to freewrite in response to the entire text. (You can share this freewriting exercise later with other readers.) Let your response include all the questions you find yourself asking and whatever else you want to say about the work you have just read.

3. Reread and reconsider. Some critics believe all reading is rereading. That is, you can't really see what a work of literature says and does until you read it for a second or third time. One way to make rereading especially productive is to do it with a partner. Take turns reading portions of the text and stop along the way to discuss problem passages and whatever else interests you.

4. Review the elements of literary works. In addition to considering your personal responses to the work, explore its formal qualities, including the following elements.

- **Plot** How predictable are the events? What are the surprises? Does the story change direction? Are there pairs or clusters of events that seem similar or contrasting? What is the central conflict of the story? Are there events that don't fit?

- **Characters** What meanings are suggested by their names? their physical descriptions? their way of talking (especially repeated phrases)? their actions? the way they change or don't change? what they say about others? what others say about them?

- **Setting** Where and when does the story take place? What sort of mood or atmosphere is created by descriptions (romantic, sinister, dangerous, and so on)? How does the setting affect events? What connections seem suggested between physical environment and psychological events?

- **Point of view** From whose point of view is the story told? How much does the narrator know? What is the narrator's attitude toward the story's events and the various characters?

- **Language and imagery** What words or phrases seem to be repeated through the text? Are there any noticeable repetitions of images or figures of speech? Do any objects or events seem to have symbolic value? Does the author make use of unusual words or phrases? Does the verbal style of the text call attention to itself in any way?
- **Theme and ideology** Does the text address any universal problem or experience? Does it seem to teach a lesson, to have a "moral"? Does it show something about human nature or human relationships, individual psychology or group psychology? Does the work reflect any particular set of beliefs or ideology?

5. Find a focus for analysis and criticism. What interests you most about the work? Does it raise a compelling problem? Are you intrigued by a character? Does the author's style or approach to the subject interest you? One or more of the following activities may help you progress from your responses and reflections to a more formal critical analysis.

Exploratory Activities

- **Pick a key passage** Identify one sentence or short passage that you regard as important or problematic. Freewrite for about ten minutes on why that particular passage is significant to an understanding or appreciation of this work.
- **Brainstorm** List as many statements as you can about the text. If you need help getting started, consider the following categories: issues readers disagree about; unsolved problems in understanding the text; discoveries you have made; critical observations you have encountered.
- **Text rendering** If several students are studying the same text, gather together and have each student read aloud phrases or sentences that stand out as memorable, significant, or problematic. It is useful to hear what passages were selected by various readers. If someone else recites a passage you had picked, don't hesitate to repeat it. Often a text can be heard best when it is read in a number of different voices.

Here are the statements Sherman wrote after discussing "Harrison Bergeron" with his classmates. Throughout this workshop, you will follow Sherman's process in writing his critical analysis.

PROBLEM
SOLVING

How can I progress from a simple response to a more formal critical analysis?

Everybody thinks this is a hilarious story. I think it's funny, too, but I'm not sure I like it. I think it's snobbish and elitist.

Disagreements about theme: Does it show what can happen when you take the idea of equality too far? Or is it about how stupid the government can be when it tries to guarantee equal opportunity? Some people say both of these are the same theme. I'm not sure.

Disagreements about setting: Some people say the setting in the future shows us the direction in which we are going. I think it might also be read as a comment on the present. For example, what influences exist today that encourage us all to think, dress, and act alike? Do we see them as positive or negative influences? Are we even aware of these influences? What aspects of society encourage individuality? How do equal-opportunity laws and affirmative-action programs influence us to conform? to be individuals?

Problem in interpretation: I wonder if this story can be read as an attack on affirmative action programs, or even on the minority people's struggle for equality. Do I think this way because I'm an African American myself?

Barbara Karant, artist

6. Compose possible thesis statements. Focus your writing by choosing a single controlling idea or problem to investigate. Write two or three thesis statements that define topics in which you have some genuine interest. Your thesis statement may present a critical position you will support, identify an interpretive problem you propose to analyze, or briefly state some insight about the text.

Writing
—TIP—

If you have trouble finding something to say about your chosen text, try to think of a second text with which you can compare or contrast it.

COMPUTER
—TIP—

Save your statements and your freewriting in a word-processing file. This will give you a "data base" to draw on when you begin to draft your essay.

Sherman wrote the following thesis statements about Kurt Vonnegut's story.

ONE STUDENT'S PROCESS

"Harrison Bergeron" is a story set in the future in order to show us a current trend in our society taken to a ridiculous extreme. It is therefore a work of social commentary on contemporary American society.

The plot of "Harrison Bergeron" is unrealistic but effective as a satire on current trends in American society.

Vonnegut's story mocks a positive and healthy social movement and reveals a lack of respect for what equal opportunity and affirmative action are intended to achieve.

7. Select a topic or thesis. Share your most promising thesis statements with a small group of classmates and discuss ideas for developing each topic or thesis into an essay. Feel free to change your anticipated topic as a result of discussion or to adopt a topic proposed by another student. Sherman decided to proceed with his third thesis statement.

8. Develop a plan. Once you have selected a focus for your paper, you may wish to get together with a partner and explain to each other your plans with respect to the questions below. Feel free to ask for further explanations and to give and take suggestions.

- What do you intend to write about?
- What do you see as your key point?
- How do you propose to support or explain your key point?
- Who is likely to read your essay?
- What do you want your readers to understand or feel after reading your piece?

You can also use an outline or tree diagram to organize your ideas. These devices can help identify how ideas are related, what points you need to address, and how to fit together all your ideas and supporting evidence.

9. Gather supporting information. Write a list of all the evidence you can think of or find in support of your thesis; or, if you prefer, use a cluster rather than a list. When you think of evidence that would refute or be inconsistent with your view, write it down too. Try to figure out how you can use the disconfirming evidence to help you revise or clarify your thesis.

D RAFT AND DISCOVER

1. Begin drafting. Use your writing plan or outline to guide you, but don't let it prevent you from developing new ideas or using evidence you hadn't thought of before. If your outline isn't helping you, change it or ignore it.

 Writer's Choice If you haven't made an outline yet, should you make one at this point? If you have made one, should you follow it, revise it, or discard it?

2. Organize your draft. It is generally useful to begin your analysis with a brief summary or retelling of the text (not a detailed plot summary). Then define the question you will address in your essay. Be sure to include the title and author of the work in your introduction. In the body, address the issues you want to discuss, supporting them with references and exact quotations from the text as well as other evidence. Your conclusion should summarize the points you have made and forcefully state your conclusion or critical position.

3. _Show_ as well as _tell_. Show your readers what passages, turns of plot, or other evidence from the text lead you to make the claims you are making. Explain how the evidence makes your point of view a reasonable one. Some or all of the following strategies may help you explore your text.

Strategies

- **Comparison and contrast** Compare characters, issues, or methods of expression used in the text with other texts. Also compare your initial thoughts about the text with your thoughts after several readings.
- **Paraphrase and summary** These are important tools for explaining key passages concisely and effectively in your own words.

HANDBOOKS
FOR HELP & PRACTICE

Constructing Writing, pp. 362–369

Types of Elaboration, pp. 397–399

Using Source Materials, pp. 495–499

Writing —TIP—

If you are having trouble getting started, begin in the middle of your essay with something you know you want to say. Go back later and write the beginning.

- **Quotation** Use direct quotations to present passages that are essential to the understanding of the text or of your position. Quotations can also give your readers a feel for the writer's style and approach. However, don't rely too heavily on quotations. *Your* interpretation is what counts.

In the following passage from his first draft, notice how Sherman presents a critical statement and backs it up with a specific reference from the story.

Carnival, Binche, Belgium

ONE STUDENT'S PROCESS

Equally disturbing is Vonnegut's picture of a world that has reached "equality." His model of equality is represented by Hazel Bergeron. She sits entranced by the TV, unable to remember why tears are running down her cheeks. The disturbing message here is that to be equal, all people must be made stupid.

PROBLEM

S O L V I N G

What haven't I said yet that still needs to be said?

4. Learn from your writing. As you write and reread what you have written, you are likely to clarify and change your ideas. Use your new insights to improve your essay. Don't let your desire to argue for a particular thesis lead you to misrepresent the story or what you really think. If what you see is complicated and contradictory, say so. Intellectual honesty is more important than intellectual neatness.

5. Step back from your draft. When you have completed a rough draft, put it aside. Then read it to yourself two or three times, and get responses from two or more peer readers. The best way to get such responses is to read your essay aloud to your peers and ask them to respond orally and with written notes. They may also want to read your draft themselves. Ask questions such as the following.

Questions for Yourself

- What am I really trying to say here? Have I made clear my main point (thesis) or the problem I'm writing about? Can I put it in a nutshell for myself?

- Does my thesis accurately represent my understanding (however complicated or contradictory) of the work or does it oversimplify or misrepresent what I know? Have I ignored or avoided evidence that doesn't fit my thesis?

- Does my essay have a clear focus and stick to it?

- Do I use appropriate quotations from the text to explain my ideas?

Questions for Your Peer Readers

- Do I tell you enough about the text so you know what I'm talking about? Do I tell you more than you need or want to know? Is there anything about the plain facts of the text that you would like me to clear up?

- Can you say back to me briefly the points you hear me trying to make in my paper?

- Can you think of additional evidence to support—or to argue against—my point of view?

- Is there anything in my paper that confuses you or seems beside the point?

- Is there anything in my paper that is a new idea for you or that helps you to think about the text in a new or interesting way?

- Are there any phrases or sentences in my paper that stand out for you?

R E V I S E   Y O U R   W R I T I N G

1. Evaluate your responses. Review your own thoughts and the responses of your peer readers. Also keep in mind the following guidelines, which are often used for evaluating critical analyses.

HANDBOOKS
FOR HELP & PRACTICE

Incorporating Peer Responses,
p. 425

Quotation Marks,
pp. 824–828

Standards for Evaluation

An effective critical analysis . . .

- chooses a single controlling idea to investigate.
- presents evidence from the text to support critical, evaluative, and interpretive statements.
- integrates appropriate quotations smoothly.
- is organized clearly and logically.

2. Rework your draft. Consider the changes you want to make, and then rework your draft. Sherman made these changes to one paragraph of his draft in response to suggestions from peer readers.

ONE STUDENT'S PROCESS

George's explanation (which we can trust, since

George is presented as mentally gifted) of the impor-
                                        purpose and
                            failure to recognize an important
tance of handicaping shows Vonnegut's stupidity when
point about   laws
it comes to understanding equal-opportunity. Neither

handicaps, nor the Affirmative-Action rules that Von-
           seems to be
negut is warning against, serve to eliminate
        e   p
compitition. It can also be argued that handicaping ac-
         ^   e
tually increases compitition. For example, in sports,
                       ^
such as golf and horse racing where handicaps are ac-
                                    e
tually used, competition is insured by making the
            a   ^
contestents more equal. Equally disturbing is Vonnegut's
        ^   l
picture of a word that has reached "equality." His model
                   ^
of equality is represented by Hazel Bergeron.

, who is described as having "average intelligence, which meant she couldn't
think about anything except in short bursts."

In fact, they increase competition by making sure it is based on real ability and
not on race or social class.

Isn't this a little harsh?

Can you support this point?

Good analogy! I never thought about it that way.

You could support this point by quoting Vonnegut's description of Hazel.

3. Proofread your work. Before you submit your paper to your teacher or make it publicly available, make sure that it isn't marred by any distracting errors in grammar, usage, or mechanics.

LINKING
GRAMMAR AND WRITING
Integrating Quotes into a Text

When quoting a passage a line or two long, put quotation marks around it and insert it into the main body of your paper. When quoting a longer passage, block and indent it without quotation marks. However, include any quotation mark found in the literary passage itself. Notice that in the longer quote below, the quotation marks belong to Vonnegut's story, not to the student analysis.

SHORT QUOTATION:

His model of equality is represented by Hazel Bergeron, who is described as having "average intelligence, which meant she couldn't think about anything except in short bursts."

LONG QUOTATION:

George replies that he would be committing an act that would threaten the whole structure of their society:

> "If I tried to get away with it," said George, "then other people'd get away with it—and pretty soon we'd be right back to the dark ages again, with everybody competing against everybody else. You wouldn't like that, would you?"

For additional help with integrating quotes, see Grammar Handbook 40, "Apostrophe and Quotation Marks," on pages 824–825.

Grammar
—TIP—

Don't "improve" quotes by correcting the author's or the characters' grammar. If the literary text contains an error in mechanics, write *sic* after it in brackets.

PUBLISH AND PRESENT

HANDBOOKS
FOR HELP & PRACTICE

Responding to Others,
pp. 425–426
Sharing Writing,
pp. 427–428

- **Gather student essays on particular works or authors.** Bind them into collections that future students can then refer to. Keep these collections in the classroom, or have them shelved in your school library. You can choose to organize the collections according to works, authors, themes, genres, or other categories.
- **Pass essays around the class.** Get together with the students who have written about the same literary work or author to share insights. After each student has had an opportunity to read a variety of essays, discuss the issues and problems different students have addressed.
- **Exchange essays with students in another class.** Find a class that is studying the works of literature treated in your critical analyses. Notice the differences and similarities in the critical treatments of the works in the two classes.
- **Publish by reading your essay aloud.** Work in a small group where all students can read their essays. Take time for a discussion after each reading, so that your group becomes familiar with the different viewpoints expressed. If possible, read your essay aloud to the whole class.
- **Save your essay in your writing portfolio.** You may want to review your essay later to see if your critical position has changed.

On "Harrison Bergeron"

Sherman Brown

Kurt Vonnegut, Jr.'s "Harrison Bergeron" is for many readers (and for most first readings) a hilarious science-fiction story satirizing the tendency of our society to provide equal opportunity for everybody. It depicts a society of the future in which a government official known as the Handicapper General enforces laws that require people with special talents or natural gifts be handicapped (with weights on their legs, for example, to make the graceful more clumsy, or earphones that blast unnerving sounds into the ears of unusually intelligent people to prevent them from thinking clearly) so they can be "average" like everybody else. As a satire the story mocks human behavior in order to point out the dangers in taking certain social programs too far. In this case the story seems to want to celebrate individual talent and warn against what might happen to a society if government efforts to ensure equal employment opportunities for everybody were to be taken to their most ridiculous extreme.

Vonnegut seems to take the position that equal-opportunity efforts and affirmative-action rules will lead to mediocrity for everyone. In my view, Vonnegut's story mocks a positive and healthy social movement and reveals a lack of respect for what equal opportunity and affirmative action are intended to achieve.

Vonnegut's attitude is particularly evident in one scene. Hazel Bergeron suggests that her husband, George (whose unusual physical strength and intelligence require him to wear a number of handicapping devices), secretly reduce the weight of his handicap for a few hours each day so he could get some rest. George replies that, aside from risking a large fine and imprisonment,

Introduces the reader to the text that will be analyzed

Presents a single problem to investigate

he would be committing an act that would threaten the whole structure of their society:

> "If I tried to get away with it," said George, "then other people'd get away with it—and pretty soon we'd be right back to the dark ages again, with everybody competing against everybody else. You wouldn't like that, would you?"

Integrates quotations to explain his critical position

George's explanation of the purpose and importance of handicapping shows Vonnegut's failure to recognize an important point about equal-opportunity laws. Neither handicaps nor affirmative-action rules serve to eliminate competition. In fact, they increase competition by making sure it is based on real ability and not on race or social class. Handicapping can actually increase competition. For example, in sports such as golf and horse racing handicaps ensure competition by making the contestants more equal.

Equally disturbing is Vonnegut's picture of a world that has reached "equality." His model of equality is represented by Hazel Bergeron, who has "average intelligence, which meant that she couldn't think about anything except in short bursts." Moreover, shortly after her physically and mentally gifted son is kidnapped by the government (for being too talented), she sits entranced by the TV, unable to remember why tears are running down her cheeks. The disturbing message here is that to be equal, all people must be made stupid. Yet the purpose of equal opportunity is not to bring talented people down to the level of others. It is to allow all people an equal chance to use their abilities and talents.

Presents supporting evidence from the text

Vonnegut's story may be superficially funny, but his humor depends on a snobbish and elitist outlook that ridicules important goals for a democratic society. Taken to its extreme, the attitude toward human beings that is expressed in "Harrison Bergeron" is, therefore, even more dangerous than the most extreme version of the movement for social reform that the story satirizes.

Clearly summarizes the critical position

LEARNING FROM YOUR WRITING PROCESS

WRITER TO WRITER

One part of writing well is writing something that can be read well. . . . You say what you have to say. But you have to learn to say it in such a way that the reader can see what you mean.

Kurt Vonnegut, Jr., novelist and short story writer

1. Reflect on your writing. When you submit your paper to your teacher or classmates, or place it in your writing portfolio, attach to it an introductory note or preface for the reader. In your preface, discuss how you came to select the topic, why you chose the text you chose (if you had a choice), how your view of the text or its author changed in the course of your work on this paper, and how you came up with the major ideas you presented. Also comment, if you wish, on how satisfied or dissatisfied you are with your final draft and what you would change if you were to revise it again.

FOR YOUR **PORTFOLIO**

2. Apply your skills. Apply your skills now to a critical reading of one of the following "texts."

- **History** Write an essay based on your critical reading of a chapter of an American history text covering Columbus's "discovery" of America. As you analyze the chapter, consider how it might be read by a Native American or by a Scandinavian descendant of the Vikings.
- **Literature** Write an essay based on your critical reading of "Adam," another short story by Kurt Vonnegut, Jr. How does it compare to "Harrison Bergeron" in its style and techniques, underlying values, and theme?
- **The arts** Write an essay based on your "reading" of a film, TV show, art exhibit, concert, or popular song.
- **Sociology/education** Write an essay based on your "reading" of a school assembly or school election.
- **Other applications** Use the suggestions on pages 258–266 to write a personal response to art or a parody that incorporates your critical insights into a text.

Personal Response

F EMILY WERE HERE TODAY

BY WENDY CHAMBLESS

Have you ever been so affected by a work of art or an artist that you had to do something to express your feelings? Perhaps you called a friend to tell him how strongly you felt about a painting, or you wrote a letter to an author to say how much her book meant to you.

This poem is one high-school student's personal response to the poet Emily Dickinson and her work. As you read it, think about how the student has portrayed the poet and what the writer has revealed about herself.

If Emily were here today
the women in the supermarket would laugh at her
   for always
wearing white (even in the winter??)
and one or two might tactlessly question her
   "right" to do
so
and
the people of Amherst would call her neurotic
   and make her
the butt of local jokes
and
the board of education would laugh at her
   self-education and
hold her until she produced a diploma
and
the congregation would scorn her for
   refusing to see the
light
and even her family might wonder about her
   fear for their lives.

In desperation they might give her medication
    to calm her
or send for help
Freud would say she had Thanatos instincts and
    recommend
psychoanalysis
and
with a single word a critic might crush her
    butterfly wing
thoughts
and she would be silent
never bothering to mail another "letter to the world."
Or worse yet, nobody would notice.

Think AND *Respond*

How does Wendy Chambless feel about Emily Dickinson? How does she seem to feel about the modern world and its attitude toward people who are different? How do you know? Why do you think the writer chose to express her response in a poem? Would you ever choose a similar medium for a personal response?

Emily Dickinson,
Amherst College Library

257

INVITATION TO *Write*

"If Emily were here today" is one student's personal response to the poet Emily Dickinson. Write your own personal response to a piece of literature or music, a painting, or an individual artist.

Writing a formal review of a work of art or an artist is only one way of responding to something or someone that has affected you. At times, you may want to respond in a more personal, subjective way—a way that reveals something about you as well as about your subject. There are many forms suitable to this kind of response. For example, you might write a journal entry exploring your reactions to a poem or short story, an essay about the values expressed in a popular song, or a humorous article or parody that pokes fun at the style of a certain artist or writer.

DEVELOPING YOUR PERSONAL RESPONSE

HANDBOOKS
FOR HELP & PRACTICE

Personal Techniques,
pp. 339–342
Specific Details,
p. 398
Unity/Coherence,
pp. 401–414
Evoking Peer
Responses,
pp. 423–424
Writing Voice,
pp. 445–446

1. Choose a work of art or an artist. Think about the paintings, music, or works of literature that have impressed you deeply. Also consider artists, composers, and writers you have been most affected by. List all the names that come to mind. As you gather possible subjects, jot down your personal reactions to those that trigger the strongest response. Include some of the details you might mention in a personal response.

2. Explore your reactions. Allow time for your responses to develop. Reread the literature, reexamine the painting, or keep listening to the music you have selected. If you want to respond to an artist, review what you know about him or her. You may also want to enrich your understanding by reading parts of a biography. As you reconsider the details or different aspects of your subject, record each new thought, feeling, question, and insight.

Abstract Expressionist
painting (detail), by
Jackson Pollock

3. Choose an appropriate form.   Consider the possibilities before
you begin writing. In addition to the options already mentioned,
you might want to create an imaginary interview with a writer or
composer, or write a poem or story about an important event in an
artist's life—something you imagined or an event that actually happened. Think about your responses, then choose the form that is
most suitable for expressing your feelings and insights.

Writing
——**TIP**——
**At each stage of
the process, be
sure to choose
words that express
your genuine
feelings.**

DRAFTING YOUR
PERSONAL RESPONSE

1. Use your notes.   If you are writing from a journal entry, you
may simply have to explain more fully what you were thinking and
feeling. If you are writing an essay or story, find an angle, a point of
view, or a plot structure to help you express your reaction and
insights.

2. Mention specific details.   No matter what form you have chosen for your response, be sure to use specific details to describe the
artist or work of art. Notice how the details Wendy Chambless used
in her poem helped you to imagine how Emily Dickinson would be
understood if she were alive today.

3. Create devices that reflect your goals. As you write, think about how to dramatize your personal responses and realizations. For example, if you want to suggest that a writer's concerns are genuinely important, you might have characters in your story respond very seriously to them.

 Writer's Choice Is the format you chose working for you, or do you want to try another approach to express your reactions?

REVIEWING YOUR PERSONAL RESPONSE

1. Go back to your prewriting notes. Return to the notes you made as you explored your initial responses. Does your writing clearly express your most important reactions? If not, revise until it honestly reflects your thoughts and feelings.

2. Ask a classmate to respond to your work. Use questions like these to invite suggestions: In your own words, how would you express my responses to this artist or work of art? Have I made the reasons for my reactions clear? Have I included enough details to support my response? Are any parts of my writing troublesome or confusing? Have I left out anything important?

PUBLISHING AND PRESENTING

- **Create a poster.** Use your written response as the main element of a poster about a work of art or an artist. Create a collage, a photo montage, original drawings, or other visuals to illustrate or expand on your ideas.
- **Dramatize your response for your class.** Perform your response on your own or with classmates. Use variations in tone of voice and gestures to make your writing come alive.
- **Form a readers' circle.** Join several other writers to read your responses aloud. Discuss the suitability of the form each writer selected.
- **Compile an anthology.** Work with other students to compile an anthology of personal responses. Think of a unifying theme and create a title for your collection.

On the Lightside

JARGON

So you want to be a cartoonist. Then you had better learn the lingo. You may know how to use *speech balloons* to present *dialogue,* but do you know the distinctions among *thought balloons, idea balloons,* and *maladicta balloons?* Are you ready for the challenges of *jarns, quimps, grawlix,* and *nittles?* Can you create *spurls, squeans,* and *plewds?* How about *blurgits* and *waftarom?*

Every trade or profession has its jargon—the words and phrases that have special meanings to those on the inside but often sound like a foreign language to outsiders. Jargon can provide people with a common vocabulary or a specialized shorthand to describe the terms, tools, procedures, and concepts of their work. However, it also can be used to confuse.

As the cartoon on this page shows, cartoonists can be quite creative in creating jargon. Yet humor is the main tool of the cartoonist, and humor often comes from taking things to extremes. So it's not surprising that cartoonists have gone a bit overboard with their jargon. Although you won't find many of these terms in the dictionary, the words are real. They were created in an attempt by the National Cartoonist's Society to establish a standard language for cartoonists. The words typify one of the common traits of jargon. They look impressive, even if they're baffling.

261

Parody

ENDREMIA
AND
LIASON

by Robert Benchley

Do you remember the first time you read Greek or Roman mythology? The stories may have been interesting, but there was a bewildering array of gods and goddesses, many assigned to duties of uncertain significance.

The author of "Endremia and Liason" has exaggerated these elements of myths to create a parody—a work that makes fun of another work through exaggeration. As you read, decide which other elements of mythology are being parodied.

Endremia was the daughter of Polygaminous, the God of Ensilage, and Reba, the Goddess of Licorice. She was the child of a most unhappy union, it later turned out, for when she was a tiny child her father struck her mother with an anvil and turned himself into a lily pad to avoid the vengeance of Jove. But Jove was too sly for Polygaminous and struck him with a bolt of lightning the size of the Merchants Bank Building, which threw him completely off his balance so that he toppled over into a chasm and was dashed to death.

In the meantime, Little Endremia found herself alone in the world with nobody but Endrocine, the Goddess of Lettuce, and her son Bilax, the God of Gum Arabic, to look after her. But,

RED LICORICE GODDESS

as Polygaminous (her father; have you forgotten so soon, you dope?) had turned Endremia into a mushroom before he turned himself into a lily pad, neither of her guardians knew who she was, so their protection did her no good.

But Jove had not so soon forgotten the daughter of his favorite (Reba), and appeared to her one night in the shape of a mushroom gatherer. He asked her how she would like to get off that tree (she was one of those mushrooms that grow on trees) and get into his basket. Endremia, not knowing that it was Jove who was asking her, said not much. Whereupon Jove unloosed his mighty wrath and struck down the whole tree with a bolt of lightning which he had brought with him in case Endremia wouldn't listen to reason.

This is why it is never safe to eat mushrooms which grow on trees, or to refuse to get into Jove's basket.

Think AND Respond

Which elements of mythology were parodied in this story? Why do you think the author kept shifting from the formal, flowery style we associate with mythology to the style of current, casual speech? Begin thinking of pieces of writing, drama, art, or music that have failed to impress you. Which elements might you exaggerate to create a parody?

INVITATION
— TO —
Write

"Endremia and Liason" parodies Greek and Roman myths in a way that shows that the author questions their relevance to modern readers. Write your own parody of a work whose relevance or value you question.

You can parody anything from a literary work to a popular song, a TV show, a movie, an advertisement, or a cartoon strip. Writing a parody involves the same thought processes that you use when writing a literary review: you must identify your responses and discover which aspects of the piece have triggered them. It is those aspects that you will exaggerate to achieve the humor in your parody. In addition, you must analyze the style of the piece so that you can imitate it.

CREATING YOUR PARODY

HANDBOOKS
FOR HELP & PRACTICE

Comparison-Contrast Charts,
p. 357
Understanding Style,
pp. 444–445
Types of Language,
pp. 450–451
Figurative Language,
pp. 453–455

1. Choose a work to parody. List at least five works that you have found silly, pompous, or overrated, or whose style or content you think has been overdone. Then identify the elements of style or content that you could exaggerate. Choose one from the list.

2. Analyze your response. Write the name of the work at the top of a clean sheet of paper. On the left side of the sheet, list the effects that the work has on you. On the right side, note the elements of the work that have created each effect. For example, the author of "Endremia and Liason" might have listed *confusion* on the left side and *many odd, hard-to-read names* on the right side.

3. Plan the humor. After you finish your list, decide how you could poke fun at the elements you listed. The author of "Endremia and Liason," for example, may have listed the following strategies:

- Create ridiculous names.
- Give the gods and goddesses absurd domains.
- Exaggerate the violence.

- Create odd transformations.
- Point up the flowery language by dropping in modern phrases.
- Add a meaningless moral.

4. Decide the form and content of your parody. The form of your parody should usually be like the form of the piece being parodied (song, comic strip, TV script, or story, for example). However, you can choose a different form to create additional humor. The myth, for instance, could have been parodied by writing it as a melodramatic soap opera.

5. Use freewriting techniques. Take five or ten minutes to practice imitating and exaggerating the elements that you will parody. Loosen your imagination and let your ideas flow freely through your pen, pencil, or keyboard.

DRAFTING YOUR PARODY

1. Start subtly. Begin your parody with at least one line that is an imitation, not an exaggeration, of the style of the original. Then alternate imitation and exaggeration for comic effect, as the author of "Endremia and Liason" does. Include the best lines and phrases from your freewriting practice.

2. Keep key elements in mind. Notice how "Endremia and Liason" captures key elements of a traditional myth in a few paragraphs. Humor is often strongest when condensed, so you may find it useful to imagine that you are making a miniature of the original.

3. Conclude strongly. To end your parody, use a line that is both funny and pointed. Your ending should help make a final statement about your attitude toward the original piece.

Writing
—TIP—

If you run out of steam in the middle of your draft, go back to the original. Reread a part you especially dislike or think silly, and then freewrite for five minutes, exaggerating the elements of that part.

REVISING YOUR WRITING

1. Share your parody with someone. Guide his or her responses with questions like "What is being parodied?" and "What is the point of the parody?" If your classmate is unsure of either answer, you may need to go back and more clearly convey either your response to the piece or the elements of the piece that led to your response.

2. Check your tone. Do the proper names and words you have chosen create an appropriately humorous, exaggerated tone? If not, you may want to use a thesaurus to help you replace some of the words in your draft with humorous or exaggerated synonyms.

The movie *Spaceballs,* a parody of *Star Wars*

3. Proofread your parody. After making changes, proofread for grammar and mechanics. Be especially careful to check usage of any unfamiliar constructions you are imitating. Also, check the spelling of unusual words you have chosen for their humorous effect. If your parody includes made-up words, be sure their spelling and usage are consistent.

PUBLISHING AND PRESENTING

- **Submit your parody to a periodical.** Send a copy of your work to your school newspaper or literary magazine or to a national humor magazine that publishes takeoffs and parodies, such as *Mad* or *National Lampoon.*
- **Create a humor anthology.** With a group of classmates, collect and organize humorous writing by students and teachers. If possible, illustrate your anthology. Produce copies and distribute them to students, faculty, and parents.
- **Perform your parody.** Use readers' theater or devise a skit to present your parody to your own or another class.
- **Save your parody in your writing portfolio.** Read your parody in a month or two. See whether your response to it, or to the original, has changed.

Sentence

Elaborating on Compound-Complex Sentences

Using compound-complex sentences gives writers the freedom to combine clauses and phrases in a wide variety of ways to elaborate on ideas. Compound-complex sentences can convey a great deal of information concisely and add richness and rhythm to writing.

Notice that each model contains at least two independent clauses and one subordinate clause, and some contain phrases to further elaborate on ideas.

MODELS

1. I used my foot simply BECAUSE I couldn't use my hands, BUT it did not make me feel proud or unique.
   Christy Brown, *My Left Foot*

2. The east-bound train was ploughing through a January snow storm; the dull dawn was beginning to show gray WHEN the engine whistled a mile out of Newark.
   Willa Cather, "Paul's Case"

3. He told me all this later, BUT I've put it down here with the idea of exploding those first wild rumors about his antecedents, WHICH weren't even faintly true.
   F. Scott Fitzgerald, *The Great Gatsby*

A. Combining Sentences Combine each set of sentences below into one compound-complex sentence, using the coordinating and subordinating elements in parentheses to connect clauses, as shown in the example.

Example
   a. Every night, hundreds of planes fly over Holland and go to Germany
   b. the earth is so plowed up by the bombs (WHERE)
   c. every hour hundreds and thousands of people are killed. (AND)

Combined
   Every night, hundreds of planes fly over Holland and go to Germany, where the earth is so plowed up by the bombs, and every hour hundreds and thousands of people are killed. **Anne Frank, *The Diary of Anne Frank***

1. a. For a few minutes she ran, going down to the water and then swiftly back
   b. it could touch her bare feet (BEFORE)
   c. then she dropped luxuriously to the sand and lay there (AND)
   Shirley Jackson, "Island"

2. a. It was about eleven o'clock at night
   b. she was walking home alone (AND)
   c. a boy ran up behind her and tried to snatch her purse (WHEN)
   Langston Hughes, "Thank You, M'am"

3. a. He was about to leave Winesburg to go away to some city
   b. he hoped to get work on a city newspaper (WHERE)
   c. he felt grown up (AND)
   Sherwood Anderson, "Sophistication"

4. a. The boardwalk ended
   b. he moved a little ahead of me (AND)
   c. we descended a sloping path toward our first class (AS)
   John Knowles, *A Separate Peace*

B. Imitating Sentences Imitate the structure of each model, using your own content. Slash marks show clause breaks.

1. Each biscuit held a square of salt side bacon in its top / AND / AS it baked, / the fat oozed down and encased it in a kind of glazed tastiness.
   Conrad Richter, "Early Marriage"

2. There was a fog in the square /, AND / WHEN we came close to the front of the cathedral, / it was very big / , AND / the stone was very wet.
   Ernest Hemingway, *A Farewell to Arms*

3. Catherine had loaded her oilcloth satchel with the leftovers from Sunday dinner /, AND / we were enjoying a breakfast of cake and chicken / WHEN gunfire slapped through the woods.
   Truman Capote, "The Grass Harp"

4. WHEN I worked nights, / I wrote during the day / ; / WHEN I worked days, / I wrote during the night. **Richard Wright, *American Hunger***

C. Expanding Sentences Elaborate each sentence by adding various kinds of phrases or clauses. Start your phrases with the bracketed words. After you finish, compare your expanded sentences with the original sentences on page 329.

Example   When he entered his department, he had slowed down [to. . .], and he walked quietly [across. . .] [to. . .], [wearing. . .].

Expanded   When he entered his department, he had slowed down to his customary gait, and he walked quietly across the room to the W20 file, wearing a look of studious concentration. **James Thurber, "The Catbird Seat"**

1. The music box was in the corner [where. . .], and, [touching. . .], she brought from it one remote, faintly sweet, jangle of a note.
   Shirley Jackson, "The Little House"

2. The old woman watched him with her arms folded across her chest, [as if. . .], and the daughter watched, [her head. . .] and [her fat helpless hands. . .]. **Flannery O'Connor, "A Good Man Is Hard to Find"**

3. Earlier, when Barry had left the house [to. . .], an overnight frost had still been thick [on. . .], but the brisk April sun had soon dispersed it, and now he could feel the spring warmth [on. . .] [through. . .]. **Leslie Norris, "Shaving"**

4. [In. . .], the man would keep to the chimney sweep's footholds across the roof [until. . .], and then he would pry the window up and drop, [soft as a . . .], [onto. . .]. **Kay Boyle, "The Soldier Ran Away"**

Application Choose one of the compound-complex sentences below and imitate it. Then use your imitation as the first sentence of a paragraph. As you complete your paragraph, include several other compound-complex sentences. Notice the rhythm that these sentences bring to your writing, and notice how they clarify the relationships among things or ideas.

1. I know a guy who had been a combat medic in the Central Highlands, and two years later he was still sleeping with all the lights on.
   Michael Herr, Dispatches

2. My hosts were absolutely ignorant when it came to Mexican food; they thought my tortillas were delicious. **Sandra Cisneros, "Straw Into Gold"**

3. In the beginning, before I ever thought consciously of writing, there was my own name, and there was, doubtless, a certain magic in it.
   Ralph Ellison, "Living with a Name"

Grammar Refresher For more about compound-complex sentences, see Handbook 32, pages 633–634.

Sketchbook

Test your cross-cultural awareness:

1. Seven is a lucky number in the United States, but an unlucky number in Ghana, Kenya, and Singapore.
   a. true
   b. false

2. In the United States, a lemon scent suggests freshness, but in the Philippines it is associated with illness.
   a. true
   b. false

3. If you ask for directions, in which country or countries are you likely to get an answer such as "not very far," regardless of the distance?
   a. Mexico and the Soviet Union
   b. Lebanon and Japan
   c. Japan
   d. Paraguay and Pakistan
   e. Canada

4. When shaking hands, which of the following is true?
   a. In France, a handshake consists of a light grasp and a quick, crisp shake of the hand.
   b. In China, a pumping handshake conveys pleasure.
   c. Among Arabs, a handshake is limp and long.
   d. Among South African blacks, a handshake is followed by clenched thumbs, than another handshake.
   e. all of the above

What do you know about other cultures?

Additional Sketches

What historical event do you wish you could have witnessed? Why?

Write a page that might have appeared in a journal kept by a famous scientist or inventor.

(Answers: 1. a; 2. a; 3. d; 4. e)

Reports

Guided Assignment

RESEARCH REPORT

Related Assignment

GENEALOGICAL RESEARCH

You have the key to a treasure that millions of people had been toiling to collect for a thousand years and more. The treasure is the knowledge humanity has accumulated bit by bit over the course of history. The key is your ability to do research. Almost any question that might occur to you or come up in a conversation can be answered if you know where to look. Research is the science of looking for information. That is why research may play a part in almost every kind of writing, from fiction to news reporting. In this workshop you will sharpen your research skills by using them to write a research report and to study your family history.

Research Report

THE UNDER-GROUND RAIL-ROAD

CHARLES L. BLOCKSON

T hrough research, you can travel far into unfamiliar territory. Your search for information can open up new worlds to you, help you understand complex subjects, or help you explore in depth subjects that have a special significance for you. Historian Charles L. Blockson traced the network of people and paths that helped American blacks escape from slavery. As you read the following excerpt from a magazine article he wrote, notice how his personal interest sparked his research.

T hough forty years have passed, I remember as if it were yesterday the moment when the Underground Railroad in all its abiding mystery and hope and terror took possession of my imagination. It was a Sunday afternoon during World War II; I was a boy of ten, sitting on a box in the backyard of our home in Norristown, Pennsylvania, listening to my grandfather tell stories about our family.

"My father—your great-grand-father, James Blockson—was a slave over in Delaware," Grandfather said, "but as a teenager he ran away underground and escaped to Canada." Grandfather knew little more than these bare details about his father's flight to freedom, for James Blockson, like tens of thousands of other black slaves who fled north along its invisible rails . . . in the years before the Civil War, kept the secrets of the Underground Railroad locked in his heart until he died.

So did his cousin Jacob Blockson. . . . But Jacob told William Still, a famous black agent of the Underground Railroad in Philadelphia, the reasons for his escape: "My master was about to be sold out this Fall, and I made up my mind that I did not want to be sold like a horse. . . . I resolved to die sooner than I would be taken back."

Years after that backyard conversation with Grand-father, I read Jacob's words in Still's classic book, *The Underground Rail Road,* and saw the name of my great-grandfather written there too—and thus authenticated my family's passage upon the Underground Railroad. In Still's book I found accounts of the heroism of the fugitive slaves and that of the men and women, black and white, North and South, who helped them flee from bondage at the risk of their own lives, fortunes, and personal liberty. For the Underground Railroad was no actual railroad of steel and steam. It was a network of

paths through the woods and fields, river crossings, boats and ships, trains and wagons, all haunted by the specter of recapture. Its stations were the houses and the churches of men and women—agents of the railroad—who refused to believe that human slavery and human decency could exist together in the same land.

The scholar Edwin Wolf II captured the essence of my ancestors' experience when he wrote that *The Underground Rail Road* is filled "with tales of crated escapees, murdered agents, soft knocks on side doors, and a network as clandestine and complicated as anything dreamed up by James Bond."

As a historian attempting to research the Underground Railroad, I have found, with a mixture of admiration and chagrin, that this atmosphere of secrecy endures. So much is uncertain. . . . No one knows how many fled from bondage along its invisible tracks: As many as 100,000 between 1830 and 1860? As few as 30,000? Probably no one will ever know. What we do know is a mere fragment of the whole, but it is enough. Ordeals may have gone unrecorded and names may have been forgotten, but such records as have survived in the memories of men like my grandfather and in the memoirs of those who risked all for freedom and brotherhood make it clear that the flight to freedom on the Underground Railroad was an epic of American heroism.

Think AND Respond

Charles Blockson mentions personal recollections and books he used during his research. What other types of sources do you think he used? Blockson's research was motivated by a deep personal interest. What are some subjects in which you have a deep interest and which you would like to research?

Underground Railroad, 19th century engraving

INVITATION
TO
Write

Charles Blockson brought research alive with his personal insights about his subject. Now it's your turn to write a research report that examines a subject in depth and presents your insights about it.

Writing a research report is like solving a mystery. You begin with an idea or a theory and a list of questions. Then you conduct research, uncovering clues and tracking down answers. Finally you write, analyzing the information you've gathered and solving the mystery by revealing not only who, what, where, and when but also why and how.

A research report is similar to other types of informative writing you may have done. However, it is also unique in several respects. A report may be longer—perhaps ten to fifteen pages long, depending on your subject—and it requires that you glean information from a number of reliable sources. Still, when you write a research report, you need to do more than assemble other people's ideas and information. You need to analyze and synthesize them, adding your own thinking to the mix.

HANDBOOKS
FOR HELP & PRACTICE

Sharing Techniques, pp. 346–347

Focusing a Topic, pp. 349–352

Applying Graphic Organizers, pp. 353–360

PREWRITE AND EXPLORE

1. Look for ideas.   What subjects intrigue you? Let personal interest be your guide in finding a subject for your research report. Even if your teacher assigns a general topic, it's important to find your own personal angle on it. Try one or more of the following activities to help you identify a topic you care about.

Exploratory Activities

Freewriting   What are your interests? What puzzles you? What do you wish you knew more about? Freewrite about subjects, issues, and ideas you might like to explore in depth.

- **Using current events** With a group of classmates, make a list of news events. Then discuss the social, political, or historical issues associated with these events. Brainstorm report ideas that these issues suggest.
- **Clustering** Write and circle a specific subject or a broad area of interest on a sheet of paper. Around it, jot down any related ideas that occur to you. Circle these and branch out to more ideas related to them. Keep branching out in this way as long as you can.
- **Reading literature** American literature can be a source of ideas about the history, character, and values of the American people. Think of works such as *Moby-Dick* by Herman Melville, *Narrative of the Life of Frederick Douglass, an American Slave,* and *The House of Mirth* by Edith Wharton. What report ideas do they suggest to you?

 Writer's Choice After completing your exploratory activities, you may wish to share the ideas you generate with several other people and ask for their comments and suggestions.

2. Select a topic. Review the subjects you came up with on your own or in discussion with your peers and choose the one you most want to learn about. Perhaps you'd rather use one of the ideas you generated for the Sketchbook on page 270; the "Apply Your Skills" section on page 305 lists other options.

3. Narrow your topic. Doing some preliminary reading on your general topic in reference works—such as encyclopedias and specialized dictionaries—and scanning the tables of contents and the indexes of relevant books can help you see how your subject can be divided into smaller, more manageable parts. You might also find a unique angle on your topic by clustering or by asking "What if" questions about it. Remember that you are not bound to the narrowed topic you select now. You may always refine your topic as you research and learn more about it.

If you can't answer yes to the following questions, you may need to find a different focus for your report.

- Does the topic matter to me? Will it hold my interest?
- Is there enough information available on the topic?
- Is the topic narrow enough to be developed in a report of the assigned length?

Students in Craig Shapiro's American-studies class were assigned to write research reports drawing upon both history and literature. In this workshop you will follow Craig's progress as he selected, researched, and wrote about his topic. Craig brainstormed with his classmates and made a list of possible topics for his report. He then evaluated them in the chart shown below.

ONE STUDENT'S PROCESS

Possible Research Report Topics	Comments
How Edward Bellamy's novel <u>Looking Backward</u> influenced the presidential election of 1892	too narrow, few sources
History of computers in the workplace	better for computer class
Novels about the Civil War	too broad
Soldiers in American literature	not focused enough

Craig felt that the last topic in his chart held the most promise, and he decided to pursue it. He remembered that he had enjoyed reading Stephen Crane's *The Red Badge of Courage,* a novel about a young soldier in the Civil War. Craig therefore decided to research the Civil War and compare the experiences of real soldiers with the experience of Henry Fleming, Crane's fictional hero.

PROBLEM
S O L V I N G

How can I give my topic a unique angle?

4. Establish a goal. Determine what you want to accomplish by researching and writing about your topic. Are you on a personal quest for information about the subject, as Charles Blockson was when he researched the Underground Railroad? Do you want to prove a point, answer a compelling question, or draw a conclusion about a perplexing subject? Your personal goals can help keep you focused, but they may change during the writing process.

5. Consider your purpose. Let your purpose for writing guide you through the research, writing, and revising stages of your process. Identifying a purpose may also help you find the best angle on your topic. The chart on the next page lists examples of purposes and writing topics.

Purpose of Paper	Example of Topic
To inform	The life and times of the novelist Stephen Crane
To analyze	The maturation of Henry Fleming in *The Red Badge of Courage*
To compare and contrast	Similarities and differences between Crane's hero and real Civil War soldiers
To examine causes and effects	Early influences on Stephen Crane

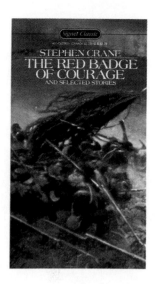

6. Write a statement of controlling purpose. Before beginning your research, you will need to formulate a **statement of controlling purpose**—a sentence that tells, as precisely as possible at this stage, what your paper will be about. Your controlling purpose will keep you moving in the right direction as you do your research, organize your material, and write your paper. It will help you identify useful sources and see the difference between relevant and irrelevant information.

Keep in mind, however, that your controlling purpose may change as you alter or refine your topic during the research stage. Later, when you've completed your research and are getting ready to organize your information into an outline for your report, you will use your statement of controlling purpose as the basis for your thesis statement. Here is the statement Craig wrote to guide his work:

> I will analyze the accuracy of the portrayal of Henry Fleming, the hero of Stephen Crane's novel *The Red Badge of Courage,* by comparing and contrasting Henry's experience with the experiences of real Civil War soldiers.

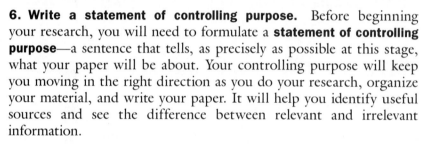

RESEARCH YOUR TOPIC

1. Prepare to gather information. Before you begin looking for sources in the library, make a list of questions you want your research to answer. Craig's list of questions is shown on the next page. Notice that all his questions relate in some way to his controlling purpose.

HANDBOOKS
FOR HELP & PRACTICE

**Reading Strategies,
pp. 494–495**

**Source Materials,
pp. 495–502**

**Library and
Research Skills,
pp. 503–513**

**Outline Form,
pp. 844–845**

PROBLEM
S O L V I N G

What questions
do I want
my research
to answer?

•What types of experiences and emotions did actual
   Civil War soldiers have?
•How did Civil War soldiers react to these experiences
   and emotions?
•Did soldiers' attitudes change during battle? If so, how?
•How did soldiers' expectations of battle and their
   actual experiences differ?
•Does the character of Henry Fleming in <u>The Red Badge
   of Courage</u> have the same experiences, emotions, and
   attitudes as the average Civil War soldier?
•How did soldiers manage their fear?

2. Begin your research. First, consult one or more good encyclopedias for articles on your subject. These articles will give you a general overview of the subject and may suggest directions for further research.

Keep in mind that you may not find suitable articles in an encyclopedia if you've already narrowly focused your topic. Therefore, look for articles on the broader subject of which your topic is a part. Craig Shapiro, for example, couldn't find any articles comparing Henry Fleming's experience with the experiences of actual Civil War soldiers. He could, however, find articles on the war itself, and these gave him valuable background information.

3. Explore different types of sources. Look for information in a variety of books and periodicals. You might check to see if there is a **bibliography**, a specialized reference work listing books and articles on a subject, that deals with your specific topic. You'll find additional books on your topic listed in the library's card or computer catalog and relevant articles listed in annual indexes such as the *Readers' Guide to Periodical Literature* and the *New York Times Index*. You may also wish to explore less obvious sources of information. Personal interviews, recordings, and television and radio programs can provide you with fresh and original material for your report.

Research
TIP

Ask the librarian
if there are any
specialized reference books that
deal with your
topic. He or she
may also be able
to suggest other
library resources.

4. Use primary and secondary sources. All sources of information can be classified as primary sources or secondary sources. **Primary sources** provide direct, firsthand information about subjects and events. Original letters, literary works, speeches, journals, and historical documents—such as the Constitution—are all primary sources. **Secondary sources** provide indirect or secondhand information. Most books and articles in magazines, encyclopedias, and newspapers are secondary sources. Craig was lucky to find excerpts from original letters written by Civil War soldiers (primary sources) in books that contained analyses of the war (secondary sources).

5. Evaluate your sources. The guidelines below can help you determine whether the sources you find contain useful and accurate information.

TECHNOLOGY
TIP

Page 880 of the Access Guide explains how to make the most of the electronic resources that may be available to you at your library.

Evaluating Source Materials

- **Is the author an unbiased authority?** Someone who has written several books or articles on your subject and whose name is included in relevant bibliographies may be considered an authority. However, try to determine to what extent an author's point of view is biased. Be sure to read works written from a variety of viewpoints, especially if your topic is a controversial one.

- **Is the source up-to-date?** Depending on your subject, a source's publication date may make a difference in the quality and timeliness of its data. Using recently published books and articles is particularly important in fields that are constantly changing, such as computers, science, and medicine. In such a field, a source published in 1974 will probably not be as relevant or accurate as one published last year.

- **Where was an article published?** If an article's title sounds promising, consider the kind of publication it appears in. In general, popular-interest magazines and tabloid newspapers are not suitable sources for a report.

- **For what audience is the source intended?** You may find books or articles that have been written about your topic for young readers. Because these often present information in an oversimplified form, they are not suitable sources for research reports. Sources of a highly complex, technical nature may also be inappropriate for your purposes.

6. Keep searching for information. Try searching the library's card or computer catalog again, using different key words to describe your topic. You might also check whether the books and articles you found on your topic contain bibliographies of resources the authors used in conducting their own research. One or more of these resources may contain information you need.

7. Make source cards. For each source you find, record complete publication information on a three-by-five-inch index card. You will need this information when you credit the source for ideas in your report and when you create a Works Cited list. The guidelines below tell you what information you should record for three common types of sources.

Research ━ TIP ━

Basic Forms for Works Cited Entries, on pages 291–293, can help you see what information you should include on source cards for a wider variety of source types.

Guidelines for Source Cards

- **Books** Write the author or editor's complete name, the title, the name and location of the publisher, and the copyright date.

- **Magazines and newspapers** Write the author's complete name, the title of the article, the name and date of the magazine or newspaper, and the page number(s) of the article.

- **Encyclopedias** Write the author's complete name (if given), the entry title, and the name and copyright date of the encyclopedia.

You may also want to include on each source card a library call number and a note about where you found the source, in case you ever need to find the source again. It's more important, however, to number each source in the upper right-hand corner of the card for easy reference during note taking. When you use sources that you will need to credit, note their source-card numbers on your note cards instead of rewriting the title and author each time. Three of Craig's source cards are shown on the next page.

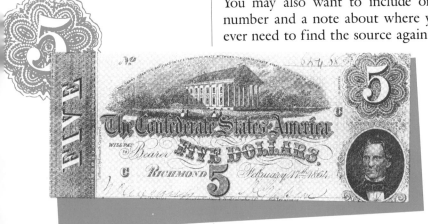

Source Card for Book

Source number (1)

Author   Book title
Catton, Bruce. <u>This Hallowed Ground</u>.

Garden City: Doubleday, 1956.
City of publication/Publisher/Copyright date

Location of source   973.7
School Library   Library call number   C297t

Source Card for Encyclopedia Entry

(3)

Entry title   Encyclopedia title
"Civil War." <u>Encyclopedia Americana</u>.

1990 ed.
Copyright date

School Library

Source Card for Magazine or Newspaper Article

(2)

Article title
Benfey, C. E. G. "The Courage of Stephen

Crane." <u>The New York Review of Books</u>
       Name of publication
19 Mar. 1989: 20–23.
Date of publication/Page number(s)

Public Library

8. Read your sources and take notes. As you review your sources, keep your controlling purpose and your research questions in mind. Closely read only those parts of your sources that are relevant to your topic. Use the following techniques to take notes when you find suitable material.

- **Quotation**   Copy from the original text word for word, including all punctuation. Use quotation marks to signal the beginning and the end of the quotation. Copy the author's exact words when you think they would enhance a point you plan to make in your report.
- **Paraphrase**   Restate the material in your own words. A paraphrase is approximately the same length as the original. Use this method when your notes need to be very detailed.
- **Summary**   Record the main idea of a passage in your own words. A summary is about one-third the length of the original. Use this method when you want to remember a general idea.

If your notes are accurate and complete, writing your report will be easier. See Handbook 23, pages 495–502, for more information about writing quotations, paraphrases, and summaries and about using them effectively in your writing.

The following guidelines can help you take notes efficiently.

Guidelines for Note Taking

- Use a separate four-by-six-inch index card for each idea, quotation, or piece of information. At the top of each card, write a brief heading that indicates the note's main idea. Later, you can group your cards according to their main ideas and arrange them into a logical order to guide your draft.

- In the upper right-hand corner of each note card, record the number of the corresponding source card.

- Indicate whether the material is a quotation, a paraphrase, a summary, or an idea of your own. This will help you to remember whether the idea needs to be credited to a source.

- Record the number of the page on which you found the material in your source. This information is essential for giving proper credit to the source in your report; you'll also need the page number if you want to go back to the source to verify a fact or a quotation or to gather more information.

- As you take notes, remember to keep your controlling purpose and research questions in mind, so that you record only relevant information. However, you should also keep an open mind as you learn about your topic; you may wish to revise your controlling purpose, add questions to your list, and use new material you find.

Research
— TIP —

Make the most of the time you spend reviewing your sources. In a book, the table of contents and the index can steer you toward useful sections. Headings in bold type signal key passages in articles.

U.S. soldiers began wearing this style of hat, called a forage cap, in 1858. In hot weather, soldiers would keep their heads cool by putting green leaves inside the cap.

Here is a note card Craig wrote as he read one of his sources.

Source number 7

Feelings About Battle   Main idea

Most soldiers felt restless, nervous, and impatient before battles
began. One soldier wrote that nothing "brings . . . such crucial
trial as the throbbing emotions that immediately precede the
clash of arms." 339   Page number

(Summary and quotation)   Type of note

9. Write a thesis statement. At this point you should have a
more precise idea of what you want to accomplish in your writing.
Recast your statement of controlling purpose as a **thesis statement**
that expresses the main idea you will develop in your report. A
thesis statement may indicate the organizational pattern you will
follow and reflect your perspective and tone.

Remember Craig's controlling purpose:

> I will analyze the accuracy of the portrayal of Henry Fleming,
> the hero of Stephen Crane's novel *The Red Badge of Courage,*
> by comparing and contrasting Henry's experience with the ex-
> periences of real Civil War soldiers.

Craig reread *The Red Badge of Courage* and examined a variety of
primary and secondary sources that focused on the human side of
the Civil War. He discovered that Stephen Crane's depiction of
Henry Fleming was accurate and realistic after all. Here is Craig's
first thesis statement:

> Henry Fleming, the hero of *The Red Badge of Courage,* is a
> realistic portrait of a Civil War soldier.

Craig felt, though, that this thesis statement was incomplete. It
didn't say how he would prove his point, and it didn't convey what
he hoped to accomplish in his writing. Craig revised his thesis statement again; this is the final draft he incorporated into the first
paragraph of his report:

> By examining the memoirs of Civil War soldiers and comparing
> them with Fleming's experiences, one can see that Stephen
> Crane's novel is an accurate portrayal of a soldier's emotions
> and actions during the war.

Writing
═TIP═

A thesis state-
ment tells the
main idea of a
piece of writing in
the same way that
a topic sentence
tells the main
idea of a para-
graph. See Hand-
book 8, page 381,
for more informa-
tion on thesis
statements; Hand-
book 10, page
401, has more in-
formation on topic
sentences.

10. Organize your information. It's a good idea to create an organizational plan, or outline, before you begin to write. Outlining is a particularly important step in writing a research report. It requires you to review the information you've gathered, weed out all the unnecessary details, and see your report as a "story" with a beginning, a middle, and an end.

Begin organizing your information by grouping your note cards according to their main ideas. Then arrange your groups so that there is a logical flow from one to the next. Keep in mind that your outline represents a plan you can follow as you write; you are always free to change your plan as you draft, however, and you may find yourself revising your outline several times before you're satisfied with the final draft of your report. Guidelines for standard outline form and models of sentence and topic outlines can be found in the Appendix, pages 844–845.

Here is part of Craig's topic outline. He used comparison-and-contrast order and order of importance to group his details.

Writing TIP

You may wish to graphically sketch out your ideas (in a cluster map, a time line, or a tree diagram, for example) before you draft an outline.

1. Begin writing.   Using your outline as a guide, begin setting your ideas down on paper. Remember that each topic and subtopic in your outline should represent one or more paragraphs in your report; your note cards should have the facts and details you need to support your ideas. As you draft, you may begin to have second thoughts about your thesis, or main idea. That's because you continue to learn about your subject as you write about it; therefore, feel free to change your thesis statement and your outline as your ideas about your subject develop.

Writer's Choice   What happens if you find that you don't have all the information you need and that your note cards don't tell the whole story? You may either stop drafting and do more research or go on to another section of your outline and do additional research when you're ready.

2. Support your analysis.   When you write a report, you need to do more than just restate the information you find in a number of reliable sources. You need to make inferences, analyze and interpret evidence, synthesize material, and draw a reasonable conclusion. Therefore, use the facts, statistics, examples, and other evidence you've gathered to support your own original ideas.

3. Avoid plagiarism.   The only material in your report that you do not need to credit, or document, is information that is considered common knowledge—information that many people have—and your own interpretations and ideas. You therefore need to credit the sources of all direct quotations, paraphrases, and summaries you use in your writing. If you neglect to do so, you will be committing **plagiarism,** the dishonest—and unlawful—presentation of someone else's words or ideas as your own. You can credit your sources by means of footnotes, end notes, or parenthetical documentation. Check with your teacher to see which method you should use.

HANDBOOKS
FOR HELP & PRACTICE

Introductions/
Conclusions,
pp. 378–390

Unity/Coherence,
pp. 401–414

Using Source
Materials,
pp. 495–502

The artist Edwin Forbes documented the Civil War for the *Illustrated Newspaper.* He drew the common soldier at rest as well as vivid battle scenes.

4. Document your sources. Parenthetical documentation is the most common way of crediting sources in the body of a paper. In this method of documentation, a detailed list of sources—including publication information—appears at the end of the report (in a Works Cited list), and parenthetical notes in the text provide readers with specific details about where each piece of information was found. Therefore, provide a reference to a source and give page numbers in parentheses following each quotation, paraphrase, or summary you use. Follow these guidelines for parenthetical documentation; you can consult the final draft of Craig's report, pages 295–303, for examples.

Guidelines for Parenthetical Documentation

- **Work by one author** Put the author's last name and the page reference in parentheses: (Barson 32–33). If you mention the author's name in the sentence, put only the page reference in parentheses: (32–33).

- **Work by more than one author** Put the author's last names and the page reference in parentheses: (Niemann and Farr 8). If a source has more than three authors, give the first author's last name followed by *et al.* and the page reference: (Baker et al. 321).

- **Work with no author given** Give the title (or a shortened version of it) and the page reference: ("Civil War Memoirs" 398).

- **One of two or more works by the same author** Give the author's last name, the title or a shortened version, and the page reference: (Sohn, War Novels 56).

- **Two or more works cited at the same place** Use a semicolon to separate the entries: (Lane 30; Hall 91).

---

5. Double-check your report's overall structure. Your report should have a compelling introduction that captures readers' attention. A thesis statement that reveals the main point of your writing may also be part of the introduction. The body of the report should develop the thesis in a series of logically organized paragraphs, and the conclusion should summarize your research and leave your readers with a lasting impression. Your thesis statement—rewritten in different words—may also be part of your conclusion.

6. Set your completed draft aside for a few days. Take a break to get some distance from your writing. Then reread your draft and have a peer read it. The questions below can guide your review.

R E V I E W   Y O U R   W R I T I N G

Questions for Yourself

- Have I written a clear thesis statement? Have I developed and supported it in the body of my report?

- Have I fully developed each of the main points in my outline? Where do I need to add more information?

- Have I included material that does not relate to my overall purpose? What information should be deleted?

- Have I developed my ideas in a logical order? How can I organize my ideas more effectively?

- Have I used direct quotations appropriately? Are any too long? Would paraphrasing some of the quotations make my report easier to read?

- Are all my facts and quotations accurate? Have I correctly documented my sources?

- Have I achieved my overall purpose and goals for the report? What changes might I make to achieve these goals?

- If this research report is a response to an assignment, have I met the requirements of the assignment?

Questions for Your Peer Readers

- What did you like most about my report? What did you like least?

- Describe the subject and purpose of my report in your own words.

- Does the order in which I've presented my ideas make sense? Which parts, if any, seem confusing or out of place?

- Which parts of my report, if any, feel incomplete? What kinds of information should I add? What can I leave out?

- Did my introduction make you want to read the rest of the report?

- Does my conclusion successfully sum up the report?

Lee Accepts the Surrender Terms, by Tom Lovell

©National Geographic Society

REVISE YOUR WRITING

HANDBOOKS
FOR HELP & PRACTICE

Art of Revision,
pp. 416–421
Peer Response,
pp. 422–426

Grammar
TIP

When you refer to your sources in your report, underscore book titles and put quotation marks around article titles.

1. Evaluate your responses. Think about the reactions you had to your draft and the opinions your readers expressed about it. What changes do you want to make? Keep in mind that a research report usually has certain characteristics.

Standards for Evaluation

An effective research report . . .

- contains a statement of thesis and purpose in an introduction that stimulates readers' interest.
- uses evidence and details from a variety of sources in the body of the report to develop and support the thesis.
- effectively integrates quotations into the text to support the writer's ideas.
- correctly credits the sources of all direct quotations and paraphrases and summaries of other people's ideas.
- follows a logical pattern of organization and includes appropriate transitions between paragraphs.
- ends with an effective, satisfying conclusion.
- includes a properly formatted Works Cited list with complete publication information for all the sources credited in the report.

2. Problem-solve. When you've decided what changes you want to make, rework your draft.

Here is how Craig Shapiro changed one part of his report after he received feedback from a peer reader.

ONE STUDENT'S PROCESS

Many soldiers believed that the courageous would
survive, ~~the coward would die.~~ *and* ~~A soldier could be~~ *ly*

comforted (even in defeat) by his own courage (Linderman 61). ~~The strange thing is that Crane never fought~~
¶Many soldiers thus tried to hide their true fears and go into the fight as
~~in a battle, though he seemed to know exactly how real~~
bravely as possible.

~~soldiers felt.~~ One of these real soldiers was Elbridge
who felt that he had to "go into the blaze,"
Capp. Like Henry, Elbridge said to himself "I must face

the danger" (Capp 135). Others resolved to let death

solve their problems. One of these soldier*s* said, "I'm
(Hinman 400).
willin ter die . . . but I don't want ter be no coward".
"I
Another Private, Sam Watkins, said that he had made up
my " (234). ~~thought~~ *"that it would be better to get*
his mind to die. Henry too ~~had decided in his own mind~~
killed directly
~~that he would prefer to die in battle~~ and end his trou-

bles (Crane 25). He was like so many other soldiers

who thought it better to fall facing the enemy than to

act like a coward (Wiley, <u>Billy Yank</u> 68). ¶The descrip-
immediately before and during the battle
tions of Henry's feelings are consistent with the

accounts of both <u>f</u>ederal and <u>c</u>onfederate soldiers.

Your point about Crane is striking all right, but it seems to interrupt the flow.

Did they really say the same words?

I like the "real speech"—it gives flavor.

Could you use direct quotations here?

This sounds like a topic for a new paragraph.

3. Prepare your Works Cited list. Gather the source cards for every source you have cited in your report, and use them to compile your Works Cited list. This final list of sources contains publication information about all the sources you actually cited in your report. It also provides a list of references for the benefit of those who wish to investigate your topic further. Sources that are not actually cited in the report should not be included. The following guidelines are general rules for setting up your list.

Guidelines for a Works Cited List

- On a separate piece of paper, center the heading *Works Cited* and double-space between the heading and the first entry. Double-space each entry, and double-space between the entries.

- Begin the first line of each entry at the left margin; indent all subsequent lines five spaces.

- Arrange all entries alphabetically by the last name of the author or editor. If no name is given, alphabetize the entry according to the first word in the source's title. If the first word is *A, An,* or *The,* alphabetize according to the second word of the title.

- Alphabetize two or more sources by the same author according to the first words in their titles. Give the author's name in the first entry only; after that, replace the author's name with three hyphens followed by a period (---.).

- Punctuate your entries correctly; use the examples on the following three pages for punctuation guidelines.

- If you wish, you may break your Works Cited list into sections for the different types of sources you used. Centered subheadings for the sections might be *Books, Articles,* and *Other Sources;* each section should be alphabetized separately.

- Use shortened names of book publishers. For example, "Little" is used for Little, Brown and Company.

The following basic forms of entries will help you to use correct punctuation and to list sources with different elements.

Basic Forms for Works Cited Entries

Whole Books

A. One author

Conynham, David P.   The Irish Brigade and Its Campaigns.
      Gaithersburg: Olde Soldier, 1989.

B. Two authors

Gilbert, Sandra M., and Susan Gubar.   The Madwoman in the
      Attic: The Woman Writer and the Nineteenth Century
      Literary Imagination.   New Haven: Yale UP, 1979.

UP is an abbreviation of "University Press."

C. Three authors

Heppelwhite, Charles W., Jeannette M. Meyerhoff, and Gerhardt B.
      Kassenbaum.   The Effects of High Technology on Smokestack
      America: An Introspective.   Litchfield: Litchfield, 1988.

D. Four or more authors

Gatto, Joseph, et al.   Exploring Visual Design.   2d ed.
      Worcester: Davis, 1987.

Et al. is an abbreviation of a Latin phrase meaning "and others."
You can use *et al.* instead of listing all authors.

E. No author given

Literary Market Place: The Directory of American Book
      Publishing.   1990 ed.   New York: Bowker, 1990.

F. An editor, but no single author

Saddlemyer, Ann, ed.   Letters to Molly: John Millington Synge to
      Maire O'Neill.   Cambridge: Harvard UP, 1984.

This form may be used when you have cited several works from a
collection. Instead of writing separate entries for each work, you
may write one entry for the entire work, listing the editor or editors
first.

G. Two or three editors

Chipps, Genie, and Bill Henderson, eds.   Love Stories for the
      Time Being.   Wainscott: Pushcart, 1987.

Parts Within Books

Page numbers of selections follow publication dates in entries for parts within books and for articles and reviews in magazines, newspapers, and journals.

H. A poem, short story, essay, or chapter in a collection of works by one author

Angelou, Maya. "Remembering." Poems. New York: Bantam, 1986. 11.

I. A poem, short story, essay, or chapter in a collection of works by several authors

Welty, Eudora. "The Corner Store." Prose Models. Ed. Gerald Levin. San Diego: Harcourt, 1984. 20–22.

J. A novel or play in a collection of novels or plays published under one cover

Serling, Rod. Requiem for a Heavyweight. Twelve American Plays. Ed. Richard Corbin and Miriam Balf. New York: Scribner's, 1973. 299–327.

Crane, Stephen. The Red Badge of Courage. The Red Badge of Courage and Other Stories. New York: Dodd, 1979. 238–375.

Magazines, Newspapers, Journals, Encyclopedias, and Reviews

K. An article in a quarterly or monthly magazine

Batten, Mary. "Life Spans." Science Digest Feb. 1984: 46–51.

L. An article in a weekly magazine

Powell, Bill. "Coping with the Markets." Newsweek 27 Apr. 1987: 54.

M. A magazine article with no author given

"How the New Tax Law Affects America." Nation's Accountants 24 Sept. 1986: 66–69.

N. An article in a daily newspaper

James, Noah. "The Comedian Everyone Loves to Hate." New York Times 22 Jan. 1984, sec. 2: 23.

O. An editorial in a newspaper

"Is America Set for the Hypermarket?" Editorial. <u>Chicago Tribune</u> 4 Jan. 1988, sec. 1: 10.

If no author is given, begin with the title.

P. An article in a journal

Aumiller, Emily P. "<u>Lord of the Flies</u> as a Musical." <u>English Journal</u> 71.8 (1982): 32.

The volume number, the number of the issue, the date, and the page reference follow the title of the journal.

Q. An encyclopedia article

Faulk, Odie B. "Western Frontier Life." <u>The World Book Encyclopedia</u>. 1993 ed.

If the article is unsigned, begin the entry with the title.

R. An unsigned, untitled review

Rev. of <u>Harry and Son</u>. <u>American Film</u> Mar. 1984: 78.

S. A signed, titled review

Ludlow, Arthur. "Glass Houses." Rev. of <u>Rolling Breaks and Other Movie Business</u>, by Aljean Harmetz. <u>Movies</u> Aug. 1983: 76.

Other Sources

T. An interview

Farquharson, Reginald W. Personal interview. 26 May 1988.

U. A published interview

De Niro, Robert. "A Walk and a Talk with Robert De Niro." By Peter Brant and Ingrid Sischy. <u>Interview</u> Nov. 1993: 90–94.

V. Information in private files

Students of Paul D. Schriener. "Of Our Lives: A history of the 1960's and 1970's." Dept. of Social Studies, Munster High School, 1981.

W. CD-ROM

<u>The Civil War CD-ROM</u>. CD-ROM. Indianapolis: Guild P of Indiana, 1996.

4. Proofread your report. As you reread your final draft slowly and carefully, correct any errors you might have made in grammar, spelling, and mechanics. Double-check the accuracy of your quotations by proofreading them against your note cards, or against the original sources if you have them on hand. Then make a clean final copy of your report, following the Modern Language Association's guidelines for manuscript preparation, listed below.

MLA Manuscript Guidelines

- **Typing or printing** Type your final draft on a typewriter, or if you are using a word processor, print out a letter-quality copy. Do not justify the lines. If you have to write your final copy by hand, use dark blue or black ink and make sure your handwriting is neat and legible. Use only one side of the paper.

- **Paper** Use 8½-by-11-inch, white, nonerasable paper.

- **Margins** Except for page numbers, leave one-inch margins on all sides of the paper. Indent the first line of each paragraph five spaces from the left margin. Indent set-off quotations (those of more than four lines) ten spaces from the left margin. Do not indent long quotations from the right.

- **Spacing** The entire paper—including the heading and title on the first page, the body of the paper, quotations, and the Works Cited list—should be double-spaced.

- **Heading and title** One inch from the top of the first page and flush with the left margin, type your name, your teacher's name, the course name, and the date on separate lines. Below this heading, center the title on the page. Do not underline the title, put it in quotation marks, or use all capital letters.

- **Page numbers** Number all pages consecutively in the upper right-hand corner, one-half inch from the top. You may type your last name before the page number to identify your work in case a page is misplaced.

5. Present your paper, then save it in your portfolio. The members of one or more of your classes may be interested in the topic of your paper. Consider using illustrations, graphs, models, or music to add interest to your oral presentation. Alternatively, you could turn your report into an electronic multimedia presentation. For help, see pages 887–889 of the Access Guide.

Craig Shapiro

Ms. Campbell

American Studies

21 May 1994

The Realistic Portrait of Henry Fleming

in Crane's <u>The Red Badge of Courage</u>

American fiction often portrays the real-life experiences of a given period in history. Herman Melville's
<u>Moby-Dick</u>, for example, accurately depicts life on a
whaling boat in the nineteenth century. Looking closely
at a fictional character may provide the reader with a
clear and accurate view of that character's era. Stephen
Crane's novel <u>The Red Badge of Courage</u> presents just
such a view through the character of the Civil War soldier Henry Fleming. By examining the memoirs of Civil
War soldiers and comparing them with Fleming's experiences, one can see that Stephen Crane's novel is an
accurate portrayal of a soldier's emotions and actions
during the war.

Henry Fleming, like many actual Civil War soldiers,
wasn't sure how well he would perform in battle. He
thought that "the only way to prove himself was to go
into the blaze, and then figuratively to watch his legs
to discover their merits and faults" (Crane 14). Many
Civil War soldiers had the same feelings as Henry. Bell
Wiley, a historian who has done extensive research on
the common private in the Civil War, wrote that soldiers

Provides thesis statement

Supports key idea by showing comparison of war experiences

Provides parenthetical
documentation with
title

were more concerned with the question of how they would stand up in battle than they were with the chance of being wounded or killed (<u>Billy Yank</u> 68). One private wrote, "I have a mortal dread of the battle field, for I . . . am afraid that the groans of the wounded & dying will make me shake. . . . I hope & trust that strength will be given me to stand up & do my duty" (Wiley, <u>Common Soldier</u> 56). The historian Gerald F. Linderman found concern with courage in the journals and letters of soldiers; one said, "If he shows the least cowardice he is undone. His courage must never fail" (7).

Provides details
that support the
paragraph's topic
sentence

This emphasis on courage served an important purpose, according to Linderman. The courageous soldier believed that his "inner qualities" would carry him through the "increasingly depersonalized mass warfare." Many soldiers believed that the courageous would survive and the cowardly would die. Even in defeat a soldier could be comforted by his own courage (61).

Incorporates parts of
quotations

Many soldiers thus tried to hide their true fears and go into the fight as bravely as possible. One of these real soldiers was Elbridge Capp. Like Henry, who felt that he had to "go into the blaze," Elbridge said to himself, "I must face the danger" (Capp 135). Others resolved to let death solve their problems. One of these soldiers said, "I'm willin ter die . . . but I don't want ter be no coward" (Hinman 400). Another private, Sam Watkins, said, "I had made up my mind to die" (234).

Henry too thought "that it would be better to get killed
directly and end his troubles" (Crane 25). He was like
so many other soldiers who thought it better to fall
facing the enemy than to act like a coward (Wiley,
Billy Yank 68).

The descriptions of Henry's feelings immediately
before and during the battle are consistent with the
accounts of both Federal and Confederate soldiers. Before
facing fire for the first time, Henry "was in a fever of
impatience" (Crane 24). Most soldiers experienced this
same feeling. One wrote that nothing "brings . . . such
crucial trial as the throbbing emotions that immediately
precede the clash of arms" (Hinman 339). Another private said that "the knowledge of an impending battle
always sent that thrill of fear and horror" (Capp 140).

Once the firing started, however, Henry's feelings, as
well as those of most soldiers, changed. Henry had been
advised that a man changed in battle, and he found that
it was true (Crane 24). Before he went into action,
Henry's main concern was for himself. After the battle
opened, however, his outlook changed. "He suddenly lost
concern for himself, and forgot to look at a menacing
fate" (Crane 30).

Civil War veterans also responded to the war in
ways they hadn't anticipated. One private wrote,
"Strange as it may seem to you, but the more men I
saw killed the more reckless I became" (Wiley, Billy

Uses exact quotation
to support writer's
point

Uses transitions to
connect main ideas

Provides accurate,
solid information
about the topic

Yank 71). Henry Morton Stanley, the famous explorer, wrote, "We plied our arms, loaded, and fired, with such nervous haste as though it depended on each of us how soon this fiendish uproar would be hushed" (354). Oliver Norton, a Pennsylvania infantryman, wrote, "I acted like a madman. . . . The feeling that was uppermost in my mind was a desire to kill as many rebels as I could" (91). Another soldier, like Henry, wished to grapple face to face with his enemies: "I was mad. . . . How I itched for a hand-to-hand struggle" (Wiley, Billy Yank 72).

Gradually, a feeling of unity—oneness—with the army, the corps, and the regiment manifested itself in both the average Civil War private and Henry Fleming. Sergeant Thomas H. Evans, a member of the regular army, said that an "abandonment of self" emerged in battle (43). Similarly, throughout Crane's novel Henry refers to himself as "part of a vast blue demonstration" (10). When he first came under fire, Henry experienced a feeling common to many Civil War soldiers:

> He felt that something of which he was a part—a
> regiment, an army, a cause, or a country—was in
> a crisis. He was welded into a common person-
> ality which was dominated by a single desire.
> For some moments he could not flee, no more
> than a little finger can commit a revolution
> from a hand. (Crane 30)

Incorporates quotations within text

Indents long quotation

On the other hand, flight from the battlefield was not uncommon among Civil War soldiers. In fact, "there was a considerable amount of malingering, skulking, and running in every major battle" (Wiley, Common Soldier 26). Soldiers who fled from the field of battle, however, were generally beset with a conflict between their bodies and their souls. William Hinman says that a soldier had to "go through a struggle . . . between his mental and physical natures" (398). Hinman describes that struggle as follows:

> The instinct of . . . [the physical nature] at such a time—and what soldier does not know it?—was to seek a place of safety, without a moment's delay. To fully subdue this feeling by the power of will was not . . . such an easy matter as might be imagined. . . . [S]ome could never do it.   (398)

Soldiers who ran tried to rationalize their actions. Henry justified his flight from battle this way:

> He had fled, he told himself, because annihilation approached. [He] was a little piece of the army. He considered the time, he said, to be one in which it was the duty of every little piece to rescue itself if possible. Later the officers could fit the little pieces together again, and make a battle front. If none of the little pieces were wise enough to save themselves from the flurry of death at such a time, why, then, where would be the army? It was all plain that he had proceeded according to very correct and commendable rules. (Crane 39)

Supports key idea by comparing problems of desertion

Uses ellipses to indicate missing material

Uses brackets to distinguish writer's paraphrase from exact quotation

Gives relevant
examples

Provides smooth
transition

Henry again tried to prove to himself that running
was the right thing to do by throwing a pine cone at
a squirrel. When the squirrel fled rather than let the
missile strike him, Henry felt that "Nature had given
him a sign" (Crane 41).

Actual combatants who ran from battle gave less
symbolic, yet similar, excuses. Some would self-inflict
wounds; others would leave the front on the pretense of
a broken musket, helping a wounded comrade, being ordered to do some special task by an officer, illness, or a
"call of nature"; many never returned (Wiley, Billy Yank
86). A hospital steward stumbled on some skulkers at
the Battle of Cedar Mountain and recorded the following:

> Some of these miserable wretches . . . muttered
> that they were not to be hoodwinked and
> slaughtered.
>
> "I was sick, anyway," said one fellow, "and felt
> like droppin' on the road."
>
> "I didn't trust my colonel," said another; "he
> ain't no soldier."
>
> "I'm tired of the war, anyhow," said a third,
> "and my time's up soon; so I shan't have my head
> blown off."   (Townsend 493)

One soldier who deserted his comrades at the Battle of
Corinth said on his return that he had not run but had
been detailed to guard a water tank. His comrades never let
him live it down (Wiley, Billy Yank 87–88). Another soldier,

nicknamed "Spinney," said he had run because he
thought that the bullets were calling his name
(Goss 148).

Whether they fled or fought valiantly, many soldiers
were surprised by the realities of combat. At first,
Henry "had the belief that real war was a series of
death struggles with small time in between for sleep
and meals" (Crane 10). He learned later, however, that
battle took up very little time in a soldier's life. He also
thought that "Secular and religious education had oblit-
erated the throat-grappling instinct" (Crane 10).
However, when the Confederates were attacking for the
first time and Henry "wished to rush forward and
strangle with his fingers," he realized that this thought
was wrong too (Crane 31).

Many actual soldiers also experienced a difference
between their expectations and the realities of battle.
Henry Morton Stanley wrote, "It was the first Field of
Glory I had seen in my May of life, and the first time
that Glory sickened me with its repulsive aspect and
made me suspect it was all a glittering lie" (357). Sam
Watkins wrote, "I had heard and read of battlefields . . .
but I must confess that I never realized the 'pomp and
circumstance' of the thing called glorious war until
I saw this" (42). Some were so naive that they were
surprised that the enemy was firing bullets (Watkins
42; Stanley 353). This difference between the untrained

Uses parenthetical
documentation
correctly

Supports key idea by
comparing differences
between expectations
and realities of war

Provides information
from a variety of
sources

Credits two sources
in one reference

soldier's image of war and the realities of combat is well portrayed in <u>The Red Badge of Courage.</u>

Under the stress of combat, both Henry Fleming and many actual Civil War soldiers rapidly matured. Henry's attainment of maturity was both quick and dramatic. Early in the novel, Henry felt the need to make excuses to escape the reality of his cowardice, but by the end of the book, Henry was able to look upon his feats, both bad and good, objectively. He thought that he "could look back upon the brass and bombast of his earlier gospels and see them truly" (Crane 109). Earlier, when Henry had been walking with a wounded soldier called "the tattered man," Henry felt guilty and embarrassed because he himself had no wound, while everyone around him had a "red badge of courage" (Crane 46). To escape his guilt and embarrassment, Henry ran from the tattered man, feeling that he "could have strangled" his wounded companion (Crane 52). By the end of the novel, however, Henry realized that the tattered man had actually been trying to help him, and he felt guilty for deserting this man, who had cared for him and aided him (Crane 108). When Henry had outgrown the selfishness of immaturity, he could finally say of himself, "He was a man" (Crane 109).

Henry's attainment of maturity was also common to many young soldiers. Bell Wiley writes, "One of the most interesting things about the boy soldiers was the speed with which they matured under the stress and strain of army life" (<u>Billy Yank</u> 301). Sam Watkins wrote that early in the war,

> we wanted to march off and whip twenty Yankees. But we soon found that the glory of war was at home with the ladies, not upon the field of blood and . . . death. . . . I might say the agony of mind were very different indeed from the patriotic times at home. (21)

Before Henry matured, he was nervous and afraid of how the strain of battle and the threat of death would affect him. After he had "become a man," however, Henry could say matter-of-factly that "he had been to touch the great death, and found that, after all, it was but the great death" (Crane 109).

Detail from painting of a drummer boy writing a letter during the Civil War.

Like many actual soldiers, Henry gains a final understanding of the meaning of life and death from his experiences during the war. Henry's diverse emotional experiences, his growth to maturity, and his eventual feeling of unity with his comrades all parallel the experiences that actual Civil War soldiers recorded in their letters and diaries. These parallel experiences reveal that <u>The Red Badge of Courage</u> is an accurate representation of real life under the conditions of the Civil War.

Concludes by summarizing main ideas and restating the thesis

Works Cited

Capp, Elbridge. <u>Reminiscences of the War of the Rebellion</u>. Nashua: Telegraph, 1911.

Commager, Henry S. <u>The Blue and the Gray</u>. Vol. 1. Indianapolis: Bobbs, 1950.

Crane, Stephen. <u>The Red Badge of Courage</u>. New York: Norton, 1976.

Evans, Thomas H. "There Is No Use Trying to Dodge Shot." <u>Civil War Times Illustrated</u> Aug. 1967: 43.

Goss, Warren Lee. "Why Don't You Get Behind a Tree." <u>Battles and Leaders of the Civil War</u>. Ed. Ned Bradford. New York: Appleton, 1956. 141–50.

Hinman, William. <u>Si Klegg and His Pard</u>. Cleveland: Hamilton, 1982.

Linderman, Gerald F. <u>Embattled Courage: The Experience of Combat in the American Civil War</u>. London: Free, 1987.

Norton, Oliver. <u>Army Letters</u>. Chicago: Deming, 1903.

Stanley, Henry Morton. "Henry Stanley Fights with the Dixie Grays at Shiloh." Commager 351–57.

Townsend, George A. "A Camp of Skulkers at Cedar Mountain." Commager 493–94.

Watkins, Sam R. <u>Company Aytch</u>. New York: Macmillan, 1962.

Wiley, Bell Irvin. <u>The Common Soldier of the Civil War</u>. Gettysburg: Historical Times, 1973.

---. <u>The Life of Billy Yank</u>. Indianapolis: Bobbs, 1951.

WRITER TO WRITER

The important thing is not to stop questioning. Curiosity has its own reason for existing. One cannot help but be in awe when he contemplates the mysteries of eternity, of life, of reality. It is enough if one tries merely to comprehend a little of this mystery every day. Never lose a holy curiosity.

Albert Einstein, physicist and author

1. Reflect on your writing. Having completed your research paper and read papers written by others, you are in a good position to reflect on the writing process you have been through. Ask yourself questions such as the ones below. Record any useful thoughts and ideas in your writing log.

FOR YOUR
PORTFOLIO

- What was the biggest problem I encountered during my writing process? What solutions did I find? How can I improve my writing process next time?
- How did my process for writing a research paper differ from the processes I used in doing other types of writing? Did I do more planning before beginning to write? Was the planning of a different type? Did I do enough planning before beginning to write?

2. Apply your skills. Try one or more of the following activities.

- **Cross-curricular** Jot down interesting questions that come up during class discussions in your history and science classes. Choose one that is left unresolved, research an in-depth answer, and present it in a detailed paper or oral report.
- **Literature** What book would you say has had the greatest impact on human history? Choose one work of fiction, such as Harriet Beecher Stowe's *Uncle Tom's Cabin,* or of nonfiction, such as Charles Darwin's *The Origin of Species.* Research how this book was written and how it affected history, and write a paper reporting your results.
- **Related assignments** Follow the suggestions on pages 306–308 to write a genealogical research report.

Related
ASSIGNMENT

INVITATION
TO
Write

Write a history of your family based on genealogical research.

PROFESSIONAL
M O D E L

One of the oldest residents of the city as well as one of the best known women in the state was laid to rest Monday, May 29. Mrs. Elizabeth Selden was buried from her residence, 455 Champlain Avenue. She leaves three daughters, Mrs. Griffin of Wichita, Kan., Mrs. Senora Yerby and Mrs. Mamie Carroll of this city, besides many other relatives and friends. Mrs. Selden had been a resident of this city for the past fifty years.

Chicago Defender, June 10, 1916

HANDBOOKS
FOR HELP & PRACTICE

Chronological Order,
pp. 363–364
Questioning,
pp. 392–394
Interviewing,
p. 369
**Sources of
Information,**
pp. 512–513

This simple obituary provides a wealth of information about the history, or **genealogy,** of a family. Such details as the woman's address and the names of her daughters would be valuable clues to a researcher seeking to document the family tree.

Doing genealogical research involves identifying your ancestors and gathering information about them. Many of the techniques you used in completing the guided assignment in this workshop can be applied to genealogical research. There are, however, some research strategies that apply specifically to genealogical research.

1. Talk to family members. Begin by consulting your immediate family. Then reach out to grandparents, uncles and aunts, cousins, more distant relatives, and longtime family friends. Ask them for specific information—such as dates, addresses, and documents— relating to your ancestors, but also inquire about other memories that might lead you to interesting and unexpected information.

2. Examine family documents. Look at family photographs, scrapbooks, written records, and documents for clues about names, places, and dates.

3. Examine newspapers and books. As the obituary entry about Mrs. Selden shows, newspaper obituaries and other articles can provide names, dates, addresses, and other facts that can help you in your research. Also consult books of local history for information.

Cambodian-American children learn traditional Cambodian dances, an important way of celebrating their culture.

4. Examine public records. Public documents such as federal census reports, county death certificates, and other official records can provide factual information. These records are kept by federal archives, county clerks, and many libraries. Ask your local librarian to suggest where to find these records. Your librarian also may be able to direct you to a library or another institution that specializes in genealogical research.

5. Write your findings. There are several ways you can transform your geneological research into an interesting family history. One way is to write a narrative history of your family. If you choose this

St. Patrick's Day, by Helen Fabri Smagorinsky, 1984.

approach, search through your research for the most interesting details you have uncovered. Recall amusing, sad, exciting, or important anecdotes that reveal important information about your family. Keep in mind that you want your family history to be more than just a random collection of names, dates, and incidents.

Another approach you can take is to create a family tree. Make your family tree as visually interesting as you can. Choose some method of highlighting the most important information you have to relate—occupations, experiences, personalities, and so on. You could write brief paragraphs of explanation to elaborate on your most compelling research.

6. Publish your findings.   You may wish to prepare copies of your family history for the members of your family and for the people who helped you with your research. You also might consider submitting your findings to a local historical or genealogical society.

Sentence

Reviewing Sentence Composing Skills

In the preceding sentence composing exercises, you have studied how professional writers vary their sentence structures and use elaboration to add detail, substance, and style to their writing.

Skill 1: Inverting Subjects and Verbs (pages 113–115)

                                    v   s

Twenty feet below him was a pool, ringed, crystal clear, and motionless as glass.   **James V. Marshall, *Walkabout***

Skill 2: Using Compound Subjects and Verbs (pages 113–115)

                            s   s   v

Compound   Uncle John and the preacher were curled in the middle
Subjects   of the truck, resting on their elbows, and staring out the back triangle. **John Steinbeck, *The Grapes of Wrath***

                          s v   v

Compound   It ran wildly in circles, biting at its tail, spun in a frenzy,
Verbs   v

          and died.   **Ray Bradbury, "There Will Come Soft Rains"**

Skill 3: Elaborating on Simple Sentences (pages 141–143)

      s   v

Alfred peeked at their faces, black and sweating in the semicircle around him.   **Robert Lipsyte, *The Contender***

Skill 4: Splitting Subject and Verb (pages 141–143)

           s

A succession of loud and shrill screams, bursting suddenly from the

                        v

throat of the chained form, seemed to thrust me violently back.
      Edgar Allan Poe, "The Cask of Amontillado"

Skill 5: Varying Sentence Types (pages 171–173)

Simple   All the actors and singers of any importance stayed
Sentence   there.

Compound Sentence	All the actors and singers of any importance stayed there /, and / a number of the big manufacturers of the place lived there in winter.
Complex Sentence	All the actors and singers of any importance stayed there / when they were in the city.
Compound- Complex Sentence	All the actors and singers of any importance stayed there / when they were in the city /, and / a number of the big manufacturers of the place lived there in winter. **Willa Cather, "Paul's Case"**

Skill 6: Elaborating on Compound Sentences (pages 203–205)

My tongue was swollen and sore [from drinking scalding hot tea],

AND the tip of my nose ached [from frostbite].

Richard E. Byrd, *Alone*

Skill 7: Elaborating on Complex Sentences (pages 235–237)

[One evening in fall,] George ran [out of his house] [to the library]

WHERE he hadn't been [in years].

Bernard Malamud, "A Summer's Reading"

Skill 8: Elaborating on Compound-Complex Sentences (pages 267–269)

He told me all this later, BUT I've put it down here [with the idea]
[of exploding those first wild rumors] [about his antecedents],

WHICH weren't even faintly true.   **F. Scott Fitzgerald, *The Great Gatsby***

A. Imitating Sentences The sentences below, from John Steinbeck's novel *The Grapes of Wrath,* are a mix of the four sentence types. Using your own words, write a sentence that imitates the structure of each model sentence. Show elaboration where it has been added to the models.

1. To the red country and part of the gray country of Oklahoma, the last rains came gently, / and / they did not cut the scarred earth.

2. A gentle wind followed the rain clouds, driving them on northward, a wind / THAT softly clashed the drying corn.

3. A day went by, and the wind increased, steady, unbroken by gusts.

4. In the gray sky a red sun appeared, a dim red circle / THAT gave a little light, like dusk, / and / AS that day advanced, / the dusk slipped back toward darkness, / and / the wind cried and whimpered over the fallen corn.

5. Pa half filled the hole, / and / then he stood panting with the effort / WHILE Uncle John finished it.

6. The tenant men squatted down on their hams again to mark the dust with a stick, to figure, to wonder.

7. In the morning, the dust hung like fog, / and / the sun was as red as ripe new blood.

8. Men stood by their fences and looked at the ruined corn, drying fast now, only a little green showing through the film of dust.

9. Casy sat on the ground beside the fire, feeding in broken pieces of board, pushing the long boards in / AS the flame ate off their ends.

10. Inside, one man, the truck driver, sat on a stool and rested his elbows on the counter and looked over his coffee at the lean and lonely waitress.

11. WHEN Joad heard the truck get under way, gear climbing up to gear and the ground throbbing under the rubber beating of the tires, / he stopped and turned about and watched it / UNTIL it disappeared.

12. The nose, beaked and hard, stretched the skin so tightly / THAT the bridge showed white.

13. A large red drop of sun lingered on the horizon and then dripped over and was gone, / and / the sky was brilliant over the spot / WHERE it had gone, / and / a torn cloud, like a bloody rag, hung over the spot of its going.

14. On the right-hand side a line of wire fence strung out across the cotton field, / and / the dusty green cotton was the same on both sides, dusty and dry and dark green.

15. A little bit ahead he saw the high-domed shell of a land turtle, crawling slowly along through the dust, its legs working stiffly and jerkily.

16. WHEN the monster stops growing, / it dies.

17. The small unpainted house was mashed at one corner, / and / it had been pushed off its foundations / SO THAT it slumped at an angle, its blind front windows pointing at a spot of sky well above the horizon.

18. The evening light was on the fields, / and / the cotton plants threw long shadows on the ground, / and / the molting willow tree threw a long shadow.

19. The sun had lowered / UNTIL it came through the angled end windows now, / and / it flashed on the edges of the broken glass.

20. The cat lifted a paw and inspected it, flicked its claws out and in again experimentally, and licked its pads with a shell-pink tongue.

B. Identifying Sentence Types   For each sentence in Exercise A, identify its type: simple, compound, complex, or compound-complex.

Applications   Each of the following paragraphs is built on certain types of sentences. Notice how the sentence structures affect the writer's style and help convey the meaning of each paragraph. Then follow the instructions to write a paragraph of your own in the style of each model.

1. Simple and Compound Sentences

> A single knoll rises out of the plain in Oklahoma, north and west of the Wichita Range. For my people, the Kiowas, it is an old landmark, and they gave it the name Rainy Mountain. The hardest weather in the world is there. Winter brings blizzards, hot tornadic winds arise in the spring, and in summer the prairie is an anvil's edge. The grass turns brittle and brown, and it cracks beneath your feet. There are green belts along the rivers and creeks, linear groves of hickory and pecan, willow and witch hazel. At a distance in July or August the steaming foliage seems almost to writhe in fire. Great green and yellow grasshoppers are everywhere in the tall grass, popping up like corn to sting the flesh, and tortoises crawl about on the red earth, going nowhere in the plenty of time.   **N. Scott Momaday, *The Way to Rainy Mountain***

Write a paragraph describing an outdoor scene. For your first sentence, imitate the structure of the first sentence of the model. Then continue your description in the style of the model, using a variety of simple and compound sentences.

2. Compound and Compound-Complex Sentences

> I worked at the cafe all spring and in June I was called for temporary duty in the post office. My confidence soared; if I obtained an appointment as a regular clerk, I could spend at least five hours a day writing.
>
> I reported at the post office and was sworn in as a temporary clerk. I earned seventy cents an hour and I went to bed each night now with a full stomach for the first time in my life. When I worked nights, I wrote during the day; when I worked days, I wrote during the night.
>
> **Richard Wright, *American Hunger***

Write a paragraph describing a situation you have been in, such as the work experiences this author describes. For your first sentence, imitate the structure of the first sentence of the model. Then continue your description in the style of the model, using a variety of compound and compound-complex sentences.

3. Complex and Compound-Complex Sentences

> The snakeskin had unkeeled scales, so it belonged to a non-poisonous snake. It was roughly five feet long by the yardstick, but I'm not sure because it was very wrinkled and dry, and every time I tried to stretch it flat it broke. I ended up with seven or eight pieces of it all over the kitchen table in a fine film of dust. The point I want to make about the snakeskin is that, when I found it, it was whole and tied in a knot. Now there have been stories told, even by reputable scientists, of snakes that have deliberately tied themselves in a knot to prevent larger snakes from trying to swallow them—but I couldn't imagine any way that throwing itself into a half hitch would help a snake trying to escape its skin.
>
> **Annie Dillard, *Pilgrim at Tinker Creek***

Write a paragraph describing a plant, animal, or object. For your first sentence, imitate the structure of the first sentence of the model. Then continue your description in the style of the model, using a variety of complex and compound-complex sentences.

Sketchbook

Bali

Tulamben

Writing postcards can be chal-
lenging because you must express your thoughts
in a very limited space. Send a postcard home
from some exotic location. It might be someplace far away ("Greetings from Tahiti;" "Greetings from Australia") or from someplace
close to home ("Greetings
from the laundromat;"
"Greetings from the parking
lot"). Draw a box the size
of a postcard and write
within the box. Try to say
something as interesting
and meaningful as you
can in that space.

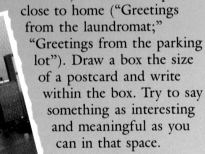

Additional Sketches

What advice do you have for a teenager moving into your
community?

Compare and contrast the teaching styles of two teachers you
have had.

Writing for Assessment

Guided Assignment

WRITTEN EXAMS

Sooner or later, you may have to take a writing proficiency test as part of your high-school education. Proficiency tests measure how skillfully you can handle a specific writing task in a limited amount of time. The writing and thinking strategies you have studied in the preceding workshops can help you write assessment essays that are clear, logical, and to the point. This workshop will help you think constructively about writing for assessment and give you an opportunity to practice your writing skills.

Written Exams

JA

SUNDAY | MON

When you participate in a writing assessment, you are expected to show your skill in organizing and presenting ideas in response to a specific prompt. The prompt contains the clues that tell you how to proceed.

The writing prompts that follow are like ones you may find on proficiency tests. As you read these prompts, think of the strategies you could use to respond to them.

Write a letter describing your favorite meal to a teenage student in a foreign country. Assume that the student is not familiar with the American diet. In your description, use vivid sensory details so that the student can easily picture and "taste" your meal.

13

20

20/345

The Student Council in your school has proposed a new grading system called "grade-weighting." In this system, students who take more difficult classes earn more credit for those classes than students in "regular" courses. Write an article for the school newspaper explaining the advantages and disadvantages of this system.

27

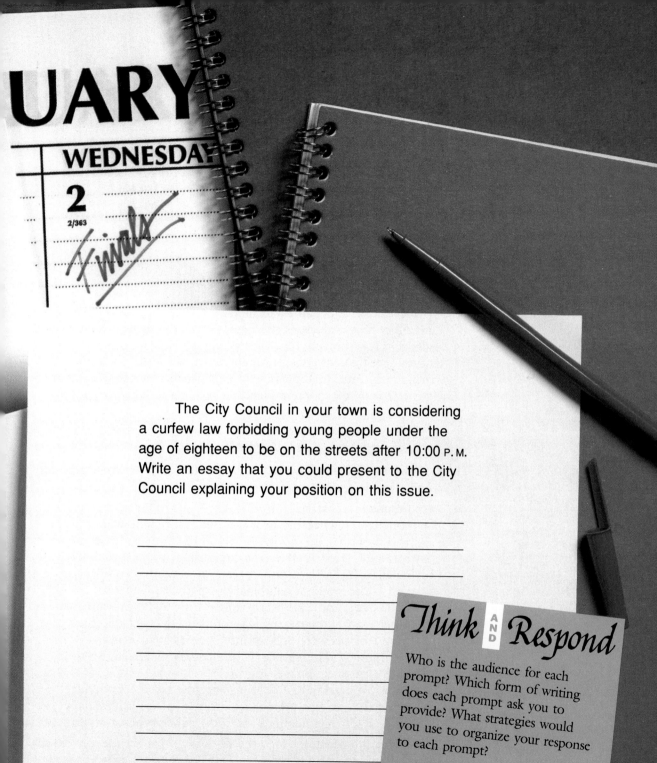

The City Council in your town is considering a curfew law forbidding young people under the age of eighteen to be on the streets after 10:00 P.M. Write an essay that you could present to the City Council explaining your position on this issue.

Think AND *Respond*

Who is the audience for each prompt? Which form of writing does each prompt ask you to provide? What strategies would you use to organize your response to each prompt?

INVITATION
— TO —
Write

To get into an advanced writing class, you need to prove that you will be able to meet its challenges. The teacher will assess your abilities by evaluating an essay you write weighing the advantages and disadvantages of working after school.

Writing assessments can be intimidating, but they don't have to be. Remember that evaluators, teachers, and administrators give writing assessment tests because they are looking for evidence of your personal writing development and your ability to analyze and think through a writing task. You can improve your performance by carefully examining the writing prompt and planning your response accordingly.

PREWRITE AND EXPLORE

HANDBOOKS

FOR HELP & PRACTICE

Writing Activity,
pp. 333–335
Shaping Writing,
pp. 361–369
Thesis Statements,
p. 381
Types of
Elaboration,
pp. 397–399
Problem Solving,
pp. 487–489

1. Read the prompt carefully.   Proficiency test prompts generally require you to make several basic writing decisions.

- **Purpose**   Why are you writing? What are you trying to accomplish? Generally, in a writing assessment your purpose will be either to *inform* or *persuade* your audience.
- **Strategy**   How will you accomplish your purpose? Do you need to use description, narration, analysis, comparison and contrast, or a combination of these?
- **Audience**   For whom are you writing? The prompt may specify an audience, which could be one person, such as a friend or teacher, or a group, such as your classmates or community. The choice of audience will affect the tone and level of language you use.
- **Form**   What kind of writing are you asked to provide? Does the prompt ask for an essay, a letter, a newspaper article, a set of guidelines, or some other type of writing?

2. Analyze the prompt.   Find the key words that are the cues to the specific thinking and writing skills you need to use. Key words include *analyze, describe, discuss, explain, interpret,* and *summarize.*

Think about the types of information you need to present and how you will need to organize your ideas. Your strategy will depend on the type of response you are writing.

Strategies

- **Descriptive response** If you are asked to *describe, show, share,* or *tell about* your subject, identify the subject's major characteristics. Then gather specific sensory details to describe these characteristics. Use a logical method of presenting your description, such as top to bottom, left to right, near to far, or most important to least important.

- **Informative exposition response** If you are asked to *analyze, explain, interpret, inform, give steps, summarize,* or *discuss* your subject, break down the subject into its parts by identifying steps in a sequence, causes and effects, or problems and solutions. Then gather details to explain each step or feature of the subject. Arrange the steps of a sequence in chronological order, or use a method of organization that presents the relationship among the features of your subject.

- **Comparison and contrast response** If you are asked to *compare, evaluate, classify, examine similarities and differences,* or *examine advantages and disadvantages,* list the qualities that can be compared or contrasted. Examine the similarities and differences, advantages and disadvantages, or pros and cons of your subject. Use the block method, addressing all the characteristics of one item and then all the characteristics of the other, or the point-by-point method, addressing each characteristic of both items one by one, to organize your response.

- **Persuasive response** If you are asked to *persuade, convince, give reasons,* or *choose a position,* decide on your position and gather facts, reasons, and opinions to support it clearly and convincingly. If the issue has two sides, discuss both sides and then give solid reasons to support your choice. Keep your audience in mind, choosing reasons and arguments that appeal directly to that audience.

PROBLEM SOLVING

What kind of information should I present? How should I organize it?

3. Plan your response. Some students find it helpful to jot down words and phrases quickly without worrying about logical order. Then they organize their notes by numbering them. Others like to make notes in a modified outline form.

Nathan planned his answer to the prompt on page 318 by first making his basic writing decisions. Then, he organized information into two lists, one titled *Advantages* and the other titled *Disadvantages*. Finally, he numbered the items in his lists to show their order of importance.

ONE STUDENT'S PROCESS

Purpose: inform
Strategy: compare and contrast
Audience: teacher of advanced writing class
Format: essay

Advantages:		Disadvantages:	
more money to spend	1	less time for personal	
experience	4	relationships	3
independence	2	less time for homework,	
learn to budget time	3	grades may slip	1
		fatigue	2

4. Develop a thesis statement. A thesis statement that contains your main idea and shows that you understand the prompt can keep you on track as you write. Nathan wrote this thesis statement.

ONE STUDENT'S PROCESS

Although students who work after school can encounter problems balancing school, work, family, and recreation, the advantages of having an after-school job outweigh the disadvantages.

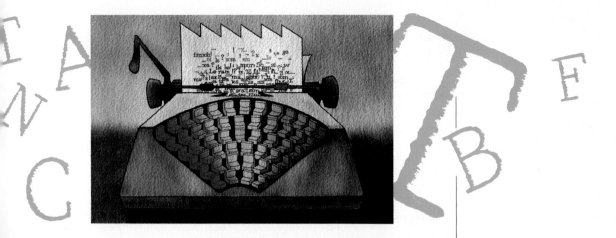

DRAFT AND DISCOVER

1. Organize your draft. Compose your response in three parts: introduction, body, and conclusion. The introduction should include your thesis statement and present a brief preview of the points you will be covering. The body should contain a separate paragraph for each point you make, and each point should be supported with appropriate facts, details, and opinions. Include transition words and phrases. The conclusion may restate your thesis statement using different words, summarize the main points, draw a conclusion about the importance of the points you made, make a recommendation, or state an opinion. Aim for a strong, solid conclusion.

2. Write to your audience. Choose a tone and style that are appropriate for your audience. However, some assessments are designed to measure how well you use standard, formal English. Avoid informal language.

3. Reread your draft. Once you have completed your draft, take time to look it over and ask yourself questions such as the following.

Review Your Writing

- Does my writing respond directly to the prompt?
- Have I considered the needs of my audience?
- Have I written my response in the proper form?
- Have I organized my response effectively?

HANDBOOKS
FOR HELP & PRACTICE

Introductions/
Conclusions,
pp. 378–390
Formal/Informal
English,
p. 449
Writing for Essay
Tests,
pp. 530–531

Writing
—TIP—

As you write your response, ideas about one section of your essay may occur to you as you are writing another section. Take notes as you write so that you won't forget the ideas.

Written Exams   **321**

Written Exams   **321**

HANDBOOKS
FOR HELP & PRACTICE

Unity/Coherence,
pp. 401–414
Art of Revision,
pp. 416–421

Grammar
—**TIP**—

Evaluators look for clear, correct sentences. Although you write quickly during an assessment, make sure all your sentences express complete thoughts and contain both a subject and a verb.

1. Evaluate your response. You won't have much time to change what you have written, but you should take the time to reread the prompt and be sure you have understood and responded to the key words. Also review your prewriting notes to make sure you included all your key points. You can strike out passages you don't need or insert additional words or lines.

As you review your writing, keep in mind that you are writing specifically for evaluation and that your evaluators will be looking for the following characteristics.

Standards for Evaluation

An effective test response . . .

- contains an engaging introduction, a well-elaborated and richly detailed body, and a strong conclusion.
- uses the appropriate strategy or strategies (such as description, narration, analysis, comparison and contrast, persuasion, or a combination) to achieve its purpose.
- uses a tone and level of language appropriate to its audience.
- uses transitions to link one idea to the next.

Nathan had only a little time to review his response. Here are the revisions he made to one section of his essay.

ONE STUDENT'S PROCESS

Earning
⌃Extra income is probably the best reason to work af-

ter school⌒and the reason most teen-agers do it. Ten

hours a week at minimum wage produces about $70 of

extra income every two weeks, money that you can

                                                   to
spend on music, movies, clothes, or⌃save for college.

2. Proofread your work. Look for errors in spelling, grammar, and punctuation, and correct these neatly.

NAME <u>Nathan Klein</u>   GRADE <u>11</u>

In the 1990s it is expensive to be a teenager, and as a result many teenagers now work after school to earn weekend money or to earn money for college. Although students who work after school may have problems balancing school, work, family, and recreation, the advantages of having an after-school job outweigh the disadvantages.

There
Their are some good reasons to take a job after school. Earning extra income is probably the best reason to work after school. Ten hours a week at minimum wage produces
can produce
almost $100
about $70 of extra income every two weeks, money that you
to
can spend on music, movies, or clothes, or to save for college. Having extra income produces other benefits--most teenagers begin to feel more independent because they are more self-supporting, and they often feel trusted and respected for doing a job right. In addition, working ten to fifteen hours a week teaches high school students how to budget time. They have to do homework at a certain time because they know that later they'll go to work and after that they'll be too tired to study. Working also teaches students to consider their priorities and to cut out some time-consuming activities like talking on the phone or just hanging out. Finally, an after-school job provides much-
for
needed experience to high school students, who often learn to get along with a boss and co-workers and perhaps even

Contains an engaging introduction

Provides a clear thesis statement in the introduction

Contains a well-elaborated and richly detailed body

acquire some useful and transferable job skills, like operating a cash register.

Of course, there are disadvantages to working after school. Working students have less free time and are forced to plan their days carefully; this planning usually results in giving up some activities in order to make time for homework. Sometimes the extra money is so attractive that student workers end up working more hours than they should--and then they skip or skimp on homework, causing their grades to suffer and putting them in academic jeopardy. Working divides the energies of students; it's hard to juggle the demands of teachers who want students' full attention, the employer who is paying for the student's time, friends still want to have fun, and family time is also necessary. Juggling all these people and activities can cause stress, fatigue, burn-out, and sometimes illness. Being stretched too thin in personal relationships is especially difficult for a young person, and friendships and family relationships can suffer.

Working after school, however, can be liberating since it provides money, independence, and experience. But the student who doesn't establish priorities and think about what he or she is doing can work too many hours or plan poorly, and in the long run damage an academic record, friendships, and family relationships. Working can be a part of a teenager's life, but it should never be the most important part.

Uses an appropriate strategy—comparison and contrast

Uses a tone and level of language appropriate to its audience

Contains a strong conclusion

You've seen how one student responded to a prompt. Now it's your turn. Write a response to one of the prompts that follows or to a prompt your teacher gives you.

Prompt 1 Write a journal entry describing your idea of the perfect room. Draw a picture in words that includes details about the room's layout, furniture, and accessories.

• **Prompt 2** The School Board is hiring a new teacher for your school. Explain in a letter to the School Board what makes an excellent teacher. Use specific examples from your experiences and memories to show board members the kind of teacher you believe they should employ.

• **Prompt 3** Assume that you believe your school needs more parking spaces for students. Draft a petition in which you try to persuade your principal to see your point of view and act on it.

• **Prompt 4** Imagine that you could travel back to the 1700's and meet with a group of colonists disgruntled about British rule. Write a list of instructions they could follow to break away from Britain and form a new nation across the sea.

• **Prompt 5** Your community is trying to decide between building a new fire station or a library on a plot of vacant land. Write an editorial for your community newspaper in which you discuss the two options; express your preference for one of them, and convince your readers that yours is the better choice.

On the Lightside

THE SUFFIX -O

For years you have studied suffixes and prefixes and how they are used to build words. Yet you probably have missed a versatile, if unofficial, suffix. Add -o to many root words and bingo! You have a new word.

When you add -o to ordinary nouns and adjectives, you get *weirdo, cheapo, neato, nutso,* and *wacko.* Match -o with clipped forms, and you get *combo* and *ammo.* The British are fond of *righto,* and *cheerio.* The Australians have contributed *bucko, kiddo,* and *boy-o.*

One of the most recent inventions is *blendo. Blendo* is a term that has been used by architects to describe a style that takes design features from adjacent buildings and blends them together. That way a new building can fit in with its neighbors, regardless of how diverse in appearance they might be. Interior designers have used the term to

describe a style made up of a radical blend of differing materials, colors, textures, and forms.

What the -o contributes to *blendo* and other words is not so much a new meaning as a new flair. Unlike other suffixes, -o is not really a functional addition, and the words it forms seldom rise above slang usage. But put an -o on the end of a word and whammo! It gains a distinctive ring.

Sentence

Author's Expansions

You have used your sentence composing skills to complete sentences begun by professional writers. Now look at the sentences they wrote. What qualities do your sentences share? What differences do you see? Whose sentences do you prefer?

Elaborating on Sentences, Exercise A, pages 79–80

1. She looked up every few minutes, sitting in the shadow of the wagon, facing the direction in which he had gone.
2. The snake, tightly coiled, vibrated his rattles in a prolonged hiss.
3. On weekends his Rolls-Royce became an omnibus, bearing parties to and from the city between nine in the morning and long past midnight, while his station wagon scampered like a brisk yellow bug to meet all trains.
4. She just stood there a long time, looking at me, trying to figure me out, the way mothers are always doing, but should know better.

Elaborating on Sentences, Exercise C, page 81

1. Arriving at the used-up haystack, the boy leaned against the barbed wire fence.
2. Slowly and conscientiously, he ate all of the wedge-shaped strips of fish.
3. With one cat in her lap and another licking an oatmeal bowl on the table, Loma sat drinking coffee and reading a book of theater plays.
4. Atticus switched on the ceiling light in the livingroom and found us there, frozen still.
5. Aunt Pearl got busy quieting them down, feeding them breakfast, helping Charlene make the lunch sandwiches.

Elaborating on Simple Sentences, Exercise B, page 142

1. Her big brown eyes, like berries that had ripened, were warmer, softer.
2. The ashes, so light and dry, smelled raw, rain-wet.
3. For a minute or two, the hand, with its writhing fingers, protruded out of the floor.
4. Down below, in the garden beds, the red and yellow tulips, heavy with flowers, seemed to lean upon the dusk.

Elaborating on Compound Sentences, Exercise A, pages 203–204

1. Dvoira, the dark-uddered cow, was out in the field behind the hut, and Yakov went out to her.
2. The sun was gone behind the westward mountain now, but still it glowed brilliantly on the oaks and on the grassy flat.
3. The past and the future are cut off; only the present remains.
4. Wanting to make some kind of noise in the silence, she coughed, and the small sound moved dustily into the darkness of the house.

Elaborating on Compound Sentences, Exercise C, page 205

1. Her hands trembled among the hooks and eyes, and her eyes had a feverish look, and her hair swirled crisp and crackling under the comb.
2. His hands relaxed; the fork fell to the ground; his head lowered.
3. The lights dazzled his eyes, and then a truck crashed into his belly, and a baseball bat blasted the side of his head.
4. The morning of June 27th was clear and sunny, with the fresh warmth of a summer day; the flowers were blooming profusely, and the grass was richly green.
5. His eyes were entranced, and he could sense the wary, watchful evil outside the brush house; he could feel the dark creeping things waiting for him to go out into the night.

Elaborating on Complex Sentences, Exercise C, page 237

1. In the dark little attic room, Henry Crowfoot turned over and wearily punched the pillow, which was hot and lumpy and smelled of old foam rubber.
2. I used to have a cat, an old fighting tom, who would jump through the open window by my bed in the middle of the night and land on my chest.
3. Upon the half decayed veranda of a small frame house that stood near the edge of a ravine near the town of Winesburg, Ohio, a fat little old man walked nervously up and down.
4. If our father was of royal blood and we were royal children, our father was certainly the only person in the world who knew it.

Eventually we'd hear a rumble on the tracks and then see a searching eye of light bearing down on us. Quickly we'd leap to our feet and get as close to the tracks as we dared, plugging our ears as the train ground to a stop in front of us, its metallic clamor deafening, its cars looming in the night like visitors from another world. As we stood there, we could see people moving back and forth inside the lighted windows. If we were outside a Pullman car, we might catch a glimpse of someone seated next to the window, staring wordlessly back at us. I wondered why everyone wasn't asleep. A frowsy-haired woman with a brown felt hat pinned to her greying curls looked like someone I might know, but didn't. Two young boys, jumping on their seats and pounding silently on the glass, could have been the Evans kids down the street, but weren't. They were strangers, separated from us not only by thick glass but by chance, being whisked away from their old lives to new ones. I felt the pull of the future, of adventure waiting for them and someday for me.

Elaborating on Compound-Complex Sentences, Exercise C, pages 268–269

1. The music box was in a corner where it had always been, and touching it gently, she brought from it one remote, faintly sweet, jangle of a note.

2. The old woman watched him with her arms folded across her chest as if she were the owner of the sun, and the daughter watched, her head thrust forward and her fat helpless hands hanging at the wrists.

3. Earlier, when Barry had left the house to go to the game, an overnight frost had still been thick on the roads, but the brisk April sun had soon dispersed it, and now he could feel the spring warmth on his back through the thick tweed of his coat.

4. In rain or snow, or through fog, or in brilliant, icy weather, the man would keep to the chimney sweep's footholds across the roof until he reached the skylight, and then he would pry up the window and drop, soft as a cat, onto the trunk below.

Writing Handbook

Sketchbook

AM 11.30

11:30 A.M.
a jar of strawberry jam
a football field

What could these three unrelated items possibly have in common? You could find out by telling a story about them. Have a classmate name a time of day, a common object, and a location. Then tell a story that starts at the time specified and involves the object and the location named.

Additional Sketches

Write everything you remember happening one month ago today.

Describe something you saw when you were feeling a strong emotion. Don't describe what *caused* the emotion; concentrate instead on the object, scene, or person you happened to be observing. Notice how your feelings affect your description.

Analyzing the Writing Activity

Writing is basically thinking on paper. One very useful critical thinking strategy is **analysis**—breaking something down into its parts and then looking at the parts individually. Analysis is useful at every stage of the writing process but especially during prewriting, when you break the task into its parts, or variables. There are six writing variables: topic, form, purpose, personal goals, audience, and voice. You will need to address each variable at some point each time you write, but there are no strict rules about when to do so. Furthermore, you can change your mind about any variable at any point in the process.

Writing Variable	Definition	Examples
Topic	what you will write about	history of magic, personal experience, Vietnam War
Form	the shape of a piece of writing	personal narrative, expository essay, poem, letter
Purpose	reason for writing	to express yourself, to inform, to describe, to analyze, to persuade, to entertain
Personal Goals	specific goals that you want the writing to accomplish	to explore an interest, to communicate an idea, to create enthusiasm for a subject
Audience	the people for whom you are writing	your classmates, your relatives, your boss, readers of a magazine or newspaper
Voice	the attitude you take toward your topic	formal, informal, objective, subjective, comic, ironic, angry

RESPONDING TO THE WRITING ACTIVITY

Different writing activities involve different responses to the writing variables.

Writing on Your Own When you write on your own, you are free to choose all your writing variables, and you can make these choices at any time. As a result, writing on your own can be great fun. However, this freedom can also be a source of confusion. Where do you begin? When writing on your own, you usually begin with a single idea—a character, a setting, a mood, or a purpose—and then build on it. Simply let yourself go. Experiment with different combinations of the writing variables the way a chemist might experiment with different combinations of chemicals. Write and think freely. You can change your mind as much and as often as you like!

Doing Assigned Writing When you are given a writing assignment in school, some of the major writing decisions may already be made for you. For example, you may be assigned a topic—write about Reconstruction after the Civil War—or a form—write a sonnet. Ask yourself which variables have already been determined for you and which ones you need to determine on your own.

Suppose that your biology teacher writes the following writing assignment on the chalkboard.

> Choose one of the species mentioned in Chapter 9 of your textbook ("Invertebrates"). Do some research in the library, and write a report on this species. Give a complete taxonomic description of this invertebrate, a description of its habitat, and a brief discussion of its behavior.

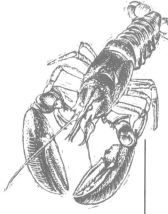

A Pantry Ballet (for Jacques Offenbach), sculpture by Joseph Cornell

The Nelson-Atkins Museum of Art, Kansas City, Missouri (Gift of the Friends of Art) F77–34

334 Writing Handbook

First, make sure that you understand all the components of the assignment. If you don't know what is meant by "invertebrates," "a complete taxonomic description," or "habitat," consult your biology textbook or a dictionary. You will also have to find out what the teacher means by *behavior*—eating habits, mating, aggression, territoriality, nesting, or all of these behaviors.

After you understand the assignment, assess the writing variables that are already given. In this case, your general **topic** is assigned—an invertebrate—but you need to limit that topic to focus on a particular invertebrate, such as the American lobster or the banana slug. The **form** of the paper is a research report with notes and references. The **purpose** of the paper will be to inform, and the **audience** will be your teacher. You are free to decide what personal goals you can fulfill with the writing and whether you want to assume the voice of a particular speaker. For example, do you want the paper to sound objective and matter-of-fact, or do you want it to sound like an enthusiastic celebration of some life form?

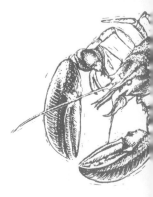

ANALYZING THE WRITING COMMUNITY

One of the most useful aspects of writing is that it helps you explore yourself. As you put your ideas on paper, your purpose and personal goals begin to take shape. When you are writing for yourself, you are an audience of one. You can experiment as much as you like with language, voice, and form until you find an approach that best expresses your goals.

WRITER TO WRITER

One of the purposes of writing is not simply to state a fact or point or [to] write on a piece of literature, but to give the reader a glimpse into the author's personality.

**Debbie Henderson, student
De Soto, Texas**

However, much of what you write must meet the expectations of a larger audience in school, in the workplace, or in the society in which you live. Always keep in mind, when making decisions concerning variables, that your primary purpose in writing is to help your readers understand your ideas. To do this, you must have a clear idea of what your audience expects.

Academic Classes   In writing for any class, ask yourself the following questions:

1. For this assignment, am I writing for myself, for other students, for teachers, or for outside judges?
2. Are there specific formats that are commonly used or required?
3. What voice (for example, objective and authoritative or emotional and personal) is expected in this discipline?
4. What variety of language (for example, formal or informal; scientific or conversational) is required or most appropriate for this assignment or this discipline?

Science and history classes, which emphasize facts, often require writing that informs or analyzes. Your chemistry teacher might ask you to explain in a lab report what happens when sulfur and oxygen are mixed. Your teacher would expect you to assume an objective voice and report your observations in accurate, scientific language. However, you would most likely use a completely different voice if you were describing the experiment (which creates quite an unpleasant smell) in a note to a friend.

Your history teacher might ask you to describe and analyze the factors that led to United States involvement in Vietnam and then to prepare a presentation for the class, taking a position on the subject.

Your purpose (to persuade) and your audience (other students) have been defined for you, but you still can choose how you will present your information. You might interview a Vietnam veteran or write a formal, persuasive essay based on newspaper or magazine articles from that time. Your voice might be that of an objective reporter or that of an angry protester. Any position, however, would have to be supported by facts that other readers and writers would find convincing.

Literature classes also require extensive analytical and persuasive writing. A teacher might ask you to write an essay analyzing a character in a story—for example, the lawyer in Herman Melville's "Bartleby the Scrivener." The purpose, audience, and form are all defined for you. You would assume an objective voice and base any comments about the character only upon what is actually in the story. Now suppose the teacher asks you instead to write an essay telling what you think might happen to a character after the end of the story. Because the teacher is asking you to create some events based on your opinion, the voice you use in the essay can be entirely of your own choosing.

In general, literature classes provide you with a broader range of variables to choose among during the course of a year than other classes. Forms can vary from the essay to verse. Formal, analytical writing is balanced by creative writing and personal response journals.

However, most classes do provide opportunities for various types of writing. Students engaged in long-term biology experiments for a science fair competition might use the journal form to record impressions and data. Their audience would be themselves; their language might be informal; their voices would be their own—those of students discovering something. Later, they would assume the voices of scientific researchers and convert their accumulated data into a formal essay for the judges. Or they could write a poem, for themselves, expressing an emotional reaction to a scientific observation.

Beyond School   The writing you do in school is only the beginning of writing activities that you will continue throughout your adult life.

Many people enjoy writing on their own and never stop keeping journals, composing poems, and writing letters. Some people—and you may be one of them—choose professional writing careers, devoting their lives to publishing poems, stories, novels, plays, essays, or news articles.

Even if you aren't a professional writer, you still need to develop writing skills that your job might require. Businesspeople often get assignments from their supervisors to produce memos, press releases, or promotional copy. Sales managers should be able to report changes in their marketing strategies in reaction to buying trends. Their audience might be corporate executives; their purpose might be to persuade. Police officers must be able to file accident reports in language that lawyers, victims, defendants, and juries can clearly interpret. These are the adult equivalents of assigned writing. Therefore, these professionals must analyze requirements and expectations the same way you do for class assignments.

You will also discover that writing for tests doesn't end with school. Essay questions often appear as part of job applications or entrance examinations, and many jobs require essay examinations for promotion.

Writing
—**TIP**—

Writing on your own, for your own purposes, on a regular basis, is the best way to become a competent writer.

Practice Your Skills

A. Think of a time when you did some writing on your own (not for school). Freewrite for a while about your experience. What prompted you to write? What was your writing experience like? Which of the writing variables did you think consciously about? What was your final product like? If you feel comfortable doing so, share your account of your writing experience with your classmates.

B. Consider the following writing prompts. What are the key words in them? Which writing variables are addressed by each prompt? For each variable, what information do you have? Which variables are *not* addressed and would have to be determined by you? What questions would you have to ask to clarify the prompt?

- Literary Contest, Geraldine Ferraro High School: Award of a $250.00 book certificate and a $1,000.00 college or vocational-school tuition payment for the best short story by a high-school student. Stories must be original. They must be typed, double-spaced, and no longer than 2,000 words. Entries due July 4.
- Oral Report (be prepared to give it next Wednesday): Brief biography of a figure of pre-Civil War era (Dred Scott, Stephen Douglas, Harriet Tubman, Henry Clay, etc.). Can be presented in alternate form (skit, story, poem, etc.). Emphasize person's character and accomplishments. Time limit for presentations: ten minutes.

C. Imagine that you are taking a writing proficiency test as part of a test for receiving a high-school diploma. The following writing prompt appears on the test.

> Describe a typical day at your high school to a teenage student from a foreign country. In your letter to the student, describe activities, courses, and features of a typical day.

Sit down and write an answer to the question, in a testlike situation. Allow yourself one small piece of scrap paper and twenty-five minutes in which to write your complete answer.

D. Imagine that you are the manager of a fast-food restaurant. You must submit a monthly report evaluating your employees, summarizing any problems that you have observed and suggesting practical solutions. Who is your audience? What is your purpose? What form will you use? What voice and language are appropriate? Now write the report, making up "facts" to fulfill your purpose.

Finding a Writing Topic

Have you ever read a great book or seen a great movie and thought, "I wonder where the writer got that idea?" Fascinating ideas are not all that common, but they are not exceedingly rare either. By learning a few techniques to stimulate creative thinking, you can regularly come up with ideas for writing that will capture other people's imaginations.

PERSONAL TECHNIQUES

To generate ideas—to retrieve and assemble information from inside you and around you—you may need only to focus your attention. Techniques for focusing attention on the world around you and the one inside your head include recalling and reflecting, observing, imaging, and using knowledge inventories and trigger words.

Recalling and Reflecting According to the ancient Greeks, Mnemosyne, the goddess of memory, was the mother of all the arts. The ancient Greeks knew, as we know today, that an individual's unique impressions of the world are stored in memory. You can get the most out of your memories and turn them into writing ideas by recalling and reflecting. When you **recall,** you bring to mind the sights, sounds, smells, tastes, and feelings of an earlier time. When you **reflect** on something you have recalled, you ask yourself questions about its significance. You associate your recollections with present-day experiences and observations to generate new ideas.

"Hank You're reflecting!"

Finding a
Writing Topic   **339**

Reflecting on something that you have recalled revives a memory and helps generate writing ideas. For example, suppose you recall a time when you were with your brother at a circus. As you focus on your memory, details come to mind—the crackling of the tent canvas far above you, the boom of the ringmaster's voice, and the sound of the organ music. After the recollection comes reflection. You wonder if the circus still creates magic for children the way it did for you and your brother. You then may decide to write an essay comparing a world where families can sit in a living room and watch performers on television with a world where families go out to watch a circus live.

Observing The technique of **observing** involves paying close attention to your environment. Professional writers realize how important it is to keep all their senses alert at all times. A screenwriter entering a restaurant, for example, might automatically register the scene for future use in a film. After observing the overall picture, the writer zeros in on numerous details. The following are some mental notes that the screenwriter might make.

General Scene	crowd, noise, delicious smells, waiters rushing around, muffled sounds from kitchen
Main Parts	helpful waiters, indecisive customers, chattering voices, clattering dishes
Details	harried servers, clamoring customers, sweating brows, a spilled bowl of soup, calls of "Waiter!"
Writing Idea	Opening scene—harried waiter, customer yells at him. Waiter drops to his knees and starts doing mock bows to customer. Manager comes rushing over. Waiter hands towel to manager, takes off bow tie, drops it in customer's soup, and says, "I quit!" Close-up of bow tie floating in pea soup; dissolve to waiter, in bathing suit, floating in ocean under Caribbean skies.

For your own writing, there are certain strategies you can use to become an acute observer. Think about the distinguishing features of your subject. List these characteristics under headings for each of the five senses. Ask yourself how the subject looks, smells, sounds, tastes, or feels. Then observe such details as your subject's composition, location, condition, function, importance, duration, and value.

Imaging When you think about events in your past or daydream about the future, you probably call up images in your mind. Certainly, such images appear in the dreams you have when you are asleep. One valuable way of gathering ideas for writing is to make a conscious attempt to call up mental images. This technique is called **imaging,** or visualizing. It is often used by artists attempting to draw things that are not directly in front of them; it is also used by writers attempting to describe such things in words.

Imaging can be a useful tool for coming up with ideas about things you have not actually experienced. For example, if you were writing a science-fiction story set in a school of the future, you might work on the setting of the story by visualizing. You could begin by picturing in your mind a present-day school. Close your eyes, think about the school, and imagine walking through it, looking into rooms, heading up and down corridors. Then start adding far-out, futuristic elements to your mental image. Eventually, you will have a picture in your mind of a school of the future.

The technique of visualizing is a valuable tool of the imagination. However, the imagination does not depend entirely on visualization. You can, for example, imagine things being different from what they are simply by asking "What if" questions. (See "Questioning," pages 342–343 in this handbook.)

Conducting a Knowledge Inventory When considering a writing idea, you'll probably find it helpful to call to mind what you already know. Chances are you will be astonished at how much you already know about your subject. One way to explore your own knowledge of a subject is to complete a **knowledge inventory.** This is simply a list of everything you can think of that you know about a topic. Use questions like the following to jog your memory:

- What do I already know about _____?
- What are the major parts or divisions of _____? What are the details of each part?
- Have I ever seen or experienced _____? What did it look or feel like? What impression did it leave?
- What unusual things have I noticed about _____?
- How do I feel about _____? Why?
- How do my friends and other people seem to feel about _____?
- Have I read about _____? In what books or magazines? What did I learn?
- Have I studied _____ in school? What did I learn there?
- What unanswered questions do I have about _____? What do I want to find out more about?

COMPUTER TIP

A word processor can be especially helpful for conducting a knowledge inventory. Type your questions first. Then you can easily move from one question to another as answers occur to you.

Using Trigger Words Words that stimulate the mind to produce images are called **trigger words.** You can find trigger words by flipping through a dictionary or browsing through textbooks, encyclopedias, or magazines. Words like the following trigger stimulating images or concepts and might serve as springboards to writing ideas.

acrobat	ribbon	meadowlark	hero
confection	taxicab	outback	lieutenant
doorbell	vulture	quintuplet	nurse
frangipani	banquet	saddlebag	patio
insect	corncob	tea	revenge
marble	dragon	bluefish	semaphore
octave	gecko	dewdrop	urchin
palisade	jukebox	fiddle	zinnia

There are two ways of making profitable use of trigger words. The first is by thinking of one or more uncommon meanings of a word. The word *hero,* for example, is used in certain parts of the country to name a supersandwich (which may require an appetite of heroic proportions). Another technique is to think of certain words as metaphors. A vulture, for example, is a bird that feeds on the flesh of dead animals. Metaphorically, though, *vulture* could refer to anyone who profits from the misfortunes of others.

W R I T E R   T O   W R I T E R

Every good paper starts with one idea which is expanded upon.

Anthony Figliolini, student
Watertown, Massachusetts

GENERAL TECHNIQUES

Questioning You know how important it is to use your senses to observe the world around you. You also know that your mind uses stored knowledge in generating ideas. How do you start the process of using stored knowledge to form new ideas?

Writer Arthur Koestler described creative questioning as a learning process in which the same person is both teacher and pupil. He meant that the creative writer first asks questions about what he or she observes and then answers those questions. To stimulate creative thinking, try asking unusual, even silly questions that begin with the words "What if."

You could ask, "What if animals resented the stereotypes we apply to them?" This might lead you to ask, "What if a cat said, 'I'm not really selfish and arrogant, and I really try to be sensitive to human needs'?" Such questions might lead you to a unique approach to the issue of stereotyping.

Questioning is also very helpful in developing and elaborating ideas. Specific techniques are discussed in "Approaches to Elaboration," pages 391–396.

Browsing Casually leafing through reading materials—**browsing**—often stimulates ideas. Suppose, for example, that you want to write a short story that involves a hospital situation. You might browse through a medical dictionary or a self-help health book at your library. One of the illnesses described in the resource might interest you. You might decide to write about a character who has this illness and about the way he or she gets through it and returns to health with the help of the medical staff at the hospital.

You can even browse aimlessly through the library or through bookstore shelves. You might find a source of topics in reference books or periodicals or in books about general subject areas that interest you.

Clip Files Sometimes when you browse through a magazine or a newspaper, you may come across an article you want to keep for future reference. If the magazine or newspaper belongs to you, you might want to clip it out and file it in an ideas file. If the source is not yours, photocopy the material. Once you've gathered a number of clippings, or **clips,** you may decide to arrange them by subject.

Remember to write the name, date, page number, and other information on the clip. That way, you can quote from the article and give credit to the source. In addition, you may not use the article for a long time. You'll want to know how old the information is when you do use it.

Gleaning Pay attention to what is going on around you, and you may find ideas in unexpected places. Writers develop antennae for events or subjects of interest being discussed around them. You don't want to "eavesdrop"; privacy is an important component of civilized life. However, you can overhear interesting conversations when they take place in public places, as in restaurants or at parties.

Finding a
Writing Topic   **343**

When you **glean,** you gather bits and pieces of information that you can use later in your writing. Gleaning can be done at any time and in any place. Like a bird collecting leaves and shreds of cloth, you collect ideas, first examining them for strength and quality, and then carefully storing them away for future use.

WRITING TECHNIQUES

Several writing techniques can help you discover ideas or expand on ones you gather through the methods just discussed. These techniques include freewriting, looping, listing, and using a journal.

Freewriting and Looping When you **freewrite,** you write about a general topic for a given period of time without paying attention to grammar, mechanics, or logic. Do not lift your pen from the paper; make yourself continue writing even if you wander away from the subject. When you are stumped for an idea, you can use freewriting to loosen up and to discover some new subjects or new angles on a subject that you already know you want to write about. The following is an example of one student's freewriting.

The Nantucket Treatment Center for people pathologically incapable of selecting an even halfway good movie at a video store.

UELEY

> one of those master video stores opened up a few blocks from our house.—Its amazing in there!—rows and rows of boxed movies. Everything from new releases to old silent movies, travelogues, and "how-to" tapes—just about anything you could ever want! Pretty soon no one will ever have to go anywhere or do anything—just plop a tape into a machine & head to the 1920's . . . (or to Africa) . . . or to Mars, for that matter. Might be a story here . . . living your life through tapes. What if some kind of disease wiped everybody out and there was this guy who survived and he spent all his time looking at videotapes of the world back where there were people. pretty wild story.

The writer of the freewriting example wanders freely from one aspect of the topic to another. However, the writing is fairly focused—focused enough, in fact, that it might be shared with peers or with a teacher. Sometimes you may want to do freewriting that is just for you—completely private—in which you really let yourself go. Let your mind wander from topic to topic, writing anything that pops into your head, but writing just as fast as you can for ten minutes or so. Then go back over what you've written and see if you can mine it for ideas.

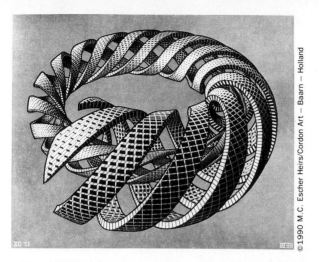

©1990 M.C. Escher Heirs/Cordon Art – Baarn – Holland

A variation of freewriting is called **looping.** As in freewriting, choose a subject and write about it for a set period of time, such as five or ten minutes. Then determine what your best idea was or where you seemed to be heading. Turn this information into a new subject for a second "loop" of freewriting. Repeat the loop at least three times. By the end of your looping experiment, you should have zeroed in on a starting place for writing.

Listing List-making can be a simple way to generate a specific topic if you have a general idea of what you want to write about. A list can also help you organize what you already know, find out what you don't know, and build a framework for later writing. By asking questions about the list, as in the example below, you can often come up with possible ideas for writing.

> Movies of Steven Spielberg
> *Close Encounters of the Third Kind*   *E.T.*
> *The Color Purple*   *Jaws*
>
> *Check:* Other movies? Any TV episodes? Movies produced, but
>   not directed? Short features? Awards? Professional history?
>   Personal background?

Using a Journal The best way to record what you observe and think is to keep a journal. A journal can be a powerful writing tool, useful for many purposes, such as the following.

- a diary for recording the events in your life
- a place for private expression of your wishes, ambitions, hopes, secrets, and dreams

Writing
—**TIP**—

Don't put off making a list because you are missing some information. An incomplete list is a good beginning.

- a sourcebook for writing ideas
- a place to put your opinions of other people's ideas
- a place to explore parts of your own life
- a place to list questions you would like to answer in writing
- a place to record your responses to literature—a "reader's log"
- a laboratory for trying out ideas, writing styles, and types of writing
- a learning log for recording what you learn in your classes, from books, from other people, and from your experiences

Here is an excerpt from the notebooks and journals of the famous poet, essayist, and anthropologist Loren Eiseley:

> There is something intensely pathetic about harmless animals dying alone. I shall never forget coming across the University of Kansas campus one summer evening and finding a dying turtle dove on the walk. I lifted up the dying bird, whose eyes were already glazing, and placed it on the flat roof of a nearby shed, where it might at least be safe from dogs or cats. . . . It was hopeless. In the last light of evening I hurried away asking myself questions I did not want to ask. Was there a nest? Were there young? . . . I did not go that way again in the morning. I knew too well what I would find.
>
> **Loren Eiseley, *The Last Notebooks***

In this journal entry, Eiseley accomplished several things. He recorded an event from his life. He expressed privately his feelings about that event. He may even have tried out a writing style—recording his moment-by-moment reactions to the sight of the dying bird. Eiseley was a professional writer, yet sometimes he wrote only for himself.

SHARING TECHNIQUES

Even though writing is most often thought of as a solitary activity, writers benefit greatly from sharing ideas with one another. Other people can provide a valuable perspective throughout the writing process, especially at the beginning when you are attempting to come up with ideas.

When you exchange ideas with other writers, you can often wed their ideas to yours to produce some third idea that is better than either one by itself. An idea that doesn't work for you may work for someone else, or someone else's discarded idea may be just the missing piece you were looking for.

Two sharing techniques you can use to generate ideas are brainstorming and discussion. If you work with other writers regularly, consider establishing a centrally located file for ideas.

Brainstorming When you **brainstorm,** you suggest multiple approaches to a problem without stopping to fine-tune or criticize any particular approach. Unlike freewriting, brainstorming is typically done orally with other people. Simply present a problem or question and ask people to respond to it freely. Every idea—no matter how bizarre it seems—is acceptable as long as it makes an attempt to answer the question or solve the problem.

Discussion Through **discussion,** writers can share information with one another and solve problems together. Like brainstorming, discussion is a group process, but it is a little more formal. Sometimes there is an assigned leader who keeps the discussion on track. The discussion leader also helps the group define key terms, tries to referee the conversation so every member can contribute, and summarizes the main points when the discussion is ended.

No two discussions are exactly alike. However, there are some important points to remember for any discussion about writing.

- Stick to the topic.
- Listen to the other speakers.
- Respond to what the other speakers say.
- Do not talk while other people are talking.
- Take notes on what is said.

GRAPHIC DEVICES

You can use **graphic devices** to find and develop ideas for writing, either alone or in combination with other techniques such as observing or questioning. See Writing Handbook 4, "Applying Graphic Organizers," pages 353–360.

Practice Your Skills

After completing each of the following activities, record your writing ideas in your journal, or write them on a page to be saved in your writing portfolio. Later, when you need a subject to write about, refer to your collection of writing ideas.

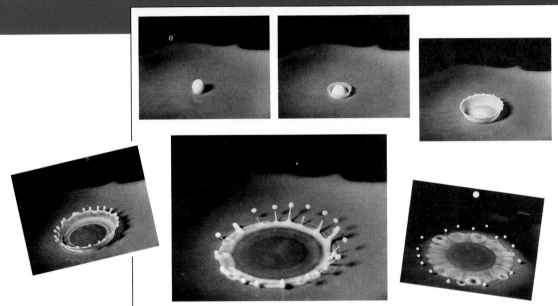

A single moment in time can have a great impact on future events.

1. Choose a single moment in your life, preferably one that occurred years ago. Think of a single sound, smell, taste, or sight from that moment. Try to create a vivid picture of the moment in your mind. Then freewrite about what you have remembered. List possible writing topics suggested by your freewriting.

2. Observe a plane, a train, a boat, or some other form of transportation. List your sensory observations about it. Then think about how it has changed in the last fifty or one hundred years. Conduct a knowledge inventory to investigate what you already know about the past and present forms of this mode of transportation. Then imagine how it might evolve in the future. Based on your sensory observations, your knowledge inventory, and your imaging, come up with at least three different writing ideas—for a factual piece, a persuasive piece, and a literary work such as a poem or short story.

3. Many people include quotations from other sources in their journals. Then they write their own reactions to each quotation. Choose one of the following examples—or find one of your own—and use the quotation as the focus of a discussion or a freewriting session. When you are finished, make a list of writing topics suggested by the discussion or the freewriting.

"Make haste slowly." Caesar Augustus
"The less of routine, the more of life." Bronson Alcott
"When in doubt tell the truth." Mark Twain

Focusing a Topic

Generating interesting writing ideas is an important stage in anyone's writing process. Ideas, however, nearly always need to be refined, or focused. When you focus a writing idea, you zero in on one particular aspect of the idea that you want to explore and develop.

Sometimes, focusing an idea means narrowing its scope. At other times, focusing may mean expanding the boundaries of an idea. In either case, an idea that is well focused is more likely to lead to coherent, compelling writing.

There are three main reasons for focusing a writing topic: to develop a topic that satisfies your general purpose and meets specific goals, to develop a topic you can treat comfortably and completely within an allotted space, and to develop a topic that will be suitable for its intended audience. When you have focused your topic in these three areas, you can begin elaborating on it and generating the details that will bring your writing to life.

Purpose and Goals   What is your general purpose for the writing you're beginning? Do you want to inform your readers about some scientific phenomenon? Will you entertain your audience with a humorous short story or a dramatic scene for the stage? Perhaps you want to persuade your readers to rally around some cause or point of view. Your general purpose may be dictated by a writing assignment you've been given, or it may be a personal choice.

Once your general purpose is clear, begin thinking about your specific goals. Suppose you've been asked to write a report for your earth science class. You decide to write about volcanoes—but what aspect of volcanic activity will you focus on? How volcanoes are formed? Volcanic disasters throughout history? The formation of volcanic islands in the Pacific Ocean? Volcanic activity on other planets? As you zero in on a particular aspect of volcanoes, your specific writing goals will become clearer and your topic will become more focused.

Length   When you are writing for yourself, you may not be concerned about length. You can just continue for pages and pages, thinking of numerous concrete and vivid details to support and elaborate your topic. For example, Thomas Wolfe worked on one novel for many years and produced thousands of pages of manuscript. He was simply writing for his own enjoyment. Later when he wanted to publish the book, it had to be drastically edited.

On some occasions, you will write in response to a classroom prompt, such as an assignment to write a five-page report on plate tectonics and earthquake activity for your earth science class. At other times, you will write in response to a publication prompt, such as a request from the editor of your school newspaper to cover the homecoming weekend's festivities and write a 500-word news article. In each of these writing situations and others like them, you will begin your writing process with a specific length in mind. You must focus your topic so that you can treat it completely and comfortably in a piece of that length. Otherwise, your subject will appear too broad or too narrow.

Suppose, for example, you have been asked to write a short article about pollution for the school paper. The topic has to be covered in 200 words—about two column inches in your paper's newsletter format. You decide that you really can't do justice to a broad topic like pollution in such a short piece. So you decide to choose one aspect of pollution and cover it in some detail.

You might choose to write about packaging material. You could make the point that we need to find alternatives to plastic; you could then tell about a mail-order firm that recently started packaging its products with real popcorn instead of those styrofoam chips that have been nicknamed "popcorn." Real popcorn is cheaper, biodegradable, and even reusable as cattle feed.

Audience Who's going to be reading your writing? Adults? Teenagers? Young children? Does your audience know quite a bit about your subject, or are they relatively uninformed? The answers to these questions will also help you to focus your topic. If your audience is sophisticated and informed, you may want your topic to be quite detailed or technical. If your audience is new to your subject, your topic may have to be a bit more general so that you can include necessary background material. Try freewriting a profile of your audience, and use that profile to help you shape your topic.

W R I T E R   T O   W R I T E R

To become a writer, you have to understand the reader. Put yourself in the reader's shoes.

Jamie Boothman, student
Seattle, Washington

HOW TO LIMIT OR
EXPAND A TOPIC

As you focus your topic, you may decide that you need to limit or expand it. How do you accomplish that? Three simple and effective ways to limit or expand a topic are questioning, brainstorming, and using graphic devices.

Questioning   Asking questions about your topic will often result in a list of related topics. Some of those topics will be narrower than your original topic, and some will be broader. When using this technique, give particular attention to questions that begin with *who, what, when, where, why,* and *how.* Such questions will usually result in narrower topics or details that can be used to expand a topic.

Suppose, for example, you were interested in writing about the Special Olympics. You might ask the following questions.

> *Who* started the Special Olympics?
> *Who* can participate?
> *Where* are the competitions held?
> *When* are they held?
> *How* are the competitions conducted?
> *What* similarities are there between the Special Olympics and the regular Olympics? What differences are there?
> *Why* were the Special Olympics created? (This question might make a good writing topic in itself.)

You can also ask questions that get at aspects of the topic that are most important to you. Here are some examples.

> What detail, moment, example, issue, or aspect of this topic matters most to me? Why?
> What incidents or events related to this topic matter to me? Why?

Brainstorming   Sometimes other writers can help you identify specific aspects of your topic. Suppose, for example, you present the broad topic of photography to your brainstorming group. One person might think of careers in photography—photojournalism, portraits, police photography. Another might mention particular photographers such as Ansel Adams, Alfred Stieglitz, or the local portrait photographer in your town. A third might think of technology and bring up strobe lights, high-speed film, stop-action, and digital retouching.

Writing
—TIP—

Questioning can also help you to organize your ideas and details prior to drafting. Organize the questions and their answers in the order you wish to write about them.

Focusing
a Topic   **351**

Each of these people has a particular insight into photography because of his or her experiences. You benefit from all these experiences, even though you may not have had them yourself. From the topics mentioned, you might choose portrait photography, using a local portrait photographer as an example. Then you might research portrait photography at your local library, using both books and periodicals.

Using Graphic Devices Graphic devices can help you look at a topic and separate it into different facets. Graphic devices include techniques such as charting, clustering, and mapping. See "Applying Graphic Organizers," pages 353–360.

Practice Your Skills

A. Choose one of the broad topics from the list at the left, and match it up with a writing format from the list at the right. Then narrow the topic to suit the format by using questioning, brainstorming, or a graphic device.

Topic	**Writing Format**
entertainment	• three-page short story
fashion	• 15–20-page research paper
Europe	• one-paragraph filler in a news-
sports and fitness	paper (maximum of 200 words)
science	• three-paragraph essay to demon-
lifestyles	strate your writing ability to a
books and ideas	prospective employer
health and nutrition	• five-minute oral report
careers	
environment	
outer space	
wild animals	

B. Select one of the following narrow topics. Broaden the topic to suit a 2,000-word article for a school newspaper by using questioning, brainstorming, or a graphic device.

- the work of a school cafeteria employee
- a popular television situation comedy
- buying a used car
- a review of a recent book or movie
- the current won-lost record of a school team
- growing roses
- your after-school job
- filling out college applications

Applying Graphic Organizers

Often, when you are writing, a visual representation, or **graphic device,** can help you see clearly what you want to say. You can use graphic devices at any stage of the writing process to explore and organize ideas.

W R I T E R   T O   W R I T E R

Let's see the very thing and nothing else.
Let's see it with the hottest fire of sight.

Wallace Stevens, poet

DEVICES FOR

EXPLORING IDEAS

Cluster Maps   Cluster maps, tree diagrams, and spider maps are three kinds of cluster diagrams you can use if you're exploring ideas related to or associated with a central idea. To make a **cluster map,** write your main idea or topic in a circle in the middle of a sheet of paper. Mentally explore that idea and think of related ideas. Write them down as they occur to you, circle them, and connect them to the main idea with lines. Next, treat each related idea as a new main idea; write down associated ideas near each one and circle them.

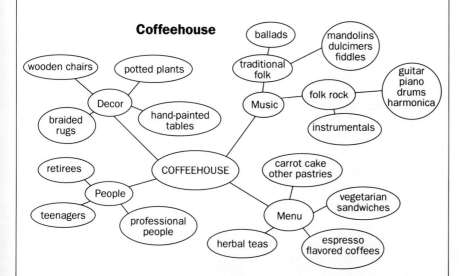

Similar to a cluster map, a **tree diagram,** or **spider map,** is most useful for breaking a topic or idea into its parts. Write the main idea at the top or bottom of a piece of paper. Then think of subordinate ideas and write these below or above your main idea, connecting them with lines that are like the "branches" of a tree or "legs" of a spider. Then, just as you do when clustering, think of ideas related to your subordinate ideas and again connect them with lines.

The process of breaking a broad, general topic down into narrower, more specific parts can help you limit and focus your ideas. Suppose you are assigned to write a paper for your health class pertaining to nutrition. Since nutrition itself is too broad a topic to tackle in one paper, you need to narrow your focus. The following tree diagram breaks nutrition down into smaller topics. Note that this process can lead to a variety of writing topics. For example, you may choose to write about the effects of the WIC program on infant mortality, or on the economics of malnutrition in countries where kwashiorkor is prevalent.

Topics Related to Nutrition

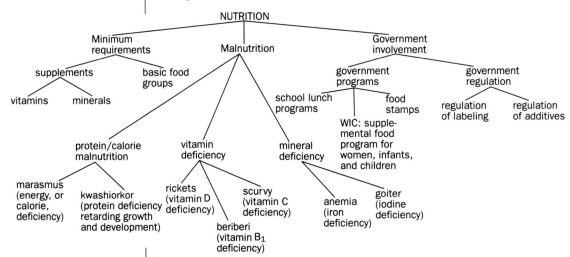

Observation Charts You can use **observation charts** to record information you gather through your five senses. Choose a topic for exploration—a place or an event, for example. Next, list the five senses as headings for columns. Then either remember or imagine your experience in that place and list beneath each heading what you see, hear, taste, touch, or smell. One student recalled the details of her visit to a county fair in the following observation chart.

County Fair				
Sight	**Sound**	**Touch**	**Taste**	**Smell**
lights of the Ferris wheel and other rides	calls of the barkers	soft, dry sheep's wool	salty popcorn and peanuts	bitter odor of livestock pens
crowds of people	fast-talking jumble of the auctioneer	splintery wood of fence around bullpen	spicy pizza by the slice	sour lemons
sheep, pigs, and cattle	heavy footsteps of animals shifting in their pens	slick metal pole on merry-go-round	tangy lemonade	fresh-mown hay
tents	roar of the crowd		sweet homemade cherry pie	
game booths	calliope music	rough cow's hide	juicy corn on the cob	
cowboys	crack of a whip			

Pro-and-Con Charts You can explore and compare the positive and negative aspects of some idea or course of action by creating a **pro-and-con chart.** Such a chart enables you to better understand all sides of an issue. Begin your pro-and-con chart by dividing a sheet of paper into two columns. Label the column on the left *Pro* and the column on the right *Con*. Then, spend some time considering your idea or course of action. You could do some freewriting to help clarify your thinking. Ask yourself questions like the following about your idea or course of action: What are its advantages and disadvantages? How is it a help? How is it a hindrance? What parts of it will prompt favorable reactions? unfavorable ones? Fill in your responses under the appropriate heading.

Suppose you have an older sister who is away at college. She has written a letter to you to say that she can't decide whether to continue studying for a professional career in ballet or to enter business school. Before answering her letter, you might make a pro-and-con chart like the one shown on the next page.

Pursuing a Career in Ballet

Pro	Con
She loves ballet.	Very few dancers make it to the top.
She has studied for a long time and invested a lot already.	Dancing is a hard, low-paying occupation.
She is very talented.	A professional dance career is short.
Even if she doesn't dance in a troupe or company, she can still teach dance at a high school or university.	

DEVICES FOR
ORGANIZING IDEAS

Analysis Frames   You can use an **analysis frame** to break down a subject into its component parts. The simplest way to construct an analysis frame is to write the subject at the top of a chart, then list its parts as column headings underneath the subject head. Summarize the characteristics of each part in the appropriate columns.

For example, if you were assigned to write a report on personal computer peripherals—equipment that can be attached to a computer to increase its capabilities—you might make an analysis frame like the one shown below to help you analyze and organize your information.

Peripherals for Personal Computers

Input Devices	Output Devices	Storage Devices
keyboard	dot-matrix printer	standard hard disk drive
mouse	laser printer	optical disk drive
scanner	color printer	removable disk drive
digitizing camera	plotter	WORM (write once, read many) drives
sound digitizer	reproduction proof or film printer	
video capture board		

Category Charts You can use a **category chart** to classify objects or ideas according to their qualities, characteristics, or membership in a group. Note how types of media are displayed according to their category in the following chart.

Types of Media

Audiovisual Media		Print Media	
radio	films	books	posters
television	audiocassettes	newspapers	billboards
facsimile	photographs	magazines	letters
or fax	slides or	pamphlets	newsletters
machines	transparencies		
videotapes			

Comparison-and-Contrast Charts Comparison-and-contrast charts and Venn diagrams are useful for organizing ideas in terms of their similarities and differences. To make a **comparison-and-contrast chart,** write the objects or ideas to be compared in the title of the chart and then summarize the results of your comparison in columns headed *Similarities* and *Differences.*

If you were writing a paper on moviemaking, you might decide to compare and contrast film and video. To organize your ideas in preparation for writing, you might create a comparison-and-contrast chart like the one below.

Film and Video

Similarities	Differences
Combine audio and visual elements in one medium	Video equipment less expensive
Still frames at high speed give impression of movement	Development and duplication not a problem with video
Can be used for making movies—traditional narrative style	Quality of film higher
Involve complicated, expensive editing procedures and equipment	Film can be projected on a big screen for large audiences; video must be projected on a television monitor

Venn Diagrams You can also graphically explore similarities and differences by using **Venn diagrams.** This graphic can help you see objects and ideas both as a whole and in relation to other things. To use a Venn diagram, draw two intersecting circles, one for each idea you are comparing. List common characteristics in the intersecting region and the characteristics unique to each in the circle outside this area. The following diagram shows the similarities and differences between hockey and soccer.

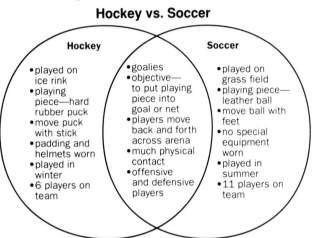

Hockey vs. Soccer

Hockey
- played on ice rink
- playing piece—hard rubber puck
- move puck with stick
- padding and helmets worn
- played in winter
- 6 players on team

(intersection)
- goalies
- objective— to put playing piece into goal or net
- players move back and forth across arena
- much physical contact
- offensive and defensive players

Soccer
- played on grass field
- playing piece— leather ball
- move ball with feet
- no special equipment worn
- played in summer
- 11 players on team

Flowcharts You can use a **flowchart** to help you organize the stages in a process or the steps necessary to complete an activity. The stages or steps are listed in order and are connected by arrows that show direction of movement. Flowcharts, like the one shown below that is commonly used by businesspeople and computer scientists, often use an oval to stand for "start" or "stop," a diamond for a decision or question, and a rectangle for an action.

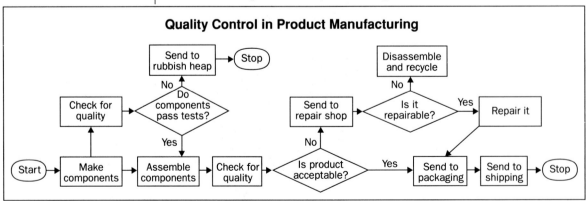

Quality Control in Product Manufacturing

Start → Make components → Assemble components → Check for quality → Do components pass tests?
- No → Send to rubbish heap → Stop
- Yes → (up to) Check for quality

Is product acceptable?
- Yes → Send to packaging → Send to shipping → Stop
- No → Send to repair shop → Is it repairable?
  - No → Disassemble and recycle
  - Yes → Repair it

Inductive-Reasoning Frames An **inductive-reasoning frame** lists separate facts or examples that support a general statement or conclusion. To make an inductive-reasoning frame, make a numbered list of specific facts and then draw an arrow to the conclusion you make. Watch how you word your conclusions; they must be based only on the evidence you provide.

Mathematicians and Their Work

Fact 1: René Descartes invented analytic geometry while still in his teens.

Fact 2: Sir Isaac Newton laid the foundations for elementary differential and integral calculus while in his early twenties.

Fact 3: Carl Friedrich Gauss invented a famous technique of mathematical analysis, the least squares method, while in college, and while still in his twenties made major contributions to geometry, algebra, and number theory.

Fact 4: Augustin Louis Cauchy made important contributions to geometry and to the theory of calculus while in his teens and twenties.

Fact 5: Évariste Galois published two major mathematical papers at eighteen and made important contributions to algebra, number theory, and group theory before his death at age twenty.

Fact 6: Bertrand Russell began formulating his derivation of arithmetic from symbolic logic while in his twenties.

Fact 7: While in his early twenties, John von Neumann made numerous major discoveries in both pure and applied mathematics and proposed a new definition of ordinal numbers that was universally adopted.

▼

Conclusion: Many mathematicians have made major contributions to their discipline while still in their youth.

Time Lines   A **time line** is useful for organizing information chronologically. To make a time line, draw a line, place times or dates along it, and write in events along the line at the times or dates when they occurred. If you were planning to write a family history, for example, you might plot important events on a time line to help organize the information you gather. Note how one student created the following time line of events in the history of her family.

1914 Grandpa Jack arrives at Ellis Island from Poland with his family. He was four years old.

1932 Grandparents on both sides of family marry on the same day, opposite sides of Chicago.

1940 Mom born

1942 Dad born

1964 Mom and Dad meet in a rainstorm, marry three months later.

1975 I am born.

1982 Grandpa Jack dies. Grandma moves in with us.

1989 I start high school.

| 1910 | 1920 | 1930 | 1940 | 1950 | 1960 | 1970 | 1980 | 1990 |

Writing
—TIP—

You don't have to limit yourself to the graphic devices discussed in this lesson. You might create devices of your own that can help you select, organize, or elaborate on ideas at any stage of the writing process.

Practice Your Skills

Choose three ideas from the following list and create two graphic devices related to each. The first graphic in each case should be either a cluster map, tree diagram or spider map, observation chart, or pro-and-con chart—graphics that help you explore topics. Next, based on the information you glean from that graphic, create another graphic related to the topic to organize your ideas—either an analysis frame, category chart, comparison-and-contrast chart, Venn diagram, inductive-reasoning frame, or time line. Develop your skills by choosing six different graphic forms.

- forms of entertainment
- effects of pollution
- sports
- education
- family
- pursuing a career in _____ (use any career you may be interested in)
- public funding of artists
- forms of energy

Shaping Your Writing

When contractors begin constructing a building, they work from complete, careful plans drawn up by architects. When you write, you, too, can choose to plan everything beforehand, deciding on a limited topic, a purpose, and an audience, making careful notes, and then organizing your information. However, you also can do some or most of your planning later, during the drafting process itself. You can simply plunge into a first draft and let the shape of your writing emerge as you continue to explore your ideas. In short, you can plan forward, plan backward, or do a combination of the two. The choice is yours.

ENVISIONING THE STRUCTURE

Generally speaking, the more complex your writing project, the more useful it is to plan ahead. For example, a research paper usually requires quite a bit of planning. You'll probably want to plan how you'll manage your time and use the library to find the sources you need. However, even in the case of a research paper, you might begin simply by doing some free-writing to show you what you already know about the topic and help you identify areas of the topic you may want to explore further.

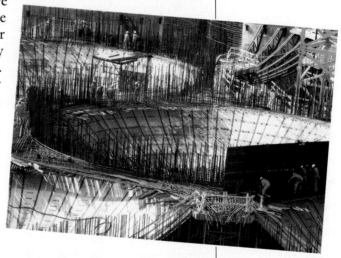

Even if you don't have a well-developed plan before writing, you may want to establish your writing purpose early in the process. Doing so will help you become invested in your writing, which means taking responsibility for your message and creating something that is personally meaningful.

Some writers find it useful to make outlines as part of the planning process. For information about preparing an outline, see Workshop 9, "Research Report," page 272–305.

Writers organize and structure their ideas throughout the writing process. When a piece of writing is well constructed, its ideas are linked together naturally and firmly, leading the reader from one idea to the next.

What is the best way to organize your writing? Of the many possible organizations, the best choice for a particular piece of writing usually is dictated by the material itself. As you write, ask yourself, "How is this idea connected to the next idea? What statement would naturally follow this one?"

WRITER TO WRITER

Every essay must have a shape. You can ask a question in the first paragraph, discussing several different answers to it till you reach the one you think is convincing. You can give a curious fact and offer an explanation of it. You can take a topic that interests you and do a descriptive analysis of it. . . . There are many other shapes [that] essays can take.

Gilbert Highet, essayist and literary scholar

In a given piece of writing, you will probably use a number of types of organization. Your piece may have an overall structure—chronological order, for example—but it may require spatial organization for some ideas and arrangement by order of importance for others. The following are some types of organization writers often use, as their material dictates.

Main Idea and Supporting Details In this type of organization, details support a main idea the way walls support a roof. You organize your material by first stating a main idea and then developing it with details, such as facts, examples, and reasons. In a single paragraph, your main idea may be stated in a topic sentence. In longer pieces of writing, your main idea may be expressed in a one-or-two-sentence thesis statement in your introduction. The paragraph at the top of the next page begins with a topic sentence stating the main idea; the sentences that follow provide examples, or supporting details.

COMPUTER
TIP

Word-processing programs allow you to move sentences and paragraphs around easily so that you can structure your ideas most effectively.

Writing
TIP

The position of a topic sentence in a paragraph may vary. Handbook 10, pages 401–403, contains more information on topic sentences. Handbook 8, page 381, has more information on thesis statements.

Support groups are an effective means by which people can overcome serious personal problems. For example, Alcoholics Anonymous has been very successful in helping people overcome addiction to alcohol. The philosophy and methods of this group have been applied to help people with other addictions as well. Overeaters Anonymous helps people deal with the tendency to eat too much, and Smokenders and Freedom from Smoking help people to overcome addiction to tobacco.

Chronological Order Another common form of organization is chronological order, or order of occurrence. This is the natural method for organizing narratives, both fictional—such as a short story—and nonfictional—such as a biography, a history, an accident report, or even a letter telling about last week's events. The following nonfiction passage is organized in chronological order.

Out of the dark she came, a vast, dim, white, monstrous shape, directly in the *Titanic*'s path. For a moment Fleet doubted his eyes. But she was a deadly reality, this ghastly thing. Frantically, Fleet struck three bells—something dead ahead. He snatched the telephone and called the bridge: "Iceberg! Right ahead!"

Hanson W. Baldwin, "R.M.S. Titanic"

Much writing that is structured chronologically, especially non-fiction such as the preceding model, begins with the first event and proceeds, step by step, to the last event. Writers, however, may vary strict chronological order to insert informative statements that clarify the events being described. The following model illustrates one such variation called **flashback**—a recalling of past events.

> Finally, I reached the hospital, parked under the "Doctors Only" sign in the restricted parking area, and struggled toward the emergency room, where I spotted two boys, ten to twelve years old, quietly playing chess as they waited for someone. Suddenly, the pain and fear that had consumed me vanished, and understandably enough, all I could think of was playing chess with my brother Dennis on the night Grandpa died. The time was ten years ago. The place was that very waiting room. Knowing how much we wanted to see him one last time, Aunt Mary had promised to get us into Grandpa's room, and she kept her promise—in fact, we walked in just in time to hear his last words. Now, in the emergency room, as I remembered those words, I smiled and turned to the nurse at the admissions desk. The pain and the fear were gone.

The flashback begins with the second sentence of the paragraph and continues through the third-to-the-last sentence. The writer returns to the present in the last two sentences.

Spatial Order   If your ideas are related by their position in space, you can order them spatially in several ways, such as the following.

top to bottom	left to right	zoom in
bottom to top	right to left	zoom out
inside to outside	near to far	
outside to inside	far to near	

Zoom in and zoom out are camera techniques that you can use to create a powerful visual experience for your reader. If you are using a zoom-in organization, you begin by describing a panoramic view, such as a city skyline, and progressively focus on finer and finer details of that scene, for example, a single building, a room in that building, and finally, the subject of your writing—a person in that room. Zoom-in and zoom-out organization can be particularly effective in introducing or concluding a piece of writing.

Another variety of spatial order is **order of impression.** In this organization, you create a physical description by beginning with the image that has the most powerful effect, moving on to the next most powerful, and so on. Notice how the writer combined far-to-near organization with order of impression in the following description of a restored clipper ship sailing into port.

> The huge white sails loomed like low clouds sitting on the horizon. As the clipper ship moved slowly toward us, the tall, graceful timbers supporting the sails created a floating forest on the ocean. A building made of oak, gleaming with years of hand-rubbing and lacquer, then floated slowly into view, and the sunburned faces of the crew came into focus more clearly with each wave, until they became distinct individuals.

Organization by Degree Sometimes the relationship among your ideas will be a specific characteristic they share. If you were writing about presidential candidates, for example, you might choose to focus on their leadership qualities and experience. You can organize this type of writing by ranking the candidates by the degree of common quality, beginning with the one that has either the most or the least of that quality. You can use almost any characteristic to organize a piece of writing by degree. Here are some examples:

- A report about gemstones could be organized from least valuable to most valuable
- An essay about jellyfish could be organized from least harmful (nonpoisonous) to most harmful (extremely poisonous)
- An editorial about ways to control toxic emissions could be organized from most effective to least effective

Two very common types of organization by degree are organization by **order of importance** and organization by **familiarity.** The following outline for a piece about Thomas Edison's inventions is organized by order of importance according to the author's view of the impact of Edison's inventions on society.

Edison's Inventions
   I. The electric light
  II. Motion pictures
 III. The phonograph
 IV. The alkaline storage battery

Inverted-Pyramid Organization   The inverted pyramid is a type of organization by degree—from more to less important—and is the traditional method for organizing a newspaper article. This organization offers busy readers, who often only have time to scan the paper, the most important information in the headline and first paragraph of each article. When using the inverted pyramid order, you begin by presenting, in a paragraph of one to three sentences, all the basic information needed to describe the event you are writing about—the who, what, where, when, why, and how. Then, in the rest of the article, you present the details of the story in order of importance.

Consider the following excerpt from an article in the *New York Times:*

Civil War in Liberia Threatening To Divide West African Neighbors

ABIDJAN, Ivory Coast, Aug. 28—The eight-month-old civil war in nearby Liberia is threatening to become a wider conflict as neighboring West African countries begin to take opposing sides, African and Western diplomats said today.

Troops from Nigeria and four smaller West African countries have established control over the port area of the Liberian capital Monrovia in the three days since they landed there, and the 3,000 men are reportedly advancing toward the Government-controlled stronghold in the city's densely populated center.

Each paragraph consists of one sentence, a style common in newspaper writing. The first paragraph gives the broad, general picture—*when* the event was reported (August 28); *where* the report originates (Abidjan); *where* the civil war is taking place (Liberia); *what* is occurring (other West African countries are taking sides in Liberia's civil war); and *who* the sources of information are (African and Western diplomats). The *why* and *how* may appear elsewhere in the article. Note how the second paragraph elaborates on the *what* and gives supporting details—citing a specific action by Nigeria and other "neighboring countries" of Liberia. The subsequent paragraphs in the article present progressively less important supporting details.

Comparison-and-Contrast Order   If you want to show the similarities or differences between two subjects, use comparison-and-contrast order. You can organize a comparison in three basic ways—by subject, by similarities and differences, and by features.

1. When organizing by subject, discuss one subject completely before you discuss the other. For example, in comparing and contrasting traditional and organic farming methods, you might first describe all the aspects of traditional farming and then all those of organic farming.

2. When organizing by similarities and differences, describe all the similarities of your subjects first and then describe all the differences (or vice versa). For example, you might organize the report on traditional and organic farming by first describing the similarities between the planting and sowing schedules of both farming methods and then explaining the differences in fertilizing and pest control.

3. You could also organize your comparison by features, comparing and contrasting each subject with respect to specific characteristics. For example, you might choose to discuss the specific features of farming: planting, weeding, fertilizing, watering, and harvesting. You could begin by describing the similarities and differences between traditional and organic planting, then between traditional and organic weed control, and so on, feature by feature, for both types of farming.

Order by Classification and Division   If your subject has a number of different components, one of the simplest ways to organize your writing is to categorize the components into groups according to their characteristics, or membership in particular classes. For example, if the subject is inventions used in warfare throughout the ages, such as the spear, the shield, the stirrup, the bow, gunpowder, the tank, the ICBM, and the stealth bomber, you might choose to classify them by their age—are they prehistoric, ancient, medieval, or modern?

Cause-and-Effect Order   Life can be thought of as a continual series of causes and effects. When its temperature falls below 32° F, water freezes. When a baby is hungry, it cries. Historical, economic, political, and scientific events can often be evaluated in terms of cause and effect.

In a cause-and-effect chain, a particular cause creates an effect. That effect then becomes the cause of another effect, and so on. For example, the threat of war may cause oil prices to rise. An increase in oil costs will cause an increase in the price of gasoline. A price hike in gas can then cause an increase in the cost of shipping goods to market, which, in turn, can cause the price of groceries to rise.

Even in a cause-and-effect chain, each cause may have multiple effects; likewise, each effect may have multiple causes. Use the following patterns when you apply cause-and-effect organization in your writing.

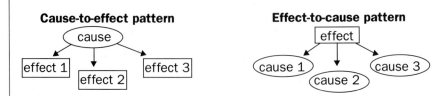

Cause-to-effect pattern

cause → effect 1, effect 2, effect 3

Effect-to-cause pattern

effect → cause 1, cause 2, cause 3

For example, if you were writing about how a company's relocation affected its employees, you could use a cause-to-effect organization to describe how the move (the cause) had different effects on employees. One employee relocated with her family; another employee decided not to move and to change his career instead; and a third did not relocate but found a better job in the same field.

Dialectic Organization (Thesis/Antithesis/Synthesis) In this form of organization, you first discuss an idea (the thesis), then its opposite (the antithesis), and finally present a combination of the two (the synthesis). Because it presents two sides of an issue and then a conclusion, this approach is especially useful in persuasive or argumentative writing. For example, if you wanted to write about the threat to owls living in a forest owned by a logging company, you might first explain the company's position—the land belongs to them and timber is in demand. Then you could describe the environmentalists' position—owls should be protected. Finally, you could propose a compromise that synthesizes both positions, such as cutting timber selectively, leaving enough to maintain the owls' habitat.

Inductive and Deductive Organization If you are presenting an argument for adopting a particular position, you might consider using either inductive or deductive organization. **Inductive organization** first presents specific facts and then ends with a general conclusion based on those facts. **Deductive organization** begins with a general statement and then makes specific statements that can be inferred from that general statement.

If you were writing an article to persuade readers to consider starting businesses based on their hobbies or personal interests, for example, you might use inductive organization. First, you could describe how Steven Jobs started Apple Computers in his garage or how Debbi Fields started Mrs. Fields Cookies. Then, from these facts, you could draw the conclusion that successful businesses can develop from very humble beginnings. Other topics might suggest a deductive organization. For example, if you were writing about the population explosion, you might first state that the population of the developing world will more than double by the end of this century. Then you might describe the consequences of this growth, such as widespread hunger, more warfare in developing countries, and an increased need for foreign aid.

Practice Your Skills

A. Read the excerpt from *Farther Off From Heaven* in Workshop 5, "Examining Changes," pages 146–158. What method of organization does William Humphrey use for this essay? Why do you think it is, or is not, effective?

B. Read the following descriptions of compositions. In a small-group discussion, explore at least two possible ways of organizing each. For some, you may decide to use several types of organization, or you may want to suggest an original method.

1. An editorial explaining to readers why it is important for them to be active in local government
2. A story about the life and adventures of Jacques Cousteau, the marine scientist
3. A composition that explains the general philosophies of Democrats and Republicans in American politics
4. An essay for your earth-science class on the different types of rocks (or fossils) that can be found in your community
5. A review of a novel or a television program
6. A report for a biology class on the human digestive system
7. A fable
8. A description of a local museum or park
9. A press release announcing your school's Thanksgiving canned-food drive to benefit shelters for the homeless
10. A proposal to open school athletic facilities for use by community residents during the summer
11. An analysis of the sources of air pollution
12. A campaign speech for someone who is running for student council
13. A eulogy for a friend or for a famous figure who recently died
14. A letter sent to a prospective employer, along with a résumé, as part of a job application
15. A poem about the dreams of a mother as she rocks her baby to sleep

Writing
TIP

Don't feel compelled to use any form of organization exclusively. You can combine several different methods or even invent your own to suit your material.

Using Collaborative Planning

The old saying "Two heads are better than one" is true when it comes to generating new ideas and solutions to problems. It can also be true for the initial planning stages of the writing process. While you will not always want or be able to plan your writing fully before you begin, a writing plan can be quite useful to guide your work. You may prefer to work alone on your writing plan, or you may find that working with someone else doing **collaborative planning** can be exciting and inspiring. Verbalizing your plan and talking through your ideas with someone else helps you stand back, see the big picture, and test your ideas before you produce a product.

PLANNING AND THE
PLANNER'S BLACKBOARD

A writing plan should focus on the topic, purpose, audience, and form of the writing. Using a **planner's blackboard** like the one shown below can help you and your collaborating partner determine these variables. Keep in mind that the arrows on the blackboard indicate that there is a dynamic interplay among the variables in your writing—a change or adjustment to one also affects the others.

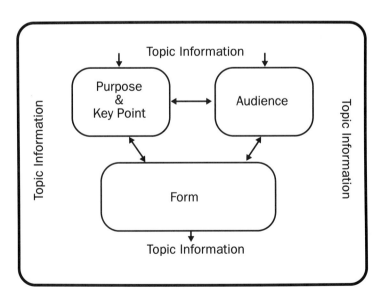

Like the graphic devices in Writing Handbook 4, the planner's blackboard allows you to visualize and graphically display the decisions you make about the purpose, audience, and form of your writing. The topic itself provides the backdrop. When you make a writing plan using the blackboard, you move back and forth among the variables as the arrows indicate.

The planner's blackboard is an excellent aid to collaborative planning. Writers can use the blackboard as a reminder to think about all the variables as they explain their writing plan to a partner. Collaborating partners can also use the blackboard to help them listen intelligently, and direct their questions as they encourage other writers to explore and develop their plans.

GETTING SUPPORT FOR YOUR WRITING PLAN

During collaborative planning a good listener can help you strengthen your writing plan and connect your topic to your purpose, audience, and form. Your partner can encourage you by noting what works well, asking questions, making suggestions, and responding as a reader might to help you test your plan.

Here is an example of the kind of dialogue that takes place during a collaborative-planning session. Notice how the writer, Tanya, clarified her purpose in the process.

Mary: Let's talk about what kind of form you're going to use for your writing.

Tanya: I don't think I want this to be really formal, you know, like having an introduction followed by a paragraph, and finally followed by my conclusion.

Mary: You think it'll be more free-flowing, more like a response statement?

Tanya: Probably. I don't see myself saying, "This is what I mean, and I feel this and in conclusion this and this." It's more like, "This is what I'm thinking and I'm not sure it's really valid, but here it is."

Mary: So your purpose is to explore?

Tanya: Yes. I have a point, but I can't be conclusive.

Mary: Okay, well, have you thought about your audience? Maybe they'd want you to be more definite.

Tanya: Maybe, but the exploration could be fun for them, too.

Writing
—TIP—

You may begin writing with a formal plan or begin with little planning and use the writing process to discover your topic, purpose, audience, and form.

Collaborative
Planning   **371**

Mary: Yes, I see what you mean. You'll have to be sure to include enough details so they can share your experience, though.

Tanya: Right. That's what I have to concentrate on.

This sample planning session also illustrates the different roles the writer and the partner play in collaborative planning.

The Role of the Writer You, the writer, are the authority in the collaborative planning process. You direct the process and do most of the talking as you and your listener focus on your writing plan. Your goal should be to confirm your good ideas, strengthen any weak ideas, and explore the range of writing possibilities.

The planner's blackboard will help you become more aware of your own ideas and writing process. At the same time, it prompts you to explore your goals and discover connections among your writing ideas.

The Role of the Collaborating Partner Collaborating partners help writers develop and elaborate on their writing plans. The partner's role is to listen, keeping the goals of the planner's blackboard in mind. Partners are not critics; their job is not to find fault or tell the writer how to proceed. A partner can ask the following questions to help a writer develop a writing plan.

1. Listen carefully and reflect, or repeat, what you heard. Say something like, "What I hear you saying is _____ . Am I hearing you right?"
2. Ask the planner to elaborate. "You just said _____ . Tell me more about what you mean or why you said that."
3. Ask about the key parts of the blackboard that the planner has explained only in a sketchy way. "If your purpose is _____ , how are you going to accomplish it? What are your other goals?"
4. Ask from time to time how different parts of the plan are connected, especially when you see possible links or problems. "If your key point here is _____ , how do you think your readers will respond to that?" "Is there any link between your purpose and the form you plan to use?" If you spot potential problems, point them out; brainstorm possible solutions together.

Practice Your Skills

A. Suppose you have been asked by your science teacher to write a report on any topic in biology or natural history. Choose one of the following general topics or come up with one of your own as the backdrop for a writing plan.

amphibians	genetics
birds of prey	parts of the brain
cell division	photosynthesis
circulatory system	poisonous snakes
endangered species	respiration
fossil hunting	viruses
regeneration	glaciers

You will probably want to focus, or limit, your topic somewhat. Create a writing plan based on your topic, taking all the writing variables into consideration. Then use the planner's blackboard to do collaborative planning with a partner. Finally, compare your original writing plan with the revised plan you made with your partner. Discuss the differences between the two plans and decide which one you would use if you were writing a draft.

B. Suppose that someone has asked you to help do collaborative planning for a short story about a rafting trip. The writer's plan is simply to write a short story based on her own rafting experience on the Penobscot River in Maine. Her main point is that when someone successfully faces a physical challenge, she may gain confidence in other areas. Use the planner's blackboard as a reminder and write an imaginary dialogue in which you ask questions and make comments as the writer explains her plan.

Writing
—TIP—
As you support a writer in collaborative planning, jot down ideas as they occur to you. That way, you will not have to interrupt the writer, and you can go back and consider the ideas later.

Collaborative
Planning   **373**

WRITING
H A N D B O O K
7

Drafting as Experimentation and Discovery

One of the most inviting aspects of writing is that you don't have to know what you want to say before you begin. You can just start **drafting**—getting your ideas on paper so you can work with them. When you draft, you don't have to worry about your choice of words, or about anything else for that matter. Instead, you can focus on capturing meaning. Writing is the making of meaning.

In fact, the ideal state in which to start writing is confusion, not certainty. Use drafting to explore your confusion—to raise questions and to explore answers to them. Realize that as you draft and revise, your ideas will come into sharper focus. Start with a sense of where you are heading and allow your writing to guide the way.

Many people make the mistake of thinking that writing is for communicating what they already know and are sure of. Then, when they draft and find themselves uncertain about something, they stop writing altogether. It's much better to keep writing and explore what is unclear to you.

When you write, you use two entirely different thinking processes—creative and critical. In the early stages of drafting, try to let your creativity flow and experience the excitement of writing. You will have time later to examine your draft critically.

Drafting can help you discover ideas that are worth researching further—ones about which you'll need to gather more information. Here's how one student writer discovered while drafting that he needed to do further research.

> Capable of leveling skyscrapers in seconds, earthquakes are among the most powerful natural disasters known. Records show that the most severe earthquake measured by the Richter scale was an 8.9 during a quake that rocked Japan in 1933. *(What exactly does an 8.9 reading mean? And what is the Richter scale?)*

While drafting, you also may discover a unique, personal angle on a topic that will make it more interesting. Here's how another student's drafting led to recalling a personal experience.

> School clubs are important. In clubs, students can develop skills and interests that receive little attention in the classroom. And in clubs students can develop friendships. *(When I was a freshman, I was new in town and didn't know anyone. The kids had their own little cliques. Then I went to a meeting of the astronomy club. Suddenly I found kids just like me, kids who were willing to "let me in.")*

Letting your ideas flow while drafting can heighten your personal insights and intellectual awareness. So remain open to new ideas as you write, and enjoy the discovery process.

Drafting Styles

You can start drafting anywhere. You can work from the conclusion backward, from the body outward to the introduction and conclusion, or from the beginning straight through to the end.

Although most good writers follow certain general patterns—such as writing a draft, getting feedback from others, rereading their work, and then rewriting—there is no single right pattern. Different people write in different ways, and the same person writes differently in different situations. Sometimes you just want to set your thoughts free on paper. This is called raw writing, or writing an **adventuresome draft.**

Adventuresome Drafts In raw writing you write down quickly all your thoughts about a topic. This method can be effective when you know something about your topic but aren't sure how much you know or how to organize the material. When doing this type of writing, don't stop to worry about form, style, audience, or even purpose. Once your first adventuresome draft is done, you can go back to it and mine it for ideas that you can use later in a more careful, revised draft.

Many of the greatest writers—John Steinbeck and Thomas Wolfe, for example—worked this way. They got all their ideas out first and then refined their organization and language.

Careful Drafts Other fine writers work differently, using a very structured, controlled approach. Henry James, for example, did careful drafts, completely mapping out the plot to each story before beginning to write. Writing a careful draft means planning in great detail what you are going to say and how you are going to say it. You might plan by using an outline or by writing a set of prewriting notes on paper or index cards.

W R I T E R   T O   W R I T E R

Outlining your essay will greatly improve your organization and coherence.

Eric Strom, student
San Marcos, California

When writing a careful draft, you can start with the body, the introduction, or the conclusion. However, in contrast to adventure-some drafting, you work very slowly, getting each part the way you want it and connecting it to what precedes and follows it.

Intermediate Drafts Most writers draft in a way that is somewhere between adventuresome and careful. You often begin with a topic, a general organization, and a few key ideas. As you draft, you weave together these ideas and, if you remain open, you will find that you also discover new ones.

An excellent way to write such an intermediate draft is **bridge-building,** because it allows you to connect your ideas as you write. Ask yourself how you can get from idea A to idea B and what details you need to provide to make that connection clear. When drafting a short story or a personal narrative, for example, bridge-building is particularly useful, since you discover what you want to say as you go along.

Writing
—— **TIP** ——

As you draft, be alert to phrases, words, or ideas that may suggest possible titles for your work.

Collection of Whitney Museum of American Art. Purchase. 42.15

Joseph Stella. *The Brooklyn Bridge: Variation on an Old Theme.* 1939. Oil on canvas.

Drafting and Revision

Because drafting involves discovery and change, it usually overlaps with revision. Some writers revise and shape all of their work as they draft. Others write a few paragraphs, stop and revise one, and then write a few more without stopping to revise them. Still others forge ahead, full steam to the end, and revise later on. Again, choose the method that works for you.

Drafting When You Can't Revise   You may not always have time to revise your draft before submitting it. Make an informal outline of your main ideas on a piece of paper. When you begin to write, cover the essential points first. In subsequent paragraphs, expand upon these points by providing details and additional information. See "Constructing Your Writing," pages 362–369, and "Types of Elaboration," pages 397–399 for more help in writing well-planned and -developed drafts.

Knowing When to Stop   Usually, writers do several drafts before moving on. Between drafts you may want to take a break so that you can see your writing with a fresh eye. You may also share your work with a peer reader who can be objective and give you feedback. As you learn more about your own writing process you'll know when it's time to stop drafting and begin fine-tuning your style.

COMPUTER
TIP

If you input your draft on a computer, format the page with triple spacing and a short line—about forty-five characters. When the draft is printed on paper, you will have plenty of room to pencil in changes and insertions.

Practice Your Skills

A. Meet with other students in a small group and discuss each of the following questions.

1. For which writing activity would you do more up-front planning—a short story or a research paper? Why?
2. Which method of drafting does each person in your group usually use? Does your approach ever vary?
3. Have you ever changed your topic as you were drafting? Why? Share your experience with your classmates.
4. Do you usually start with the body, the introduction, or the conclusion of a piece of writing? Why?

B. Imagine that you will write a science-fiction short story, a letter to the editor urging your community to vote against building a nuclear power plant, and a research report on the history of the United Nations. Explain to a partner how your drafting process would differ for each piece of writing. Then draft and revise one of these topics.

Writing Introductions and Conclusions

Although you can begin drafting your writing anywhere in the piece, at some point you will need to write a beginning and an ending. The types of beginning, or **introduction,** and ending, or **conclusion,** you use will depend on the kind of writing you are doing and on what you want to say.

Peanuts: Reprinted by permission of UFS, Inc.

NONFICTION INTRODUCTIONS

Although all writing must begin somewhere, not all pieces have actual introductions. For example, some narratives open by simply jumping into the middle of the action of the story, without any preliminaries. This is called beginning *in medias res,* a Latin phrase meaning "in the middle of things."

However, most pieces of nonfiction writing do have introductions. Like beginnings *in medias res,* introductions usually serve to capture the reader's interest. Many also either suggest or directly state the topic or main idea of the piece. In journalism, the first paragraph, or introduction, is called a lead, because it leads the reader into the rest of the piece. The following are some common methods for introducing a piece of nonfiction.

Present a Startling, Unusual, or Interesting Fact or Opinion One way to capture a reader's attention is by saying something surprising or shocking. George Orwell, the author of such classic novels as *1984* and *Animal Farm,* was a master of the startling introduction. On the next page are the opening lines from two of his essays.

> As I write, highly civilized human beings are flying overhead, trying to kill me.
>
> **George Orwell, "England, Your England"**
>
> In Moulmein, in Lower Burma, I was hated by large numbers of people—the only time in my life that I have been important enough for this to happen to me.
>
> **George Orwell, "Shooting an Elephant"**

W R I T E R   T O   W R I T E R

> The best writing, in my opinion, pulls the reader in with an exciting beginning.
>
> **Chris Converse, student**
> **Birmingham, Alabama**

Relate an Anecdote An anecdote is a very brief story that makes a specific point or evokes a particular response, such as surprise, horror, or laughter. David Quammen, a writer for *Outside* magazine, begins one of his essays with the following story.

> One evening a few years ago I walked back into my office after dinner and found roughly a hundred black widow spiders frolicking on my desk. I am not speaking metaphorically and I am not making this up: a hundred black widows. It was a vision of ghastly, breathtaking beauty, and it brought on me a wave of nausea. It also brought on a small moral crisis— one that I dealt with briskly, maybe rashly, in the dizziness of the moment, and that I've been turning back over in my mind ever since.
>
> **David Quammen, "The Face of a Spider: Eyeball to**
> **Eyeball with the Good, the Bad, and the Ugly"**

Begin with a Description A vivid, detailed description can make a wonderful introduction, setting the mood and stimulating the reader's interest.

Writing Introductions
and Conclusions   **379**

In the following example, notice how the writer uses description to emphasize how exotic her subject is.

▼

The jungle conversation is a monotonous drone of cicadas, punctuated by monkey chatter. High in the canopy, hooting gibbons move like living pendulums. Contemptuous of gravity, a young gibbon free-falls fifty feet, at last curling long, graceful fingers around a limb just above the forest floor.

A green lizard sits frozen, an emerald brooch on white tree bark. Suddenly it springs into the humid air, opens two thin membranes and glides gracefully through a slit in the dark, rich curtain of the jungle.

Nancy Sefton, "Indonesia"

Draw an Analogy An analogy is a comparison between your subject and something very different. For example, the writer of the following essay begins by comparing automobiles to apples. Note, also, that she makes use of a traditional saying—another technique commonly used in introductions.

▼

One bad apple can spoil a whole basket. The same is true of automobiles and air quality. Just 10 percent of all vehicles on U.S. roadways are spewing out half the automobile-emitted carbon monoxide pollution that fouls our cities' air.

**Deborah Erickson, "Remote Possibility: Infrared
Pollution Sensor Could Be Clean-Air Catalyst"**

Ask a Question Sometimes you may wish to put your main idea in the form of a question, as the writer of the following piece about prehistoric food preservation did.

▼

If you think you have problems storing leftovers, consider an Ice Age hunter faced with a ton of leftover mastodon. A typical mastodon kill yielded about 2,000 pounds of edible meat. How did ancient hunters store so much meat and protect it from scavengers?

University of Michigan, "Leftover Mastodon"

Include a Quotation A well-chosen quotation may be just what you need both to introduce your topic and to give it the credibility that primary sources and authorities can provide. Notice how the writer of the following piece used a quotation to make her point economically and effectively.

▼

> You have only to take one look at Lorin Adkins to know why he says things like: "No wealth is greater than your health." His trim, muscular 79-year-old body tells the rest of the story.
> **Jan Elerman, "World Class at 79"**

Begin with a Thesis Statement An introduction to a piece of nonfiction—a persuasive essay, a literary analysis, an explanation, an essay for assessment, or a report, for example—often includes a **thesis statement,** one or two sentences that clearly state the main idea of the writing that follows. A thesis statement may also convey the writer's point of view and signal the paper's overall organization. Thesis statements may be woven into introductions that use any of the techniques described in this handbook. Here are three examples of thesis statements for nonfiction essays:

> The most difficult job in professional sports is officiating the games. Referees need excellent vision, great physical strength and endurance, and a thick skin to protect them from the verbal barbs they receive from unfriendly crowds.

> Although some people believe that television has silenced conversation in the evenings, I believe that television programs give us something to talk about.

> In his novel *1984,* George Orwell critiques totalitarian society through the character of Winston Smith.

Other Types of Introductions The examples you've just looked at are some of the most common ways of introducing a piece of writing. Here are a few techniques that are used less often but are no less effective.

You can promise the reader some benefit, as Russell Baker does in "Little Red Riding Hood Revisited." Baker begins his humorous retelling of the story by saying, "In an effort to make the classics accessible to contemporary readers, I am translating them into the modern American language."

**COMPUTER
TIP**

If your software has "split-screen" capability, keep your thesis statement on the screen at all times to help you avoid straying from your main idea.

Writing Introductions
and Conclusions   **381**

You can begin by taking a stand, as Henry David Thoreau does in "Resistance to Civil Government." These are his opening sentences: "I heartily accept the motto, 'That government is best which governs least. . . .' Carried out, it finally amounts to this . . . 'That government is best which governs not at all.' "

You might even address the reader directly. In the first paragraph of "The Battle with Mr. Covey," a chapter in his autobiography, Frederick Douglass writes, "You have seen how a man was made a slave; you shall see how a slave was made a man."

Remember, the ways to introduce your writing are limited only by your imagination.

NONFICTION CONCLUSIONS

A good conclusion should continue to hold the interest you captured in the introduction to your writing and leave your reader with a sense of closure and resolution. It also typically has the following characteristics.

- It follows logically from the material you have presented in your piece of writing.
- It does not introduce new, unrelated material.
- It leaves the reader with something to think about.

There are as many ways to conclude your writing as there are to introduce it. Here are some of the most common methods for concluding a piece of writing.

Restate the Thesis One particularly effective way of concluding a piece of writing is to restate your thesis, or main idea, in different words. In "Autobiographical Notes," for example, James Baldwin explains how he came to be a writer and what his early ambitions were. He ends with this sentence: "I want to be an honest man and a good writer."

Summarize the Ideas in the Body Paragraphs Another way to conclude a piece of writing—especially one in which you present a substantial amount of information, make a series of points, describe a process, or present a critical review—is by summarizing the main ideas of the paragraphs. First, you might summarize the main idea of the whole piece. Then you can restate, in a sentence or two, the main idea of each body paragraph, presenting the information in the order in which it appeared in the body. In the following example, note that each sentence corresponds to a major idea.

All these examples show that more and more people are finding it possible to work at home for themselves. Accountants, writers, graphic artists, designers, marketing consultants, lawyers, sales people, and many, many others are finding home-based work to be just the thing for them. New communications technologies, such as modems, fax machines, and overnight mail services, make work from home more feasible than it was in the past. Among the many benefits of working at home are flexible hours, comfortable surroundings, and a great measure of independence.

Marilyn Shepherd, "Home Work"

Generalize About the Information You Have Presented The purpose of many pieces of writing is to prove a point, to show why a course of action would or would not be appropriate, or to explain or support a policy. A good way to conclude such a piece of writing is to draw a general conclusion—a generalization.

For example, scientist Lewis Thomas used a generalization to conclude his essay discussing whether or not we should be trying to contact intelligent beings in other parts of the universe.

Writing
——**TIP**——
Choose a concluding technique carefully, since it will affect the final impression you make on your reader.

Writing Introductions
and Conclusions   **383**

> Perhaps we should wait a while, until we are sure we know what we want to know, before we get down to detailed questions. After all, the main question will be the opener: Hello, are you there? If the reply should turn out to be Yes, hello, we might want to stop there and think about that, for quite a long time.
>
> **Lewis Thomas, "Ceti"**

Make a Prediction One way to keep your reader thinking after reading your piece is to end with a prediction.

LITERARY
M O D E L

> By perseverance and fortitude, we have the prospect of a glorious issue; by cowardice and submission, the sad choice of a variety of evils—a ravaged country—a depopulated city —habitations without safety, and slavery without hope—our homes turned into barracks and bawdy houses for Hessians, and a future race to provide for, whose fathers we shall doubt of. Look on this picture and weep over it! And if there yet remains one thoughtless wretch who believes it not, let him suffer it unlamented.
>
> **Thomas Paine, "Common Sense"**

Issue a Call for Action One effective way to end your piece of writing is to urge the reader to take some action.

PROFESSIONAL
M O D E L

> Let us act this year, so that in 2001 we can look our children and our grandchildren in the eye and say, "Here, we made the world a better place for you. We continued the tradition of the forty thousand generations of humans who came before us. Do the same for your children."
>
> **Carl Sagan, "1984 and 2001: A New Year's Resolution"**

Ask a Question Another way to leave your reader thinking is to write a conclusion that contains a question. In the next example, the author uses an analogy of several bags to show the pointlessness of being preoccupied with the color of another person's skin.

▼

In your hand is the brown bag. On the ground before you is the jumble it held—so much like the jumble in the bags, could they be emptied, that all might be dumped in a single heap and the bags refilled without altering the content of any greatly. A bit of colored glass more or less would not matter. Perhaps that is how the Great Stuffer of Bags filled them in the first place—who knows?

Zora Neale Hurston, "How It Feels to Be Colored Me"

End with a Quotation A concluding quotation can lend an immediacy and personal perspective that make a lasting impression.

▼

All the MMU [Manned Maneuvering Unit] veterans agreed that the experience of being a human satellite [walking in space] is difficult to describe because it's not like anything on Earth. . . . [According to former astronaut Robert Stewart] "During the *Apollo* missions, one guy was orbiting the moon and was on the far-side-of-the-moon orbit. He was out of touch literally with all humanity, the rest of the universe. Now *that's* real solitude."

Alcestis Oberg, "Space Walking"

Relate an Anecdote You can also use a compelling anecdote, or brief story, to make a concluding point.

▼

One day when I was about seventeen, I was walking through a park toward my best friend's house, wearing a full-length yellow sundress. A little girl asked her father as I walked by, "Daddy, is that Snow White?" Her father's reply was, "Yes, I think it might be." I just smiled at the little girl as she stared at me open-mouthed. I kept walking to my friend's house, wondering about the difference between fantasy and lies. I guess if little girls are allowed to believe that a chubby man who helps sell toys for department stores is Santa Claus, they might as well be allowed to believe that a teenager in a long yellow dress is Snow White! For myself, I'd rather kids were told the truth. There's enough to wonder about in the world without making up lies— even little snow-white ones.

NARRATIVE INTRODUCTIONS AND CONCLUSIONS

A **narrative** is a piece of writing that tells a story. It can be imaginary, as in a short story, or real, as in a newspaper account. Several special types of introductions and conclusions work particularly well for narratives.

Narrative Introductions

Set the Scene Narratives often begin by setting the scene of the upcoming action. Notice how John Steinbeck uses imagery and alliteration to create a vivid description.

About fifteen miles below Monterey, on the wild coast, the Torres family had their farm, a few sloping acres above a cliff that dropped to the brown reefs and to the hissing white waters of the ocean. Behind the farm the stone mountains stood up against the sky. The farm buildings huddled like clinging aphids on the mountain skirts, crouched low to the ground as though the wind might blow them into the sea. The little shack, the rattling, rotting barn were gray-bitten with sea salt, beaten by the damp

wind until they had taken on the color of the granite hills. Two horses, a red cow and a red calf, half a dozen pigs, and a flock of lean, multicolored chickens stocked the place. A little corn was raised on the sterile slope, and it grew short and thick under the wind, and all the cobs formed on the landward sides of the stalks.

John Steinbeck, "Flight"

Describe the Main Character Consider beginning your narrative with a description of the main character. Eudora Welty used carefully chosen details to help readers form a mental picture of her character.

> It was December—a bright frozen day in the early morning. Far out in the country there was an old Negro woman with her head tied in a red rag, coming along a path through the pinewoods. Her name was Phoenix Jackson. She was very old and small and she walked slowly in the dark pine shadows, moving a little from side to side in her steps, with the balanced heaviness and lightness of a pendulum in a grandfather clock. She carried a thin, small cane made from an umbrella, and with this she kept tapping the frozen earth in front of her. This made a grave and persistent noise in the still air, that seemed meditative like the chirping of a solitary little bird.
>
> **Eudora Welty, "A Worn Path"**

Introduce the Central Conflict Many stories are about the working out of some conflict, or struggle. Often writers begin their stories by introducing that conflict.

> The thousand injuries of Fortunato I had borne as I best could; but when he ventured upon insult, I vowed revenge. You, who so well know the nature of my soul, will not suppose, however, that I gave utterance to a threat. At length, I would be avenged; this was a point definitely settled—but the very definiteness with which it was resolved precluded the idea of risk. I must not only punish with impunity. A wrong is unredressed when retribution overtakes its redresser. It is equally unredressed when the avenger fails to make himself felt as such to him who has done the wrong.
>
> **Edgar Allan Poe, "The Cask of Amontillado"**

Introduce a Major Symbol Some writers like to start a story with an image that they will later develop into a major symbol. For example, in James Hurst's story "The Scarlet Ibis," the ibis, a type of bird, comes to symbolize all people and creatures that are rare, exotic, and fragile. Hurst begins his story by both setting the scene and introducing the symbol from which the story takes its name.

> It was in the clove of seasons, summer was dead but autumn had not yet been born, that the ibis lit the bleeding tree. The flower garden was stained with rotting brown magnolia petals and ironweeds grew rank amid the purple phlox. The five o'clocks by the chimney wall still marked time, but the oriole nest in the elm was untenanted and rocked back and forth like an empty cradle. The last graveyard flowers were blooming, and their smell drifted across the cotton field and through every room of our house, speaking softly the names of our dead.
>
> **James Hurst, "The Scarlet Ibis"**

There are many other ways to begin a story. As pointed out at the beginning of this handbook, you can begin in the middle of things *(in medias res)* with some central action, and then go back and describe the events that lead up to this action. You can also use a combination of methods. In his classic story "The Devil and Tom Walker," for example, Washington Irving begins with two paragraphs that not only describe the setting but also introduce the main characters, the central conflict, and the major symbols of the story. As you write your introduction, experiment with several of the methods or with a combination of methods that will help draw your readers into your narrative. Then, when you revise, choose the introduction that is most effective.

Narrative Conclusions

Just as special types of introductions are most effective for narratives, so are certain types of conclusions.

Present the Last Event Many times a story simply ends with the last in a series of events. This type of conclusion is particularly common in short stories and novels.

> Through the window I saw Tom Wells come out of his bungalow, staring first up at the circling fighters and then down at the DC-4. He shrugged his arms into his old sheepskin jacket and began to run toward me over the grass.
>
> **Dick Francis, *Flying Finish***

End with a Climactic Event The climax is the point of highest suspense or tension in a story. A writer may decide to end a story at this moment of heightened tension. In a classic example of such a conclusion, Frank Stockton ends his short story "The Lady, or the Tiger?" at the height of emotional conflict for a young man whose jealous lover must decide between condemning him to death or giving him up to another woman. The reader never finds out which course the woman chooses.

> Her decision had been indicated in an instant, but it had been made after days and nights of anguished deliberation. She had known she would be asked, she had decided what she would answer, and, without the slightest hesitation, she had moved her hand to the right.
>
> The question of her decision is one not to be lightly considered, and it is not for me to presume to set myself up as the one person able to answer it. And so I leave it with all of you: Which came out of the opened door—the lady, or the tiger?
>
> **Frank Stockton, "The Lady, or the Tiger?"**

Provide a Resolution Unlike Stockton, most writers choose to resolve a story's conflict with an episode or thought that follows the climactic event. Such a conclusion, or resolution, does not necessarily eliminate surprise or suspense for the reader. For example, the short story "An Occurrence at Owl Creek Bridge" has a sudden, surprising conclusion. Throughout the story, the central character, Peyton Farquhar, has tried to escape death by hanging. Thinking he has really escaped, he reaches his home and leaps into the arms of his beloved; at that moment, the conflict is suddenly resolved.

> As he is about to clasp her, he feels a stunning blow upon the back of the neck; a blinding white light blazes all about him with a sound like the shock of a cannon—then all is darkness and silence!
>
> Peyton Farquhar was dead; his body, with a broken neck, swung gently from side to side beneath the timbers of the Owl Creek Bridge.
>
> **Ambrose Bierce, "An Occurrence at Owl Creek Bridge"**

Practice Your Skills

A. Two of the thesis statements below need to be revised. Rewrite them so that each clearly states a main idea and reveals a plan of organization or a point of view. Then write an introductory paragraph or a conclusion for each of the three topics, using the techniques described in this handbook. Include the thesis statement in your introduction or rephrase it for your conclusion.

1. There are responsibilities of citizenship that all people over the age of eighteen share.
2. Teenagers need to have their own spending money. Even if they work after school, they can still do their homework. Having money teaches people how to be responsible with it.
3. Movies are never entirely boring. Unlike a bad play, which is intolerable if the script is poor and the acting is embarrassing, a bad movie can be salvaged by a beautiful score, exciting special effects, or an unusual setting.

B. Write an introduction or a conclusion to one of the pieces of nonfiction described below. Make sure that your main idea or purpose is clearly stated.

1. A speech to the local school board, arguing that tryouts for sports teams should be eliminated so that all students are free to participate in the sports of their choice
2. A personal profile of your favorite teacher, friend, or community leader for the school literary magazine
3. An editorial for or against whale and dolphin exhibitions in aquariums around the country

C. Read the following scenarios for short stories, or use your imagination to create a scenario of your own. Freewrite about different ways of beginning and ending the stories. Then share your ideas with your classmates in a group discussion.

1. *Setting:* a large suburban high school
   Characters: six high school students
   Conflict: A high school junior is pressured to join a social group, but she faces a difficult decision: although she likes the people in the group, she must give up two of her childhood friends in order to join.
2. *Setting:* a potato field
   Character: a middle-aged farmer
   Conflict: The farmer checks on her potato plants and discovers pea-green slime bubbling up from a hole in the ground.

Elaboration: Developing Writing Topics

As a writer, you can elaborate on important concepts by providing specific information that illustrates your point. Elaboration helps readers understand your idea by providing convincing or vivid support, in much the same way that details added to a roughly sketched drawing often make the picture more realistic, memorable, or meaningful. The details you choose to support your topic allow you to explore your personal interests and make the topic your own.

While elaboration can occur at any point in the writing process, many people like to work out their ideas in great detail during prewriting. They come up with a topic, with main ideas related to the topic, and with specific details related to these main ideas early in the writing process. Then, and only then, do they begin writing. However, elaboration need not occur only during prewriting. Many people find that as they draft, dozens of ideas for elaboration occur to them. Sometimes they also discover that there are gaps in their material, and they add additional information to fill these gaps. Elaboration also happens frequently during revision. As writers read over their drafts, they often find ideas that seem weak and that need additional support. Elaboration is, therefore, a key revision technique.

Elaboration adds details like the detail in the elaborate ceremonial dress of the Quapaw Tribe, Quapaw, Oklahoma.

APPROACHES TO ELABORATION

The technique of questioning, as well as various other information-gathering techniques, are useful ways of collecting details. In addition, you can use any of the methods for finding and focusing ideas described in Writing Handbooks 2 and 3 or graphic devices discussed in Writing Handbook 4 to find details you can use in elaborating on your topic.

Questioning

Action Questions Action questions—those beginning with the words *who, what, where, when, why,* or *how*—are especially helpful when you need details to describe an event. The following are some action questions beginning with the five *W*'s and *H*:

1. *Who?* Who is, was, or will be responsible? Who else is, was, or will be involved?
2. *What?* What is happening? What has happened? What might happen?
3. *Where?* Where does, did, or will it happen? What is the place like?
4. *When?* When does, did, or will it happen?
5. *Why?* Why did, does, or will it happen? What is, was, or will be causing it? What is, was, or will be its purpose?
6. *How?* How does, did, or will it happen? How does, did, or will it work?

   The **action pentad** shown below represents another method of questioning a subject that involves action.

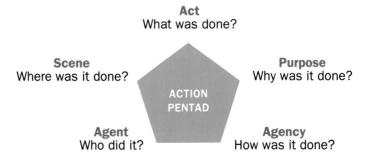

Act
What was done?

Scene
Where was it done?

Purpose
Why was it done?

ACTION
PENTAD

Agent
Who did it?

Agency
How was it done?

Category Questions One approach to analyzing a subject is by asking **category questions** to explore the various ways in which it can be classified. Think of as many different categories, classes, or groups as you can to which the subject might belong. For example, is the subject a physical object? An event? A place? An opinion or a position on an issue? Category questions can also focus on many aspects of an idea, such as how it relates to other ideas, where the idea comes from, and what is already known about it. The chart on the next page presents a list of categories and related questions.

Definition

- How does the dictionary define it? How would I define it?
- To what group does it belong?
- What are some specific examples of it?
- What are its parts? How might they be divided?

Comparison

- What is it similar to? In what ways?
- What is it different from? In what ways?
- What is it better than? In what ways?
- What is it worse than? In what ways?

Cause and Effect

- What causes it?
- What effects does it have?
- What is its purpose?
- When might it happen again?

Conditions and Events

- Is it possible? Why or why not?
- Is it practical? Why or why not?
- Has it happened before? When? How?
- Who has done or experienced it?

Documentation

- What facts or statistics do I know about it?
- What laws are there about it?
- What have I seen, heard, or read about it?
- What do people say about it?
- What saying, proverb, song, or poem do I know about it?
- How could I find out more about it?

Invention Questions To see your subject from a different angle, try asking yourself questions based on suggestions made by the Greek philosopher Aristotle about 2,300 years ago. Aristotle's twenty-eight techniques, known as methods of Aristotelian invention, originally were intended to give guidance in developing persuasive arguments. These methods are still used today to stimulate creative thinking. The following chart lists some of Aristotle's most useful methods. Any of these techniques can help you elaborate on topics for writing.

Techniques for Invention

- Compare and contrast your subject with other things. Find ways in which your subject is unique.
- Think of synonyms for your subject and of their implications or connotations.
- Consider how your subject changes over time.
- Relate the subject to yourself.
- Define your subject; think of the different meanings of words used to name it.
- Think of the parts of your subject.
- Look for examples of your subject. Think of what your examples have in common or how they differ and see if you can generalize from them.
- Look for causes and effects, pros and cons.
- Look for analogies and draw conclusions about your subject based on your analogies.
- Contrast the actual or current state of your subject with its possible state.
- Consider common opinions concerning your subject and whether these opinions are factually based.

Gathering Information

There are basically three sources you can consult for answers to the questions you have generated about your topic: yourself—dialoguing; other people—interviewing; and resource materials—the library.

Dialoguing Of course, writers use dialogue to bring out the personalities of their fictional characters and to advance the action of their stories. However, a writer can also use dialogue to develop writing ideas in various ways.

- Interview yourself about the topic and write down both your questions and your answers. Be sure to ask follow-up questions to help you access all that you know.
- Hold a dialogue between two parts of yourself and explore your contradictory feelings. Have your confident side encourage your insecure side to try something new; or imagine that you're in the middle of running a marathon. Your tired legs are trying to convince your mind to let them rest.
- Take on the roles of two characters (or even of one character and one abstract idea or inanimate object). For example, you could generate ideas about the nuclear arms race by imagining a dialogue between Abraham Lincoln and Mahatma Gandhi. You could generate ideas about forestry and conservation by writing a dialogue between a lumberjack and a fir tree.

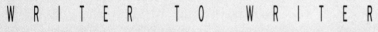

W R I T E R   T O   W R I T E R

The advice I would give to another writer is to concentrate, but let your mind run wild with thoughts.

Laura Corrado, student
Northfield, Illinois

Don't worry too much about whether the conversation makes sense. Just start the dialogue and get ready to be surprised as new ideas surface.

Dialoguing can be particularly helpful for developing ideas for persuasive writing because it requires you to consider more than one side of an issue.

Interviewing   Interviewing is one of the best ways to gather current information about a topic. Writers, especially journalists, often quote the people they interview in their articles, and these quotes add variety and authenticity to their writing. When you're writing about current events, interviews are particularly important. People who are witnesses to an event can give you facts and firsthand impressions that will enliven your story.

You may choose to interview a person who belongs to a certain profession or is an expert in a field you wish to write about. Your interview will go smoothly if you do some research and prepare your questions in advance. The expert will then be convinced of your sincere interest and will give you the information you need. Also, your own prior knowledge of the subject will enrich the interview. When incorporating information gathered from an interview in your writing, be sure to quote the person's words accurately, or to paraphrase or summarize his or her ideas. See "Using Source Materials in Writing," pages 495–502, for more information.

Using Library Resources   Reference works, such as encyclopedias, almanacs, dictionaries, and collections of short biographies, can be found in a separate section of your library. These references can help you find the specific details you need. It's useful to review a reference book quickly when you're looking for information. You can begin by skimming—moving your eyes quickly over the pages, noting titles, topic sentences, and highlighted words or phrases. By skimming, you can evaluate the work to see if it will be useful to you without reading more than you need.

If you find that you want to review the material more carefully, you can scan by moving your eyes quickly across the pages looking for specific words or phrases about your subject. When you come across a passage that contains such key words or phrases, stop and do in-depth reading, reading carefully to find the information you need. See "Strategies for Reading and Using Source Materials," pages 494–502 and "Library and Research Skills," pages 503–513 for additional information.

TYPES OF ELABORATION

What kinds of details do you use to elaborate on a given topic or main idea? The answer depends on the purpose, audience, and form of your writing. Sometimes, as in an academic report, facts and statistics are the most useful details. At other times, as in a story or essay, sensory details will be more appropriate. Other types of details that you can use for elaboration include incidents, specific examples, quotations, opinions, and graphic aids.

Facts and Statistics   A fact is a true statement that can be proved with reference materials or with firsthand observation. Statistics are facts expressed in numbers. The writer of the following paragraph used facts and statistics to elaborate on the topic of nuclear power.

> According to the 1990 Universal Almanac, there were 428 nuclear power reactors around the world in 1989. Twenty-six nations in that year were generating electricity from nuclear power plants. In eleven nations nuclear power produced over 30 percent of all electricity, and in three nations—Belgium, France, and South Korea—nuclear power plants produced over 50 percent of all electrical energy.

Sensory Details   When you develop an idea through description, you may want to use details that appeal to the senses of sight, smell, taste, touch, or hearing. As you read, pay attention to the sensory images in the following paragraph.

> The sounds of tag beat through the trees while the top branches waved in contrapuntal rhythms. I lay on a moment of green grass and telescoped the children's game to my vision. The girls ran about wild, now here, now there, never here, never was, they seemed to have no more direction than a splattered egg. . . . The gay picnic dresses dashed, stopped and darted like beautiful dragonflies over a dark pool. The boys, black whips in the sunlight, popped behind the trees where their girls had fled, half hidden and throbbing in the shadows.
>
> **Maya Angelou, *I Know Why the Caged Bird Sings***

COMPUTER
TIP

If you type an initial draft of your essay before completing your information gathering, you can use the insert mode to add more details, facts, quotations, and examples as you discover them.

STUDENT
MODEL

LITERARY
MODEL

Incidents Describing an incident—an interesting or significant event—can be a good way to elaborate on an idea. In the excerpt below, Annie Dillard uses an incident to illustrate how difficult it can be really to see, and then accurately describe, any particular aspect of nature.

> My eyes account for less than one percent of the weight of my head; I'm bony and dense; I see what I expect. I once spent a full three minutes looking at a bullfrog that was so unexpectedly large I couldn't see it even though a dozen enthusiastic campers were shouting directions. Finally I asked, "What color am I looking for?" and a fellow said, "Green." When at last I picked out the frog, I saw what painters are up against; the thing wasn't green at all, but the color of wet hickory bark.
>
> **Annie Dillard, _Pilgrim at Tinker Creek_**

Specific Examples Sometimes a main idea can be supported with one or more specific examples. The following paragraph is from a paper in which a student argues that cartoons can have literary or journalistic merit. The writer provides two specific examples of cartoonists who have received Pulitzer Prizes—awards given for excellence in literature, journalism, and music—to support his position.

> Most people associate the Pulitzer Prize with excellence in serious literature or reporting. However, the prize is also awarded to cartoonists. For example, in 1986 Jules Feiffer won the Pulitzer for his cartoons in New York's _The Village Voice._ In 1989, Jack Higgins won the prize for his cartooning in the _Chicago Sun-Times._ Given our all-too-human tendency to take ourselves too seriously, it is fitting that a prestigious prize should go to people who teach us how to laugh at ourselves.

Quotations You can use quotations in various ways. For example, a quote from an expert may give greater weight—and add credibility—to a point that you've made. You can also use quotations to introduce new ideas or details. The writer of the following paragraph uses a quote from a highly regarded novelist to support her main idea—that artistic temperaments must find expression.

STUDENT
· · · · · · · · · · · ·
M O D E L

> Some people have universal messages to convey, things to express to all of humanity. Such people, artists, need to find an art form—writing, music, visual arts—through which to send their messages. As Toni Morrison observed, "And like any artist with no art form, she became dangerous." That is, without an artistic outlet, emotional pressure may build and turn into anger or violence.

Opinions Wishes, dreams, judgments, and proposals—all are forms of opinion. Opinions are often used for elaboration. In the following paragraph, the opinion expressed in the first sentence is supported by several other opinions that follow. Each sentence in the paragraph is what is known technically as a statement of obligation. A statement of obligation tells what the writer believes should, must, or ought to be done.

STUDENT
· · · · · · · · · · · ·
M O D E L

> If we are really serious about the health of our citizens, then we ought to act now to correct some of the abuses in food labeling and advertising. We should stop manufacturers from using the label "natural" on products full of man-made chemicals. We should stop them from labeling foods "lite" that contain nothing but empty calories, often in the form of sugar. We should stop them from plastering "no cholesterol" on the front of products that are full of saturated fats. We should require that the percentage of fat and sugar in every product be posted, clearly, on food labels. Only by doing such things can we counteract the subtly deceptive advertising that is making America, oddly enough, both overweight and undernourished.

Graphic Aids Sometimes a graphic aid can support a main idea even more effectively than words can. Common graphic aids include bar graphs, pie charts, maps, tables, and time lines. For example, suppose that you are writing a report on the effect a mandatory recycling program would have on your community and on the life span of the landfills in your region. You could research what percentage of buried garbage is glass, paper, metal, and plastic, and graph your results in a pie chart. You also could add to your paper a bar graph showing examples of how costs of recycling compare with revenues from the sale of recycled materials.

Practice Your Skills

A. Choose three of the following main ideas. Follow the suggestions in parentheses to come up with new ideas to support or develop each statement you select.

1. Knowledge of science is essential to understanding events in the modern age. (Browse through some news magazines and newspapers to find specific examples of events and discoveries that can be fully understood only by people with at least some scientific knowledge.)
2. Not only is the population of the earth growing rapidly, most of this growth is occurring in the poorest countries on the planet. (Look into some almanacs or encyclopedia yearbooks to find facts and statistics to support this statement.)
3. No real friend will encourage you to do things that will bring you harm. (Use your own knowledge, information from a group discussion, dialoguing, or information that you gather through freewriting or clustering.)
4. My favorite [painting, sculpture, sport, automobile] is _____ . (Fill in the blanks. Then use questioning, charting, brainstorming, freewriting, or personal observation to gather details.)
5. A number of government officials, as well as ordinary citizens, oppose the proposed [city ordinance, school re-zoning, new highway, tax increase]. (Choose any issue relevant in your community. Then look through newspapers to find articles, editorials, and letters to the editor that pertain to your topic. Interview elected officials and city residents for more information. Use quotations carefully to add details and to support your main points.)

Fresh Gasoline,
by Noboru Tsubaki,
1989

B. Imagine that you are going to use the following information in a writing assignment. Create a bar chart or table you might include in your finished product.

The American Chamber of Commerce Researchers Association reports on the cost of living in various cities in the United States. The United Nations reports on the cost of living of its personnel in cities around the world. Each report is based on a cost of living index. The overall average is 100, and each city's index is a percentage of the average. In 1988, the cost of living index for Boston was 164.8. For New York it was 154.5. For Chicago it was 122.3. For Atlanta, it was 108.9. For Dallas it was 104.1. For Omaha, Nebraska, it was only 92.5. In Baghdad, it was 116 and in Managua, 68.

Unity and Coherence

To communicate ideas clearly, your writing should flow effortlessly from one idea to the next. The qualities that create an impression of smoothness and logic in writing are known as unity and coherence.

Writing has **unity** when all the details are related directly to the main idea. Writing has **coherence** when all the details are connected logically to one another. **Transitional devices** help provide logical links between ideas.

METHODS FOR ACHIEVING
UNITY

Unity in writing means that all sentences support the main idea. An unrelated thought can derail readers and make them lose track of where you, the writer, are trying to take them.

Unity in Paragraphs

To maintain unity in paragraphs, check each sentence against the paragraph's topic sentence, main idea, or function. Here are some different ways to be sure you're writing a unified paragraph.

1. Write a topic sentence and supporting details. A topic sentence states the main idea of a paragraph. If you do have a topic sentence, you can easily check each sentence to make sure it supports the main idea.

2. Write a series of sentences all related to a single, implied main idea. In the following paragraph, all the sentences help support a single main idea—that students have different ideas about the perfect way to study. However, no single sentence expresses this idea explicitly. Instead, the main idea is supported by the paragraph as a whole.

▼

> Some people are happiest studying in groups. Others are happier studying alone. Some students study better when they wait till the last minute and do their work under pressure of a time limit. Others study better if they begin well ahead of a deadline and work slowly and steadily toward their goal.

Writing
—**TIP**—

Writing a topic sentence is just one way to help ensure that a paragraph will be unified. You don't have to have a topic sentence in every paragraph.

STUDENT
· · · · · · · · · · · ·
M O D E L

3. Delete unrelated ideas. One way to achieve unity is simply to delete any material not related to your main idea, or to replace it with material that is related during revision.

Topic sentence

Sentences related to topic sentence

Sentence not related to topic sentence—should be deleted or moved to another paragraph

Grandma Moses began painting in her seventies, and in the last two decades of her life became one of the best-known American painters. While the painting style of Grandma Moses was termed "primitive" because she had never had an art lesson, people appreciated the sincerity and humanity of her work. Her colorful paintings depicted simple scenes of American farm life, based on her own experiences in New York and Virginia. This truly American artist continued producing numerous paintings until her death at the age of 101. Another famous painter of that time was Andrew Wyeth.

Out for Christmas Trees, by Grandma Moses 1946

Copyright ©1973, Grandma Moses Properties Co., New York

4. When necessary, create two paragraphs from one. Notice that the paragraph below lacks unity because it really deals with two main ideas. The best way to fix this problem is to create two separate paragraphs, each about a single idea.

> In science-fiction movies, insects and other creatures often achieve the size of skyscrapers and threaten the existence of humans. During the 1950's and 1960's, Hollywood and Tokyo could not produce enough such films. Giant scorpions, ants, spiders, lizards, octopuses, lobsters, and birds (some as large as the Empire State Building) crawled, swam, flew, and generally ate their way across the movie screens of the world. ¶Often the reason given in the films for the amazing growth of these monstrous antagonists was a nuclear accident or some chemical formula created by a mad scientist. However, such increases are actually physically impossible. When a creature doubles in size, its volume and weight quadruple. An ant the size of a dog would literally be crushed by its own weight— crushed flatter than one of Godzilla's victims.

Unity in Description

When you write a descriptive paragraph, you need to be especially concerned about unity. A good description relies on creating a unified impression rather than a unity of ideas. Consider the following example.

> The table in the corner of the terrace glittered, an unexpectedly formal island of glass and silver in the darkness. It was lit by one tall lamp with a dark shade; the light flowed downwards, concentrated on the white cloth, and was then reflected up, lighting our faces strangely . . . against the surrounding darkness.
>
> **John Fowles, *The Magus***

Notice the words and phrases that support the picture developing in your mind: *glittered, glass, silver, lit, lamp, light, white, reflected, lighting.* All of these words convey an image of brightness and light.

Coherence in writing means that the ideas flow from one to the next without awkward breaks or gaps in logical organization. In a coherent paragraph, the sentences are connected logically. You can achieve such connections through the use of parallel structures and punctuation. You can also use transitional words to show the logical order of your ideas, and you can use pronouns, synonyms, and repeated words to show that statements made in separate sentences refer to the same things.

Transitional Devices

The major method of achieving coherence within a paragraph is by using transitional words or phrases. Occasionally, two ideas are so obviously connected that no transitional device is needed, as in these sentences.

LITERARY
M O D E L

> "We could go out to the park and have breakfast outdoors."
> I looked out the open door.
>
> **Ernest Hemingway, *A Farewell to Arms***

More often, however, you need to add a special word or phrase to show how two ideas are connected. Consider the following.

PROFESSIONAL
M O D E L

> Officials still can't explain how the tambequi [a carnivorous fish] got to Oregon, where it's illegal to sell anything even resembling a piranha. *Fortunately for Oregon*, the fish are not likely to survive a single winter in the Pacific Northwest.
>
> ***Oregon's Agricultural Press***

In this example, "Fortunately for Oregon" shows the relationship between the idea of the first sentence and the idea stated in the second.

Though all transitions show relationships, there are many different kinds of relationships and thus many different kinds of transitional words and phrases. Some common transitional words show relationships of time or place. Others show logical relationships, such as cause and effect, similarity, degree, or contrast.

Time or Sequence   When you are telling a story or describing a process, you will often choose to connect your ideas with words that refer to time or sequence (the order of events). Some common transitional words that refer to time are *before, during, after, earlier, later, soon, first, next, then,* and *finally.* The following paragraph shows how transitions of time or sequence can be used to connect ideas.

Notice how the transitional words *soon, first, then,* and *during* provide coherence.

> *Soon* after seven I went to Mummy and Daddy and then to the sitting room to undo my presents. The *first* to greet me was you, possibly the nicest of all. *Then* on the table there were a bunch of roses, a plant, and some peonies, and more arrived *during* the day.
>
> **Anne Frank, *The Diary of a Young Girl***

Place   When writing a visual description, you can connect your ideas with words that show spatial relationships. These words include *left, right, above, around, beneath, near,* and *under.* The following paragraph shows how transitional words that indicate spatial relationships can be used to connect a paragraph.

> The room was long with windows *on the right-hand side* and a door *at the far end* that went into the dressing room. The row of beds that mine was in *faced the windows* and another row, *under the windows, faced the wall*. If you lay on *your left side* you could see the dressing room door. There was another door *at the far end* that people sometimes came in by. If any one were going to die they put a screen *around the bed* so you could not see them die, but only the shoes and puttees of doctors and men nurses showed *under the bottom of the screen* and sometimes at the end there would be whispering.
>
> **Ernest Hemingway, *A Farewell to Arms***

Degree   When presenting ideas of unequal importance, you can connect your ideas with words that express degree. Examples include *better, best, more, most, even more, worse, worst, less,* and *least.* The following paragraph shows how transitional words that indicate degree can be used to provide coherence.

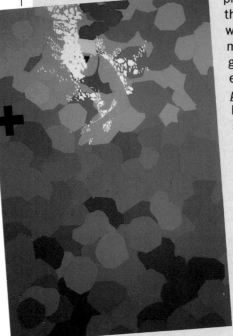

At first, learning to swim seemed like something I just had to do because it was one of the requirements of being a complete person. As time went on, though, I realized that the water was like a whole new world for me to explore. The confidence I got from conquering this new environment became _more important_ than the security of knowing that I had this basic life skill. But the _most important_ feeling that swimming gave me —_more important_ than confidence and a sense of security— was a feeling of freedom. I felt that I could go anywhere and do almost anything that anyone else could. I was a multi-environment creature now—no longer a prisoner of land.

Similarity and Difference The following transitional words show relationships of similarity and difference: _as, like, and, again, too, also, likewise, equally, similarly, another, moreover, in addition, in the same way,_ and _equally important._ Notice the transitions of comparison and contrast that connect ideas in the following paragraph.

When I was growing up, I sometimes had my own room and sometimes shared a room with my sisters. I felt _the same way about_ my sisters whether I said goodnight to them in the next bed or before I closed my door. _However,_ I felt _differently about_ myself when I could close the door and have my own space. _Similarly,_ now that I am an adult, whenever I really need to delve deep into my thoughts, I try to find somewhere to be alone.

Cause and Effect   Some words that show cause and effect are *once, since, therefore, as a result, because, besides, consequently,* and *so.* The following paragraph shows how transitions of cause and effect can be used to connect ideas.

▼

> One of the keys to raising output on a sustainable basis is protecting the resource base. _With cropland becoming scarce,_ future food security depends on safeguarding it both from conversion to nonfarm uses and from erosion that reduces its inherent productivity. Nearly a decade ago, U.S. Assistant Secretary of Agriculture Rupert Cutler observed that "asphalt is the land's last crop." _Once productive cropland is lost_ to suburban development, shopping malls, or roads, it is difficult to restore it to food production.
>
> **Lester R. Brown et al., "Outlining a Global Action Plan"**

PROFESSIONAL
M O D E L

Note that the phrases "With cropland becoming scarce" and "Once productive cropland is lost" both imply causality. (In this context, *once* means "as a result of.")

Other Relationships   In addition to the uses shown above, transitions can signal that an example is coming up, that the material following the transition is being emphasized, or that additional information or explanation is being given.

Transitions That Introduce Examples

as	for example	for instance
like	such as	to illustrate
that is	namely	in particular

Transitions That Signal Emphasis

indeed	in fact	in other words

Transitions That Signal More Information

in addition	besides	furthermore
moreover	also	as well

Transitions That Signal Explanation

for example	that is	in other words

Notice how the transitions in the paragraph below lead you from one idea to the next.

Penguins go to great lengths to establish families, and the male penguin shares parenting responsibility equally with the female. _For example_, after the female lays the eggs, the male guards them for five weeks while the female hunts the ocean for food. The male has to sit on the eggs faithfully to protect them from predatory birds, and he rarely abandons his brood. _Furthermore_, the male shows his loyalty to the female when she returns. Before he goes off to stretch his legs and take a swim, he brings the female a stone. The male penguin is monogamous and highly protective of his young. _In other words_, he is a faithful "husband" and a devoted father.

Word Chains

Although many transitions connect two or more ideas by describing the relationships between them, some transitions connect ideas by repeating key words or referring to the same idea again in different words.

Repetition Skillful repetition of key words can tie ideas together and give your work coherence. For example, notice how the repetition of the word _grass_ forms a kind of chain and serves to link the sentences that follow.

The sun lay on the _grass_ and warmed it, and in the shade under the _grass_ the insects moved, ants and ant lions to set traps for them, grasshoppers to jump into the air and flick their yellow wings for a second, sow bugs like little armadillos, plodding restlessly on many tender feet. And over the _grass_ at the roadside a land turtle crawled, turning aside for nothing, dragging his highdomed shell over the _grass_.

John Steinbeck, _The Grapes of Wrath_

Pronouns As you know, pronouns refer back to nouns or forward to nounlike words. They can help give your writing coherence by referring to a key word again and again. The following passage uses pronouns to provide coherence.

> Fourteen passengers, with the captain, remained on board, resolving to trust their fortunes to the *jolly-boat* at the stern. We lowered *it* without difficulty, although it was only by a miracle that we prevented *it* from swamping as *it* touched the water. *It* contained, when afloat, the captain and his wife, Mr. Wyatt and party, a Mexican officer, wife, four children, and myself.
>
> **Edgar Allan Poe, "The Oblong Box"**

LITERARY
M O D E L

Grammar
——**TIP**——

Make sure all your pronouns have clear, unambiguous antecedents.

Synonyms and Near Synonyms Sometimes you may decide to take a different approach to repetition—thinking of different ways to refer to the same thing. The following paragraph shows how synonyms and near synonyms can be used to provide coherence. Richard Adams uses "half-darkness" as a synonym for *night,* and "a peaceful sound" as a near synonym for *bubbling.*

> They met with no more adventures that *night*, moving quietly along the edges of the fields under the *dim light* of a *quarter moon.* The *half-darkness* was full of sounds and movement. Once Acorn put up a plover, which flew round them, calling shrilly, until at length they crossed a bank and left it behind. Soon after, somewhere near them, they heard the unceasing *bubbling* of a nightjar—*a peaceful sound,* without menace, which died gradually away as they pushed on.
>
> **Richard Adams, *Watership Down***

LITERARY
M O D E L

Parallel Structures

Another way to achieve coherence is by the use of parallel structures. This simply means using similar grammatical structures or sentence patterns for ideas that are equal or similar. For example, the following sentences use parallel structures to create transitions between similar ideas.

> She was a beautiful baby. She blew shining bubbles of sound. She loved motion, loved light, loved color and music and textures.
>
> **Tillie Olsen, "Here I Stand Ironing"**

LITERARY
M O D E L

Unity and Coherence **409**

Note how Tillie Olsen uses parallel structures by beginning each sentence with the word *she* and a verb. Also note her parallel repetition of the verb *loved* in the third sentence. By using parallel structures in this way, Olsen conveys to readers that the ideas are all related to the main idea—*She was a beautiful baby.*

You can sometimes enhance parallelism in your writing by using semicolons. For example, notice how the semicolon is used in the following examples to separate items with similar grammatical structures. Because the punctuation indicates how the material is related, it makes for coherence through parallelism.

> Karate is a sport; it is also a philosophy of life.

> The beach party was a disaster from start to finish: Teddy got the beach blanket wet; Manuel squashed the sandwiches; Marcy forgot her bathing suit.

At times, you can emphasize the coherence of your writing by using colons. This punctuation mark shows that the material that follows gives further information about the idea that precedes it. In the second example above, you can see how the colon, as well as the semicolons, makes for parallelism and indicates to readers how the information is related.

ACHIEVING UNITY AND COHERENCE IN COMPOSITIONS

Just as you work to achieve unity and coherence when you write a single paragraph, you need these qualities in longer compositions. In a unified paragraph, each sentence is related to the main idea of the paragraph; so too, each paragraph of a longer composition must be related to the main idea of the whole piece. Coherence works much the same way. Just as each sentence in a coherent paragraph should follow logically from the one that precedes it, so in a coherent composition each paragraph should follow logically from the one before.

In order to create unity and coherence in longer compositions, you can use the same techniques you use to create these qualities within single paragraphs. For example, to create unity in a composition you must make sure that each paragraph, detail, example, or illustration clearly contributes to the main idea or purpose of the composition. Notice that the composition that follows has a simple pattern: the first paragraph introduces the main idea and the following paragraphs support this idea. All the supporting paragraphs are tightly linked to the main idea.

Likewise, to create coherence in a composition you must make sure all the paragraphs of the composition develop logically from one to another. The major way you can create coherence in a longer composition is by using transitional devices to connect paragraphs to one another and to give coherence to the composition as a whole. Notice how the following composition uses various transitional devices to create coherence.

Waking in the morning while my brain is still fuzzy and before my eyes are really open, my sharpest sense seems to be my hearing. The first sound I hear is my cat purring loudly in my ear from where she has curled on my pillow for the night. Then there's the soft whir of my electric clock on the bedside table. But these are just the preliminaries to my morning symphony of sound.

Things really get going as I tune into my mother making breakfast: the slam of the fridge; water running in the sink; the clatter of the dishes and silverware on the table; the clink of metal against metal as she beats the eggs in a metal bowl for scrambled eggs.

Then the range of my hearing broadens. "Have a good day, dear," my mother says to my father, who replies with his usual indistinct "Umph" as he swallows his last bit of coffee and gives her a quick kiss. The back door slams, and I hear the car door crack shut and the revving of the motor.

Finally, the last note of the symphony: "Sara, Sara, time to get up now." My mother wakes me to toast and eggs, and the rest of my senses come alive. My ears will not be as keen again for the rest of the day.

Practice Your Skills

A. Revise the following paragraphs to correct problems in unity and coherence.

1. Langston Hughes was very much aware of the proud history of African Americans, and he encapsulated this history in a magnificent poem entitled "The Negro Speaks of Rivers." This poem is as good as—maybe better than—Hughes's poem "Song of a Black Girl." The poem makes reference to great African cultures and to the rivers associated with them—the cultures that grew up along the banks of the Congo, the Nile, and finally the Mississippi. Hughes speaks for African Americans collectively when he writes, "I've known rivers:/Ancient, dusky rivers./My soul has grown deep like the rivers." Another great poet of the Harlem Renaissance was Arna Bontemps.

2. The computer has had a long and interesting history. In the 1970's, Steven Jobs and Stephan Wozniak, working in a garage, created the first highly successful personal computer—the Apple®—and the era of personal computers began. The first computer ever conceived was a calculating machine dreamed up by the Englishman Charles Babbage in the mid-nineteenth century. Then, in the early part of the twentieth century, a brilliant English mathematician, Alan Turing, worked out the mathematical basis for modern computing, using a binary code of 1's and 0's. The abacus used by the ancient Chinese was a kind of computer used for simple arithmetic. Next came the Princeton math professor John von Neumann, who in the 1930's and 1940's created the concept of a stored program. Finally in 1946, the first modern computer, the ENIAC, was built—a computer that filled a large room. From that time on, computers got smaller and smaller. First came the mainframes, then the minis, and at last, personal computers and workstations.

B. Read the following pairs of sentences that come at the end of one paragraph and begin the next. The sentences in each pair are linked by a transitional device. Find the device in each pair and tell what kind it is.

1. Since the beginnings of astronomy, scientists have been paying close attention to Earth's closest neighbor—Mars.

   Mars is quite similar to our own planet.

2. The next step in aviation came around 1900 when German engineers designed the zeppelin.

   By 1910, the zeppelin was providing passenger service.

The abacus is an accounting instrument that has been used by the Chinese for centuries.

3. Our precinct's low turnout for the last national elections seemed to indicate a growing sense of political apathy.

> Yet, record numbers voted in the local elections because of their concern over the zoning issue.

4. The school's on-the-road driving lessons have proven valuable.

> Another benefit is the classroom instruction on rules of the road.

5. By 7:00 P.M. hockey practice was over.

> Consequently, I went into the locker room to shower and dress.

6. The rain rapidly began to fall on the campsite, creating panic among the picnickers.

> They began to gather up their lunches and hurriedly shove them into their hampers.

7. The robin had built its nest in the maple tree.

> Below on the ground were a family of chipmunks who had built a burrow under the garage.

8. Throughout the tropical forest, the other animals could hear the angry sounds of the hungry dinosaur.

> The giant reptile was getting nearer and nearer to the time when he would have to eat again.

C. Copy the following passages. Underline the transitional words and phrases in each. Then discuss with your classmates the function that each transition serves. Discuss both transitions that show relationships and transitions that repeat or refer. Note that each of these paragraphs contains a number of different kinds of transitions, including pronouns, repeated words, and synonyms.

1. Teachers recall the beguiling freedom and charm of younger children's work and wonder what happened. They deplore what they see as "tightness" and "lack of creativity" in students' drawings. The children themselves often become their own most unrelenting critics. Consequently, teachers frequently resort to crafts projects such as paper mosaics, string-painting, drip-painting, and other manipulations of materials.

   As a result, most students do not learn how to draw in the early and middle grades. Their self-criticism becomes permanent, and they very rarely try to learn to draw later in life.
   Betty Edwards, *Drawing on the Right Side of the Brain*

2. It is not too much to speak of the court's decision [*Brown* v. *Board of Education of Topeka,* the decision that ruled school segregation unconstitutional] as a new birth of freedom. It comes at a juncture in the affairs of mankind when this reaffirmation of basic human values is likely to have a wonderfully tonic effect. America is rid of an incubus which impeded and embarrassed it in all its relations with the world. Abroad as well as at home, this decision will engender a renewal of faith in democratic institutions and ideals.

The Washington Post, May 19, 1954

3. When atoms combine to form a solid, you can picture the result as being something akin to a large Tinker-Toy structure. The atoms themselves are represented by the spheres where the sticks come together, while the sticks themselves represent the forces which hold the atoms in place. Depending on the type of material and the number of different types of atoms involved, these structures can get very complicated. The forces between atoms in the structure can be generated in a number of different ways. For example, electrons can jump from one atom to another, leaving the original atoms with a net positive charge and the final one with a net negative charge. In this case, simple electrical attraction holds the material together. The atoms in ordinary table salt are bound together this way. Alternately, atoms may share electrons, a process which creates an attractive force. Most organic materials are held together by this process. Intermediate situations, in which electrons are partly exchanged and partly shared, can also arise.

James S. Trefil, *A Scientist at the Seashore*

D. Read the following summary of a composition. Each statement represents a paragraph. Describe the techniques you would use to revise the paragraphs to make the composition more unified and coherent.

> MAIN IDEA: Gradually, scientists are discovering the secrets of the animal world.

1. In 1952, a scientist named T. H. Bullock discovered that rattlesnakes can "see" with their eyes closed.
2. The snake used two dimples between its nostrils and its eyes.
3. The rattler can locate its prey with its eyes blindfolded.
4. Some scientists study plants, and others study animals.
5. These dimples are heat sensitive, so that the snake can locate its prey and also determine its shape and size.
6. The frog has a useful vision sense, too. It can block out objects that are neither a threat nor a goal.

BEARS TRAMPLE VIOLETS

When we root, root, root for the home team, who are we really supporting? To judge by their names, it is everything from fearsome beasts to flowers.

Sometimes, we cheer vicious predators—Lions, Tigers, and Bears—on to victory. Other times it's gentler flora and fauna, such as Buckeyes, Sycamores, and Violets, or Beavers, Ducks, and Cardinals. The world of nature also contributes many reptiles and insects, such as Rattlers, Horned Frogs, Hornets, and Yellowjackets.

Humans have not been left out. There are ethnic groups (Fighting Irish and Ragin' Cajuns), and all sorts of Cowboys and Indians. Occupations are well represented, with Boilermakers, Packers, Engineers, and Lumberjacks. So is crime, with a wide range of Pirates, Vandals, Bandits, and Raiders. Natural disasters—Hurricanes, Cyclones, and Earthquakes—have their place, as do all the colors of the rainbow, from Crimson, to Orangemen, to Big Green.

All of the team names make a statement. Often the statement is aggressive, since most team sports are aggressive activities. Sometimes the names are commemorative—the Cleveland Browns were not named after the color, but after the team founder, Paul Brown. Some statements are even antiestablishment. Students at the University of California at Santa Cruz voted to call their team the Banana Slugs to protest the "football mentality" at other schools.

©1990 TFC, INC.

The famous San Diego Chicken, Ted Giannoulas, is credited with pioneering the mascot craze in 1974. He remains a major box office draw for his unique comedy act.

The Art of Revision

Novelist
Joyce Carol Oates

Revision is not only an art, as Joyce Carol Oates suggests, but it
is also somewhat of a science that involves a number of distinct
activities. The following mnemonic can help you remember them.

- **R**eread your draft.
- **E**valuate it.
- **V**iew it as your audience might.
- **I**ncorporate new material.
- **S**earch for problems with your old material.
- **E**liminate those problems.

You don't have to wait until you've completed a draft to begin
revising: Revision is an ongoing part of the writing process. For
example, before you begin a draft, you may change your writing
plan or prewriting notes. During drafting, you will pursue new ideas
and modify your material accordingly; and after you finish the
draft, you will review your writing, again rethinking and restructur-
ing it as necessary.

Before completing your revision, set aside the draft for a day or
two so that you can return to it with a fresh eye. Also remember
that no two writers will make the same decisions, and there is no
correct approach to revision.

As you revise, you will focus on content, form, grammar, usage,
and mechanics. Although each type of revision involves a different
kind of thinking, in practice writers often revise content, review
form, and proofread for mechanical errors simultaneously.

Revising for Content

When you rethink the content of your writing—your most important task—you do whatever is necessary to make sure that

your work has a clear focus or main idea; ideas that are developed completely; and no unnecessary or irrelevant material. Consider the following criteria in evaluating your writing.

Checklist for Rethinking Content

- Have I discovered what is important about my topic? Have I expressed this focus or main idea clearly?

- Have I incorporated adequate detail? Are there weak or general ideas that I could replace with strong, specific ones?

- Are there ideas that I should add to help my readers better understand my message?

- Is there material that is unnecessary, irrelevant, or confusing?

Focus specifically on content as you read the following first draft of a student essay.

> The Gettysburg Address is one of the most famous speeches in American history. It was delivered at the dedication of a national cemetery at Gettysburg a few months after the battle of Gettysburg. The featured speaker at the ceremony was Edward Everett, one of the country's foremost orators.
>
> The ceremonies at Gettysburg began at ten o'clock in the morning. Edward Everett spoke for two hours. He spoke without looking at his manuscript, using gestures and raising and lowering his voice to make his points. People said he was his "classic best."
>
> After Everett finishes, Lincoln rose. He was on his feet less than three minutes. His speach did not sound like much since the audience seemed disapointed.
>
> Many people criticized the speech. A reporter from the Chicago Tribune was among the few to recognize the greatness of the occasion. He said that "the dedicatory remarks by President Lincoln will live among the annals of man."

You may note, as the writer did, that she had not clearly stated her main idea—the contrast between Everett's and Lincoln's speeches and the fact that few people at first realized the greatness of Lincoln's words. She therefore decided to add a clarifying sentence to her first paragraph. She realized that her main idea would be clearer if she added a supporting detail to the final paragraph in which she described the audience reactions to Lincoln's address. She also realized at this stage that other structural and mechanical errors still remained to be corrected.

Revising for Structure

When you revise for structure, you rework the form of your draft so it presents the ideas in a logical order, deals with a single major idea in each paragraph, and contains transitions that make the relationships between ideas clear. Ask yourself the following questions.

Checklist for Reworking Structure

- Are my ideas logically connected to one another? Would moving paragraphs or sentences make the relationships between my ideas clearer?
- Does each paragraph deal with one major idea or serve one major function?
- Are there places where I should add transitional words, phrases, or sentences to make sentences and paragraphs flow more smoothly and logically?
- Do my sentences repeat words or phrases needlessly? Can I combine any sentences to improve the grace and rhythm of my writing?

In reviewing the structure of her piece, the writer of the sample essay on the Gettysburg Address decided that the information about Edward Everett in her first paragraph actually belonged in the second paragraph. She also decided she needed a transitional phrase in her third paragraph to make clear her main point—the contrast between Everett's speech and Lincoln's. To make the sequence of events clearer, she also added the transitional word *afterwards* in her last paragraph. Finally, she combined several sentences with repeated words to make her writing more graceful. The revised draft on page 420 shows how she incorporated these content and structural changes into her revised piece.

Revising for Mechanics

Refining the mechanics, or proofreading your writing, adds the finishing touch to your work and prevents readers from being distracted from your ideas by errors in grammar, usage, or mechanics. Review your work with the following questions in mind.

Checklist for Refining Mechanics

- Have I used punctuation marks and capitalization correctly?

- Have I checked the spellings of all unfamiliar words?

- Have I used proper grammar? Do all my subjects and verbs agree? Have I corrected run-ons and sentence fragments?

- Is my usage correct? Have I used words with the correct meanings in their proper contexts?

When proofreading, keep a dictionary and a style book (such as the Grammar and Usage Handbook of this textbook) on your desk so that you can check items about which you are unsure. You will also find it helpful to use standard proofreading marks such as those in the following chart to indicate your changes. These symbols make it easy for you or anyone who reads your draft to understand how you want your draft corrected.

Proofreading Marks

∧	Insert a letter or word	⌒	Close up
⊙	Insert a period	¶	Begin a new paragraph
≡	Capitalize a letter	∧	Insert a comma
/	Make a capital letter lowercase	∿	Transpose the position of letters or words
ℯ	Delete letters or words		

You may choose to proofread as you write and revise, or save proofreading for your last draft.

COMPUTER
TIP

Word processing programs offer spelling checkers. Use them to help you identify misspelled words in your writing.

When the writer of the essay about the Gettysburg Address finished revising for content and structure, she proofread her piece, correcting several mechanical errors. All of these corrections are included in the edited copy shown below.

Abraham Lincoln's The Gettysburg Address is one of the most famous
At first, however, few people realized how momentous it was.
speeches in American history. It was delivered at the
dedication of a national cemetery at Gettysburg a few
months after the battle of Gettysburg. The featured
speaker at the ceremony was Edward Everett, one of
the country's foremost orators.

The ceremonies at Gettysburg began at ten o'clock
He
in the morning. Edward Everett spoke for two hours.
He spoke without looking at his manuscript, using
gestures and raising and lowering his voice to make
his points. People said he was at his "classic best."

d
After Everett finishes, Lincoln rose. He was on his
After Everett's two-hour oration,   Lincoln's   was unimpressive, and
feet less than three minutes. His speach did not
e   p
sound like much since the audience seemed disa-
Afterwards,
pointed. Many people criticized the speech. A reporter
from the Chicago Tribune was among the few to recognize the greatness of the occasion. He said that
"the dedicatory remarks by President Lincoln will live
Secretary of State Seward
among the annals of man."   commented, "His speech was not
equal to him."

Abraham Lincoln,
by George Peter
Alexander Healy

Practice Your Skills

Read the following paragraphs and revise them. Discuss your revisions with a small group, and compare the different ways group members revised each paragraph.

1. In the 1960's, a schoolteacher in kettering, England began tracking Soviet satellites with his students. They used some complex mathematical techniques, such as those required to determine apogees—just for fun—to see if they could detect a pattern in the flights. Mr. Perry's students liked mathematics but their favoriet subject was history. Mr. Perry and his students never expected that what they were doing would get any attenshun outside of their little school.

2. Perry was overwalmed with phone calls from top secret government officials and Journalists. The schoolboys had inadvertently gotten involved in an international spy thriller. It turned out that the information that Mr. perry and his students had gathered was very important to defense officials in the United States, they had actually found the location of a new Soviet satellite launching pad. They had also cracked a secret code formula and recognized that the purpose of the soviet satellites was survellence.

WRITING
HANDBOOK
12

Peer Response

All writers have their own approaches to revision. Some prefer to wait until their work is completely drafted before beginning to self-edit. Others rewrite constantly, often rewording the same section several times before moving to a new idea or chapter. During an interview in 1963, Ernest Hemingway said that before he began writing each day, he always rewrote what he had written the previous day. He recalled rewriting the last page of *A Farewell to Arms* thirty-nine times before it satisfied him. Then he read through the entire manuscript, making additional changes before sending it on to his editors for their suggestions.

The FAR SIDE Cartoon by Gary Larsen reprinted by permission of Chronicle Features, San Francisco, California

After self-editing, most writers still need the fresh eye and emotional distance of other readers to feel assured that their ideas are as clearly expressed as possible. Professional writers turn to their editors. In the classroom, you can turn to your peers. In asking other people to respond to your work, you are not giving up control of your writing. You are in charge. You can follow the advice of your peer reader or not, as you please.

WRITER TO WRITER

When I finish my first draft, I read the piece to see if it flows smoothly and makes sense. Then I have someone else read and critique it.

April Hicks, student
Jackson, Mississippi

An honest reader is precious to a writer. However, your reader needs to feel free to react honestly. If you can make your needs clear—mainly that you want your reader to react as an audience and not as a "fixer"—then his or her reactions, or lack of reaction, will be valuable. For example, if you don't get a laugh when you think you should, maybe you should rethink your writing.

422 Writing Handbook

If you can clearly tell your reader what you need him or her to respond to in your writing, you will be more likely to get a useful response. Here are some approaches to "directing" your reader:

Sharing with No Response   You can ask your reader just to listen as you read your piece aloud: "Please listen. Don't respond. Just let me read this to you." Believe it or not, you can tell a lot about your writing just by reading it aloud. It helps to have someone listen to you, even when he or she doesn't respond, because you are more aware of what you're saying when you have an audience. It may be particularly useful to you to have your reader simply listen silently when you have just started exploring ideas. At that stage, you may be feeling insecure—too unsure for criticism. Another time when you may not want response from your reader is when you are completely finished with a piece. You may just want to share it because you're proud of it. You don't want to make any more changes.

Requesting Only Positive Responses   Sometimes you may want your reader to respond to only the things he or she likes. You'll enjoy this kind of response, and it will also be useful to you. By listening carefully to what works for your reader, you may also be able to discover what doesn't work. For instance, if several readers don't mention an example that you thought was really effective, you may decide to reconsider it.

Sharing to Establish Clear Purpose   When you are trying to get a clear picture of your main ideas and themes, ask your reader questions like these: What do you hear as the main idea in my essay or the main feeling or theme in my story? What other ideas or themes do you hear? Through peer response, you might find out whether your writing says what you think it says. You might also hear some new ideas that will take you in interesting directions.

Getting a Response to Your Ideas   Ask your reader to talk to you about *what* you've said, not *how* you've said it. Pose questions such as these: What are your ideas on this topic? Do you agree or disagree with me? What more do you need to know? Answers to these questions can reveal whether or not you have succeeded in engaging your readers' interest in your ideas and whether or not your ideas make sense. By asking readers to respond to your ideas you may gain new insights that will help you clarify or expand your ideas.

Requesting Analytic Responses to Specific Features If there are particular aspects of your writing that concern you, say to your reader, "There are certain things about my piece that I want to focus on. Please tell me about . . . ." Then you can point to various features of your piece. For example, you might ask for help on something concrete and specific like sentence structure: Would you check this piece over to see if you can find any ways in which I can improve the variety of my sentences? Or you might ask for help on something more general like organization: Do you think my organization is logical? Do my examples help support my main idea?

Here are other types of questions you might consider asking your peer reader.

1. Is my language clear?
2. Are there enough examples?
3. Did I persuade you or at least make you question your position?
4. Does my organization seem logical? Does it lead you along without making you feel lost or off balance?
5. Do the paragraphs seem to work well as paragraphs?
6. I really feel nervous writing to this person, but I want to seem calm and confident. Have I managed to do that?

Requesting "Movies of the Reader's Mind" Say to your reader, "Let me stop you every few minutes as you read my piece. I want to find out what's going on in your mind—moment to moment—as you read."

For example, you might stop your reader, and he or she might respond, "Well, I was really caught up in what you were saying in the first couple of paragraphs in your story. Then when I started to read this paragraph, I became frustrated. I could see that I wasn't going to get any more description about Sam's feelings when he found out about his sister. I'd really like to know whether he feels guilty or angry or whatever."

One variation on this technique is to read your piece aloud, stop in the middle, and ask, "What are you thinking or feeling now?" Another variation involves giving the reader your work and asking him or her to stop after each page to write a reaction on a separate piece of paper.

This type of response is probably the most trustworthy of all response methods. You're not asking readers what they think is good or how they think you should change the piece. You are asking for the actual reactions—the facts. You can draw your own conclusions about how well your writing works.

One word of caution: You shouldn't ask for this kind of response unless you and your reader really trust each other. You need to be able to let your reader respond honestly and perhaps say something negative like, "I felt you were being somewhat unfair in your piece."

Readers sometimes get stuck at the level of general, unhelpful responses, such as "I pretty much like it" or "I didn't get too interested." If this happens, try to coax a more specific response. For example, ask where he or she began to lose interest.

INCORPORATING PEER RESPONSES

There is no simple way to evaluate responses to your writing. Different readers will always respond differently to the same piece of writing; in fact, the same reader may respond differently to the same piece of writing at different times. Therefore, look for consistent responses—things you hear, in different words, more than once. Take each reader's reactions with a grain of salt until you've heard all the responses.

Remember that you're in control of your writing. You can just listen without quarreling about what your peer readers say. Once you get used to listening to reader responses, this process can be deeply satisfying. Although you may not agree with everything eventually you will learn to evaluate your reader's comments in terms of how they relate to your purpose and to your personal goals. Use their responses to help determine what you want to say, to gain perspective, to find new ideas, and to clarify the content that you have written.

RESPONDING TO OTHERS' WRITING

When responding to other people's writing, think of how you would want them to respond to yours. In other words, be constructive. Try to think of gentle, encouraging ways to frame your criticisms. For example, instead of saying, "This organization makes no sense to me," you might say, "What if you reorganized your ideas so that the connection between these two paragraphs is clearer?" Try to be specific and to avoid simply making negative comments.

COMPUTER TIP

If you write in a computer lab, leave a printout of your first draft beside your computer. Everyone moves around the lab in round-robin fashion, reading the drafts and typing comments into the computers. This anonymity helps promote honest responses.

Remember that it's important to respond to what is good in a piece of writing, too. Suppose a writer has selected an exciting topic but hasn't developed it very well. Praise the writer for choosing an interesting topic, then suggest ways that he or she could make the piece of writing appeal more to the reader by using vivid details, examples, or incidents. If the idea is good, but the execution is inadequate, propose possible solutions.

Practice Your Skills

A. Read the following negative comments about a piece of writing. Discuss with your classmates how the same points might be made more constructively.

1. What were you thinking about when you wrote this example? It doesn't prove your point at all.
2. Boy, you really can't spell!
3. Your paper is totally disorganized. I can't follow your train of thought. What are you talking about?
4. This idea is so off the wall! How in the world did you ever come up with something like that?
5. Your paragraphing is really bad, and I don't see any transitions here.

B. Consider the following piece of student writing. In a small group, practice responding to this piece in each of the six ways described in this handbook. Then revise the piece of writing based on the group's comments.

> At the end of the nineteenth century, everybody was excited about flying machines. Balloons had been around for a while. In 1870, the French used them to take messages out of Paris during the German invasion.
>
> There was a glider in 1853, invented by Sir George Cayley. Otto Lilienthal, the German aviator, perfected the art of gliding before his death in an accident in 1896.
>
> An American physicist, Samuel Pierpoint Langley, almost managed to get off the ground in a powered glider. As we all know, the Wright brothers were the first to successfully fly in a powered glider. Or airplane. Their flight, on December 17, 1903, lasted only 59 seconds; the flight covered 852 feet. However, as modest as it was, the little hop was a turning point in transportation history.
>
> Nowadays a trip by airplane is boring and romance comes when you take a train.

Sharing and Publishing

Once you have completed a piece of writing, what happens to it? If it is something personal, you might put it in your journal or file it away in a special place. However, if your writing is meant for an audience, you might consider one or more of the following ideas.

Ways to Share Your Writing

You can share your writing in several general ways: informal sharing, self-publishing, and formal publishing.

Informal Sharing

- Discuss your notes, outline, or draft with someone else.
- Have another person sit at your word-processing terminal to read what you've done and to type in comments.
- Have someone take your material, read it, and make marginal comments before returning it to you.
- Schedule a writer's conference with your teacher, bringing a piece of writing or your complete portfolio.
- Form a writing exchange group with other class members who are working on similar projects. Share your work and discuss methods of moving ahead with your assignments.

Self-Publishing

- Use a photocopier or mimeograph machine to make copies of your work for friends, relatives, and classmates.
- Photocopy your writing onto an acrylic transparency and put it on an overhead projector.
- Present your work orally in a report, a speech, a reading, an interpretation, or a dramatic performance.
- Include your work in a letter to a friend or relative.
- Transmit your work to others using a facsimile machine.
- Save your writing on a computer diskette and give it to others who have access to a compatible machine.
- Make your writing part of a poster, collage, or bulletin board.
- Use a computer-paging-layout program to produce well-designed copies of your work to give to others.
- Make a videotape or audio cassette recording of your work.
- Create your own book, magazine, or newspaper.

**Format require-
ments differ. Check
the requirements
before submitting
your work to a
teacher or a
publication.**

Formal Publishing

- Submit your writing to the school newspaper by expressing an opinion in a letter to the editor or a movie review.
- Consult the editor or advisor of the yearbook to find out the requirements for becoming a contributing writer. Or find out how to join the staff.
- If your school has a literary magazine, try submitting some of your poems, stories, and essays.
- Check your local newspapers for the type of material they accept. Many accept letters to the editor, longer personal commentaries, and articles of local interest.
- Enter your writing in a contest. *The Atlantic Monthly, English Journal,* National Federation of Press Women, National Council of Teachers of English, Poetry Society of America, *Redbook,* and *Scholastic Magazines* all sponsor writing contests. Contact each organization for details.
- Try the open market by finding out requirements for submissions to magazines. Check at your library for books such as *Market Guide for Young Writers* and *Writer's Market.*

PREPARING MATERIALS FOR SHARING OR PUBLISHING

Before sharing or publishing your material, you will probably want to **format** it, that is, put it into final form. The format you choose will depend on the type of writing and the audience. For informal sharing, your handwritten notes will probably be fine. However, for formal sharing, you should probably prepare your work on a typewriter or word processor, using standard double-spaced format, with your name and the page number in the upper right-hand corner of each page and a ¾-inch margin all around.

If you are interested in designing your own books or newsletters, you might want to investigate some sources in the library on layout and graphic design. **Layout** is the process of dividing up a page into rows and columns with space for pictures and art. **Graphic design** is the art of determining how all the elements on a printed page will appear. Layout and graphic design are made easier by the many word-processing programs and special page-layout programs designed for computers. If you want to design your own publication, consult a computer dealer or the manuals for specific programs.

Crafting Better Sentences

You practice good craftsmanship when you pay careful attention to details. This is especially true with writing. Focusing on such details as the quality of individual sentences will help you improve your writing immeasurably. To improve your sentences, be particularly alert for those that present ideas incompletely or unclearly or that use imprecise or unnecessary words.

CORRECTING EMPTY SENTENCES

Empty sentences are ones that say too little. Two kinds of empty sentences are those that contain circular reasoning and those that contain unsupported opinions.

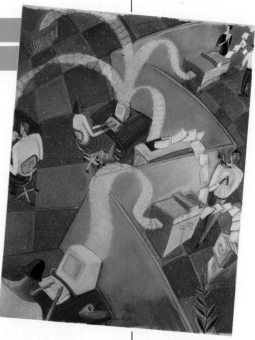

Avoiding Circular Reasoning Statements that do nothing more than restate the same idea in different words are empty sentences. These sentences are the result of circular reasoning. Circular reasoning occurs because a writer has not carefully thought out the relationship between ideas and, therefore, cannot clearly express the relationship in writing.

Circular   Thomas à Becket and Henry II often quarreled because they did not get along well.

Strategy   In effect, the sentence says that Becket and Henry quarreled because they quarreled. To produce a meaningful statement, supply reasons.

Revised   Thomas à Becket and Henry II often quarreled because, as Archbishop of Canterbury, Becket upheld the rights of the church against Henry's royal power.

Avoiding Unsupported Opinions A statement that is not supported by facts, reasons, or examples serves only to reflect the writer's opinion. Such a sentence is empty because it does not advance an argument or add to the knowledge of the reader. The writer should develop an unsupported opinion with evidence or delete the sentence.

Unsupported	Cave formations are really interesting.
Strategy	Add facts and examples to create an effective sentence.
Revised	Cave formations that have been carved out by acid rainwater take on the interesting shapes of vertical shafts, pits, and hollow oval tubes.

Practice Your Skills

A. Read the following sentences and identify examples of circular reasoning or unsupported opinion. Rewrite the sentences to correct the faults.

1. Most of the people who live in India are Hindus, but not all of the people who live there are.
2. America should build a permanent space station soon because building one would be good for our country.
3. Thomas Edison's inventive genius was of great value.
4. Reggae became a popular form of music in the Caribbean, since it has qualities of rhythm and melody that made it well liked.
5. Prehistoric cave dwellers feared many natural phenomena because they had great distrust of things they feared.

B. Revise the following paragraph by rewriting or, in some cases, deleting the empty sentences. Not every sentence in the paragraph requires revision.

The Gulf Stream is a warm ocean current that flows from the Gulf of Mexico along the eastern coast of the United States. It is an important navigational feature for sailors. However, when Columbus discovered America he was not aware of the Gulf Stream because he was uninformed about it. Five years later, when Sebastian Cabot sailed the western Atlantic, he too was ignorant of this current. Cabot made a curious observation that was unusual. Some of the supplies

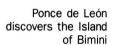

Ponce de León discovers the Island of Bimini

in the ship's hold below deck fermented. Cabot did not understand why this happened because he didn't know what caused the spoilage. He did not connect this phenomenon with the warmer temperatures of the water in the Gulf Stream. In fact, it was not until 1513 that the seafaring world learned of the stream. In that year Ponce de León described a Florida current that proved to be the swift beginning of the Gulf Stream. Clearly, Ponce de León made an important discovery.

REVISING OVERLOADED SENTENCES

Examine the following two sentences, which make a similar point.

It is life near the bone where it is sweetest.

Rather than surrounding yourself with possessions and seeking change in your scenery or appearance just for the sake of change, create a life that is simple and constant, for that is where life is sweetest.

The first sentence, by writer Henry David Thoreau, has clarity and force. The second sentence is not as effective as the first because it tries to say too much. It is **overloaded.** Overloaded sentences contain:

- unrelated details,
- too many ideas, or
- ideas that are loosely or awkwardly strung together.

Omitting Unrelated Details When unrelated details appear in a sentence, they interrupt the flow of thought. Help your reader to follow the main idea by deleting any detail that is not closely related to this idea.

Overloaded	Aldous Huxley, who used to live in Britain, said, "The most distressing thing that can happen to a prophet is to be proved wrong. The next most distressing thing is to be proved right."
Strategy	Delete the irrelevant clause about Huxley having lived in Britain.
Revised	Aldous Huxley said, "The most distressing thing that can happen to a prophet is to be proved wrong. The next most distressing thing is to be proved right."

Separating Ideas Everyone has had the experience of trying to pack too many ideas into a single statement. Such a sentence can cause the writer to forget his or her original thought. As a result, the reader may become confused trying to follow that thought.

Overloaded	Basketball was invented in 1891 by James A. Naismith, who was a YMCA instructor who needed an indoor game for winter play, so he nailed peach baskets at either end of a gymnasium and used a soccer ball for play.
Strategy	Separate ideas and combine sentence parts.
Revised	Basketball was invented by YMCA instructor James A. Naismith, who needed an indoor game for winter play. He nailed peach baskets at either end of a gymnasium and used a soccer ball for play.

Separating the ideas in one overloaded sentence into two or more sentences allows the reader to grasp each individual idea in turn. When you find an overloaded sentence in your own writing, follow these steps:

1. Look for the main idea.
2. Identify the details that are related to the main idea.
3. Identify any secondary ideas.
4. Break each idea into separate sentences, and cluster related details around each subject-verb combination.
5. Drop irrelevant details.

Revising Loosely Connected Sentences Sometimes a sentence becomes overloaded because the writer strings a number of ideas together by placing *and*'s between clauses. As a result, no one idea stands out; there seems to be no organization. You can revise such a loosely connected sentence in two ways.

1. If there are too many ideas for one sentence, divide the groups of connected ideas into two or more sentences.
2. Find the logical connections between ideas. Replace *and* with a more appropriate connective, or transition, where necessary. The best way to determine what connectives to use is to divide your sentence into its separate ideas and then determine the relationships between those ideas. Some useful transitional words are *because, then, but, later, before,* and *consequently.*

Writing
—TIP—
In revising loosely connected sentences, ask yourself if the ideas are connected closely enough to be in one sentence, and, if so, what the connection is.

Overloaded	By the turn of the century, N. C. Wyeth was a well-known commercial artist and his illustrations for *Treasure Island* brought him fame and a handsome income and he preferred painting landscapes and still lifes.
Strategy	Divide into two sentences. Then replace *and* with *but* to show contrast of ideas.
Revised	By the turn of the century, N. C. Wyeth was a well-known commercial artist. His illustrations for *Treasure Island* brought him fame and a handsome income, but he preferred painting landscapes and still lifes.

Practice Your Skills

A. Revise these sentences, omitting unrelated details and adding words if necessary to create new sentences or to combine ideas.

1. When skin has been moderately sunburned it becomes damaged, and it may take a long time to return to normal, which may be from four to fifteen months.
2. The earth's most abundant form of animal life finally has a zoo of its own, and it is located at the Smithsonian Institution in Washington and is called the Insect Zoo.
3. The service-station attendant told us that Mac's Garage would repair our odometer, which registered 26,000 miles.
4. The nasturtiums did not grow, and the gardener used nitrogen, and when that did not work he used peat moss, and he learned that the peat moss was effective only when it was worked into the soil.
5. People no longer fear old age, and they stay healthy and active with diet and exercise, and they remain useful members of society.

B. Revise the ineffective sentences in the following paragraph.

> Pennsylvania Dutch artisans have contributed significantly to American history and culture with a variety of art forms and with inventions such as the Conestoga wagon and the Pennsylvania rifle, which helped America win the West. Their distinctive art style is known for its colorful, decorative motifs. Evidence of this artistic ability, in the form of hex signs, covers many Pennsylvania Dutch barns, which are very sturdily built. Artistic talent is also evident in their great love of music and this love is most apparent in their church music, especially choirs and one of the most famous is the Bach choir.

USING WORDS PRECISELY

In addition to the unclear presentation of ideas, imprecise words can make your sentences hard to understand. Make your writing exciting and your meaning clear by choosing your vocabulary with care.

Using Specific Rather than General Words

A general word can refer to many different things. It is usually better to use specific terms rather than general ones. Consider this example:

> The dance was especially impressive.

This sentence doesn't say much. The reader might ask, "Which dance?" and "In what way was it impressive?" The words used in the sentence lack a specific, clear-cut meaning.

For example, *dance* can refer to many events, from a classical dance on stage to a free-form dance to rock-and-roll music in a high-school gym. *Ballet, rumba, waltz, cha-cha,* and *tap* are all specific words to describe particular dances.

Likewise, the word *impressive* can mean many things. If the sentence were rewritten in the following way, then the reader would have a far better understanding of what aspects of the dance the writer was impressed by.

> The Brazilian rumba was colorful and rhythmic.

In this sentence, the writer replaced a general noun and a general adjective with more specific words to create a far more vivid and meaningful sentence.

Choosing Specific Modifiers   Sometimes you can enhance verbs and nouns with specific modifiers. Using strong, vivid adjectives and adverbs will make your writing engaging for your readers. Writers often lose the opportunity to make their writing more effective by choosing vague or "empty" modifiers. Words such as *beautiful, nice,* and *really* don't have specific meanings. These words express only general approval or disapproval. The reader looks for stronger evidence—concrete words to show why or how something affected the writer.

Empty Modifiers to Avoid

good	bad	really	cute
awesome	exciting	great	fine
super	terrible	pretty	fun
interesting	fantastic	boring	nice

Empty Modifier   This orange juice tastes *awful.*
Specific Modifier   This orange juice tastes *bitter* and a *little rotten.*

Notice that the empty modifier *awful* has been replaced with **sensory details.** An excellent way to make your writing clearer is to use words that refer to things that can be seen, touched, tasted, heard, or smelled.

Showing, Not Telling   Using specific verbs, nouns, and sensory adjectives in your writing will enable you to show your observations and ideas to the reader rather than simply telling the reader about them. Look for sensory details as you compare the following two descriptions.

1. We went slowly and carefully through the cave. It was dark, damp, and scary.

2. Drops of water hung from the walls and ceiling and splashed onto the floor of the cave. As we ducked our heads and felt our way through the slimy passage, beams of sunlight faded and shadows disappeared in the heavy blackness. Sounds were unnaturally amplified and seemed to come from all directions at once.

Stalactites and stalagmites in Onandaga Cave, Missouri

Notice how the second passage actually leads you through the cave with verbs such as *hung, splashed, ducked, felt, faded,* and *disappeared.* In addition, the writer's use of sensory adjectives such as *slimy* and *heavy* permits you to feel the cave's damp environment rather than simply read about it.

To write vividly and powerfully, nouns and verbs are your best tools. Though strings of modifiers may accurately describe your subject, they will be far less evocative and informative for your reader.

Notice how the following two sentences describe the same scene but create completely different effects.

Effective   The hallway glistened with moonlight reflecting from the mirror propped near the window.

Less Effective   It was beautiful and magical, filled with bright, glistening light.

The first sentence uses verbs and nouns to create a clear and specific image. In contrast, the second sentence relies on modifiers and forms a vague picture that could be describing a crystal ball or a French horn rather than a hallway.

When selecting verbs to show, not tell, action verbs are far more powerful and precise than state-of-being verbs. They help create a vivid picture in the mind of the readers.

State-of-Being Verb	The girl was proud of her mathematics project.
Action Verb	When she completed the mathematics project, the girl *leaned* back, *beaming* for all to see.

Notice that the dull verb *was* has been replaced with the vivid, specific verb *leaned* and the verbal *beaming*. Other words have also been added so that the sentence shows the girl's pride rather than simply tells about it.

Practice Your Skills

A. Rewrite each sentence below to achieve clarity. In sentences 1–3, concentrate on replacing weak verbs or rewriting the sentences to eliminate state-of-being verbs. In sentences 4–6, concentrate on replacing general and vague nouns and modifiers. Also remember to use words that appeal to the senses.

1. John felt bad after history class.
2. Samantha played baseball well.
3. She left the room angrily.
4. Mom said we should think about how lucky we are.
5. The sunrise was beautiful.
6. Riding a train through the countryside can be relaxing.

B. Revise the following paragraphs to make them clearer and more effective. To do so, choose specific words. Also add details where appropriate and, where possible, show rather than tell.

1. We ran down the apartment building stairs. I could smell cooking as I passed a door. I was happy to have some free time before supper. We went outside and crossed the street to the basketball court. There were some kids there already, so we weren't sure what to do.
2. From the water came a man's voice. He was lying on his surfboard and paddling. There was something in the water. The bathers all moved farther up the beach. There they were, all together, looking out over the water.

Correcting Redundancy

Wordiness may arise from **redundancy,** the needless use of words with similar meanings. Careful reading can help you easily spot and delete words that unnecessarily repeat an idea.

Wordy	Picasso's style is often imitated by modern artists of today.
Revised	Picasso's style is often imitated by modern artists.

Redundancy occasionally arises from the unnecessary repetition of the word *that*.

Wordy   Alonzo Babers knew *that* if he failed to win the race *that* the United States would not win a gold medal.

Revised   Alonzo Babers knew *that* if he failed to win the race, the United States would not win a gold medal.

Using too many modifiers is another type of redundancy that makes your writing hard to read.

Wordy   My roommate and fellow counselor at camp last summer was a really nice, sweet, generous, and companionable guy, but when it came to helping out with chores, he was completely and utterly useless.

Revised   My roommate and fellow counselor at camp last summer was a really companionable guy, but when it came to helping out with chores, he was utterly useless.

Another problem involves the repetition of a word or phrase. Correct repetition by using a synonym, substituting a pronoun for a noun, or rewriting the sentence.

Wordy   During prime time there are more silly situation comedies than there are serious dramas and news programs. Many of these silly situation comedies are simply boring.

Revised   During prime time, silly situation comedies outnumber serious dramas and news programs. Many of these sitcoms are simply boring.

Reducing Sentences

Often you can enhance your style by reducing sentences, that is, by making them more compact and effective. As you revise, look for opportunities to turn longer sentences into shorter ones. Look for opportunities to change:

- a clause to a phrase,
- a clause to an appositive, or
- a phrase to a single modifier.

Clause   Swift wrote *Gulliver's Travels*, <u>*which is a satire.*</u>
Appositive Swift wrote *Gulliver's Travels*, <u>*a satire.*</u>

Phrase   One of the old programs <u>*on radio*</u> was recently revived.
Modifier One of the old <u>*radio*</u> programs was recently revived.

For more information on using appositives and modifiers, see "Appositives and Appositive Phrases," pages 601–602, and "Understanding Modifiers," pages 736–743.

Practice Your Skills

Eliminate wordiness in the following sentences.

1. No one knows who or whatever has just been making the spherical, circular patterns in English fields recently.
2. The senator answered all of the questions unhesitatingly and without any reservations.
3. Wordsworth, who is one of the Lake poets of England, is often called a poet of nature.
4. The report, which was long and tedious, was delivered to an audience that was altogether bored.
5. The lion tamer understood that if the lion tamer made the tiger from Siberia angry that it would only make the situation worse.
6. The blunder, which was mine, will cost me both time and money.
7. The chemists performing the experiment discovered that an essential factor that was necessary to the success of the experiment was the temperature of the chemicals.
8. The bylaws state that a quorum must be present to vote, and two-thirds of the membership is needed for a quorum.
9. The start of the Renaissance had its beginning during medieval times, which covered the period between A.D. 1400 to 1600.
10. The essential requirements necessary for election to the presidency are clearly outlined in the Constitution, which tells a candidate everything he or she needs to know.

CLARIFYING WORD AND
SENTENCE RELATIONSHIPS

Be aware of the relationships among words within your sentences. To clarify your writing, avoid awkward beginnings and misplaced modifiers. Also look for correct subordination of ideas, for a close relationship between subject and verb, and for parallelism between sentence parts.

Avoiding Awkward Beginnings

Words placed at the beginning of a sentence have the greatest impact on your reader. Certain phrases create awkwardness without adding meaning to the sentence. Some of these expressions are *the fact that, what I believe is, what I want is, being that, the reason that,* and *in my opinion.* As you revise, look for and delete the awkward expressions that weaken your writing.

Placing Modifiers Together

Placement of words and phrases is important in achieving sentence clarity. Keep in mind several common placement problems.

Misplaced Modifiers When a modifier is separated from the word it modifies, it is misplaced. Instead, place it close to the word it modifies. A single adjective is usually placed immediately before the word it modifies. An adjective phrase is usually placed immediately after the word it modifies. A misplaced phrase may appear to modify the wrong word and thus confuse your reader.

Confusing	The boys were warned about reckless driving *by the coach.*
Revised	The boys were warned *by the coach* about reckless driving.

Dangling Modifiers A dangling modifier is one that does not seem to be reasonably related to any word in the sentence. Sometimes this error produces unintentional humor.

Confusing	*Changing the tire,* the car rolled down the hill.
Revised	*As I was changing the tire,* the car rolled down the hill.

Subordinating Ideas Correctly

The main clause in a sentence states the main idea. Writing in which all ideas are expressed as main ideas is not effective, because it implies that all ideas are of equal value. You can use clauses and phrases to indicate which ideas are of greater and lesser importance.

Using a Clause You can indicate a less important idea by using a subordinate clause. A subordinate clause can never stand alone; it must be connected with the main clause by a subordinating conjunction such as *when, because, after,* and *although.*

Weak	Last night we were watching TV, and our cat rushed into the room and sprang onto the set.
Revised	Last night we were watching TV when our cat rushed into the room and sprang onto the set.

Using a Phrase   As another alternative, you can improve the connection between your ideas by converting a clause into a participial phrase that modifies one word in the main clause of your sentence.

Weak   Jake was pinned under the fallen sycamore tree, and he shouted for help.

Revised   Pinned under the fallen sycamore tree, Jake shouted for help.

Details of lesser importance can also be subordinated by using appositives.

Weak   The video recorder is a useful teaching aid, and it makes our science lessons more exciting.

Revised   A useful teaching aid, the video recorder makes our science lessons more exciting.

When you use subordination, be careful not to confuse the subordinate idea with the main idea. **Upside-down subordination** results when you incorrectly place the main idea within a subordinate clause or phrase.

See "Phrases and Clauses," pages 599–639, for more information on using phrases and clauses correctly.

Practice Your Skills

Revise these sentences, removing awkward beginnings, placing modifiers correctly, and subordinating ideas reasonably.

1. The fact is that when it is winter in the United States, it is summer in Australia.
2. What you call a squeeze play is one in which the batter bunts to score a runner from third base.
3. It is a myth that Lincoln wrote the Gettysburg Address while traveling to Gettysburg on the back of an envelope.
4. After biting the mail carrier, I sold my dog.
5. Apply ice to an injury, and that will help reduce inflammation.
6. Veterans Day was once called Armistice Day, and it is a legal holiday.
7. The reason that the quarterback threw the football out-of-bounds was due to the fact that he wanted to stop the clock.
8. I spotted a wild buffalo sitting in my car.
9. Sarsaparilla is an old-fashioned soda, and you can still buy it in some remote areas.
10. In the Hawaiian Islands, the climate is temperate, and the temperature varies as little as ten to twelve degrees throughout the year.

Keeping Related Sentence Parts Together

Readers have certain expectations about the way a sentence will be constructed. For example, they expect certain elements will be kept together: subject and verb, verb and complement, and parts of the verb phrase. If these parts are widely separated, your sentences will be hard to read and understand.

Awkward The visitor to Rome *was,* as she toured the city, *struck* by its mixture of ancient and modern architecture.

Revised As she toured the city, the visitor to Rome *was struck* by its mixture of ancient and modern architecture.

Colosseum
Rome, Italy

Practice Your Skills

Revise these sentences, bringing related sentence parts together.

1. Surgeons and their assistants, instead of using sterile rubber gloves, used to scrub their hands with a harsh antiseptic.
2. A nurse at Johns Hopkins Hospital when she scrubbed with the antiseptic was always breaking out in a rash.
3. Dr. William Halstead, since he wanted to keep the nurse on his staff, devised his own solution to her problem.
4. He made plaster casts of the nurse's hands, and had a rubber company mold from the casts thin rubber gloves.
5. He himself was, by 1893, wearing the gloves in surgery.
6. Rubber gloves, because they were more sterile than the best-scrubbed hands, were quickly adopted by other surgeons.
7. Of course, individually molded gloves were, after the demand became great, no longer made.

8. Manufacturers then began to create, following the laws of supply and demand, standard sizes at reduced cost.
9. Halstead created, as a result of a nurse's allergy, a safer surgical environment.

Keeping Sentence Parts Parallel

Parts of a sentence that serve a similar function should be made parallel in structure. Notice the parallelism in the sentence below.

> I wonder sometimes if my father knew how much more I learned from *observing* him than from *listening* to him.

After reading this sentence aloud, read the following version.

> I wonder sometimes if my father knew how much more I learned from observing him than when I listened to him.

In the first sentence, the likeness of form helps you recognize the likeness of content and function. In the second passage, the use of dissimilar forms to express parallel ideas causes confusion and impedes your understanding.

Practice Your Skills

Correct the faulty parallelism in the following sentences. Rewrite the sentences.

1. Charlie Chaplin's film character "The Little Tramp" was known for his derby hat, his baggy pants, bamboo cane, and the way he had a shuffling walk.
2. My baby brother is plump, fair, and has light hair.
3. Queen Victoria spent her adult life raising nine children and as the ruler of the British Empire for sixty-four years.
4. The storm cut off the lights, stopped the pump, and the furnace stopped going.
5. Helen Keller's parents were concerned about her and if they could help her development.
6. Dave tried playing football in the afternoon and his homework at night.
7. Cottonseed oil is used in steel making, and linseed oil to make paint.
8. Mavis Lindgen, who ran a marathon at age seventy-one, and Floyd Parsons, playing 117 hockey games at age sixty-nine, were both active seniors.
9. Ms. Johnson's duties were hiring personnel and sometimes to evaluate programs.
10. He was an actor with a funny face but who hated comedy.

Refining Your Voice and Style

Everyone uses language differently. Yet, somehow, you are immediately able to recognize many voices, identifying the tone, accent, pronunciation, phrasing, and word choice that distinguish individuals. These differences in the way people express themselves are part of what make up **voice.** Writers also have distinctive voices, or ways of using language. If your language seems comfortable and normal to you in your writing, then you are writing in your own voice.

Occasionally, you may be required to write in a way that makes you feel slightly uncomfortable—for example, when writing a formal report or a business letter. Even in these situations, it's a good idea to use your own voice to write your first draft. When you use your own voice, you often think and write more productively. After you've articulated your ideas in a draft, you can revise the language to give it the appropriate voice.

UNDERSTANDING STYLE

The way you walk, talk, dress, and even sign your name—all contribute to your unique, personal style. In writing, too, you have a style, an individual way of choosing words and putting sentences and ideas together. Your writing style is what distinguishes your writing voice from everyone else's. That style may vary, depending on what you are writing, but it will always reflect who you are.

WRITER TO WRITER

Style is the hallmark of a temperament stamped upon the material at hand.

André Maurois, French novelist

Listed below are several elements that work together to create style.

- **Sentence Structure** How long or short your sentences are, how you vary sentence types, how you order the words in your sentences—these aspects of sentence structure mark your writing style.

- **Diction**   Your word choice reflects your style. Do you choose the informal word *begin* or the more formal *commence?* Do you usually choose words with positive or negative connotations?
- **Imagery**   Do you generally describe things in a straightforward, objective way? Do you draw on figurative language to color your descriptions?
- **Mechanics**   Would you be unable to write without using dashes? Are you fond of the semicolon? Your use of punctuation is also part of your style.
- **Tone**   What is your attitude toward your subject? Are you critical, nostalgic, detached? The way you feel about your subject influences the language you use.

DEVELOPING YOUR WRITING VOICE

Your voice will naturally change and mature as you grow as a writer. Compare the following five-line passages from two poems by Robert Frost. The first was written when Frost was sixteen, the second when he was thirty-nine. How do the voices of the two passages differ?

I found that wing broken today!
For thou art dead, I said,
And the strange birds say.
I found it with the withered leaves
Under the eaves.
      Robert Frost, "My Butterfly"

When I see birches bend to left and right
Across the lines of straighter darker trees,
I like to think some boy's been swinging them.
But swinging doesn't bend them down to stay
As ice storms do.
      Robert Frost, "Birches"

LITERARY
M O D E L

In the first passage, Frost is clearly not speaking in his own natural voice. He is imitating the archaic language and the tone of deep melancholy of Romantic poetry he has read. In the second passage, Frost's writing has matured considerably. He speaks in ordinary, conversational English and writes a much more intimate poem.

It's a good idea for you to experiment with different voices. Try out voices the way you might try out different styles of clothing until you find the one that is best suited to you.

There are many ways to experiment with different voices. One way is to imitate other writers. Choose a writer whose work you really enjoy, read a paragraph or two, and try to analyze what gives those passages their particular "flavor." Then try to write paragraphs of your own that have a similar sound.

You might also decide to change various aspects of your writing systematically. For example, use longer sentences with more clauses and phrases in one draft. Then use short, simple sentences in another. Use abstract words in one draft; in another, use only words that refer to things you can sense.

Through imitating other voices and experimenting with your own, you will discover ways of phrasing and structuring sentences that seem natural for you. You may start working these new ideas into your writing on a regular basis. In this way, your voice will grow and change. If you keep a writing portfolio, you'll be able to go back to older pieces and track this development.

CHOOSING DIFFERENT VOICES

Developing and experimenting with your own writing voice will enable you to write comfortably in many different situations and to create a variety of characters in your fiction. For example, you may want to tell a story from the point of view of a ninety-year-old woman whose native language was Chinese. You must decide not only how she would see the world, but also what kinds of words and grammatical structures she would use to express her ideas. A character's voice will not necessarily be the same as your own voice. Being familiar with your voice, however, gives you the freedom to develop voices for many different characters without losing control of your writing.

Even when you're doing nonliterary writing, you might decide to use a voice different from your own. For example, if you were writing an investigative piece for the school newspaper, you might use a voice that is objective and authoritative, like that of an experienced newspaper reporter. If you were writing an editorial, however, your voice could be cynical or sardonic. Always be sure that the voice you choose is appropriate for the writing situation.

Practice Your Skills

A. Read the following passages. Then briefly describe the voice in each passage and identify the elements that contribute to the writer's style. Decide whether the writer is using his own voice, or a character's voice. (Hint: Think about what kind of person might be speaking in each case.)

1. Downstairs we came out through the first-floor dining room to the street. A waiter went for a taxi. It was hot and bright. Up the street was a little square with trees and grass where there were taxis parked. A taxi came up the street, the waiter hanging out at the side. I tipped him and told the driver where to drive, and got in beside Brett. The driver started up the street. I settled back. Brett moved close to me. We sat close against each other. I put my arm around her and she rested against me comfortably. It was very hot and bright, and the houses looked sharply white. We turned out onto the Gran Via.

Ernest Hemingway, *The Sun Also Rises*

2. Now this is the point. You fancy me mad. Madmen know nothing. But you should have seen me. You should have seen how wisely I proceeded—with what caution—with what foresight — with what dissimulation I went to work! I was never kinder to the old man than during the whole week before I killed him. And every night, about midnight, I turned the latch of his door and opened it—oh, so gently! And then, when I had made an opening sufficient for my head, I put in a dark lantern, all closed, closed, so that no light shone out, and then I thrust in my head. Oh, you would have laughed to see how cunningly I thrust it in! I moved it slowly—very, very slowly, so that I might not disturb the old man's sleep. It took me an hour to place my whole head within the opening so far that I could see him as he lay upon his bed. Ha!—would a madman have been so wise as this!

Edgar Allan Poe, "The Tell-Tale Heart"

Refining Your
Voice and Style   **447**

3.   The key word with growing children . . . seems to be communication. If you're a lip-reader of any repute whatsoever, you have no problem. However, if you must compete with local disc jockeys which feed hourly through their earplugs, this could get pretty sticky. We have solved this problem by buying time on the local station and reporting personal messages: "We moved last week." "Daddy's birthday is in September."

Erma Bombeck, *Giant Economy Size*

B. The following passages are from two essays entitled "Why I Write" by different writers. In a small-group discussion, compare and contrast the voices of the two passages.

1.   From a very early age, perhaps the age of five or six, I knew that when I grew up I should be a writer. Between the ages of about seventeen and twenty-four I tried to abandon this idea, but I did not with the consciousness that I was outraging my true nature and that sooner or later I should have to settle down and write books.

George Orwell, "Why I Write"

2.   Of course I stole the title for this talk from George Orwell. One reason I stole it was that I like the sound of the words: *Why I Write*. There you have three short unambiguous words that share a sound, and the sound they share is this: I, I, I.

In many ways writing is the act of saying *I,* of imposing oneself upon other people, of saying *listen to me, see it my way, change your mind*. It's an aggressive, even a hostile act. You can disguise its aggressiveness all you want with veils of subordinate clauses and qualifiers and tentative subjunctives, with ellipses and evasions—with the whole manner of intimating rather than claiming, of alluding rather than stating—but there's no getting around the fact that setting words on paper is the tactic of a secret bully, an invasion, an imposition of the writer's sensibility on the reader's most private space.

Joan Didion, "Why I Write"

C. Choose two of the passages from Exercise A and write paragraphs in which you imitate their voices. Afterward, reflect on your writing experience. How did the pieces of writing that you produced differ from your usual writing? Were they better? worse? Did you learn any new techniques that you might use in the future? If so, what are the techniques and how could you incorporate them in your own writing?

Levels of Language

To create a meaningful experience for your reader, you must choose language appropriate to your audience and purpose.

FORMAL AND INFORMAL ENGLISH

Formal English is language that is suited to serious speeches, scholarly journals, legal documents, business reports, and textbooks.

▼

PROFESSIONAL
MODEL

In such an expression as "We must listen to both sides of every question," there is an assumption, frequently unexamined, that every question has, fundamentally, only two sides. We tend to think in opposites, to feel that what is not "good" must be "bad" and that what is not "bad" must be "good."

S.I. Hayakawa, *Language in Action*

In the model notice the serious tone, lack of contractions, and long, complex sentences.

Informal English, also known as **colloquial English,** is the language of conversation, informal talks, personal letters, and sometimes newspapers and magazines. In the following passage, note the casual tone, simple vocabulary, contractions, and variety of sentence lengths.

▼

PROFESSIONAL
MODEL

"Where's my pet monkey Mimi?" squeaked an elderly woman. . . . "Someone's stolen my wallet, and I can't buy myself a train ticket home," moaned a lanky teenager. For the two officers stationed at the Ochanomisu police box in the heart of Tokyo, the complaints were typical. Within fifteen minutes they had soothed the woman with a promise to be on the lookout for her pet (it was found) and lent the penniless youth 560 yen ($2.33) from a special emergency fund. . . ."

Time Magazine

Writers often combine formal and informal English, which allows them to maintain an appropriate tone without becoming monotonous.

As a writer or speaker, you can choose from special varieties of language that include idioms, slang, euphemisms, clichés, jargon, and gobbledygook. Use this language cautiously; it can interfere with clarity and may be inappropriate.

WRITER TO WRITER

Proper words in proper places make the true definition of a style.

Jonathan Swift, British essayist and novelist

Writing
TIP
When you first draft a piece of writing, you may use somewhat informal language. As you review your writing, your purpose and audience may require a more formal approach.

Idioms An **idiom** is an expression whose meaning differs from the meanings of the individual words. Some common idiomatic expressions are "putting you on," "a hard-and-fast rule," and "a drop in the bucket." Avoid using idioms when they may cause confusion, such as when communicating with nonfluent speakers of English.

Slang Both newly coined expressions and established words and phrases that have acquired new meanings make up the **slang** vocabulary. Slang often begins within a subculture and comes into general use, although it is usually short-lived. Slang is appropriate only for informal speaking and writing or in dialogue.

Euphemisms A **euphemism** is an expression that is less direct— and some would say, less offensive—than the word it replaces. For example, the term *deceased* is a euphemism for *dead*. Sometimes euphemisms are used out of courtesy, but often they simply cover up the truth. For example, the term *antipersonnel weapon* is a euphemism for a weapon designed to kill people.

Clichés A **cliché** is an expression that was once fresh and powerful but has lost its impact from overuse. Some common clichés are "explore every avenue," "working my fingers to the bone," and "in the final analysis." Clichés may be used as verbal shorthand, but effective writers and speakers avoid them or turn them into original expressions.

Jargon   Specialized vocabulary, called **jargon,** is used by people in a particular field of endeavor. For example, a physician who refers to the "etiology of myocardial infarctions" is using medical jargon to describe the cause of heart attacks. Most fields of endeavor have their special jargon, which may range from slang to formal. Baseball players speak of sliders and knuckleballs; scuba divers speak of buoyancy compensators and second-state regulators. If you must use jargon when writing for nonspecialists, make sure that you define terms that are likely to confuse readers.

Gobbledygook   Self-important language characterized by overloaded sentences and vague, abstract, uncommon, or technical words is called **gobbledygook.** It is often found in technical, legal, or business documents and is usually the result of a misguided attempt to impress the reader. Sometimes, however, it is used deliberately to obscure meaning.

> The dealer and/or his/her authorized representative, from the effective date shown, for the period of time of the contractual agreement described herein, agrees to repair or replace (or reimburse if unable to repair or replace) the listed covered component parts of the vehicle described herein.

Put simply, what this means is: "If any of the following parts of your car break down while this contract is in effect, the dealer agrees to fix the parts, replace them, or reimburse the owner for them." Unless you are writing a satire or parody, you should avoid gobbledygook by using language that is simple and direct.

DIALECTS

A **dialect** is a variety of language used by people from a particular place or by members of a particular social group. Dialects can differ from one another in pronunciation, in grammar, and in vocabulary.

Since the early part of this century, widespread communication through the media—television and radio—have reduced regional differences in dialect in the United States. However, certain regions or cultures still have a distinctive style of speech. Speaking and writing in dialect is not incorrect. However, it may or may not be appropriate for a particular audience or purpose. Dialect that sounds quite natural in casual conversation, for example, may not be appropriate for schoolwork or business communication.

Levels of
Language   **451**

Practice Your Skills

A. Revise the following extremely informal draft, making it more formal. Also correct any errors that you find in spelling, grammar, usage, or mechanics.

> The Amazon is, like, this really long river. I mean, it's really, really long—3,300 miles or so in all. In places its so big its like an inland ocean. It flows from these mountains in Peru called the Andes, across the whole country of Brazil, to the Atlantic ocean. For most of the way, the water is all crummy because its so full of plant matter. All this plant matter makes the waters of the Amazon a dynamite breeding place for fish. In fact, most of the varieties of tropical fish sold in fish stores in the good old U S of A come from that river!

B. Read the following passage. Identify at least one example of jargon and one idiom. Also identify ways Huck's dialect differs from yours in pronunciation, in grammar, and in vocabulary.

> I struck for the light, but as soon as he turned the corner I went back and got into my skiff and bailed her out, and then pulled up shore in the easy water about six hundred yards, and tucked myself in among some wood-boats; for I couldn't rest easy till I could see the ferryboat start. But take it all around, I was feeling ruther comfortable on accounts of taking all this trouble for that gang, for not many would 'a' done it. I wished the widow knowed about it. I judged she would be proud of me for helping these rapscallions, because rapscallions and deadbeats is the kind the widow and good people takes the most interest in.

> **Mark Twain,** *The Adventures of Huckleberry Finn*

C. Rewrite the following passages of gobbledygook, turning them into simple, straightforward English.

1. In accordance with federal statute, we request that you please extinguish all smoking materials in the appropriate receptacles before embarkation aboard this flight. Failure to comply will result in detention and prosecution.

2. Invariably, experience has shown that the ramifying consequences, or "fruits," as it were, of one's labors tend to be commensurate with prior preparatory activities, or which one must especially note, as of particular importance in this regard, that activity commonly known, in the vernacular of the agricultural trade, as "the sowing of the seed."

Figurative Language and Sound Devices

Good writing not only conveys information, it also creates experiences. As a writer, one of your tasks is to try to weave a web of language that catches readers up in your writing, creating the feeling that they are actually there.

Chop Suey,
by Edward Hopper

USING LANGUAGE
IN SPECIAL WAYS

When writers say something that is not meant to be taken literally, they are using **figurative language.** Different types of figurative language you can draw on to create rich, sensory language experiences for your readers include imagery, simile, metaphor, personification, symbolism, and hyperbole.

Imagery An **image** conveys a sensory experience—a sight, sound, taste, touch, or smell—that enriches your message. Whenever possible, use concrete images to show rather than tell your reader what you mean. Compare the examples on the following page.

Telling   When spring comes in the Arctic, the ice begins to melt and make sounds.

Showing   When spring comes in the Arctic, vast floes of ice begin to melt, slowly, drop by drop. Patches of blue water emerge. Light glistens from thousands of rivulets, and the melting ice moans softly as it dwindles away.

Simile   A **simile** is a comparison between two unlike persons or things. It always contains the word *like* or *as*. A simile can have a powerful effect on readers because it forces them to experience a familiar object in an unfamiliar way. Consider the following examples.

> As cruel a weapon *as* the cave man's club, the chemical barrage has been hurled against the fabric of life.
> **Rachel Carson, *Silent Spring***

> Sounds were indistinct, the atmosphere *like* cotton wool.
> **Maurice Herzog, *Annapurna***

In the first example, the concrete image of a cave man's club reinforces the destructive impact of chemical pollutants. In the second example, the tangible image of cotton wool gives the reader a concrete way of imagining how thin mountain air feels at extremely high altitudes.

Metaphor   A **metaphor** is an implied comparison between two unlike persons or objects. A metaphor is similar to a simile and can have the same power. However, there is one difference: a metaphor does not use the words *like* or *as*. Consider the following example.

> White swan of cities, slumbering in thy nest
> So wonderfully built among the reeds.
> **Henry Wadsworth Longfellow, "Venice"**

Longfellow likens Venice, a city built on a network of canals, to a swan sleeping in its nest. Both Venice and the swan are white, surrounded by vegetation, and rest on water. The metaphor also suggests that the city shares the swan's elegance and grace.

Personification   The technique of attributing human qualities to animals and inanimate objects is called **personification.** Notice how the poet e.e. cummings used this technique very effectively in the following excerpt.

> nobody, not even the rain, has such small hands
> **e.e. cummings, "somewhere i have never traveled, gladly beyond"**

Writing
—TIP—
Let your imagination work for you. Enter the scene you are describing and look around— sniff, taste, touch, listen.

Personification is often used to project human feelings onto animals and things.

> In time, two of my ospreys were nudged by love and began to
> install new equipment in the great nest on my point.
> **John Steinbeck, "My War with the Ospreys"**

Hyperbole Exaggeration used to achieve a particular effect is called **hyperbole.** Notice how Walt Whitman uses hyperbole to convey the sense of awe he feels when he contemplates the wonder of life, even the life of so humble a creature as the mouse. This hyperbole is effective precisely because of the disparity between the mouse and the "sextillions of infidels."

> And a mouse is miracle enough to stagger sextillions
> of infidels. **Walt Whitman, "Song of Myself"**

Symbolism A **symbol** is an image whose meaning goes beyond the literal denotation of the word. For example, the skull and crossbones is a traditional symbol of poison, piracy, or death. The ever-changing moon is a traditional symbol of inconstancy in love. Symbolism is an especially important technique in poetry, but it is also used in prose. You can make use of traditional symbols in your writing, or you can create your own. Observe the original symbols Washington Irving used in this passage from his famous American short story.

LITERARY
M O D E L

About the year 1727, just at the time that earthquakes were prevalent in New England, and shook many tall sinners down upon their knees, there lived near this place a meager, miserly fellow, of the name of Tom Walker. He had a wife as miserly as himself: they were so miserly that they even conspired to cheat each other. . . . They lived in a forlorn-looking house that stood alone, and had an air of starvation. A few straggling savin trees, emblems of sterility, grew near it: no smoke ever curled from its chimney; no traveler stopped at its door.

Washington Irving, "The Devil and Tom Walker"

The desolate farm with its forlorn-looking house, its smokeless chimney, and its straggling savin trees symbolizes the desolate spiritual and emotional lives of the inhabitants.

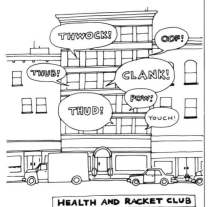

HEALTH AND RACKET CLUB

USING SOUND DEVICES

You can make your writing richer by employing devices that capitalize on the sounds of words. Devices that are particularly useful are onomatopoeia, alliteration, consonance, and assonance.

Onomatopoeia The use of words or phrases that sound like what they denote is called **onomatopoeia.** Words such as *snap, hiss, crackle, zing, meow, caw,* and *murmur* are all onomatopoeic. Notice how Robert Frost uses onomatopoeic words to reproduce the sound of a buzz saw.

> The buzz saw snarled and rattled in the yard. . . .
> **Robert Frost, "Out, Out—"**

Alliteration The repetition of initial consonant sounds is called **alliteration.** Annie Dillard uses the repetition of the *b* sound in the following sentence to emphasize the fragility of a butterfly.

> Each monarch butterfly had a brittle black body and deep orange wings limned and looped in black bands.
> **Annie Dillard, *Pilgrim at Tinker Creek***

Consonance A third type of sound device, **consonance,** occurs when consonant sounds are repeated in the middle of or at the end of words. Note the repetition of sounds in the following examples of consonance.

> a hint of motion within   the most ice-like kiss

Like alliteration, consonance often helps to convey the meaning of the sentence by emphasizing certain sounds. In the following passage, Ray Bradbury uses the consonance of the *r* sound to emphasize certain words and echo both the sound and the harshness of destruction.

> The crash. The attic smashing into kitchen and parlor. The parlor into cellar, cellar into sub-cellar.
> **Ray Bradbury, "There Will Come Soft Rains"**

Assonance A sound device related to consonance, **assonance** repeats vowel sounds, usually within words that are close to each other. Study the following examples of assonance.

> moaning and groaning   a red felt headdress
> snap, crackle, and rattle   about the house

Assonance may be used separately or jointly with alliteration or consonance to enhance the reader's experience. In the following line, the *er* sound suggests the rustle and the whirr sound of swinging on a tree.

One could do w<u>or</u>se than be a swing<u>er</u> of b<u>ir</u>ches.

Robert Frost, "Birches"

Other sound devices that writers often use include rhyme and regular rhythm. Feel free to experiment with all of these techniques in your own writing.

Practice Your Skills

A. Identify the figure of speech used in each example as *Simile, Metaphor, Personification,* or *Hyperbole.*

1. Her clear-looking eyes, with fine little rays of brown in them, like the spokes of a wheel, were full of approval for Stephen.
   Katherine Anne Porter
2. O serpent heart, hid in a flow'ring face.   **William Shakespeare**
3. And this love . . . would live forever.   **Alice Walker**
4. Farmers heap hay in stacks and bind corn in shocks against the biting breath of frost.   **Margaret Walker**
5. A whirring like insects from the refrigerator . . .   **Rumer Godden**
6. When Dawn spread out her finger tips of rose . . .   **Homer**
7. He had failed everything; and what he hadn't failed, he hadn't taken yet. (Undoubtedly, F's had even been penciled in for the next year.)
   Bill Cosby
8. For Christmas I bought the cook a cookbook. She promptly fixed it and we had it for dinner last night. It was the first decent meal we had in three weeks.   **Groucho Marx**

B. Find examples of onomatopoeia, alliteration, consonance, assonance, and rhyme in the following lines.

And the silken, sad, uncertain rustling of each purple
   curtain
Thrilled me, filled me with fantastic terror never felt
   before. .   **Edgar Allan Poe**

C. Bring the following scene to life by using imagery and sound devices.

The kitchen was a mess, and I could barely hear the telephone ringing over the sounds from the stereo. Yes, Beau was home. Yes, indeed.

Narration and Point of View

As you have learned from every story you have created and every report you have composed, writing is all about making choices. One choice you can make that has profound effects on the nature of your work is the choice of a point of view.

UNDERSTANDING POINT OF VIEW

The **point of view** of a piece of writing is the perspective from which it is told. The three different points of view correspond to the grammatical concept of person in pronouns: **first-person**—*I* and *we;* **second-person**—*you;* and **third-person**—*he, she,* and *it.* The point of view from which you write defines your relationship to your subject. First-person point of view brings immediacy to your writing, while third-person point of view can create an objective distance. Second-person point of view uses the imperative tone in giving directions, commands, or requests and is most often used in nonfiction writing.

Point of View in Nonfiction

First-Person Point of View In nonfiction writing, the first-person point of view is used whenever you want to tell about your own ideas or experiences. This point of view is used, for example, in personal essays, in most letters, and in most autobiographies or memoirs. See Workshop 1, "Memoir," pages 22–34. The following is an example of nonfiction writing from the first-person point of view.

> [I] also wrote plays, and songs, for one of which I received a letter of congratulations from Mayor La Guardia, and poetry, about which the less said, the better. My mother was delighted by all these goings-on, but my father wasn't; he wanted me to be a preacher. When I was fourteen I became a preacher, and when I was seventeen I stopped.
>
> **James Baldwin, "Autobiographical Notes"**

W R I T E R   T O   W R I T E R

> I write in the first-person, or about myself. I know that when I'm writing about myself, my information is always right.
>
> **Beth McCarron, student**
> **Northfield, Illinois**

Third-Person Point of View The third-person point of view is used in biographies and, generally, in nonfiction writing in which the emphasis is on what is being told rather than on the teller. The following is a passage from an article about Ellis Island in New York.

James Baldwin,
novelist and essayist

> Close to 900,000 came through Ellis in 1907, its peak year. And that included only steerage passengers—the great majority. They were barged or ferried to Ellis from Manhattan piers, while first- and second-cabin passengers were cursorily processed on shipboard.
>
> For 17-year-old Myron Surmach from Ukraine, Ellis Island marked the first day of a long life in America. He came in 1910 intending to work for a few years in the Pennsylvania coal mines, then return to his homeland.
>
> **Alice J. Hall, *National Geographic***

Second-Person Point of View The second-person point of view is used almost exclusively in nonfiction, and then only in special circumstances, as when giving directions or instructions. Technical writing is often done in the second person. Benjamin Franklin used the second-person point of view in one part of his autobiography,

Narration and
Point of View   **459**

when he made a list of virtues in the form of commands to himself. Notice that the "you" that is the subject of each sentence is implied.

1. TEMPERANCE. Eat not to dullness; drink not to elevation.
2. SILENCE. Speak not but what may benefit others or yourself; avoid trifling conversation.
3. ORDER. Let all things have their places; let each part of your business have its time.

Benjamin Franklin, *The Autobiography*

Point of View in Fiction

First-Person Point of View Fiction writing from the first-person point of view tends to be immediate and forceful. Everything is seen from the perspective of the character who is telling the story.

My father's family name being Pirrip, and my Christian name Philip, my infant tongue could make of both names nothing longer or more explicit than Pip. So, I called myself Pip, and came to be called Pip.

Charles Dickens, *Great Expectations*

One of the joys of first-person fiction writing is that you get to assume the identity, or **persona,** of someone else, to speak with his or her voice and to have his or her thoughts, emotions, and reactions. In the passage above, Charles Dickens speaks as Pip, a straightforward, sensible boy looking back at his infancy. At the same time, when you write fiction in the first person, you must limit yourself to what your persona can see, hear, or experience.

Third-Person Point of View When writing fiction in the third person, an author can choose between two forms, based on the scope of the narrator's knowledge. If the narrator's knowledge comes from the perspective of a single character, then the story is being told from a **third-person limited point of view.** In the following passage, the point of view is limited to the perspective of the boy Arnold. All the action is seen through his eyes. Only that which he senses is described; Eugene's actions are presented only as Arnold sees them.

Arnold drew his overalls and raveling gray sweater over his naked body. In the other narrow bed his brother Eugene went on sleeping, undisturbed by the alarm clock's rusty ring. Arnold, watching his brother sleeping, felt a peculiar dismay; he was nine, six years younger than Eugie, and in their waking hours it was he who was subordinate. To dispel emphatically his uneasy advantage over his sleeping brother, he threw himself on the hump of Eugie's body.

"Get up! Get up!" he cried.

Gina Berriault, "The Stone Boy"

If the narrator's knowledge extends to the internal experiences of all the characters, then the story is being told from a **third-person omniscient point of view.** The word *omniscient* simply means "all-knowing." In the following passage, a young man and woman are falling in love. Because the narrator is speaking from the third-person omniscient point of view, he or she can describe the feelings and motivations of the characters. As a result, the reader gets a relatively objective view of both characters.

L I T E R A R Y
· · · · · · · · · · · ·
M O D E L

When the moment of sophistication came to George Willard, his mind turned to Helen White, the Winesburg bander's daughter. Always he had been conscious of the girl growing into womanhood as he grew into manhood. Once on a summer night when he was eighteen, he had walked with her on a country road and in her presence had given way to an impulse to boast, to make himself appear big and significant in her eyes. Now he wanted to see her for another purpose. He wanted to tell her of the new impulses that had come to him. He had tried to make her think of him as a man when he knew nothing of manhood, and now he wanted to be with her and to try to make her feel the change he believed had taken place in his nature.

As for Helen White, she also had come to a period of change. What George felt, she in her young woman's way felt also. She was no longer a girl and hungered to reach into the grace and beauty of womanhood.

Sherwood Anderson, *Winesburg, Ohio*

EXPERIMENTING WITH POINT OF VIEW

Sometimes your choice of point of view is straightforward. You are likely to choose the first person to tell a personal story, the second person for the step-by-step directions of a recipe, and the third person point of view for a biographical account.

Sometimes, however, you may wish to experiment, choosing an unusual point of view to make your writing more interesting. The following are some possibilities.

1. Tell someone else's story using the first-person point of view. This is done, for example, by people who ghostwrite autobiographies for other people and sometimes by people who write fictionalized accounts of other people's lives.
2. Tell about an event you experienced, but use the third-person point of view, making yourself into a character in the story.
3. Try writing a short story from the point of view of a first-person narrator who can see inside other characters' minds.
4. Try writing a first-person account from the point of view of a non-human "character"—an animal, for example, or a mountain. This is often done in poetry.
5. Try adopting the point of view of someone who is very much unlike you or who has a unique perspective. William Faulkner did this when he told part of his novel *The Sound and the Fury* from the point of view of a mentally handicapped adult.
6. Try telling a story from different points of view. Have different characters report on the same events.
7. Write from the point of view of an "unreliable narrator." That is, make your narrator someone who is insane, as Edgar Allan Poe often did, or who is untrustworthy or a liar.

UNDERSTANDING VANTAGE POINT

Vantage Point—the physical location from which the speaker stands in relation to the ideas, events, and characters in the writing—is related to point of view. The choices you make about vantage point can have a strong effect on your writing. For example, Charles Dickens as Pip might describe an escaped convict as if he were spying on the convict from behind a gravestone. The place behind the gravestone would then be his vantage point and would affect both the description and its tone.

If you were to describe Yosemite Canyon in Northern California, you might choose to describe it from the air.

> The canyon dips into the earth, making a dark, velvety impression in the green landscape. Slicing through the depths of the canyon are the shining ribbons of water that are its rivers and waterfalls.

Instead, you might choose to describe the canyon from the vantage point of a raft in the canyon river.

> The canyon rises above the gorge, its steep, slick walls throwing threatening shadows on the fast-running water. The roar of the river is deafening. A glimpse of blue sky far above relieves the claustrophobic feeling of enclosure.

Practice Your Skills

A. Read the following paragraphs and discuss the point of view and the narrator in each. How are they different? How are they similar? What effect does each narrator's choice of point of view have?

1. From the first years to which my memory stretches, I have been a disappointed woman. When, with my brothers, I reached forth after the sources of knowledge, I was reproved with, "It isn't fit for you; it doesn't belong to women." Then there was but one college in the world where women were admitted, and that was in Brazil.
    Lucy Stone, "Disappointment Is the Lot of Women"

2. The colonel's son was twelve the winter he started to make the pipe rack for his father. He was a handsome, dark-eyed boy, with a voice as high and clear as a choir boy's, and a quickness, a nimbleness, about him that was in his mind as well as in his flesh. He had a skill for carpentry and mechanics in his fingers, and he could shoot game as expertly as any man his father hunted with.
    Kay Boyle, "The Soldier Ran Away"

B. Choose one of the unusual points of view listed on page 462. Do a piece of writing using this point of view.

C. Choose an unusual vantage point from which to write a paragraph about something familiar—such as your street corner from underneath a manhole cover.

Writing
—TIP—

When you are writing from an unusual point of view, stop several times during the writing process and ask yourself, "Could my narrator have experienced this?"

Using Dialogue

Dialogue is simply conversation transcribed to the written page. Dialogue creates a sense of immediacy and does more than any other single technique to breathe life into a piece of writing. Instead of telling your readers what the fictional characters said, let the readers listen to the actual conversation. Instead of paraphrasing what people say in an interview, let the people speak for themselves.

USING DIALOGUE IN NONFICTION

Nonfiction—writing that deals with real people and actual events—includes histories and biographies, essays and magazine articles, interviews, accident reports, and speeches. Nonfiction writers often try to liven up their writing by using dialogue to show as well as tell what people are doing and feeling. Notice how John McPhee uses dialogue to help the reader experience life on a Wyoming ranch in the early 1900's.

There was a pack of ferocious wolfhounds in the country, kept . . . for the purpose of killing coyotes. The dogs seemed to relish killing rattlesnakes as well, shaking the life out of them until the festive serpents hung from the hounds' jaws like fettucine. The ranch hand in charge of them said, "They ain't happy in the spring till they've been bit. They're used to it now, and their heads don't swell up no more. . . ."

One summer afternoon, John Love was working on a wood-pile when he saw two of the wolfhounds streaking down the creek in the direction of his sons, whose ages were maybe three and four. "Laddies! Run! Run to the house!" he shouted. "Here come the hounds!" The boys ran, reached the door just ahead of the dogs, and slammed it in their faces.

John McPhee, _Rising from the Plains_

USING DIALOGUE IN FICTION

Fiction—imaginary prose narratives—includes short stories, novels, legends, tall tales, and myths. Dialogue can perform a variety of functions in fiction, including revealing character, presenting information, advancing the plot, and creating a mood. Notice how Garrison Keillor uses dialogue to portray the relationship between a boy and his mother and create a comic mood.

▼

"Why do you stay in your room all the time?" his mother asked him one morning as he stood at the kitchen counter, spreading peanut butter on a hamburger bun.

"I'm not in my room now, am I?"

"No."

"So then I don't stay in my room _all the time_, do I?"

"Well, a lot of the time."

"I sleep in my room. There's a lot of time right there. You want me to sleep on the living room couch?"

"Oh, Johnny."

One reason he stayed in his room was the sheer number of _Oh, Johnnys_ he heard when he came downstairs.

Garrison Keillor, _Lake Wobegon Days_

Writing TIP

When writing dialogue, put the words each character speaks in quotation marks. Also, begin a new paragraph each time the speaker changes.

In the following passage, notice how skillfully science-fiction writer Ray Bradbury uses dialogue to set the scene, establish a mood, and present information.

▼

"Unbelievable," Eckels breathed, the light of the Machine on his thin face. "A real Time Machine." He shook his head. "Makes you think. . . . "

"Of course, it's not our business to conduct escapes, but to form safaris. . . . All you got to worry about is—"

"Shooting my dinosaur," Eckels finished it for him.

"A *Tyrannosaurus Rex.* The Tyrant Lizard, the most incredible monster in history. Sign this release. Anything happens to you, we're not responsible. Those dinosaurs are hungry."

Eckels flushed angrily. "Trying to scare me!"

"Frankly, yes. We don't want anyone going who'll panic at the first shot. Six safari leaders were killed last year. . . ."

Ray Bradbury, "A Sound of Thunder"

U SING DIALOGUE IN DRAMA

▼

Matt: A guy the other day—I eat at this cafeteria, I talk to a lot of nutty guys—

Sally: I don't want to hear another story, I—

Matt: No, no, no, this is not like that. I came down here to tell you this. This guy told me we were eggs.

Sally: Who? You and me?

Matt: All people. He said people are eggs. Said we had to be careful not to bang up against each other too hard. Crack our shells, never be any use again. Said we were eggs. Individuals. We had to keep separate, private. . . .

Sally: And you think he's right or you think he's wrong?

Matt: *(up and pacing)* Well, it's all right there in his analogy, ain't it? What good is an egg? Gotta be hatched or boiled or beat up into something like a lot of other eggs. Then you're cookin'. I told him he ought not to be too afraid of gettin' his yolk broke.

Lanford Wilson, *Talley's Folly*

Dialogue is the major component of drama and so must provide nearly all the information about the characters and action. There are a variety of ways of punctuating dramatic dialogue. As in the passage you just read, however, speaker tags come generally at the beginning of a line of dialogue. Stage directions are enclosed in parentheses and convey information about gestures, tone of voice, costumes, scenery, and props. A speaker's lines end with a dash when that speaker is interrupted by another. See "Dramatic Scene," pages 102-106.

Here are a few ideas to consider when you write dialogue, whether for nonfiction, fiction, or drama.

Dallas Museum of Fine Arts, Foundation for the Arts Collection, gift of Mr. and Mrs. James H. Clark

The Beginning of the World, by Constantin Brancusi, 1920

Guidelines for Writing Dialogue

- Try to make your characters sound natural. Remember that people often use contractions and sentence fragments when they speak. They also use different dialects, depending on where they grew up.

- Include the tone in which your characters speak. Words may be mumbled, screamed, droned, whispered, or sobbed.

- Read your dialogue aloud when you finish and listen carefully to the way the characters talk. Do they sound like real people? If not, revise.

Practice Your Skills

Read the following passage from a short story by Washington Irving. Then rewrite it using dialogue to present information and show the action. Replace references to "conversation," "anecdotes," and "accounts" with the words of the characters themselves.

> We had been disappointed this day in our hopes of meeting with buffalo, but the sight of the wild horse had been a great novelty, and gave a turn to the conversation of the camp for the evening. There were several anecdotes told of a famous gray horse, which has ranged the prairies of this neighborhood for six or seven years, setting at naught every attempt to capture him. . . . Equally marvelous accounts were given of a black horse on the Brazos, who grazed the prairies on that river's banks in Texas. For years he outstripped all pursuit.
>
> **Washington Irving, "Camp of the Wild Horse"**

Using Dialogue **467**

Creating Character and Setting

Think of a short story that had a powerful impact on you. What do you remember most about it? Perhaps you think of a powerful setting, such as the dark dungeon and sharpened steel blade in Edgar Allan Poe's "The Pit and the Pendulum." Perhaps you recall a memorable character, like Walter Mitty in James Thurber's "The Secret Life of Walter Mitty."

In a powerful piece of fiction, one element of the narrative, such as character or setting, usually dominates. Yet, although one element usually prevails, all the elements must work together. Although Poe's prisoner in "The Pit and the Pendulum" is faceless, the tone of the character's comments accentuates our terror as we experience the slashing pendulum of the setting through his eyes.

Character and setting are two elements of fiction that often play dominant roles and need to be carefully created.

WRITER TO WRITER

My favorite part of writing is being able to create any type of environment or situation for the character.

Josh Smith, student
Birmingham, Alabama

CHARACTER

Some writers say that while they may create characters, once "born," the characters take on lives of their own. Therefore, don't feel you have to know everything about a character as you begin to write. You will develop your characters as they interact with other elements of the story—setting, plot, mood, and other characters.

Ways to Create a Character

Here are some ideas for planting a seed that may emerge into a full-grown character.

Clustering Think of someone you know or can imagine. Write the person's name in the center of your paper, and circle it. Draw lines from this circle out to others that contain details about the character, such as where he or she lives or what he or she might say.

To create a complete character with a history, values, and personality, try freewriting an interview with the character. Ask these questions.

1. What do you do on a typical day?
2. Tell me about your friends.
3. If you could have one wish, what would it be?
4. What are you most afraid of? Why?

Unusual Combinations Combine a real or imaginary person's characteristics with those of someone else. For example, imagine news anchor Dan Rather walking like Charlie Chaplin's little tramp. Freewrite about this composite individual.

If your character were a vegetable, what kind would he or she be? What kind of tree? These "loosening" mechanisms show you the fascinating people in your imagination.

Ways to Present Characters

Description, dialogue, and narration (the primary types of writing in fiction) can each serve as a vehicle to reveal character.

Description Describing personal traits is one way to show what a character is like. In this passage from "A Summer's Reading," Bernard Malamud shows his main character as a quitter with many excuses.

George Stoyonovich was a neighborhood boy who had quit high school on an impulse when he was sixteen, . . . This summer was a hard time for jobs and he had none. Having so much time on his hands, George thought of going to summer school, but the kids in his classes would be too young. He also considered registering in a night high school, only he didn't like the idea of the teachers always telling him what to do.

Bernard Malamud, "A Summer's Reading"

LITERARY
M O D E L

Dialogue   One of the best ways to reveal character is with **dialogue,** what the characters say. We learn about people through listening to what they say and, more importantly, to how they speak. Consider the following passage from Flannery O'Connor's "The Life You Save May Be Your Own." Mr. Shiftlet has just appeared on the old woman's porch.

> "Lady," he said, "nowadays, people'll do anything anyways. I can tell you my name is Tom T. Shiftlet and I come from Tarwater, Tennessee, but you never have seen me before: how you know I ain't lying? How you know my name ain't Aaron Sparks, lady, and I come from Singleberry, Georgia, or how you know it's not George Speeds and I come from Lucy, Alabama, or how you know I ain't Thompson Bright from Toolafalls, Mississippi?"
>
> **Flannery O'Connor, "The Life You Save May Be Your Own"**

Writing
TIP

In your everyday conversations, pay attention to *how* people speak. Call on these traits of speech in creating your fictional characters.

Mr. Shiftlet's ability to get and keep the old woman off-balance, as well as his Southern origins and level of education, are introduced very effectively in this piece of dialogue.

Narration   Through the relating of events, **narration,** the writer can also reveal the personality of his or her characters. What people do, the way they react to events, conveys important information. In James Thurber's "The Secret Life of Walter Mitty," Mitty launches into a daydream every time someone starts yelling at him. Mitty's reaction shows him to be an escapist.

SETTING

A story that creates a strong sense of setting—of time and place—can be just as powerful as one in which character or plot dominates.

Ways to Create Setting

Some techniques that you can use to create a setting include clustering, charting, freewriting, and sketching.

Clustering   Write your imaginary place and time in the center of a piece of paper. Name details about the setting, and write them in circles that you draw outside the central circle. For example, you might list details such as stale, dry air and a calendar for the year 2025. These details might be the beginning of a story about an underground community in the future.

Charting Make a chart with headings for each of the five senses—sight, hearing, touch, taste, and smell. Then, in each column, list particular sights, sounds, feelings, tastes, and smells associated with the time and place you want to write about.

Freewriting Close your eyes and imagine yourself in a time and place that you've experienced or can imagine. Using sensory details, describe that time and place.

Sketching Make some sketches of your setting. A floor plan of a house can be useful for a story that takes place inside. A rough map of an imaginary neighborhood that you're writing about can help you create your setting and keep it straight.

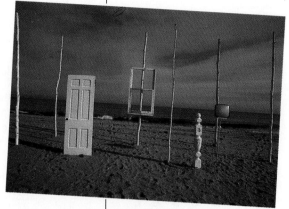

Beach Scene #2,
by Micheal de Camp

Ways to Present Setting

Like character, you can establish setting through description, dialogue, and narration.

Description One of the most commonly used methods of presenting setting is with description. Effective description uses concrete nouns—for example, *violin* instead of *instrument*—and usually appeals to more than one of the five senses. Consider the following passage from "A Wagner Matinée." In it, Willa Cather appeals mainly to the sense of sight and touch as she describes the setting of a symphony concert.

▼

> The matinée audience was made up chiefly of women. One lost the contour of faces and figures, indeed any effect of line whatever, and there was only the colour of bodices past counting, the shimmer of fabrics soft and firm, silky and sheer; red, mauve, pink, blue, lilac, purple, écru, rose, yellow, cream, and white, all the colours that an impressionist finds in a sunlit landscape, with here and there the dead shadow of a frock coat.
>
> **Willa Cather, "A Wagner Matinée"**

LITERARY
M O D E L

Creating Character and Setting **471**

Dialogue Setting can be indirectly conveyed through dialogue. For example, suppose a character in a story talks like this.

> Aye, Goody Shepherd. The cows are melked, and I be ready to feed the chickens now.

You can tell that the time is probably about two hundred years ago, when people still used the term *goody* to address women. The cow milking and the chicken feeding suggest that the setting is a farm, and the speech—pronunciations like *melked,* for example—indicates an old, rural dialect.

Narration Though its primary purpose is to advance plot, the relating of events can also convey setting. Consider the following passage from Stephen Crane's short story "A Mystery of Heroism."

> When a piece was fired, a red streak as round as a log flashed low in the heavens, like a monstrous bolt of lightning. The men of the battery wore white duck trousers, which somehow emphasized their legs; and when they ran and crowded in little groups at the bidding of the shouting officers, it was more impressive than usual to the infantry.
>
> **Stephen Crane, "A Mystery of Heroism"**

Notice how this narration paints a dramatic scene for the reader at the same time that it advances the events of the plot.

Practice Your Skills

A. Create a fictional character by following these steps.

1. Choose any four people in your life, and list their first names on a sheet of paper. Make a chart for each person, listing his or her physical appearance, clothing, values and beliefs, profession or usual activities, and habits or mannerisms.
2. Make up names for two fictional characters. For each character, blend the characteristics of two of the people from your real life. Make a chart for each character, just like the charts you made for the real people, including details from the first charts.

B. Write an introductory paragraph establishing a setting that one of the characters you created might inhabit. Use one of the methods described in this handbook to create a strong sense of time and place.

Developing Your Vocabulary

Pneumonoultramicroscopicsilicovolcanoconiosis. What does this word mean? Like a miner unearthing mineral deposits, with a little digging you can uncover the meanings of words you are seeing for the first time.

You can break this intimidating word into manageable parts: *pneumono* ("of the lungs"), *ultra* ("very"), *microscopic* ("small"), *silico* ("relating to silicon"), *volcano* ("vent through which gases escape"), *coni* ("cone-shaped"), and *osis* ("diseased condition"). From its parts, you can infer something about its meaning. In fact, *pneumonoultramicroscopicsilicovolcano-coniosis* is a lung disease caused by inhalation of very fine silicate particles.

By developing your knowledge of word parts and their meanings as well as words and their definitions, you can improve your speaking, reading, and writing skills.

INFERRING WORD MEANINGS FROM CONTEXT

The sentence or passage in which a word appears is called its **context.** Often you can determine the meaning of an unfamiliar word by analyzing its context. You may have to reflect on the entire passage in which the word appears to draw a conclusion about, or **infer,** its meaning.

Inference from Specific Context

Several types of context clues will help you determine the meaning of an unfamiliar word. Among these clues are *definition and restatement, example, comparison and contrast,* and *cause and effect.* The table on the next page defines and illustrates these context clues and indicates the key words that signal them.

Context Clue	Key Words
Definition and Restatement The writer places a definition or restates the word after the word itself. A *rapier* is a slender, two-edged sword.	in other words or this means which is to say that is
Example The writer follows an unfamiliar word with an example. The speaker's words were *derogatory.* For instance, he charged the opposing candidate with insensitivity to the problems of the homeless.	such as like especially for instance other this, these for example
Comparison The writer compares an unfamiliar word to a familiar word. This change in policy could have as *cataclysmic* an effect on the downtown area as an earthquake would.	like as in the same way resembling similar to likewise
Contrast The writer uses familiar words to tell what an unfamiliar word does not mean. Mrs. Wane introduced Judge Jones in glowing terms, although her private remarks had been *disparaging.*	but although on the other hand as opposed to on the contrary unlike
Cause and Effect The writer relates an unfamiliar word to familiar words in a cause and effect relationship. Since he lied under oath, the witness was charged with *perjury.*	because since therefore consequently as a result

Inference from General Context

Often the context clues to the meaning of an unfamiliar word will appear in later sentences in a paragraph, and the clues will be less obvious than those discussed so far. Be alert not only for key words signaling context clues, but also for clues suggested by the structure of the paragraph and by the relationship of the main idea and supporting details.

Inference Based on Structure   The structure of a passage can give a clue to the meaning of a word. For example, a repeated sentence pattern may suggest associations between words, as in the following example.

> High inflation foreshadows an economic slowdown. High unemployment *portends* less spending for consumer goods.

The verb *portends* is linked with the verb *foreshadows* by the parallel structure of the sentences, providing a clue to its meaning.

As a special type of parallel structure, a list also can enable you to determine the meaning of an unfamiliar word from your knowledge of other words in the list.

> On one game farm you can see a herd of elephants, a *pride* of lions, and a pack of wolves in their natural habitats.

The words *pride, herd,* and *pack* are linked in structure and meaning.

Inference Based on Main Idea and Supporting Details   One way to understand an unfamiliar word is to ask yourself questions such as these: Does the main idea of the passage offer a clue to the meaning of the word? Do any supporting details, including descriptive words and phrases, individually or collectively suggest the meaning of the word? Ask these questions as you read the following passage and determine the meaning of the italicized word.

> Behind the auction barn was a corral for *feral* horses. One could hear them halfway across town, kicking and snorting whenever someone approached, opposing their unnatural captivity with natural savageness and fury.

The meaning of the word *feral* is suggested in the phrases *unnatural captivity* and *savageness and fury.* In addition, the second sentence gives supporting details about the actions of the feral horses, describing them as kicking, snorting, and unused to people. You can infer, therefore, that *feral* means "wild."

Practice Your Skills

A. For each sentence below, use context clues to choose the word that is closest in meaning to the underlined word.

1. He had lived a life of <u>rectitude</u> in the service of the public, but his biographer uncovered some private wrongdoings.
   - (A) luxury
   - (B) virtue
   - (C) triumph
   - (D) difficulty
2. Like a latter-day Benedict Arnold, the <u>perfidious</u> general was caught red-handed selling secrets to a foreign agent.
   - (A) traitorous
   - (B) highly decorated
   - (C) methodical
   - (D) courageous
3. To operate in the black, a private college must have a sizable <u>endowment;</u> that is, it must supplement tuition income with income from private donors.
   - (A) administration building
   - (B) private donations
   - (C) alumni organization
   - (D) government grant
4. The optometrist, unlike the <u>ophthalmologist,</u> cannot prescribe drugs or perform surgery.
   - (A) dental technician
   - (B) one who fits glasses
   - (C) M.D. eye specialist
   - (D) pharmacist
5. Pewter is a combination of copper, tin, and antimony. This <u>alloy</u> is quite soft and presents some problems to the metalsmith.
   - (A) mixture of metals
   - (B) hardware
   - (C) bowl
   - (D) chemical
6. Because of the <u>dearth</u> of jobs in their country, many people emigrated to America.
   - (A) increase
   - (B) abundance
   - (C) scarcity
   - (D) agricultural
7. The mime troupe, the dramatic club, and other local <u>thespians</u> will convene Saturday for a day-long workshop.
   - (A) organizations
   - (B) singers
   - (C) Greeks
   - (D) actors
8. Within the atom are particles like the <u>positron</u> that exist for only a very short time.
   - (A) brief moments
   - (B) subatomic particle
   - (C) atom
   - (D) experiment
9. A cow is a <u>herbivore;</u> that is, it feeds on plants.
   - (A) botanist
   - (B) cannibal
   - (C) mystic
   - (D) vegetarian
10. The pears she had picked looked <u>succulent,</u> although there were many still on the tree that were hard and unripe.
    - (A) green
    - (B) hard
    - (C) juicy
    - (D) large

B. For each italicized word below, write a definition based on context clues. Check your answers in a dictionary.

1. Cells use hormones—*insulin,* for example—to order other cells to respond to such conditions as too much sugar in the blood.
2. Eventually it should be technically possible to make limitless copies, or *clones,* of desirable microorganisms.
3. *Lysosomes* also serve as cell janitors, aiding in the removal of old or defective cells from the system.
4. Some scientists say that cancer is caused by *mutations*—alterations in the DNA of a cell.

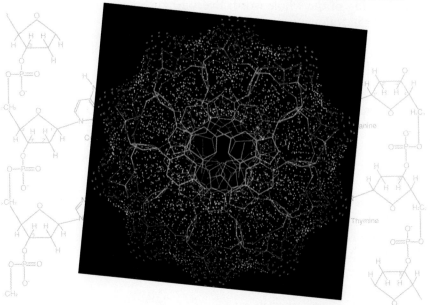

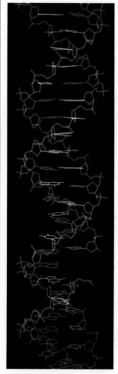

Cross section (left) and side view (above) of computer-generated images of DNA

C. The following passages are from the works of professional writers. Study the context of each italicized word and write a definition. Then check your definitions in a dictionary. Be prepared to discuss the clues that led you to your definition.

1. There are long periods of silence when one hears only the *winnowing* of snipe, the hoot of a distant owl, or the nasal clucking of some amorous coot.
   Aldo Leopold
2. Now, returning from my *foray* into the grasshopper meadow, I was back where I started, on the bank that separates the cottage from the top of the dam.
   Annie Dillard
3. A bramble caught hold of her skirt, and checked her progress. When she began to *extricate* herself it was by turning round and round, and so unwinding the prickly switch.
   Thomas Hardy

4. Gauss was in many ways an *enigmatic* and contradictory personality. The only son of working class parents, he rose to become the leading mathematician of his age, yet he lived modestly and avoided public notice. His demeanor was mild, yet he was an aloof, politically reactionary and often unyielding man who asked only that he be allowed to continue his creative work undisturbed.   **Ian Stewart**

ANALYZING WORD PARTS

If you know one part of a word, sometimes you can figure out the meaning of the whole word. Every English word includes one or more of the following parts.

Prefix	a word part that is added to the beginning of another word or word part
Suffix	a word part that is added to the end of another word or word part
Base Word	a complete word to which a prefix and/or suffix can be added
Root	a word part, often of Greek or Latin origin, to which a prefix and/or a suffix may be added; roots cannot stand alone.

Prefixes

Most of the prefixes used to form English words have more than one possible meaning. However, each of the prefixes in the list below has just one primary meaning. These prefixes, therefore, are reliable clues to the meanings of the words in which they appear.

Prefixes with a Single Meaning

Prefix	Prefix Meaning	Example
auto-	for or by itself	autonomous
bene-	good	beneficial
com-, con-	with, together	concurrent
dys-	bad, abnormal	dyslexia
equi-	equal	equilateral
intro-	into	introduce
mal-	bad	malform
mis-	wrong	misinform
mono-	one, single	monotone
poly-	many	polyglot
pre-	before	premature

In contrast, some common prefixes have more than one possible meaning. Examples are listed below.

Prefixes with Multiple Meanings

Prefix	Prefix Meaning	Example
ab-, a-	not	atypical
	away	abscond
	up, out	arise
ad-	motion toward	adapt
	addition to	adjoin
	nearness to	adhere
amphi-	both kinds	amphibian
	around	amphitheater
counter-	opposite, contrary to	counterclockwise
	complementary	counterpart
de-	opposed to, away from	deflect
	down	descend
	reverse action of, undo	defrost
dis-	opposite of	disqualify
	lack of	dispirit
	away	dislodge
em-, en-	to put or get into	encapsulate
	to make, cause	enrapture
	in, into	embrace
	to add emphasis	enliven
hypo-	under	hypodermic
	deficient in	hypothyroid
il-, im-, in-, ir-	not	irresistible
	in, into	inject
	very	illustrious
pseudo-	fictitious	pseudonym
	falsely similar to	pseudoscience
re-	back	recall
	again	restart
super-	over and above	superstructure
	very large	supertanker
trans-	across	transcontinental
	beyond	transnational

Suffixes

Most suffixes that are useful for determining word meaning appear in nouns and adjectives. Some **noun suffixes,** such as those listed below, are used only to make nouns from other parts of speech. Try to think of other words formed from these suffixes.

Noun Suffixes That Make Abstract Words	
Suffix	**Example**
-ance, -ence	sustenance, turbulence
-ation, -ition	machination, nutrition
-ice	malice, avarice
-ism	chauvinism, idealism
-ty, -ity	frailty, geniality

Many noun suffixes, however, add a specific meaning to a word rather than creating a particular part of speech. Some of these suffixes are listed below.

Noun Suffixes with Single Meanings		
Suffix	**Suffix Meaning**	**Example**
-archy	form of government	monarchy
-cide	killer, killing	germicide
-fication	act or state of making or causing	ratification
-ics	science or skill	athletics
-itis	inflammation	appendicitis

The following noun suffixes signify an agent, one who does something.

Noun Suffixes Indicating an Agent	
Suffix	**Example**
-ant, -ent	commandant, student
-er, -or	biographer, dictator
-ician	technician
-ist	pianist

Adjective suffixes often have quite specific meanings and, for that reason, can provide reliable clues to the meanings of unfamiliar words.

Adjective Suffixes with Specific Meanings

Suffix	Suffix Meaning	Example
-able, -ible	capable of being, or having qualities of	comfortable, legible
-atory	of, characterized by	accusatory
-fic	causing or producing	horrific
-most	most	foremost

Each of the adjective suffixes in the chart below means "full of" or "having."

Adjective Suffixes Meaning "Full of" or "Having"

Suffix	Example
-acious	audacious
-ent	insistent
-ose	verbose
-ous	felicitous

Several adjective suffixes have the meaning "pertaining to." These suffixes can also mean "connected with," "tending to," or "like."

Adjective Suffixes Meaning "Pertaining to"

Suffix	Example
-aceous	herbaceous
-al	original
-ant	vigilant
-ative	demonstrative
-ic, -ical	caloric, historical
-ive	protective
-like	lifelike

Practice Your Skills

A. For each word below give the meaning first of the prefix and then of the whole word. Check your answers in a dictionary.

1. dysfunction
2. preindustrial
3. deregulate
4. monorail
5. malpractice
6. compromise
7. disinterested
8. irreconcilable
9. misadventure
10. counterbalance
11. advantage
12. reinstitute
13. equiangular
14. amoral
15. polynomial

B. Add a prefix to each of the following words to form a new word. Check your answers in a dictionary.

1. religious
2. upholster
3. tension
4. cover
5. franchise
6. perfect
7. hypnosis
8. rich
9. nourished

C. For each italicized word below, give the meaning of the prefix and then of the word. Check your answers in a dictionary.

Trial by jury is one of the pillars of our *contemporary* legal system. United States law provides that citizens selected to serve on a jury for a criminal trial be *impartial* regarding the case. The jurors listen to the testimony of the witnesses and the arguments of the lawyers. The judge explains the laws that apply to the case, seeking to prevent any *irrelevant* thinking. Then the jurors discuss the case, weighing the evidence as *dispassionately* as possible, and deliver their verdict. We are all the *beneficiaries* of the jury system.

Paul Newman as attorney Frank Galvin in *The Verdict*, 1982.

D. For each of the words below first give the meaning of the suffix and then of the whole word. Use a dictionary if necessary. Then use each word in a sentence.

1. genocide	6. contemptible	11. envious	16. nationalism
2. guileless	7. arthritis	12. avoidance	17. fallacious
3. permanence	8. anarchy	13. comatose	18. arboreal
4. prolific	9. bulbous	14. unification	19. statuette
5. valorous	10. cherubic	15. formative	20. superintendent

E. Use a noun suffix meaning "agent" to make new words related to those listed below.

1. politics	4. editing	7. geology	10. magic
2. psychiatry	5. statistics	8. photography	11. auditing
3. biology	6. conducting	9. attending	12. presiding

F. Determine the meaning of each word in italics by studying the suffix and the context of the word. Check your answers in a dictionary.

1. A half-dozen mean-looking *buccaneers* boarded the ship and proceeded to rob the crew of their possessions.
2. As the finishing touch to her model of the Spanish ship, Amy added a *diminutive* Christopher Columbus.
3. In the battle of Valley Forge, General Washington showed himself to be a superb *tactician*.
4. The fact that the remains of the pharaohs are still well preserved attests to the advanced state of the art of *mummification* in ancient Egypt.
5. This new *herbicide* will kill all the weeds in the field without hurting the fish in the pond.
6. When the guards filled the moat and pulled up the drawbridge, the castle was all but *impenetrable*.
7. As a student of *aesthetics*, Frank was concerned less with whether a piece of art was genuine than with why it was considered beautiful.
8. Senator McNally had a *soporific* way with words that put half his audience to sleep before he had finished his remarks.
9. As the debate on censorship proceeded, it appeared that the main argument between the opponents was *semantic;* they could not agree on the meaning of "free speech."
10. On the day the students were to elect a new student-body president, Sarah, who was favored to win, felt *magnanimous* toward her hard-running opponent and treated him to a hamburger and a milk shake at lunch.

Word Roots and Root Families

If you remove the prefix and suffix from a long word, you are sometimes left with a word part that cannot stand alone. For example, deleting the prefix and suffix from the word *introspection* leaves the word part *spec.* Such a word part is a **root.**

Identifying the root or roots on which an unfamiliar word is constructed can help you understand what the word means. Consider, for example, the word *cryptic.* This word may appear unfamiliar, but if you remove the suffix *-ic,* you reveal the word *crypt.* If you know that *cryptos* is the Greek word for *secret* or *hidden* and that *-ic* is an adjective suffix, you can figure out that *cryptic* means "secretive."

A group of words that has a common root is called a **word family.** For example, all of the words in the following word family are derived from the Latin root *vid,* or *vis,* which means "see."

vista	visionary	evidence
video	providence	visor
envision	invisible	visualize

Learning the meaning of one root can enable you to determine the meanings of the entire family of words in which the root occurs.

Many English words are derived from Greek or Latin roots, such as those listed on the following pages.

Greek Roots and English Derivatives

Root	Meaning	English Word
anthrop	human	anthropology
bibl	book	Bible
bio	life	biology
chron	time	chronological
cosmo	world, order	cosmic
crac, crat	govern	democratic
dem	people	demography
dynamo	power	dynamic
ethno	race, nation	ethnic
gen	birth, race	genetic
geo	earth	geology
gram	something written	grammar
homo	same	homogenized
hydr	water	hydrant
iatr	heal	psychiatry
log	word, thought	logical
logy	study of	criminology
micro	small	microchip
neo	new	neophyte
neuro	nerve	neurotic
nom, nym	name	nominate
osteo	bone	osteopath
pan	all, entire	pandemonium
patho	suffering, disease	pathetic
phil	love	philanthropist
phobe	fear	phobia
phon	sound	phonics
pneum	air, breath	pneumatic
poli	city	police
poly	many	polygamy
psych	breath, soul, mind	psychology
soph	wise, wisdom	sophist
syn, sym	with	synchronize
techne	art, skill	technology

If hydr- means water, is this hydrart?

Latin Roots and English Derivatives

Root	Meaning	English Word
amicus	friend	amicable
animus	mind, spirit	animate
cred	believe	credulity
corpus	body	corporation
dorm	sleep	dormitory
gratia	kindness, favor	gratitude
junct	join	junction
jus, juris	law, right	justice
juvenis	youth	rejuvenate
mandare	command	mandatory
multus	much, many	multiplicity
opus, operis	work	operate
pon, pos, posit	place, put	compose
scrib, script	write	conscript
solus	alone	solitary
stat	stand, put in place	stationary
tempus	time	temporal
terminus	end, boundary	terminal
tract	pull, move	contract
ven	come	convene
vid, vis	see	visible
volve	turn, roll	evolve

Writing TIP

After you have analyzed a word's meaning, check the definition in a dictionary.

Practice Your Skills

A. Identify the Greek or Latin root or roots in each of the following words. (Some words have more than one root.) Give the meaning of the root or roots and the word. Use a dictionary if necessary.

1. gratuity
2. ethnology
3. phobic
4. neurology
5. Polynesia
6. credence
7. temporary
8. symbiosis
9. demagogue
10. microfilm
11. terminate
12. hydroelectric

B. Listed below are pairs of words from the same word family. For each pair, identify the Greek or Latin root. Then add at least two other words from the same family.

1. microbiology
   meteorology
2. philosophy
   bibliophile
3. sympathy
   synchronize
4. polyphonic
   monopoly
5. jury
   justice
6. synonym
   antonym
7. claustrophobia
   necrophobia
8. deposit
   reposition

Critical Thinking and the Writing Process

The word *critical* comes from the Greek verb *krinein* meaning "to discern or judge." To think critically is to think analytically. The skills and techniques of critical thinking can help you write more intelligently, in a logical, fair-minded, and perceptive manner.

STRATEGIES FOR PROBLEM SOLVING

You may encounter a problem at any point in your writing process, a problem that you need to solve before you can move on. Critical thinking strategies can help you both identify and solve the problem.

Identifying the Writing Problem

You have to make sure you understand the nature of your writing problem before trying to solve it. Identifying a problem is a three-step process.

Step 1 Define the problem by asking two goal-oriented questions: What is the situation like now? What will the situation be like when the problem is solved?

Step 2 State the problem as clearly as you can, in a single sentence if possible.

Step 3 Explore the problem in detail. If possible, analyze the problem graphically with a sketch, a diagram, a chart, or a map. Discuss the problem with others. Freewrite to see where that leads.

Kurt Vargo. © 1991

Solving the Writing Problem

Once you have identified a problem, you can apply one of the following problem-solving strategies.

Trial and Error Brainstorm to come up with a list of possible solutions to the problem. Evaluate each solution, and predict its outcome. If a solution looks unworkable, eliminate it from the list. Then try the feasible solutions one at a time, beginning with the solution that seems either the most straightforward or the most likely to work.

Application: Suppose you have a speech to write. You have a topic, but you are not sure of what to do next. You can start by listing three possible ways to proceed.

1. You could go to the library to find a collection of famous speeches. Perhaps you could use one of them as a model.
2. You remember a personal essay you once wrote on the same topic. Perhaps you could turn the essay into a speech.
3. You could freewrite and/or consult with peers.

After reviewing several speeches, you decide that option 1 is not for you. You don't want to imitate anyone; you want to be original. That leaves you with options 2 and 3. Start with the second option, because it is the most straightforward.

Divide and Conquer   Divide the problem into manageable segments, and then work on each segment independently.

Application: You might encounter problems with organization when writing up a complicated scientific experiment. A solution might be to break the information down into logical steps and then work on each step separately.

Calling on Past Experience   Think of similar problems that you have solved in the past. Evaluate past solutions to determine if they can be applied to the new situation.

Application: Suppose you want to write a potential employer to ask for an interview. Your problem is that you aren't sure how to begin and what tone and format to use. The solution is to examine other business letters you have written to get ideas for the structure of your request letter.

Simplifying   Writers sometimes get into trouble by trying to do everything at once. If this ever happens to you, try asking yourself questions such as the following: Am I trying to cover too much material? How can I simplify my task? What information is essential to my purpose? What information can I leave out?

Application: In writing an advertisement for your favorite brand of athletic shoes, for example, you can easily get bogged down in details such as price, comfort, and durability. At times like these, it is best to keep things simple. An advertisement is most effective when it conveys a single message. Concentrate on one goal—perhaps that the shoes are the most comfortable available.

What-If Questions All writers run into a dry spell from time to time. One way to start the ideas coming again is to ask questions beginning with the words "What if . . . ?"

> *Application:* If you want to write a short story, but are having trouble finding an idea, begin by asking "what-if" questions about anything that comes to mind and see what happens. For example, you might ask: What if there were still huge herds of buffalo roaming free on the Great Plains? What if U.S. astronauts had discovered a lost civilization on the moon? What if the polar icecap starts to melt?

Two Heads Are Better Than One Writing is a solitary business, but other people can help you achieve your goals, especially when you approach them with particular requests.

> *Application:* Your friends might be able to help you focus on a suitable idea to begin a speech, for example.

Pros and Cons Writing involves choices of all kinds, and it is not always obvious which approach will prove most effective. A pro-and-con chart can often help you out of this dilemma.

> *Application:* In choosing a topic for a science report, for example, you may have two great ideas, but can't decide between them. The solution could be to make a chart listing the pros and cons of each topic and then to choose the topic with the most pros.

Practice Your Skills

With three or four classmates, discuss the following writing problems and their possible solutions.

1. You are taking an essay test in an English class. One of the writing prompts on the test is this: Briefly describe some recurring themes among the Elizabethan writers we have studied. How could you use the divide-and-conquer strategy to organize your answer?
2. You have three ideas for the conclusion of a screenplay for a situation comedy that you have written for your English class. How might the trial-and-error strategy help you decide which idea to use?
3. You and your friends are putting together a theatrical skit for a street carnival. How could you use the calling-on-past-experience method to come up with a writing idea for the skit?
4. You have to write a paper for your psychology class on a topic dealing with differences between men and women. How could you use the simplification strategy to come up with a suitable topic?
5. You are trying to write a detective novel, and you want the story to take place in the White House. Use the what-if strategy to come up with ideas for the plot.

W R I T E R T O W R I T E R

Shouting is not a substitute for thinking, and reason is the salvation of freedom.

Adlai Stevenson, politician

STRATEGIES FOR
PERSUASIVE WRITING

Critical thinking is particularly important in persuasive writing, in which the writer presents reasons to support an idea that is open to debate. Essentially, there are two different kinds of persuasive writing, **persuasion** and **argumentation.** In persuasion, the writer's purpose is to convert the reader to a certain way of thinking. For example, a politician might write a speech detailing reasons why the electorate should vote for him or her. In argumentation, the writer explains a position without expecting the reader to act. For example, an essay exam in an English class may ask a question such as, "Was Shakespeare's Hamlet a procrastinator?" Such a question asks for argumentation, not persuasion.

To argue persuasively, you must be able to draw conclusions from the facts and opinions available to you. Two strategies that help make this possible are induction and deduction.

Inductive Thinking Strategies

Induction is a form of logical argument in which you reason from the specific to the general. You begin with a set of specific facts, examine the facts for logical connections, and use that information to create a generalization. Here is an example of induction.

Inductive Reasoning: From the Specific to the General

Specific fact	The fishing industry and the gray seal compete for the same fish.
Specific fact	The Canadian fishing industry used to kill gray seals in great numbers.
Specific fact	By 1940, the seals were on the verge of extinction.
Specific fact	The Canadian government ordered a halt to the slaughter.
Specific fact	The population of gray seals is now between 50,000 and 100,000.
Generalization	Prompt intervention can usually succeed in rescuing an endangered species from extinction.

Application: Inductive thinking is an excellent technique for devising a major point, or thesis, to support an argument. For example, if you want to write an essay discussing conflicting claims that you often see in advertisements for over-the-counter cold remedies, you might begin by gathering the following specific facts.

- One cold remedy promises fast relief from the discomforts of a cold.
- A second promises fast relief from headaches, chills and fever.
- A third purports to be the most effective cold remedy on the market.

After evaluating these claims and counterclaims, you might come up with the following thesis statement for your essay.

> Because pharmaceutical companies make extravagant claims for their cold remedies, the consumer must examine the scientific evidence that supports those claims before evaluating the products.

Writing
— TIP —

In revising your persuasive writing, make sure the conclusion you have drawn follows logically from the specific facts you presented and no other facts are needed.

Deductive Thinking Strategies

Deduction is a form of logical argument in which you reason from the general to the specific. Here are two examples of deduction.

Deductive Reasoning: From the General to the Specific

Generalization	All mammals have an internal mechanism to regulate their body temperature.
Specific fact	Whales are mammals.
Specific conclusion	A whale has an internal mechanism to regulate its body temperature.
Generalization	All mathematics courses taught in college require computer skills.
Specific fact	Statistics is a mathematics course taught in college.
Specific conclusion	Statistics requires computer skills.

Application: Deductive reasoning can be particularly helpful in drafting a composition. After you have chosen a topic you can begin to investigate it and gather material using an inductive process. You can then develop your thesis deductively, beginning with your general conclusion and providing your audience with enough details to prove your point. For example, if you were writing a story set in rural South Dakota during the 1930's Dust Bowl, you would first gather facts about the environmental and economic conditions at the time. Then you would develop your central conflict and characters by providing specific details that reveal the characters' unique responses to those conditions. You will continue to use both reasoning processes as you clarify your ideas.

Practice Your Skills

Complete one or both of these activities, as your teacher directs.

1. Gather material for a magazine article about being a teenager in the 1990's. Using your observations and experiences, list the specific ideas, opinions, attitudes, habits, concerns, modes of dress, and activities of today's teenagers. Then make a generalization that covers several of these aspects. Use your generalization as the thesis statement for an essay.
2. Suppose that you are writing a play. One of the characters was a Navy pilot during World War II and flew commercial airplanes for twenty-six years. What specific conclusions about this character can you deduce from these general facts? List your deductions. Then write a brief character sketch telling about the character in detail.

Sketchbook

Every year, the Bulwer-Lytton Fiction Contest awards prizes for intentionally bad writing. The contest, named after an inept nineteeth-century novelist, "honors" such characteristics of poor writing as mixed metaphors, overdone imagery, and preposterous figures of speech. Here is one winning entry:

Dolores breezed along the surface of her life like a flat stone forever skipping along smooth water, rippling reality sporadically but oblivious to it consistently, until she finally lost momentum, sank and, due to an overdose of fluoride as a child which caused her to suffer from chronic apathy, doomed herself to lie forever on the floor of her life as useless as an appendix and as lonely as a five-hundred pound barbell in a steriod-free fitness center.

Now it's your turn. Try your best to do your worst.

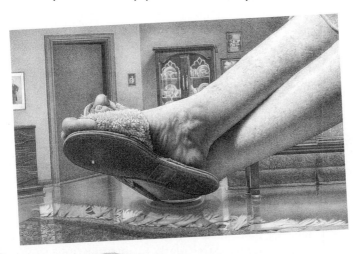

Additional Sketches

Write a description of yourself from the point of view of a grandparent.

Would you write the story of your life as a comedy, a tragedy, a mystery, or some other literary form? Explain your choice.

Strategies for Reading and Using Source Material

Much of your success in and out of school depends on your ability to understand and use what you read. Specific strategies can help you read effectively and incorporate information you glean from your reading into your writing.

APPLYING READING STRATEGIES

Reading strategies are obviously important in school, but they are also important on the job. People in most careers find that they need to read continually—to study manuals, reports, memoranda, specifications, and other written sources. The following strategies can help you read more efficiently throughout your life.

Preview Before reading closely, take a broad overall look at the material to get a general idea of its contents. Begin by reading the first two paragraphs, the first sentence of subsequent paragraphs, the last two paragraphs, and any information presented in special type—such as captions, headings, and boldfaced words—or in graphics, such as photos, graphs, diagrams, and charts.

Take notes as you read Writing down information in your own words as you read engages more of your attention and helps you remember what you read.

Predict Make guesses about what will come next in your reading. Predicting is especially useful when you're studying literature.

Question Before reading, make a list of questions to which you expect to find answers as you read. Write down the answers as you find them. Add new questions to your list as they occur to you.

Identify main ideas Main ideas often appear as the topic sentences of paragraphs, particularly in introductions or conclusions. Remember that main ideas are sometimes implied rather than directly stated. As you find or infer main ideas, jot them down.

Identify relationships As you read, look for passages that state or imply relationships between things or ideas, such as sequence, cause and effect, part to whole, spatial order, and order of importance.

Make Inferences   You are making an inference when you draw a conclusion based on your observations or prior knowledge of the world. For example, if you read in a short story that a character wakes up in the morning and sees that the street is wet, you infer that it rained during the night, even though the writer doesn't say so directly. Note important inferences you glean from your reading in your learning log. (See "Strategies for Problem Solving," pages 487–489.)

Respond with your own ideas and opinions   As you read, write down your own ideas and opinions about the material. Think critically; challenge the author by thinking of possible exceptions or of different points of view.

Review what you have read   Review your notes and organize them into separate lists, such as questions and answers about the reading, main ideas, key terms and their definitions, and ideas or opinions you want to follow up at a later date.

Summarize and paraphrase   Simplifying a reading selection by restating it in your own words will help you learn and remember what you read. Guidelines for paraphrasing and summarizing can be found on pages 497–501.

USING SOURCE MATERIALS IN WRITING

In addition to being good strategies for reviewing and understanding what you read, paraphrases and summaries are two ways of incorporating what you read into your writing. A third way is to use direct quotations.

Using Direct Quotations

You may wish to incorporate a direct quotation from a source into your writing when the material is especially well said or when you want to support or prove your own ideas.

It's very important that you credit, or document, your source to avoid plagiarism. It is often enough to name the source and its author in the sentence preceding the quotation. In a more formal piece of writing, such as a research report, you almost always need to give a parenthetical reference after the quotation and provide publication information for the source in a Works Cited list.

If the sentence introducing the quotation contains the author's name, follow the quotation with the page number on which it appears in the source. However, if the sentence introducing the quotation does not include the author's name, put the author's last name before the page number in the parenthetical reference.

> For example, Benjamin Whorf wrote that "the Hopi language is seen to contain no words, grammatical forms, constructions, or expressions that refer directly to what we call 'time,' or to past, present, or future" (50).

> One influential linguist claimed that "the Hopi language is seen to contain no words, grammatical forms, constructions, or expressions that refer directly to what we call 'time,' or to past, present, or future" (Whorf 50).

A full source citation, such as the following, should be included in the Works Cited list.

> Whorf, Benjamin Lee. "An American Indian Model of the Universe." <u>International Journal of American Linguistics</u> 16 (1950): 50–72.

See "Research Report," pages 286 and 290–293, for more information on parenthetical documentation and Works Cited lists.

Avoiding Plagiarism

When you use someone else's words or ideas without documenting the source, you are guilty of **plagiarism.** Plagiarism is a form of stealing; it is unlawful, and it can carry severe penalties. Avoid accidental plagiarism by making source cards and taking careful notes when you are conducting research. For each source you consult, write complete publication information on a three-by-five-inch index card. Give each card a source number. When you take notes, always put quotation marks around direct quotations, and indicate whether other notes are paraphrases, summaries, or ideas of your own. For more information about using source cards and note cards to help you keep track of your sources and document them correctly, see "Research Report," pages 280–283.

When you write, follow these guidelines:

• **Document all direct quotations.** Make sure that you have copied each quotation word for word and that the punctuation is the same as in the original.

Grammar
━━ TIP ━━

When you are directly quoting from an original source, use ellipses to indicate omissions of material. (See page 815 for additional information.)

- **Document information you glean from your sources.** This includes all ideas and expressions that you didn't think of yourself but that you copied, paraphrased, or summarized.
- **Do not document common knowledge.** Information is considered common knowledge if it can be found in several different sources or if it is knowledge that many people have.

Writing a Paraphrase

When you paraphrase, you express the main idea, the supporting details, and the tone of someone else's material in your own words. A paraphrase simplifies a selection but does not necessarily shorten it. You can use a paraphrase to adapt material for a report or to help you understand what you read. When you use a paraphrase in your writing, you must always credit the source of the ideas.

Read the paragraph below. The steps described on the following pages will help you paraphrase it.

PROFESSIONAL
M O D E L

> When computer involvement is heavy, the distortion of time and drive for perfection while on the computer are unlike any experience young people have had before. In sports, one is limited by sore muscles or physical weariness. There are cues to tiredness in other activities such as practicing music, reading, or just playing "pretend" games. The attention span is naturally broken by stiff fingers, tired eyes, or a shift in imagination. Working with computers, the limit is mental exhaustion. Children, like adults, do not readily recognize the signs of mental fatigue. If they don't stop working, they experience a kind of depletion. Only by being alone can they recuperate.
>
> **Craig Brod, *Technostress***

1. Locate the main idea. Look at the selection as a whole to determine the main idea. Next, put the main idea into your own words. In the above paragraph about computers, the main focus is the weariness that comes with heavy computer use. You might paraphrase this idea as follows to give focus to the writing of your final paragraph.

> Young people do not recognize the unfamiliar signs of mental tiredness from computer work, so they may keep working until they feel drained and need to be alone to recover.

2. List supporting details. Include all the points and arguments that support the central meaning of the selection. Arrange them in the same sequence as in the original, but put them in your own words. The supporting details in the passage on the previous page include the following.

1. Heavy computer involvement creates a distortion of time and a drive for perfection.
2. In sports, playing music or games, and reading, there are physical signs of exhaustion, such as tired fingers or eyes, that will cause the person to stop the activity.
3. The tiredness associated with computers is mental exhaustion, which is less easily noticed, and therefore, does not induce people to rest.
4. If people work beyond the point of mental exhaustion, they feel depleted and need to be alone to recuperate.

3. Determine the tone. A paraphrase must accurately convey the tone of the selection—the attitude of the author or speaker. In the selection by Craig Brod, notice the use of rather formal wording in phrases such as "computer involvement" and "one is limited." The writer also reveals serious concerns with the hazards of computer work. The following paraphrase misinterprets the tone of the selection, and distorts the meaning and purpose of the piece.

> A bleary-eyed teenager, striving to perfect a computer program, may feel hungry for dinner when it's really time for breakfast! The youngster might not be so oblivious in sports, where sore muscles or tiredness would bring on a quick trip to the sidelines. He or she might also enjoy an afternoon catnap when tired of practicing music, reading, or playing games. But computers tire the brain.

4. Rethink the vocabulary. Replace difficult words in the original with simpler, more familiar synonyms. For example, you can replace *recuperate* in the original with *recover*, *depleted* with *drained*, *fatigue* with *tiredness*, and *cue* with *sign*. Be careful not to distort the writer's tone, however.

The following paragraph, written by a student, is the paraphrase of the selection by Craig Brod. Notice that the writer followed the same order of ideas that Brod did and successfully captured the tone and meaning of the original passage. Also note that it is approximately the same length as the original.

A young person who becomes extremely absorbed in computer work often has two unfamiliar experiences. While feeling a strong desire for perfection in the computer work, the person's sense of time becomes deformed, or twisted out of shape. In other activities, such as sports or reading, young people recognize the signs of tiredness. Muscles may become weary, eyes tire, or the attention simply shifts. However, the tiredness associated with computers is mental—not easily noticed by a young person. The young computer operator who continues beyond this point will soon feel extremely drained. Recovery requires time alone.

5. Revise the paraphrase. Reread your paraphrase and make revisions, making sure that the material is in your own words and that you have shortened long sentences and used simple vocabulary. Be certain that it expresses the idea of the original and uses a similar tone. Finally, proofread your paraphrase for errors in spelling, grammar, usage, and punctuation. You should use standard English, regardless of the type of language used in the original.

Practice Your Skills

Paraphrase the following selection.

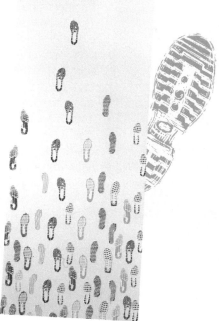

"Tracking is the process of answering a series of questions about a beast and its interactions with the environment," he [Tom Brown, world-famous tracker] observes. Reading a print in detail takes years of study, adds Brown. He relies on "pressure releases," specific spots in any print that reveal how the foot interacted with the soil. He points out, for instance, that as a person ages, his or her bones change. Brown can "read" the status of a person's muscles and skeleton, and hence the person's age, by studying two specific spots in the footprint: the outside edge of the foot and a hook-shaped motion of the ball of the foot, in conjunction with the person's stride.   **Richard Wilkomir**

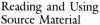

Writing a Summary

Like a paraphrase, the **summary** of a selection (also called a **précis**) presents someone else's ideas in different words. However, whereas the paraphrase is about the same length as the original, the summary shortens a passage to about one-third of its original length, capturing only its essential ideas. Writing summaries, then, can help you review what you have read and adapt complex material for inclusion in a research paper. In incorporating summarized material, be sure to credit the author whose ideas you use. See page 496 of this handbook for correct citation style.

Though shorter than the paraphrase, the summary has the same basic structure. Using your own words, include important points in the same order as the original and be sure to convey the correct main idea and tone.

As you read the following paragraph, think about how you might summarize it. Then follow the steps to see how one student proceeded.

PROFESSIONAL
. . . .
M O D E L

Tavern sign, lion
(19th century)

Lions and tigers are always associated together in the minds of the zoo or circus goer, yet in temperament and appearance the two could hardly be more different. The lion is a naturally lazy, and a ponderous beast; the tiger, with its broad, powerful shoulders and immensely strong hind limbs, is like a huge and impressively powerful spring and has a seventeen-foot leap. It is a very nervous, highly strung animal, and hates shouting or sharp words of command. . . . Its hearing is sharp, and its sense of smell far more acute than the lion's—and it can attack from the crouching position or even when lying down, so quick are its reactions. Unlike the lion, which fights with one front paw at a time (the other it uses to keep its balance), the tiger fights, almost boxes, with both paws at a tremendous speed, using its hindquarters to propel it forward. In the wild, the tiger is a natural climber and will often lie along a branch or sit on a rock. This habit means that it learns to climb onto its [circus] tub far more quickly than the lion. More cunning and more daring than the lion, the tiger is generally quicker to learn. It is also a more cynical creature, cannot be bluffed as easily as the lion, and requires different handling.

Peter Verney, *Here Comes the Circus*

1. Identify the main idea and important points. Determine the main idea and identify the important points in the original passage. In this selection the first sentence expresses the basic idea—the contrast between lions and tigers. Notice how the paragraph develops by presenting important points of difference between the two animals.

W R I T E R   T O   W R I T E R

The most valuable of all talents is that of never using two words when one will do.

Thomas Jefferson, statesman

---

2. Reduce the information. A summary should be about one-third the length of the original. To reduce the information, eliminate unnecessary details, examples, anecdotes, and repetitions. Once you have identified the important points and reduced the information, write the summary in your own words. Remember to express the important points in the same order as the original. Following is the summary one student wrote.

▼

Although people think of lions and tigers as similar, there are important differences between them. The lion is lazy and slow compared with the strong, agile, and more keen-scented tiger. Nervous and quick to react, the tiger can attack from a crouch and, unlike the lion, fight with both front paws. Being a natural climber, the tiger can learn to mount a circus tub faster than the lion. More daring than the lion and cleverer, the tiger is quicker at learning tricks. The tiger presents a different problem in training, however, being harder to bluff.

3. Revise the summary. Reread the first draft of your summary, checking it against the original to make sure that all important points are included. Eliminate any unnecessary details. Remember that separate details in the original can be appropriately combined in the summary. Make sure that your summary is about one-third the length of the original passage. Finally, proofread your summary for clarity, accuracy, and errors in spelling, grammar, usage, and punctuation.

S T U D E N T
· · · · · · · · · · · ·
M O D E L

Reading and Using
Source Material **501**

Practice Your Skills

Summarize the following selections.

1.   Not often does a literary work inspire a series of films. It is rare indeed that one becomes a continuing screen effort to the point that, in effect, it establishes careers for a large number of actors. But that is exactly what Edgar Rice Burroughs's *Tarzan of the Apes* has achieved.

    ERB's fantastic creature has . . . directly affected more lives than any character in fiction. "How much would heredity," ERB mused on a sleepless night in 1911, "influence character if the infant were transplanted to an entirely different environment and raised there?" For his fictional experiment, he put a babe of the English nobility into the jungles to be brought up by apes. " . . . and the boy-child was called Tarzan, which is ape-talk for 'white skin.'"

    Little did ERB realize then the potential of his fictional hero. He could not have guessed that Tarzan would become an international figure, idolized by millions. He could not have known that his brainchild would make him wealthier than in his most satisfying dreams. In fact, he thought the story poor and doubted its salability, until *All-Story Magazine* purchased it in 1912 for seven hundred dollars.

Gabe Essoe

2.   There is one activity of dolphins which, while not confined to them, never ceases to astonish us. I am referring to their games and to their love of play. Many other species of animals love to play—cats are a notable example—but dolphins, by the powers of observation they display and by the ingenuity they show, lead us to attribute to them a behavior not unlike our own. Perhaps it is because they show signs of a sense of humor while playing. . . .

    All trained dolphins seem to take pleasure in performing their stunts, but they also love to play among themselves. They sometimes spend hours throwing a fish, or a piece of cloth, or a ring. . . .

    We know that such behavior is not inspired by the boredom of captivity, and that it does not result from training, for dolphins also play when they are at liberty in the sea. They push any floating object before them—a piece of wood, or, like Opo, an empty bottle.

    Dolphins also love to surf, and they allow themselves to be carried on the crests of waves, just as human surfers do. (In Florida, on at least one occasion, dolphins actually joined human surfers.) And, like humans, they wait for a particularly big wave.

Jacques-Yves Cousteau and Phillipe Diolé

Library and Research Skills

The excitement of discovering answers to your questions and realizing that those answers lead to even more questions is what makes research so rewarding. However, not knowing how to find the information you need can be frustrating. Because a great deal of your research time will be spent in libraries, learning procedures for using the library will enable you to make use of its resources most effectively.

THE CLASSIFICATION OF LIBRARY MATERIALS

You probably are already familiar with the two divisions libraries use to classify books—fiction and nonfiction.

Fiction

In most libraries novels are arranged in alphabetical order by the author's last name. Multiple books by the same author are shelved alphabetically by title. Short stories may be shelved either with novels by the author's last name or in a separate section at the end of the fiction books. Some libraries shelve short-story collections in the nonfiction section.

Nonfiction

Nonfiction, or factual material, is organized by either the Dewey Decimal System or the Library of Congress Classification. The **Dewey Decimal System** is the method most libraries use to classify nonfiction books. Memorizing the categories on the chart that follows will enable you to go directly to the sections of the library where the resources you need are shelved.

Dewey Decimal Classifications

000–099	General Works (encyclopedias, bibliographies)
100–199	Philosophy (conduct, psychology)
200–299	Religion (the Bible, mythology, theology)
300–399	Social Science (law, education, economics)
400–499	Language (grammars, dictionaries, foreign languages)
500–599	Science (mathematics, biology, chemistry)
600–699	Technology (medicine, inventions, cooking)
700–799	The Arts (painting, music, theater, sports)
800–899	Literature (poetry, plays, essays)
900–999	History (biography, geography, travel)

The **Library of Congress** classification, or **LC,** another method of classifying nonfiction materials, is used by libraries that house more material than the Dewey Decimal System can handle. The LC system uses twenty-one broad categories, designated by letters of the alphabet. Subcategories are indicated by a second letter. For example, *N* is the designation for fine arts; painting, a subcategory of fine arts, is labeled *ND*. Individual books are numbered within each subcategory. Libraries using the LC system usually post charts identifying the categories and directing users to the appropriate shelves. Note that fiction books are not included in this classification system.

Sections of the Library

Libraries have separate sections for storing different types of resource materials.

Stacks Libraries have two kinds of stacks, or bookshelves: open and closed. You can browse in **open stacks** until you locate the book with the call number you are seeking. In contrast, users do not have access to **closed stacks.** To use materials shelved there, you must fill out a call slip with the call number, title, and author of the book and have a librarian obtain the book for you. Most libraries have separate stacks for nonfiction, fiction, biography, and reference works.

Periodicals The periodical section contains recent magazines and newspapers. A librarian can tell you how to obtain back issues.

Writing
—TIP—

Browsing through open stacks or the periodicals section of your library can be a good way to find ideas for writing.

Nonprint Materials Libraries usually have a separate section for materials such as photographic reductions of printed material stored on microfilm or microfiche. Such sections have machines used to read microfilm and microfiche. They also stock audiovisual materials such as filmstrips, movies, recordings, videocassettes, and art prints.

Vertical File Many libraries have vertical files, file cabinets in which printed matter is stored in alphabetical order by subject. Materials that you might find in a vertical file include pamphlets, brochures, reprints, clippings, and photographs.

Special Sections Some libraries have special sections for rare or unique books, genealogy information, local history, or audiovisual materials.

Once you understand how libraries organize resource materials, you can concentrate on finding the sources you need. Several search tools can help you locate the material easily.

SEARCH TOOLS: CATALOGS AND INDEXES

Catalogs and indexes are the nucleus of any library. Use them to survey quickly the range of material available on your subject.

Card Catalog

The card catalog provides three types of listings for every nonfiction book in the library—by subject, by title, and by author. Fiction books are often listed only by author and title. Recently, many libraries have replaced or supplemented the card catalog with a computer catalog. The computer catalog contains the same information that a card catalog does, with the advantage of quick and efficient scanning of resources. It also provides features such as a printed list of books available on your subject, including notations indicating whether a book has been checked out or is available in another library. See page 880 of the Access Guide for a discussion of computer catalogs.

In both card and computer catalogs, every listing for a nonfiction book includes a call number, which appears in the upper left-hand corner of a nonfiction catalog card or in the first part of a computer listing. This call number consists of the Dewey Decimal number or LC letter code that gives the location of the book.

Indexes

Indexes are reference books that provide alphabetized listings of names, places, subjects, titles, or authors of works or first names of works. Each listing in an index is followed by the titles of reference works that contain information on the subject. Below is a brief description of several indexes that can help you structure your research.

Readers' Guide to Periodical Literature The *Readers' Guide* is an index to articles published in a wide variety of periodicals. Suppose, for example, that you were preparing an exhibit on trends in toys since World War II and needed information about the rise and fall of sales of hula hoops in the 1950's. Skimming the subject in the bound volumes of the *Readers' Guide* for each year of the 1950's will provide you with a list of articles on the subject. You can then locate the magazines you need. For a more current topic, you would consult the unbound *Readers' Guide* issues for the current year. In the following sample entries from the *Readers' Guide,* notice that topics are listed by both author and subject. Also note the information that identifies the magazine and cross-references to other entries.

TECHNOLOGY
TIP

There are also several computerized and on-line indexes you can use. For more about electronic reference sources, see pages 880–882 of the Access Guide.

Excerpt from the *Readers' Guide*

Subject Entry —

Marshall Plan
   Did the Marshall Plan work too well? S. Jenkins. il

Name of Magazine — *U S News World Rep* 102:13 Je 8 '87 — Date
   Diplomacy's splendid achievement. M. Whitaker, il

Volume Number — *Newsweek* 109: 47 Je 8 '87
   Marshall arts. H. Fairlie, *New Repub* 196:7-8 + Je 15 '87
   Perils of policy: the Marshall Plan only worked once. W. Pfaff. *Harpers* 274:70-2 My '87

Marshals Service (U.S.) *See* United States. Marshals Service — Cross-Reference

Marshes
      See also
      Bayous
      Everglades (Fla.)
      Honey Island Swamp (La.)

Author Entry — **Marston, Ray**
   Logic-gate fundamentals. il *Radio-Electron* 58:50-4 Ap '87

The New York Times Index This index lists chronologically every subject covered in *The Times* each year and gives a brief abstract of each article. Suppose, for example, that you wanted to learn more about the famous Watergate hearings of the Nixon era. To find newspaper articles written at the time, you might use *The New York Times Index*.

Granger's Index to Poetry Have you ever needed a copy of a poem whose title you couldn't remember? In *Granger's,* you can look up the first line, author, or title of a poem and find a list of books that contain the poem. The excerpt in the box shows the listings in *Granger's* for Robert Frost's "Stopping by Woods on a Snowy Evening." The abbreviations used to indicate the books in which this poem may be found are explained in the front of the index.

Excerpt from *Granger's Index*

Stopping by Woods on a Snowy Evening. Robert Frost. AmPP; AP; BiP; BoNaP; CABA; CMop; CoBMV; FaBoCh; FaBV; FaFP; FaPON; FF; FPL; Gojo; GrPl; HAP; HBMV; HeIP; HoPM; InPK; InPS; LiTA; LiTM; MasP; MoAB; MoAmPo; MoShBr; MoVE; MP; NePA; NIP; NoAM; NOBA; BoP; NTCP; OBCA; OxBA; PAI; PDV; PoRA; PoSC; PrIm; RHPC; SCV; SiSoSe; SoSe; SUS; TAP; TiPo; TreFS; TrGrPo; TwAmPo; TwCP; UnPo; ViBoPo; WHA "Woods are lovely, dark and deep, The," *sel.* TRV

Literary Indexes Similar to *Granger's,* literary indexes such as the *Short Story Index* and the *Play Index* help you locate books that contain a particular literary work.

GENERAL AND SPECIALIZED REFERENCE WORKS

Becoming familiar with the reference area of the library will probably contribute more to the quality and efficiency of your research than anything else you can do. General reference works, such as dictionaries, encyclopedias, yearbooks, atlases, and almanacs, are marked with an *R* or *REF* above the call number and are shelved in a separate room or section. You can use these sources to survey an entire topic or isolate specific facts.

Dictionaries

Two kinds of general dictionaries you will use in research are unabridged and abridged.

Unabridged Dictionaries These reference works, such as the *Oxford English Dictionary* or *Webster's Third New International Dictionary,* contain longer, more detailed entries than do abridged dictionaries; in addition, they list a large number of uncommon words. For example, you could use an unabridged dictionary to find the meaning of a Shakespearean word such as *compt*—"trimmed," "polished," or "in good condition."

Abridged Dictionaries These shortened dictionaries provide a quick reference for definitions, spellings, pronunciations, and usage. An example of an abridged dictionary is *Webster's New World Dictionary of the American Language.*

Specialized Dictionaries

Several dictionaries treat a specific aspect of the language, such as rhyme, slang, idioms, phrases, abbreviations, etymologies, and usage. If you are looking for a word to rhyme with *duress* and *stress,* for example, a general dictionary will not be adequate. You will need to consult a dictionary of rhymes.

Thesaurus This dictionary of synonyms and antonyms is very helpful to a writer looking for a fresh word to substitute for an overused one, or for a synonym with just the right connotations. *Roget's Thesaurus in Dictionary Form* is an example of a standard thesaurus.

Special-Purpose Dictionaries Special-purpose dictionaries deal with music, medicine, law, foreign languages, biography, and many other subjects. They can add that special spark of interest to a report or allow you to use specialized terms confidently. Suppose you were preparing an essay on constitutional rights and you wanted a comprehensive explanation of *habeas corpus.* You would find a more complete definition in a law dictionary than in a general dictionary.

Encyclopedias

Encyclopedias may cover general or specialized subject areas. There are several types of encyclopedic references.

General Encyclopedias   Encyclopedias are collections of articles on a broad range of subjects, arranged alphabetically in volumes. Because they provide this breadth of coverage, encyclopedias cannot also offer depth. Each article gives only a survey of a topic. Familiarize yourself with the various sets of encyclopedias in your library and consult the encyclopedia yearbooks for updated information on selected topics. Also investigate the *Encyclopaedia Britannica.* This work is composed of three parts: the *Propaedia,* or outline of knowledge and guide to the encyclopedia; the *Micropaedia,* which serves as an index and short-entry encyclopedia; and the *Macropaedia,* which contains knowledge in depth.

Specialized Encyclopedias   Special encyclopedias are available for the fields of art, history, science, mathematics, literature, hobbies and many other subjects. For example, if you were writing an in-depth report on parenting instincts in primates of the wild, you could consult a special encyclopedia, such as the *International Wildlife Encyclopedia,* for comprehensive information.

Almanacs, Yearbooks, and Atlases

Published annually, almanacs and yearbooks are sources of current facts and statistics as well as matters of historical record in government, economics, sports, and other fields. For example, if you were preparing an argument for a debate, you might find the statistics in an almanac or yearbook to support your contentions about recent Republican fiscal policy.

Atlases are books of maps that also contain global demographic statistics and information about weather, geography, and other related subjects. For example, a source such as the *National Geographic Atlas of the World* would be a good book to consult for data on the effect of geography on the history of island nations.

TECHNOLOGY
TIP

If you use an electronic encyclopedia, atlas, or almanac, find out if it is downloaded from a CD-ROM or if it is on-line. On-line encyclopedias are especially useful if you need up-to-date statistics or facts on a current subject. For more about electronic reference materials, see pages 880–882 of the Access Guide.

Geographical dictionaries are good sources for information about place names and geographical locations.

Biographical References

You can research a noted person's life by consulting one of the many excellent biographical reference sources that are available. You can also read full-length biographies about the person. To use biographical sources effectively, it helps to know the nationality of the person and whether or not he or she is living.

If you need only simple facts such as the date of birth or the career history of a person, a special dictionary such as *Webster's Biographical Dictionary* would be a good source. If you need to gather more complete information about a person, consult sources such as *Who's Who* and *Current Biography* for living subjects and sources such as *Dictionary of American Biography* for historical figures.

Full-length biographies offer the most complete treatment of a person's life and accomplishments. Library placement of biographies varies. Some libraries include biographies in the 900 Dewey Decimal category and mark each with a three-digit number beginning with 92. Others create a separate biography section and mark each book with a *B* and the first letter of the last name of the person the book is about. Familiarize yourself with the system used to categorize biographies in your library.

Literary Reference Works

Literary research may involve a variety of tasks. You may need to learn about writers and their works or investigate some aspect of literary history. Occasionally you will need to identify a quotation or locate a poem or short story. Literary reference works meet all these needs.

Books About Authors There are many reasons for consulting a literary reference work. For example, you might investigate the life of Willa Cather in order to understand its effect on her work. Sources such as *Twentieth Century Authors, Contemporary Authors,* or Benet's *The Reader's Encyclopedia* will tell you that Willa Cather grew up in Red Cloud, Nebraska, and that her parents were Bohemian immigrants. More extensive entries in *American Writers: A Collection of Literary Biographies* and *Writers at Work* draw a connection between Willa Cather's own experiences and those of the pioneer heroines in her novels. A variety of biographical references are available for authors from various parts of the world. To look up information on an author, you will usually need to know the author's complete name and the time period when he or she lived and wrote.

Book Review Digest *Book Review Digest* provides professional reviews arranged alphabetically by author. For example, if you were responsible for writing the book reviews in your school newspaper, you could use the *Digest* to compare your views with those of professional reviewers. You might even incorporate an interesting quotation from a professional's review in your article.

Cyclopedia of Literary Characters Organized alphabetically by title, with separate author and character indexes, this work identifies the main characters in 1,300 novels, dramas, and epics from world literature. For example, as you are watching the evening news, one public figure calls another a "Uriah Heep." Who was Uriah Heep? A glance at the listing "Uriah Heep" in the character index of the *Cyclopedia of Literary Characters* leads you to a listing for Charles Dickens's *David Copperfield* and the information that Heep was a hypocritical embezzler who professed loyalty to the very people he was cheating.

W R I T E R   T O   W R I T E R

I quote others only the better to express myself.

Montaigne, French essayist

Books of Quotations You may already be familiar with *Bartlett's Familiar Quotations* as a source for identifying quotations, lines of poetry, and well-known sayings. This work allows you to search for a quotation by author as well as by subject or first line. *Bartlett's* also contains a short section with often-quoted passages from religious works, such as the Bible, the Koran, and the Book of Common Prayer.

Bergen Evans's *Dictionary of Quotations* is another useful source. It extends beyond *Bartlett's* to include the comments of many contemporary figures. Notice how the following excerpt from the *Dictionary of Quotations,* gives not only the source of the quotation but also two earlier versions and sources. The earlier versions are shown in italic type.

Other Literary Sources   Your library offers many reference works on the history of literature. Among them you will find *Scribner's American Writers* and the Oxford Companion Series. Suppose that you have read Shakespeare's *Henry IV* and that you are writing a character study of Sir John Falstaff. You know that Falstaff appears in other Shakespearean plays, but how can you quickly learn which ones? You will find this kind of information in *The Oxford Companion to English Literature.* Other alphabetically arranged entries include short biographies of authors; discussions of literary movements, awards, and lists of winners; and explanations of literary allusions.

OTHER SOURCES
OF INFORMATION

Good research means leaving no stone unturned. This may require that you go beyond the library to contact various organizations or individuals for information.

Experts   Often you can find just the information you need by interviewing someone who is an authority on your subject. This person might be a professional in your community or a friend or acquaintance who knows a great deal about your subject.

The U.S. Government   The government may provide needed information that would be difficult to obtain elsewhere. The Government Printing Office and many governmental agencies publish material on a multitude of subjects. If, for example, you need to know the federal safety regulations for playground equipment in order to help construct a community play area, begin by checking the *United States Government Organizations Manual.* The brief descriptions of each agency will tell you whom to consult for specialized information. Then look at the *Selected List of U.S. Government Publications* to learn what pamphlets or brochures you can obtain. If these are not available in the library, send for them yourself. Your congressional representative also may be a source of federal documents.

Organizations and Associations When researching a topic, ask yourself, "Who could help me? Who might care?" The answer may suggest organizations or special-interest groups—such as the American Heart Association or Literacy Volunteers—which could provide you with excellent free materials, suggest community programs, and even supply speakers. Names of organizations may be found in the *Encyclopedia of Associations.*

Practice Your Skills

A. Use the specialized reference works in your library to respond to the following items. List the reference work you consulted for each item.

1. Who is Merlin, and in what literary work(s) does he appear?
2. What is the setting of Stephen Vincent Benét's poem "John Brown's Body?"
3. What are the birth and death dates for Blaise Pascal?
4. How can you obtain a passport?
5. When did Sir Edmund Hillary climb Mount Everest?
6. Why were Ogden Nash's poems so popular?
7. Who was the first man to go into space?
8. In which time zone is Las Vegas, Nevada?

B. Find as many sources and versions as you can for the following quotations: (1) "A house divided against itself cannot stand." (2) ". . . ask not what your country can do for you; ask what you can do for your country."

C. Using the *Readers' Guide* and *The New York Times Index,* list five recent articles about the relationship between cholesterol levels and diet. Then list five individual experts, government sources, or associations you might contact for more information on this subject.

D. Beginning by consulting the card catalog in your library, list three sources other than encyclopedias that provide information on the French and Indian War. Include a biography as one of your sources. Describe what steps you took to find your other sources, including any false or extra steps.

TECHNOLOGY
——— TIP ———

Many government agencies and institutions, along with private associations, now have sites on the Internet. For more about accessing these sites, see pages 881–882 of the Access Guide.

Public Speaking

Many people have jobs that involve giving speeches—lawyers, museum guides, politicians, public relations professionals, salespeople, and teachers. People also give speeches quite often outside the workplace—at town or city council meetings, at meetings of clubs and associations, and at gatherings of friends and family. Learning to speak well in public is, therefore, extremely practical.

Portrait of John F. Kennedy ©1967, by James Wyeth

TYPES AND METHODS
OF PUBLIC SPEAKING

Most speeches fall into one of three categories. **Informative speeches** provide information. These range from simple announcements to full-fledged oral reports or lectures. **Persuasive speeches** include all speeches in which the speaker attempts to persuade the audience to adopt a position or to take some action. Sales demonstrations and political campaign speeches are examples of persuasive speeches. **Occasional speeches** are speeches made in conjunction with special occasions: to introduce featured speakers or performers; to present or acknowledge honors, awards, or gifts; or to commemorate a person or event.

Just as there are different kinds of speeches, there are also different ways of preparing and delivering them.

- **The Manuscript Method.** With this method, you write out your speech word-for-word; then read it to your audience, making sure to glance up from the page to make eye contact.
- **The Memorization Method.** You write out your speech and commit it to memory. A memorized speech can seem more immediate, spontaneous, and engaging to an audience than one that is read from a manuscript. When using this method, however, it is a good idea to have note cards as a backup.
- **The Extemporaneous Method.** With this method, you prepare an outline or note cards that give the main ideas and significant details of your speech. During delivery, you make up the exact words of the speech as you present it.
- **The Impromptu Method.** In this situation, you simply stand up and talk about the topic. This method is appropriate in meetings or in responding to a question.

SPEECH PREPARATION
AND DELIVERY

Impromptu Speeches Even an impromptu speech should have some preparation. Take a moment to organize your thoughts in your head. Ask yourself what the main idea is that you want to express. Then think of several supporting statements that you can make. Finally, think of how you want to introduce your comments—perhaps with a question, with a joke, with a reference to something said by another speaker, or with a reference to the questions, issue, or occasion at hand.

Manuscript, Memorized, and Extemporaneous Speeches For more formal speeches, one of the following methods, or some combination of them, is most effective.

1. Treat the preparation of the speech as you would any writing or research assignment. Focus your topic, gather information, organize it, experiment with your ideas in various drafts, and then write a final draft. Pay particular attention to creating an effective introduction and conclusion.

2. Memorize or outline your speech. If you choose to memorize your entire speech, or just the introduction and conclusion, work by looking at one small section, then looking away to repeat the lines. When that section is memorized, continue until the memorization is complete. If you choose to outline your entire speech or just the body of it, work from your written copy, making an outline that includes all of your main heads and supporting details.

3. Practice. To enhance your confidence and ensure a successful speech, give a dress rehearsal for friends or family members.

4. Do a self-critique, and work on specific elements of your delivery. As you practice, work on specific verbal and nonverbal elements of your presentation. Think about these verbal elements.

- **Pace**   Is your delivery too fast or too slow?
- **Articulation**   Are you pronouncing your words crisply?
- **Volume**   Will the audience be able to hear you?
- **Tone**   Are you conveying the proper emotion?
- **Pitch and intonation**   Are you using the rise and fall of your voice to emphasize your meaning?
- **Stress**   Are you emphasizing important words and phrases?
- **Pausing**   Do you pause for effect before or after important points or laugh lines?
- **Dynamic variation**   Are you effectively varying your pace, articulation, volume, tone, pitch, and stress?

Nonverbal elements to think about include the following:

- **Eye contact**   Are you looking at the audience?
- **Gestures and facial expressions**   Do these expressions reinforce what you are saying?
- **Posture and body language**   Are you standing up straight, but comfortably? Do you appear confident?

5. Prepare any props you might need. Some speakers make effective use of visual aids, such as charts, graphs, maps, or handouts.

6. Deliver your speech. Begin by pausing, taking a breath, and looking at your audience. During your speech, pace yourself. Don't rush. Allow yourself to pause briefly when you feel nervous or feel you have made a mistake. Maintain eye contact with your audience.

Reprinted by permission of NEA, INC.

SPEAKER TONIGHT

YOU'LL DO FINE.. JUST REMEMBER TO SPEAK SLOWLY, MAINTAIN EYE CONTACT, AND WAG YOUR TAIL NOW AND THEN.

© 1990 by NEA, Inc.   THAVES 10-11

Practice Your Skills

A. After the explosion of the space shuttle *Challenger,* in January 1986, President Ronald Reagan delivered a speech written by his chief speech writer, Peggy Noonan. Read the speech and then answer the questions that follow it.

Ladies and gentlemen, I'd planned to speak to you tonight to report on the State of the Union. But the events of earlier today have led me to change those plans. Today is a day of mourning and remembering.

Nancy and I are pained to the core by the tragedy of the shuttle *Challenger.* We know we share this pain with all of the people of our country. This is truly a national loss. . . . We mourn seven heroes: Michael Smith, Dick Scobee, Judith Resnik, Ronald McNair, Ellison Onizuka, Gregory Jarvis, and Christa McAuliffe. We mourn their loss as a nation together.

For the families of the seven, we cannot bear, as you do, the full impact of this tragedy. But we feel the loss and we are thinking about you so very much. Your loved ones were daring and brave and they had that special grace, that special spirit that says, "Give me a challenge and I'll meet it with joy." They had a hunger to explore the universe and discover its truths. They wished to serve, as they did. They served all of us.

We have grown used to wonders in this century. It's hard to dazzle us. But for twenty-five years the United States space program has been doing just that. We've grown used to the idea of space, and perhaps we forget that we've only just begun. We're still pioneers. They, the members of the *Challenger* crew, were pioneers.

And I want to say something to the school children of America who were watching the live coverage of the shuttle's takeoff. I know it is hard to understand, but sometimes painful things like this happen. It's all part of the process of exploration and discovery. It's all part of taking a chance and expanding man's horizons. The future doesn't belong to the fainthearted. It belongs to the brave. The *Challenger* crew was pulling us into the future, and we'll continue to follow them.

I've always had great faith in and respect for our space program and what happened today does nothing to diminish it. We don't hide our space program. We don't keep secrets and cover things up. We do it all up front and public. That's the way freedom is, and we wouldn't change it for a minute.

We'll continue our quest in space. There will be more shuttle flights and more shuttle crews, and, yes, more volunteers,

Challenger crew:
Back row from left:
Ellison Onizuka,
Christa McAuliffe,
Gregory Jarvis, and
Judith Resnik.
Front row from left:
Michael Smith,
Dick Scobee, and
Ronald McNair

more civilians, more teachers in space. Nothing ends here. Our hopes and our journeys continue. . . .

There's a coincidence today. On this day 390 years ago, the great explorer Francis Drake died aboard ship off the coast of Panama. In his lifetime, the great frontiers were the oceans, and a historian later said, "He lived by the sea, died on it, and was buried in it." Well, today, we can say of the *Challenger* crew their dedication was, like Drake's, complete.

The crew of the space shuttle *Challenger* honored us by the manner in which they lived their lives. We will never forget them, nor the last time we saw them, this morning, as they prepared for their journey and waved goodbye and "slipped the surly bonds of Earth" to "touch the face of God."

1. If you were delivering this speech, what emotions would you communicate in what parts of the speech?
2. In what places would you pause for effect? In what places would you accelerate your pace?
3. Where would your volume increase? Where would it decrease?
4. What words and phrases would you choose to deliver with particular emphasis?
5. What words in this speech would you have to check the pronunciation of?

B. Choose any topic you are interested in and prepare a five- to ten-minute speech on this topic. Practice your speech and deliver it to your class. As other students present their speeches, take notes on the verbal and nonverbal elements of their delivery.

College and Career Preparation

When selecting a career or field of study, you must decide what subjects you are most interested in and then create a plan of action that will allow you to incorporate these subjects into a specific and unique goal. The best way to do this is to think about your general interests and abilities and then narrow them down to a very particular focus.

While some people know what career they want to pursue from an early age, most people discover the field that suits them best only after much time and, often, trial and error. Even after embarking on educational and career paths, people often change directions to pursue new and more satisfying routes.

One useful way to assess your career options is to talk to your guidance counselor about completing an **interest inventory.** The inventory asks you to consider your preferences in a number of areas, such as work environment, salary levels, physical activity, intellectual challenge, and predictability of work routine. The inventory also assesses your verbal and mathematical aptitudes. By addressing these issues and answering questions specifically designed to help students clarify interests, you will be better prepared to make thoughtful and sensible decisions about your future.

OBTAINING CAREER AND COLLEGE INFORMATION

After determining your skills and interests, the next step is to acquire information about the careers and schools that match up with those career goals. The basic step in planning a career is establishing the type of educational preparation you will need. First, decide which type of institution caters to your interests. Consider the following possibilities: a vocational school, a traditional four-year college, a junior college, military training, or an apprenticeship program.

The following list describes excellent sources of information:

1. Guidance, college, and career counselors These individuals can provide a wealth of reference materials and employment information. Counselors can also help you determine the type of education you need to attain your goal.

2. College catalogs and bulletins Obtain these through the mail, at the library, or from your school guidance counselor. If necessary, consult out-of-town telephone directories at the library.

3. The *Dictionary of Occupational Titles* and the *Occupation Outlook Handbook* These books contain material on thousands of jobs, including information about working conditions, salaries, and the prospects of future employment. Both are available in most counseling offices and libraries.

4. *The College Handbook*, guidebooks produced by Barron's Educational Services, Inc., and Peterson's Guides These and other similar books contain descriptions of colleges, including the size of the student body, programs, tuition, financial aid, and admission requirements. Look for college reference books in counseling offices, libraries, and bookstores.

5. School and community libraries Use your library research skills to locate some books and articles on specific careers or schools.

VISITING COLLEGES

If college is part of your future plans, you can gain important information about the schools that interest you by visiting the campuses. Write or call ahead of time to set up an information interview. A college visit provides an opportunity for you to discover the "flavor" of a school and to determine whether you would feel comfortable there. Encourage a parent or close relative to accompany you on the visit, especially if it is away from your city.

Interviews

In an information interview, you can inquire about academic and extracurricular programs, financial aid, and other issues that concern you. Since some institutions require formal interviews as part of the application process, an informal interview will give you valuable experience.

Before your interview, study the college catalog to glean basic information about the school that can help you determine what to ask the interviewer. Make notes or tag the pages with points you want to discuss. For a successful interview, whether informal or formal, follow the guidelines listed in the box that follows.

Interview Guidelines

- **Control your nervousness.** Answer questions with confidence, focusing on valuable attributes and experiences.

- **Present a good appearance.** Groom yourself well, and dress neatly and appropriately.

- **Arrive promptly for your interview.** Demonstrate reliability and responsibility by arriving on time.

- **Be courteous.** Greet the interviewer with a friendly introduction and handshake. When the interview is over, thank the interviewer for his or her time.

- **Take your time answering questions.** If necessary, tell the interviewer that you need to collect your thoughts before responding. Answer questions completely and concisely.

- **Follow up the interview.** Indicate your interest and courtesy by sending a thank-you note to the interviewer.

Questions You May Be Asked   During the interview, be prepared to answer questions such as those listed below. Speak positively about yourself and answer every question thoroughly.

Interview Questions

- In what subjects did you receive your best and worst grades? Why? What is your class rank?

- What subjects do you like best and least? Why?

- What extracurricular activities have you participated in?

- What is your possible college major? Why have you chosen this field of study?

- What books have you read this year? Tell me about them.

- If you could not attend college, what would you do?

- What hobbies or interests do you have?

- What are your goals?

- How would your good friends describe you?

- What attributes do you feel a successful person needs?

Writing
— TIP —

Remember to use standard business-letter format and strategies when writing a follow-up note to an interviewer.

Questions to Ask Remember that one purpose of the interview is to give you the opportunity to accumulate information. Ask questions that indicate your interest in the school and that cannot be answered by reading the college catalog. The following list may give you ideas for questions.

Questions to Ask the Interviewer

- What cultural activities are available on or near the campus?
- What is the attitude of the community toward the college?
- What intramural sports programs and fitness facilities exist?
- Are there study rooms in the dorms? Quiet hours?
- How does the college rank academically in my primary area of interest?
- Are there fraternities and sororities? Can freshmen join?
- Is student housing guaranteed? What alternatives exist?
- Do most students stay on campus over the weekend?
- What kinds of campus work opportunities exist?
- Are there exchange programs or special internships?

Activities to Include in Your College Visits

Be sure to allow time before or after your interview to walk around the campus. This is an excellent way to get a feeling for the academic and social atmosphere of the school. Try to allow a full day at each college you are seriously considering. Include as many of the following activities as possible.

1. Tour the campus. Take advantage of any guided tours that are available but spend some time on your own as well.
2. Explore the library and student union to see what these facilities have to offer. These are also excellent places to observe students and faculty and to get a sense of the campus atmosphere.
3. Sit in on a class. Be sure you have the instructor's permission.
4. Talk to students and townspeople about the college. Obtain copies of the school and local newspapers.
5. Visit a freshman dormitory, cafeteria, and other facilities that interest you, such as the art department or the microbiology lab.

Following a visit, take time to write down your impressions of the college. Perhaps you might want to make an evaluation form, using criteria such as "The academic program is well suited to my needs," "I like the atmosphere," and "My chances of being accepted are good." You can rate each category on a scale of 1 to 5, and rank the college on the factors that are important to you.

APPLYING FOR ADMISSION

The United States has nearly 3,000 colleges that are enormously diverse in terms of reputation, cost, facilities, programs, requirements, and financial aid available. You are shopping for one that suits your needs most perfectly.

As you narrow your choice of colleges, consider such factors as your high-school grades, class rank, entrance-examination scores, the teacher recommendations you're likely to get, and any special abilities or talents that would enhance your prospects.

Read the college catalog carefully to determine what requirements you must meet for admission. Colleges may require any or all of the materials in the list that follows.

1. A completed application form
2. Transcripts of courses and grades from your high school
3. Scores on the SAT, ACT, or other college entrance exams
4. An application fee
5. An essay to demonstrate your writing abilities
6. Letters of recommendation
7. An interview

To fill out an application form, read each line carefully before responding. To avoid errors, you may want to photocopy the form or write your answers on a separate piece of paper before filling out the actual form. Type or write legibly in black ink. Submit your application and other requested information in ample time to meet the deadline.

Begin the application process early. One rule of thumb regarding deadlines is to have all your applications finished before you sit down to Thanksgiving dinner in your senior year. Though applications can certainly be written after that time, this date allows you to be considered for early admission programs.

Practice Your Skills

A. Make a list of your interests, abilities, and the kind of environment in which you think you would be more productive. Come up with at least two study or career paths for yourself. If you wish, discuss them with a guidance counselor.

B. Read through the catalog of a school you are interested in. Write several questions about the school that aren't covered in the catalog.

C. With your choices from Exercise A in mind, review the *Occupation Outlook Handbook*. Make notes about what changes in the next ten years might affect the professions you have in mind.

Writing Business Letters

The most familiar and commonly used type of business communication is the letter. A business letter incorporates many of the elements of persuasive writing. Whether you are requesting information, applying for a job, ordering a product, or seeking a refund, your letter represents an attempt to win the reader's agreement or cooperation. How can you get the reader to agree with your message and do what you request?

FORMS OF BUSINESS LETTERS

The conventions that govern the format of business letters have evolved over the years to meet two basic communication needs: convenience and courtesy. You need to know the format requirements of a business letter, or you run the risk of losing your reader before the letter is even read.

Six Parts of a Letter Every business letter has six basic parts. These parts work together to help you present information in an organized and predictable way.

1. The **heading** includes the address of the writer and the date.
2. The **inside address** identifies where and to whom the letter is being sent. Whenever possible, direct your correspondence to a specific person by name. If you are writing to a local company or organization, you can phone to find out to whom you should send your letter.
3. The **salutation** follows the inside address. If you do not know the person's name, address the department or positions within the company or organization. The following forms are acceptable.

   Dear Mr. Rodriguez: Dear Sir or Madam:
   Dear Mrs. Schlegel: Dear Customer Service Department:
   Dear Ms. Jefferson: Dear Editor:

4. The **body** contains the central message of the letter.
5. The **closing** should be appropriate to the audience and occasion of your letter. Some common closings follow.

Formal	Businesslike	Less Formal
Yours respectfully,	Yours truly,	Sincerely,
Respectfully yours,	Very truly yours,	Sincerely yours,

6. The **signature** should be handwritten in ink.

P.O. Box 68
Wilton, AL 35187
November 16, 1991

Jason Woemack, Service Manager
Woemack Motors
467 Main Street
Mobile, AL 36601

Dear Mr. Woemack:

The paint job performed by your company on my 1990 Plymouth is inadequate. Your paint-shop supervisor, John Singer, will verify that the job was not completed satisfactorily.

The instructions on my order and on invoice number 6634-P state that both the hood and the right front quarter panel were to be repainted. However, when I arrived to pick up the car, only the hood had been done. Unfortunately, I was unable to leave the car at the shop because I needed it for work.

I have enclosed a copy of the invoice. As you will note, I did pay for the complete job, which totaled $184.36. Therefore, I expect that the quarter panel will be painted at no additional charge.

Please contact me to arrange a date for completion of this job. I may be reached on weekdays after 3:00 P.M. My number is 555-9743.

Sincerely,

Cynthia Lopez

Cynthia Lopez

Full-Block and Modified-Block Forms Business letters are most often presented in either a full-block or modified-block form. In full block, all parts of the letter begin at the left margin, and paragraphs are not indented. In modified block, the heading, closing, and signature are aligned near the right margin. Paragraphs are indented.

TYPES OF BUSINESS LETTERS

There are several different types of business letters, each with its own particular purpose. The following information will help you when writing each kind.

Letters of Request These letters are used to gain information about schools, employment opportunities, and specific products or services. In addition, letters of request are often used to gather information for research projects.

When you write a letter requesting information, begin by stating specifically what information you need, as well as when and why you need it. If more than one piece of information is needed, you may wish to include an itemized list in the body of your letter. Make it as easy as possible for the reader to reply.

Letters Ordering Products If you wish to order a product through the mail and no order form is available, you can write an order letter. Describe clearly the merchandise you wish to order; include all relevant details, such as the item's exact name, size, color, model number, quantity, unit price, and total price. Tell how you are paying for the order, and make certain that you include any sales tax, handling charges, or other fees that may apply. If you are enclosing payment, say so in your letter and state the amount. Keeping a duplicate copy of your letter is essential for following up if there is a delay in filling your order.

Letters of Complaint, Adjustment, or Appreciation Occasionally, you may have to write a letter to resolve a conflict or to settle a claim. Begin by stating your purpose; then describe the product or service ordered, including all relevant dates and prices. Clearly identify the problem, such as a wrong model, damaged or incomplete goods, late delivery, or poor service. Finally, explain what action you would like the company to take to resolve your complaint. Include photocopies of all relevant documents—such as receipts and money orders—with your letter. Be sure to make duplicate copies of everything you send for your own records.

If, on the other hand, you are especially pleased with a product or service, you can write a letter of appreciation. Besides being a welcome expression of thanks, such letters provide valuable feedback to companies about how their products or services are received.

Letters of Opinion These letters usually present opinions about current events or public issues and may recommend a specific course of action. They are often written to newspaper or magazine editors, or to government officials at local, state, or national levels.

In writing a letter of opinion, you need to identify clearly your topic and your point of view. You should briefly state your main points, support them with factual evidence, and maintain a reasonable tone. (See "Persuasive Essay," pages 208–222.)

Writing
—**TIP**—

Ask a peer reader to respond to your letter, looking specifically for clarity and appropriate tone.

Though business letters are written to achieve a variety of purposes, all effective letters share these characteristics: they efficiently get their message across, and they establish a positive, polite, and businesslike tone.

Stating Your Message What you have already learned about the writing process will help you to convey your message successfully. Use prewriting strategies to identify your purpose and audience and to organize your material. As you write the first draft of your letter, follow these general guidelines.

1. Begin by stating your purpose simply and concisely.
2. Provide any necessary information or details related to the purpose of the letter.
3. Conclude the letter by asking the reader to take whatever action will accomplish your purpose.

Revise your letter for clarity and brevity—it is in your own best interest to make your letter easy to understand. Make certain that your message is well organized and that it contains all necessary content. Edit ruthlessly to eliminate any unnecessary details. Finally, carefully proofread for proper grammar, punctuation, and spelling. This is one form of writing in which it is especially important to maintain rigid standards.

Creating a Positive Tone The reader's impression of you will be largely determined by the tone you adopt, for your tone conveys a message about what kind of person you are. The image of yourself that you communicate in your writing needs to reflect the same kind of qualities that people appreciate in face-to-face encounters. Your letter needs to show that you are considerate and sincere.

Use simple, straightforward language; avoid using the stiff and unnatural language that immature writers mistakenly view as sophisticated. A sentence such as "Enclosed herein is a receipt of the bill of lading granted to me" is a poor substitute for "I have enclosed a shipping receipt." Reading your letter aloud will often help you to detect language that sounds affected or forced.

Finally, you should always strive to convey your message in a positive manner. Emphasize what can be done to resolve your problem or achieve your goal; do not belabor the negative side of the situation. When there is a choice between using positive or negative forms of statements, use the positive, because that is more likely to elicit a positive response. Consider the difference between the following two examples.

> I am returning this sweater because the seams fell apart after it had been worn only twice. I don't suppose that I can have a replacement, even though the sweater wasn't made right. I've never seen such shoddy workmanship.

> I am returning this almost-new sweater. As you can see, the seams have come apart, though there are no signs of wear. I have been very pleased with prior merchandise and service I have received from your company. May I please have a replacement?

The Letter, by Mary Cassatt, 1891

Practice Your Skills

A. Write for two of the free government publications listed below. Follow the full-block form for one letter and the modified-block form for the other. Mail your letters to Consumer Information Center-D, P.O. Box 100, Pueblo, CO 81002. Be sure to include the item number and publication description in your request and to clearly indicate the address to which the material should be sent. Check your letters to make sure they are clear and courteous.

1. *Endangered Species.* Item no. 574R.
2. *Quackery—The Billion Dollar "Miracle" Business* (information on how to protect yourself from various types of health fraud). Item no. 529R
3. *Plain Talk About Stress.* Item no. 564R.
4. *How to Take Weight Off Without Getting Ripped Off.* Item no. 543R.

B. Imagine that you have just received a letter from the Bruiser Collection Agency stating that you owe $1,796 for clothing purchased at the posh Gilded Seams boutique. You have often looked longingly in the windows of the Gilded Seams, but never even dared go into the boutique. Write a letter to the collection agent, Rocky N. Forcer, to explain that you never made such purchases. The collection agency's address is 2010 W. Bicipital Lane, Jersey City, NJ 07304. Be sure that the tone of your letter is polite and businesslike and that you communicate in a positive manner what can be done to remedy the situation.

Assessment Skills

Regardless of your career or college plans, you will be required to write for many tests—standardized college board or placement tests in addition to essay tests for your academic classes. Following are strategies you can use to prepare for all these tests.

WRITING FOR ESSAY TESTS

To do well on essay tests, you must be able to apply the steps in the writing process as quickly and skillfully as possible. Analyzing various types of essay questions and developing strategies for responding to them can help you present your knowledge most effectively. The major types of essay questions and suggested strategies are discussed below.

Explanation   In this type of question, you must clarify the components of a problem, a relationship, a process, or the meaning of a term. Always use examples to support an explanation. To identify explanation questions, look for the key words *describe, explain,* or *discuss.*

Comparison/Contrast   Comparison/contrast questions ask you to explore the similarities and differences between two subjects. To identify these questions, look for the key words *compare* and *contrast.* If only the word *compare* appears in the question, clarify whether you need to discuss only similarities or both similarities and differences.

Definition/Description/Identification   In these types of questions you must show that you understand and can explain the distinguishing characteristics of a subject. Be sure that the characteristics you identify apply uniquely to this subject. To identify these questions, look for the key words *identify* and *define.*

Interpretation   Interpretation questions require that you consider the significance of a subject in the context of your total knowledge and explain it in your own words. Look for the key word *interpret.*

Analysis   In answering analysis questions you must break something down into its component parts and examine these parts to determine the meaning of the whole. Be sure to identify all the parts of the subject. Look for the key word *analyze.*

Summarization This type of question asks you to give a condensed version of a process, an event, or a sequence. Briefly cover only the most important points.

Once you have determined what kind of essay question you are answering, do some quick planning. For example, jot down notes or make a rough outline. Then develop your main points, in sequence, completely but concisely.

Practice Your Skills

Read the following essay test questions that deal with the antebellum South. Then identify the questions according to type and explain how you would go about answering them.

1. Compare and contrast the experiences of house slaves with those of field slaves in the antebellum South.
2. Analyze the effects of emancipation on the Southern economy.

TAKING STANDARDIZED TESTS

In contrast to classroom tests, which measure particular knowledge, standardized academic tests are designed to assess general academic abilities.

Types of Standardized Tests Aptitude tests evaluate how well prepared you are to do college-level academic work. The two most widely used aptitude tests are the Scholastic Aptitude Test (SAT) and the American College Testing examination (ACT).

The SAT is being revised during the early 1990's and the new format and questions will be phased in over several years. Check with your school counselor to make sure you have the most recent information. The SAT currently consists of two sections—one that measures verbal abilities and one that measures mathematical abilities. Each section is scored on a scale of 200–800. The Test of Standard Written English (TSWE) is given along with the SAT to measure your ability to recognize and use standard written English.

The ACT consists of four sections: English usage, mathematics usage, social studies reading, and natural sciences reading. Each section is scored on a scale of 0–36.

Some colleges also require applicants to submit an achievement test score in specific subject areas. The College Entrance Examination Board (CEEB) offers fourteen achievement tests in areas including foreign languages, history, and mathematics.

Preparing for Standardized Tests You can prepare for aptitude tests by studying the types of questions they contain and practicing the skills they measure: vocabulary, reading, computation, critical thinking, and English usage. These strategies can help.

- Work on increasing your vocabulary.
- Read widely on your own.
- Write often and examine your language carefully.
- Study the practice materials made available to you.
- Prepare yourself mentally as well as physically. Think of the test as an opportunity, not an obstacle.

UNDERSTANDING STANDARDIZED TEST QUESTIONS

The following questions are typical of those that appear on SAT or ACT tests or on College Entrance Examination Board achievement or assessment tests.

Antonym Questions Antonym questions give you a word and ask you to choose the word whose meaning is most nearly opposite.

 APATHY: (A) indifference   (B) wrath   (C) zeal
            (D) expression   (E) bewilderment

To answer an antonym question, use the following strategies.

1. Do not be thrown off by synonyms such as *A* in the above example.
2. Eliminate the obviously incorrect choices.
3. Choose the word that is *most* opposite in meaning. The correct answer to the sample would be *C—zeal*.

Practice Your Skills

Write the letter of the word that is most nearly opposite in meaning to the given word.

1. WILT: (A) prevent   (B) drain   (C) expose
   (D) revive   (E) stick
2. ISSUE: (A) dilute   (B) revolve   (C) depend
   (D) substitute   (E) retract
3. PREMEDITATED: (A) spontaneous   (B) conclusive
   (C) disruptive   (D) vindictive   (E) strenuous
4. SUMMARIZED: (A) bracing   (B) accented
   (C) detailed   (D) animated   (E) disconcerting

Analogy Questions Analogy questions give you two words that are related in some way. You need to determine this relationship and identify the pair of words that is related in the same way.

ADVERTISING:SELLING::   (A) reporting:informing
(B) marketing:research   (C) training:helping
(D) creating:destroying   (E) discovering:exploring

Follow these strategies in answering analogy questions.

1. Create a sentence that contains the words and shows their relationship.

    Advertising is a way of *selling* to the public.

2. Find the pair of words among the answer choices that could logically replace the given pair in your sentence.

    Reporting is a way of *informing* the public.

    None of the other choices expresses the same relationship.

3. Recognize the types of relationships, such as those listed below, that can be expressed in analogies.

Types of Analogies

Type	Example
action to object	PLAY:CLARINET
cause to effect	SUN:SUNBURN
item to category	IGUANA:REPTILE
object to purpose	PENCIL:WRITING
object to its material	CURTAINS:CLOTH
part to whole	PAGE:BOOK
time sequence	RECENT:CURRENT
type to characteristic	DANCER:AGILE
word to antonym	ASSIST:HINDER
word to synonym	PROVISIONS:SUPPLIES
worker to product	ARTIST:SKETCH
worker to workplace	CHEF:KITCHEN
word to derived form	ACT:ACTION

Practice Your Skills

Select the lettered pair that best expresses a relationship similar to the one expressed in the original pair.

1. HEIGHT:MOUNTAIN::   (A) depth:trench   (B) shade:tree
   (C) weight:age   (D) speed:highway   (E) mineral:mine
2. LEAVE:LINGER::   (A) manipulate:manage
   (B) warrant:employ   (C) surprise:astonish
   (D) cease:prolong   (E) flout:violate
3. APPAREL:PERSON::   (A) plumage:bird   (B) prey:animal
   (C) water:fish   (D) insignia:officer   (E) scenery:theater
4. SONG:RECITAL::   (A) author:bibliography
   (B) episode:series   (C) coach:team
   (D) intermission:play   (E) poetry:prose

Sentence-Completion Questions   A sentence-completion question is a sentence with words missing. Your job is to select the word or words that best complete the sentence.

> A band of gorillas builds a _____ camp each night after a day of _____ for the berries and leaves that make up their diet.
>
> (A) solid . . . trading   (B) sturdy . . . roaming
> (C) interesting . . . seeking   (D) makeshift . . . foraging
> (E) circular . . . farming

To answer sentence-completion questions, use these strategies.

1. Read the sentence carefully, noting key words or phrases. Words that signal sequence, such as *after* in the question above, give clues to the relationships.
2. Eliminate choices that make no sense, that are grammatically incorrect, or that contradict some part of the sentence.
3. In an item with two blanks, your answer must correctly fill *both* blanks.
4. Use logic to decide between two reasonable choices. In the example above, both *B* and *D* will complete the sentence. However, since the camp is remade each night, it is probably *makeshift,* and the gorillas are *foraging* for food.

Practice Your Skills

Choose the best words to complete the following sentences.

1. He claimed that the document was _____ because it merely listed endangered species and did not specify penalties for harming them.
   (A) indispensable   (B) inadequate   (C) punitive
   (D) aggressive   (E) essential

Writing
—**TIP**—

Use context clues to help you answer sentence-completion questions.

2. The author makes no attempt at _____ order; a scene from 1960 is followed by one from 1968, which, in turn, is followed by one from 1964.

(A) an impartial   (B) an innovative   (C) a motley
(D) a chronological   (E) an extemporaneous

3. The ability to estimate distance comes only with _____; a baby reaches with equal confidence for its bottle or the moon.

(A) tranquility   (B) talent   (C) experience
(D) assurance   (E) distress

4. She undertook a population census of the island with the _____ , if not always the enthusiastic support, of the authorities.

(A) objection   (B) elation   (C) suspicion
(D) acquiescence   (E) elimination

Reading-Comprehension Questions   Reading-comprehension questions assess your ability to interpret written material. You may be asked to pick out the central idea, recall a specific detail, draw a conclusion from the information given, determine the meaning of a word, identify the mood of the passage, or determine specific techniques that the writer has used.

To answer these questions, use the following strategies.

1. Before you read the passage, read all the questions.
2. Skim the passage, getting a feel for its main idea.
3. Read the passage again, with the questions in mind.
4. Read all the answer choices. Choose the best answer based on the material in the passage, not based on your opinion.
5. Notice the author's reasoning, tone, and style.

Practice Your Skills

Read the following passage. Then choose the best answer to each of the questions.

Mars revolves around the Sun in 687 Earth days, which is equivalent to 23 Earth months. The axis of Mars's rotation is tipped at a 25° angle from the plane of its orbit, nearly the same as Earth's tilt of about 23°. Because the tilt causes the seasons, we know that Mars goes through a year with four seasons just as Earth does.

From Earth, we have long watched the effect of the seasons on Mars. In the Martian winter, in a given hemisphere, there is a polar ice cap. As the Martian spring comes to the Northern Hemisphere, for example, the north polar cap shrinks, and material in the planet's more temperate zones darkens. The surface of Mars is always mainly reddish, with darker gray areas that, from Earth, appear blue-green. In the spring, the darker regions spread. Half a Martian year later, the same process happens in the Southern Hemisphere.

One possible explanation for these changes is biological: Martian vegetation could be blooming or spreading in the spring. There are other explanations, however. The theory that at present seems most reasonable is that each year during the Northern Hemisphere springtime, a dust storm starts, with winds that reach velocities as high as hundreds of kilometers per hour. Fine, light-colored dust is blown from slopes, exposing dark areas underneath. If the dust were composed of certain kinds of materials, such as limonite, the reddish color would be explained.

1. According to the author, seasonal variations on Mars are a direct result of the
   (A) proximity of the planet to the Sun.
   (B) proximity of the planet to Earth.
   (C) presence of ice caps at the poles of the planet.
   (D) tilt of the planet's rotational axis.
   (E) length of time required by the planet to revolve around the Sun.

2. It can be inferred that, as spring arrives in the Southern Hemisphere of Mars, which of the following is also occurring?
   (A) The northern polar cap is increasing in size.
   (B) The axis of rotation is tipping at a greater angle.
   (C) A dust storm is ending in the Southern Hemisphere.
   (D) The material in the northern temperate zones is darkening.
   (E) Vegetation in the southern temperate zones is decaying.

English-Usage Questions   Standard English-usage questions require you to identify usage errors, such as incorrect verb tenses, improper agreement between pronouns and antecedents, lack of parallel structure, and incorrect use of idioms.

In each sentence, four words or phrases are underlined and lettered. Choose the one underlined part that needs to be corrected. If the sentence contains no error, choose *E*.

He spoke <u>bluntly</u> and <u>angrily</u> to <u>we spectators</u> <u>who had</u>
         A   **B**   **C**   **D**
<u>gathered</u> on the sidewalk. <u>No error</u>
                              E

Apply the following strategies in answering English-usage questions.

1. Read the entire sentence through completely.
2. Check to see if its parts are in agreement.
3. Check the grammatical construction of the sentence.
4. Look for misuse of modifiers and other words.
5. Remember, the error occurs in an *underlined* part of the sentence. In the example sentence, *C* is incorrect. The pronoun *us* should follow the preposition.

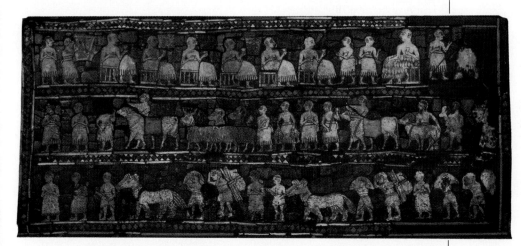

The Standard of Ur, Sumerian, 3rd mill. B.C. British Museum, London

The English-usage questions on the ACT differ somewhat from those on the SAT. The following are typical ACT usage questions.

The <u>Sumerians</u> produced particularly
     1
noteworthy sculptures. The early works, which date from about 3000–2500 <u>bc,</u> communicate deep emotional
 2
and spiritual <u>intense</u> but show no
     3
marked skill in modeling.
Although later works show evidence of improved modeling skills, they <u>were lacking</u> the inspiration and vigor
  4
of the earlier works.

1. A. No change
   B. sumerians
   C. Sumer people
   D. sumer people
2. F. No change
   G. BC
   H. b.c.
   J. B.C.
3. A. No change
   B. intensely
   C. insensitivity
   D. intensity
4. F. No change
   G. have lacked
   H. lack
   J. had lacked

Practice Your Skills

Write the letter of the underlined part that must be changed to make the following sentences correct. If there is no error, write E.

1. Most people listen to the weather forecast every day, <u>but</u> they
   A
   know <u>hardly nothing</u> <u>about</u> the forces <u>that influence</u> the
   B   **C**   **D**
   weather. <u>No error</u>
   E

2. <u>Him</u> and <u>the other</u> delegates <u>immediately</u> accepted the
   A   **B**   **C**
   resolution <u>drafted by</u> the neutral states. <u>No error</u>
   D   **E**

3. The foundations <u>of</u> psychoanalysis were established by Freud,
   A
   who <u>begun to</u> <u>develop</u> his theories <u>in</u> the late 1880's. <u>No error</u>
   B   **C**   **D**   **E**

4. In her novels, Nella Larson <u>focused on</u> the problems of young
   A
   black women <u>which</u> <u>lived in</u> Europe and America <u>during</u> the
   B   **C**   **D**
   1920's. <u>No error</u>
   E

Sentence-Correction Questions In a sentence-correction question, the underlined portion of the sentence contains an element that is wordy, unclear, awkwardly phrased, grammatically incorrect, ambiguous, or illogical.

Below the sentence are five versions of the underlined part. You choose the best version. If you think that sentence is correct as written, choose *A*. Here is a typical example.

> The shorter bear-paw snowshoes are the best choice if you are looking for <u>an easy to lift and maneuver model.</u>
> (A) an easy to lift and maneuver model.
> (B) a model that is easy to lift and maneuver.
> (C) an easy model as far as lifting and maneuvering goes.
> (D) a model with ease of lifting and also maneuver.
> (E) an easily lifted and also maneuvered model.

To answer sentence-correction questions, use these strategies.

1. Think of a way to rephrase the underlined portion before you look at the choices.
2. If you have trouble deciding between two choices, read each version in the context of the entire sentence. In the example above, the underlined phrase is awkward, and *B* represents the best choice for correction.

Practice Your Skills

Select the answer that replaces the underlined words to create the most effective sentence. Select *A* if the original is correct.

1. Because dodo birds could not <u>fly, so they were killed</u> by the hogs and monkeys brought to the islands by the explorers.
   (A) fly, so they were killed
   (B) fly, they were killed
   (C) fly and they were killed
   (D) fly, and this allowed them to be killed
   (E) fly, killing them

2. Performing before an audience for the first time, <u>fear suddenly overcame the child and she could not remember her lines.</u>
   (A) fear suddenly overcame the child and she could not remember her lines.
   (B) the lines could not be remembered by the child because she was overcome by fear.
   (C) the child was suddenly overcome by fear and could not remember her lines.
   (D) the child was suddenly overcome by fear, and consequently not remembering her lines.
   (E) suddenly the child was overcome by fear, and consequently not remembering her lines.

3. Violin makers know that the better the wood is seasoned, the <u>better the results for the tone of the instrument.</u>
   (A) better the results for the tone of the instrument.
   (B) better the tone of the instrument.
   (C) better the result is for the instrument's tone.
   (D) resulting tone will be better.
   (E) result will be a better instrument tone.

4. Although today many fabrics are made from synthetic fibers, at one time <u>all natural fibers were used in their manufacture.</u>
   (A) all natural fibers were used in their manufacture.
   (B) all fabrics were made of natural fibers.
   (C) they were making them all of natural fibers.
   (D) they made fabrics of all natural fibers.
   (E) their manufacture was of all natural fibers.

5. Written in 1873, <u>the author did not publish her book until 1924.</u>
   (A) the author did not publish her book until 1924.
   (B) not until 1924 was the author's book published.
   (C) the author's publishing her book did not occur until 1924.
   (D) the author's book was not published until 1924.
   (E) book publishing was not until 1924.

Construction-Shift Questions These questions appear in the English Composition Test given by the College Entrance Examination Board. You will be asked to rephrase a sentence according to specific instructions and then to study five answer choices to see which one fits into the revised sentence correctly. Look at the example construction-shift question below.

> In these early works, van Gogh's compassion for the poor miners of Belgium is clearly shown.
>
> Begin the sentence with *These early works*
> (A) compassion of van Gogh   (B) show of compassion
> (C) clearly show   (D) had shown clearly
> (E) were shown to evidence

Construction-shift questions challenge you to think of alternative ways of expressing an idea. If you can make more than one good sentence, choose the one that best fulfills the following criteria: retains original meaning of sentence, is most natural sounding, is expressed in standard written English, and is most concise and gracefully constructed.

The rephrased example sentence would read, "These early works clearly show van Gogh's compassion for the poor miners of Belgium." *C* is, therefore, the correct answer.

Practice Your Skills

Change the following sentences according to the instructions; then choose the answer that best fits within the revised sentence.

1. Some working environments are so rigid and so confining that little room is left for expressions of individual identity.
   Begin the sentence with *The rigidity and confinement*
   (A) so that little room   (B) leave little room
   (C) and leaving little room   (D) and little room to
   (E) because they left little room to
2. For centuries the Chinese did not feel any need for a police system, relying instead upon a strong tradition of family discipline.
   Insert *had such* after *Chinese*
   (A) so they relied   (B) that they felt no
   (C) because they relied   (D) and not feeling   (E) from relying
3. Astrology seems to be an intuitive art instead of an exact science.
   Substitute *seems more* for *seems to be*
   (A) than an intuitive   (B) and more exact
   (C) than being exact   (D) and less intuitive   (E) than an exact

Critical Listening and News Reporting

Our knowledge of the world is determined, to a great extent, by what we hear on TV or read in newspapers or magazines. Therefore, it is essential that we respond critically to this information.

DEVELOPING
LISTENING SKILLS

Listening skills are especially important for staying informed about current events. There are two different types of listening: **two-way listening,** which gives you an opportunity for response—to stop the speaker, ask questions, and clarify meaning; and **one-way listening,** in which you cannot respond to the speaker. With this type of listening, you have only one chance to grasp the information. The guidelines on the next page, which may be applied to both kinds of listening situations, will help you listen more accurately and efficiently and respond critically to what you hear.

JUST A NORMAL DAY AT THE NATION'S MOST IMPORTANT FINANCIAL INSTITUTION...

KAL ©1990, Cartoonists & Writers Syndicate

Critical Listening
and News Reporting **541**

- **Keep an open mind.** Be open to what others have to say. Try not to let your own feelings and views interfere with your ability to listen to the ideas of others. Guard against selective listening, hearing only what you want to hear or what you expect the speaker to say.

- **Stay focused on the topic.** As a listener, think about why the topic is important to you, especially when the presentation seems dry or uninteresting. Remember that your mind can work faster than the speaker's voice, so keep your mind busy by thinking about what is being said.

- **Identify the purpose and main ideas.** Knowing the speaker's purpose will help you recognize the main ideas. Pay particular attention to the introduction and conclusion. Also note the speaker's volume, gestures, and intonation, which often are used to emphasize main ideas. Notice how the supporting details develop and explain the main ideas.

- **Anticipate and predict to stay on track.** In a well-prepared and presented talk, what has come before is a good predictor of what will come later. As you listen to what the speaker is saying, you should get a clear impression of the direction in which the speech is going. Listen carefully for those topics which you expect the speaker to cover. Listen as if you were engaged in an unspoken dialogue with the speaker.

- **Review and summarize.** Keep track of main ideas that have been presented. If possible, take notes, but don't let note taking get in the way of your listening. After listening, it is often useful to summarize in your own words what has been said.

Practice Your Skills

Pay careful attention to your listening experiences over the next several days. List these experiences as they occur, and classify them as one-way or two-way listening. Examine your own role in each listening situation. Write a paragraph or two to evaluate your strengths and weaknesses as a listener. Consider whether applying any of the listening guidelines could help you improve your skills.

Nowhere are your listening skills more important than in evaluating news reports. To develop and maintain a critical perspective when you listen to the news, keep the following points in mind.

1. The whole story has not been told. Because of time restrictions, news broadcasts on television and radio present summaries and simplified explanations of events. Make a habit of asking yourself questions such as "What facts may have been deleted?" "What other information do I need?"

2. Most issues and problems are not as simple as they appear. News reports often rely on simple "black-and-white" contrasts and ignore shades of gray. Reports about conflicts in the Middle East, for example, frequently contrast only two opposing sides. In reality, most conflicts have more than two sides, and many of the people involved are less extreme than the way they are depicted on the news.

3. Strong emotions or visual images can fool you. News reports often present highly emotional words and pictures. Don't let your understanding of an event be unduly influenced by its emotional impact. Appreciate the strong feelings surrounding a news event, but always try to focus on the facts—the reality of the event.

4. Question news reports that seem too good or too bad to be true. Reporters working on "breaking" news stories sometimes offer unverified information in their rush to present the story. That's why early reports of injury or death in a disaster often prove to be wildly exaggerated or why preliminary reports of scientific breakthroughs later prove to be much less dramatic. Critical listeners dismiss such speculation and wait for the facts.

5. News reports may contain hidden editorializing. Hidden editorializing means that subjective opinion is disguised as objective reporting or that only selected facts or elements of a story are presented. One reporter may say, "The President faced a barrage of questions about his role in the recent fiasco in the Middle East." Another may say, "The President calmly defended the Middle East policies of his administration, though he regretted recent problems." The first implies that the President was wrong; the second, that he was right. Both reporters may have allowed personal opinions to influence their choice of language.

Practice Your Skills

Create a list of questions about a current event that you would like to learn more about. Then listen to at least two television reports about the event. How many of your questions were answered in the reports? Write a paragraph on whether it is a good idea to rely exclusively on television for news.

Right: Fir tree forest in Appalachian Mountains destroyed by acid rain. Below: Poverty-stricken Nicaraguan child

IDENTIFYING PERSUASIVE APPEALS

Unlike news reports, which generally try to be informative and objective, editorials, political commercials, and feature stories are often strongly persuasive. Editorial commentators try to shape your opinion about issues and events, political campaigners seek your support, and people being interviewed try to present themselves in a flattering light.

Understanding the Language of Persuasion

Developing an awareness of the following persuasive techniques will help you to listen critically to speeches and interviews and to identify misleading information.

Denotation and Connotation   Consider the difference between the following statements: "John Knots is a shrewd negotiator," and "John Knots is a crafty negotiator." The **denotative** meanings of these statements are the same; each refers to John Knots's expertise as a negotiator. Yet their **connotative** meanings are dramatically different, for shrewd and crafty carry different associations and suggest different behaviors. Don't let connotations interfere with your critical evaluation of what you hear.

Loaded Words   Loaded words carry strong connotations. Words with powerful positive connotations, such as *dedication,* are sometimes called **purr words.** Loaded words with powerful negative connotations, such as *pigheaded,* are called **snarl words.** Beware of loaded words used to cloud information or manipulate emotions.

Vague or Undefined Terms   Some words have floating meanings, the connotations of which vary from person to person. Judgmental words such as *right* or *wrong* or labeling words such as *conservative, liberal,* or *radical* are actually vague terms. Unless a speaker clearly defines such words in context or supports them with concrete examples, his or her statements will be meaningless.

Qualifiers   Qualifiers can allow people to make claims that are misleading without actually being false. For example, a corporate spokesperson seeking voter approval for a corporate headquarters in the community might claim that the project *"could* mean as many as 500 new jobs." That claim would be accurate even if the project actually created only five new jobs. Listen carefully for qualifiers such as *nearly, most cases, almost* and *virtually.*

Unfinished Claims   When a political leader announces that annual expenditures have been reduced by ten percent, you are hearing an unfinished claim. To finish the claim, the speaker would need to tell you what the reduction was being compared with and how the figure was determined. Ten percent from the preceding year? From five years ago? From the twenty percent increase that she supported initially? Whenever you hear an unfinished claim, ask yourself what information is needed to finish it. Evaluate the claim after you have determined the missing information. If that information is not available, dismiss the claim.

Recognizing Types of Persuasive Appeals

There are a number of different strategies that speakers use to make persuasive appeals.

Appeals to Authority   In this type of appeal, the listener is asked to rely on the judgment of others. Such appeals may be presented in the form of **testimonials,** statements from "experts" or celebrities, who attest to the merits of a person, product, or service.

Sometimes appeals to authority refer to **polling results.** Be skeptical of polls unless the speaker gives specific information indicating that the sampling was done scientifically. To be reliable, polls must include a large and representative population, ask unbiased questions, and accurately report results and their statistical significance.

Appeals to Emotion   Emotional appeals sometimes contain very little information. Instead they might appeal to our fear of rejection; yearning for adventure; or desire for security, power, or religious truth.

Appeals to Reason or Common Sense   This type of appeal implies that if the listener is a reasonable person, he or she will believe or do or think just what the speaker wants. Whenever you find yourself being appealed to as a "reasonable person," think critically about the factual evidence that is part of the appeal. Is it relevant? Is it documented? Have important details been omitted?

Appeals by Association   These are appeals to people's desires to be socially accepted. In statements such as "Everyone likes ice cream," persuaders are using **bandwagon appeal.** They are urging you to step in line with the crowd.

One variation on bandwagon appeal is called **plain-folks appeal,** in which ordinary, average people are shown to support a product or candidate. The opposite of plain-folks appeal is known as **snob appeal.** Rather than appealing to your need to be like everyone else, advertisers who use snob appeal are focusing on your need to be distinctive and set apart.

Another type of appeal by association is known as **transfer.** In this approach, a company or campaign manager tries to transfer the positive feelings associated with certain images to its product or candidate. For example, flags and pictures of family members are often used to symbolize a candidate's devotion to country and family.

Judging the Evidence

After you listen carefully to a speaker's use of persuasive language and identify the type of appeal used, you need to evaluate the evidence he or she offers to support the claims. The following guidelines will be useful to you in judging the evidence.

- **Separate fact from opinion.**   A fact is a statement that can be proved. An opinion is a statement that cannot be proved; usually it is a person's view or judgment of a subject. Consider the following examples.

Fact   Plankton, the microscopic organisms found in oceans, can be harvested for food.

Opinion   Plankton should be developed as a primary food source for underdeveloped countries.

TV lawyer Perry Mason was famous for sifting through facts to find the truth.

- **Evaluate the facts.**   Facts can be verified by personal observation, by reference to a recognized expert, or by reference to an authoritative written source, such as an encyclopedia.
- **Recognize bias.**   Some of the signals of bias have already been discussed: loaded language, vague or undefined terms, misused qualifiers, and unfinished claims. Another signal of bias, called **stacking the evidence,** occurs when someone deliberately ignores facts that would refute his or her opinion. **Misquoting** or **quoting out of context** may also indicate bias.
- **Evaluate opinions and reasoning.**   An opinion that is well supported by statements of fact is probably sound. However, make sure to evaluate the logic linking the facts and opinion. (See "Strategies for Persuasive Writing," pages 490–492.)
- **Consider other points of view.**   Before responding to a speech containing a persuasive appeal, consider other points of view by gathering evidence from reliable sources.

Writing
—**TIP**—

Watch for missing or misused transitions. These can signal faulty reasoning.

Critical Listening
and News Reporting **547**

Practice Your Skills

A. Spend an evening as a television "monitor." Listen to the local and national news programs and any current-events programming. Pay special attention to commercial advertising. Listen for examples of testimonial, polling results, appeal to emotion, plain-folks appeal, snob appeal, and other persuasive appeals. Write a paragraph analyzing each technique you identify, focusing especially on how it misleads or persuades.

B. Identify the persuasive appeals in the following statements and indicate what additional information you would need to evaluate them critically.

1. Almost everyone gave the speaker a standing ovation.
2. Senator Lowe presented a radically progressive program for tax reform.
3. Three-fourths of the people polled do not support the President's policy.
4. No thoughtful person could watch this travesty of justice without joining in the protest.
5. If you care about your family's future, support your local educational-television station with a generous donation.

On the Lightside

THE INTERROGATIVE PUTDOWN

The form [Question-Statement] has been identified by R. W. Prouty of Westlake Village . . . ; I think, though, that Prouty's term—the Question-Statement—is inadequate to suggest its underlying wickedness. Perhaps it could be more accurately called the Interrogative Putdown. . . . My wife almost always resorts to the Interrogative Putdown to let me know that I have done something stupid, such as driving past our turnoff on the freeway again. What she usually says is: "Where are you going?"

This suggests genuine curiosity. She had been expecting me to take the usual turnoff but I have gone past it, and now, excited by the prospect of adventure, she simply can't wait to find out where I'm taking her. How exciting, she seems to imply, to have an unpredictable mate!

Of course I know the old Interrogative Putdown when I hear it. I'm not fooled by its mask of innocence. What she really means is, "Well, you've done it again, boy. You're really getting absent-minded."

Naturally she doesn't wish to come right out and say I'm getting absent-minded, because absent-minded is a code word for senile, which ordinary kindness does not allow her to say. So she simply says, "Where are you going?" and the message is received.

Just the other evening I asked her, after sampling an unfamiliar dish: "This is *chicken?*" I'm sure she recognized it at once as an Interrogative Putdown, meaning that I knew very well it was chicken but I didn't like the way it was prepared and I didn't want her to try it again.

Her answer was very clever, neither openly resentful nor belligerent, yet it offered me . . . no chance for a follow-up. She might have said, for example, "What do you think it is?" That would have been a Counter-Interrogative Putdown, meaning "Are you such a clod you don't know chicken when you taste it?"

But alas, what she actually said was: "Does the stereo really have to be that loud?"

Simply brilliant. Not only was it a Counter-Interrogative Putdown meaning "Are you deaf?" (i.e., senile) but a non-sequitur as well. The old one-two. There was nothing to do but turn down the stereo and eat my dinner. Whatever it was.

Jack Smith

549

Ocean Park No. 29, by Richard Diebenkorn, 1970. Dallas Museum of Art, gift of the Meadows Foundation Incorporated

Grammar and Usage Handbook

ASSESSMENT

Directions One or more of the underlined sections in the following sentences may contain errors of grammar, usage, punctuation, spelling, or capitalization. Write the letter of each incorrect section, then rewrite the item correctly. If there is no error in an item, write E.

> **Example** Before the crash <u>of the *hindenburg,*</u> travel in <u>lighter-</u>
> A B
> <u>than-air</u> vehicles <u>seems</u> to be the <u>wave of the future.</u> <u>No error</u>
> C D E
>
> **Answer** A—of the *Hindenburg,* C—seemed

1. The <u>name Muhammad</u> is <u>more</u> common <u>than any</u> given name in the <u>world today.</u>
   A   B   C   D
   <u>No error</u>
   E

2. <u>In 1980,</u> according to the *Book of Lists*, the <u>most extravagantest</u> price ever paid for a
   A   B
   painting was 6.4 <u>million dollars; however,</u> by 1990 Impressionist paintings were
           C
   regularly being sold <u>for fourty and fifty</u> million. <u>No error</u>
          D   E

3. Three people have been elected <u>president</u> of the <u>United States</u> with <u>less</u> popular votes
            A   B   C
   than <u>their opponents:</u> John Quincy Adams, Rutherford B. Hayes, and Benjamin
      D
   Harrison. <u>No error</u>
        E

4. In <u>atomic fission</u> the <u>nucleus</u> of a radioactive <u>element such as uranium</u> is <u>splitted</u> into
      A   B   C   D
   two more or less equal parts. <u>No error</u>
             E

5. It was first <u>thought that</u> the nomadic <u>people who have spread throughout the world</u> were
        A   B
   originally from <u>Egypt;</u> consequently, they are called <u>"Gypsies."</u> <u>No error</u>
        C   D   E

6. In the history of American music, there <u>have been</u> a long line of <u>great blind</u> <u>performers,</u>
               A   B   C
   including Ray Charles, Terri Gibbs, <u>Doc Watson, and Stevie Wonder.</u> <u>No error</u>
               D   E

7. The Bill of <u>rights</u> <u>are</u> the first ten <u>amendments</u> to the <u>Constitution of the United States.</u>
        A B   C   D
   <u>No error</u>
   E

8. Eric von Stroheim, <u>who</u> many people consider one of the <u>greatest</u> early film directors,
   A   B
   adapted Frank Norris's novel *McTeague* as a nine-hour film called *Greed,* but it was
   C
   shown only once in <u>it's</u> entirety. <u>No error</u>
   D   E

9. Before motion pictures were <u>developed,</u> Edward Muybridge was one of the first <u>to ask</u>
   A   B
   how the <u>principals</u> of photography might be applied to <u>motion?</u> <u>No error</u>
   C   D   E

10. Although <u>these sort of thing</u> went out of fashion <u>later,</u> after 1943, when Eugene <u>O'Neill's</u>
    A   B   C
    daughter married Charlie Chaplin against <u>his</u> will, O'Neill never saw her or mentioned her
    D
    name again. <u>No error</u>
    E

11. <u>In A.D. 1099</u> <u>Christian crusaders</u> fought Jews and Moslems, thus establishing a kingdom
    A   B
    in <u>Jerusalem. That</u> lasted about <u>one hundred</u> years. <u>No error</u>
    C   D   E

12. The Grand Canyon of the <u>Colorado River,</u> along with the Painted Desert, the Petrified
    A
    <u>Forrest,</u> and Meteor Crater, <u>draw</u> thousands of tourists each year to <u>Arizona,</u> the 48th
    B   C   D
    state. <u>No error</u>
    E

13. <u>After the Hundred Year's War Edward II of England</u> must have <u>felt bad</u> when he <u>became</u>
    A   B   C   D
    the first national ruler to go bankrupt. <u>No error</u>
    E

14. It <u>couldn't hardly</u> have been anything <u>but a coincidence</u> when, <u>in 1911,</u> three men
    A   B   C
    in London were hanged for the murder of a man at Greenberry Hill; their names were
    <u>Green, Berry and Hill.</u> <u>No error</u>
    D   E

15. In Kentucky <u>its</u> against the law for a <u>man who is married</u> to buy a <u>hat unless</u> his wife is
    A   B   C
    present to supervise <u>him</u> shopping. <u>No error</u>
    D   E

16. One of the youngest rulers in history <u>were</u> Mary, Queen of <u>scots,</u> who became <u>queen in</u>
    A   B   C
    1542 at the age of <u>one week.</u> <u>No error</u>
    D   E

17. The Red River's source is in New Mexico, and the White Rivers is in Arkansas, but
        A   B   C
    both flows into the Mississippi. No error
         D   E

18. Dr. Seuss, the children's author, might not seem to have much in common with James
               A   B
    Joyce, but both Joyce and he had an early book rejected by more than twenty
     C   D
    publishers. No error
           E

19. In her book *The Geographical History of America,* Gertrude Stein says, "In the
                                              A
    United States there is more space where nobody is than where anybody is," but she don't
                                                      B   C
    mention the places where everybody is, such as New York City. No error
                            D   E

20. In a four-way contest, Abraham Lincoln was elected President of the United States in
         A   B
    1860 with only thirty nine percent of the popular vote. No error
     C   D   E

21. In 1978 three men entered a housewares store to shoplift, however, they were
                                        A
    aprehended immediately after the crime, not having noticed that the store was hosting a
       B   C   D
    convention of store detectives. No error
                        E

22. Early in his career, Charlie Chaplin developed his "Little Tramp" character after
                                        A   B
    stagehands laughed at his tripping accidentally over a stage prop and tipping his hat in
                                   C   D
    apology. No error
          E

23. Marx and Engel's major writing, the *Communist Manifesto,* was only a forty-page
     A   B   C
    pamphlet; however, it's influence has been felt by nearly everyone in the modern world.
                          D
    No error
     E

24. William of Orange became King of England in 1689 when Parliament offered the crown
                                A   B   C
    jointly to his wife Mary and he. No error
                   D   E

25. Panama hats, with their closely woven straw and black bands, is a product of the
       A   B   C
    south american country of Ecuador. No error
       D   E

Sketchbook

He: "Hi, how're you doin'?"

She: "Not bad. I'm still trying to figure out how to get ready for three tests in one week, and my date for the dance just backed out, but other than that I'm OK. And you?"

He: "OK, but—"

But what? What's bothering him? Continue this dialogue. See where it takes you. Remember, you can have one person ask the other a question even if you don't have an answer in mind. Just ask; then see what the other person comes up with. Take care to use quotation marks and other punctuation marks correctly.

Additional Sketches

Where would you go if you could take a trip anywhere in the world? Write the itinerary for your dream trip. Be sure to use capitalization and punctuation correctly.

Imagine a humorous character who constantly interrupts himself or herself with digressions, irrelevant remarks, and out-of-sequence details. Write a message that this character might give to a friend, showing his or her difficulty in getting to the point. Use dashes and parentheses to indicate shifts in thought.

Review of Parts of Speech

THE PARTS OF SPEECH

By this time, having studied English for many years, you are familiar with the eight parts of speech in the English language. This lesson will serve both as a review and as a diagnostic and teaching lesson.

To review the parts of speech, do the following exercise and check your answers with the key on page 577. If you find that you need more practice, study the part or parts in this lesson that provide the help you need. You will find definitions, explanations, and exercises for each part of speech: noun, pronoun, verb, adjective, adverb, preposition, conjunction, and interjection. Use the Application and Review on pages 576–577 to recheck your skills.

Finally, as you do the exercises in this lesson, keep this important rule in mind.

The part of speech of any particular word is determined by the function of the word in the sentence.

For example, what part of speech is the word *dance?* The question cannot be answered until the word is seen in context: *The dance is on Friday. Please dance with me. The dance class begins at nine.* These examples illustrate that, depending on its function, *dance* can be be a noun, a verb, or an adjective.

Diagnostic Exercise   Write the italicized words from the following literary excerpt. After each word write what part of speech it is. Check your answers with the key on page 577.

(1) *At* the top of Richmond Lane lived Amy's *friend* Tibby, a *prematurely sophisticated* blond *tot,* best remembered for having drawled *conversationally* to Mother, when she, Tibby, was only six *and still* missing her front teeth, "*I* love your hair, Mrs. Doak." (2) When Tibby and Amy *were* eight, Amy brought home yet another *straight-A* report card. (3) Shortly *afterward,* Mother *overheard* Tibby say exasperatedly to Amy, "How can *you* be so smart in school and so dumb *after* school?" (4) In fact, *as* the years passed, after-school became Amy's *bailiwick,* and she was *plenty* smart at *it.*

(5) *When* Amy wasn't playing with Tibby, she played with her dolls. (6) *They* were a hostile crew. (7) Lying rigidly in

Writing Theme
Childhood

their *sickbeds,* they *shot at* each other a *series* of haughty expletives. (8) She had picked *these* up *from* Katy Keene comic books; Katy Keene was a *society* girl with a great many clothes. (9) Amy *pronounced* every consonant of *these* expletives. . . .

(10) "I'll *show* you, you vixen!" cried a flat-out and *staring* piece of buxom *plastic* from *its* Naturalizer shoe box.
(11) *"Humph!"*

Annie Dillard, *An American Childhood*

Nouns

A noun is the name of a person, place, thing, quality, or action.

Nouns can be classified in several ways. All nouns can be placed in at least two categories, and some can be placed in more than two.

A **concrete noun** names something perceptible to the senses—sight, hearing, smell, touch, and taste—such as *cat, cotton, pickle.*

An **abstract noun** names something that is not perceptible to the senses, such as an idea, quality, emotion, or state: *happiness, safety, jealousy, being.*

A **common noun** names one or all the members of a class: *camera, glass, soldier, theory, women, mechanics, bears, rules.*

A **proper noun** names a particular person, place, thing, or idea. A proper noun always begins with a capital letter and may consist of more than one word: *Amadeus Mozart, France, Lake Michigan, Memorial Day, Christianity.*

Writing
—TIP—

Use precise nouns, such as *telescope* rather than *instrument,* to give your readers a vivid picture.

A **compound noun** contains two or more elements that have individual meanings. A compound noun may be spelled as one word, as separate words, or as a hyphenated term: *jackpot, dining room, Oak Street, well-being, sister-in-law.* Consult a dictionary when in doubt as to the form of a compound noun.

A **collective noun** denotes a collection of persons or things that are regarded as a unit: *team, flock, band.* It takes a singular verb when it refers to the collection as a whole; it takes a plural verb when it refers to the members of the group as separate persons or things.

Grammar Note   The *-ing* form of the verb is often used as a noun. When used as a noun, this form is called a **gerund.** *Snorkeling* can be dangerous. Chris did the *washing.* For more information about gerunds, see Grammar Handbook 32, "Phrases and Clauses," pages 599–641.

Practice Your Skills
CONCEPT CHECK

Nouns   Write the italicized nouns in the following literary excerpt. Identify each noun by type: Concrete, Abstract; Common, Proper; Compound; Collective. All nouns belong to two categories; some will belong to three.

(1) Only once did I have a small bit of my share of *success.* (2) On a single *occasion* Kosloff gave *exercises* in *pantomime.* (3) He suddenly stopped the *class* and called me out from my *position* in the back of the *room.* (4) I demonstrated the exercise to a hushed and watching *group.* I did, of course, the best I could, trembling a little. They applauded. (5) *Kosloff* beamed on me. (6) He told *Uncle Cecil* that I showed the finest *talent* for pantomime of any *pupil* he had ever taught. (7) This *remark* was naturally not repeated to me until long after.

(8) My well-filled curriculum—*classes, homework, tennis,* piano, *editing*—was ordered with just one *thought:* to make room for the dance practice. (9) I rose at six-thirty and I studied and practiced at breakneck *concentration* until six in the *evening* when I was at last free to put on dancing *dress* and walk—to Mother's *bathroom.*

(10) All through the lonely, drab exercises beside Mother's tub, without music or *beat,* proper floor or mirror, I had the *joy* of looking forward to dinner with *Father.* . . .

Agnes De Mille, ***Dance to the Piper***

PRONOUNS

A pronoun is a word used in place of a noun or another pronoun.

The noun to which a pronoun refers is called its **antecedent**.

Tom said he and Ian will go. (*Tom* is the antecedent of *he*.)

Pronouns can be classified into seven categories.

Personal Pronouns

A personal pronoun is a pronoun that denotes the person speaking, the person spoken to, or the person or thing spoken about. Pronouns have person, number, gender, and case.

Person A pronoun that refers to the person speaking is a **first-person** pronoun; to the person spoken to, a **second-person** pronoun; and to the person or thing spoken about, **third-person**.

Number A pronoun referring to one person, place, thing, or idea is called **singular**. A pronoun referring to more than one is **plural**.

Gender Personal pronouns in the third-person singular have gender. A pronoun is **masculine, feminine,** or **neuter** depending on whether it refers to a male, a female, or to an animal or a thing.

Case A personal pronoun has three cases, or forms, that indicate its function in the sentence: **nominative, objective,** and **possessive**.

Writing —TIP—

In writing, make sure that every personal pronoun you use has a definite, clear antecedent.

Singular Personal Pronouns

	Nominative	Possessive	Objective
First Person	I	my, mine	me
Second Person	you	your, yours	you
Third Person	he, she, it	his, her, hers, its	him, her, it

Plural Personal Pronouns

	Nominative	Possessive	Objective
First Person	we	our, ours	us
Second Person	you	your, yours	you
Third Person	they	their, theirs	them

The personal pronouns in the possessive case are also known as **possessive pronouns.** The forms *my, your, her, his, its, our,* and *their* function as adjectives; they are used to modify nouns. *That is my document.* The forms *mine, yours, hers, his, its, ours,* and *theirs* function as nouns; they are used in place of a noun. *That document is mine.*

For more information, see Grammar Handbook 35, "Pronoun Usage."

Reflexive and Intensive Pronouns

The reflexive and intensive forms of a pronoun are made by adding the suffix *-self* or *-selves.* Although these two types of pronouns look identical, they are used in different ways. Neither, however, can be used without an antecedent.

Reflexive and Intensive Pronouns

First Person	myself, ourselves
Second Person	yourself, yourselves
Third Person	himself, herself, itself, themselves

Basket Dance, by Pueblo artist Oqwa Pi

A **reflexive pronoun** is a pronoun used as the direct object of a reflexive verb; the object is identical with the subject.

Kristen judges *herself* too harshly.

An **intensive pronoun** is used in apposition to a noun or pronoun to increase its force.

King Arthur *himself* designed the famous Round Table.

Demonstrative Pronouns

A **demonstrative pronoun** specifies or singles out the person or thing referred to: *this, that, these,* and *those.*

> *This* is the primer you should use to prepare the wood.
> Are *those* the pages assigned for today?

Interrogative Pronouns

An **interrogative pronoun** is used to ask a question: *who, whom, whose, which,* and *what.*

> *Who* ordered stir-fried vegetables?
> *Which* is the more difficult course—physics or chemistry?

Indefinite Pronouns

An **indefinite pronoun** does not refer to a specific person or thing. An indefinite pronoun usually does not have an antecedent.

> *Someone* left the phone off the hook, so I couldn't call you.
> *Most* of the schools were closed because of the snowstorm.

Most indefinite pronouns are always singular or always plural. A few, however, can be singular or plural, depending on the context.

Commonly Used Indefinite Pronouns

Singular			Plural	Singular or Plural	
another	everybody	no one	both	all	most
anybody	everyone	nothing	few	any	none
anyone	everything	one	many	more	some
anything	much	somebody	several		
each	neither	someone			
either	nobody	something			

Relative Pronouns

A **relative pronoun** introduces a subordinate clause and always has an antecedent: *who, whom, which, what, that.*

> Schliemann was the *archaeologist who* discovered Troy. (The relative pronoun *who* refers to the antecedent *archaeologist.*)
> The Giants are the *team that* won the most games. (The relative pronoun *that* refers to the antecedent *team.*)

Martina Navratilova

Writing
—**TIP**—
Choose lively action verbs to hold your reader's interest.

Practice Your Skills

CONCEPT CHECK

Pronouns Write the pronouns in the following sentences, and identify each as *Personal, Reflexive, Intensive, Demonstrative, Interrogative, Indefinite,* or *Relative.*

1. Many of the sports enthusiasts here play tennis, but they don't consider themselves professionals.
2. I myself enjoy the game because it is an individual sport that requires precise skill and fast reflexes.
3. The French introduced tennis in the 1100's or 1200's, but they hit the ball with their hands instead of with racquets.
4. The British developed the modern game, renaming it lawn tennis.
5. Which is the most famous tennis tournament? Wimbledon is, of course.
6. Before 1968, only amateurs, including young Martina Navratilova herself, were allowed to play at Wimbledon.
7. After 1968, most were professionals and were seeded, or scheduled to play, according to rank and reputation.
8. Seeded players do not play one another early in the tournament.
9. What do you know about players who are good enough to be seeded?
10. Those are the players who usually distinguish themselves at tennis tournaments.

VERBS

A verb is a word or phrase that expresses an action, a condition, or a state of being.

The two main categories of verbs are action verbs and linking verbs.

Action Verbs

An **action verb** expresses an action. The action may be physical or mental.

Physical Action	Sharon *winced* at the sound of the siren.
	The potter *created* a graceful pitcher from the shapeless lump of clay.
Mental Action	Phillip *considered* all his options.
	Sam and I *recognized* the old man in the wheelchair from the party.

Linking Verbs

A **linking verb** does not express action. Instead, it links the subject of a sentence to a noun, pronoun, or adjective in the predicate.

> Judge Bianca *is* also a professor at Lee University. (*Is* links the predicate nominative, *professor,* with the subject, *Judge Bianca.*)
> Sumiko *looked* dejected after the winners were announced. (*Looked* links the predicate adjective, *dejected,* with the subject, *Sumiko.*)

The most common linking verb is *be*. Other linking verbs include sensory verbs (*sound, taste, appear, feel, look, smell*) and verbs that express condition (*become, remain, seem, stay, grow*).

Some verbs can function as both linking verbs and action verbs.

Linking Verb	Action Verb
Carey *grew* silent.	We *grew* eggplants last summer.
Kim *felt* ill.	Aida tentatively *felt* her bruised arm.

Auxiliary Verbs

An **auxiliary verb** is used with another verb to indicate voice, mood, or tense. A main verb and its auxiliaries are called a **verb phrase.**

Auxiliary	+	Main Verb	=	Verb Phrase
was		planning		was planning
is		seen		is seen
will have		finished		will have finished
would		survive		would survive

The most frequently used auxiliaries are forms of *be* and *have*. These are other common auxiliaries:

must	may	shall	could	would
might	can	will	should	do

Often the auxiliary verb and the main verb are separated by other words. In the example below, note that the contraction *n't* is not part of the verb.

> We *had* just *arrived*.   *Did*n't you *meet* Helene?

Transitive and Intransitive Verbs

Action verbs may be transitive or intransitive. A **transitive verb** is one that takes a direct object. The verb expresses an action that is carried from the subject to the object. An **intransitive verb** is one that does not take an object.

Transitive	**Intransitive**
Mom *painted* the ceiling.	The concert *began* early.
Someone *rang* the bell.	The workers *left* at noon.

A few verbs are only transitive; others, only intransitive. Many verbs, however, are both transitive and intransitive.

Transitive	**Intransitive**
The trio *sang* folk songs.	We *sang* along.
I *could*n't *see* the signal.	I *could*n't *see* clearly.
The boy *flies* a kite.	Birds *fly*.

Grammar Note Linking verbs are always intransitive, because they do not take objects.

For more information on verb usage, see Grammar Handbook 33.

Practice Your Skills

A. CONCEPT CHECK

Verbs Write the verb or verbs in each sentence below. Label each as *Action* or *Linking*. Also identify each action verb as *Transitive* or *Intransitive*. Be careful not to confuse the verb with a gerund, participle, or infinitive.

1. In the fifth century A.D., barbarian Visigoths attacked Rome.
2. The Visigoths would not withdraw until the Romans gave them precious commodities.
3. Alaric, the Visigoth leader, demanded large amounts of gold, silver, and silk, as well as 3,000 pounds of their most valuable possession—pepper!
4. The Romans became inconsolable when they contemplated the loss of the pepper.
5. In the past, Roman finances had suffered greatly from unprofitable trading for the exotic black spice from the East.
6. According to Pliny, a Roman historian, the country was losing the equivalent of $25 million a year in Oriental trade.
7. Nevertheless, the aristocrats of Rome were adamant; they would not surrender their most important status symbol.
8. Rome fell, and Europe plunged into the Dark Ages, but pepper was still valuable nine hundred years later during the Renaissance.
9. Peppercorns became substitutes for precious metals and currency and served as payment for taxes and rent; Italian merchants held a monopoly on the pepper trade.

10. Other Europeans grew tired of the exorbitant prices; they were desperate and they were determined as they sought a new route to the East and its pepper.

B. REVISION SKILL

Eliminating Wordiness Sometimes writing can be strengthened by substituting an action verb for a longer phrase that includes a *be* verb. Eliminate wordiness in the paragraph below by substituting strong verbs for longer *be* verb phrases.

Wordy   Often people are in disagreement about what is of value.
Revised   Often people disagree about what is of value.

> In the early civilization of the Sudan, salt was equal to gold in value. Some groups were in control of large salt deposits while others were owners of gold mines. Each was in need of the other's riches, so they traded. Salt was also of influence in the economy of ancient Rome. Each soldier and civil servant was the recipient of a ration of salt known as a *salarium.* In fact, our word *salary* is a derivation from *salarium.*

C. APPLICATION IN WRITING

A Personal Credo A personal credo is a statement about what you believe to be of value. Write a short paragraph that describes what you believe to be of value. Use a variety of action and linking verbs in your paragraph.

ADJECTIVES

An adjective is a word that modifies a noun or a pronoun.

An adjective changes the meaning of a noun or pronoun by limiting, qualifying, or specifying. It answers one of these questions:

Which one?   *this* fossil, *another* book, *those* computers
What kind?   *silver* ornaments, *huge* serving, *lively* writing
How many?   *three* rings, *some* exhibitors, *few* volunteers
How much?   *enough* help, *abundant* harvest, *little* chance

As shown in the above examples, an adjective usually precedes the word it modifies. Sometimes for variety, however, a writer places the adjective after the noun.

> Jenny, *petite* and *blonde,* wrestled the runaway calf to the ground.

Writing
TIP

Use imaginative adjectives—such as *arctic* weather, rather than *cold* weather—to engage your reader.

Predicate Adjectives   A **predicate adjective** is an adjective that follows a linking verb; it always modifies the subject of the sentence.

The answer seems *obvious*.   We were *ecstatic*.

Proper Adjectives   Proper adjectives are derived from proper nouns and are always capitalized: *Swiss* cheese, *Talmudic* scholar.

Other Words as Adjectives   Many words that are generally thought of as other parts of speech can also function as adjectives. These include nouns and several of the demonstrative, interrogative, relative, and indefinite pronouns.

The present and past participles of the verb may also function as adjectives.

The *ensuing* argument forced the legislature to send the bill back to committee. (*Ensuing* is a present participle functioning as an adjective and modifying the noun *argument*.)

Other Parts of Speech as Adjectives	
Nouns	*wall* clock, *computer* table, *plastic* toy
Pronouns	*my* coat, *this* whistle, *which* students, *few* jobs
Participles	*spinning* top, *crushed* flower, *well-washed* jeans

Articles

The articles *a, an,* and *the* are considered adjectives because they modify the nouns or noun phrases they precede. The article *the* is called the **definite article** because it specifies a particular person, place, thing, or group.

A and *an* are the **indefinite articles.** They indicate that a noun is not unique but is one of many persons, places, things, or groups. Use *a* before a word that begins with a consonant sound. Use *an* before a word that begins with a vowel sound. Remember, it is the sound, not the spelling that determines the correct choice.

a unicorn	*an* honorary degree
a history book	*an* unknown quantity
a telephone	*an* invitation

Note that when a noun modified by *a* or *an* is repeated in a piece of writing, it becomes particular and is preceded by *the*.

We saw *a* dog trotting along. *The* dog was black.

Practice Your Skills

A. CONCEPT CHECK

Adjectives For each of the sentences in the following literary excerpt, write the adjectives and tell which words they modify. Remember to look for predicate adjectives and for other parts of speech that are functioning as adjectives. Do not list articles.

(1) Becky effortlessly skated ahead to the lift shed. (2) The encumbered motion of walking on skis, not natural to him, made Ethan feel asthmatic: a fish out of water. (3) He touched his parka pocket, to check that the inhalator was there. . . . (4) The clock on the lodge wall said a quarter to noon. (5) The giant thermometer read two degrees above zero. (6) The racks outside were dense as hedges with idle skis. (7) Crowds, any sensation of crowding or delay, quickened his asthma; as therapy he imagined the emptiness, the blue freedom, at the top of the mountain. (8) The clatter of machinery inside the shed was comforting, and enough teen-age boys were boarding gondolas to make the ascent seem normal and safe. (9) Ethan's breathing eased. Becky proficiently handed her poles to the loader points up; her father was always caught by surprise, and often as not fumbled the little maneuver of letting his skis be taken from him. (10) Until, five years ago, he had become an assistant professor at a New Hampshire college an hour to the south, he had never skied; he had lived in those Middle Atlantic cities where snow . . . is only an encumbering nuisance, a threat of suffocation.

John Updike, "Man and Daughter in the Cold"

B. APPLICATION IN WRITING

Personal Narrative As you have learned, adjectives aid a writer in adding detail. Recall a situation that was awkward for you or for someone you know. You might wish to record or list some of the details of the incident before beginning to write. Then recount the situation in the form of a personal narrative. Use adjectives to supply detail.

ADVERBS

An adverb modifies a verb, an adjective, or another adverb.

Adverbs tell *where, when, how,* or *to what extent* about the words they modify.

Where?	waddled *away,* sank *lower,* rode *east*
When?	shipped *yesterday,* arrived *early,* slept *late*
How?	opened *slowly,* rocked *ceaselessly,* hummed *softly*
To what extent?	*completely* ruined, *very* sorry, *really* pleased

Adverbs that modify adjectives or other adverbs by adding emphasis are often called **intensifiers.** Words like *too, extremely, truly, really,* and *actually* add strength, or intensity, to writing just as vivid colors give intensity to a painting.

Adverbs that specify place are called **directive adverbs.** Many adverbs may be combined with verbs to make idioms: *give up, break in, set off.* An **idiom** is a phrase that has a meaning as a whole but cannot be understood from the meanings of the individual words. Negatives such as *not* and *never* are also adverbs. For more about adverbs, see Grammar Handbook 36.

Practice Your Skills

CONCEPT CHECK

Adverbs For each of the following sentences, write the adverbs and tell which word or words they modify.

1. Architecturally, Venice is one of the most beautiful cities in the world.
2. The handsome old city's buildings and decorations, from Byzantine to Renaissance, show quite clearly and proudly the city's great heritage.
3. Famous works of the Venetian school of painting and art are widely represented in the palaces, public buildings, and churches.

Writing
—**TIP**—

Adverbs aid precision by expanding and focusing verbs.

Writing Theme
Venice

---

4. Tourists never fail to include on their itineraries a stop at centrally located St. Mark's Square.
5. When visiting the square, one must not miss two strikingly beautiful structures.
6. On the east side is St. Mark's Cathedral, first constructed in A.D. 828 and later rebuilt on several occasions; next to it, the Doges' Palace stands magnificently beside a canal.
7. Venice is most closely identified with its famous Grand Canal, which winds lazily for approximately two miles, dividing the city into two nearly equal parts.
8. Although many extremely tightly wound streets penetrate the city, a very popular and truly typical method of transportation is the gondola.
9. The gondola, a flat-bottomed boat, glides almost effortlessly across the usually peaceful canal waters.
10. One of Venice's most romantic images is that of the gondolier singing to two young lovers as he navigates the canal with his slender oar.

PREPOSITIONS

A preposition is a word that indicates the relation of a noun or pronoun to some other word in the sentence.

A preposition always introduces a phrase, called a **prepositional phrase,** which consists of the preposition, a final noun or pronoun, and any modifiers. The noun or pronoun that ends the phrase is the **object of the preposition.** The preposition, then, relates the object to some other word in the sentence. This word may be a noun, pronoun, verb, adjective, or adverb.

> Most *of* the computers *in* our lab were donated *by* large manufacturers. (The preposition *of* relates the object *computers* to the pronoun *most; in* relates the object *lab* to the noun *computers; by* relates the object *manufacturers* to the verb *donated.*)
>
> Juan bounded *up the broad steps.* (*Up the broad steps* is the prepositional phrase; *steps* is the object of the preposition *up; the* and *broad* are modifiers of the object. *Up* relates the object *steps* to the verb *bounded.*)

A **compound preposition** is a phrase that functions as a preposition. Examples include such phrases as *according to, in place of, because of, in regard to,* and *prior to.*

Writing
TIP

Select prepositions that accurately convey the relationship between words or ideas.

Commonly Used Prepositions

about	before	down	of	to
above	behind	during	off	toward
across	below	except	on	under
after	beneath	for	onto	underneath
against	beside	from	out	until
along	between	in	outside	up
among	beyond	inside	over	upon
around	but	into	past	with
as	by	like	since	within
at	despite	near	through	without

For more information on prepositional phrases, see Grammar Handbook 32, "Phrases and Clauses."

Practice Your Skills

CONCEPT CHECK

Prepositions For each of the following sentences, write the prepositions and their objects.

1. In the late 1500's, Elizabethan plays were performed in both public and private buildings.
2. Public theaters were constructed without roofs and were built around central courtyards.
3. There were no artificial lights, so performances were held during daylight hours.

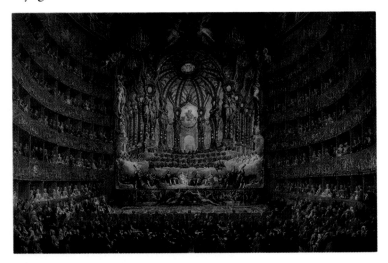

A Musical Fete, by Giovanni Pannini

4. According to many scholars, the poorer spectators, known as groundlings, stood along the edge of the raised stage and viewed the play.
5. Wealthier playgoers sat comfortably inside the galleries above the groundlings.
6. Because the stage projected into the courtyard, the actors were surrounded on three sides by the audience.
7. An upper stage hung like a balcony at the back of the main stage.
8. If a play included ghosts or spirits, they could appear and disappear through a trapdoor in the main stage.
9. In regard to scenery, scholars note that little was used except such props as thrones, swords, and tents.
10. If the spectators were not enjoying a performance, they threw objects at the actors, pulled them off the stage, and fought among themselves; nevertheless, they loved the theater.

Queen Elizabeth I, by Nicholas Hilliard

CONJUNCTIONS

A conjunction is a word that is used to connect sentences, clauses, phrases, or words.

In the following examples, the conjunctions are shown in boldface type. The elements they connect are shown in italics.

We can *bake* **or** *broil* the fish.
Close the door, **but** *leave the window open.*
Neither *Paul* **nor** *Ann* was on time.
The watch was repaired **while** *we waited.*
Alan ran **as if** *he were in great danger.*

There are three kinds of conjunctions: coordinating, correlative, and subordinating. Conjunctive adverbs also function as conjunctions.

Coordinating Conjunctions

A **coordinating conjunction** is used to connect elements of equal rank.

Coordinating Conjunctions						
and	but	or	for	so	yet	nor

Correlative Conjunctions

Correlative conjunctions are always used in pairs. The structures of the elements used after correlative conjunctions should be parallel, as in the example below.

Correlative Conjunctions

both . . . and	neither . . . nor	whether . . . or
either . . . or	not only . . . but (also)	

Incorrect   Both the sheriff and deputy pursued the thief tirelessly.
Correct   Both *the sheriff* and *the deputy* pursued the thief tirelessly.

Subordinating Conjunctions

A **subordinating conjunction** is used to connect clauses of unequal rank. The subordinate clause is usually an adverb clause—one expressing time, place, degree, manner, condition, cause, or purpose.

┌──INDEPENDENT──┐ ┌──────SUBORDINATE──────┐
The audience gasped when the phantom appeared in the mist.
(The subordinating conjunction *when* introduces an adverb clause expressing time.)

Subordinating Conjunctions

Time	after, as, as long as, as soon as, before, since, until, when, whenever, while
Manner	as, as if
Place	where, wherever
Cause or Reason	because, since
Condition	although, as long as, even if, even though, if, provided that, though, unless, while
Purpose	in order that, so that, that

For more about clauses, see Grammar Handbook 32, "Phrases and Clauses."

Conjunctive Adverbs

A **conjunctive adverb** is an adverb used as a coordinating conjunction. It serves to carry the sense from one clause to another.

> I had no umbrella; *nevertheless,* I walked out into the rainy night.
>
> Ian was late for class; *furthermore,* he'd lost his homework.

Conjunctive Adverbs

accordingly	finally	indeed	still
also	furthermore	moreover	then
besides	hence	nevertheless	therefore
consequently	however	otherwise	thus

Punctuation Note A conjunctive adverb is usually preceded by a semicolon and followed by a comma.

Practice Your Skills

CONCEPT CHECK

Conjunctions Write each conjunction and identify it as *Coordinating, Correlative, Subordinating,* or *Conjunctive Adverb.* Some sentences have more than one conjunction.

Writing Theme
Diving for Treasure

1. Some people argue that sunken shipwrecks should not be open to exploration by treasure divers, but the issue is open to debate.
2. Many divers insist that as long as they exercise reasonable caution they should have the right to dive anywhere.
3. Archaeologists feel that because so many wrecks are like time capsules, they should be protected and valued like museums.
4. Many amateur divers are only interested in treasure; consequently, they often damage or destroy archaeologically valuable sites.
5. Nevertheless, many wrecks might remain undiscovered if divers are not given a free hand.
6. On the other hand, neither the fact that wreck sites are frequently dangerous nor the fact that they offer a strong temptation to inexperienced divers can be overlooked.
7. Treasure diving is very expensive; therefore, few people ever make money from it.
8. Mel Fisher did find a fortune diving for treasure when he discovered the *Nuestra Señora de Atocha,* yet he also found tragedy.

9. Fisher's search cost him eight million dollars; moreover, it tragically also cost several lives.
10. There must be some way to protect both the interests of divers and the interests of archaeologists, but the dilemma remains unresolved.

INTERJECTIONS

Writing **TIP**

Use interjections sparingly for greatest effect.

Writing Theme
The Appointment

An interjection is a word or group of words used to express sudden feeling. It has no grammatical relation to any other word in the sentence.

Strong interjections are followed by exclamation points. Milder interjections are followed by commas. Any part of speech may be used as an interjection.

Wow! I won!   *Well,* I've heard everything now.

Practice Your Skills

DRAFTING SKILL

Using and Punctuating Interjections The dialogue below might have taken place in a busy movie director's office. From the list below, choose an appropriate interjection and add the correct punctuation.

Stop	Hello	Oh	Sorry	Never
Surprise	Impossible	Well	Honestly	Sure

1. **Actor:** _____ Miss Ferrara. I am Mr. Fox, and I have an appointment with Mr. Spielberg at noon.
2. **Secretary:** _____ Mr. Spielberg never takes appointments before two o'clock.
3. **Actor:** _____ why don't you just ring his office and check?
4. **Secretary:** _____ He asked not to be interrupted.
5. **Actor:** _____ we'll see about that. I'll ring him myself.
6. **Secretary:** _____ Give me that phone this instant, young man.
7. **Actor (into telephone):** _____ Mr. Spielberg, is it necessary to have your secretary stand guard over your office? We have an appointment today.
8. **Secretary:** _____ If you persist, I'm going to have to take stern measures.
9. **Actor:** _____ When I said it was Michael J. Fox, he told me to come right in.
10. **Secretary:** _____ Michael J. Fox or not, I don't believe you and I'm calling security immediately.

On the Lightside

ACRONYMS AND ABBREVIATIONS

When President Franklin Delano Roosevelt set up the TVA, the WPA, and other New Deal programs called by their initials, one political opponent complained about the resulting "alphabet soup." By using acronyms and abbreviations, FDR popularized the now-widespread process of forming new words.

Acronyms and abbreviations are made by combining the initial letters or syllables of series of words. In abbreviations, such as TVA for Tennessee Valley Authority and WPA for Works Progress Administration, each letter is pronounced individually. In acronyms, such as *scuba* for *self-contained underwater breathing apparatus,* a group of letters is pronounced as a word.

Although examples can be found as far back as ancient Hebrew scriptures, an explosion of acronyms and abbreviations has occurred in the twentieth century. Roosevelt's New Deal led the way by naming government agencies. World War II brought such words as *radar* for *radio detection and ranging,* and *jeep* from G.P. for *general purpose vehicle.*

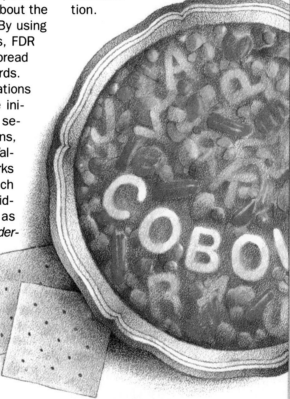

Companies and organizations use acronyms and abbreviations as a preferred form of identification.

One example of this is NOW for National Organization for Women. Acronyms are a popular means of shortening technical and scientific terms. *Laser* is easier on the tongue than *light amplification by stimulated emission of radiation.*

GRAMMAR
HANDBOOK
30

Writing Theme
Unusual Origins

A. Word Usage In each of the following sentences, determine how the italicized words or phrases are used. Identify the use of each as a *Noun, Pronoun, Verb, Adjective, Preposition, Conjunction,* or *Interjection.*

1. The idea for a *self-developing* camera first occurred to Edwin Land *as* he traveled around New Mexico in 1943 *as* a tourist.
2. He began to think *seriously* about *it* when his small daughter asked, *"Gee,* why do we have to wait so *long* to see the pictures?"
3. Listening attentively to *her,* Land *pictured* the *added* fun people would have with their cameras *if* they could see the photo *immediately.*
4. *Land* accepted his *daughter's* challenge and began experiments *that* would eventually lead to the growth of a large and successful corporation.
5. He already knew a great *deal* more *about* cameras than most people did and *had patented* several devices that *were sold* to Eastman Kodak.
6. His *first* invention was a *polarizing* filter that he created *while* he was still a freshman at *Harvard University.*
7. *So impatient* was Land to work on his inventions that he left college *before* graduating.
8. Along with a *Harvard* professor, he formed Land-Wheelwright Laboratories in 1932, *and* the *two* of them worked out of a Boston basement.
9. *This* led to the *formation* of Polaroid Corporation, where he *first* worked on his *long-sought* goal of reducing headlight *glare.*
10. *Fortunately,* thanks to his daughter's question, Land *found* other goals, and several *years* later he produced the first *developing* process *inside* a small, inexpensive camera.

B. Parts of Speech In each of the following sentences, identify the part of speech of the italicized word. Then write a new sentence on any subject, using the word as the part of speech indicated in parentheses.

1. *Humor* is not what it used to be. (verb)
2. When we think of humor, we think of comedy, but people a thousand years ago were *more* likely to think of humor in connection with health. (adjective)
3. The Latin word for humor means "moisture," and early *Roman* doctors believed the human body contained four basic humors. (noun)
4. A person's health was determined by the *balance* of the four humors. (verb)

5. These humors were said to correspond to *body* fluids, and they were classified according to the following colors: red, yellow, white, and black. (noun)
6. Physicians believed an excess of the red humor, which was *blood,* to be the cause of fevers. (adjective)
7. They often treated fevers by drawing blood from the patient *until* they believed the balance of humors had been restored. (preposition)
8. By the 1700's, *this* concept of humor was associated not only with illness but also with unbalanced, foolish, or exaggerated behavior. (pronoun)
9. Humor thus became a favorite subject for writers of comedy, because comedy, according to Renaissance theories, *inspired* audiences to correct their own irrational or immoral conduct. (adjective)
10. Now a new association between humor and health is being explored by modern researchers investigating the possibility that laughter speeds up the *healing* process and may even prolong life. (verb)

Answer Key for the Diagnostic Exercise

1. At—prep.
   friend—noun
   prematurely—adv.
   sophisticated—adj.
   tot—noun
   conversationally—
       adv.
   and—conj.
   still—adv.
   I—pronoun

2. were—verb
   straight-A—adj.

3. afterward—adv.
   overheard—verb
   you—pronoun
   after—prep.

4. as—conj.
   bailiwick—noun
   plenty—adv.
   it—pronoun

5. When—conj.

6. They—pronoun

7. sickbeds—noun
   shot—verb
   at—prep.
   series—noun

8. these—pronoun
   from—prep.
   society—adj.

9. pronounced—
       verb
   these—adj.

10. show—verb
    staring—adj.
    plastic—noun
    its—pronoun, adj.

11. Humph—interj.

The Parts of a Sentence

SUBJECTS AND PREDICATES IN SENTENCES

Sentences make statements, ask questions, give commands, or show strong feelings. Every sentence must express a complete idea.

A sentence is a group of words that expresses a complete thought.

A complete sentence has two basic parts: a subject and a predicate.

The subject is the person, place, thing, or idea about which something is said.

The predicate tells something or asks something about the subject.

Subject	Predicate
Ice	melts.
The ice on the pond	melts fast in the spring sun.
Who	is figure skating on the pond?

The **complete subject** includes all the words that identify the person, place, thing, or idea the sentence is about. The **complete predicate** includes all the words that tell or ask something about the subject.

Each complete subject contains a **simple subject,** and each complete predicate contains a **simple predicate** (the verb). The simple subject, usually called the **subject,** names exactly whom or what the sentence is about. The subject may be one word or a group of words, but it does not include modifiers. The verb tells what the subject does or is. It may be one word or several words, but it does not include modifiers.

In the following sentences, the complete subject and the complete predicate are separated by a vertical line. The simple subject and the verb are in bold type.

> The **entrance** to the ancient tomb | **was covered** with sand and rocks.
> **It** | **was** almost invisible to the unaided eye.

Sentence Diagraming   For information on diagraming subjects and verbs, see page 859.

Compound Sentence Parts

In a sentence, the subject, the verb, or both can be compound.

A **compound subject** is two or more subjects that share the same verb. The subjects are joined by a conjunction.

A **row** of trees *and* a **clump** of bushes blocked our view.

A **compound verb** has two or more verbs that share the same subject. The verbs are joined by a conjunction.

The crowd **cheered** *and* **shouted** for the candidate.

Sentence Diagraming For information on diagraming sentences with compound parts, see page 861.

Practice Your Skills

CONCEPT CHECK

Subjects and Predicates Copy each sentence. Draw a line between the complete subject and the complete predicate. Then underline the (simple) subject once and the verb twice.

1. Pearl Bailey made her show-business debut in 1933.
2. Pearl and her brother reached stardom on Broadway.
3. This vibrant woman was known and was loved around the world as a singer and entertainer.
4. Bailey gained fame both as a diplomat and as an author.
5. President Reagan and President Bush appointed her to terms as special advisor at the United Nations.
6. Her position at the UN took her all over the world.
7. Strong humanitarian concerns and philosophical interests led her back to school in 1978.
8. She entered Georgetown University and earned an undergraduate degree in theology.
9. Authorship of an autobiography, *Talking to Myself,* was Pearl Bailey's next achievement.
10. This remarkable woman remained active until her death at 72 in 1990.

Pearl Bailey

SUBJECTS IN DIFFERENT TYPES OF SENTENCES

A sentence may be classified according to its purpose: (1) to make a statement; (2) to ask a question; (3) to give a command, request, or direction; or (4) to express strong feeling or excitement.

The most common sentence pattern in English places the subject before the verb. When this order is reversed (inverted), the subject is harder to find. This part of the chapter will explain the four types of sentences and point out unusual subject-verb patterns.

Declarative Sentences

The **declarative sentence** expresses a statement, a fact, a wish, an intent, or a feeling. Most declarative sentences have normal subject-verb order. However, a writer may invert this order for special emphasis.

Normal Order	Then, suddenly without any warning, a searing wind <u>swept</u> across the prairie.
Inverted Order	Then, suddenly without any warning, across the prairie <u>swept</u> a searing <u>wind</u>.

Declarative Sentences with *There* or *Here*   In sentences that begin with *there* or *here,* the subject usually follows the verb. *There* or *here* can function either as an adverb or an expletive. In these situations an **expletive** is a word that helps get the sentence started but has no other grammatical function.

Adverb	There <u>is</u> the tennis <u>racket</u> you've been searching for all morning.
Expletive	There <u>must be</u> some <u>solution</u> to the growing number of endangered species.

Interrogative Sentences

The **interrogative sentence** asks a question and ends with a question mark. The subject may come after, before, or in the middle of the verb.

> Where <u>is</u> the <u>nation</u> of Tonga?
> <u>What</u> <u>caused</u> the power blackout?
> <u>They</u> <u>are</u> here already?
> <u>Have</u> <u>you</u> finally <u>finished</u> scraping off the old paint?

Sentence Diagraming   For information on diagraming interrogative sentences, see page 859.

Imperative Sentences

The **imperative sentence** is used to give a command, to make a request, or to give a direction. An imperative sentence usually ends with a period. However, if it expresses a strong feeling, it may end with an exclamation point. The subject of an imperative sentence is usually understood to be the pronoun *you*.

(<u>You</u>) <u>Take</u> the train on Track 2 to Union Square.
(<u>You</u>) Please <u>reply</u> by October 15.
<u>You</u>, <u>run</u> for help!

Sentence Diagraming   For information on diagraming imperative sentences, see page 859.

Exclamatory Sentences

The **exclamatory sentence** expresses strong feeling or excitement. Sentences of the other three types can be considered exclamatory when they express strong feeling. An exclamatory sentence ends with an exclamation point unless it begins with an interjection. In that case the exclamatory sentence can end with either an exclamation point or a period.

What a beautiful dive Carleen made!
Isn't the view breathtaking!
(You) Help, call an ambulance!
Ouch, that iodine stings.

Practice Your Skills

A. CONCEPT CHECK

Sentence Types   Number your paper from 1 to 8. Identify each sentence in the following literary passage as *Declarative, Interrogative, Imperative,* or *Exclamatory,* and name the punctuation mark that belongs at the end.

(1) Is it not crystal clear, then, comrades, that all the evils of this life of ours spring from the tyranny of human beings (2) Only get rid of Man, and the produce of our labor would be our own (3) Almost overnight we would become rich and free (4) What then must we do (5) Why, work night and day, body and soul, for the overthrow of the human race (6) That is my message to you comrades: Rebellion (7) I do not know when that Rebellion will come, it might be in a week or in a hundred years, but I know, as surely as I see this straw beneath my feet, that sooner or later justice will be done (8) Fix your eyes on that, comrades, throughout the short remainder of your lives

George Orwell, *Animal Farm*

B. PROOFREADING SKILL

Correcting End Punctuation   Rewrite the passage below, correcting all types of errors and supplying all appropriate end punctuation.

> Do the talking animals in *Animal Farm* remind you of similar characters Today's beloved Muppets and cartoon characters such as the cat Garfield and the tiger in "Calvin and Hobbes," are part of a long history of entertainment and advise provided by talking animals
>
> aesop's fables are more than two thousand years old, but the lessons taught by stories such as "The Fox and the Crow" and the "tortoise and the Hare" still apply to people today Can you think of some rabbit characters that talk have you ever considered that Bugs Bunny, the White Rabbit in *alice's adventures in wonderland,* and Aesop's hare might all be part of a literary tradition What pleasure and wisdom they all have brought us

C. APPLICATION IN WRITING

Creating a Scene   Write a short scene in which the central character is an animal who is able to think and talk. You may choose to use your own pet as a character.

Writing
—— **TIP** ——
Keep your reader's attention by varying sentence types and subject placement, where appropriate.

COMPLEMENTS

Mikhail dances. This sentence expresses a complete thought with just a subject and a verb. In many sentences, however, other words are needed to complete the meaning of the verb. These words are called complements.

> **A complement is one or more words that complete the meaning of the verb.**

You will study four kinds of complements: direct objects, indirect objects, objective complements, and subject complements.

Direct Objects

A **direct object** is a word or group of words that receives the action of the verb in a sentence. The direct object answers the questions *whom* or *what* about the verb.

> Mayor Young praised *Janet* for her work with homeless people. (praised *whom?*)
> Ed copied a *portrait* by Gainsborough. (copied *what?*)

A direct object can be a single word, as in the preceding sentences, or it can be a phrase or a clause.

>Carla enjoyed *having you here in El Paso.* (phrase)
>Yoshiko disliked *what you said about the town.* (clause)

A direct object can also be compound.

>Susan B. Anthony advocated *abolition* and women's *suffrage.*

Direct Object or Adverb? Do not mistake an adverb after an action verb for a direct object. An adverb answers the question *where, when, how,* or *to what extent.*

>The car struck a *pillar.* (direct object—struck *what?*)
>The storm struck *quickly.* (adverb—struck *how?*)

Sentence Diagraming For information on diagraming direct objects, see page 860.

Practice Your Skills

CONCEPT CHECK

Direct Objects Write the following sentences, underlining the verb once and the direct object twice. Remember that a direct object can be compound.

1. Born in Harlem, civil rights organizer Robert Moses earned two degrees in philosophy from Harvard.
2. Moses found employment and security as a mathematics teacher in a private school.
3. In 1961, Moses's conscience brought him to the South to work for civil rights.
4. Racial tension had turned parts of the South into ugly battlegrounds.
5. Despite federal law, African Americans still lacked many rights.
6. Moses's plan included mobilizing civil rights workers from the North.
7. His "educational summer project" in 1964 drew over a thousand college students southward.
8. They believed strongly that black voters should be educated and registered.
9. A newly formed Freedom Democratic Party sent 68 delegates to the 1964 Democratic National Convention.
10. These delegates achieved a major breakthrough in equal representation for African Americans in the voting process.

Writing Theme
Civil Rights

Robert Moses,
civil rights leader

The Parts of
a Sentence   **583**

Indirect Objects

An action verb can have an indirect object as well as a direct object. An **indirect object** is a word or group of words that tells *to whom, to what, for whom,* or *for what* the action expressed by the verb is performed. A sentence can have an indirect object only if it has a direct object. As you can see in the following sentences, the indirect object (I.O.) always comes before the direct object (D.O.).

> We told the *reporter* our *story.* (*Reporter* is the indirect object. It answers the question *to whom?*)
> Dad wrote the *airline* a *letter* of complaint. (*Airline,* the indirect object, answers the question *to what?*)

Notice that an indirect object is not preceded by the prepositions *to* or *for.* When a noun or pronoun is preceded by *to* or *for,* that noun or pronoun is the object of the preposition.

> Lee offered *Grant* his sword in surrender. (*Grant* is the indirect object.)
> Lee offered his sword in surrender to *Grant.* (*Grant* is the object of the preposition *to.*)

Sentence Diagraming For information on diagraming indirect objects, see page 860.

Practice Your Skills

CONCEPT CHECK

Identifying Complements Label three columns *Verb, Indirect Object,* and *Direct Object.* For each sentence, write the verb and any objects in the appropriate columns. Watch for compound verbs and objects.

1. Tobacco smoke can cause smokers and nonsmokers serious health problems.
2. Smoking can give people cancer and emphysema.
3. Laws in many states now deny users of cigarettes, cigars, and pipes the right to smoke in enclosed public places.
4. The breaking of such laws can cost offenders fines or jail terms.
5. Japanese leaders once handed smokers stiff prison sentences.
6. Many of the world's airlines now ban smoking or give nonsmokers special sections.
7. Many companies assign employees who smoke separate work areas.
8. New programs are teaching smokers habit-breaking techniques.
9. Concerned nonsmokers often offer smoking friends warnings and gentle reminders about their use of tobacco.
10. The Surgeon General has set us a goal of a smoke-free nation.

Objective Complements

An **objective complement** is a noun or an adjective that follows the direct object and identifies or describes that object. The objective complement can be compound. Only the following verbs and their synonyms take objective complements: *appoint, call, choose, consider, elect, find, make, keep, name, think.*

> The victory made the *players heroes.* (*Players* is the direct object; *heroes* is the objective complement.)
> The press called the *victory historic.* (*Victory* is the direct object; *historic* is the objective complement.)

Jesse Owens, winner of four gold medals in the 1936 Olympic Games in Berlin, Germany

Subject Complements

A **subject complement** is a noun, a pronoun, or an adjective that follows a linking verb, such as *be,* and identifies or describes the subject. Like an objective complement, a subject complement can be compound. (For information on linking verbs, see page 563.) There are two types of subject complements: *predicate nominatives* and *predicate adjectives.*

Predicate Nominatives A **predicate nominative** is one word or a group of words that follows a linking verb and renames, identifies, or refers to the subject of the sentence. Predicate nominatives are either **predicate nouns** or **predicate pronouns.**

> Those people are *refugees.* (predicate noun)
> This aisle seat is *mine.* (predicate pronoun)

Predicate Adjective A **predicate adjective** is an adjective that follows a linking verb and modifies the subject of a sentence.

Beth was *proud* yet *humble* when she accepted the award.

Sentence Diagraming For information on diagraming subject complements, see page 861.

Practice Your Skills

A. CONCEPT CHECK

Objective and Subject Complements Identify each italicized word as *Objective Complement, Predicate Nominative,* or *Predicate Adjective.*

1. Galileo Galilei was not the first *person* to use a telescope on the skies, but he was *clever* enough to see other practical applications for the invention.
2. The seaport of Venice was an unwalled *city*; thus, it was *vulnerable* to attack from the sea.
3. Venice's rulers thought Galileo's telescope an excellent warning *device*, and they made it an important *part* of the city's defense.
4. Galileo was somewhat *unethical*, though, in suggesting that he was the *inventor* of the telescope.
5. Galileo was *embarrassed* when Dutch telescopes arrived in Venice; the Venetian authorities, however, considered his scientific discoveries so *important* that they overlooked his claim.

B. APPLICATION IN WRITING

A Description Galileo's telescope penetrated the mysteries of the night sky. Write a paragraph describing the sky outside your window on a clear night. What feelings do the moon and stars evoke?

CHECK POINT
PAGES 578–586

Divide your paper into two columns. For each sentence, write its *complete subject* in one column and its *complete predicate* in the other. Underline and identify any *Indirect Object* (write *I.O.* above it), *Direct Object (D.O.), Objective Complement (O.C.),* or *Subject Complement (S.C.).*

1. Travel brochures give you a description of Kathmandu, Nepal, nestled in a soft green valley at the foot of the Himalayas.
2. Many foreign visitors consider this 1,200-year-old capital city of Nepal a modern-day Shangri-La.

Writing
TIP

Use various kinds of complements to add detail to your sentences.

3. Set on the banks of the Baghmati River, Kathmandu harbors both the best and the worst features of an ancient city.
4. The streets are noisy and thick with dust.
5. The city is friendly to residents and tourists, however.
6. Its large international hotels offer guests every possible modern comfort and convenience.
7. A foreigner can wander the narrow streets freely without fear.
8. People in this city of Hindu and Buddhist temples consider their statues gods but hang their laundry out to dry right beside them.
9. Kathmandu's people celebrate the changes of the seasons with colorful festivals.
10. During the autumn festival called Indra Jatra, the city's residents elect a young girl the representative of the goddess Dēvi.

AVOIDING SENTENCE FRAGMENTS

You know that a sentence must have both a subject and a verb and express a complete thought. A sentence fragment does not express a complete thought and often lacks a subject, verb, or both.

A sentence fragment is only part of a sentence.

In some fragments either the subject or the verb is missing.

Fragment	Summoned local farmers to battle. (Who or what summoned the farmers? The subject is missing.)
Sentence	*Sybil Ludington,* a colonial New York teenager, summoned local farmers to battle in 1777.
Fragment	Sybil, whose father commanded a regiment of colonial militia. (What did Sybil do? The verb is missing.)
Sentence	Sybil, whose father commanded a regiment of colonial militia, *sped* through the night on horseback and *called* the scattered farmers to duty.

In other fragments both the subject and all or part of the verb are missing.

Fragment	A British force on the march from Danbury. (Who did what to the British force? The subject and verb are missing.)
Sentence	The *regiment confronted* and *defeated* a British force on the march from Danbury.

The Parts of
a Sentence   **587**

Fragment	Praised by leaders of the Revolution for her gallant ride. (Who was praised? The subject and part of the verb are missing.)
Sentence	Young *Sybil was* praised by leaders of the Revolution for her gallant ride.

Sentence fragments can be the result of an incomplete thought or incorrect punctuation.

Fragments Resulting from Incomplete Thought

Sentence fragments can occur when your thoughts come faster than you can put them on paper. You may write a second thought before completing the first, or you may leave out an important part of a sentence. For example, you may intend to express the following complete thoughts:

> Eun Lee used several rolls of film at the carnival. After it had closed, he developed the film. The next day he sold ten of his photos to the *Telegraph*.

As your thoughts race ahead, however, you may write something like the following:

> Eun Lee used several rolls of film at the carnival. *After it had closed*. The next day he sold ten of the photos to the *Telegraph*.

This passage contains a confusing fragment: *After it had closed*. Readers may think you meant to say that Eun Lee took the pictures of the carnival after it had closed. Carefully proofread what you have written to eliminate such fragments.

Practice Your Skills

A. CONCEPT CHECK

Sentence Fragments On a piece of paper, write *Sentence* after the number of each complete sentence. Change each fragment to a sentence by adding or inserting words. Change punctuation where necessary.

1. Krakatoa, one of many Indonesian island volcanoes.
2. Towered more than 6,000 feet above the sea.
3. In 1883 a series of powerful eruptions shook the island.
4. During the summer of 1883 the volcanic activity.
5. On August 26 came the most violent eruption to date.
6. A black cloud of steam and ash 17 miles into the air.

Experienced writers occasionally use deliberate fragments to establish mood or create realistic dialogue. If you try this technique, be sure your meaning remains clear.

Writing Theme
Nature's Power

7. The climactic explosion occurred on August 27 at 10 A.M.
8. The sound of the blast was heard 2,000 miles away in Australia.
9. Vast amounts of dust and ash thrown 50 miles into the air and deposited over 300,000 square miles of territory.
10. Total darkness in the surrounding region for two and a half days.
11. Created spectacular sunsets throughout the world for a full year.
12. The foundations of the island collapsed as tons of supporting matter spewed into the air.
13. Causing a series of devastating tidal waves.
14. Just after the first great explosion, a wave 120 feet high hit the coastal towns of Java and Sumatra.
15. Almost 36,000 lives lost in that one great wave.

B. REVISION SKILL

Correcting Sentence Fragments Write a paragraph based on the sentences and fragments that follow. Add transitions and details as needed.

Floods were driving people from their homes. Ruined by water and mud. River mud through the doors and windows. Cleaning up afterward took great patience and courage. The lifework and savings of many completely gone, washed away in the floodwaters. Volunteers aid to many flood victims. Some buildings swept away in the raging floodwaters. A few residents thinking of starting over somewhere else. A new start right along the river edge. Flood control by replanting forests on the sides of the mountains.

The Parts of
a Sentence   **589**

Fragments Resulting from Incorrect Punctuation

A complete sentence begins with a capital letter and ends with a period, a question mark, or an exclamation point. The words between the capital letter and the end punctuation mark must express a complete thought. Many fragments are caused by the **period fault.** This fault occurs when writers insert end punctuation before they have finished writing a complete thought.

Fragment	Georgia O'Keeffe painted animal skulls. While living in New Mexico.
Sentence	Georgia O'Keeffe painted animal skulls while living in New Mexico.
Fragment	Although major crustal movements cause severe damage. Smaller earthquakes are hardly noticed.
Sentence	Although major crustal movements cause severe damage, smaller earthquakes are hardly noticed.

Practice Your Skills

A. CONCEPT CHECK

Sentence Fragments   Each of the following items contains a fragment error. Make each fragment part of the sentence by changing punctuation and capitalization.

1. When Andrew Jackson was elected President in 1828. A major turning point in American politics was reached.
2. Jackson's election signaled a shift in power. Away from wealthy property owners in highly organized parties.
3. Born on the Carolina frontier. Jackson was the first President from west of the Appalachians.
4. The son of poor Irish immigrants. He became an orphan at fourteen.
5. He and his brother were captured by the British. During the Revolutionary War.
6. Jackson later served as a justice of the State Supreme Court of Tennessee. And as a general in the War of 1812.
7. An impressive figure, tall, gaunt, and craggy. He was nicknamed "Old Hickory" by his followers because of his toughness.
8. During Jackson's presidency. Land opened in the West and a great westward movement began.
9. As a result of his strong reform actions. Andrew Jackson gained renown as a champion of the people.
10. This man from a poor background. Started a major reform movement that later became known as Jacksonian Democracy.

B. DRAFTING SKILL

Combining Sentences and Fragments Combine each sentence in Column A with a fragment from Column B. Make ten new sentences in all. Use appropriate punctuation and be sure your new sentences make sense.

Column A

1. Students gather in small groups.
2. They make last-minute promises and garner support.
3. The competition for votes is fierce.
4. This morning there was a disturbance.
5. A slate of candidates and their supporters staged a march.
6. They stomped through the halls.
7. The marchers dispersed quickly.
8. I confess I'd be surprised.
9. Advertising seems more important than substantial ideas.
10. School atmosphere can be a reflection.

Column B

a. Of the world at large.
b. Chanting slogans and waving signs.
c. Whispering urgently to each other.
d. If the entire slate weren't elected.
e. Among the candidates.
f. As the student elections draw nearer.
g. Right before Home Room.
h. Before the organizers were identified.
i. Even in high-school elections.
j. To rally voters to their cause.

C. PROOFREADING SKILL

Finding Sentence Fragments Rewrite the following passage, correcting all types of errors. Be alert to sentence fragments.

Although Abraham Lincoln had never held a prominent natonal office. He won the Republican nomanation for President. Leaders in the South had threatened that the southern states would secede from the Union. If northern voters elected Lincoln. Sixty percent of the people voted for Lincoln. He easily won election with 180 electoral votes. The southerners made good on there threat. Before Lincolns' inauguration as President on March 4 1861. South carolina and six other states of the South had left the Union and formed the Confederate States of America. The opening shots of the Civil War were fired. When troops of the Confederacy attacked fort Sumter.

Writers sometimes do not use an end mark to signal where one sentence ends and another begins. The result of this omission is a run-on sentence.

A run-on sentence is two or more sentences written as though they were one sentence.

Run-on   The doctor cut off the sleeve of my shirt then she cleaned the deep gash in my arm.

Correct   The doctor cut off the sleeve of my shirt. Then she cleaned the deep gash in my arm.

Comma Fault or Comma Splice

A **comma fault** or **comma splice** occurs when a writer joins two complete sentences with a comma instead of separating them with a correct end mark. The result is the most common type of run-on sentence.

Comma Fault   Debby arrived much too early, her new watch was running twenty minutes fast.

Correct   Debby arrived much too early. Her new watch was running twenty minutes fast.

Comma Fault   Where is the new tape player I left on the table, has someone taken it?

Correct   Where is the new tape player I left on the table? Has someone taken it?

Correcting Run-on Sentences All the sample run-on sentences were corrected by rewriting them as two separate sentences. At times, though, the two or more related ideas in a run-on sentence can be combined in one compound sentence. Three methods of combining ideas follow.

1. You can combine related ideas into one sentence by using a comma and a coordinating conjunction.

Run-on   Liz blurted out her opinion on the crime problem, she regretted it immediately.

Correct   Liz blurted out her opinion on the crime problem, *but* she regretted it immediately.

Writing
═TIP═

Using *and* too often to join clauses can make your writing seem childish. Vary your ways of joining clauses.

2. You can combine related ideas by using a semicolon. Notice that when a semicolon is used, no conjunction is needed.

Run-on Take public transportation, it saves gas.
Correct Take public transportation; it saves gas.

3. You can combine related ideas by using a semicolon and a conjunctive adverb followed by a comma.

Run-on The weather bureau has predicted severe thunderstorms, the space shot will have to be postponed.
Correct The weather bureau has predicted severe thunderstorms; *consequently,* the space shot will have to be postponed.

Notice that each correct sentence above is a compound sentence with two independent clauses.

Practice Your Skills

A. DRAFTING SKILL

Eliminating Run-on Sentences   Complete each sentence by adding an independent clause beginning with the word(s) in parentheses. Use semicolons and commas where necessary.

1. Television is one of our most important means of communication. (however)
2. It can cover events anywhere in the world. (for instance)
3. Television cameras have even gone into space with the astronauts. (and)

In 1960, television played an important role in the debate between Richard M. Nixon and John F. Kennedy.

The Parts of
a Sentence   **593**

4. More than 98 percent of all homes in the United States have at least one television set. (furthermore)
5. Most American TV programs are meant for entertainment. (but)
6. Research shows that on average a television set is in use in each home for seven hours a day. (as a result)
7. Television advertising is a billion-dollar industry. (and)
8. Television is becoming increasingly important in political campaigns. (therefore)
9. Political advertising on TV has been the subject of criticism. (consequently)
10. Critics say that political ads are too often negative and unfair. (but)

B. REVISION SKILL

Correcting Run-on Sentences   Correct each run-on sentence below, using one of the following methods: (1) a period and a capital letter, (2) a semicolon alone, (3) a comma and a coordinating conjunction, or (4) a semicolon and the conjunctive adverb *however, nevertheless,* or *therefore* followed by a comma.

1. It's a stormy Saturday night in winter, it's a perfect time to read a mystery story.
2. The invention of the detective story is credited to Poe many of its leading practitioners today are women.
3. Perhaps the most famous mystery writer of all is Dame Agatha Christie, her complex puzzlers have entertained millions of readers.
4. Christie's fictional sleuth Hercule Poirot is always confronted by any number of colorful suspects he manages to solve "locked-room" mysteries.
5. Countless readers are fiercely devoted to the exploits of Poirot others revere Christie's Miss Marple.
6. Miss Marple lives a quiet country life, somehow she always finds herself involved in solving some serious crime.
7. Dorothy L. Sayers is one of Agatha Christie's many literary heirs, Sayers's Lord Peter Wimsey mysteries have been dramatized on television.
8. Some American mystery writers have created tough detectives in gritty settings these hard-boiled characters have often found their detective work entangled with a love interest.
9. Once this species of detective was uniformly male, now writers such as Sara Paretsky have added memorable hard-boiled females to their ranks.
10. So on the next stormy, wintry night, choose the detective you most admire and settle in for a suspenseful evening of reading can you beat the sleuth to the solution?

A scene from the movie *Death on the Nile,* by Agatha Christie

Revise the following fragments and run-ons to make them complete sentences. If the statement is complete, write *Correct.*

1. American states all have mottoes, many people in a state may not understand the meaning of the motto.
2. One example, California.
3. Some people know that the state's motto is *Eureka* they do not know what *Eureka* means.
4. Some of them may even come from Eureka, California. Without knowing the meaning of their town's name.
5. *Eureka* is Greek, it means "I have found it."
6. Why did California's legislators vote to adopt *Eureka* as their state's motto?
7. There is a story about Archimedes, the ancient Greek mathematician, he discovered the principle of specific gravity.
8. The story is that Archimedes sat down in the bathtub one day the water overflowed onto the floor.
9. He startled his neighbors. By running down the street dripping wet, shouting, "Eureka!"
10. He had come to a startling realization about the volume of a solid, irregularly shaped object. Such as his own body.
11. Could be determined by measuring the volume of water that it displaced.
12. It is, of course, much easier to measure water than to measure a Greek mathematician.
13. *Eureka* has come to be used in many situations. In which someone discovers something remarkable.
14. The early history of California full of such remarkable discoveries.
15. Probably the one the legislators had in mind was the discovery of gold in the California hills.
16. That event changed the state's history forever, California never looked back.
17. Of course, California is not the only state. That has taken its motto from the wisdom of the ancient Greeks or Romans.
18. Oklahoma's motto, *Labor omnia vincit,* is Latin it means "Labor conquers all things."
19. The motto of North Carolina is *Esse quam videri,* or "To be, rather than to seem," this means that all of us should be more concerned with what we really are than with what other people think we are.
20. The Latin motto of Arkansas sums up the concept of democracy. In the words *Regnat populus*, or "The people rule."

The Parts of
a Sentence

595

GRAMMAR
HANDBOOK

31

Writing Theme
Following Convictions

A. Writing Different Kinds of Sentences Identify each sentence as *Declarative, Interrogative, Imperative,* or *Exclamatory.* Then rewrite the sentence as the type named in parentheses. Change wording as needed. Use correct punctuation.

1. Whew, the streets of this city are like a furnace in August! (Declarative)
2. Will you please turn up the air conditioner? (Imperative)
3. I don't know how we'd survive these dog days of summer without one. (Interrogative)
4. Look at those children playing in the street. (Interrogative)
5. What a brazen thing they're doing, opening the fire hydrant like that! (Declarative)
6. It's a disgrace that they're allowed to do that. (Exclamatory)
7. Why don't you call in a complaint? (Imperative)
8. At least lean out the dining room window and ask the children to stop. (Interrogative)
9. Don't they look as if they're having a good time out there? (Declarative)
10. It won't do any real harm to let them cool off—just this once. (Exclamatory)

B. Identifying Complements Copy the following literary passage. Underline all complements. Identify each complement by writing one of the following above it: *D.O. (Direct Object), I.O. (Indirect Object), O.C. (Objective Complement), P.N. (Predicate Nominative), P.A. (Predicate Adjective).* Some types of complements appear more frequently than others.

(1) Children are naturally active and somewhat materialistic, but they are not incurably purposeful. (2) Their activity has a fanciful quality and is harmless although often destructive to property.

(3) We teach our child many things I don't believe in, and almost nothing I do believe in. . . . (4) We teach cleanliness, sanitation, hygiene; but I am suspicious of these practices. (5) A child who believes that every scratch needs to be painted with iodine has lost a certain grip on life which he may never regain, and has acquired a frailty of spirit which may unfit him for living. (6) The sterile bandage is the flag of modern society, but I notice more and more of them are needed all the time, so terrible are the wars.

(7) We teach our child manners, but the only good manners are those which take shape somewhat instinctively, from a feeling of kinship with, or admiration for, other people who are

behaving in a gentle fashion. (8) Manners are a game which adults play among themselves and with children to make life easier for themselves, but frequently they do not make life easier but harder.
E.B. White, *One Man's Meat*

C. Correcting Fragments   Rewrite the following paragraph. Correct all fragments by joining them to complete sentences.

On a memorable day in a recent October. Naomi Thompson Clinton of Columbia, South Carolina, acted with great courage. To save the life of Harold Martin. A truck driver. Martin's tractor-trailer collided with another truck. Carrying drums of gasoline. Several of the drums rolled onto the highway. Bursting into flames. Martin was thrown from his truck into the fire. Instantly, Clinton rushed to his aid. Dragging him out of the inferno. And smothering the flames on his clothing. By risking her own life. She was able to save the life of the imperiled truck driver. Martin was taken to the hospital. With only minor burns and injuries. In recognition of her courageous action, Clinton received a medal. From the Carnegie Hero Fund Commission.

D. Correcting Run-on Sentences   Rewrite each of these run-ons as two sentences, or use any method discussed on pages 592–593.

1. Abraham Lincoln was bitterly opposed to the institution of slavery, his opinions on the subject were clear and forceful.
2. He spoke against the "monstrous injustice of slavery," he felt it made the American republic hypocritical.
3. Lincoln recalled a trip along the Ohio River the sight of slaves chained together on the shore had deeply disturbed him.
4. Lincoln the human being hated slavery Lincoln the President was at first reluctant to oppose it officially.
5. He feared that an abolitionist stance might antagonize the border slave states, they might secede from the Union.
6. However, on January 1, 1863, he issued the Emancipation Proclamation it declared all slaves in the Confederacy free.
7. Lincoln's proclamation applied to the Confederate states the loyal slave states were not affected.
8. It directly freed fewer than 200,000 slaves however, during the war it was of enormous symbolic value.
9. The proclamation inspired the Thirteenth Amendment, Lincoln did not live to see its ratification.
10. Lincoln was shot to death in 1865 his assassin was John Wilkes Booth, a Confederate sympathizer.

The Parts of
a Sentence   **597**

On the Lightside

COLORFUL ENGLISH

Since the founding of our country, the names of colors have brightened the colloquial expressions of each generation of Americans. Take *greenhorn,* for example.

Radioactive Cats, by Sandy Skoglund

Originally, the word—spelled *greynhorne*—referred to an animal with immature horns, which were susceptible to a particular fungus that gave them a greenish cast. The term later came to mean "an inexperienced and often gullible person" and was used to refer to a new immigrant who was not familiar with the local ways.

Today *pink* has widely varying meanings. For example, the term can suggest perfect health, as in "You're in the pink." Also, because the international Communist movement is associated with the color red, pink can mean a political radical with communist sympathies.

Over time an expression may acquire new and unrelated meanings. Consider the different meanings of *red-eye.* The term has long referred to thick ham gravy. In addition, in both world wars, members of the U.S. armed forces used the word *red-eye* for ketchup. Now a person can refer to "catching the red-eye," a cross country flight that leaves one coast late at night and arrives at the other early in the morning. The expression was inspired, no doubt, by the appearance of the sleepless passengers.

Phrases and Clauses

PREPOSITIONAL PHRASES

A phrase is a group of related words that does not contain a verb and its subject. A phrase functions as a single part of speech.

A prepositional phrase consists of a preposition, its object, and any modifiers of the object. A prepositional phrase acts as a modifier in a sentence.

> The dog squeezed *under the low wooden fence*. (The prepositional phrase acts as an adverb modifying the verb *squeezed*.)

The object of a preposition is always a noun, a pronoun, or a word or group of words used as a noun.

> Kevin relieved the tension by *laughing*. (*Laughing* is a verb form acting as a noun. *Laughing* is the object of *by*.)
> Give the tickets to *whoever wants them*. (*Whoever wants them* is a noun clause. It is the object of *to*.)

The object of a preposition is sometimes compound. The parts of a compound object are joined by a conjunction.

> The allied forces repelled the invaders with *guns and bayonets*.

A sentence can include more than one prepositional phrase.

> The *Concorde* cruises *at twice the speed of sound*.

Sometimes two or more prepositional phrases can modify the same word.

> We arrived *at the hotel in the morning*.

At other times, one prepositional phrase modifies the object of the prepositional phrase that comes before it.

> I especially like the painting *of the sunflowers in the blue vase*.

Adjective Phrases

When a prepositional phrase modifies a noun or a pronoun, it acts as an adjective and is called an **adjective phrase.**

Writing
——TIP——
Using prepositional phrases is one way to add detail to your writing.

An adjective phrase usually comes directly after the noun or the pronoun it modifies.

> The quarrel *between Joe and him* became heated. (modifying a noun)
> Anyone *with a pass* may board now. (modifying a pronoun)

Adverb Phrases

When a prepositional phrase modifies a verb, an adjective, or an adverb, it acts as an adverb and is called an **adverb phrase.** An adverb phrase that modifies a verb can appear anywhere in a sentence. If an adverb phrase modifies an adjective or another adverb, it usually appears near the word it modifies.

> *On Tuesdays,* Ted has band practice. (modifying a verb)
>
> Myra was extraordinarily lucky *in her stock-market investments.* (modifying an adjective)
>
> I telephoned Alys soon *after her graduation day.* (modifying another adverb)

Sentence Diagraming   For information on diagraming prepositional phrases, see page 862.

To review the use of commas with prepositional phrases, see Handbook 38, page 786.

Practice Your Skills

CONCEPT CHECK

Prepositional Phrases Rewrite these sentences. Then underline each prepositional phrase and identify it as an *Adjective Phrase* or an *Adverb Phrase.*

1. Three years ago, the Kearny dump, with its ten tons of garbage, was closed to landfill use.
2. The 110-foot mound of New Jersey garbage now plays host to grasshoppers, field mice, and other insects and small rodents.
3. Soon, those fifty-seven acres of garbage in the Hackensack Meadowlands will become a work of art.
4. Artist Nancy Holt and a team of landscape architects will supervise this unusual transformation of a common landfill into Sky Mound.
5. The result of their work will be a modern version of Stonehenge.
6. Huge steel structures will align with the sun, moon, and stars as a frame for solstices and equinoxes.

7. Features of Sky Mound will include grassy knolls, gravel paths, and a pond stocked with fish.
8. In one year, over 100 million commuters will get a good view of Sky Mound from highways and commuter trains.
9. Development of the site into a wildlife refuge and a methane-recovery system is a by-product of the Sky Mound project.
10. Before long, raccoons, cottontail rabbits, grasshoppers, and field mice will be breeding in the wildlife refuge.

APPOSITIVES AND APPOSITIVE PHRASES

An appositive is a noun or a pronoun that is usually placed immediately after another word in a sentence to identify it or to provide more information about it.

The poet *Nikki Giovanni* explained her writing techniques.
Dr. Barnard, *the surgeon,* will speak to you in a few minutes.

The appositive and its modifiers form an **appositive phrase.** The modifier of an appositive may be a single word, a phrase, or a clause.

The queen presented the trophy, *a tall silver cup with ornate handles.* (The noun *cup* is the appositive that identifies *trophy.* The adjectives *tall* and *silver* and the adjective phrase *with ornate handles* modify the appositive *cup.*)

Appositives occasionally precede the noun or pronoun to which they refer.

A strong runner, Mai Li is expected to win the 500-meter race tomorrow afternoon.

Appositives and appositive phrases can be essential or nonessential. **Essential appositives** are needed to make the meaning clear.

The writer *J. D. Salinger* has led a very secluded life. (Without the appositive, the intended meaning will not be clear.)

Nonessential appositives add extra meaning to a sentence in which the meaning is already clear.

Lord Tennyson, *a poet laureate of Great Britain,* is buried in the Poet's Corner of Westminster Abbey.

Writing
TIP

Set off a nonessential appositive with commas; do not use commas with an essential appositive.

Whether an appositive is essential or nonessential is sometimes determined by particular circumstances. Compare these sentences.

Our son Mike is a senior in high school. (essential)
Our son, Mike, is a senior in high school. (nonessential)

In the first sentence, the appositive is essential because Mike has a brother; in the second sentence, Mike is the only son.

Sentence Diagraming   For information on diagraming appositives and appositive phrases, see page 864.

Practice Your Skills

CONCEPT CHECK

Appositives and Appositive Phrases   Write the following sentences and underline all the appositive structures. If an appositive is a literary title, underscore only once. Add commas as needed.

1. The years from 1945 to 1951 the post-World War II era were significant in the growth of the American theater.
2. Some of the most respected plays of Eugene O'Neill, Tennessee Williams, and Arthur Miller American theater giants opened on the Broadway stage.
3. During this brief time span, Arthur Miller had two major successes *Death of a Salesman* and *All My Sons*.
4. The themes of Miller's plays issues of human responsibility appealed strongly to the American public.
5. The Eugene O'Neill play *The Iceman Cometh* opened to great critical acclaim.

Scene from the movie
A Street Car Named Desire, by Tennessee Williams

602 Grammar Handbook

6. Tennessee Williams a most prolific and poetic writer contributed *A Streetcar Named Desire* and *The Glass Menagerie.*
7. These well-established playwrights were joined by important newcomers such as Carson McCullers author of *The Member of the Wedding.*
8. The legendary actors Marlon Brando, Rex Harrison, and Jessica Tandy also appeared on Broadway during this period.
9. In these years a happier time than America had known for decades the musical theater flourished.
10. Consequently, this time a brief half-dozen years reflected growth in the American theater that has never been surpassed.

VERBALS AND VERBAL PHRASES

A **verbal** is a verb form that functions in a sentence as a noun, an adjective, or an adverb. A verbal, its modifiers, and its complements form a **verbal phrase.**

Verb Forms	The leaves *are trembling* in the wind.
	The butter *has melted.*
Verbals	*Trembling* is a perfectly normal, instinctive reaction to fear.
	We stepped over the puddles that had formed from the *melted* ice.
Verbal Phrases	*Trembling in terror,* the children ran from the house.
	We gazed sadly at our snowman, *melted by the hot sun.*

In this part of the lesson, you will learn about the three kinds of verbals and verbal phrases: *infinitives, participles,* and *gerunds.*

Infinitives and Infinitive Phrases

An **infinitive is a verb form made up of the word *to* and the base form of a verb. An infinitive functions as a noun, an adjective, or an adverb.**

Noun	*To fly* was Amelia Earhart's ambition. (subject)
	She loved *to fly.* (direct object)
	Her lifelong dream was *to fly.* (predicate nominative)

Adjective	Laurence Richardson is the man *to contact.* (modifies the noun *man*)
Adverb	The entire high school band turned *to watch.* (modifies the verb *turned*)
	The midnight movie was scary *to watch.* (modifies the adjective *scary*)
	The sun goes down too quickly *to watch.* (modifies the adverb *quickly*)

Sometimes forms of the infinitive can include one or more auxiliary verbs.

> Miguel was relieved *to have arrived.*
> Pat was angry *to have been tricked.*

At times, an infinitive does not begin with the word *to.*

> Will you help us *move?* (Will you help us *to move?*)
> They did not dare *leave.* (They did not dare *to leave.*)

An infinitive, its modifiers, and its complements form an infinitive phrase.

When the subject of an infinitive phrase is a pronoun, the pronoun must be in the objective case.

> We planned for *Kayla to follow later.*
> We planned for *her to follow later.*

Sometimes the subject of an infinitive phrase follows a verb directly. Do not mistake the subject of the phrase for the direct object of the verb. In such a case, the entire infinitive phrase functions as the direct object.

> The landlord thought *us completely to blame.*

Since the infinitive in an infinitive phrase is a verb form, it can be modified by adverbs and adverb phrases.

> The doctor needed *to work quickly.* (The adverb *quickly* modifies the infinitive *to work.*)
> The rescue-team volunteers began *to dig with all their might.* (The adverb phrase *with all their might* modifies the infinitive *to dig.*)

Like other verb forms, the infinitive in an infinitive phrase can have complements.

> Suzanne intended *to give you the keys.* (*You* is the indirect object of the infinitive *to give,* and *keys* is the direct object.)

Anita's greatest desire was *to be captain.* (*Captain* is a predicate nominative after *to be.*)

Alex knows how *to appear confident.* (*Confident* is a predicate adjective after *to appear.*)

An infinitive phrase, like an infinitive, can act as a noun, an adjective, or an adverb.

Noun	*To save lives* is a paramedic's chief duty. (subject)
Adjective	That is not the way *to settle an argument.*
Adverb	Joan worked long hours *to earn her college tuition.*

Experienced writers do not usually insert words between *to* and the verb. This creates a **split infinitive,** a form that is generally awkward.

Awkward	Wise consumers try *to promptly pay their bills.*
Better	Wise consumers try *to pay their bills promptly.*

Usage Note Although strict grammarians may object to split infinitives, some sentences sound better when *to* and the verb are separated by the modifier: The coach tried *to* really *understand* her players.

Sentence Diagraming For information on diagraming infinitives and infinitive phrases, see page 864.

Practice Your Skills

A. CONCEPT CHECK

Infinitive Phrases Write the following sentences and underline the infinitive or the infinitive phrase in each sentence.

Writing Theme
The Thought Process

1. Most people know that in moments a computer can solve problems that a human would take years to solve.
2. Indeed, to make certain mathematical computations was impossible before the development of computers.
3. However, people often do not realize that there are many mental tasks a computer can't begin to do.
4. In fact, some things that a child can do quickly would take the fastest computer several days to complete.
5. To understand the difference between human thought and computer "thinking," one must understand algorithms.
6. An algorithm is, quite simply, a method used to solve a problem.
7. To work on a problem, a computer always needs a method; it can't accomplish anything without one.
8. Humans, however, try to work things out by using trial and error.

9. The way this trial and error process works to narrow options quickly is one of the mysterious aspects of human intelligence.
10. A computer might need to try millions of solutions to a problem that a human brain could solve after a dozen trials.

B. APPLICATION IN LITERATURE

Infinitives   Write the infinitives or infinitive phrases in each of the following quotations. Then write *Noun, Adjective,* or *Adverb* to show how each infinitive or infinitive phrase is used.

1. As a species, we have everything in the world to learn about living.
   Lewis Thomas
2. To err is human, to forgive divine.   **Alexander Pope**
3. Oh! they're too beautiful to live, much too beautiful!
   Charles Dickens
4. To have great poets, there must be great audiences, too.
   Walt Whitman
5. To endure is greater than to dare; to tire out hostile fortune; to be daunted by no difficulty; to keep heart when all have lost it; to go through intrigue spotless; to forgo even ambition when the end is gained—who can say this is not greatness?
   William Makepeace Thackeray
6. The truth is found when men are free to pursue it.
   Franklin D. Roosevelt
7. A story with a moral appended is like the bill of a mosquito. It bores you, and then injects a stinging drop to irritate your conscience.   **O. Henry**
8. Let sleeping dogs lie—who wants to rouse 'em?   **Charles Dickens**
9. To be, or not to be: that is the question.   **William Shakespeare**
10. Fortunately, [psychoanalysis] is not the only way to resolve inner conflicts. Life itself remains a very effective therapist.
    Karen Horney, M.D.

C. PROOFREADING SKILL

Correcting Phrases   Rewrite the following passage, correcting any spelling, punctuation, and capitalization errors. Pay special attention to split infinitives and to essential and nonessential appositives.

> "Computer compulsives" people who love to work with computers at home or at work often feel impatient with the slower pace of real life. Psicologists have found computer compulsives to be intolerant of others behavior—behavior that is uncertain, off the subject, or irrelevant. These computer lovers

don't seem able to comfortably accept any answers other than *yes* or *no* from those around them their family or friends. Computer compulsives seem to always want eficient communication that is simply and immediately clear and to communicate with other computer literates people who are also madly in love with these machines. One psicologist reports that such computer compulsives are likely to usually ignore or avoid people who talk to slowly or in general terms. Computer compulsives interest is less in communicating than in "interfacing" interacting to give and recieve information.

Participles and Participial Phrases

A participle that functions as an adjective is another type of verbal.

There are two forms of the participle: the **present participle** (*taking*) and the **past participle** (*taken*). The past participle can be used with auxiliary verbs, as in *having taken, being taken,* and *having been taken.*

Modifying a Noun	The *grinning* Cheshire cat gazed down at Alice.
	Having been reelected, the President could again devote his energy to governing the country.
Modifying a Pronoun	*Stumbling,* he just managed to save himself from a fall during the last seconds of the game.

Present participles and past participles are often used with auxiliary verbs to form verb phrases. Do not mistake the participle in a verb phrase, which is a verb, for the participle used as an adjective, which is a verbal.

Verb	Our flight has been *canceled.*
Verbal	We missed our *canceled* magazine subscriptions.

A participial phrase consists of a participle, its modifiers, and its complements.

A participle can be modified by an adverb or an adverb phrase.

> *Swimming strongly against the current,* Sherry finally reached the shore. (The participle *swimming* is modified by both the adverb *strongly* and the adverb phrase *against the current.*)

Because a participle is a verb form, it may have complements.

> *Having rejected his first plan,* Jonathan began work on another one. (In the participial phrase, *plan* is the direct object of the participle *having rejected.*)

Writing
━TIP━

Use a comma after a participial phrase that comes at the beginning of a sentence.

Writing
——**TIP**——
Set off a nones-
sential partici-
pial phrase with
commas. No com-
mas are used with
essential parti-
cipial phrases.

Participial phrases, like appositive phrases, are either essential or nonessential. An **essential participial phrase** is one that must be included to make the intended meaning of a sentence clear. A **nonessential participial phrase** is one that adds additional information to a sentence in which the meaning is already clear.

Essential   Those people *sitting around the large conference table* are the ambassadors from the Central American countries. (The participial phrase explains exactly *which* people are meant.)

Nonessential   The ambassadors, *sitting around a large conference table,* discussed the crisis. (The participial phrase provides information that is not needed to make the intended meaning clear.)

Sentence Diagraming   For information on diagraming participles and participial phrases, see page 863.

Practice Your Skills

CONCEPT CHECK

Participles and Participial Phrases   Rewrite each of these sentences, underlining the participle or participial phrase in each. Then write the noun or pronoun the participle or participial phrase modifies. Add commas if necessary.

1. Safety in the workplace is usually associated with industry, but the painting profession carries its share of occupational hazards.

Bullfight in a Divided Ring, by Francisco de Goya (c. 1810–1812)

2. Lead and other compounds used in paints have long posed a threat to the working artist.
3. For example, having studied the life of Francisco de Goya carefully, experts have concluded that he suffered from illnesses related to his work.
4. Striking suddenly and leaving him partially blind and deaf, Goya's illness was a mystery at the time.
5. The ailing painter was forced to stop work for two years.
6. Reduced exposure to paints alleviated the symptoms.
7. Studies of Goya's working habits indicate that he used enormous amounts of lead white and a mercury compound.
8. In addition, the grinding process he used to produce his own pigments added to the toxic lead levels.
9. Looking at the evidence in the light of today's medical knowledge, historians of both art and medicine believe that Goya suffered extensive nerve damage from his work materials.
10. They also believe that this damage was a major factor in the changing mood and character of his painting.

Gerunds and Gerund Phrases

The gerund is a verb form that ends in *-ing* and always acts as a noun.

A gerund can be a subject, an object, a predicate nominative, or an appositive.

Subject	*Swimming* is good exercise.
Direct Object	Maria does not enjoy *cooking*.
Predicate Nominative	His chief job is *painting*.
Appositive	The winter sports *skiing* and *skating* are enjoyed by many Canadians.

A gerund phrase consists of a gerund with its modifiers and complements.

Because it is a verb form, the gerund in a gerund phrase can be modified by adverbs, adverb phrases, or both.

> *Working steadily through the night* enabled the technician to restore phone service. (The adverb *steadily* and the adverb phrase *through the night* modify the gerund *working*.)

Because a gerund functions as a noun, it can be modified by an adjective or an adjective phrase. A single adjective usually appears before the gerund. An adjective phrase often follows the gerund. Note the position of modifiers on the following page.

Quick thinking by the world leaders prevented a dangerous crisis. (In the gerund phrase, the adjective *Quick* and the adjective phrase *by the world leaders* both modify the gerund *thinking*.)

Since the gerund is a verb form, it can have complements of various types, such as direct objects, indirect objects, predicate nominatives, and predicate adjectives.

Giving Jerry the tickets created the confusion. (In the gerund phrase, *Jerry* is the indirect object of the gerund *giving,* and *tickets* is the direct object.)

Becoming an astrophysicist fulfilled Angela's dream. (*Astrophysicist* is a predicate nominative after the gerund *becoming*.)

Lee tried to keep from *appearing nervous.* (*Nervous* is a predicate adjective following the gerund *appearing*.)

Like a gerund alone, a gerund phrase always acts as a noun.

Subject	*Talking in the theater* is rude.
Predicate Nominative	Clare's hobby is *restoring antique cars.*
Object of a Preposition	By *paddling hard,* the canoeist managed to avoid the falls.
Appositive	His biggest shortcoming, *always being late,* got him into trouble.

Sentence Diagraming For information on diagraming gerunds and gerund phrases, see page 863.

Practice Your Skills

A. CONCEPT CHECK

Gerund Phrases Write the gerund or gerund phrase in the following sentences.

1. Retelling the legend of Billy the Kid is a favorite occupation for writers of stories, novels, and films.
2. Behind all the killing, everyone seems to believe, there must surely be a human drama of pathos and dignity.
3. As a result, most writing about the events of his life has been highly romanticized.
4. Born William Henry McCarthy in Manhattan, Billy began living a life of crime at the age of twelve.
5. He fell in with a gang of troublemakers whose major activities in the Southwest were shooting and cattle rustling.
6. It wasn't long before killing became a habit with Billy.

7. He was credited with shooting more than twenty men.
8. Remarkably, people back East in the cities loved reading about the small young man with the fast gun.
9. Portraying Billy as the "Robin Hood" of the frontier became common with dime-novel authors of the day.
10. By covering his exploits with glamour, writers turned the story of a vicious murderer into a Wild West legend.

B. REVISION SKILL

Revising Awkward Structures Rewrite the following sentences by replacing the italicized word or phrase with a gerund or gerund phrase to improve the sentences. Use the hints in parentheses.

Example   *To whitewash the Old West* and romanticizing its heroes is a process that has gone on for years. (subject of the sentence)

Revision   Whitewashing the Old West and romanticizing its heroes is a process that has gone on for years.

1. Writers have worked hard at creating a myth and *to present the Old West in a romantic light.* (object of the preposition *at*)
2. *The history of the Old West when you read it* often gives the impression of a beautiful wilderness settled by proud, rugged pioneers. (subject of the sentence)
3. If films were accurate, only one ability, *to work with determination,* enabled European men to settle the West. (appositive)
4. *To ignore* African Americans, women, Hispanics, and Asian Americans was common. (subject of the sentence)
5. Later, American attitudes started changing and slowly *reflect* the absence of bias. (compound direct object)
6. Today, some historians charge one man *who created that false picture.* (object of the preposition *with*)
7. In the 1800's, a single essay by Frederick Jackson Turner, in which he depicted brave, independent men transforming a wilderness into an American paradise, may have been the *point at which the distortion began.* (predicate nominative)
8. Turner largely ignored the enormous role of women *who opened the frontier to settlement.* (object of the preposition *in*)
9. Furthermore, *the term frontier, when you define it* as "the meeting point between savagery and civilization," as Turner did, was a gross insult to Native Americans. (subject of the sentence)
10. *That we blame* one man for a century of myth and fiction is probably unfair, but Turner's essay did greatly influence the literature that followed. (subject of the sentence)

C. APPLICATION IN WRITING

A Tall Tale Exaggeration also plays a part in the literature of the West. Invent a hero or a heroine and write a tall tale about his or her western adventures. Use gerunds to tell about the character's remarkable abilities, such as roping or riding.

USING PHRASES CORRECTLY

Careful use of phrases is essential to good, clear writing. It should always be obvious to the reader what word is being modified, and the modifying phrase should always appear as close as possible to that word.

Misplaced Modifiers

Sometimes modifiers cause confusion because they are awkwardly placed in a sentence. If a phrase seems to modify the wrong word, it is called a **misplaced modifier.**

Misplaced *Turning plump and red,* the gardener watched his tomatoes. (The participial phrase *turning plump and red* seems to modify *gardener.*)

Clear The gardener watched his tomatoes *turning plump and red.* (The participial phrase *turning plump and red* clearly modifies *tomatoes.*)

612 Grammar Handbook

Misplaced	Melting snow caused floods *from the mountains* that covered the valley. (The prepositional phrase *from the mountains* seems to modify *floods*.)
Clear	Melting snow *from the mountains* caused floods that covered the valley. (The prepositional phrase *from the mountains* clearly modifies *snow*.)
Misplaced	*Charging up the hill,* the words "Remember the *Maine!*" were shouted by the Rough Riders. (The participial phrase *charging up the hill* seems to modify *words*.)
Clear	*Charging up the hill,* the Rough Riders shouted the words, "Remember the *Maine!*" (The participial phrase clearly modifies *Rough Riders*.)

Dangling Modifiers

Sometimes a phrase does not seem to be logically related to any word in a sentence. Such a phrase is called a **dangling modifier** because it "hangs loosely" without an apparent connection to the sentence. Dangling modifiers may be prepositional phrases, participles or participial phrases, or infinitives or infinitive phrases.

In order to correct a dangling modifier, you need to supply the word being modified. Notice how supplying the missing word being modified clarifies the meaning of the following sentences.

Dangling	*Laughing with jubilation,* the last final exam was finished. (The modifier is dangling. The word being modified is missing.)
Clear	*Laughing with jubilation,* the class finished the last final exam. (Adding the word *class* to the sentence makes the meaning clear.)
Dangling	*Standing at the summit of the mountain,* the view was spectacular. (The participle is dangling. The word being modified is missing.)
Clear	*Standing at the summit of the mountain,* the hikers admired the spectacular view. (Adding *the hikers* makes the meaning clear.)
Dangling	*To ascend the thirty-foot granite chimney,* skill, daring, and reliable equipment are needed. (The word being modified is missing.)
Clear	*To ascend the thirty-foot granite chimney,* the climbers needed skill, daring, and reliable equipment. (Adding *the climbers* makes the meaning clear.)

Absolute Phrases An absolute phrase contains a noun modified by a participle. An absolute phrase has no grammatical connection with the rest of the sentence in which it occurs and does not function as any part of speech. Sometimes, however, an absolute phrase relates to the rest of the sentence by indicating circumstance, reason, or time, as shown in the following examples.

Circumstance	*Their throats parched,* the lost travelers wandered aimlessly in the scorching desert heat.
	The defendant angrily denied the charges, *his dark eyes flashing.*
Reason	*Our business finished,* everyone shook hands with one another.
	The post office having closed early, Dominique looked around for a mailbox.
Time	*The day's work done,* I turned out the light and started my long trip home.
	The gypsy moths having left at last, Carlos surveyed the denuded forest.

Since an absolute phrase does not modify a word in another part of the sentence, it cannot be misplaced or dangling.

Practice Your Skills

A. CONCEPT CHECK

Misplaced and Dangling Modifiers Rewrite the following sentences, eliminating misplaced and dangling modifiers. If a sentence is correct and contains an absolute phrase, write *Absolute*.

1. Without ever visiting the islands, a few words of Hawaiian are familiar to most people.
2. Words such as *aloha* have entered the English language and even can be found in English dictionaries over the years.
3. Classified as a Polynesian language, missionaries in the nineteenth century were the first to compile dictionaries of Hawaiian.
4. The language never before recorded in writing, Hawaiian children had learned about their history and culture only through the spoken word.
5. Passing stories from generation to generation, a rich oral tradition had been maintained.
6. In order to convert the people, the language was written down by the missionaries.
7. To record the sounds of the Hawaiian language in writing, the Roman alphabet was used.

8. The language now having been recorded, the missionaries used both English and Hawaiian to convert the people to Christianity.
9. Known at the time as the Sandwich Islands, daily life was quickly changed by these Western influences.
10. Struggling for control, the islands were fought over by many foreign countries.
11. The islands in the middle of the nineteenth century came under U.S. control.
12. The Department of Public Instruction in all schools outlawed the use of the Hawaiian language.
13. Ordering the use of English, teachers and students were prohibited from speaking Hawaiian, even on the playgrounds.
14. Recognizing the futility of restricting the use of Hawaiian, the law was repealed in 1986.
15. To learn the Hawaiian language, a few schools have established programs for children.

B. PROOFREADING SKILL

Misplaced and Dangling Modifiers Rewrite the following paragraph, eliminating all misplaced or dangling modifiers. Also correct all spelling, punctuation, and capitalization errors.

American English is rapidly becoming a popular language in most parts of the World, used for conducting business in this high-tech age. Motivated by the flexibility of American English, the language spoken in the United States is used by people everywhere to some extent. The words *hi* and *OK* mean the same in Taiwan, Italy, and Brazil as they do in Iowa and north Carolina. Sometimes when American English becomes commonly used abroad, meanings, pronunciations, and grammatical usage change drastically. For example, the word *salvage* means "to save" in the United States, but in the Philipines it means "to execut someone." The invitation "Let's hiking," although ungrammatical in American english, is fine in Japan Sometimes American English words and expressions are simply borrowed. Visiting a business office in Germany, for example, *Der Boss* for *the boss* might be heard. Some of our foreign friends are not eager to accept American English words and phrases, or Anglicisms, into their countrys vocabulary. the French Academy, guardian of pure french, objects to the invasion of such phrases as *le weekend* and *le shopping* as substitutes for the french equivalents. Thinking about the impact of American English abroad, the language will continue to serve the needs of international business and industry.

A. Write the phrase or phrases in each of the following sentences. Tell whether each is an *Appositive Phrase,* an *Infinitive Phrase,* a *Prepositional Phrase,* a *Gerund Phrase,* or a *Participial Phrase.* Keep in mind that a prepositional phrase may be part of a verbal.

1. Dancing as a cultural activity probably started with ancient religious ceremonies.
2. Moving into other areas of human life, it later became a form of recreation and entertainment.
3. Dancing flourished at peasant fairs and in royal courts.
4. At court, professional entertainers danced to amuse royalty.
5. Then, in 1581, Catherine de Médicis, mother of the king of France, asked her favorite court musician and dance master to create an entertainment for a wedding.
6. The magnificent spectacle resulting from this royal request lasted for six hours.
7. Lacking a stage, the performers danced in a great hall, surrounded by their audience.
8. Most dance historians consider this performance to be the beginning of ballet.
9. For the next three centuries, dancing as an art form grew in sophistication and popularity.
10. Ballet had no challenger in this area until the twentieth century brought a new form, modern dance, to delight the audiences of the world.

B. Write each italicized phrase and identify it as one of the following: *Prepositional Phrase, Appositive Phrase, Infinitive Phrase, Participial Phrase,* or *Gerund Phrase.*

1. The truest expression *of a people* is in its dances and music. The body never lies.
   Agnes De Mille
2. *Dancing in all its forms* cannot be excluded from the curriculum of all noble education: dancing with the feet, with ideas, with words, and, need I add that one must be able to dance with the pen?
   Friedrich Nietzsche
3. Then you died *on the prairie,* and scorned all disgraces,/O broncho that would not be broken of dancing.
   Vachel Lindsay
4. I realized there was no character—whether a sailor, or a truck driver, or a gangster—that could not be interpreted *through dancing.*
   Gene Kelly

5. *To learn to dance* is the most austere of disciplines.   **Havelock Ellis**

6. I wandered lonely as a cloud/That floats on high o'er vales and hills,/When all at once I saw a crowd,/A host, of golden daffodils;/Beside the lake, beneath the trees,/*Fluttering and dancing in the breeze.*   **William Wordsworth**

7. It is not enough *to want to be a dancer* in order to be able to become one. Here the body has the first and final word.
   Eugene Gilson

8. We love to dance that new one *called the Civil War Twist.* The Northern part of you stands still while the Southern part tries to secede.   **Dick Gregory**

9. Dancers work and live from the inside. They drive themselves constantly, *producing a glow that lights not only themselves, but audience after audience.*   **Murray Louis**

10. The value of dance, *its greatest value,* is in the "intangibles."
    Ted Shawn

C. Read the following sentences carefully, and rewrite them to correct any misplaced or dangling modifiers. Write *Correct* if the sentence has no errors.

1. Generally known as a unique contribution to the world of art and entertainment, people think that the modern musical originated in America.

2. Yet, looking closely at history, the origins of the musical lie in England.

3. Actually, John Gay's *The Beggar's Opera* is considered the first musical produced in 1728.

4. Musical comedy did not really develop until the 1880's in America in its present form.

5. Having enjoyed their songs and jokes for a long time, vaudeville and music hall performances were enthusiastically attended.

6. Then came the musical revue, with songs tied together loosely by a theme rather than a plot.

7. Having a plot filled with songs, characters in the next musicals were poorly developed.

8. Writing these often highly entertaining musicals, early performances were created by people like the brilliant writer and humorist P. G. Wodehouse.

9. Many people feel that *Oklahoma!* with its serious subject matter, well-developed characters, and complex plot, introduced the era of the modern musical.

10. Finally, many classical musicians added their talents to the Broadway stage like Leonard Bernstein as modern musicals grew in sophistication.

CLAUSES

A clause is a group of words that, unlike a phrase, contains a verb and its subject. The two kinds of clauses are **independent clauses** and **subordinate clauses.**

Independent Clauses

A clause that can stand alone is an independent clause.

Each of the sentences below has two independent clauses. The subject of each independent clause is underlined once; the verb is underlined twice.

> Princess Elizabeth married Prince Philip of Greece in 1947, and she became Queen of England five years later.
> Originally, she had little chance of ascending to the throne of England, but her uncle, the Duke of Windsor, renounced the throne in 1936.

Each of the clauses in the sentences can stand alone as a sentence because it expresses a complete thought.

> Princess Elizabeth married Prince Philip of Greece in 1947.
> She became Queen of England five years later.
> Originally, she had little chance of ascending to the throne of England.
> Her uncle, the Duke of Windsor, renounced the throne in 1936.

Subordinate Clauses

A clause that cannot stand alone as a sentence is a subordinate clause.

The following subordinate clause has a subject and a verb. Nevertheless, it cannot stand alone as a sentence because it does not express a complete thought.

> When Charles had gone . . . (What happened then?)

Since a subordinate clause functions as a single part of speech, add an independent clause to form a complete sentence. In the sentence below, the independent clause is underlined.

> When Charles had gone, a long silence filled the room.

Notice that a subordinate clause often begins with an introductory word, such as *when* in the example above.

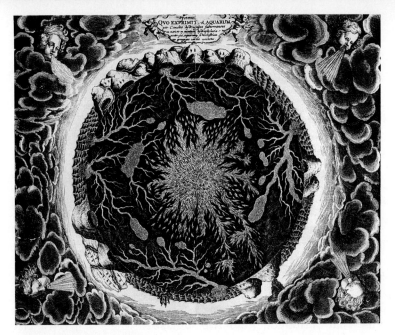

17th century print of a cross section of the earth showing the central fire of a volcano.

Practice Your Skills

CONCEPT CHECK

Independent and Subordinate Clauses Write the subject and verb of each independent clause in the following sentences. Write out each subordinate clause.

1. When a volcano near the town of Armero, Colombia, erupted in 1985, it started a series of mudslides.
2. The mudslides completely destroyed Armero, and 23,000 people in the area died.
3. Alberto Nuñez fled from Armero while the volcano was erupting.
4. Twenty-four days passed before Nuñez could return to the town.
5. As Nuñez looked around, he saw the deserted town in ruins.
6. His own home was completely submerged in mud, but the house next door was only partially buried.
7. To Nuñez's amazement, he noticed that smoke was rising from the chimney of the neighboring house, which belonged to María Rosa Echeverry, age sixty-six.
8. Nuñez found Señora Echeverry inside; she had survived for twenty-four days on small amounts of barley, raw sugar, and rice.
9. She was rescued when Nuñez noticed wisps of smoke from the fire that she had built to keep insects away.
10. The lucky woman was glad to see Nuñez because she had run out of food a few days before his arrival.

The three kinds of subordinate clauses are **adjective clauses, adverb clauses,** and **noun clauses.**

Adjective Clauses

An adjective clause is a subordinate clause that is used as an adjective to modify a noun or a pronoun.

An adjective clause, like an adjective, answers the questions *What kind of?* or *Which one?* Usually, the adjective clause immediately follows the noun or pronoun it modifies.

> Juanita has a machine *that counts and rolls coins.* (What kind of machine?)
> This is the park *where I once played.* (Which park?)

Words That Introduce Adjective Clauses Many adjective clauses begin with one of these **relative pronouns:** *who, whom, whose, that,* and *which.* The relative pronoun relates the adjective clause to the noun or pronoun it modifies. The modified word is the antecedent of the relative pronoun. An adjective clause that begins with a relative pronoun is sometimes called a **relative clause.**

The relative pronoun in an adjective clause can act as the subject, the direct object, the object of a preposition, or a modifier, as shown in the examples below.

Subject	Thomas Jefferson was the man *who wrote the Declaration of Independence.* (The relative pronoun *who* is the subject of the verb *wrote.*)
Direct Object	Esther is probably not someone *whom you can trust.* (The relative pronoun *whom* is the direct object of the verb *can trust.*)
Object of a Preposition	The cause *for which we are asking help* is a worthy one. (The relative pronoun *which* is the object of the preposition *for.*)
Modifier	The family *whose home burned down* is living with us for a while. (The relative pronoun *whose* modifies the noun *home.*)

Not all adjective, or relative, clauses begin with relative pronouns. Some begin with the relative adverb *after, before, since, when, where,* or *why.* A **relative adverb,** like a relative pronoun, relates the adjective clause to the word it modifies. In addition to serving as an introductory word for an adjective clause, the relative adverb modifies the verb within the clause.

> The Roaring Twenties was the time *when the flappers danced the Charleston and listened to ragtime.* (The adjective clause modifies the noun *time.* The relative adverb *when* introduces the clause and also modifies the verbs *danced* and *listened.*)

In some adjective clauses, the introductory relative pronoun or adverb can be dropped.

> You are just the one *I want to see.* (The relative pronoun *whom* has been dropped.)

Essential and Nonessential Clauses Like some phrases, adjective clauses may be essential or nonessential. An **essential adjective clause** is one that must be included to make the meaning of a sentence complete.

> Eleanor of Aquitaine was a powerful woman *who married two kings during her life.* (The intended meaning of the sentence would be incomplete without the clause.)

A **nonessential adjective clause** is one that adds extra information to a sentence the intended meaning of which is already complete and clear.

> The movie *Empire of the Sun, which I did not see,* was based on a true story.
> The producer of *Empire of the Sun* was Steven Spielberg, *whose father was an electronics engineer.*

Sentence Diagraming For information on diagraming adjective clauses, see page 865.

Practice Your Skills

A. CONCEPT CHECK

Adjective Clauses Write the adjective clause in each sentence, and underline the introductory relative pronoun. If the introductory word has been omitted, write *Omitted.*

1. Superstitions that center on good luck symbols have been with us since prehistory.
2. The rabbit's foot, which is even today considered a lucky charm, has existed since 600 B.C.

Writing
TIP

In formal writing use *that* to begin essential adjective clauses. Use *which* to begin nonessential adjective clauses.

Writing Theme
Luck

3. The hare, which is born with its eyes open, was thought to have special powers.
4. It was the foot that was believed to confer those powers.
5. Somehow this superstition was transferred to the rabbit, whose eyes are firmly closed at birth.
6. Another lucky item, the horseshoe, is an amulet the fourth-century Greeks may have originated.
7. Millions of Europeans and Americans, who believed in its power to bring good luck, hung horseshoes over their doorways.
8. One of the strangest superstitions is the idea that the larger half of a chicken's clavicle brings luck.
9. The Etruscans, who believed in the divine soothsaying powers of the chicken, began the custom of pulling the "wishbone."
10. Finally, thanks to agricultural science, four-leaf clovers, which were once rare, are now a dime a dozen.

B. DRAFTING SKILL

Adding Adjective Clauses Complete the sentences by adding an adjective clause that expresses the idea in parentheses. Include a relative pronoun or a relative adverb, and use commas if necessary.

1. Charles Lindbergh acquired the nickname "Lucky Lindy" from an adoring world. (Lindbergh flew from New York City to Paris alone in 1927.)
2. This was a tremendous feat. (The feat captured the imagination of people of all ages and nations.)
3. Lindbergh left college after one year to attend a flying school. (He had shown an interest in flying at an early age.)
4. In 1926, after a year in the Army aviation program, he purchased a World War I Curtiss. (He fondly referred to this plane as "Jenny.")
5. The successful solo transatlantic flight brought great recognition and fame to Lindbergh. (The flight was a competitive venture sponsored by a St. Louis businessperson.)
6. Lindbergh did not have the same good fortune in all of his personal life. (Lindbergh lived up to his nickname in the air.)
7. In fact, his spectacular fame and fortune resulted in a devastating tragedy. (The tragedy was one of the most publicized crimes of the time.)
8. In 1929, Lindbergh had married Anne Morrow and had moved to Englewood, New Jersey. (This is where their son was born.)
9. At the age of two, the Lindbergh child was kidnapped and killed. (The child was, of course, greatly loved by his parents.)
10. To escape the publicity, Charles and Anne moved to Europe. (They had no privacy after this tragedy.)

C. APPLICATION IN WRITING

A Myth Choose some ordinary object to be a good luck charm. Then write a short explanation of how it came to be lucky. Begin your myth with the following: "The _____ , which is very lucky, was once only ordinary." Use adjective clauses.

Adverb Clauses

An adverb clause is a subordinate clause that is used as an adverb to modify a verb, an adjective, or another adverb.

Modifying a Verb	Carla will explain everything *when she finally gets here tomorrow morning.*
Modifying an Adjective	His skating became much better *after he began to practice daily.*
Modifying an Adverb	Dana can take you and your friends there more easily *than your mother can.*
Modifying a Participle	Satisfied with himself *after he finished the report,* Paul took a long study break.
Modifying a Gerund	Working at two jobs *while she went to college* left Julie little time for fun.
Modifying an Infinitive	Kenneth decided to study the map *before he started out on the long trip.*

Phrases and Clauses   **623**

Writing
—**TIP**—
Use a comma
after an adverb
clause that begins
a sentence.

Adverb clauses answer the following questions about the words they modify: *Where? When? Why? How? To what extent? Under what circumstances?*

> We found the boat *where Cora left it.* (found *where?*)
> *When the sirens sounded,* everyone jumped. (jumped *when?*)
> We started early *because traffic was heavy.* (started *why?*)
> Lian acted *as if she meant business.* (acted *how?*)
> My younger sister walks much faster *than most other people do.* (faster *to what extent?*)
> Employees get an extra day off *provided that they report for work on time every day for six months.* (get *under what circumstances?*)

A sentence may even have more than one adverb clause.

> *Wherever the coach went,* she inspired her players to win *because she believed in them.* (The first clause answers the question *Where?;* the second clause, *Why?*)

Words That Introduce Adverb Clauses Subordinating conjunctions usually introduce adverb clauses. A **subordinating conjunction** relates the clause to the word it modifies and also shows a specific relationship between the ideas in the sentence. Listed below are some subordinating conjunctions and the relationships they illustrate.

Subordinating Conjunctions	
Time	as, as soon as, after, before, since, until, when, whenever
Cause	because, since
Comparison	as, as much as, than
Condition	if, although, as long as, though, unless, provided that
Purpose	so that, in order that
Manner	as, as if, as though
Place	where, wherever

Elliptical Clauses Writers and speakers may drop one or more words from some adverb clauses when there is no possibility readers and listeners will be confused by the omission. An adverb clause from which a word or words have been omitted is an **elliptical clause.** The adjective *elliptical* means "marked by the omission of one or more words."

> *While driving to Nashville,* we sang country and western songs. (The words *we were* have been dropped from the clause *While we were driving to Nashville*.)
>
> Carla has been waiting *as long as you.* (The words *have been waiting* have been dropped from the clause: *as long as you have been waiting*.)
>
> *Whenever possible,* eat a balanced meal. (The words *it is* have been dropped from *Whenever it is possible*.)

Sentence Diagraming For information on how to diagram adverb clauses, see page 865.

Practice Your Skills

A. CONCEPT CHECK

Adverb Clauses Write the adverb clause in each sentence.

1. Whenever teacher Diane Gillson says "Rei!" to her students, they stand, bow slightly, and respond, "Konnichiwa."
2. This daily ritual occurs as they begin their class in Japanese.
3. They work hard at a flash-card drill until they have learned the forty-six basic *katakana* characters that represent different syllables in Japanese.
4. As if that weren't enough to learn, the language also includes Chinese characters.
5. If learning English as a foreign language seems difficult, picture Japanese characters with as many as five pronunciations and meanings.
6. The number of American students taking Japanese more than doubled in the early 1980's, even though teachers of Japanese were scarce.
7. Although Japanese is still studied by fewer than 25,000 people, it is now the seventh most popular language in the United States.
8. Though you might expect elementary, high school, and college students to show interest, many adults are also learning Japanese.
9. Wherever Japanese is taught, people are learning to read and speak the language.
10. If you decide to learn Japanese, find a good school and be prepared to study hard.

B. DRAFTING SKILL

Expanding Sentences Expand each sentence by adding an adverb clause that expresses the relationship described in parentheses.

> ***Example***   We especially enjoyed Spanish class. (*Time:* The teacher tried a new approach.)
> We especially enjoyed Spanish class when the teacher tried a new approach.

1. Some foreign language teachers are finding that more is learned and retention is better. (*Condition:* They use a technique called Total Physical Response.)
2. Using TPR, students respond physically to commands. (*Time:* The teacher presents new material.)
3. Students respond with movements, not with words. (*Cause:* Understanding the spoken word is stressed before speaking.)
4. No student is forced to speak. (*Time:* He or she is ready.)
5. Experts feel that students are learning a new language. (*Manner:* They were learning their native language.)
6. First, the teacher models an action. (*Purpose:* The student can relate the command to the needed response.)
7. The teacher continues to participate. (*Time:* The students' responses come naturally.)
8. Tests show that students learn more vocabulary. (*Comparison:* They learn with conventional techniques.)
9. In fact, they can recall large numbers of words learned the previous year. (*Time:* They return from summer vacation.)
10. It seems that moving the body while learning improves memory. (*Cause:* Movement forces the learner to concentrate.)

C. APPLICATION IN WRITING

A Scene Description   If you were a scriptwriter, what hair-raising scenes would you include in a script for an action film intended for actors who speak different languages? Write a paragraph or two in which you describe your ideas. Use adverb clauses, and try to use at least one elliptical clause.

Noun Clauses

A noun clause is a subordinate clause that is used as a noun in a sentence.

A noun clause can be used in all the ways that a noun is used: as (1) a subject, (2) a direct object, (3) an indirect object, (4) a predicate nominative, or (5) the object of a preposition.

Subject	*Where the hostages are* is being kept secret.
Direct Object	Our captain knew *where the fish were biting*.
Indirect Object	The police will give *whoever caused the accident* a ticket.
Predicate Nominative	The interesting challenge is *how you can use a modem most effectively*.
Object of a Preposition	They were talking about *who would win the Nobel Peace Prize*.

Words That Introduce Noun Clauses The introductory word in a noun clause can be a pronoun or a subordinating conjunction.

| Pronouns | who, whom, whose, which, that, whoever, whomever, what, whatever |
| Subordinating Conjunctions | how, that, when, where, whether, why (See subordinating conjunctions on page 572.) |

Some of the words that introduce noun clauses also introduce adjective and adverb clauses. To avoid mistaking one clause for another, study the sentence and decide how the clause functions.

> Seeing *where her ancestors had their home in Africa* moved Winnie deeply. (See *what?* The clause acts as a direct object of the gerund *seeing* and is a noun clause.)
> Here is the exact spot *where Joey found the box of gold coins*. (*Which* spot? The clause acts as an adjective and modifies the noun *spot*.)
> A new family lives *where the Segals used to live*. (Live *where?* The clause acts as an adverb and modifies the verb *lives*.)

Usage Note Writers and speakers frequently drop the introductory word *that* from a noun clause.

> No one told the media *the press conference had been canceled*. (The introductory word *that* has been dropped from the clause.)

Be careful to retain *that* after verbs such as *see, feel, think, learn,* and *say* when omitting them would change the meaning of the sentence. Compare these sentences:

> I see you make your own decisions.
> I see that you make your own decisions.

Sentence Diagraming For information on diagraming a noun clause, see page 865.

Practice Your Skills

Writing Theme
Writing and
Publishing

A. CONCEPT CHECK

Noun Clauses Identify each noun clause and tell its function by writing *Subject, Direct Object, Indirect Object, Predicate Nominative,* or *Object of a Preposition*. If the introductory word *that* is missing from the clause, write *Omitted*.

1. We know that the appearance of magazines followed the invention of the printing press.
2. Historians even have some information about when the first magazine was printed.
3. The first German periodical gave whoever was interested lengthy articles on politics and religion.
4. As the years passed, European magazines published what was considered light entertainment.
5. However, a curious finding is that magazines had a limited market in the American colonies.
6. That, for a very long time, no magazine lasted even one year is not easy to explain.
7. Perhaps no publishers thought people would object to paying a week's wages for a monthly subscription.
8. Certainly, another contributing factor was that the mail system was poor.
9. In the late 1800's, for the low price of 15 cents, S. S. McClure provided a magazine for what became a following of devoted readers.
10. That other subscriptions cost between 25 and 35 cents gave the popular magazine, called *McClure's,* an advantage.

B. CONCEPT CHECK

Noun Clauses Write the noun clause in each sentence and identify its function as *Subject, Direct Object, Indirect Object, Predicate Nominative,* or *Object of a Preposition*.

1. Did you know that a column called "Straight Dope" appears in many newspapers?
2. Many readers wonder who the author of the column really is.
3. Editor Ed Zotti swears someone named Cecil Adams writes "Straight Dope."
4. The editorial office of the Chicago *Reader* is supposedly where Cecil writes the popular column.
5. However, Ed Zotti cannot explain why Cecil is never there.
6. People are suspicious about why no one has ever seen or talked to Cecil.

7. That Zotti vigorously denies authorship of "Straight Dope" suggests a solution to the mystery of Cecil's true identity.
8. Whoever actually writes the column claims to be "the world's smartest human being."
9. Readers send questions about all kinds of subjects to whoever the columnist is.
10. For example, Cecil tells readers whether cats are smarter than dogs and countless other "facts."

THE STRUCTURE OF SENTENCES

In Grammar Handbook 31, you learned that sentences are sometimes classified according to their purpose: declarative, interrogative, imperative, and exclamatory. Now you will learn about and use sentences that are classified by their structure—by the number and kinds of clauses they have. According to this classification system, there are four kinds of sentences: **simple, compound, complex,** and **compound-complex.**

Simple Sentences

A simple sentence is a sentence that has one independent clause and no subordinate clauses.

Some important paintings are being restored.

Although a simple sentence has only one independent clause, it can have several phrases as well as compound parts.

Some important paintings *in the Sistine Chapel in Rome* are being restored *by skillful laborers.* (prepositional phrases)
The Sistine Chapel *paintings* and a famous Leonardo da Vinci *masterpiece* in Milan are being restored. (compound subjects)

Compound Sentences

A compound sentence is a sentence that has two or more independent clauses that are joined together.

The independent clauses in a compound sentence can be joined by (1) a comma and a coordinating conjunction such as *and, but, or, nor, for, so,* or *yet;* (2) a semicolon; or (3) a semicolon and a conjunctive adverb followed by a comma.

The invitation was tempting, *but* we could not accept it.

Erica played The Boss's new album; it's his best yet.

The agents found the strongbox; *however,* the secret documents were not inside.

Sentence Diagraming For information on diagraming simple and compound sentences, see pages 859 and 866.

Movie still from *Our Town,* Thornton Wilder's classic story of life in a small New England town.

Writing Theme
Cities and Towns

Practice Your Skills

A. CONCEPT CHECK

Simple and Compound Sentences Identify the structure of each quotation by writing *Simple Sentence* or *Compound Sentence*. If the sentence is simple, identify any compound parts.

1. Divine Nature gave the fields, and human art built the cities.

   Varro (116–27 B.C.)

2. We stopped at Awazu and arrived at the Royal City after dark on the second day of the Finishing month.

   Takasue's daughter, author of the *Sarashina Diary*

3. Whether in the pastoral joys of country life or in the labyrinthine city, we Americans are always seeking. **Carson McCullers**

4. Saigon was called the Paris of the Orient by the French, and like her sister city in Europe, she was sultry and sulky, brash and noisy.

   Le Ly Hayslip

5. The towns were Dos Cabezas, a clutch of houses under worn twin peaks like skulls, and Wilcox, clean and orderly.

William Least Heat Moon

6. It couldn't have happened anywhere but in little old New York.

O. Henry

7. There is no solitude more dreadful for a stranger, an isolated man, than a great city. **Pierre Claude Boiste**

8. Boys and girls together, me and Mamie O'Rourke,/Tripped the light fantastic on the sidewalks of New York. **James W. Blake**

9. Athens might be very very beautiful, but the Salonika railroad station was not. **Emma Lathen**

10. I was born in Paris and have always lived there. **Simone de Beauvoir**

B. DRAFTING SKILL

Achieving Sentence Variety Combine the following odd-numbered pairs to form simple sentences with compound parts. Combine the even-numbered pairs to form compound sentences. Use the words in parentheses to join the sentences; add necessary punctuation.

1. According to legend, European settlers paid twenty-four dollars for Manhattan. They got a real bargain. (and)
2. This twenty-two-mile island suffers from crime, pollution, and gridlock. It enjoys more financial, educational, and cultural activity than anywhere else in the country. (but)
3. No city is more American. It has so many interesting ethnic communities with cultures from around the world. (yet)
4. Indeed, New York City is a city of paradoxes in many ways. This quality only makes it more appealing. (and)
5. Manhattan is the economic center of the city. It is the cultural center as well. (and)
6. Broadway, for example, is the bright, shining center of America's commercial theater. Small, shabby storefront theaters are the real artistic focus of New York City drama. (however)
7. Fifth Avenue, with its elegant stores, is an important part of Manhattan. Wall Street, with its financial institutions, is also an important part. (and)
8. Land in Manhattan is affordable only for the wealthy. Central Park, encompassing hundreds of acres, is open to the poorest citizen. (nevertheless)
9. Thousands of tourists explore New York City every year. They discover its wonderful diversity. (and)
10. Through the years, millions of immigrants left home to settle in New York City. Each was filled with hope symbolized by the Statue of Liberty. (for)

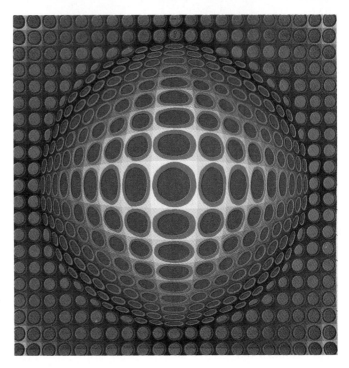

Writing
——**TIP**——

**Skillful writers
are careful to
place the main
idea in the inde-
pendent clause
and the less im-
portant idea in
the subordinate
clause.**

Complex Sentences

A complex sentence is a sentence that has one independent clause and one or more subordinate clauses.

One Subordinate Clause	"Doonesbury" is one comic strip *that I read in the paper daily.*
More Than One	Each of the astronauts *who had landed on the moon* made many personal appearances *after they returned to Earth.*

The subordinate clause in a complex sentence always functions as either a noun or a modifier. If it is a modifier, the subordinate clause modifies a word in the independent clause.

> A jigsaw is the tool *that you need.* (The clause modifies the noun *tool.*)
> *If the rain continues,* the wheat will rot. (The clause modifies the verb *will rot.*)

If the subordinate clause in a complex sentence acts as a noun, it is usually one of the basic parts of the independent clause. It can be the subject, object, complement, or object of a preposition in the independent clause.

What you heard about the foreign-exchange program is untrue. (The noun clause acts as the subject of *is,* the verb in the independent clause.)

Talia claims *that you deliberately locked her out of the house last Monday.* (The noun clause acts as the direct object of the verb *claims.*)

The amount that you will have to pay will be *whatever the jury decides.* (The noun clause acts as the predicate nominative after the linking verb *will be.*)

Lilia is concerned about *what happened yesterday.* (The noun clause acts as the object of the preposition *about.*)

In each sentence above, the subordinate clause is a part of the independent clause; the two cannot be separated. Nevertheless, each sentence has one independent clause and at least one subordinate clause. Therefore, all the sentences are complex sentences.

Sentence Diagraming   For information on diagraming complex sentences, see page 866.

Compound-Complex Sentences

A compound-complex sentence is a sentence that contains two or more independent clauses as well as one or more subordinate clauses.

Each of the following compound-complex sentences has two independent clauses, which are underlined once, and one subordinate clause, which is underlined twice.

Amalia is the one who finally solved the problem, but she is modest about her abilities.

Try the job with the publishing company; however, don't blame me if you dislike it.

Sue hopes that she will be a judge; it is her most cherished goal.

The independent clauses in a compound-complex sentence can be joined in one of three ways: (1) by a coordinating conjunction preceded by a comma (as in the first example above), (2) by a conjunctive adverb preceded by a semicolon and followed by a comma (as in the second example), or (3) by a semicolon alone (as in the third example).

The subordinate clauses either modify a word in one of the independent clauses or act as a noun within one of the independent clauses.

Writing
─TIP─

Skillful writers engage the reader by using a variety of sentence types.

Examine the compound-complex sentence below.

We came up the walk, and Hiroshi noticed that the front door, which we had closed and locked, was wide open.

Independent Clause 1	We came up the walk.
Independent Clause 2	*Hiroshi noticed that the front door,* which we had closed and locked, *was wide open.*
Subordinate Clause 1	that the front door was wide open (The clause is part of the second independent clause.)
Subordinate Clause 2	which we had closed and locked (The clause is part of the first subordinate clause.)

Sentence Diagraming   For information on diagraming compound-complex sentences, see page 866.

Practice Your Skills

A. CONCEPT CHECK

Sentences   Write one of these terms to identify each sentence: *Simple, Compound, Complex,* or *Compound-Complex.*

Writing Theme
Aspirations

(1) In the evening after supper George left the house and wandered in the neighborhood. (2) During the sultry days some of the storekeepers and their wives sat in chairs on the thick, broken sidewalks in front of their shops, fanning themselves, and George walked past them and the guys hanging out on the candystore corner. (3) A couple of them he had known his whole life, but nobody recognized each other. (4) He had no place special to go, but generally, saving it till the last, he left the neighborhood and walked for blocks till he came to a darkly lit little park with benches and trees and an iron railing, giving it a feeling of privacy. (5) He sat on the bench here, watching the leafy trees and the flowers blooming on the inside of the railing, thinking of a better life for himself. (6) He thought of the jobs he had had since he had quit school— delivery boy, stock clerk, runner, lately working in a factory— and he was dissatisfied with all of them. (7) He felt he would someday like to have a good job and live in a private house with a porch, on a street with trees. (8) He wanted to have some dough in his pocket to buy things with, and a girl to go with, so as not to be so lonely, especially on Saturday nights. (9) He wanted people to like and respect him. (10) He thought about these things often but mostly when he was alone at night.

Bernard Malamud, "A Summer's Reading"

B. CONCEPT CHECK

Sentence Structure Identify each sentence as *Compound, Complex,* or *Compound-Complex.* Then write each subordinate clause and identify it as a *Noun* or a *Modifier.*

1. Little Goldie Mabovitch, whose family left Russia in 1906, grew up in Milwaukee, Wisconsin.
2. She became a teacher, but teaching is not what saved her a place in history.
3. Few would have guessed that this Midwestern schoolteacher would become a world leader.
4. In 1921 Goldie and her husband Morris Myerson emigrated to Palestine, and they joined a kibbutz, or settlement.
5. Adjusting to life in Palestine was challenging; however, she was soon active in the kibbutz.
6. She was the representative to the Histadrut, which was a large organization of all the trade unions.
7. On May 14, 1948, the State of Israel was proclaimed, and Goldie Myerson was one of the people who signed its declaration of independence.
8. Of course, the history books record her as Golda Meir, who became Israel's fourth prime minister.
9. From 1969 to 1974, she served her young country, but a war that could not be stopped by her diplomacy cut short her term.
10. Her courage was not recognized until after her death; doctors discovered that she had suffered from leukemia for twelve years.

AVOIDING PHRASE AND CLAUSE FRAGMENTS

As you have learned, a **sentence** expresses a complete thought. It must contain a subject and a predicate.

Phrases as Fragments

Writers sometimes mistakenly use phrases as if they were sentences. However, since a phrase has neither a subject nor a verb, it cannot be a sentence.

Fragment	The bell rang wildly. *At the appointed hour.*
Sentence	The bell rang wildly at the appointed hour.

A series of prepositional phrases may also be mistaken for a sentence, but because it lacks a subject and a verb, it is a **fragment.**

Fragment	The dancers performed awkwardly. *During the first few rehearsals of the routines for the new musical.*
Sentence	The dancers performed awkwardly during the first few rehearsals of the routines for the new musical.

A noun and an appositive fragment may be mistaken for a sentence. However, such a group of words has no verb, so it cannot be a sentence.

Fragment	Sue Mathews, *an outstanding sports writer.*
Sentences	Sue Mathews is *an outstanding sports writer.*
	Sue Mathews, *an outstanding sports writer,* awarded the championship trophies.

Writers sometimes also mistake verbal phrases for sentences because the verbals that begin the phrases look like, and in some ways function like, verbs. Study the following participle, gerund, and infinitive fragments, and note the several ways in which they can be connected with sentences.

Fragment	*Locked out of his car* (participial phrase)
Sentences	*Locked out of his car,* Ernesto could not get to the airport. (The phrase is used as a modifier.)
	Isamu was *locked out of his car* at the mall. (The participle is used as the main verb of a verb phrase in a sentence.)

Fragment	*Taking the train to New York City* (gerund phrase)
Sentences	Takana enjoys *taking the train to New York City.* (The phrase is used as the direct object.)
	Taking the train to New York City could be an adventure. (The phrase is used as the subject.)

Fragment	Chuck had a plan. *To take a shortcut through the cemetery.* (infinitive phrase)
Sentences	Chuck had a plan. It was *to take a shortcut through the cemetery.* (A subject and a verb are added to the phrase.)
	Chuck's plan was *to take a shortcut through the cemetery.* (The phrase is used as the predicate nominative.)

Subordinate Clauses as Fragments

Because a subordinate clause has a subject and a verb, it may be confused with a sentence. However, the subordinating conjunction that introduces such a clause makes it a fragment.

Sentence	We waited patiently for information about the overdue train.
Subordinate Clause	*While* we waited patiently for information about the overdue train, . . .

Placing an end mark after or before a subordinate clause will not make it a sentence. A subordinate clause is always a fragment unless it is joined with an independent clause.

Fragment	*After the game started.* The players forgot their fears.
Sentence	After the game started, the players forgot their fears.

Another way to correct a subordinate clause fragment is to rewrite the clause as a sentence.

Fragment	Six huge tapestries hung on the castle wall. *All of which are priceless.*
Sentence	Six huge tapestries hung on the castle wall. *All of them are priceless.*

Practice Your Skills

REVISION SKILL

Eliminating Phrase and Clause Fragments Rewrite the following word groups to make them sentences instead of fragments. You will need to change punctuation and capitalization and add words.

1. Centuries ago, women in Japan were considered inferior beings. Based on Buddhist teachings at the time.
2. Later, as Confucian teachings spread. Women were taught to be obedient.
3. Meiji Tennō, emperor of Japan from 1867 to 1912.
4. He tried to modernize Japan. By changing old ideas and learning new ways from Western culture.

Writing Theme
Japanese Culture

Lotus Flower and Swimming Fish, by Watanabe Kazan. Seattle Art Museum, Sansō Collection

Phrases and Clauses   **637**

5. Five Japanese girls were sent to the United States. During the Meiji period.
6. Called the Iwakura mission of 1872.
7. The girls were supposed to learn Western ways and culture. To become models of change back in Japan.
8. One of the five girls who were sent to the United States, Tsuda Umeko.
9. When she returned to her homeland, filled with Western ideas. She discovered that she had become more American than Japanese.
10. Believing in higher education for Japanese women. She founded a women's college in Tokyo called Tsuda College.

C H E C K   P O I N T
PAGES 618–638

A. Identify the italicized word groups as *Phrase, Adjective Clause, Adverb Clause,* or *Noun Clause.*

1. Many ideas *that were little more than common sense and luck* have made millions of dollars.
2. The people *behind these ideas* were not only curious and imaginative, but they had the courage to take business risks.
3. A great idea usually requires an entrepreneur *to make it a working reality.*
4. These creative ideas, *which include biscuit mix, potato chips, and fitted sheets,* are each the result of someone's recognizing an opportunity and seeing it through.
5. Potato chips were the fluke discovery of a chef *who was trying to please a fussy customer.*
6. Another inventor, *a woman in Texas,* solved the problem of twisting and tangling sheets *at night.*
7. She simply added elastic to the corners, *creating the first fitted sheet.*
8. *When a food company employee questioned a train chef about the "instant" fresh biscuits on the table,* he discovered the secret of the first ready-made dry biscuit mix.
9. *That he got the credit instead of the chef* is not really unfair.
10. The ability to recognize the potential of an idea is *what creates million-dollar products.*

B. Combine each pair of sentences, using *coordinating conjunctions, conjunctive adverbs,* or *semicolons.* Be sure to use commas and make word changes when necessary.

1. The first patent laws in the United States were passed in 1790. The U.S. Patent Office today does a brisk business.

2. From 1860 to 1890, the office issued 440,000 patents. It issued almost three times as many from 1930 to 1960.
3. A patent is a grant of property right to an inventor. It prevents other enterprising inventors from making, using, or selling that person's invention.
4. In 1846, Elias Howe patented a sewing machine. His machine was not successful.
5. Howe failed at home. He took his wife, his family, and his ingenuity to England.
6. He sold his ideas in England. He barely managed to support his family on the money he made.
7. A surprise awaited him when he returned home. He discovered that his patented parts were used in other brands of sewing machines.
8. Howe sued the other inventors and won. He received royalties on all the sewing machines produced in the United States.
9. Not all patented inventions have been as successful as the sewing machine. Some never made it past the model stage.
10. For example, there are more than 300 patented devices to prevent snoring. The problem of snoring has not been solved for either the snorers or their unwilling listeners.

C. Rewrite the following passage, *eliminating all fragments.* Some of the sentences are correct as written but would be improved if rewritten to combine with fragments.

THE FAR SIDE By GARY LARSON

"Hey! Look what Zog do!"

Thomas Jefferson mounted his dapple gray horse and began the long, dangerous journey. Through the snow and sleet toward his beloved Monticello. Of all the magnificent houses ever built. Few were ever so much a part of the owner. The structure showing throughout the marks of Jefferson's creative genius. The bricks that formed the walls. The nails that held down the floors. And much of the furniture were made on his mountaintop plantation.

On the roof of the house was a weather vane. Turning whichever way the wind blew it. Over the main doorway of the house a great clock with two faces. One of which could be read from the porch, and the other could be read from the entrance hall. The clock could show the day of the week because of a weight. Moving a metal wheel.

In the library at Monticello, the first significant collection of books in the United States. Here too were his swivel chair and tables with revolving tops. Only two of his many ingenious inventions. In his later years, reduced to near poverty. Jefferson sold his collection of books. To pay off debts that had accumulated. While he was serving as President.

GRAMMAR
H A N D B O O K
32

Writing Theme
Art and Artists

A. Identifying Phrases and Clauses   Identify the italicized group of words in each sentence as *Adjective Phrase, Adverb Phrase, Appositive Phrase, Infinitive Phrase, Participial Phrase, Gerund Phrase, Independent Clause,* or *Subordinate Clause.*

1. Georgia O'Keeffe, *born in Wisconsin in 1887,* was different and independent even as a child.
2. It is not surprising *that she became an innovative modern artist.*
3. She was unhappy *with her first art lessons.*
4. Anyone *with a talent for copying* could have mastered those classes.
5. *Sketching casts of hands and torsos,* however, was not her idea of art.
6. Nevertheless, her goal was *to become a fine artist.*
7. A man named Alon Bement became her friend and teacher, for *he helped her put feelings into her paintings.*
8. In later years she said that Bement had given her an "alphabet," *the elements to work with,* so that she could create her own art.
9. Alfred Stieglitz, *whom she later married,* exhibited her paintings.
10. Today, her vivid abstracts hang *in museums all over the world.*

B. Correcting Sentence Errors   Some of the following sentences have misplaced or dangling phrases and split infinitives. Other sentences have phrases with comma errors. Rewrite these sentences correctly. If the sentence is correct as written, write *Correct.*

1. Walking through the National Gallery of Art in Washington, D.C., paintings from almost three centuries cover the walls.
2. *Squire Musters* is a portrait of a dignified man in a white wig painted by the British artist Sir Joshua Reynolds.
3. The portrait of Mrs. Cuthbert painted in 1765 by Jeremiah Theus holding a volume of sonnets hangs on another wall.
4. As decades and centuries passed, the subjects of paintings changed.
5. John William Casilear's landscapes attempt to boldly portray the wilderness.
6. Strongly influenced by the French impressionists, the subjects of Mary Cassatt's paintings include children in natural settings.
7. Thomas Eakins's paintings reveal his remarkable detail and perspective farther along in the museum.
8. The Ashcan School which appeared at the beginning of the twentieth century would have shocked Sir Joshua Reynolds.
9. Eight painters were dubbed the Ashcan School by critics of the time because their paintings reflected social issues.
10. Of course, the pop art paintings probably would have shocked those eight rebels hanging in the museum.

C. Subordinate Clauses Identify each italicized subordinate clause below as *Adjective, Adverb, Subject, Direct Object, Predicate Nominative, Object of a Preposition,* or *Object of an Infinitive.*

1. *When I experienced a distinct physical thrill in my stomach,* I knew it was my eyes telling me the painting was "right."
   Tom Wesselman
2. Art is a lie *that makes us realize the truth.*   **Pablo Picasso**
3. I can't expect even my own art to provide all the answers—only to hope *that it keeps asking the right questions.*   **Grace Hartigan**
4. According to one critic my work looks like scraped billboards. I went to look at billboards and decided *that more billboards should be scraped.*   **Mark Tobey**
5. Art produces ugly things *which frequently become beautiful with time.*   **Jean Cocteau**
6. Any art communicates *what you are in the mood to receive.*
   Larry Rivers
7. *That which takes effect by chance* is not art.   **Seneca**
8. Fine art is *that in which the hand, the head, and the heart of man go together.*   **John Ruskin**
9. All the really good ideas I ever had came to me *while I was milking a cow.*   **Grant Wood**
10. Art is a human activity having for its purpose the transmission to others of the highest and best feelings to *which people have risen.*   **Leo Tolstoy**

D. Identifying Types of Sentences   Identify the following sentences as *Simple, Compound, Complex,* or *Compound-Complex.*

1. A caricature is a distorted picture of a person or an action.
2. Caricatures, which date back to the 1500's, often ridicule people.
3. Some target famous people, and others poke fun at certain groups.
4. Today, political cartoonists use caricature freely; however, this freedom did not always exist.
5. In 1832, the French artist Honoré Daumier drew a caricature of King Louis-Philippe, who had a pear-shaped figure.
6. The drawing depicted the king as a giant pear, and although the people enjoyed it, the king did not.
7. Louis-Philippe was enraged and had Daumier imprisoned.
8. Daumier was first put into jail; then he was sent to a mental hospital.
9. The king wanted to make the point that only an insane person would oppose him.
10. The six months that Daumier spent in confinement did not dampen his spirit, for he drew many caricatures after that incident.

Directions One or more of the underlined sections in the following sentences may contain errors of grammar, usage, punctuation, spelling, or capitalization. Write the letter of each incorrect section, then rewrite the item correctly. If there is no error in an item, write E.

> ***Example*** According to <u>Charles L. Hogue</u> of the <u>Los Angeles county</u>
>   **A**   **B**
> Museum of Natural <u>History. "Knee-high</u> to a grasshopper" is about
>   **C**
> one-half <u>an inch</u>. <u>No error</u>
>   **D**   **E**
>
> ***Answer*** B—Los Angeles County C—History, "knee-high

---

1. <u>Thomas Jefferson</u> wrote the Declaration of <u>Independence. Which</u> was later <u>revized</u> by
        A   **B**   **C**
   Benjamin Franklin, John Adams, Congress, and Jefferson <u>himself.</u> <u>No error</u>
                                                                              D   **E**

2. The word *anesthesia* <u>coined in 1846 in Boston,</u> was formed from <u>greek</u> word parts
                                        A   **B**
   meaning <u>"lack</u> of <u>feeling."</u> <u>No error</u>
                   C   **D**   **E**

3. <u>Aspirin</u> is the <u>most widely</u> used <u>drug</u> in the <u>world, scientists</u> still do not know why
        A   **B**   **C**   **D**
   or how it works. <u>No error</u>
                            E

4. <u>Santa Fe's</u> official <u>name Villa Real de la Santa Fe de San Francisco de Asis is</u> one of the
        A   **B**
   <u>longest place</u> names in the <u>world.</u> <u>No error</u>
            C   **D**   **E**

5. Our sixteenth <u>president Abraham Lincoln was</u> voted the best U.S. President <u>in a 1982</u>
                          A   **B**
   <u>survey</u> of leading <u>historians, political</u> <u>scholars and</u> authors. <u>No error</u>
        C   **D**   **D**   **E**

6. <u>Originaly</u> written as a bank <u>commerical,</u> <u>"We've</u> Only Just <u>Begun"</u> became a popular hit
        A   **B**   **C**
   in the <u>1970's.</u> <u>No error</u>
              D   **E**

7. <u>Plays, written by William Shakespeare, are</u> performed <u>throughout the world</u> in such
                  A   **B**
   diverse <u>languages</u> as Japanese, Russian, <u>Italian, and</u> Hebrew. <u>No error</u>
         C   **D**   **E**

8. The <u>twenty first</u> <u>century which will begin with the year 2001</u> <u>is</u> almost upon <u>us.</u>
        A   **B**   **C**   **D**
   <u>No error</u>
    E

9. Although *Poetry* magazine was only a small Chicago <u>periodical it</u> contributed to the
            A   **B**
   early recognition of <u>such great poets</u> as <u>Frost, Pound, Eliot, Sandburg, and Edgar Lee</u>
                        C   **D**
   <u>Masters.</u> <u>No error</u>
            E

10. While some people <u>argue</u> about whether the <u>Loch Ness</u> monster exists <u>at all, others</u>
                    A   **B**   **C**
    think <u>there</u> may be more than one. <u>No error</u>
        D   **E**

11. <u>President Truman's</u> full name was Harry S <u>Truman the</u> "S" was not an <u>abreviation</u> for a
             A   **B**   **C**
    name and <u>was correctly written</u> without a period. <u>No error</u>
            D   **E**

12. Although Othello is the <u>title role</u> in the play of that <u>name. The</u> <u>villian</u> Iago has almost
                        A   **B**   **C**
    half again as <u>many lines.</u> <u>No error</u>
                D   **E**

Directions Each of the following sentences has a grammatical problem. On your paper
write the letter of the corrected sentence.

13. The Baghdad battery is an artifact that looks like a modern chemical battery found in
    the ruins of a 2,000-year-old village.
    A. The Baghdad battery is an artifact that looks like a modern chemical battery found.
       In the ruins of a 2,000-year-old village.
    B. Found in the ruins of a 2,000-year-old village, the Baghdad battery is an artifact that
       looks like a modern chemical battery.
    C. The Baghdad battery is an artifact that looks like a modern chemical battery to find
       in the ruins of a 2,000-year-old village.

14. Asking a price of $200,000 in 1980, a tropical rain forest near Sea Turtle Park in Costa Rica was offered for sale.
    A. A tropical rain forest near Sea Turtle Park in Costa Rica was offered for sale, asking a price of $200,000 in 1980.
    B. Asking a price of $200,000, a tropical rain forest near Sea Turtle Park in Costa Rica was offered for sale in 1980.
    C. Asking a price of $200,000, in 1980 a government agency offered a tropical rain forest near Sea Turtle Park in Costa Rica for sale.

15. Appearing in 1894, Joseph Pulitzer published the first full-color comic strip in his New York newspaper.
    A. Appearing in 1894 in his New York newspaper, Joseph Pulitzer published the first full-color comic strip.
    B. Joseph Pulitzer published the first full-color comic strip in his New York newspaper, appearing in 1894.
    C. Appearing in 1894, the first full-color comic strip was published by Joseph Pulitzer in his New York newspaper.

16. To put astronauts on the moon, many hours of scientific study and vast amounts of money were expended.
    A. Putting astronauts on the moon, many hours of scientific study and vast amounts of money were expended.
    B. To put astronauts on the moon, NASA expended many hours of scientific study and vast amounts of money.
    C. To put astronauts on the moon, vast amounts of money and many hours of scientific study had to be expended.

17. One can see the backward-growing hair that gives a Rhodesian ridgeback its name along its spine.
    A. The backward-growing hair that gives a Rhodesian ridgeback its name can be seen along its spine.
    B. Along its spine, the backward-growing hair that gives a Rhodesian ridgeback its name one can see.
    C. The backward-growing hair that one can see gives a Rhodesian ridgeback its name along its spine.

18. Alarmed by the mild tremors, supplies were hoarded and survival kits were bought.
    A. Supplies, alarmed by the mild tremors, were hoarded and survival kits were bought.
    B. Being alarmed by the mild tremors, supplies were hoarded and survival kits were bought.
    C. Alarmed by the mild tremors, people hoarded supplies and bought survival kits.

Sketchbook

Harnessed by Hayfever?

FREE YOURSELF QUICKLY, EFFECTIVELY.

No More Runny Nose, No More Itchy Eyes.

GET HAYFEVER RELIEF—GET

HAY*NoMore*

Copywriters in advertising agencies often use sentence fragments to add "punch" to the advertisements they write, like the newspaper advertisement above. Write your own advertisement for a similar product. Try using punchy sentence fragments to grab the reader's attention.

Additional Sketches

Playwrights use the four types of sentences to reflect the many ways in which people talk to each other and express emotion. Write the dialogue for a scene with four characters. Have each character speak in only one type of sentence (declarative, exclamatory, interrogative, or imperative).

You are walking through a park or down a busy street. What do you observe? Write two paragraphs that accurately describe your walk. Include vivid adjectives and adverbs to enhance your description.

Verb Usage

Review the basic ideas about verbs briefly before going further in this chapter. A **verb** is a word that expresses an action, a condition, or a state of being. An **action verb** expresses a present, past, or future mental or physical action. A **linking verb** does not express action; it serves as a link between the subject of a sentence and a word in the predicate that renames or modifies the subject. Grammar Handbook 30 presents more information about verbs.

Each verb has a variety of forms. Each form is constructed from one of the verb's four **principal parts:** the **present infinitive** (or **present**), the **present participle,** the **past,** and the **past participle.**

Present	Present Participle	Past	Past Participle
swim	(is) swimming	swam	(have) swum
wonder	(is) wondering	wondered	(have) wondered

The present participle of each verb above is shown with *is* before it; the past participles are preceded by *have.* When used as part of a verb phrase, these participles are always used with auxiliary verbs. For other forms of the auxiliary verbs, see Grammar Handbook 30.

Notice the *-ing* ending of the present participles. The present participle of every verb is formed by adding *-ing* to the present form. The past and past participle may be formed in more than one way. The ending of the past and of the past participle of a verb shows whether the verb is regular (*wonder*) or irregular (*swim*).

Regular Verbs

The past and past participle of every **regular verb** are formed by adding *-d* or *-ed* to the present. The majority of verbs are regular.

Present	Present Participle	Past	Past Participle
slip	(is) slipping	slipped	(have) slipped
pry	(is) prying	pried	(have) pried
panic	(is) panicking	panicked	(have) panicked
praise	(is) praising	praised	(have) praised

The spelling of the present form of some regular verbs must be changed before adding *-ing* or *-ed.* Study the spelling changes of the verbs on the previous page: *slip* (double the final consonant), *pry* (change *y* to *i* in the past and past participle), *panic* (add *k* after the final *c*), *praise* (drop the final *e*).

The American *Apollo* and Russian *Soyuz* join in space, 1975

Practice Your Skills

CONCEPT CHECK

Regular Verbs Correctly complete each sentence by writing the principal part of the verb asked for in parentheses.

1. Representatives of NASA and IKI, the Soviet space agency, have (*discuss*—Past Participle) a joint space travel venture to the planet Mars.
2. Their plans for this incredible journey have (*include*—Past Participle) the use of a two-nation crew and a jointly built space vehicle.
3. These two agencies (*propose*—Past) that the mission should begin in the twenty-first century.
4. With a similar goal in mind, scientist and writer Isaac Asimov is (*advocate*—Present Participle) a slow and careful approach to space exploration.
5. He contends that the first humans on Mars should not (*travel*—Present) directly from Earth.
6. It is best if such travelers (*arrive*—Present) on Mars directly from the moon.
7. Asimov is (*suggest*—Present Participle) a system of way stations between Earth and Mars.

8. If scientists (*establish*—Past) an Earth-orbiting space station, they should be able to use it as the first way station from which to launch vehicles to the moon.

9. Because gravity does not (*exist*—Present) on artificial satellites, space vehicles can be launched more easily from space station satellites than from Earth.

10. Once on the moon, specialists can (*construct*—Present) mining stations to supply raw materials needed to build Mars-bound rockets.

11. The moon has a weak gravitational field, so vehicles that are (*head*—Present Participle) for other planets can depart more easily from the moon than from Earth.

12. It should not be surprising that Asimov (*conclude*—Past) that the moon would make a good launching pad to Mars and to worlds beyond.

13. For centuries, scientists and space travel enthusiasts have (*speculate*—Past Participle) about a journey to Mars.

14. Scientists and dreamers alike have (*gaze*—Past Participle) in wonder at the bright red jewel in the night sky.

15. It may be that today's young people will be able to tell their children that they (*watch*—Past) the first journey to Mars unfold on their television screens.

Irregular Verbs

About sixty frequently used verbs in the English language are irregular. Unlike regular verbs, the past and past participles of **irregular verbs** are not formed by adding *-d* or *-ed* to the present. They are formed irregularly, but there are patterns to the irregularity that allow these verbs to be divided into five groups. The examples below represent each of the groups of irregular verbs presented in the sections that follow.

Present	Present Participle	Past	Past Participle
burst	(is) bursting	burst	(have) burst
flee	(is) fleeing	fled	(have) fled
wear	(is) wearing	wore	(have) worn
shrink	(is) shrinking	shrank	(have) shrunk
grow	(is) growing	grew	(have) grown

The past and past participle forms of irregular verbs may be difficult for you to remember unless you memorize them or refer to a dictionary each time you use them. To find the principal parts of an irregular verb in the dictionary, look for the present form of the verb. The principal parts will be given in the entry that begins with the present form. If you decide to memorize each irregular past and past participle, you can make your task easier by breaking down irregular verbs into the five groups shown in the rest of this section.

Group 1 The first of the five groups of irregular verbs is easiest to remember. The present, past, and past participle of each are exactly the same. The present participle is formed the same way the present participle of a regular verb is formed, by adding *-ing.*

Present	Present Participle	Past	Past Participle
bid	(is) bidding	bid	(have) bid
burst	(is) bursting	burst	(have) burst
cost	(is) costing	cost	(have) cost
cut	(is) cutting	cut	(have) cut
hit	(is) hitting	hit	(have) hit
hurt	(is) hurting	hurt	(have) hurt
let	(is) letting	let	(have) let
put	(is) putting	put	(have) put
set	(is) setting	set	(have) set
shut	(is) shutting	shut	(have) shut
split	(is) splitting	split	(have) split
spread	(is) spreading	spread	(have) spread
thrust	(is) thrusting	thrust	(have) thrust

Group 2 The past and the past participle of each verb in this group are spelled in the same way. The verb *get* has a second past participle, *got.*

Present	Present Participle	Past	Past Participle
bring	(is) bringing	brought	(have) brought
catch	(is) catching	caught	(have) caught
fight	(is) fighting	fought	(have) fought
flee	(is) fleeing	fled	(have) fled
fling	(is) flinging	flung	(have) flung
get	(is) getting	got	(have) gotten *or* got
lead	(is) leading	led	(have) led
lend	(is) lending	lent	(have) lent
lose	(is) losing	lost	(have) lost
say	(is) saying	said	(have) said
shine	(is) shining	shone	(have) shone
sit	(is) sitting	sat	(have) sat
sting	(is) stinging	stung	(have) stung
swing	(is) swinging	swung	(have) swung
teach	(is) teaching	taught	(have) taught

Writing
—TIP—

In American English the past participle *gotten* is preferred.

Verb Usage   **649**

A. CONCEPT CHECK

Irregular Verbs   Write the principal part of the verb in parentheses that completes each sentence correctly. Then write the name of the principal part.

1. Late in a sixteenth-century night, the door of the Boar's Head Tavern (burst) open with a jolting crash.
2. A pair of strong hands had (fling) a protesting gentleman into the muddy street.
3. Whimpering slightly, the forlorn fellow picked up his hat, (put) it onto his head, and limped away down the lane.
4. Inside the tavern, playwright Christopher Marlowe (catch) his breath.
5. "I trust that there are no other theater critics present," Marlowe (say), a pleasant smile belying his steely gaze.
6. "I (bid) you be frank and tell me what you think of my latest work," the playwright continued.
7. "The author is (get) concerned that there are others who don't care for his creations," quipped one patron.
8. Marlowe, his eyes darting in the offender's direction, retorted, "I ask you. What other writer is (lend) such luster to the London stage in this year of Our Lord 1590?"
9. The playwright's pointed challenge had (sting) the other patrons into a surly silence.
10. A few, fearing a new storm of wrath, had even (flee) to the comparative safety of the streets.
11. "He is (teach) his critics a lesson tonight," one onlooker growled to another.
12. "Many literary authorities say that only Marlowe's wit (cut) deeper than his sword," murmured another patron.
13. The word had (spread) to most people in the tavern that night about the fight with William Bradley.
14. As a result of that brawl, Marlowe had been snatched from the theater and (thrust) into Newgate Prison for a short stay.
15. The tavern patrons also knew that the government had (bring) him into its secret service—perhaps as a spy.
16. "A fight with Marlowe (set) you against the Queen and Sir Walter Raleigh," muttered one townsman to a friend.
17. "Will it not be ironic if Marlowe ultimately (lose) his life in the way he so often seems to spend it—in a brawl?" the friend mused prophetically.
18. Scarcely three years later, a quarrel over a tavern bill (lead) to the fatal stabbing of the first great Elizabethan dramatist.

Aphra Behn

B. PROOFREADING SKILL

Irregular Verbs   Rewrite the following passage, correcting all errors in grammar, usage, mechanics, and spelling. Pay particular attention to irregular verb forms.

The pendulum of literary fame has always swinged erratically, with certain writers shining brilliantly in one era and fading into obscurity in another. In recent year's renewed interest in the works of Aphra Behn has brung her deserved recognition. Born in 1640, Behn spent her early life in Suriname in daily touch with the institution of slavery. She was splitted between an acepted custom and the tragedy of daily life that hurt her deeply. Later as a writer, she fighted against slavery with works such as her novel oroonoko.

In 1658 Behn set sail for Engaland, where she married a dutch merchant. Later, as a widow, she might well have shut herself away in grief. Instead, patriotism lead her to holland, where she served as a spy for england. She did, however, let her dissatisfaction be known when she said, "my services have costed England nothing." In this way she spreaded word of the governments' unwillingness to pay for her services.

Returning to England in poverty, Behn thrusted herself onto London's lively literary scene. Her comic satirical plays soon caught the public's fancy. Several prominent figures found that plays such as *The city heiress* stinged and got under ones skin. As a satirist, she hit her targets unfailingly.

Today, critics have lended their support in publicizing the works of Behn—the first englishwoman to earn a living solely by writting.

C. APPLICATION IN WRITING

Imaginative Writing   Like Christopher Marlowe or Aphra Behn, imagine yourself performing some secret mission on which your government's international position may depend. Write two or three paragraphs describing some events related to your situation. Use ten or more of the irregular verbs in Group 1 and Group 2.

Group 3   The past participle of each irregular verb in this group (except *bear* and *bite*) is formed by adding *-n* or *-en* to the past form. Note the spelling of the past participle of *bear* and the spelling changes needed to form the past participle of *bite* and *swore*.

Present	Present Participle	Past	Past Participle
bear	(is) bearing	bore	(have) borne
beat	(is) beating	beat	(have) beaten
bite	(is) biting	bit	(have) bitten
break	(is) breaking	broke	(have) broken
choose	(is) choosing	chose	(have) chosen
freeze	(is) freezing	froze	(have) frozen
speak	(is) speaking	spoke	(have) spoken
steal	(is) stealing	stole	(have) stolen
swear	(is) swearing	swore	(have) sworn
tear	(is) tearing	tore	(have) torn
wear	(is) wearing	wore	(have) worn

Practice Your Skills

A. CONCEPT CHECK

Irregular Verbs   Write the past or past participle form of the verb in parentheses, whichever completes the sentence correctly.

1. During the American Revolution, Loyalists were despised because they had (swear) allegiance to the English king.
2. Divided loyalties within colonial families often (tear) the families apart.
3. For example, Benjamin Franklin's heart had (break) when his only son, William, became a Loyalist.
4. This period also brought forth colonial patriots like Patrick Henry who had (speak) out eloquently against British tyranny.
5. There were also powerful pro-American members of the British Parliament who believed in the American cause and (speak) out against the war.
6. However, men were not the only ones who had (choose) sides.
7. Ann Bates, a secret Loyalist who had (choose) to spy for the British, went to American army camps to gather information.

8. Other women, however, wished to contribute to the revolution and made the uniforms that Continental American soldiers (wear).
9. Other American women, like Deborah Sampson, had (wear) Continental uniforms to disguise themselves as men in order to fight in battles.
10. Ultimately, the revolutionaries (beat) the British and established their own government.

B. DRAFTING SKILL

Experimenting with Wording   Rewrite the following sentences, replacing the italicized verb with the correct form of its synonym in parentheses. After you have rewritten each sentence, evaluate which wording is more effective and why.

1. Achilles *cursed* under his breath as his scout described the enemy troops moving to meet the Greek soldiers and their leader. (swear)
2. With a glint of amusement in his eyes, Achilles said to his aide: "I would not have *picked* these opponents." (choose)
3. "Be more specific," he then instructed his scout. "Tell me exactly what type of armor they are *bearing on their persons*." (wear)
4. "Light armor, as though preparing for speed," reported the scout, "and they are *carrying* spears, axes, and crescent-shaped shields." (bear)
5. "Odysseus has *talked* of these women warriors before, has he not? What has he called them . . . Amazons?" queried Achilles. (speak)
6. The aide replied, "He has *testified* that they are cunning and ferocious opponents." (swear)
7. Achilles rolled his eyes and sneered, "Well, we will see how ferocious they are when Greece's finest soldiers *rip* into their ranks." (tear)
8. "Let them attack. It will be as though mosquitoes were *nibbling at* us. A few slaps and they'll be gone." (bite)
9. The meeting *split* up and Achilles' commanders ran to take charge of their troops. (break)
10. Three hours later, the able-bodied soldiers *carried* the wounded past Achilles, their spent leader. (bear)
11. He squinted across the smoky field and watched the Greek soldiers *stop* in terror as the truly ferocious Amazons swooped down upon them. (freeze)
12. With strategic brilliance, the Amazon warriors had *shattered* the ranks of the overconfident Greek troops and had sent them running. (break)
13. "The Amazon leader, Penthesilea, is *besting* my finest warriors in single combat," Achilles muttered in amazement. (beat)

Writing
—TIP—

Synonyms, words with similar meanings, add variety and richness to writing.

14. As his cowed and humbled troops looked on, he turned to them and *said* the word he hated most: "Retreat." (speak)
15. Struggling to salvage his warrior pride, Achilles vowed, "They *grab* a victory from us today, but we shall be revenged." (steal)

C. PROOFREADING SKILL

Irregular Verbs   Rewrite the following paragraphs correctly. Watch for incorrect irregular verbs as well as incorrect capitalization, punctuation, and spelling.

In 1864, president Lincoln choosed to welcome and honor Sojourner Truth at the white house. Lincoln spoke with admiration of the acomplishments of this remarkable woman. Standing proudly, She bore the President's praise with the same quiet dignity as she had beared the attacks of her oponents.

The President's comments chronicled the many hardships this daughter of slaves had bore. Early in life, she had broken the shackles of degradeing bondage and had swore dedication to the fight for freedom. Traveling across America, she had sweltered in summer and had froze in Winter, but she always had spoke her message of independence and equality for all men and women.

Often, southern sympathizers who believed in slavery broke up her meetings. In 1863, a group of men in kansas city beaten her badly. Her enemies had tore at her with slander, with insults, and with mob violence. "It is always biting away at me," she told her friends, "but I must not let it steal away my will and spirit."

Group 4   Study the spelling changes in the principal parts of the irregular verbs in this fourth group. The vowel *i* in the present changes to *a* in the past and to *u* in the past participle. Notice the two past forms of *spring*. Both are correct, but *sprang* is more common.

Present	Present Participle	Past	Past Participle
begin	(is) beginning	began	(have) begun
drink	(is) drinking	drank	(have) drunk
ring	(is) ringing	rang	(have) rung
shrink	(is) shrinking	shrank	(have) shrunk
sing	(is) singing	sang	(have) sung
sink	(is) sinking	sank	(have) sunk
spring	(is) springing	sprang *or* sprung	(have) sprung
swim	(is) swimming	swam	(have) swum

The Shipwreck of Don Juan, by Eugene Delacroix

Practice Your Skills

A. CONCEPT CHECK

Irregular Verbs   Write the correct form of the verb in parentheses to complete each sentence. Then write the name of each verb's principal part.

1. When a ship (sink) in the days before modern communication, the death of all the passengers was almost a certainty.
2. Before the era of radios and telegraphs (begin), the account of a rescued shipwreck victim might have read something like this.
3. April 13, 1834. In my recurring nightmare, the passengers on our ship have (drink) a toast at the captain's table.
4. Suddenly an alarm bell (ring), and the next second a horrific crash made the ship shudder.
5. As I awoke in the lifeboat, the nightmarish images of the shipwreck have (shrink) in the glare of the tropical sun.
6. Though we (begin) our time aboard the raft full of hope and gratitude, the passage of time has left us weary and desperate.
7. Days ago we (drink) the last of our precious water supply, and now we are hoping for rain.
8. Repeatedly the gulls have (sing) their harsh songs overhead only to draw our eyes toward a cloudless sky.
9. Hope had (spring) into our hearts once or twice when we saw the signs of ships on the horizon, but we were unable to signal them.
10. To keep our spirits up, Miss Walters (sing) sea chanteys to us.

11. As a diversion, I would have (swim) when the ocean was quiet, but the mate warned me of the danger of sharks.
12. One morning, the raft rocked suddenly as the mate (spring) to his feet.
13. One glorious word (ring) over and over in my ears: "Land! Land! Land!"
14. Within a moment, the realization had (sink) into my brain and I strained to look where he pointed.
15. Then, sharks or no, we were in the water and had (swim) several yards toward the island that loomed before us.

B. DRAFTING SKILL

Experimenting with Tense Rewrite the following diary entry to show it as an event in the past. Use the correct verb forms.

(1) Today, I, Robinson Crusoe, have begun to keep a diary of my adventures on this island far out at sea. (2) It all begins when my boat sinks during a terrible storm. (3) As I row toward land in a small dinghy, it springs a leak. (4) Then the small craft capsizes and sinks. (5) I swim toward shore, but after I swim only a short distance the water chokes me. (6) Soon the sound of the wind and waves rings shrilly in my ears.

(7) Once I am ashore, the stores salvaged from the wreck shrink rapidly in the first few days. (8) I sing to myself to fend off panic and loneliness. (9) When I drink the last of my fresh water, I know that I also need to find food and shelter. (10) Then my adventure really begins.

Group 5 The past participles of most of the irregular verbs in this group are formed by adding *-n* or *-en* to the present form. Pay special attention to the past participles of *come, do, go,* and *run*. Also, note the spelling changes needed to form the past participles of *ride, slay,* and *write*.

Present	Present Participle	Past	Past Participle
blow	(is) blowing	blew	(have) blown
come	(is) coming	came	(have) come
do	(is) doing	did	(have) done
draw	(is) drawing	drew	(have) drawn
drive	(is) driving	drove	(have) driven
eat	(is) eating	ate	(have) eaten
fall	(is) falling	fell	(have) fallen
give	(is) giving	gave	(have) given
go	(is) going	went	(have) gone
grow	(is) growing	grew	(have) grown

know	(is) knowing	knew	(have) known
ride	(is) riding	rode	(have) ridden
rise	(is) rising	rose	(have) risen
run	(is) running	ran	(have) run
see	(is) seeing	saw	(have) seen
shake	(is) shaking	shook	(have) shaken
slay	(is) slaying	slew	(have) slain
take	(is) taking	took	(have) taken
throw	(is) throwing	threw	(have) thrown
write	(is) writing	wrote	(have) written

Practice Your Skills

A. CONCEPT CHECK

Irregular Verbs Rewrite the following sentences to correct any errors in verb usage. Write *Correct* for sentences that have no verb errors.

1. It was 1939, and the lumberyard boys went home with a 23–8 victory over the boys from the dairy team.
2. No one knew it then, but those two teams in Williamsport, Pennsylvania, had wrote history.
3. Little League baseball had taken the field, and an American institution had came into being.
4. Nearly two-thirds of today's major-league players seen their first team competition in a Little League program.
5. Others who throwed, hit, caught, and ran their way through Little League include senators, astronauts, quarterbacks, actors, and rock stars.
6. Though most reactions have been enthusiastic, Little League has drawn occasional criticism.
7. In the 1950's, some people feared physical or psychological danger as a result of the pressures of competition; however, this objection give way when research studies concluded that Little League play didn't damage children.
8. Since the 1970's, when several lawsuits shaked the League, an estimated 7,000 girls have come into the program.

Little League baseball teams are now open to girls.

9. Little League baseball has grew to include 16,000 programs in thirty countries, and twenty million youngsters have rose to the challenge of the sport since that day in 1939.
10. More important than developing baseball skills, however, Little League has did its best work in providing its graduates with memories of achievement, friendship, and fun.

B. DRAFTING SKILL

Irregular Verbs During the Middle Ages, knights often entered jousting competitions with one another. Read about this type of medieval competition in an encyclopedia or history book. Then write ten sentences about an imaginary jousting event, using each of the ten verbs listed below.

1. given	3. eaten	5. threw	7. took	9. knew
2. shook	4. fell	6. ridden	8. slain	10. risen

C. APPLICATION IN WRITING

A Story Another form of competition during medieval times involved storytelling. Troubadours and traveling storytellers might be invited to compete at presenting the best story in court. Compose a brief story that you might enter in such a competition. Use a variety of verbs from this lesson in your story.

VERB TENSES

A verb has different forms to show the different times of the action expressed by the verb. These forms are called **tenses.** Speakers and writers can use different tenses to express actions that are occurring now, actions that have occurred in the past, and actions that will occur in the future. All verbs have three *simple tenses* (present, past, and future) as well as three *perfect tenses* (present perfect, past perfect, and future perfect). These simple and perfect tenses are formed by using the principal parts of a verb and combining them when necessary with the proper forms of *be, have,* and other auxiliary verbs.

Verb Conjugation

The **conjugation** of a verb is a list of all the forms of the simple and perfect tenses of the verb. The conjugation of the regular verb *walk* is shown on the following page.

Principal Parts

Present	Present Participle	Past	Past Participle
walk	(is) walking	walked	(have) walked

Simple Tenses

	Singular	Plural
Present Tense		
First Person	I walk	we walk
Second Person	you walk	you walk
Third Person	he, she, it walks	they walk

Past Tense		
First Person	I walked	we walked
Second Person	you walked	you walked
Third Person	he, she, it walked	they walked

Future Tense (*will* or *shall* + the present form)

First Person	I will (shall) walk	we will (shall) walk
Second Person	you will walk	you will walk
Third Person	he, she, it will walk	they will walk

Perfect Tenses

Present Perfect Tense (*has* or *have* + the past participle)

First Person	I have walked	we have walked
Second Person	you have walked	you have walked
Third Person	he, she, it has walked	they have walked

Past Perfect Tense (*had* + the past participle)

First Person	I had walked	we had walked
Second Person	you had walked	you had walked
Third Person	he, she, it had walked	they had walked

Future Perfect Tense (*will have* or *shall have* + the past participle)

First Person	I will (shall) have walked	we will (shall) have walked
Second Person	you will have walked	you will have walked
Third Person	he, she, it will have walked	they will have walked

Using the Simple Tenses

Certain rules govern the formation and use of the present, past, and future tenses.

The Present Tense   To make the third-person singular form of the present tense, add *-s* or *-es* to the first principal part, the present form: he *throws,* she *catches*. All other singular and plural forms of the present tense use the unchanged present form: I *throw,* you *catch,* we *throw,* they *catch*. Use the present tense to show (1) a present action, occurring at this moment, (2) a regularly occurring action, (3) a constant or generally true action.

Present Action	This milk *smells* sour.
Regular Action	The stores *close* at six on Sundays.
Constant Action	Planet Earth *circles* the sun.

To express a past action or condition as if it were happening now, use the **historical present tense.** In writing about literature, this tense is preferable.

> In the ancient Greek tragedy *Women of Trachis,* the queen accidentally *kills* her husband when she *tries* to win his love back.

The Past Tense   Add *-d* or *-ed* to the present, the first principal part, to form the past tense of a regular verb: we *talked,* they *smiled,* she *insisted,* you *tried*. For an irregular verb, use the past form in the list of principal parts of the verb: I *lent,* it *cost,* he *gave*. Use the past tense to express an action that began and ended in the past.

> Chief Osceola *led* a group of Seminoles against government troops in the 1840's and *defeated* them.

Chief Osceola

Using Present and Perfect Infinitives The **present infinitive** (to walk, to hear) and the **perfect infinitive** (to have walked, to have heard) are both used to express actions that take place at different times.

To express an action that takes place *after* another, use the present infinitive form of a verb.

Incorrect	We had hoped *to have stayed* longer in Caracas. (The use of the perfect infinitive is incorrect because the action it is meant to express happened after the action expressed by *had hoped*.)
Correct	We had hoped *to stay* longer in Caracas.

To express an action that takes place *before* another, use the perfect infinitive form of the verb.

> I feel very proud *to have served* my country in my youth.
> (The perfect infinitive is used correctly here to express an action that happened before the action expressed by the verb *feel*.)

Practice Your Skills

A. CONCEPT CHECK

Verb Tenses Write the underlined verbs in the following sentences. Identify the tense of each verb.

Writing Theme
Festivals

1. Communities all over the world <u>have held</u> fairs for centuries.
2. *Fair* <u>comes</u> from the Latin word *feria,* meaning a holiday or feast day.
3. Fair organizers <u>have categorized</u> their events as "agricultural," "trade," and "world."
4. In 1641, the government of New Netherland <u>authorized</u> the first annual fair in the American colonies.
5. By the mid-1700's, before the Revolutionary War, fairs <u>had spread</u> throughout the colonies.
6. They <u>were</u> primarily agricultural and <u>showcased</u> the things produced on colonial farms.
7. By the early twentieth century, fairs <u>had grown</u> into a major industry in the United States.
8. To appreciate a fair, simply <u>enter</u> the gate and <u>observe</u> the prize cattle, carnival midway, balloon vendors, and food booths.
9. You <u>will enjoy</u> the colorful exhibits, exciting games, and skilled entertainers.
10. By the end of the evening, you <u>will have experienced</u> a modern version of a very ancient event.

B. DRAFTING SKILL

Verb Tenses Write the verb in parentheses in the tense indicated.

1. When one thinks of New Orleans, Mardi Gras (*spring*—Present) instantly to mind.
2. French colonists (*introduce*—Past) this extravagant event to the city in 1766.
3. Earlier cultures (*celebrate*—Past Perfect) festivals that were similar to the more modern Mardi Gras.
4. In the city of New Orleans, exclusive clubs called *krewes* traditionally (*organize*—Present Perfect) parades and parties.
5. Each year, weeks before the festivities, each krewe (*select*—Future Perfect) a king and a queen to ride in the parade.
6. When these celebrations first began, only the club members (*adorn*—Past) themselves in lavish costumes.
7. Once the revelers (*see*—Past Perfect) the carnival royalty dressed in such extravagant outfits, they soon followed suit.
8. These outrageously outfitted spectators (*enjoy*—Present Perfect) many Mardi Gras parades.
9. Each time, the carnival (*become*—Present) a dazzling whirl of color and music and laughter for them.
10. With a shout of *"Laissez les bons temps rouler!"* the good times indeed (*roll*—Future) as long as the Mardi Gras exists.

C. APPLICATION IN WRITING

A Record of Events Describe a festival, such as a country fair, a Fourth of July event, or a Cinco de Mayo celebration. Record it first as a memory, then as an eyewitness account, and finally as it might be in twenty years. Which approach is most effective? Why?

PROGRESSIVE AND EMPHATIC VERB FORMS

In addition to six basic tenses, every verb has other special forms—six progressive forms and the emphatic forms of the present tense and the past tense.

Using the Progressive Forms

As the name suggests, progressive forms are used to show progress, or ongoing action. The six progressive forms are constructed by combining present and perfect tenses of *be* with a present participle.

I am walking, you are walking (present progressive)
I was walking, you were walking (past progressive)
I will (shall) be walking, you will (shall) be walking (future progressive)
I have been walking, you have been walking (present perfect progressive)
I had been walking, you had been walking (past perfect progressive)
I will (shall) have been walking, you will (shall) have been walking (future perfect progressive)

To express an action that is in progress at the present time, use the **present progressive form.**

The attending doctor in the emergency room *is treating* the child's broken arm.

The present progressive can also express an action in the future when it is used with an adverb or a group of words that indicates the future.

The celebrity's plane *is arriving* in an hour.

To express an ongoing action that happened in the past, use the **past progressive form.**

Maria Tallchief *was dancing* with the New York City Ballet during the mid-1900's.

To express an ongoing action that will take place in the future, use the **future progressive form.**

People *will be listening* to the music of the Beatles for years to come.

To express an ongoing action that began in the past and is continuing in the present, use the **present perfect progressive form.**

> Attorney Vilma Martinez *has been working* to promote civil rights causes since the 1960's.

To express an ongoing past action interrupted by another past action, use the **past perfect progressive form.**

> Native Americans *had been living* on this continent for thousands of years before Columbus came.

To express an ongoing future action that will have taken place by a specified future time, use the **future perfect progressive form.**

> By noon the peace marchers *will have been walking* for six hours.

Using the Emphatic Forms

To give force or emphasis to a verb, use the **emphatic forms** of the verb. Add the auxiliary *do* or *does* to the present tense of the verb to form the present emphatic. To form the past emphatic, add *did* to the present tense.

Present	Books about sports *sell* many copies.
Present Emphatic	Books about sports *do sell* many copies.
Past	He *gave* much time to volunteer work.
Past Emphatic	He *did give* much time to volunteer work.

The emphatic forms are used in negative statements and questions, but they do not necessarily add emphasis to such sentences.

> The hikers *did*n't *expect* to encounter snow in July.
> *Do* many immigrants *come* to the United States today?

Practice Your Skills

CONCEPT CHECK

Progressive and Emphatic Verbs Write each progressive and emphatic verb form used in the following sentences. Then write the name of the form.

1. England has been granting power to female monarchs for centuries.
2. Not until the second half of this century did a woman serve as that nation's prime minister.
3. The daughter of a grocer, Margaret Thatcher had been studying chemistry at Oxford when she became active in student politics.

4. Thatcher found out that law did interest her, so she took some part-time courses while working as a research chemist.
5. At the time Thatcher ran for Parliament, the country was suffering from numerous trade union strikes.
6. Thatcher felt then that the situation was a serious threat to the well-being of public service, and she still does denounce strong union activity.
7. Apparently the voters had been waiting for a stand such as Thatcher's, and she went on to win the leadership of the Conservative party in the Parliament.
8. Though now officially retired, Thatcher is planning to remain active in politics.
9. If she does so, by the year 2000 she will have been serving her country for forty years.
10. If her accomplishments serve as a model, perhaps other nations will be electing female leaders in the near future.

Improper Shifts in Tense and Form

Use the same tense to express two or more actions that occur at the same time.

Do not shift tenses within or between sentences unless such a change is needed to clarify meaning. Use the same tense for the verbs in a compound sentence and in a sentence with a compound predicate.

Incorrect   Congress *passes* laws, and the President *enforced* them.
Correct   Congress *passes* laws, and the President *enforces* them.

Incorrect   The U.S. Supreme Court *hears* many cases and *ruled* on their constitutionality.
Correct   The U.S. Supreme Court *hears* many cases and *rules* on their constitutionality.

Not all shifts in tense are incorrect. A shift in tense may be needed to show that actions occurred at different times.

Vincent van Gogh *had died* (past perfect) long before the world *recognized* (past) his genius.
Billions of years *will have passed* (future perfect) by the time the sun *dies*. (present)

Practice Your Skill

A. CONCEPT CHECK

Tense and Form   Each of the literary passages below illustrates how a well-known writer uses verb tenses and forms to show differences in time. List each italicized verb. Then identify the verb by writing the name of the tense, the name of the progressive form, or the name of the emphatic form. After you have finished, reread each passage to gain an appreciation of the skillful way in which the author employs verb tenses and forms to express actions that happen at different times.

1. I had been here just a year before, in mid-February, after an attack of influenza. And now I *had returned,* after an attack of influenza. It *had been raining* when I *left.*   **Max Beerbohm**

2. At that moment the boss *noticed* that a fly had fallen into his broad inkpot, and *was trying* feebly but desperately to clamber out again. . . . The boss *took* up a pen, *picked* the fly out of the ink, and shook it on to a piece of blotting paper.   **Katherine Mansfield**

3. The sun *said,* "My friend, my beloved moon, I *will miss* your constancy more than I can say. I'll long for our time together. I*'ll treasure* the time I *have* alone to think about what you *tell* me. And I'll hope that our time together is a time to talk, to discuss, maybe even have a little argument."   **Judith Stein**

4. Her mother *was perspiring* and disheveled when she *returned* with the tall stack of cutlets and wrapped them on the table. Zelda *did* not *look* up but felt keenly the woman's discomfort.
                                                                    Jess Wells

5. We commonly *do* not *remember* that it is, after all, always the first person that *is speaking.*   **Henry David Thoreau**

6. The anthropologist *had been investigating* language groups in northern Queensland. He was going to spend a few weeks in the city, at a university, before joining his wife in India. She *is* the new sort of wife with serious interests of her own.   **Alice Munro**

7. Shotwell *keeps* the jacks and rubber ball in his attaché case and *will* not *allow* me to play with them. He *plays* with them alone, sitting on the floor near the console hour after hour, chanting "onesies, twosies, threesies, foursies." . . . And when he *has finished,* when he *has sated* himself, back they *go* into the attaché case.   **Donald Barthelme**

8. Fiction *has been redefining* itself along theoretical lines. It *has* also *been advancing* its claim . . . to be understood as art, as high art, as holy art. Fiction *has helped* advance the successful claim of all the arts to be worth their candles.   **Annie Dillard**

9. I *saw* a happy man, one whose cherished dream *had* so obviously *come* true, who *had attained* his goal in life, who *had got* what he wanted, who *was* satisfied with his lot and with himself.

Anton Chekhov

10. "You *have* never *seen* our garden?" she *asked* him as they *went* down the steps. "It *is* fairly large."

Thomas Mann

B. REVISION SKILL

Consistency in Tense and Form   Rewrite each sentence to correct any unnecessary shift in tenses. If the tenses need no correction, write *Correct*.

1. The poet Emily Dickinson expressed her feelings and indicates her individuality in several ways.
2. Her poetry displayed a strange use of punctuation, and her lines reflect experimental rhyme and meter.
3. She preferred dashes instead of commas and traditional end punctuation, and she often uses capital letters inconsistently.
4. Although Dickinson's personal life is as unusual as her poetry, she didn't wish to draw attention to her differences.
5. In her mid-twenties, she withdrew from public life and had lived in almost total seclusion.
6. In seclusion, she refused to go beyond her house and garden, and she will wear only white.

The Metropolitan Museum of Art. Bequest of Miss Adelaide Milton de Groot (1876–1967). (67.187.141)

Across the Room,
by Edmund C. Tarbell,
1967

7. She had no wish for recognition, so she publishes only seven out of her 1,775 poems during her lifetime.
8. She scribbled poems on scraps of paper, wrote them on backs of envelopes, and will copy them on sheets of paper.
9. After she had sewn them into little notebooks, she stored them in her dresser drawer, where they were found by her sister after her death.
10. Perhaps many more years will pass before we totally appreciate her brilliance.

C. PROOFREADING SKILL

Improper Shifts In Tense Find the errors in the following paragraph. Be alert to improper shifts of tense and other problems in the use of tenses. Also watch for errors in capitalization, punctuation, and spelling. Then rewrite the paragraph to correct all errors.

> Who would ever guess that people in the dallas area ate more caned spinich per capita than people in any other part of the United States. This is only one of many strange consumption phenomena. For example, Hawaiians eat the most canned meat, as they has since World War II. The most prune juice is drank in Miami, and mixed vegetable juice was three times more popular in denver than anywhere else. On the other hand Syracuse, New York, produces plenty of apples but drank the least cider, and Denver is drinking the least prune juice.

C H E C K   P O I N T
PAGES 646–670

PAGES 646–670

A. Copy each italicized verb form. Label it *Present, Present Participle, Past,* or *Past Participle.*

1. The sun has just *begun* to set as you walk out onto the shore of Loch Ness.
2. A cold wind is *blowing* down the lake, stirring it into ripples.
3. A narrow but deep channel of water, Loch Ness *cuts* through the Scottish Highlands at about the 57th parallel.
4. Before working its way here, that stiff breeze probably first *sprang* up over the frigid waters of the North Sea.
5. You're thankful that you are *wearing* a suitably warm jacket.
6. Like other tourists, you *came* here to Loch Ness because of the rumors.
7. Over the years, people have reportedly *caught* sight of an extraordinary creature in this remote Scottish lake.

8. Now the lake is *drawing* thousands of curious spectators every year.
9. From fishermen in rowboats to scientists with bathyspheres, they *spread* out daily across the Loch, hoping to catch a glimpse of its mysterious resident.
10. They have *brought* sophisticated radar detection devices and mystical homemade fishing lures.
11. They *sit* for hours in their boats, peering into the blue-green depths of the Loch.
12. Speculators *fight* over the most attractive theory: is it a miraculously preserved dinosaur or a huge sturgeon?
13. When interviewed, witnesses *swore* that "Nessie" resembled the long-necked Plesiosaurus that haunted the seas during the Cretaceous Period.
14. So far, though, no one has *been* able to sight the creature clearly enough for identification.
15. This afternoon you, too, were disappointed when you *saw* nothing from your small motorboat.
16. Now the sun is down, and waves are *breaking* onto the beach.
17. As the icy wind *stings* your face, you begin to picture a cozy hearth and a hot meal.
18. You question the impulse that *drove* you to come on this unlikely quest.
19. Look there—something large and oddly graceful has *swum* out of the fog!
20. After one quick look, you find that you are *running* back to your hotel, calling for other witnesses.

B. Write the form of the verb in parentheses that will complete each of the following sentences correctly.

1. Even before tourists became interested, strange legends had (exist) telling about fabulous creatures living beneath the waters of the British Isles.
2. For years, in northern England, they told of green-haired Peg Powler who regularly (bear) children beneath the surface of the river Tees.
3. Scottish grandmothers have (sing) their charges to sleep with tales of the Selkies and Roane.
4. These peaceful fairy folk would (put) on seal skins and travel safely and easily through the waters around the British Isles.
5. When the full moon (shine), the Selkies dropped their seal disguises and danced along the seashore.
6. Travelers have always (flee), however, to avoid encounters with kelpies, or water-horses.

7. Scots believe that many folks have (lose) their lives by taking rides on these cunning, shape-changing creatures.
8. Even now, some wary types who walk by water late at night may (bite) their lips in fear.
9. According to other legends, the skinless, centaur-like Nuckelavee (slay) cattle and people alike with its poisonous breath.
10. Perhaps these legends (grow) from parents' tales, devised to keep curious children away from dangerous bodies of water—and perhaps not.

C. Write the verb in parentheses in the tense indicated to complete each sentence correctly.

1. Eating calamari is the closest most of us (*come*—Present Perfect) to meeting the legendary Kraken.
2. This tentacled monster (*make*—Past Perfect) many appearances in legend before its memorable cameo in the film *Twenty Thousand Leagues Under the Sea.*
3. Norwegian fishermen first (*report*—Past) appearances of the Kraken in the sixteenth century.
4. We can only speculate whether some (*observe*—Future) the Kraken in years to come.
5. One particular day, the soundings that the fishermen made to determine water depth (*read*—Past) only five fathoms instead of the usual fifteen.
6. The men (*row*—Past Perfect) a safe distance away before the Kraken broke the surface.

7. "If I live a century," said the captain, "I (*see*—Future Perfect) nothing else so monstrously large—a mile long at least."
8. In recent years, scientists (*identify*—Present Perfect) the Kraken as a giant squid.
9. They know that when such a large beast descends, it (*create*—Present) a huge whirlpool.
10. Probably, by the next generation, the legendary exaggerations (*cease*—Future Perfect).

D. Write the form of the verb asked for in parentheses to complete each sentence correctly.

1. It is 1922, and a British Royal Air Force pilot (*call*—Present Progressive) for a weather report.
2. He thinks something curious (*affect*—Past Emphatic) his radio.
3. A baffling series of minor accidents (*bother*—Past Perfect Progressive) the R.A.F. since World War I.
4. Headquarters (*respond*—Past Perfect Progressive) "Gremlins sur la Manche" before the baffled aviator's radio went dead.
5. By the year 2000, probably countless pilots and mechanics (*experience*—Future Perfect Progressive) the sneaky exploits of these mysterious gremlins.
6. Clearly some supernatural force (*interfere*—Past Progressive) with British navigators—why else would so many planes get lost?
7. It is true, however, that people (*attribute*—Present Emphatic) seemingly mysterious mishaps to the impish activities of spirits.
8. The Japanese, for example, (*manage*—Past Emphatic) to blame some common annoyances on unseen beings.
9. A typical explanation might be, "Don't ask who cut your sandal strap: the weasel-like Kama Itachi (*slice*—Present Perfect Progressive) with his invisible sickle again!"
10. As long as things persist in going wrong for no good reason, we (*blame*—Future Progressive) gremlins and other invisible spirits for our mishaps.

VOICE AND MOOD

When you write or speak, you select a specific verb tense to indicate the time of the action the verb expresses. You can also use the progressive and emphatic forms to express the circumstances of an action more accurately. Verbs also have certain other constructions that you can use for special purposes. Mastering these constructions can help you add precision and variety to your writing.

Active and Passive Voice

The voice of a verb indicates whether the subject is the performer or the receiver of the action the verb expresses. A verb is in the **active voice** if the subject performs the action. However, if the subject receives the action, the verb is in the **passive voice.**

Active Voice	The victors of World War II *founded* the United Nations. (The subject *victors* performed the action of founding.)
Passive Voice	The United Nations *was founded* by the victors of World War II. (The subject *United Nations* received the action of being founded.)

The verb in the active voice above has a direct object; it is a transitive verb. Notice in the example above that when this verb is changed to the passive voice, the direct object *United Nations* becomes the subject. Intransitive verbs and linking verbs cannot be in the passive voice because they do not have direct objects that can become subjects.

Retained Objects Some transitive verbs in the active voice can have both direct objects and indirect objects. When these verbs are changed to the passive voice, either of the two objects can become the subject of the sentence. The other remains an object and is called a **retained object.**

Active Voice	The proctor gave each student a copy of the test. (*Student* is the indirect object, and *copy* is the direct object.)
Passive Voice	Each student was given a copy of the test by the proctor. (*Copy* is the retained object.)
Passive Voice	A copy of the test was given each student by the proctor. (*Student* is the retained object.)

Using Voice in Writing

The active voice is more forceful and less wordy than the passive voice. To avoid vagueness and wordiness, do not use the passive voice in long passages. Also avoid using the active voice and the passive voice in the same sentence and in related consecutive sentences.

The passive voice does have legitimate uses: (1) when the writer wants to emphasize the person or thing receiving the action of the verb or (2) when the person or thing performing the action is unknown or deliberately kept anonymous.

Writing TIP

Consistently using the active voice keeps the focus of your writing on the subject in each sentence.

The returning astronauts *were honored* with a huge parade.
(The persons receiving the action are emphasized.)
Further flights of the space shuttle *were postponed* indefinitely.
(The person performing the action is unknown.)

Practice Your Skills

A. CONCEPT CHECK

Active and Passive Voice   Write the verb in each sentence. Then write *Active* or *Passive* to identify the voice of the verb.

Writing Theme
Pioneers in Music

1. The blues singer Blind Lemon Jefferson was born in Texas in 1897.
2. As a child, he absorbed the musical expressions of the work and worship around him.
3. He traveled throughout the South from Texas to Virginia in search of an audience.
4. Only rarely was he featured in vaudeville houses or traditional theaters.
5. Most often he performed his music in the streets of small towns, in front of the feed store, or in the town square.
6. His brief but influential recording career lasted from 1926 to 1929.
7. Later blues artists such as B. B. King were profoundly influenced by his song style and his unusual use of the guitar.
8. The guitar was used by Jefferson as an extension of his voice rather than simply as an accompaniment.
9. Two of his most inventive and evocative songs, "That Black Snake Moan" and "See That My Grave Is Kept Clean" still please audiences.
10. Blind Lemon Jefferson was found frozen to death in a Chicago snowstorm in 1929.

B. DRAFTING SKILL

Achieving Directness   Read the following sentences. They contain verbs in both the active and passive voices. When direct wording would improve the sentences, change the passive verbs to active verbs, deleting words as necessary.

1. Bessie Smith and Ma Rainey are considered by many historians to be the most influential female pioneers of the blues.
2. The women's recordings are marked by sophisticated, jazzy arrangements of musicians like Louis Armstrong and Fletcher Henderson.
3. Ma Rainey's blues were bred in the tent shows and vaudeville revues of the South.
4. Ma and her husband Will were advertised by playbills as "The Assassinators of the Blues."

Bessie Smith

Verb Usage **675**

5. That title conveys some of the earthy, raw power of Rainey's spell-binding performances.
6. Bessie Smith was crowned the Empress of the Blues by her adoring fans.
7. Bessie was catapulted to international stardom by recordings, film work, and stage appearances.
8. Her spirited style is best expressed in songs like " 'Tain't Nobody's Bizness If I Do."
9. Another famous song, "Nobody Knows You When You're Down and Out," evokes the artistic neglect she suffered during the Great Depression.
10. The triumphs and tragedies of Bessie Smith's life have made her a symbol of the power to overcome oppression.

Understanding and Using Mood

The term **mood** is used to designate the manner in which a verb expresses an idea. English speakers and writers can use three moods: the indicative, the imperative, and the subjunctive. The **indicative mood,** which is used most often, indicates a fact. It can be used in declarative, interrogative, and exclamatory sentences.

> Sally K. Ride *was* the first American woman in space.
> *Was* Guion Bluford the first African American to orbit Earth?

The **imperative mood** is used to give a command or make a request. The subject of a verb in this mood is always understood to be *you*.

> *Send* for this information pamphlet today.
> Kindly *include* a stamped, self-addressed envelope.

The **subjunctive mood** is used (1) to express a wish or a condition that is contrary to fact or (2) to express a command or a request after the word *that*.

> Most people would prefer that the temperatures in August *were* cooler. (expresses a wish)
> If temperatures *were* cooler, then electricity bills would be lower. (expresses a condition contrary to fact)
> The power company asked that residential users *be* conservative in their power consumption during peak hours. (expresses a command or a request after *that*)

The forms of the indicative and subjunctive moods are exactly the same, with the three exceptions listed on the following page.

1. The -s is omitted from verbs in the third-person singular.

Indicative   Dr. Carlos Sanchez *supports* our cause.
Subjunctive   We requested that Dr. Carlos Sanchez *support* our
              cause.

2. In the present subjunctive, the verb *to be* is always *be*.

Present Subjunctive   The Surgeon General has proposed that the
                       United States *be* smoke-free by the year
                       2000.

3. In the past subjunctive, the verb *to be* is always *were*.

Past Subjunctive   If I *were* rich, I would travel around the world.

Practice Your Skills

CONCEPT CHECK

Moods of Verbs   Write the italicized verb in the sentence and identify its mood.

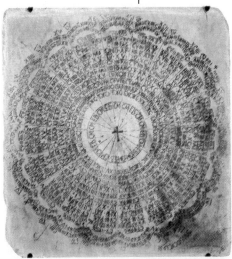

Writing Theme
Time

1. *Imagine,* if you will, a world without clocks, calendars, wristwatches, or computer date books.
2. Go back to a world where humans *depended* on the sun, the
   moon, and the cycles of nature instead.
3. *Step* with me into "The Time Zone."
4. The year is 46 B.C. and, if you *were judging* by the autumnal chill in the air, you
   would say that it was September.
5. *Look* around. You soon realize that you
   are in a Roman palace, preparing for a
   short trip.
6. The imperial scribe is speaking to you, and
   he suggests strongly that you *be* back in
   Rome on time for your appointment with
   Julius Caesar.
7. "If you *were* to be even a day later than
   January 3," he suggests with a nasty smile,
   "there would be consequences."
8. You *bow* humbly as you leave the palace,
   trying to ignore that smile.
9. You wonder, as you *walk* down the stone streets, what could take
   you away from Rome for so many months.
10. Little do you know that the Roman calendar has been getting fur-
    ther and further off for years and, if all the adjustments *were* made
    immediately, January 3 would be one week away.

Roman calendar,
6th century

Verb Usage   **677**

Because the meanings and spellings of the two verbs in each of the following pairs are so close, they can cause confusion. Learn to use *lie* and *lay, rise* and *raise,* and *sit* and *set* correctly.

Lie and Lay

Lie and *lay* are two different words and have two different meanings. Here are their principal parts.

Present	Present Participle	Past	Past Participle
lie	(is) lying	lay	(have) lain
lay	(is) laying	laid	(have) laid

Lie, an intransitive verb, means "to rest in a flat position." This verb never has a direct object.

> The island of Guam *lies* in the middle of the Pacific Ocean.
> Many sunken ships *are lying* on the floor of the ocean.

The transitive verb *lay* means "to place." It takes a direct object except when it is in the passive voice.

Active Voice Chinese workers *laid* the foundation for the Central Pacific Railroad in the 1860's.
Passive Voice The foundation for the Central Pacific Railroad *was laid* by Chinese workers in the 1860's.

Rise and Raise

Rise and *raise* are two different words and have two different meanings. Here are their principal parts.

Present	Present Participle	Past	Past Participle
rise	(is) rising	rose	(have) risen
raise	(is) raising	raised	(have) raised

The intransitive verb *rise* means "to go upward." It never has a direct object.

> Deep-sea divers *rise* slowly to the surface to prevent a condition called the bends.
> The bread *will* not *rise* because there is no yeast in it.

The transitive verb *raise* means "to lift" or "to make something go up." This verb can have a direct object except when it is in the passive voice.

The neighbors *are raising* money for the family whose house burned.

The roof *was raised* so that another story could be added to the house.

Sit and Set

Sit and *set* are two different words and have two different meanings. Here are their principal parts.

Present	Present Participle	Past	Past Participle
sit	(is) sitting	sat	(have) sat
set	(is) setting	set	(have) set

The intransitive verb *sit* means "to occupy a seat." It does not take a direct object.

A calico cat *was sitting* on the porch.
We *will sit* just behind the dugout at the baseball game.

The transitive verb *set* means "to put or place." It usually takes a direct object.

With great relief, the movers *set* the piano on the floor.
Someone *had set* a large carton on the kitchen table.

Practice Your Skills

A. CONCEPT CHECK

Commonly Confused Verbs   Rewrite each sentence, correcting any error in verb usage. If a sentence has no error, write *Correct*.

1. As you drive south on Lake Shore Drive toward downtown Chicago, the Sears Tower raises before you.
2. The world's tallest office building sets on Wacker Drive between Jackson and Van Buren streets.
3. Miracles of design and construction were needed to raise the Sears Tower to its height of 1,454 feet.
4. The placement of the sixteen thousand windows was lain out to afford workers and visitors spectacular views of the city and Lake Michigan.
5. Another engineering marvel that lays north and east of the Sears building is the John Hancock Center.
6. A combined residential and office building, the Hancock Center sits regally on North Michigan Avenue.
7. As you set in the windowed restaurant atop the Hancock, your eyes are drawn to the vast blue expanse of Lake Michigan.

Writing
TIP

Set can also be used to write in the passive voice. *The table was set.*

Writing Theme
Famous Buildings

8. When the weather warms, the lakefront beaches begin to fill with people sitting out their blankets and beach chairs.
9. They lie there soaking up the sun, eager to make up for the long winter days inside.
10. Chicago's waterfront parks have been lain out with great care.
11. Indeed, the parks lay along the lake shore like a front yard, which they have been called.
12. At times, however, the city and the lake set uneasily side by side.
13. For many years, the water level of Lake Michigan rose steadily.
14. The harsh winter winds that give Chicago its nickname rose the level of the lake even more.
15. On several occasions, the angry waters have flooded the streets and parking lots that lay adjacent to the lake.

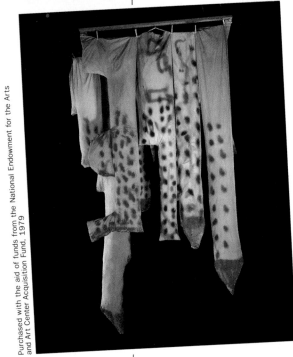

Purchased with the aid of funds from the National Endowment for the Arts and Art Center Acquisition Fund, 1979

Upside Down City, by Claes Oldenburg, 1962. Collection Walker Art Center, Minneapolis

B. DRAFTING SKILL

Using Commonly Confused Verbs   Replace the blank in each of the following sentences by writing the correct form of the verb in parentheses.

1. Some years ago, to accompany a vista of towering trees _____ up around a group of pioneers, a television soundtrack proclaimed, "The bluest skies you've ever seen are in Seattle." (rising, raising)
2. This song may have _____ a few mistaken expectations. (risen, raised)
3. Seattle _____ in a part of the Pacific Northwest that is prone to considerable precipitation. (lies, lays)
4. The city of Seattle _____ among seven hills that rise steeply from the shores of Puget Sound. (sits, sets)
5. It _____ between the Olympic Mountains to the west and the Cascade Range to the east. (lies, lays)
6. To the southeast _____ the magnificent spectacle of 14,410-foot Mount Rainier. (rises, raises)
7. _____ in the lowlands and surrounded by ocean and mountains, Seattle often becomes a basin for aerial moisture. (Sit, Set)
8. There are weeks when nature seems to have _____ a ceiling of

gray clouds like a builder _____ concrete. (laid, lain) (lying, laying)

9. In fact, because of where Seattle _____ , it often receives more than 38 inches of rain per year. (sits, sets)

10. Nonetheless, Seattle has _____ to the position of one of the most rapidly growing cities. (risen, raised)

CHECK POINT
PAGES 673–681

PAGES 673–681

A. Rewrite each of the following sentences, changing the verbs from the passive voice to the active voice.

1. The hot still air of summer has often been disturbed by the rasping calls of the cicadas.
2. That electric buzzing from the nearby trees is produced by an orchestra of green and black insects.
3. The sounds are created by rapidly vibrating plates, called timbals, on the insect's abdomen.
4. Because of its appearance in July and August, the most common cicada is referred to by entomologists as the dog-day cicada.
5. Scientists have long been intrigued by a relative known as the periodical cicada.
6. These long-lived insects are characterized by lengthy hibernations and brief mating periods.
7. A foot or so under the ground, a small chamber has been excavated by the tiny nymph cicada.
8. After an incubation period of seventeen years, the cicada is called out of the earth by a powerful natural impulse.
9. In a remarkable metamorphosis, the nymph is replaced by a gossamer-winged adult.
10. The periodical cicada is allowed only a month by its biological timetable in which to mate and give birth before it dies.

B. Identify the mood of the italicized verb in each of the following sentences as *Indicative, Imperative,* or *Subjunctive.*

1. In the 1950's, one of the most popular types of science-fiction movie *was* the "giant-insect film."
2. If this *were* the 1950's, moviegoers might be rushing out to see movies like *Tarantula* or *The Beginning of the End.*
3. In the latter, the army requests that a scientist *investigate* the destruction of a small Midwest town.
4. In measured tones, the scientist reports: "*Think* about it, General. Giant grasshoppers. Some as big as houses."

Writing Theme
Insects

Verb Usage **681**

5. In a similar thriller, *Them,* the menace to humans *is* a horde of giant ants crawling out of the Mojave Desert.
6. Viewers often felt as if they *were* part of the terror being enacted on the movie screen.
7. One message of movies such as these was "*Beware* of the uncontrollable unknown!"
8. Such movies *sprang* up at the dawn of atomic experimentation.
9. Some people felt as if they *were* victims of unstoppable progress.
10. Decades later, in their attempts to halt nuclear tests, protesters would chant, "*Ban* the Bomb!"

C. For each of the following sentences, write the correct verb form of the two verbs in parentheses.

1. Recent occurrences of Lyme disease have (raised, risen) concerns about insects in the woods.
2. It is true that an unnerving variety of ticks and fleas is (sitting, setting) on the branches that wave gently overhead.
3. These tiny predators are (laying, lying) in ambush for unwary warmblooded wayfarers.
4. They infest not only the trees that (rise, raise) above, but also the grasses that carpet the ground below.
5. A walk through the woods on a humid summer day can also (rise, raise) clouds of gnats and mosquitoes.
6. The mosquito in search of a meal will eagerly (sit, set) down on any exposed skin.
7. However, a few precautions can (lie, lay) to rest any fear of unwanted insect attacks.
8. For example, travelers who (sit, set) hats on their heads run less risk of picking up unwanted company.
9. Travelers who have (sat, set) or (lain, laid) down in the grass should briskly brush themselves off.
10. However, when the question of the effect of bee stings is (raised, risen), there is a more serious matter at hand.
11. The threat of bee stings (lays, lies) mostly in the serious allergic reactions of a few unfortunate individuals.
12. A bee sting does more than (rise, raise) a welt on the skin of these people.
13. A serious allergic reaction can cause the afflicted to (lay, lie) in the hospital for days.
14. For nonallergic persons, (lying, laying) a paste of baking soda and water on most insect bites will alleviate the itching.
15. (Sit, Set) your mind at rest—with enough care you can still safely enjoy a walk in the woods.

A. Using Verbs Correctly   Write the correct verb form for each of the following sentences.

1. If you have (swam, swum) in the ocean lately, you may have wondered about the presence of sharks.
2. Rarely have sharks actually (bit, bitten) people.
3. However, public perception of potential danger from sharks (took, taken) on exaggerated proportions after the film *Jaws*.
4. Even photographs of sharks (brung, brought) a chill of fear to some.
5. Now this antagonism toward sharks has (drove, driven) people to hunt them for sport.
6. Shark meat has also (catched, caught) the attention of gourmet chefs as a menu item.
7. Thousands of sharks are also (slew, slain) annually for their fins, which are considered a delicacy.
8. The pendulum has (swang, swung); the predator is now the prey.
9. Scientists have (spoke, spoken) about the effects of a declining shark population on the ecological balance of oceans.
10. Once the number has (fell, fallen) drastically, uncontrolled populations of certain other fish would create an imbalance.

Writing Theme
Relating to
Our Environment

B. Verb Tenses   Write the tense of the verb named in parentheses.

1. People (*become*—Present Progressive) more concerned about the effect of excess carbon dioxide in the atmosphere.
2. People (*use*—Past Perfect Progressive) far fewer CO_2-producing fuels before the Industrial Revolution than they have since.
3. A few (*know*—Past) that the research results of Svante Ahennius (*suggest*—Past Progressive) that excessive CO_2 could raise the global temperature.
4. For some time, physicists (*explore*—Present Perfect Progressive) the idea that atmospheric CO_2 traps infrared radiation.
5. In the past, scientists (*hope*—Past Perfect) that the ocean would absorb CO_2 from fossil fuels.
6. Now, however, they (*find*—Present) that CO_2 stays in the air.
7. By the time an engine has consumed a gallon of gas, it (*discharge* —Future Perfect) 5.6 pounds of carbon as CO_2.
8. Studies have shown that the quantity of CO_2 in the air (*increase*— Present Perfect) over 28 times since the 1840's.
9. It is possible that airborne CO_2 (*double*—Future) in the future.
10. By the twenty-first century, researchers (*gather*—Future Perfect Progressive) data for over two hundred years; we (*wait*—Future Progressive) to hear about some solutions.

C. Changing Verb Tenses and Forms Rewrite each sentence, following the directions in parentheses. Add or delete words as needed.

1. Ancients believed that natural elements *are controlled* by gods and goddesses. (Correct the tense of the italicized verb.)
2. The goddess Ceres was believed by the Romans to control the bounties of the harvest. (Change the verb to the active voice.)
3. Watching the lightning, the Norse knew that it *represents* the handiwork of Thor. (Correct the tense of the italicized verb.)
4. Chinese mythology thought that the source of lightning *is* Tien Mu. (Correct the tense of the italicized verb.)
5. The Chinese *believed* that lightning flashed between mirrors in her hands. (Change the italicized verb to the past emphatic.)
6. If you are a Yakut villager in Mongolia, you would pay tribute to Ai Toyon. (Correct the use of the subjunctive mood.)
7. This two-headed eagle sat on top of the world tree and sends out light. (Make the tenses consistent.)
8. Roman blacksmiths honored Vulcan for the fire that will make their work possible. (Make the tenses consistent.)
9. Providing an essential element for both survival and cultural advancement, all gods of fire were held in high esteem. (Use *having* with a past participle.)
10. Even now, the concept of fire evokes a feeling of mythic power. (Use the present emphatic.)

D. Identifying Voice and Mood Write the verb in parentheses in the voice or mood indicated.

1. Modern cultures usually (*take*—Active Voice) climate, resources, dangers, and stability into account when constructing shelter.
2. For example, in India, some houses (*build*—Passive Voice) on stilts to protect the inhabitants from the dampness of the ground.
3. In contrast, Eskimos cannot (*build*—Active Voice) wooden homes because the region they inhabit is largely above the tree line.
4. Eskimos make homes of stone, grass, or earth, and, when hunting in icy regions, they (*build*—Indicative Mood) with snow.
5. In earthquake-vulnerable Japan, logic suggests that a builder (*construct*—Subjunctive Mood) a home of light materials.
6. The roofs of Japanese homes often (*make*—Passive Voice) of light bamboo sticks, and the frame walls are paper-covered.
7. Wandering Mongolians prefer that their dwellings (*be*—Subjunctive Mood) yurts, or felt tents.
8. The comfortable, roomy yurts (*move*—Passive Voice) easily as the herders travel with their grazing animals.

Agreement of Subject and Verb

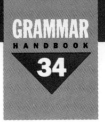

AGREEMENT IN NUMBER

The **number** of a word indicates whether it is **singular** or **plural.**

The subject and verb of a sentence must agree in number.

A singular verb is used with a singular subject; a plural verb is used with a plural subject. This grammatical accord between subject and verb is called **agreement.**

> The <u>sliding door</u> (singular) <u>opens</u> (singular) onto the back porch.
>
> The <u>French doors</u> (plural) <u>open</u> (plural) in from a balcony.

Except for the verb *be,* the form of a verb is changed to show number only in the third-person singular of the present tense.

Verbs				
Singular			**Plural**	
I	joke		we	joke
you	joke		you	joke
he, she, it, Dale	jokes		they, the lawyers	joke

When you check subject-verb agreement, note that nouns ending in *-s* are usually plural but verbs ending in *-s* are usually singular.

Singular and Plural Forms of *Be*

The forms of the verb *be* are irregular and must be memorized.

Forms of **Be**				
	Present Tense		**Past Tense**	
	Singular	**Plural**	**Singular**	**Plural**
First Person	I am	we are	I was	we were
Second Person	you are	you are	you were	you were
Third Person	he, she, it is	they are	he, she, it was	they were

WORDS BETWEEN SUBJECT AND VERB

A verb agrees only with its subject.

Sometimes one or more words come between a subject and its verb. As these examples show, intervening words do not affect subject-verb agreement.

> One of Jupiter's moons is volcanically active. (*One*, not *moons*, is the subject.)
>
> Profits, with the exception of last quarter's loss, were better than expected. (*Profits*, not *loss*, is the subject.)

The expressions *with, together with, along with,* and *as well as* are prepositions. As shown in the example above, the objects of these prepositions do not affect the number of the verb.

Practice Your Skills

CONCEPT CHECK

Agreement in Number of Subject and Verb For each of the following sentences, write the subject and the form of the verb that agrees in number with the subject.

1. Various geographical areas of the country (inspire, inspires) humorists who reflect a regional wit and humor.
2. Lifestyles, as well as characteristics of speech, (vary, varies) from one part of the country to another.
3. However, regional humor, with its witty references to American culture, (amuse, amuses) many different people.
4. The work of humorists James Thurber and Max Shulman (contain, contains) humor related to life in the Midwest.
5. The works of Woody Allen, along with early twentieth-century writer Damon Runyon, (portray, portrays) typical New Yorkers.
6. On the other hand, the dry witticisms of Garrison Keillor (spring, springs) from events in Midwestern small-town life.
7. Similarly, the stories of Mark Twain often (reveal, reveals) humorous aspects of a more rural lifestyle in Missouri.
8. Perhaps Will Rogers, with his colorful images of Texas and Oklahoma, (was, were) the wittiest Southwestern humorist.
9. Rogers, together with Twain, (is, are) thought of as typically "American" in terms of a humorous approach to writing.
10. Interestingly, these humorists, no matter how witty they are, (do, does) not always appeal to audiences in other countries.

Writing Theme
Regional Humor

COMPOUND SUBJECTS

In most cases, use a plural verb with a compound subject in which the parts are joined by *and.*

Good <u>lighting</u> and careful <u>composition</u> <u>make</u> photographs interesting.

Use a singular verb with a compound subject when the subject is thought of as a unit.

<u>Bread and butter</u> <u>is</u> always part of our evening meal.

Use a singular verb with a compound subject that is preceded by *each, every,* or *many a.*

Every <u>magazine</u> and <u>catalog</u> <u>has</u> its own computerized mailing list.

When the parts of a compound subject are joined by *or* or *nor,* use a verb that agrees with the subject nearer the verb.

Neither the <u>mayor</u> nor the council <u>members</u> <u>were</u> pleased with the press coverage. (The plural verb *were* agrees with *members,* the subject nearer the verb.)

Practice Your Skills

A. CONCEPT CHECK

Correct Subject-Verb Agreement For each of the following sentences, write the form of the verb that agrees in number with the subject.

1. Carson McCullers and Lillian Hellman, highly respected writers, (comes, come) from the South.
2. McCullers's *The Heart Is a Lonely Hunter* and *The Ballad of the Sad Café,* originally novels, (was, were) later adapted for the theater.
3. Every major character and central theme in the works of both McCullers and Hellman (reflect, reflects) the authors' intense views of the world.
4. *Grotesque* and *gothic* (is, are) terms often used to describe McCullers's characters.
5. Every story and play (focus, focuses) on characters with unusual features or personalities.
6. Psychological drama or social tension (mark, marks) Hellman's plays.

7. *The Little Foxes, Watch on the Rhine,* and *The Children's Hour,* all plays by Hellman, (feature, features) characters facing crises.
8. Neither the critics nor the public (was, were) kind to *Watch on the Rhine* when it first appeared.
9. Many a writer (has, have) faced similar rejection.
10. Hellman's memoirs—*An Unfinished Woman, Pentimento,* and *Maybe*—(reveals, reveal) the real-life dilemmas she encountered.

Above: Carson McCullers
Left: Lillian Hellman

B. APPLICATION IN WRITING

A Comparison Think of two women that you can compare. Write a paragraph about the similarities and differences between the two. In your comparison, use some sentences with compound subjects.

CHECK POINT
PAGES 685–688

A. For each of the following sentences, write the form of the verb that agrees with the subject.

1. Water travel in ancient times (was, were) slow and tedious.
2. The development of wind-powered ships (marks, mark) an important advance in the history of navigation.

3. The civilization of ancient Egypt, with its pyramids and other marvels, (is, are) credited with inventing the sail.
4. The power and classification of sailing craft (depend, depends) on the rig, or the sails with their masts and ropes.
5. Many a shipbuilder (has, have) worked on improving the rig.
6. Every designer and sailor (strives, strive) for greater speed.
7. The sails of ancient Egypt (was, were) nothing more than a square piece of cloth attached to a single mast.
8. By 500 B.C., the Phoenicians, along with the Greeks, (was, were) building ships with two masts.
9. Around A.D. 1000, sailors in the Mediterranean (invents, invent) a lateen sail for sailing directly into the wind.
10. Engines and steam power (appears, appear) as improvements in the 1700's.
11. Two centuries later, the great age of ocean liners (introduces, introduce) sea travelers to luxury.
12. Neither steam nor sails (prevails, prevail) on the seas today.
13. Instead, most pleasure craft, as well as cargo ships, (uses, use) petroleum.
14. However, dependence on petroleum (remains, remain) a problem.
15. Perhaps nuclear power and automation (holds, hold) some answers for the future.

B. Rewrite the following sentences, correcting all errors in subject-verb agreement. If a sentence is correct, write *Correct.*

1. Novels and movies, such as *Treasure Island* and *The Crimson Pirate,* has created a highly romanticized picture of pirates.
2. Every popular pirate movie or story feature either a swashbuckling hero or buried treasure.
3. At certain times in history, merchant ships and seacoast villages were quite often plundered.
4. In fact, the 1500's and 1600's is known as "the great age of piracy."
5. Neither a national flag nor ship emblems was displayed by a pirate ship, except in an effort to deceive other vessels.
6. To this day, the skull and crossbones on a black flag remain the symbol of a pirate ship.
7. Many a pirate or buccaneer are depicted as owning vast treasure.
8. In reality, a pirate, along with other legendary bandits, usually was impoverished.
9. Some pirate names of historical significance includes Jean Lafitte, who helped the Americans in the War of 1812, and Bartholomew Roberts, who was known as "Black Bart."
10. Although pirating still occurs occasionally, the modern technology of nautical defense systems provide a strong deterrent.

Some indefinite pronouns are always singular; some are always plural; and some may be either singular or plural, depending on how they are used in the sentence.

Singular Indefinite Pronouns

another	either	neither	other
anybody	everybody	nobody	somebody
anyone	everyone	no one	someone
anything	everything	nothing	something
each	much	one	

Use a singular verb with a singular indefinite pronoun.

Another of her qualities is a winning personality.
Each of the songs has a strong bass line.
Neither of those countries abides by the treaty.
Everybody on the team gets a small trophy.

Plural Indefinite Pronouns

both	few	many	several

Use a plural verb with a plural indefinite pronoun.

Few on the President's staff see him regularly.
Several of the trumpet players need new instruments.
Many of the refugees have no possessions.

Pronouns That Can Be Singular or Plural

all	enough	most	plenty
any	more	none	some

These indefinite pronouns are considered singular when they refer to nouns that name a quantity or part of something. They are considered plural when they refer to nouns that name things that can be counted. Read the following examples.

<u>Most</u> of the snow <u>has</u> melted. (*Snow* cannot be counted.)
<u>Most</u> of the leaves <u>have</u> fallen. (*Leaves* can be counted.)

Practice Your Skills
CONCEPT CHECK

Writing Theme
Drum and
Bugle Corps

Indefinite Pronouns as Subjects   For each of the following sentences, write the subject and the correct form of the verb.

1. Some of the brass players from our high school's jazz band (have, has) joined the famous Santa Fe Drum and Bugle Corps.
2. Each of them (move, moves) to California for a summer of practice.
3. Anyone under nineteen (qualify, qualifies) to join.
4. Many of the musicians (work, works) at part-time jobs to earn travel money for competitions.
5. No one (fail, fails) to feel the excitement of drum-and-bugle-corps work.
6. Few in any drum and bugle corps (miss, misses) the national competition held every August in Madison, Wisconsin.
7. Plenty of the spectators (cheer, cheers) as the competing corps line up at the edge of the field.
8. Everyone at the event (find, finds) something to applaud.
9. Most of the drum and bugle corps (has, have) a distinctive style.
10. Much of the group's creativity (show, shows) in the director's choreography for each drum and bugle corps.

The basic rules for subject-verb agreement are simple, yet certain situations can cause confusion.

Inverted Subject and Verbs

Problems in subject-verb agreement often arise when the subject of a sentence follows the verb. Most often these sentences begin with a phrase or with *there* or *here*. Inverted subject-verb order also occurs in questions that begin with *why, where, what,* or *how.*

When you write a sentence with inverted subject-verb order, look ahead to the subject in order to determine whether the verb should be singular or plural.

Incorrect	Through the air <u>floats</u> the <u>parachutists</u>.
Correct	Through the air <u>float</u> the <u>parachutists</u>.

Incorrect	There <u>is</u> some beautiful <u>geraniums</u> in the yard.
Correct	There <u>are</u> some beautiful <u>geraniums</u> in the yard.

Incorrect	Here'<u>s</u> the <u>librettos</u> for this season's operas.
Correct	Here <u>are</u> the <u>librettos</u> for this season's operas.

Incorrect	Why <u>is</u> the <u>lifeguards</u> gathered at the pool?
Correct	Why <u>are</u> the <u>lifeguards</u> gathered at the pool?

Incorrect	How <u>does</u> the different broadcast <u>media</u> maintain their objectivity?
Correct	How <u>do</u> the different broadcast <u>media</u> maintain their objectivity?

In the third example above, notice that the contraction *here's* stands for *here* and the singular verb *is.* It should be used only with singular subjects. This is also true for other contractions: *there's, what's, where's, how's, who's.*

Sentences with Predicate Nominatives

Use a verb that agrees in number with the subject, not with the predicate nominative.

Dwindling <u>resources</u> <u>are</u> one problem. (*Resources* is the subject and takes a plural verb.)

One <u>problem</u> <u>is</u> dwindling resources. (*Problem* is the subject and takes a singular verb.)

The <u>dwindling</u> of resources <u>is</u> one problem. (*Dwindling* is the subject and takes a singular verb.)

Sentences with *Don't* and *Doesn't*

In general, use the singular form *doesn't* with a singular subject and the plural form *don't* with a plural subject.

Exceptions are the singular pronouns *I* and *you;* they always take *don't.*

Singular   Doesn't the orchestra use snares, chimes, or tympani?
            It doesn't always need percussion.

Plural   Don't boa constrictors eat live mice?
            They don't eat more than one or two a week.

Practice Your Skills

CONCEPT CHECK

Other Agreement Problems For each sentence, write the correct form of the verb that agrees in number with the subject.

1. How (does, do) medical advancements improve health care?
2. As in the days of Hippocrates, the focus of medicine (is, are) still patients and their families.
3. However, out of medical experiments at universities (come, comes) new knowledge.
4. Available to the physician (is, are) numerous instruments and laboratory tests that did not even exist a decade ago.
5. A doctor's physical examination (seems, seem) the best starting point for the diagnosis of simple ailments.
6. Nevertheless, doctors (doesn't, don't) rely on just one procedure to discover illnesses.
7. (What's, What are) one of the ways diagnosis has improved?
8. At one time, X-rays (was, were) the only tool doctors had for seeing internal problems.
9. Now there (is, are) some reliance on other technologies.
10. For example, *ultrasound* (is, are) sound waves that are higher than a human can hear.
11. (Here's, Here are) advanced technology that requires skilled technicians.
12. From the return echoes of ultrasound (comes, come) important information about the eyes, heart, or abdomen.
13. (Don't, Doesn't) you have some diagnostic tests in your yearly physical examination?
14. Ultimately, analyses of test results and case histories (is, are) really the most important step in diagnosis.
15. There (is, are) nurses, technicians, and other specialists to aid the family physician.

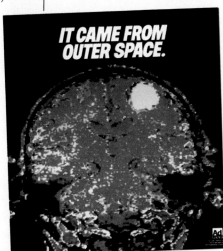

IT CAME FROM OUTER SPACE.

Digital image of a patient's skull; derived from space technology, digital imaging is a more informative and a much safer procedure than using X-rays.

Agreement of Subject and Verb   **693**

Collective Nouns as Subjects

A **collective noun** is the name of a group of people or things—for example, *committee, club, team, herd, crowd*. A collective noun takes a singular verb unless the individual members of the group are to be emphasized.

The <u>committee</u> <u>makes</u> many decisions at each meeting. (refers to group as a whole)
The <u>committee</u> <u>fight</u> among themselves. (emphasis on individual members)

The <u>team</u> <u>practices</u> every afternoon from three to five. (refers to group as a whole)
The <u>team</u> <u>were</u> practicing different shots. (emphasis on individual members)

Singular Nouns That End in *-s*

Not all nouns that end in *-s* are plural. Some nouns with a final *-s* are actually singular. They stand for only one thing and take a singular verb: *news, mumps, measles, checkers*.

<u>Mumps</u> <u>is</u> not very dangerous for small children.
Did you know that today's <u>news</u> <u>is</u> usually sent via satellite?
<u>Checkers</u> <u>is</u> my favorite game.

A few nouns with a final *-s* refer to one thing yet take a plural verb: *congratulations, pliers, scissors, trousers*.

Left-handed <u>scissors</u> <u>are</u> assembled backward.
Those <u>trousers</u> <u>are</u> very flattering.
<u>Congratulations</u> <u>are</u> due every member of the team.

Words that end in *-ics*—*athletics, civics, economics, ethics, genetics, politics*—may be either singular or plural. They are singular when they refer to a school subject, a science, or a general practice. Otherwise they are plural. Often the plural form is preceded by a possessive noun or pronoun.

<u>Politics</u> <u>is</u> everyone's business. (singular)
His <u>politics</u> <u>are</u> clearly stated in this article. (plural)

The name of a country or of an organization is singular even though it may be plural in form.

The <u>Philippines</u> <u>consists</u> of thousands of islands.
The <u>United Nations</u> <u>has sent</u> troops into some parts of the world to keep the peace.

Titles, Phrases, and Clauses as Subjects

Use a singular verb with a title.

The title of a book, play, TV show, film, musical composition, or other work of art is singular and takes a singular verb.

> <u>The Grapes of Wrath</u> <u>is</u> much more than the saga of one family.
>
> <u>The Planets,</u> by Gustav Holst, <u>moves</u> from quiet, slow strings to thunderous, blaring brass.

Any phrase or clause referring to a single thing or thought takes a singular verb.

> <u>What we want</u> <u>is</u> your support.
>
> <u>"It's later than you think"</u> <u>is</u> true for many who procrastinate.

Numerical Terms in Subjects

Words stating amounts are usually singular.

Words or phrases that express periods of time, fractions, weights, measurements, and amounts of money generally use a singular verb.

> <u>Three hours</u> <u>is</u> too much time to spend on this lesson.
>
> <u>Five-eighths</u> of a mile <u>is</u> five laps around the track.
>
> <u>Fifty cents</u> <u>seems</u> too little to charge.

If the subject is a period of time or an amount that is thought of as a number of separate units, use a plural verb.

> Seven <u>years</u> of training <u>are required</u> for that job.
>
> Twelve <u>houses</u> <u>were demolished</u> by the tornado.

Practice Your Skills

A. CONCEPT CHECK

More Agreement Problems   For each of the following sentences, write the form of the verb that agrees in number with the subject.

1. The United Nations (works, work) diligently to promote aid and understanding among nations.
2. This body of international representatives (achieves, achieve) cooperation during times of political unrest and natural disaster.
3. The members' ethics (takes, take) precedence over any other concern.
4. What has greatly helped their international efforts (is, are) improvement in communication technology.

5. *Peaceful Communications Among Nations* (demonstrates, demonstrate) the importance of mass media in international cooperation.
6. The news of a disaster (is, are) transmitted around the world in minutes.
7. Thousands of miles (is, are) a mere blink of the eye in satellite communication.
8. Thanks for such marvels (goes, go) largely to scientists who develop computer and space technology.
9. As a result of telecommunications, a trained rescue team (mobilizes, mobilize) to aid victims in a matter of hours.
10. Millions of dollars (is, are) raised for families needing shelter from a storm.
11. Tragically, a region's economics (suffers, suffer) as a result of many an earthquake or flood.
12. On a more personal level, the Peace Corps also (advances, advance) world cooperation.
13. A team (arrives, arrive) in a developing country.
14. A nation's politics (plays, play) no role in the technological help that is offered.
15. Promoting peace and understanding among nations (is, are) the Peace Corps's goal.

B. REVISION SKILL

Correcting Subject-Verb Agreement Errors Rewrite the following sentences, correcting any errors in subject-verb agreement. If a sentence is correct, write *Correct*.

1. Modern electronics have changed how people communicate.
2. A company using a computer and modem has access to multiple libraries of information.
3. Through the use of computers and modems to send data over telephone lines, efficient communications is possible.
4. "Modulator and demodulator" are what *modem* stands for.
5. Thousands of electronic "bulletin boards" across the country is actually computers with modems that exchange data.
6. Thanks is due to volunteers called SYSOP's, or system operators, for operating those bulletin boards.
7. A network of users asks questions and checks the bulletin board.
8. Graphics are posted for others to copy for their own use.
9. A team of computer operators use modems to transmit messages at different speeds.
10. At any speed, twelve pages take less time to send by modem than by even the speediest mail service.

C. PROOFREADING SKILL

Checking for Agreement Problems Proofread the following paragraphs. Then rewrite them, correcting all errors. Pay particular attention to subject-verb agreement.

A dazed crowd wander about staring at the debris. Alone on the boards of the second floor stand a toilet and a sink a tub sits firmly on a concrete slab with the house in rubble around it. Two pickup trucks in front of the house rocks with their wheels in the air. The next house don't have a roof but the house after that is untouched.

This sene of debris and chaos are a disaster. A tornaedo has struck. No one has been killed, but hundreds of people is stunned. Fortunately, there are some relief on the way. How do the Red cross help? Within a day, a crew of caseworkers begin to interview the families and provide asistance. Whatever the victims doesn't have any longer—clothes, as well as food and medicine—is donated and distributed.

The Red Cross distribute money or vouchers rather than actual goods because that helps the local economy. Many businesses appears damaged by the disaster, and they needs customers to help them rebuild. Politics play no part here: what the Red Cross provides are help and support for all.

RELATIVE PRONOUNS AS SUBJECTS

Sometimes the subject of an adjective clause is a relative pronoun (see page 561). To determine whether to use a singular verb or a plural verb in the clause, you must first determine the number of the relative pronoun. If the antecedent of the relative pronoun is plural, then the relative pronoun is plural. If the antecedent is singular, then the relative pronoun is singular.

The antecedent of a relative pronoun determines the number of the verb.

Singular   Maria is the only one of the racers who has won a trophy at every competition level. (**Who** refers to the singular antecedent *one;* therefore, the clause has a singular verb: *has won.*)

Plural   Sandra is one of the runners who race every week. (**Who** refers to the plural antecedent *runners;* therefore, the clause needs a plural verb: *race.*)

In the examples above, two words might appear to be possible antecedents of the relative pronoun. Examine such sentences carefully to determine the actual antecedent.

Practice Your Skills

A. CONCEPT CHECK

Relative Pronouns as Subjects   For each of the following sentences, write the form of the verb that agrees in number with the subject of the adjective clause.

1. The administrative and legislative segments of the government are the two branches that (is, are) described in the Constitution.
2. In the case of the Supreme Court, the size and scope, which (is, are) left to Congress to determine, are not delineated in the Constitution.
3. However, the status of the Court, which (is, are) defined by the Constitution, is independent of the will of Congress.
4. The President, whose appointments to the Court (is, are) confirmed by the Senate, determines who will serve.
5. This method of selecting Supreme Court justices is part of the system of checks and balances that (helps, help) to ensure the democratic process.

Writing Theme
The Supreme Court

6. Still, the President, rather than Congress, is the only one who (has, have) great power in determining what political and social views are represented on the Court.
7. His decision is extremely important because Supreme Court justices, who (has, have) always been lawyers, may serve as long as they wish.
8. Currently serving as Supreme Court justices are nine men and women whose responsibility (includes, include) interpreting laws and defending the Constitution.
9. The decisions that the justices of the Supreme Court (makes, make) often affect laws regulating many aspects of American life.
10. After a case is heard and a decision is made, any justice of the court who (opposes, oppose) the majority opinion may put that opposition, called a dissenting opinion, in writing.

B. APPLICATION IN WRITING

An Editorial Many newspaper editorials take a position on decisions made by the Supreme Court. Write a newspaper editorial stating your position on a certain law with which you agree or disagree. When you have finished writing, check for correct subject-verb agreement in adjective clauses.

CHECK POINT
PAGES 690–699

A. For each of the following sentences, write the form of the verb that agrees in number with the subject.

1. (There's, There are) several Chinese tales about the discovery of silk.
2. One of these stories, which (is, are) four thousand years old, tells how the princess Si Ling-Shi first noticed the silkworm.
3. Si Ling-Shi and her maid, who (was, were) sitting together in the garden, spotted a strange-looking worm in a mulberry tree.
4. "(Don't, Doesn't) it seem as if that worm were spinning a cocoon?" the maid asked the princess.
5. "How (do, does) it create that beautiful silk thread?" the astonished princess responded.
6. Both of the women (was, were) captivated by the silk cocoon and began to unravel it and put it to use.
7. The emperor's court (was, were) intrigued by the fabric that could be woven from the silk thread.
8. What amazes historians (is, are) that two thousand years elapsed before the secret of silk production was known outside of China.

Agreement of
Subject and Verb   **699**

9. None of the members of the court (was, were) willing to reveal the secret.
10. In fact, for years anyone caught stealing silkworm eggs (was, were) put to death.
11. Today, exports of silk fabric and clothing (remains, remain) an important part of China's economy.
12. (There's, There are) gorgeous, valuable items created simply by the work of silkworms.
13. The silk trade (doesn't, don't) occur solely in China any longer.
14. However, the Chinese (was, were) made wealthy from their exclusive domination of the silk trade.
15. Economics in China, over the period of several dynasties, (was, were) built in part by this delicate thread.

B. Rewrite the following sentences, correcting all errors in subject-verb agreement.

1. Why do the average person shudder when faced with a snake?
2. Some of the causes of fear is various superstitious beliefs and misunderstood facts about various kinds of snakes.
3. In many cases, hysterics are not an uncommon reaction for people who unexpectedly encounter a snake.
4. While it is true that dozens of species of snakes is poisonous, most snakes are totally harmless.
5. Our beliefs about the true nature of snakes is a mixture of fact and fiction learned as children.
6. For example, many has heard that cobras in wicker baskets are charmed by flute music played by fakirs, or snake charmers.
7. However, what captures a cobra's interest are actually the movements of the flute, not its sounds.
8. Perhaps you are not the only one who don't know that snakes cannot hear; instead of hearing actual sounds, they sense vibrations in the earth.
9. All snakes detect motion, and some of this reptile family senses warmth.
10. Interestingly, a group of scientists have been credited with using this same principle of heat sensitivity in weapons detection.
11. Another of the myths about snakes are that milk snakes, with their double rows of extremely sharp teeth, can milk cows on a farm.
12. Feeding upon mice are actually the job of harmless milk snakes.
13. Farmers doesn't usually mind the presence of milk snakes because they help control the mice population that feeds on grain.
14. Learning as much as possible about the helpful side of snakes help people act prudently when unexpectedly confronted with a snake.
15. Few ever kills humans except when cornered or frightened.

A. Correct Subject-Verb Agreement   For each of the following sentences, choose the correct form of the verb that agrees in number with the subject.

1. Fencing, along with other combative sports like wrestling, boxing, and the martial arts, (was, were) once a common self-defense technique.
2. Dueling, in Europe and in many parts of the world, (was, were) a legal way to settle personal disputes.
3. During the Middle Ages, many a disagreement or problem (was, were) decided with sword or saber.
4. Today, however, athletics (is, are) the domain where one most commonly finds sword fighting, or its modern equivalent, fencing.
5. Most of today's fencing competitors (uses, use) a long, thin sword, with a button on the end, called a foil.
6. The lunge, or forward thrust, and the parry, or defensive block, (constitutes, constitute) the most basic fencing moves.
7. Each of these precise fencing techniques (was, were) developed over centuries of military training.
8. Both lunging and parrying, which (requires, require) excellent balance, help develop muscle coordination.
9. There (is, are) many precautions taken to guarantee the safety of fencing competitors, such as wearing protective clothing and face masks.
10. Either the grace of the fencers or their close calls (holds, hold) the attention of the spectators.

B. More Subject-Verb Agreement   For each sentence below, choose the correct form of the verb.

1. What sets fencing apart from many competitive sports such as football, baseball, or track and field, (is, are) the need for only two competitors.
2. Similarly, tennis and other racquet sports such as badminton (doesn't, don't) require more than two competitors to play a match or a game.
3. The sport of tennis (is, are) really two different games—"lawn tennis" and "court tennis."
4. There (is, are) many differences between the two games, even though both are called tennis.
5. Most writing about tennis (refers, refer) to lawn tennis, whether the game is being played indoors or outdoors.
6. The United States (was, were) introduced to tennis by Mary Outerbridge, who brought the game here after seeing it played in Bermuda in 1874.

Writing Theme·
Competing
One on One

Agreement of
Subject and Verb   **701**

7. During World War II, the American public (was, were) denied the excitement of important international matches played in other countries.
8. After the war, America and Australia (was, were) dominant in the sport for almost twenty years, providing such stars as Pancho Gonzales and Maureen Connolly as well as Rod Laver and Margaret Court Smith.
9. Today, players from around the world (is, are) winners of major televised international competitions viewed by hundreds of thousands of fans.
10. Millions of dollars (is, are) earned by a few of the top tennis champions, both through product endorsements and actual cash prizes for tournaments.

C. Correcting Errors in Subject-Verb Agreement   Rewrite the following paragraphs, correcting the errors in subject-verb agreement. Some sentences contain more than one error.

(1) The practice of karate involve more than the guttural yells and "karate chops" portrayed in popular American movies. (2) The techniques of this martial art requires intense mental concentration and physical strength and flexibility. (3) Karate, with its Japanese history, are inextricably linked with Buddhism. (4) The beliefs and discipline of Zen meditation helps the *karate-ka* (person who practices karate) focus his or her energy.

(5) The *gi,* or uniform, of the *karate-ka* are made only of white cloth, which symbolize singleness of purpose. (6) The single purpose of the *karate-ka* are to grow in self-knowledge. (7) As a result, there are psychological growth that in turn enable practitioners to improve their fighting techniques.

(8) All members of a *dojo* (place where karate is practiced) shares the same purpose. (9) In the *dojo,* all—whether servers, laborers, teachers, students, executives—is equal. (10) Members of a *dojo* helps one another learn. (11) Neither their rank nor their position are shown by the belts they wear with their *gis*. (12) What these belts show are their experience. (13) Patience, courtesy, concentration, and respect is the hallmarks of this discipline.

On the Lightside

FROM NAME TO NOUN

In the nineteenth century, Jules Léotard flew through the air with the greatest of ease. This daring young Frenchman on the flying trapeze was a star in the circuses of Paris and London. He perfected

Two Little Circus Girls, by Pierre Auguste Renoir, 1879

the aerial somersault and other stunts, but he is not remembered today for his death-defying feats. Instead, he is remembered for what he wore. Jules Léotard invented a close-fitting, one-piece elastic costume that was soon copied by circus performers throughout Europe. His leotard has become a standard part of the wardrobe of acrobats, dancers, and entertainers everywhere.

Many words come from the actions, accomplishments, and even misfortunes of people. The words that are formed from names are called **eponyms.** They start as proper nouns, but over time they become so common that the capital letter is dropped. For example, *maverick* comes from Samuel A. Maverick, a Texas cattleman who upset his fellow cattlemen because he refused to brand his calves. *Pompadour* comes from a hairstyle favored by a mistress of French King Louis XV. *Dunce* can be traced to thirteenth-century philosopher John Duns Scotus, whose followers refused to accept new teachings during the Renaissance.

The names of people are behind many words, including *atlas, boycott, derringer, guillotine, guppy, lynch,* and *volt.* Eponyms live on long after the people behind them are forgotten.

Directions One or more of the underlined sections in the following sentences may contain errors of grammar, usage, punctuation, spelling, or capitalization. Write the letter of each incorrect section; then rewrite the item correctly. If there is no error in an item, write E.

Example   The first money to carry the motto <u>"In God We Trust"</u>
              <u>   </u>
                            A   **B**

<u>were</u> bank notes which <u>apeared</u> in 1864. <u>No error</u>
C   **D**   **E**

Answer   C—was D—appeared

---

1. <u>Warner Brothers studios</u> must <u>have wanted to have set</u> a record when it asked
   A   **B**
   <u>John Barrymore</u> to bestow 191 kisses on a number of beautiful señoritas in the film
   C
   <u>*Don Juan*</u>. <u>No error</u>
   D   **E**

2. Before his death <u>in 1941,</u> Robert Baden-Powell, who founded the <u>Boy Scouts,</u> <u>is</u> also a
   A   **B**   **C**
   British <u>intelligence officer.</u> <u>No error</u>
   D   **E**

3. <u>Many</u> of the <u>workers</u> building the St. Gotthard Tunnel in <u>Switzerland</u> in 1882 <u>were</u>
   A   **B**   **C**   **D**
   injured. <u>No error</u>
   E

4. The <u>lute, with</u> its descendants the sitar, violin, fiddle, guitar, and ukulele, <u>are</u> more
   A   **B**
   widely used <u>than any other</u> stringed instrument <u>in the world.</u> <u>No error</u>
   C   **D**   **E**

5. Neither <u>a large handfull</u> of potato chips <u>nor</u> a large bowl of pretzels <u>have</u> as much salt
   A   **B**   **C**
   <u>as one</u> serving of canned soup. <u>No error</u>
   D   **E**

6. If Vincent van Gogh <u>would have been able</u> to sell his paintings for what they bring
   A
   <u>today,</u> he <u>would have died</u> a billionaire <u>several times over</u> instead of a pauper. <u>No error</u>
   B   **C**   **D**   **E**

7. The <u>Sphinx,</u> a beautiful and mysterious statue, <u>sets</u> not far from where the
   A   **B**
   <u>Great Pyramid of Giza</u> <u>raises</u> into the sky. <u>No error</u>
   C   **D**   **E**

8. Though they could <u>have fled</u> before the storm <u>began,</u> Lee Trevino, Jerry Heard, and
    A B

    Bobby Nichols were all <u>struck</u> by lightning at the <u>Western Open Golf Tournament</u> in
    C D

    1975. <u>No error</u>
    E

9. <u>For camouflage</u> a bug called <u>*Fulgora lucifera* has</u> a false head that <u>lays</u> on the ground
    A B C

    and <u>resembles</u> the head of a South American alligator. <u>No error</u>
    D E

10. *Truth or Consequences* <u>were</u> first <u>seen</u> in <u>1956, making</u> it one of the <u>oldest</u> game
    A B C D

    shows on television. <u>No error</u>
    E

11. Native Americans <u>had been living</u> in what <u>is</u> now the <u>United States</u> for thousands of
    A B C

    years <u>before Christopher Columbus</u> "discovered" it. <u>No error</u>
    D E

12. <u>Although virtually every</u> man and woman in America <u>are familiar</u> with the ice-making
    A B

    properties of the freezer, few <u>is aware</u> that this machine was invented by a doctor to
    C

    provide ice for <u>fever-racked</u> patients. <u>No error</u>
    D E

13. The rattlesnake and the copperhead <u>is famous</u> for being <u>poisinous, but</u> the cobra is the
    A B

    <u>most dangerous</u> <u>venomous</u> snake. <u>No error</u>
    C D E

14. In the television <u>series, "The Many Loves of Dobie Gillis,"</u> a whole cast of future
    A

    <u>stars, including</u> Warren Beatty and Tuesday Weld, <u>were representative of</u> average
    B C

    <u>American</u> teenagers. <u>No error</u>
    D E

15. Anyone who <u>saw</u> the film <u>*Dr X,*</u> <u>has seen</u> Humphrey Bogart in a <u>horrer</u> movie. <u>No error</u>
    A B C D E

16. Marlon Brando <u>was born</u> in <u>Omaha Nebraska,</u> but he <u>don't</u> sound like a Midwesterner in
    A B C

    The Godfather. <u>No error</u>
    D E

17. Casey Jones is one of the few <u>American</u> folk <u>heros</u> who <u>was</u> real and not simply created
    A B C

    by a <u>songwriter or storyteller</u>. <u>No error</u>
    D E

18. There <u>is</u> <u>absolutely</u> no <u>"man-eating" plants</u> in the world, although some plants <u>do</u> trap
      A   **B**   **C**   **D**
    insects. <u>No error</u>
           E

19. <u>Locusts,</u> which <u>come out of</u> the ground once <u>every seventeen years,</u> <u>is</u> a serious problem
      A   **B**   **C**   **D**
    in some areas of the Midwest. <u>No error</u>
                                E

20. The American colonists declared <u>there</u> <u>independance</u> from Great Britain <u>only after</u> they
                                    A   **B**   **C**
    <u>had tried</u> every other means to gain justice. <u>No error</u>
      D   **E**

21. Giant hailstones <u>weighing</u> more than a pound each <u>begun</u> to kill cattle as they <u>falled</u> on
                     A   **B**   **C**
    the Russian village of Kostov in July <u>1923; twenty-three</u> people were killed trying to
                                          D
    save the livestock. <u>No error</u>
                     E

22. Don Quixote <u>mounted his horse</u> <u>while his squire,</u> <u>Sancho Panza,</u> <u>holds</u> the animal
                   A   **B**   **C**   **D**
    steady. <u>No error</u>
         E

23. Of one hundred crossword puzzle <u>creators who</u> contributed to two <u>New York puzzle</u>
                                      A   **B**
    magazines in <u>1970, one-fourth</u> <u>was</u> in prison. <u>No error</u>
               C   **D**   **E**

24. Neither <u>the members</u> of the <u>city council</u> nor the chairperson <u>were</u> available for questions
            A   **B**   **C**
    from <u>the press.</u> <u>No error</u>
         D   **E**

25. Although poor grades <u>could have hurted</u> <u>him, Winston</u> Churchill <u>rose</u> from the bottom
                       A   **B**   **C**
    of his class to become <u>prime minister</u> of England. <u>No error</u>
                     D   **E**

Sketchbook

Write a brief essay on the body language of walking. In your essay, use a variety of synonyms for the verb *to walk*. Explain how specific personality traits can be revealed by the way in which a person walks.

Additional Sketches

Compare and contrast the style and content of five television commercials. Use indefinite pronouns such as *none, all, many, several,* and *each,* and make sure your subjects and verbs agree.

You are a member of a jury that has been unable to reach a verdict. Explain to the judge why the members of the jury are deadlocked. Make sure your subjects and verbs agree.

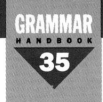

Pronoun Usage

THE CASES OF PRONOUNS

A pronoun is a word used in place of a noun. Most pronouns have a case, a form that indicates the relation of the pronoun to other words in the sentence. Pronouns in the **nominative case** are used as subjects or predicate nominatives; those in the **objective case,** as objects; and those in the **possessive case,** to show possession.

Of all the types of pronouns, personal pronouns have the most forms. (See Handbook 30, "Pronouns" for the classes of pronouns.) The forms of the personal pronouns are as follows:

Singular Personal Pronouns

	Nominative	Objective	Possessive
First Person	I	me	my, mine
Second Person	you	you	your, yours
Third Person	he, she, it	him, her, it	his, her, hers, its

Plural Possessive Pronouns

	Nominative	Objective	Possessive
First Person	we	us	our, ours
Second Person	you	you	your, yours
Third Person	they	them	their, theirs

Besides case, the form of the personal pronoun indicates number (singular or plural), person (first person—person speaking, second person—person spoken to, third person—person or thing spoken about), and gender (masculine, feminine, or neuter).

The case forms for the relative pronouns *who* and *whoever* are as follows:

Nominative	Objective	Possessive
who	whom	whose
whoever	whomever	whosever

The nominative and objective forms of most indefinite pronouns, such as *someone* or *everyone,* are identical. (For a list of indefinite pronouns, see page 561.) The possessive case ends in -'s: *someone's, everyone's.*

Several pronouns—such as *this, that, these, those, which,* and *what*—do not have cases.

In this grammar handbook, you will learn the correct way to use the various cases.

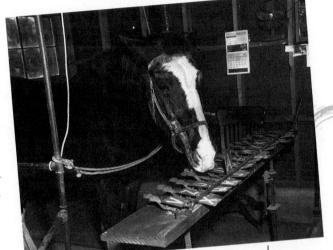

In the 1920s, an unusual invention was developed to enable Lady Wonder, the "educated, mind-reading horse," to answer questions and predict the future. Lady Wonder pecked out her answers by nudging the keys of an oversize typewriter with her nose.

Practice Your Skills

CONCEPT CHECK

Pronouns   Write the pronouns in the following sentences. Identify the personal pronouns as follows: first, second, or third person; singular or plural; and nominative, objective, or possessive case. For all other pronouns, identify only the case.

1. Anyone who has read the history of inventions knows the less-than-inspired ideas people have used to make their fortunes.
2. Many of these patented inventions might have been forgotten if they hadn't been so funny.
3. My favorite foolish invention is a hazardous alarm clock.
4. It consists of a wooden hammer suspended over the sleeper's bed and is designed to hit the sleeper over the head at the time he or she is supposed to get up.
5. The alarm might actually awaken sleepers for a brief moment before knocking them out.
6. Reading about inventions also makes me wonder whoever invented hats in the shape of umbrellas.
7. I have seen umbrella hats on television but never on anybody's head.
8. Perhaps everyone has ideas for inventions.
9. True, few of us can be geniuses like Leonardo da Vinci, whose ideas included everything from contact lenses to the helicopter.
10. Still, I wonder what inventions might be in me—or in you.

Writing Theme
Inventions

A pronoun can be used as the subject or the predicate nominative. Pronouns with these functions take the nominative case.

Pronouns as Subjects

The pronoun subject of a verb is in the nominative case.

When the subject of a sentence consists of a single pronoun, you are not likely to use the wrong form. When the subject consists of more than one pronoun or of a noun and a pronoun, however, errors in the pronoun form are more likely. To decide on the correct form of the pronoun to use in a compound subject, try each subject separately with the verb.

> Quentin and (I, me) played in the backgammon tournament.
>   (Quentin played; I played, not me played.)
> (She, Her) and Inez run a plant-watering service. (Inez runs;
>   she runs, not her runs.)

Pronouns as Predicate Nominatives

A **predicate pronoun** follows some form of the linking verb *be* and renames the person or thing that is the subject.

A predicate pronoun is in the nominative case.

The linking verb *be* used before a predicate pronoun may appear in any tense or mood; for example, *was, has been, can be, must be, might be, should be,* and *will be.*

> The person who telephoned *was* I.
> It *might have been* they who were riding on the parade float.
> The swimmer in the striped suit *should be* she.

If a sentence with a predicate pronoun sounds awkward, rewrite the sentence.

Awkward   The first performer in the talent show was *he*.
Better   *He* was the first performer in the talent show.

In informal conversation and writing, it is both common and acceptable to use the objective case of the pronoun in such sentences as *It is me* or *That was them.* In formal writing, however, use the nominative case for predicate pronouns.

Practice Your Skills

CONCEPT CHECK

Pronouns in the Nominative Case For each of the following sentences, write the correct pronoun shown in parentheses.

Writing Theme
Education

1. Shell-Flower was six years old when (she, her) and her grandfather Chief Winnemucca went to work on a California ranch.
2. It was (he, him) who had decided the Piutes of Nevada should travel to learn more about white ways.
3. The only white people (she, her) and other tribe members had known in Nevada were a few trappers and explorers.
4. Shell-Flower learned Spanish and English on the ranch; perhaps the one who gained most from ranch life was (she, her).
5. Later she spent a year living with Mormons, and it must have been (they, them) who renamed her Sarah.
6. When the Piute princess returned to her grandfather, Sarah and (he, him) decided she should attend a white school.
7. However, many parents objected to Sarah's presence; school administrators and (they, them) agreed that she should leave.
8. Nonetheless, Sarah proved that (she, her) would not give up.
9. When her father was kidnapped by an Idaho tribe, it was (she, her) who rode hundreds of miles to rescue him.
10. Perhaps her greatest achievement came in later years when her husband and (she, her) opened a school for Piute children.

PRONOUNS IN THE
OBJECTIVE CASE

Pronouns, like nouns, can function as the object of a verb, the object of a preposition, or as part of an infinitive phrase.

Pronouns as Objects of Verbs

A pronoun used as a direct or an indirect object is in the objective case.

When a verb has a compound object, try each object with the verb separately to decide which case of the pronoun to use.

Direct Object	The party invitation included Meg and (he, him). (included Meg; included him, not included he)
Indirect Object	Our neighbor gave Della and (I, me) instructions on how to care for his orchids. (gave Della; gave me, not gave I)

Pronouns as Objects of Prepositions

A pronoun used as the object of a preposition is in the objective case.

Again, when a preposition has a compound object, you may have trouble deciding which case of the pronoun to use. Try each pronoun separately in the prepositional phrase.

> I went to the Italian festival with Joe and (he, him).
> (with Joe; with him, not with he)

Usage Note In informal speech nominative-case pronouns are often incorrectly used as objects of prepositions. The preposition *between,* as in *between you and I,* is a common example. Only objective-case pronouns should be used as objects of prepositions. Thus the correct form would be *between you and me.*

Pronouns with Infinitives

An infinitive is a verb that is preceded by *to*. See pages 603–604 for more information about infinitives.

A pronoun used as the subject, object, or predicate pronoun of an infinitive is in the objective case.

Subject of Infinitive   The director asked *him to speak* more slowly. (*Him* is the subject of *to speak*.)

Object of Infinitive   Everybody wanted *to hear them*. (*Them* is the object of *to hear*.)

Predicate Pronoun   We didn't expect the swimming instructor *to be her.* (*Her* is the predicate pronoun after *to be*.)

Practice Your Skills

A. CONCEPT CHECK

Pronouns in the Objective Case For each of the following sentences, write the correct pronoun of the two in parentheses.

1. Today's program is devoted to an author new to many of (we, us).
2. Between you and (I, me), I don't think there's a better writer than the Canadian author W. P. Kinsella.
3. His stories have force, and they compel (I, me) to keep reading.
4. He is well known to (we, us) for his baseball novel *Shoeless Joe.*
5. When Phil Alden Robinson read *Shoeless Joe,* it inspired (he, him) to write and direct a movie version.
6. Hollywood producers wanted (he, him) to search for a new, catchy title.

7. The solution for Robinson and (they, them) was to name the film *Field of Dreams*.
8. If we knew Kinsella only for his baseball books, his comic tales of life on an Indian reservation would surprise (we, us).
9. Kinsella's characters are members of the Cree Tribe; home to (they, them) is the Ermineskin Reserve in central Alberta.
10. The narrator, Silas Ermineskin, gives (we, us) a look at the lives of people such as Frank Fence-post and Sadie One-wound.
11. Mad Etta is another unforgettable character; the Cree come to see (she, her) for medical and spiritual help.
12. Silas describes (she, her) as so large that she needs to sit on a tree trunk; no chair will hold (she, her).
13. Silas didn't expect the chronicler of his people's lives to be (he, him).
14. Yet he finds revelations in all that happens to (they, them).
15. Kinsella's other titles include *Dance Me Outside* and *Born Indian;* for some fascinating reading, find (they, them) in your library.

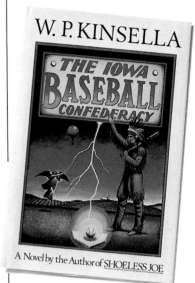

B. APPLICATION IN LITERATURE

Choosing Pronouns   For each of the following sentences, write the correct pronouns.

1. I hear America singing, the varied carols I hear . . ./Each singing what belongs to (he, him) or (she, her) and none else.
   Walt Whitman

2. Margot and (I, me) are treated as children over outward things, and (we, us) are much older than most girls of our age inwardly.
   Anne Frank

3. I was looking for myself and asking everyone except myself questions which (I, me), and only (I, me) could answer.
   Ralph Ellison

4. It was (her, she) who really made the decisions, she who was more in touch with things. . . . I enjoyed it when (we, us) sat together at the table learning about the continental shelf.   **William Trevor**

5. June and (I, me) looked at each other. Our collective had argued for six months over whether (we, us) could manage without Penny and Ray, and still there was no way (we, us) could predict what it would be like.   **Barbara Wilson**

C. APPLICATION IN WRITING

Personal Narrative   Good writers find drama in everyday events. Write a paragraph describing an ordinary day that developed into something more. Use nominative- and objective-case pronouns.

Environmental
Concerns

CHECK POINT
PAGES 708–714

For each of the following sentences, write the correct pronoun shown in parentheses.

1. Our German friends told (we, us) about a new movement in housing called *Baubiologie.*
2. We asked (they, them) to translate, and Oskar and (she, her) said the term means "biological architecture."
3. When Gretchen showed (we, us) a few articles on *Baubiologie,* I asked to borrow (them, they) because the person who knew the least about this topic was (I, me).
4. I read that *Baubiologie* relates to the Asian philosophy of *feng shui*—building in harmony with the environment—an idea that appeals to my friend and (I, me).
5. As examples, Gretchen and Oskar showed (we, us) pictures of their new homes.
6. We were amazed to discover that the builders of these beautiful homes were (they, them).
7. Following *Baubiologie,* both Gretchen and (he, him) built their houses with natural materials, such as wood, brick, and clay.
8. (She, Her) and Oskar used only paints and finishes that had no toxic chemicals.
9. *Baubiologists* suggest that people listen to (they, them) and choose home sites carefully.
10. According to (they, them), strong electric or magnetic fields and subterranean water veins should be avoided.

11. Research has convinced (they, them)—and frankly, (I, me) as well—that these conditions may cause health problems.
12. Both Oskar and (she, her) believe that sleeping on wooden beds will help (they, them) avoid harmful electrical fields.
13. (They, Them) tried to convince (we, us) that living quarters should be placed well away from the garage to avoid car exhaust.
14. Oskar encouraged (we, us) to decorate with green plants to provide (we, us) with oxygen.
15. Gretchen says that when friends visit (she, her), (they, them) are often soothed by the quiet harmony of her home.

PRONOUNS IN THE POSSESSIVE CASE

Personal pronouns that show possession are in the possessive case. The possessive pronouns *mine, yours, his, hers, its,* and *theirs* are used in place of nouns: Those black gloves are *mine. Yours* are brown. *My, our, your, his, her, its,* and *their* are used as adjectives to modify nouns: *My* gloves are black. *Your* gloves are brown.

Possessive Pronouns Modifying Gerunds

A pronoun used to modify a gerund is in the possessive case.

If the present participle (the *-ing* form of a verb) is used as a noun, it is called a gerund; if it is used as a modifier, it functions as an adjective. A gerund may be the subject or an object in a sentence. A pronoun modifying a gerund takes the possessive case. A pronoun modified by a participle is in the nominative or objective case.

> *His* disappearing in a puff of smoke was the last part of the act. (*His disappearing in a puff of smoke* is a gerund phrase used as the subject. The possessive form *his* modifies the gerund phrase.)

> Astonished, the audience saw *him* disappearing in a puff of smoke. (*Disappearing* is a participle used as an adjective to modify *him.*)

> The neighbors objected to *their* painting the house bright purple. (*Painting the house bright purple* is a gerund phrase, the object of the preposition *to.* The possessive pronoun *their* should be used before the gerund. The act of painting is the focus.)

The neighbors watched *them* painting the house purple.
(*Painting the house purple* is a participial phrase modifying *them*. The people doing the painting are focused on.)

In some sentences, either the objective or the possessive case can be used, depending on the meaning.

Imagine *his* having to spend the night in a tent.
(emphasizes action)
Imagine *him* having to spend the night in a tent.
(emphasizes person)

Practice Your Skills

A. CONCEPT CHECK

Possessive Pronouns For each of the following sentences, write the correct pronoun shown in parentheses.

1. Drama students throughout the Pacific Northwest look forward to (them, their) viewing of the Oregon Shakespeare Festival.
2. After studying the plays of Shakespeare, students are delighted to see (them, their) being brought to life by professional actors.
3. Whether they are performing *Hamlet, Twelfth Night,* or another Shakespearean work, (them, their) acting delights audiences.
4. Before the play, one member of a troupe of dancers invites you to see (him, his) singing and dancing on the green.
5. (Their, Them) agile performance of sixteenth-century dances aids (us, our) understanding of dance in Shakespeare's time.
6. A favorite experience of (me, mine) is sitting in the outdoor Elizabethan theater at sundown.
7. (You, Your) scanning the upper reaches of the theater may give you another thrill: the sight of bats flying.
8. For me, a trip to the festival isn't complete without (me, my) walking along Lithia Creek in downtown Ashland.
9. One Ashland resident claims that (him, his) drinking of its waters has improved his health.
10. (Me, My) tasting of the bitter water makes me doubt his word.

B. PROOFREADING SKILL

Pronouns Rewrite the following paragraph, correcting all errors in spelling, capitalization, punctuation, and pronoun usage.

Recently my family and me relived the experience of riding west with a wagon train on the Oregon Trail. Despite the scent of sagebrush and the seenic view of the nebraskan landscape, the trip was not easy for the pioneers—or we. We soon discovered that riding in a wagon was quite a jarring experience. In fact, a guide told my sister and I that us placing a bucket of milk on the wagon axle would result in a bucket of churned butter. Like many of the pioneers, my sister and me decided to walk the twelve-mile stretch for the day. That first night, while we were eating a supper of buffalo stew and sourdough bread, my mother and me calculated that we had covered one percent of the distanse of those who followed the trail, and us both felt a great deal of admiration for them. after only one day, we knew that we would not want to travel another ninety nine days—more than three months—to reach home.

PROBLEMS IN PRONOUN USAGE

Most problems that occur in the use of pronouns involve choosing between the nominative case and the objective case. To decide which case is needed, you must determine how the pronoun functions in the sentence.

Who and Whom in Questions and Clauses

When asking questions, the choice between *who* and *whom* often causes confusion. To decide which word to use, you must know how the pronoun functions in the question.

Who is the nominative case of the pronoun; it is used as the subject of a verb or as a predicate pronoun. *Whom* is the objective case; it is used as the direct object or as the object of a preposition.

> *Who* found the missing painting? (*Who* is the subject of *found*.)
> *Whom* did he suspect? (*Whom* is the direct object of *did suspect*.)

The pronouns *who, whoever, whom, whomever,* and *whose* may be used to introduce noun or adjective clauses. These pronouns also have a function in the clause.

Who and *whoever* are nominative forms and can act as the subject or predicate pronoun in a clause. *Whom* and *whomever* are objective forms and can act as the direct object or the object of a preposition within a clause. In deciding which pronoun to use, first isolate the subordinate clause, and then determine the function of the pronoun in the clause.

The gentleman (who, whom) Elizabeth Bennet married was Mr. Darcy.

1. The adjective clause is (*who, whom*) *Elizabeth Bennet married*.
2. In the clause, the pronoun functions as the direct object of *married. Whom,* the objective case, is correct.

He will give a reward to (whoever, whomever) finds his pet snake.

1. The noun clause is (*whoever, whomever*) *finds his pet snake.* The entire clause is the object of the preposition *to.*
2. In the clause, the pronoun acts as the subject of the verb *finds. Whoever,* the nominative case, is correct.

In determining whether to use *who* or *whom,* do not be misled by parenthetical expressions in the subordinate clause.

Carolyn is the person who, *I think,* made the suggestion. (*Who* is the subject of *made* in the subordinate clause.)

Usage Notes *Who* is acceptable in informal speech and writing, as in *Who are they playing?*

The pronoun *whose* functions as a possessive pronoun.

Buddy Holly, *whose songs include "Peggy Sue,"* was a pioneer of rock 'n' roll. (*Whose* is a possessive pronoun modifying *songs.*)

Practice Your Skills

A. CONCEPT CHECK

Who* and *Whom For each of the following sentences, write the correct pronoun shown in parentheses.

1. (Who, Whom) among us still believes the old canard that short people are somehow inferior?
2. History contains many examples of people of less than average height (who, whom) accomplished great deeds.
3. The image of David facing Goliath is an inspiring symbol to (whoever, whomever) seeks to overcome huge obstacles.
4. The diminutive Napoleon Bonaparte was the person (who, whom) dominated Europe in the early 1800's.
5. To (whoever, whomever) he met, this French general seemed to be not a man of short stature but a man of enormous ambition.
6. Even in Hollywood there were several leading men (who, whom) were shorter than their female costars.

Writing
TIP

For all formal writing, use *whom* when the objective-case form of this pronoun is needed.

Writing Theme
Individuality

7. Tiny Veronica Lake was one actress to (who, whom) Alan Ladd did not seem small; thus they were paired regularly in the 1940's.

8. James Cagney was another actor in classic films (who, whom, whose) lack of height made him seem tougher.

9. Cagney was an electrifying performer (who, whom) could dominate each scene through sheer energy.

10. (Whoever, Whomever) has seen him swagger through a room full of huge hoodlums cannot doubt his strength.

11. A filmmaker (who, whom) has achieved fame is Spike Lee.

12. Spike Lee is a writer, actor, and director (who, whom, whose) slight frame contains the talent of many people.

13. It is he to (who, whom) audiences look for the most thought-provoking images of African-American life.

14. The young woman (who, whom) the critics hailed as the best female ice skater of the early 1970's stood a mere 5'1" tall.

15. Janet Lynn's gracefully beautiful free-skating routines dazzled (whoever, whomever) watched her perform.

Napoleon Bonaparte Crossing the Alps, by Jacques-Louis David

B. APPLICATION IN LITERATURE

Who and **Whom**   For each of the following sentences, write the correct pronoun shown in parentheses.

1. It may be those (who, whom) do most, dream most.
   Stephen Leacock

2. I think somehow, we learn (who, whom) we really are and live with that decision.   **Eleanor Roosevelt**

3. We often forgive those (who, whom) bore us; we cannot forgive those (who, whom) we bore.   **Duc de la Rochefoucauld**

4. A man (who, whom) does not read good books has no advantage over the man (who, whom) can't read them.   **Mark Twain**

5. I never make the mistake of arguing with people for (whom, whose) opinion I have no respect.   **Edward Gibbon**

6. There are two kinds of egotists: those (who, whom) admit it and the rest of us.   **Laurence J. Peter**

7. There are two kinds of people in one's life—people (who, whom) one keeps waiting, and the people for (who, whom) one waits.
   S. N. Behrman

8. Parents are the last people on earth (who, whom) ought to have children.
   Samuel Butler

9. An idealist is one (who, whom), noticing a rose smells better than a cabbage, concludes that it will also make a better soup.
   H. L. Mencken

10. An intellectual is someone (who, whose) mind watches itself.
    Albert Camus

PRONOUNS USED WITH
AND AS APPOSITIVES

An appositive is a noun or pronoun that follows another noun or pronoun as an identification or explanation of that word. A pronoun can be the word identified by the appositive, or it can be the appositive itself.

Pronouns Followed by Appositives The pronouns *we* and *us* are often followed by appositives. To decide whether to use the nominative case, *we,* or the objective case, *us,* read the sentence without the appositive.

> (We, Us) volunteers distributed the posters for the fair to many neighborhood businesses. (We distributed the posters, not us distributed the posters.)
> The publicity work was organized by (we, us) volunteers.
> (by us, not by we)

Pronouns as Appositives The correct form of the pronoun used as an appositive is determined by the function of the noun with which the pronoun is in apposition.

> The co-chairpersons, *Jessica* and *I,* will set up the committees. (*Jessica* and *I* are in apposition with *co-chairpersons,* which is the subject of *will set up.* The nominative form *I* is required.)

To determine which form of the pronoun to use in apposition, try the appositive by itself in the sentence.

> Mia got the funny greeting card from two friends, Lee and (she, her). (from Lee and her, not from Lee and she)

Practice Your Skills

REVISION SKILL

Using Pronouns Correctly   Revise the following paragraph correcting all errors in pronoun usage.

(1) Stories of courage at sea often inspire we landlocked inhabitants. (2) Ida Lewis's story is really about two courageous people, her father and her, who operated Lime Rock Lighthouse on the Rhode Island coast in the mid-1800's. (3) Many people romanticize lighthouse duty; however, us land dwellers seldom realize what this life entailed. (4) Captain Lewis rescued crews from shipwrecks, and him and his family kept the signal light burning. (5) After he suffered a stroke, it was decided that both Ida and him would perform the lighthouse duties. (6) When Ida was sixteen, she assumed full responsibility for the job, a fact that may surprise us modern readers. (7) She rowed through storms and towering waves while her father watched from shore; they were two strong people, she and him. (8) One time she saved three shepherds and a sheep by rowing her living cargo, the sheep and they, safely to shore. (9) A New York reporter wrote about she and her rescues. (10) She made her last rescue at age sixty-four, showing we younger people that courage is not limited by sex or age.

PRONOUNS IN COMPARISON·

A comparison can be made by using a clause that begins with *than* or an *as . . . as* construction.

Alma is better at solving crossword puzzles *than Evelyn is*.
They have *as* many signatures on their petitions *as we have*.

The final clause in a comparison is sometimes elliptical; that is, some words are omitted from the clause. The omission of words makes it more difficult to determine the correct pronoun to use in the clause.

Alma is better at solving crossword puzzles than she.
They have as many signatures on their petitions as we.

To decide which case of the pronoun to use in an elliptical clause, fill in the words that are not stated.

> No one was more excited about riding in a cable car than he. (No one was more excited about riding in a cable car than he was.)
> The Capulets were just as quarrelsome as they. (The Capulets were just as quarrelsome as they were.)

Sometimes either the nominative case or the objective case may be correct, depending on the meaning.

> I ski with Terry more often than he. (This means "I ski with Terry more often than he does.")
> I ski with Terry more often than him. (This means "I ski with Terry more often than I ski with him.")

Reflexive and Intensive Pronouns

A pronoun ending in *-self* or *-selves* can be used intensively for emphasis. Such pronouns can also be used reflexively to refer to a preceding noun or pronoun.

> During his last lesson, Rob *himself* landed the plane. (Intensive)
> We made *ourselves* party hats. (Reflexive, indirect object)

Pronouns ending in *-self* or *-selves* cannot be used alone. Each must have an antecedent in the same sentence.

Incorrect Wendell and myself put up the decorations. (There is no antecedent for *myself.*)
Correct Wendell and I put up the decorations.

Practice Your Skills

A. CONCEPT CHECK

Pronoun Usage Choose the correct pronoun from those shown in parentheses.

1. There is no greater fan of tall tales than (I, me).
2. Between (you, yourself) and (me, myself), Davy Crockett stories are among the best.
3. Few frontier heroes had as many adventures as (he, him).
4. In one tale Davy and a raccoon got (them, themselves) into a confrontation.
5. No one but (him, himself) could claim to grin a raccoon out of a tree.

Writing Theme
Tall Tales

6. Davy's mother was also exceptional in that no one, including a steam mill, could spin as much wool as (she, her).

7. Nor could anyone except (her, herself) jump a seven-rail fence backward.

8. She could cut down a gum tree ten feet around by (her, herself).

9. Eventually, Davy's neighbors persuaded (him, himself) to run for Congress.

10. They felt no one would be better for the job than (he, him).

11. It was true he understood people like (them, themselves).

12. At first Davy found (him, himself) at a loss whenever he gave speeches.

13. However, when he told tales instead, his audiences considered (theirselves, themselves) privileged listeners.

14. Soon Davy, his pet alligator, and his pet bear found (them, themselves) on their way to Washington, D.C.

15. Historical records, not tales, tell (us, ourselves) that he served two terms in the U.S. House of Representatives.

B. APPLICATION IN WRITING

Imaginative Writing Choose an incident, real or imaginary, and write about it in the exaggerated style of a tall tale.

CHECK POINT
PAGES 715–723

Rewrite the following sentences, correcting all errors in the use of pronouns. If a sentence has no errors, write *Correct*.

Writing Theme
Arabian Nights

1. It was the Arab scholar al-Mas‘ūdī whom first mentioned the book called *Hazar Afsanak (A Thousand Legends)* in the ninth century.

2. However, him publicizing the tales doesn't mean that he was familiar with the version we know today.

3. The Arab people theirselves referred to the book as *A Thousand and One Nights*.

4. The sorcerers, thieves, and monsters who we know best as characters in *The Arabian Nights* have changed over the centuries.

5. Us referring to them as *Arabian* is actually inaccurate, since the tales also originated in India and Persia.

6. Arab storytellers who haunted the seaports and marketplaces absorbed legends from other cultures.

7. They outdid theirselves in adding to the stories.

8. Our thanks go to an unknown scholar in eighteenth-century Cairo; no one did a more thorough job of assembling the tales than him.

9. Who should Western readers thank for first bringing *A Thousand and One Nights* to their attention?

10. Antoine Galland accomplished this feat; few French traveled as widely in the Middle East as him.

11. No one knows whose translation first brought the tales to we English-speaking readers in 1706.

12. Years later, according to Sir Richard Burton, writer John Payne and him competed with each other to produce the most accurate translation.

13. An explorer, poet, mystic, and spy, Burton made hisself as famous for his adventures as for his 1885 translation of the *Nights*.

14. The African explorations of his partner John Speke and he have been the subject of several books and movies.

15. Whom among us does not know the legend of Shahrazad and the thousand and one nights?

16. No one ever had a more compelling reason to tell stories after dark than she.

17. Shahrazad was married to King Shahryar, whom had sworn to execute his wife after their wedding night.

18. Two clever women, her sister Dunyazad and her, tricked the king into listening to a series of exciting stories.

19. Since she would not finish the story before he felt sleepy, the king himself postponed her execution night after night.
20. Picture him listening to her for 1,001 nights until he fell so deeply in love he could not bear to lose her.

PRONOUN-ANTECEDENT AGREEMENT

An antecedent is the noun or pronoun to which a pronoun refers.

A personal pronoun must agree with its antecedent in number, gender, and person.

Agreement in Number If the antecedent is singular, use a singular pronoun. If the antecedent is plural, use a plural pronoun.

When the antecedent is a singular indefinite pronoun, use a singular pronoun to refer to it. The following indefinite pronouns are singular:

another	anything	everybody	neither	one
anybody	each	everyone	nobody	somebody
anyone	either	everything	no one	someone

Each (singular) of the Boy Scouts was wearing *his* (singular) bandanna. (*Each* is the antecedent of *his.*)
Everyone (singular) has a right to *his or her* (singular) opinion.

When the antecedent is a plural indefinite pronoun, use a plural possessive pronoun to refer to it: *our, your,* or *their.* The following indefinite pronouns are plural:

both   few   many   several

Both of the magazines featured the President on *their* covers.
Many of us improved *our* free-throw shooting with practice.

When the antecedent is the indefinite pronoun *all, some, any, most,* or *none,* you may use a singular or plural pronoun. The correct form depends on whether the noun in the prepositional phrase following the pronoun names something that can be counted.

Some of the silver has lost *its* luster. (cannot be counted)
Some of the racers have received *their* entry numbers. (can be counted)

In the examples on the preceding page, the indefinite pronouns are used as subjects. Note that the verb, as well as any pronouns referring to the subject, agrees in number with the subject.

Incorrect	None of the actors *has* forgotten *their* lines.
Correct	None of the actors *has* forgotten *his or her* lines.
Correct	None of the actors *have* forgotten *their* lines.

When two or more singular antecedents are joined by *or* or *nor*, use a singular pronoun.

> Either *Iris* or *Elena* will give *her* speech first.
> Neither *Will* nor *Leon* has finished *his* physics experiment.

Use the noun nearer the verb to determine the pronoun for subjects joined by *or* or *nor*.

> Neither the dogs nor the cat had eaten *its* meal.
> Neither Will nor his lab partners have finished *their* experiments.

When a collective noun is the antecedent, use either a singular or a plural pronoun, depending on whether you wish to emphasize the group as a whole or the individuals forming the group.

> The football team has *its* new plays. (the team as a whole)
> The football team have been awarded *their* letters. (the members of the team as individuals)

Agreement in Gender   A personal pronoun must agree in gender with its antecedent. *He, his,* and *him* are masculine pronouns; *she, her,* and *hers,* feminine; and *it* and *its,* neuter.

When a singular antecedent pronoun refers to a category of persons that may include both males and females, the phrase *his or her* is acceptable. In fact, many people who want to avoid sexist language prefer *his or her* to *his*.

Correct	Each diver should bring *his* aqualung.
Correct	Each diver should bring *his or her* aqualung.

Agreement in Person   A personal pronoun must agree in person with its antecedent. Be aware that the indefinite pronouns *one, everyone,* and *everybody* are in the third person singular.

Pronouns referring to these antecedents should likewise be in the third person singular: *he, his, him, she, her,* or *hers*.

Incorrect	Everyone should report to *your* cabin soon.
Correct	Everyone should report to *his or her* cabin soon.

Practice Your Skills

CONCEPT CHECK

Pronoun-Antecedent Agreement Rewrite the following sentences correcting any errors in pronoun or verb agreement. If a sentence has no errors, write *Correct.*

1. The cast is taking its places on stage.
2. Each of them are wearing their medieval costume.
3. Everyone is doing their best to make the Camelot set seem real to the audience.
4. Many playwrights who have written plays about King Arthur have based their works on *Le Morte d'Arthur* by Sir Thomas Malory.
5. One of the playwrights wrote their play because people are fascinated with the knights of the Round Table.
6. Some wrote their plays because of the story's romantic appeal.
7. Anyone wishing for magic should keep their eyes on Merlin.
8. There are two versions of how Arthur died, and both have their supporters.
9. In one version, no one who wants Lancelot to win Queen Guinevere will have their way.
10. Depending on the ending you read, either wounds from a fight with Lancelot or a battle takes their toll on Arthur.
11. Each of the endings have Mordred as their villain.
12. The lights are dimming; everyone should take your places.
13. Neither Arthur nor Lancelot have made their entrance.
14. Perhaps some of the magic will weave its way across the footlights.
15. Though centuries old, none of the tales have lost their charm.

PRONOUN REFERENCE

The noun that a pronoun replaces must be expressed or clearly understood. If the pronoun reference is vague or ambiguous, a sentence may be confusing, misleading, or even unintentionally humorous.

Unidentified and Indefinite Reference

The antecedent of a personal pronoun should always be clear.

Unidentified Reference Frequently a problem occurs when the pronoun *it, they, this, that,* or *which* is used without a clear antecedent. In many cases, the sentence has no definite referent. Often the problem can best be corrected by rewording the sentence.

Writing
—TIP—

In formal writing the pronoun *you* should be used only to mean "you the reader."

Unidentified	It says in the book that strawberries are not true fruits.
Better	The book states that strawberries are not true fruits.
Unidentified	Tell me what tapes they are putting on sale.
Better	Tell me what tapes the store is putting on sale.

Indefinite Reference Sometimes the antecedent of a pronoun may not be directly expressed; it may be implied in the context of the sentence. When the reference is vague, the problem can be corrected by adding a clear antecedent or by replacing the pronoun with a noun.

Weak	Achilles was courageous, and he showed it in many episodes in Homer's *Iliad.* (*It* does not have a clear antecedent; the noun *courage* is only implied by the adjective *courageous.*)
Better	One outstanding quality of Achilles was his courage, and he showed it in many episodes in Homer's *Iliad.*
Weak	Birdwatching is most exciting to Rob when he sights an unusual one. (There is no clear antecedent for *one.* The idea of *bird* is contained in the compound noun *birdwatching,* but part of a compound noun cannot be the antecedent of *one.*)
Better	Birdwatching is most exciting to Rob when he sights an unusual species.
Vague	We spent two hours looking at Native American art. *This* made us rush through the dinosaur exhibit. (*This* has no clear noun or pronoun antecedent.)
Better	We spent two hours looking at Native American art. This delay made us rush through the dinosaur exhibit.
Vague	I lost one contact lens, *which* blurred the TV picture. (*Which* has no clear antecedent.)
Better	Because I lost one contact lens, the TV picture looked blurred.

The pronoun *you* is sometimes used to refer to people in general, rather than to the person spoken to. Used in this way, *you* has an indefinite antecedent.

Indefinite	With some computer programs you use fewer keystrokes for basic word-processing functions than with other programs.
Better	Some computer programs use fewer keystrokes for basic word-processing functions than other programs do.

728 Grammar Handbook

Ambiguous Reference

The word *ambiguous* means "having two or more possible meanings." The reference of a pronoun is ambiguous if the pronoun may refer to more than one word. This situation can arise when a noun or pronoun falls between the pronoun and its true antecedent.

Ambiguous	Take the screens off the windows and paint *them*. (Does this mean paint the windows or screens?)
Better	Paint the screens after you take them off the windows.
Ambiguous	Sue told Ellen that she was next on the program. (Who was next—Sue or Ellen?)
Better	Ellen was next on the program, and Sue told her to get ready to go on.

Writing
— **TIP** —
When you proof-read your writing, make sure that each pronoun has a clear antecedent preceding it.

Practice Your Skills

A. CONCEPT CHECK

Pronoun Reference Rewrite the following sentences correcting unidentified, indefinite, or ambiguous pronoun antecedents.

1. Bicycling can be an enjoyable, healthful, and economical sport for people who own one.
2. However, it can put people in the hospital if they have an accident while riding a bicycle.
3. They show in a recent study that nearly 400,000 bicycle-related injuries require hospitalization each year.
4. Researchers also warn them that another half million riders suffer less serious injuries.

Writing Theme
Sports and Safety

5. Each year more of you die from bicycle accidents than from poisoning, falls, and firearm injuries combined.
6. Statistics indicate that when you wear a helmet, you reduce the risk of head injury by eighty-five percent.
7. It is ironic that many owners of bicycles also own helmets but don't use them.
8. It says in one article that in this country only two percent of bicyclists wear helmets when they ride.
9. Unfortunately, Consuela's reaction when her mother urged her to wear a helmet is typical. She told her she thought they were ugly and inconvenient.
10. Many government officials are concerned about it, and they are showing their concern by requesting a law to ensure that bicyclists wear them.

B. REVISION SKILL

Clarifying Pronoun Reference Rewrite the following paragraph, correcting all errors in unclear pronoun usage.

This indoor climber practices on a wall that she had installed in the basement of her home.

(1) Indoor climbing began in France where they have enjoyed the sport since the mid-1980's. (2) They report in several sports articles that indoor climbing is becoming one of the nation's fastest growing sports. (3) A number of colleges have installed climbing walls in their gyms, and they have become popular attractions. (4) Many sporting facilities are also erecting new walls for their patrons and some of them are eight stories high. (5) On a climbing wall, you can experience the sensation of ascending a cliff. (6) These structures simulate the crannies and ledges of a mountain's face, which makes climbing possible. (7) Climbers must scale the wall in teams to ensure their safety. (8) In most climbing facilities, they require that climbers wear helmets and safety lines. (9) Most also require partnering a climber, which means that you attend their safety line from the ground. (10) From such training, climbers learn to be patient and careful, and they demonstrate it each time they climb.

Rewrite the following sentences, correcting all problems in pronoun reference.

1. At the age of seventeen, Dorothea Lange decided to become a photographer, although she had never taken one.
2. She told her mother she had a real talent and she should not fail to develop it.
3. Soon Lange had set up her own studio for taking portraits, which was not common for a woman in the early 1900's.
4. Before the 1930's, they had large, slow-operating, eight-by-ten-inch cameras.
5. They made taking candid pictures difficult and cumbersome.
6. When better equipment became available, Lange took candid pictures of people, and it became her life's career.
7. Lange took powerful, touching photographs of poor people during the depression of the 1930's which earned her fame.
8. Her book has a careful arrangement. Its photographs tell a story by their sequence and juxtapositioning.
9. More than just photographs, it is history.
10. Lange, as well as the other photographers recording the Great Depression, took people's pictures only if they were willing.
11. Each of her photographs captures the suffering and humiliation of the poor and make their impact on the viewer.
12. She had the people look at the camera, so in each photograph it looks as if they are having their pictures taken.
13. In Lange's pictures, you see such subjects as people waiting in breadlines and migrant workers with their children.
14. If a picture turned out to be beautiful, it was nice but incidental.
15. Lange's pictures appeared in several newspapers and magazines which helped create support for government relief programs.
16. Among the company of photographers called documentarians, probably none are more celebrated than Dorothea Lange.
17. Her "Migrant Mother" is famous because it leads a life of its own; many more people have seen it than know who made it.
18. They installed the file of her photographs in the Library of Congress, and they are considered very impressive.
19. In one biography of Lange, it states that she and other depression photographers made "the most remarkable human document ever recorded in pictures."
20. They also made a significant contribution to the development of the photo essay as a genre.

WRITING
H A N D B O O K
35

Writing Theme
Discoveries
of Science

A. Choosing Correct Pronouns For each of the following sentences, write the correct form of the pronoun shown in parentheses.

1. The two reporters selected to travel to the National Radio Astronomy Observatory to research a feature article were Juanita and (I, me).
2. There were several scientists at this New Mexico observatory (who, whom) were studying the center of our galaxy.
3. Juanita and (they, them) discussed the recent discovery of evidence of a gigantic black hole at the galaxy's core.
4. Between Juanita and (I, me, myself), we filled five notebook pages with facts such as a black hole is a stellar object with a massive gravitational field.
5. At a briefing, (we, us) reporters were told that the object's gravity is so strong that light cannot escape it—hence the name.
6. An astronomer told (Juanita and I, Juanita and me) that the center of our galaxy is 25,000 light years from Earth.
7. Physicists (who, whom) were involved in the study found stellar debris around the black hole.
8. (Their, Them) measuring certain changes also revealed evidence of huge bursts of energy coming from the black hole.
9. Juanita was even more amazed than (I, me) at the implications of the discoveries.
10. The physicist to (who, whom) we spoke told us that the black hole was apparently devouring the surrounding stars.
11. According to (he, him), these energy bursts result when the black hole's gravity sucks in a neighboring star.
12. The experts (themselves, theirselves) guess that this black hole may have consumed over a million stars since the galaxy's birth.
13. Neither the physicist nor the other scientists had finished all (his, their) calculations of this phenomenon.
14. If it weren't for (their, them) skillful handling of the complicated instruments, none of their discoveries would have been possible.
15. The scientists (who, whom) will be featured in our article have added vastly to (us, our) understanding of one of the galaxy's most puzzling structures.

B. Correcting Pronoun Errors Rewrite the following sentences, correcting pronoun errors. If a sentence has no errors, write *Correct*.

1. Neither Shawna nor me really knew much about the incredible career of George Washington Carver.
2. We visited the Carver National Monument near Diamond Grove, Missouri.
3. This made us curious about his work.

4. Few people have contributed as much to the progress of agriculture in the United States as him.
5. In 1896 Booker T. Washington encouraged Carver to head his new Department of Agriculture at the Tuskegee Institute.
6. They claim in some sources that Carver built his new department literally from a trash heap.
7. Carver's students used old teacups for their mortars and reeds for pipettes.
8. But the discoveries made by Carver hisself and by his associates changed the nature of agriculture in the South.
9. Whom among us has not heard of the economic suffering caused by the cotton-devouring boll weevil?
10. Carver urged cotton farmers to diversify their crops, which improved both the economy and the ecology of the region.
11. The peanut and many other crops owe their prominence in the Southern agricultural economy to Carver's research.
12. It is reported in one source that Carver made over 300 different products from the peanut and 118 from the sweet potato.
13. Both Shawna and myself were surprised to learn that Carver made plastics, soap, and ink from peanuts.
14. Carver was truly ingenious, and it shows in his achievements.
15. In 1953 Carver was honored by the U.S. Congress, which established the Carver Monument near his birthplace in Missouri.

C. Proofreading Rewrite the following paragraphs, correcting all errors in spelling, capitalization, punctuation, and pronoun use.

The discovery of the planet neptune resulted from coincidences. Two mathematicians whom never actually saw the planet and whom worked independently are jointly credited with the discovery. Here is the plot as it occured.

The orbit of the seventh planet in the soler system, Uranus, did not seem to follow the laws of gravity. In 1843 a young British mathematician named John Adams set to work on the problem. Two years later, working with data on the orbit of Uranus, he had laid out the orbit of a more distant planet. He then submitted his work to the royal astronomer, whom ignored the young scientists ideas. Meanwhile, a noted French mathamatician, Urbain Leverrier, had come up with a nearly identical solution.

It was John Galle, another astronomer, who made what he thought was an actual sighting of Neptune. However, when his assistant and him first looked at the spot where the planet should be; they saw only a cluster of stars. By them later comparing the recent sightings with old charts, they noticed that there was indeed a "new" star—the planet Neptune.

Sketchbook

BUS STOP

In Montgomery, Alabama, Rosa Parks, a seamstress, refused to obey a bus segregation law. Her arrest helped bring about the civil rights movement.

Think of a literary or historical character with whom you identify. Write several paragraphs comparing or contrasting yourself to that character. Use adjectives and adverbs that clearly convey the ways in which you are alike and different. Use pronouns correctly.

Additional Sketches

While assisting a political candidate with his campaign strategy, you have been asked to compile a report discussing the three most important issues he faces. Use comparative and superlative modifiers to examine the importance of each issue.

You and your friends have learned that your favorite radio disc jockey will be taken off the air. Write a letter to the owner of the radio station explaining why you believe the disc jockey should be retained. Make sure that pronoun antecedents are clear and that pronoun cases are used correctly.

On the Lightside

GRAMMAR SIMPLIFIED

We Americans have only two rules of grammar:

Rule 1. The word "me" is always incorrect.

Most of us learn this rule as children, from our mothers. We say things like: "Mom, can Bobby and me roll the camping trailer over Mrs. Johnson's cat?" And our mothers say: "Remember your grammar, dear. You mean: 'Can Bobby and *I* roll the camping trailer over Mrs. Johnson's cat? . . .'"

The only exception to this rule is in formal business writing, where instead of "I" you must use "the undersigned." For example, this letter is incorrect:

"Dear Hunky-Dory Canned Fruit Company: A couple of days ago my wife bought a can of your cling peaches and served them to my mother who has a weak heart and she [almost] died when she bit into a live grub. If I ever find out where you live, I am gonna whomp you on the head with an ax handle."

This should be corrected as follows:

". . . If the undersigned ever finds out where you live, the undersigned is gonna whomp you on the head with an ax handle."

Rule 2. You're not allowed to split infinitives.

An infinitive is the word "to" and whatever comes right behind it, such as "to a tee," "to the best of my ability," "tomato," etc. Splitting an infinitive is putting something between the "to" and the other words. For example, this is incorrect:

"Hey man, you got any, you know, spare change you could give to, like me?"

The correct version is: ". . . spare change you could, like, give to me?"

The advantage of American English is that, because there are so few rules, practically anybody can learn to speak it in just a few minutes. The disadvantage is that Americans generally sound like jerks, whereas the British sound really smart, especially to Americans. . . .

So the trick is to use American grammar, which is simple, but talk with a British accent, which is impressive. . . .

You can do it, too. Practice in your home, then approach someone on the street and say: "Tally-ho, old chap. I would consider it a great honour if you would favour me with some spare change."

Dave Barry

Adjective and Adverb Usage

UNDERSTANDING MODIFIERS

Before examining the usage rules for modifiers, recall the definitions and functions of modifiers. An **adjective** modifies—that is, describes or limits—a noun or a pronoun; an **adverb** modifies a verb, an adjective, or another adverb. To decide whether a modifier is an adjective or an adverb, determine the part of speech of the word it modifies.

A *gelatinous* creature oozed out of the spaceship. (The word *gelatinous* modifies the noun *creature;* thus, *gelatinous* is an adjective.)

The creature was *transparent.* (The word *transparent* in the predicate modifies the noun *creature* in the subject; therefore, *transparent* is a predicate adjective.)

The creature slithered *slowly* across the grass. (The word *slowly* modifies the verb *slithered;* therefore, *slowly* is an adverb.)

It seemed to be a *very* intelligent being. (The word *very* modifies the adjective *intelligent;* thus, *very* is an adverb.)

Adjective and Adverb Forms

Most adjectives have no identifying form or ending. Adverbs, however, are often formed by adding *-ly* to an adjective.

Adjective	Adverb
swift	swiftly
hopeless	hopelessly
greedy	greedily

Note, however, that not every word that ends in *-ly* is an adverb. Be careful to distinguish between adverbs and adjectives such as *friendly.*

The art studio had a *lovely* view. (adjective)
Grease the pancake griddle *lightly.* (adverb)

Some adjectives and adverbs have the same form. Usually such modifiers have only one syllable.

Adjective	Adverb
a *fast* race car	grows *fast*
a *high* branch	jump *high*

Some adverbs have two forms, one with *-ly,* the other without. Choose the one that fits the level of language you are using. In formal writing as in formal speaking situations, the *-ly* form is usually more appropriate.

> On a twisting mountain road, it's best to drive *slowly.*
> The sign says "Drive *Slow.*"

> The doctor said, "Breathe *deep.*"
> After a restless night, Sara slept *deeply* all morning.

> "Come *quick!*" shouted Leon as the chicks began to hatch in the incubator.
> The ability to think *quickly* is an asset.

Modifiers That Follow Verbs

A word that modifies an action verb, an adjective, or an adverb is always an adverb. Sometimes, however, you may be tempted to place an adjective instead of an adverb after an action verb. To avoid this common error, remember that a modifier that follows and limits an action verb is always an adverb.

Incorrect	Beverly Sills sings *beautiful.*
Correct	Beverly Sills sings *beautifully.*

Unlike action verbs, which are often followed by adverbs, a linking verb is very often followed by a predicate adjective. A predicate adjective modifies the subject of the sentence.

If a modifier follows a form of the verb *be*—the most common linking verb—speakers and writers seldom have difficulty using the correct form. However, other linking verbs, such as those in the sentences below, can also be used as action verbs. Choosing a modifier in these cases becomes more difficult. Study these examples.

Linking Verb	**Action Verb**
That lake *looked* choppy.	The driver *looked* quickly in the mirror.
The medicine *tastes* bitter.	Kim *tasted* the mango cautiously.
The wind *grew* chilly.	Orchids *grow* profusely here.
The mayor *appeared* skeptical.	The document *appeared* suddenly on the screen.

To decide whether to use an adjective or an adverb, think about which word in the sentence the adjective or adverb is going to modify. If it is going to modify a noun, as in the sentences in the left-hand column above, use an adjective; if it is going to modify a verb, as in the sentences in the right-hand column, use an adverb.

Adjective and
Adverb Usage

Practice Your Skills

A. CONCEPT CHECK

Adjectives and Adverbs Write the correct modifier of the two in parentheses. Then label the modifier *Adjective* or *Adverb*.

1. The legend of Lydia Darragh is one of the (real, really) exciting stories of individual courage in the American Revolution.
2. Born in Ireland, Darragh felt (hopeful, hopefully) as she emigrated to America after her marriage.
3. In the colonies, Darragh grew (famous, famously) as a skillful and caring nurse and midwife.
4. Darragh's son joined the American army and fought (fierce, fiercely) in the Revolution, with his mother's loyal support.
5. Then, (sudden, suddenly), in December of 1777, the war entered Darragh's home when British officers appeared on her doorstep.
6. Darragh felt (indignant, indignantly), but she kept her head.
7. She listened at the door and, as soon as the coast looked (clear, clearly), she set out to warn the American army of a planned attack.
8. Darragh must have seemed (harmless, harmlessly), for she passed quickly by the British.
9. Once past, she changed her course and walked toward the American camp that was thirteen miles (distant, distantly).
10. When she met an American officer on her way, she relayed the message, and, as a result, two days later the Americans withstood the British attack (easy, easily).

The Nation Makers, by Howard Pyle (1853-1911). Collection of the Brandywine River Museum

B. REVISION SKILL

Using Adjectives and Adverbs Correctly Rewrite the paragraph, correcting any errors in the use of adjectives or adverbs. If the sentence contains no errors, write *Correct*.

(1) That sunny October day in Midland, Texas, seemed rather ordinary. (2) Then some terrible news spread rapid through the small West Texas city and, soon afterward, the world. (3) Jessica McClure, eighteen months old, had fallen

into an abandoned well in her aunt's backyard and was wedged tightly at a curve in the shaft twenty-two feet down. (4) Rescue workers dropped a microphone into the well and found that Jessica was still conscious. (5) Drilling experts furiously dug another shaft beside the one in which Jessica was trapped. (6) Ten hours after beginning, the drillers felt hopefully; they had reached a point only two feet away from Jessica. (7) Then they tunneled careful from their shaft to the one where Jessica was wedged. (8) One worker who was digging the tunnel said that Jessica seemed calmly; he said that she was humming a song. (9) Hours later, a paramedic reached Jessica and pulled her gentle through the two-foot tunnel into the rescue shaft. (10) Almost sixty hours after Jessica's fall, the weary paramedic climbed triumphant out of the rescue shaft with Jessica safe in his arms.

C. APPLICATION IN WRITING

A News Story   Write a brief news story that reports on an act of courage. You may choose an event you know of or do some brief research. Include information about where it occurred and the people who were involved. Include vivid adjectives and adverbs that will appeal to the senses of your reader.

COMPARING ADJECTIVES
AND ADVERBS

Each adjective and adverb has three forms, or degrees. The **positive degree,** the first form, is used to describe one person, place, group, thing, idea, or action.

Positive   Alpha Centauri is a *bright* star. It sparkles *brilliantly* at night.

The **comparative degree** of an adjective or adverb is used to compare two persons, places, groups, things, ideas, or actions.

Comparative   Canopus is a *brighter* star than Alpha Centauri. It sparkles *more brilliantly* than Alpha Centauri.

In your reading and writing, look for clues that signal the use of the comparative. The word *than* and phrases such as *the other one, of the two,* and *of the pair* signal that two things are being compared.

Writing
—TIP—

A strong noun or verb often can make use of a modifier unnecessary. For example, *tore* is more effective than *ran very fast.*

Adjective and
Adverb Usage   **739**

The **superlative degree** of an adjective or adverb is used to compare three or more persons, places, groups, things, ideas, or actions.

Superlative   Sirius is the *brightest* star in the night sky. It sparkles *most brilliantly* of these three stars.

Sometimes the number of items being compared is not specified. You must infer this information. For example, how would you decide which degree of the modifier to use to complete the following sentence?

Supergiants such as Betelgeuse are the (larger, largest) stars.

The context of the sentence suggests that more than two stars are being compared; consequently, the superlative form, *largest,* is the correct choice.

Usage Note   A common error is to use the superlative instead of the comparative in comparing two things. For example: "I have two children. The *oldest* is six, and the *youngest* is three." "Which team do you like *most:* the Celtics or the Lakers?" The modifiers in these sentences should be *older, younger,* and *more.*

Some modifiers are absolutes and may not be compared. For example, if something is *unique,* it is one of a kind. It cannot be *more* (or *less*) unique than something else. Other absolute modifiers include *complete, infinite,* and *total.*

Regular Comparisons

Adjectives and adverbs, like verbs, may be regular or irregular. Most modifiers are regular, and their comparative and superlative degrees are formed in one of the following two ways.

1. The comparative and superlative degrees of one-syllable modifiers are formed by adding *-er* and *-est,* respectively. This is also true of most two-syllable adjectives.

Positive	Comparative	Superlative
light	lighter	lightest
hot	hotter	hottest
wise	wiser	wisest
mighty	mightier	mightiest
few	fewer	fewest
soon	sooner	soonest

Spelling Note   For some modifiers, a spelling change must be made in the positive form before adding the comparative or superlative ending. See these examples on page 740: *hot* (double the final consonant), *wise* (drop the final *e*), *mighty* (change the *y* to *i*). Such spelling changes are found in dictionary entries for modifiers.

Usage Note *Few* (*fewer, fewest*) is used for things that can be counted: *I have a few groceries to buy.* *Less* (*lesser, least*) is used for things that cannot be counted: *There seems to be less rain this fall than there was last fall.*

2. Most two-syllable adverbs, adverbs ending in *-ly,* and all three-syllable modifiers use *more* and *most* to form the comparative and superlative.

Positive	Comparative	Superlative
ridiculous	more ridiculous	most ridiculous
cautious	more cautious	most cautious
dangerous	more dangerous	most dangerous
boldly	more boldly	most boldly
miserable	more miserable	most miserable
abstract	more abstract	most abstract
colorful	more colorful	most colorful

For negative comparisons, the words *less* and *least* are placed before the positive forms: *wrinkled, less wrinkled, least wrinkled; closely, less closely, least closely.*

Irregular Modifiers

The comparative and superlative forms of many commonly used adjectives and adverbs are irregular.

Modifiers with Irregular Forms		
Positive	**Comparative**	**Superlative**
bad	worse	worst
far	farther *or* further	farthest *or* furthest
good	better	best
ill	worse	worst
late	later	latest *or* last
little	less	least
many	more	most
much	more	most
well	better	best

Usage Note *Farther* and *farthest* compare distances; *further* and *furthest* compare times, amounts, and degrees: *The finish line is only a mile <u>farther</u>. Stay tuned for <u>further</u> developments.*

Practice Your Skills

A. CONCEPT CHECK

Comparatives and Superlatives Write each sentence with the correct comparative or superlative form of the modifier given in parentheses.

1. A week in October 1962 might have been the (perilous) period in history for humanity.
2. At the beginning of that week, United States intelligence sources reported that what Americans had feared (much) had happened.
3. The Soviet Union had secretly installed nuclear missiles on the island of Cuba, which is no (far) than ninety miles from Florida.
4. Further reports gave even (bad) news than that: the missiles were aimed at major cities in the United States.
5. During that week, nuclear war seemed (imminent) than at any other time since the development of nuclear weapons.
6. President John F. Kennedy faced the (difficult) problem any American president had ever faced.
7. He had to force Soviet Premier Nikita Khrushchev to remove the missiles in a way that was (likely) to touch off a nuclear war.
8. This crisis was (ominous) than any other since World War II.
9. However, during the next week the news became much (good) than it had been; Khrushchev had agreed to remove the missiles.
10. The Cuban missile crisis demonstrated that when dealing with nuclear weapons world leaders would have to exercise (much) caution than they had previously.

B. REVISION SKILL

Using Comparatives and Superlatives Rewrite the following sentences. Correct all of the errors in the use of comparative and superlative forms. Label sentences with no errors *Correct.*

1. In *Profiles in Courage,* John F. Kennedy tells of the pre-Civil War South's struggle to prevent the North from becoming most powerful in the Senate.
2. The South wanted to make sure there would never be less slave states than free states.
3. The attention of the nation was focused on the three more gifted parliamentary leaders in American history—Henry Clay, John C. Calhoun, and Daniel Webster.

Henry Clay supported the Missouri Compromise in an effort to avoid civil war.

4. Kennedy says that Clay had probably the greater vision of the three, hammering out three great compromises during his career that kept the Union together for forty years.

5. Pro-slavery Calhoun was most extraordinary than the other two, both physically and intellectually.

6. Of the three, it was abolitionist Webster, says Kennedy, whose political courage cost him more.

7. Webster was subjected to some of the fiercer scorn in history for supporting a Clay compromise that made concessions to the South, but in the end probably saved the Union.

8. Two years later, following the publication of *Uncle Tom's Cabin,* by Harriet Beecher Stowe, abolitionist sentiment became more intense and swept the country.

9. After reading Stowe's compelling description of the slaves' suffering, the public became least willing to compromise on the issue of slavery.

10. Many pros and cons were weighed in deciding whether or not individual states had the right to legalize slavery, but today's citizens agree that the injustice of slavery was the most important factor.

C. APPLICATION IN WRITING

A Proposal Imagine that you are part of a committee to plan some event or activity. The committee is split into two opposing groups. Describe the task you are faced with and write a compromise proposal. Explain which side wanted the seating to be *more* accessible from the dance floor and which wanted the *less expensive* band, and so forth.

Writing Theme
National Parks

A. Write the correct form of the modifier given in parentheses. Then label the modifier *Adjective* or *Adverb*.

1. The Olympic National Park reigns (magnificent, magnificently) over the Olympic Peninsula of western Washington State.
2. The park is one of the world's (better, best) examples of nature's beauty and diversity.
3. In a (real, really) short distance, visitors can travel from ocean shores through rain forests and up into glacier-covered mountains.
4. The coastal lands and rain forests were invaded by European culture by 1592 and have since undergone (farther, further) development, but the rugged interior is largely undisturbed.
5. In 1909, President Theodore Roosevelt ensured that much of the area would remain forever (beautiful, beautifully) when he designated it a National Monument.
6. By 1938, the Olympic National Park had been converted into one of the (more, most) stunning components of the National Park System.
7. Along the fifty-seven miles of rugged coastline, the ocean pounds (relentless, relentlessly) on the shore to produce sea stacks and sculptured arches.
8. Among the delights of the coast are tide pools, even though every year they contain (less, fewer) examples of sea life.
9. The Olympic Mountains rise (dramatic, dramatically) from the water's edge, intercepting moisture-laden clouds from the Pacific that dump their loads on the western slopes.
10. The result is one of the (rarer, rarest) occurrences in nature—the temperate rain forest.

B. Write each sentence with the correct comparative or superlative form of the modifier given in parentheses.

1. Can you think of anything (remarkable) than donning scuba gear or snorkle equipment for a day in the park?
2. Just a little (far) off the Florida coast than the three-mile continental border lies a living coral reef.
3. Totally underwater, it comprises what may be the (more) unusual park area in the U.S.
4. Although the federal park system refers to it as Key Largo Coral Reef Preserve, Floridians use the (much) familiar name of John Pennekamp Coral Reef State Park.

5. Marine biologists consider it perhaps the (good) site in the world to study coral growth.
6. However, the creation of the park in 1960 grew out of a (serious) concern than the study of ocean life.
7. The (ill) threat to the survival of the area came from curio vendors who harvested barge loads of sponges.
8. (Little) harmful, but still a problem, were spearfishing enthusiasts.
9. Today, snorklers can swim among species such as the silvery spade fish or the (colorful) blue and gold queen angelfish.
10. They can view firsthand a (great) variety of tropical fish than can be found in any pet store.

C. Correct any error in the use of the adjective or adverb in italics in the following sentences. If a sentence has no error, write *Correct*. Then write the word that is modified by each adjective or adverb.

1. Everglades National Park is the *immensest* subtropical wilderness of all the national parks.
2. A segment of a one-million-acre area, the park looks *mysteriously* and *beautifully,* as though it were another world.
3. Starting at Lake Okeechobee, water flows *slow* through the saw grass marsh toward the Gulf of Mexico.
4. *Further* to the south along the coast lies the area known as Ten Thousand Islands.
5. Jungle-like plant life includes numerous kinds of trees, the *taller* of which is the mangrove, often reaching heights of seventy feet.
6. Visitors can view the area from trails, and in some places they can walk *farther* out into the swamp on long boardwalks.
7. Some of the *more* unusual animal life in the world can be seen in this concentrated area.
8. One of the *oddest* creatures is the manatee or sea cow.
9. Some of the wildlife in the Everglades has been *near* lost to hunters.
10. Creation of the park has stemmed many of the *worse* problems.

USING COMPARISONS
CORRECTLY

When making comparisons, certain constructions can become confusing and can lead to errors. To avoid two of the most common comparison errors—double comparisons and illogical comparisons—keep the following guidelines in mind.

Double Comparisons

The comparative degree of a modifier is formed either by adding -er to the positive form or by placing *more* before the positive form. Using both -er and *more* at the same time is not correct. Similarly, the superlative degree of a modifier is formed either by adding -est or by using *most*. Using both is not correct.

Incorrect	Metal is *more stronger* than plastic.
Correct	Metal is *stronger* than plastic.
Incorrect	What is the *most cheapest* fare to Vancouver?
Correct	What is the *cheapest* fare to Vancouver?

Illogical Comparisons

1. The word *other* or *else* is used to compare an individual member with the rest of its group.

Illogical	Our team has scored more points than any team in the league. (Is our team not in the league?)
Clear	Our team has scored more points than any *other* team in the league.
Illogical	Elena is as talented as anyone in the cast of the play. (Is Elena not in the cast?)
Clear	Elena is as talented as anyone *else* in the cast of the play.

2. The word *than* or *as* is required after the first modifier in a compound comparison.

Illogical	Obviously, Natalie is as sympathetic if not more sympathetic than Joyce.
Clear	Obviously, Natalie is as sympathetic *as,* if not more sympathetic than, Joyce.
Clear	Obviously, Natalie is as sympathetic *as* Joyce, if not more sympathetic.
Illogical	Dimitri had as much reason to be optimistic if not more than I did.
Awkward	Dimitri had as much reason to be optimistic *as,* if not more than, I did.
Clear	Dimitri had as much reason to be optimistic *as* I did, if not more.
Illogical	Your chances of getting into college are as good if not better than Bert's.
Clear	Your chances of getting into college are as good *as* Bert's, if not better.

7-1 © 1985 Universal Press Syndicate

"That's him! That's the one! . . . I'd recognize that silly hat anywhere!"

3. Both parts of a comparison must be stated completely if there is any chance of misunderstanding.

Unclear	I phone him more than Naomi. (more than you phone Naomi or more than Naomi phones him?)
Clear	I phone him more than Naomi *does*.
Clear	I phone him more than *I phone* Naomi.
Unclear	The Red Sox beat the Yankees more often than the White Sox that year.
Clear	The Red Sox beat the Yankees more often than the White Sox *did* that year.
Clear	The Red Sox beat the Yankees more often that year *than they beat* the White Sox.
Unclear	The income of a doctor is higher than a nurse.
Clear	The income of a doctor is higher than *that* of a nurse.
Clear	A doctor's income is higher than a *nurse's*.

Practice Your Skills

A. CONCEPT CHECK

Correct Comparisons Rewrite the following sentences to make the comparisons clear and correct. If there are no problems in a sentence, write *Correct*.

Writing Theme
Film Stars

1. The great film comedian W. C. Fields was as strange if not stranger than the characters he played.
2. One of his most oddest habits concerned money.
3. Fields made as much during his career as any star in Hollywood, but somehow it all seemed to disappear.
4. The pudgy actor with the bulbous nose and semi-permanent squint seemed to love bank accounts more than his family and friends.
5. During the course of his career, he told a close friend, he opened more than seven hundred different accounts.
6. He opened accounts in small towns and large, often putting more money into a bank in South Waterhole than Los Angeles.
7. When Fields died, his executors launched a most thoroughest search for his assets; they were unsuccessful.
8. His heirs were as industrious if not more than his executors, but they, too, failed.
9. Of course, you might think, "What could be more easier than notifying all the banks in the country to check their records for W. C. Fields's name?"
10. The problem is that Fields's imagination was more vivid than his executors; all of the accounts were in different false names.

Adjective and
Adverb Usage   **747**

B. PROOFREADING SKILL

Correcting Comparisons Rewrite the paragraph to correct errors in spelling, mechanics, and the use of comparisons.

Boris Karloff is as famous, if not more famous, than any other acter for playing monsters and villains in horror movies. Karloff chose the most horrifying roles he could find Some critics say that he terrified more moviegoers than any villain in the history of film, including Lon chaney (*The Wolf Man*) and Bela Lugosi (*Dracula*). Karloffs fame as a horror star spread quick after he played the monster in *Frankenstein*. To film audiences, each of his succeeding roles became more terrifyingly than the one before it. However, his true personality was far gentler and kindlier than the characters he played.

SPECIAL PROBLEMS WITH MODIFIERS

The following guidelines will help you learn the correct use of several confusing modifiers.

This and *These*; *That* and *Those*

The adjectives *this* and *that* modify singular nouns; *these* and *those* modify plural nouns. In the following examples, notice that the words *kind, sort,* and *type* signal that the singular adjective *this* or *that* should be used.

Incorrect	*Those* kind are more expensive.
Correct	*That* kind is more expensive.
Incorrect	*These* sort of shoes hurt my feet.
Correct	*This* sort of shoe hurts my feet.

Usage Note Following *this (that) kind (sort, type),* use the singular form of the noun: *this kind of glove* (not *gloves*).

Them and *Those*

Those can function as either a pronoun or an adjective. *Them* is always a pronoun and should never be used as an adjective.

Incorrect	Where did you put *them* tools?
Correct	Where did you put *those* tools? (adjective)
Correct	Where did you put *them?* (pronoun)
Correct	*Those* are my tools. (pronoun)

Bad and Badly

Bad is an adjective that is used before nouns and after linking verbs. *Badly* is an adverb.

> A *bad* fuel pump delayed the launch. (adjective)
> I felt *bad* (not *badly*) about losing. (adjective)
> The mudslide damaged the homes *badly*. (adverb)
> It was a *badly* executed plan. (adverb)

Usage Note Notice that no hyphen is used between an adverb that ends in *-ly* and a following adjective.

Good and Well

Good is an adjective used to modify nouns and pronouns.

> That is a *good* suggestion.

Sometimes *good* may be used as a predicate adjective after a linking verb.

> The cool rain felt *good* after the hot day.

Well can be used as a predicate adjective after a linking verb. As an adjective, *well* means "in good health."

> After a long illness, Mark seemed *well*.

Well can also be used as an adverb to modify an action verb. When used as an adverb to modify an action verb, *well* means "expertly" or "properly."

> Consuela played *well* at the concert last night.

The Double Negative

It is not correct to use two or more negative words to express a single negation. This redundancy is called a **double negative.**

Incorrect	We do*n't* know *nothing* about photography.
Correct	We do*n't* know *anything* about photography.
Correct	We know *nothing* about photography.
Incorrect	We do*n't* have *no* information.
Correct	We do*n't* have *any* information.
Correct	We have *no* information.
Incorrect	We did*n't* see *none* of the events.
Correct	We did*n't* see *any* of the events.
Correct	We saw *none* of the events.

The words *hardly, barely,* and *scarcely* function as negatives and should not be used with other negative words.

| *Incorrect* | There was*n't hardly* anyone at the concert. |
| *Correct* | There was *hardly* anyone at the concert. |

| *Incorrect* | I could*n't barely* hear the music. |
| *Correct* | I could *barely* hear the music. |

| *Incorrect* | The flaw was*n't scarcely* visible. |
| *Correct* | The flaw was *scarcely* visible. |

The expressions *can't help but* and *haven't but* are double negatives that should be avoided.

| *Incorrect* | This defeat *can't help but* hurt his pride. |
| *Correct* | This defeat *can't help hurting* his pride. |

Incorrect	I *haven't but* a few minutes to talk.
Correct	I *have but* a few minutes to talk.
Correct	I *have only* a few minutes to talk.

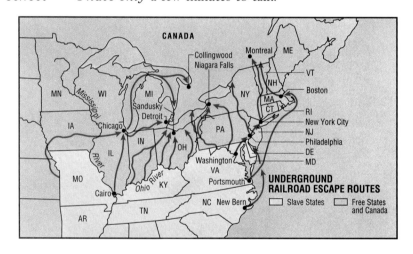

Practice Your Skills

A. CONCEPT CHECK

Special Problems with Modifiers   Write the correct word or phrase given in parentheses.

1. In the annals of American history, few have been braver than (those, them) people who participated in the Underground Railroad.
2. In operation between roughly 1830 and 1860, the Underground Railroad (was no, wasn't no) actual railroad of steel and steam.

3. (These, This) kind of railroad was a network of paths through woods and fields, river crossings, boats, trains, and wagons.
4. Its stations (were nothing, weren't nothing) more than houses, churches, and other ordinary buildings.
5. Its agents were men and women who (couldn't help pitying, couldn't help but pity) enslaved human beings and who risked imprisonment to help free them.
6. The passengers were black men and women who looked forward to escaping bondage but who felt (bad, badly) about leaving friends and relatives behind.
7. (Them, Those) people who traveled the railroad escaped to free Northern states, Canada, Mexico, or the Bahamas or Cuba.
8. Harriet Tubman was one who used (this, these) system of routes and sanctuaries to escape to free territory.
9. After Tubman gained her own freedom, she wanted to help the people in bondage who were treated (bad, badly).
10. She returned to free (them, those) slaves who needed her help.
11. As a conductor on the Underground Railroad, she did a (good, well) job, eventually leading more than 300 fugitives to freedom.
12. None of the fugitives she assisted were (never, ever) captured.
13. Though Tubman's success is well known, no one knows how (well, good) the Underground Railroad succeeded as a whole.
14. Estimates of the number of escaped slaves range from 30,000 to 100,000, and historians cannot evaluate the railroad's achievements using (that, those) sort of imprecise information.
15. It is difficult to be more accurate because, even today, one (can scarcely, can't scarcely) uncover information about the number of blacks who used the Underground Railroad.

Harriet Tubman, at the risk of her own life, led many slaves to freedom.

B. REVISION SKILL

Using Modifiers Correctly   Rewrite the following sentences to correct errors in the use of modifiers. If the sentence has no errors, write *Correct*.

1. Most people don't hardly realize how unusual some Civil War military strategies were.
2. One of these kind of strange tactic was introduced in 1864 to help the Confederate cause.
3. In that year, twenty raiders were told they could serve the Confederacy good by robbing banks.
4. Apparently, the Confederate soldiers didn't feel badly about engaging in criminal activity; they headed north immediately.
5. In hardly no time, they had slipped through Union lines to rendezvous in Vermont.

6. Them soldier-thieves then robbed the First National Bank of St. Albans of $54,000, which they turned over to the Confederacy.
7. These sort of unorthodox maneuver was not solely the province of the South.
8. The North thought it might be well to use balloons.
9. Though at first Lincoln and his advisers barely paid any attention to the plan suggested by Thaddeus S. Lowe, hot air balloonist, they eventually saw some merit in it.
10. Even them people who had laughed at Lowe had to admit that making reconnaissance balloon trips and taking the first aerial photographs proved useful to the Union cause.

C. PROOFREADING SKILL

Using Modifiers Correctly   The following paragraph contains errors in spelling, punctuation, and the use of modifiers. Rewrite the paragraph, correcting all of these errors.

> The news from the battlefield near the small town of gettysburg sounded badly to President Lincoln. The weary leader hoped them rebels would loose the battle and rejoin the Union. The troops on both sides had fought brave and good according to the dispatches, the victory of the Union armies could not help but please the President. Yet, he grieved deep for the thousands of young Confederate and Union men killed or maimed in the bloody struggle. Looking at the names on the long lists of casualties, Lincoln may have thought, We can't forget none of the brave men whose names are listed here. In any event, Lincoln went to Gettysburg and gave a speech honoring them. After he finished speaking, hardly no sound could be heard from the audience. Lincoln thought they disliked the speech. That, however, was not true. The memirable speech had moved the listeners so deep that they were unable to applaud.

C H E C K   P O I N T
PAGES 745–752

Some of the following sentences contain errors in the use of modifiers. Rewrite these sentences to correct the errors. Label the sentences with no errors *Correct*.

1. Trees may prove to be most important than any other resource.
2. They are as useful, if not more useful than, any living organism.
3. One can't help but be aware that for thousands of years trees have provided foods, fibers, medicines, and most important, wood.

4. However, many people don't realize that trees are major producers of life-giving oxygen.
5. At the same time, them silent sentinels take in the carbon dioxide that may be a factor in global warming.
6. In one year, a tree inhales as much carbon dioxide, if not more, than a car produces on an 11,300-mile trip.
7. Meanwhile, it exhales enough oxygen to keep a family of four breathing good for a year.
8. Most of us know that trees are the most largest of all plants; the most tall grow higher than thirty-story buildings.
9. However, are we aware that these kind of plants are also the oldest living things on earth?
10. The tree that is older than any tree is a bristlecone pine called Methuselah.
11. These type of trees are found in the Inyo National Forest in California.
12. One can't help but be amazed at the fact that Methuselah is 4,700 years old.
13. The rangers at Inyo have not marked the tree and won't never tell visitors where the real Methuselah stands.
14. They fear that people would treat Methuselah bad, trampling the root system and peeling off pieces of bark for souvenirs.
15. Rangers fear that them people would eventually kill Methuselah with their thoughtlessness.
16. Both intentionally and unintentionally, we are killing the trees on earth more faster than we should.
17. For example, the rain forests of Brazil are not doing good as a result of irresponsible cutting.
18. In addition, logging companies, which often have government approval, are cutting the great forests of the United States as fast, if not faster, than those in Brazil.
19. At the present rate of cutting, there aren't but thirty years left before those forests are gone forever.
20. In fact, the United States logs more than any country in the world.
21. Then, too, ozone and acid rain may be causing as much damage to the forests as the lumber industry.
22. Of the northwestern red spruce that are taller than 2,500 feet, half of those that seemed well in 1960 are now dead.
23. In an American city, a tree's chances of dying are better or at least as good as its chances of surviving.
24. For every one of them trees planted, four die—certainly a startling statistic.
25. One can't help but wonder whether, by killing our most precious resources, we are killing ourselves, too.

GRAMMAR
HANDBOOK
36

Writing Theme
Perseverance and
Accomplishment

A. Choosing Correct Modifier Forms   Write the correct form of the modifier given in parentheses.

1. There are those who (can hardly, can't hardly) believe that great fortunes can be made through intelligence alone.
2. For (this, these) kind of person, Simón Patiño is a startling and enlightening example.
3. Patiño was born a (poor, poorly) Spanish-Indian peasant in Bolivia in 1862.
4. As an adult, he got a job working as a clerk in a store and got along about as (good, well) as others in his town.
5. Then, one day, Patiño's boss sent him on what was to be the (more important, most important) errand of his life.
6. A prospector had run up a (real, really) large bill and the store owner wanted it collected.
7. Patiño eventually found the prospector, but the man didn't have (no, any) money.
8. However, the prospector convinced Patiño that the deed to one of his mines was (as good, as good as), if not better than, the $250 he owed.
9. When Patiño went back to town, after giving the prospector a receipt, he (couldn't help feeling, couldn't help but feel) proud of his decision and the deal he made.
10. His boss, on the other hand, decided that any more of (these kind of deals, this kind of deal) would jeopardize the business itself.
11. Patiño was fired and told he owed the store owner 250 dollars; he went home feeling (bad, badly) about losing his job.
12. However, Patiño believed in the prospector much more strongly than (his boss, his boss did), and Patiño now owned the mine.
13. Patiño realized that, as automobiles and tin cans became more popular, his tin mine was worth almost as much as (any, any other) kind of mine.
14. His intelligence, judgment, and faith paid off (good, well).
15. Before he died, Simón Patiño was one of the five (wealthier, wealthiest) people in the world.

B. Correct Modifier Usage   The following sentences contain errors in the use of modifiers. Rewrite these sentences correctly.

1. Williaminia Fleming—born Williaminia Stevens in Dundee, Scotland—didn't start out to be no astronomer.
2. Though she taught for five years in her youth, a life of training minds wasn't hardly her goal.

3. When she was married, Fleming gave up her teaching easy and moved to Boston with her husband.
4. However, her marriage failed, and soon Fleming had to earn a living as would any woman on her own.
5. Fleming took a job as a housekeeper, because the pay for a housekeeper was higher than a teacher.
6. Her employer was Professor Edward C. Pickering of Harvard, one of the most finest astronomers of the time.
7. One day, in a rage at one of his research assistants, Pickering declared that his housekeeper could do more better.
8. Fleming apparently felt as confidently as her boss did.
9. She left the domestic staff and went happy to the observatory.
10. Once Fleming started work, Pickering couldn't help but see that she had great talents.
11. He began to rely more on his high-school-educated assistant than his Harvard colleagues.
12. In time, the "Pickering system" for classifying the stellar spectrum became the reliabler "Pickering-Fleming" system.
13. Pickering proved himself more fairer than most of his male colleagues when he insisted that Fleming's name appear with his own on articles published in astronomical journals.
14. During her career, Fleming discovered almost all of the 107 so-called Wolf-Rayet stars and more of the "novae" stars than any astronomer.
15. In 1906, she became the first American woman elected to the Royal Astronomical Society, an honor the young Scottish bride of twenty-nine years before couldn't hardly have imagined.

C. Application in Literature   Read each of the following quotations carefully, and choose the correct word or phrase from the two in parentheses.

1. Educators have argued that there must be a sequence to learning, that perseverance and a certain measure of perspiration are (indispensable, indispensably) . . . and that learning to be critical and to think (conceptual, conceptually) and (rigorous, rigorously) do not come (easy, easily) to the young.   **Neil Postman**
2. There are only two or three human stories, and they go on repeating themselves as (fierce, fiercely) as if they had never happened before.   **Willa Cather**
3. Anyone can hold the helm when the sea is (calm, calmly).   **Livy**
4. What we (ardent, ardently) wish, we believe.   **Edward Young**
5. The (greatest, greater) part of a writer's time is spent in reading, in order to write; a man will turn over half a library to make one book.   **Samuel Johnson**

Directions   One or more of the underlined sections in the following sentences may contain errors of grammar, usage, punctuation, spelling, or capitalization. Write the letter of each incorrect section; then rewrite the item correctly. If there is no error in an item, write E.

Example   Mata Hari, who many people have described as the
     A
most famous German spy of World War I, had a daughter, Banda
         B   **C**
MacLeod, who worked as a double agent for the Allies in World
        D
War II. No error
        E

Answer   A—whom

---

1. It is <u>ten times</u> as easy <u>to make</u> a hole-in-one <u>while playing golf</u> <u>than it is</u> to roll a perfect
        A   **B**   **C**   **D**
   game in bowling. <u>No error</u>
                        E

2. The <u>youngest</u> player <u>who</u> we know played in the <u>major leagues</u> was Joe Nuxhall of the
       A   **B**   **C**
   <u>Cincinnati Reds,</u> a fifteen-year-old pitcher. <u>No error</u>
        D   **E**

3. Dueling <u>is legal</u> in the <u>South American country</u> of Uruguay as long as both duelers <u>are</u>
            A   **B**   **C**
   blood <u>donors.</u> <u>No error</u>
          D   **E**

4. When his subjects <u>disguised theirselves</u> so <u>thoroughly</u> behind fashionable facial hair that
                      A   **B**
   police <u>could not identify</u> criminals nor wives their husbands, the king objected to <u>them</u>
           C   **D**
   wearing false beards. <u>No error</u>
                            E

5. <u>Us Americans</u> certainly <u>have</u> a tendency to <u>exagerate;</u> a ten-gallon hat, for example, really
      A   **B**   **C**
   <u>holds</u> three-quarters of a gallon. <u>No error</u>
      D   **E**

6. Some of the <u>most great</u> figures in history and literature—<u>Samuel Johnson, Clara Barton,</u>
                  A   **B**
   <u>Abraham Lincoln, Louisa May Alcott, Winston Churchill</u>—filled their <u>lifes</u> with
                                                                          C
   achievement <u>in spite of</u> severe clinical depression. <u>No error</u>
                  D   **E**

7. The animal that can <u>best</u> reproduce human speech <u>is</u> not the parrot <u>or the myna,</u>
   $\quad$ **A** $\qquad\qquad\qquad\qquad$ **B** $\qquad\qquad\qquad$ **C**
   but the <u>remarkably</u> versatile dolphin. <u>No error</u>
   $\qquad$ **D** $\qquad\qquad\qquad\qquad\qquad$ **E**

8. <u>Whom</u> would imagine you <u>could catch</u> fish in the <u>Sahara</u> by digging through the sand
   $\quad$ **A** $\qquad\qquad\qquad$ **B** $\qquad\qquad\qquad$ **C**
   <u>to underwater streams?</u> <u>No error</u>
   $\qquad$ **D** $\qquad\qquad$ **E**

9. English <u>contains more</u> words <u>than any language,</u> but there <u>are few</u> people <u>who</u> use more
   $\qquad\qquad$ **A** $\qquad\qquad$ **B** $\qquad\qquad\qquad$ **C** $\qquad\qquad$ **D**
   than a small fraction of them. <u>No error</u>
   $\qquad\qquad\qquad\qquad\qquad$ **E**

10. The wind in <u>Chicago, which</u> is called the <u>"Windy City,"</u> is <u>far less gusty</u>
    $\qquad\qquad$ **A** $\qquad\qquad\qquad\qquad$ **B** $\qquad\qquad$ **C**
    <u>than Great Falls,</u> Montana, or a dozen other cities. <u>No error</u>
    $\qquad$ **D** $\qquad\qquad\qquad\qquad\qquad\qquad$ **E**

11. <u>Japan, West Germany and the United Kingdom</u>—none of <u>them</u> countries <u>is</u> the
    $\qquad\qquad\qquad$ **A** $\qquad\qquad\qquad\qquad\qquad\qquad$ **B** $\qquad\qquad$ **C**
    leading trading partner of the <u>United States; that</u> honor belongs to Canada. <u>No error</u>
    $\qquad\qquad\qquad\qquad$ **D** $\qquad\qquad\qquad\qquad\qquad\qquad\qquad$ **E**

12. Benjamin Franklin didn't see <u>no harm</u> in <u>it but</u> kite-flying <u>is illegal</u> in Washington, <u>D.C.</u>
    $\qquad\qquad\qquad\qquad$ **A** $\qquad$ **B** $\qquad\qquad$ **C** $\qquad\qquad\qquad$ **D**
    <u>No error</u>
    E

13. In his famous <u>book *Gulliver's Travels,*</u> Jonathan Swift described the <u>moons of Mars</u>
    $\qquad\qquad$ **A** $\qquad\qquad\qquad\qquad\qquad\qquad\qquad$ **B**
    very <u>accurately,</u> considering that the book <u>was written</u> in 1726. <u>No error</u>
    $\qquad$ **C** $\qquad\qquad\qquad\qquad\qquad$ **D** $\qquad\qquad$ **E**

14. If the people in early portrait photographs appear <u>stiffly,</u> they <u>were probably reacting</u> to
    $\qquad\qquad\qquad\qquad\qquad\qquad$ **A** $\qquad\qquad$ **B**
    the clamp that held them in position long <u>enough for</u> an unblurred picture
    $\qquad\qquad\qquad\qquad\qquad$ **C**
    <u>to be registerred</u> on the plate. <u>No error</u>
    $\quad$ **D** $\qquad\qquad\qquad$ **E**

15. In the <u>United States</u> each of two <u>states—Missouri and Tennessee—</u>shares <u>their border</u>
    $\qquad$ **A** $\qquad\qquad\qquad$ **B** $\qquad\qquad\qquad$ **C**
    with eight other <u>states.</u> <u>No error</u>
    $\qquad\qquad$ **D** $\qquad$ **E**

16. Eddie Gaedel, at a <u>hieght</u> of three feet seven inches, <u>was the shortest man</u> ever to play
    $\qquad\qquad$ **A** $\qquad\qquad\qquad\qquad\qquad$ **B**
    <u>professional baseball;</u> he also had <u>the least times</u> at bat. <u>No error</u>
    $\quad$ **C** $\qquad\qquad\qquad$ **D** $\qquad\qquad\qquad$ **E**

17. Since students at Cambridge <u>were not allowed</u> to keep dogs <u>in their rooms,</u> the
                              A   **B**
    <u>poet Lord Byron</u> came up with something <u>more better;</u> he kept a bear. <u>No error</u>
      C   **D**   **E**

18. Some of the <u>anceint</u> firs and <u>cedars in</u> the Olympic rain forest <u>are</u> <u>as tall if not taller</u>
                  A   **B**   **C**   **D**
    <u>than</u> a twenty-five story building. <u>No error</u>
    E   **E**

19. <u>There's</u> no reason to feel <u>bad</u> if someone calls you a <u>*nonesuch;*</u> the word is
      A   **B**   **C**
    <u>complimentary,</u> suggesting that there is no one else like you in the world. <u>No error</u>
      D   **E**

20. <u>Sixty-eight-year-old</u> Edward Payson Weston <u>broke</u> his own <u>record—set when he was</u>
      A   **B**   **C**
    twenty-eight—by walking from Portland, Maine, to Chicago, Illinois, in <u>fewer</u> than
                                                                            D
    twenty-six days. <u>No error</u>
                      E

21. The <u>most expensive</u> animal product in <u>history</u> is <u>alicorn, or unicorns horn,</u> a thing that
          A   **B**   **C**
    <u>does not exist.</u> <u>No error</u>
      D   **E**

22. James Whistler painted his mother, and August Bartholdi <u>sculpted his. Of</u> the two,
                                                            A
    Bartholdi's mother draws the <u>biggest</u> crowds; she was the model for the
    B   **C**
    <u>Statue of Liberty.</u> <u>No error</u>
      D   **E**

23. <u>There are</u> more than 450 active <u>volcanoes</u> in the <u>world, but</u> 80 of them are not visible to
      A   **B**   **C**
    the naked eye; <u>them</u> are the ones that are underwater. <u>No error</u>
                    D   **E**

24. The first automobile accident <u>ocurred</u> in <u>New York City on</u> May 30, 1896, when an
                                    A   **B**
    automobile <u>hit a bicycle;</u> neither the driver of the car nor the bicycle rider lost <u>his</u> life.
                C   **D**
    <u>No error</u>
      E

25. <u>Of all mammals,</u> the one with the <u>longer</u> life span is neither the <u>elephant nor the wale,</u>
      A   **B**   **C**
    but the <u>human being!</u> <u>No error</u>
             D   **E**

Sketchbook

Think of common superstitions that many people believe. Do you have any superstitions of your own? Write a brief essay that explains any superstitious beliefs you have, or why you don't believe in superstitions. Use a variety of sentence types and structures.

POGO

Copyright, 1989, OGPI. Distributed by Los Angeles Times Syndicate.
Reprinted by permission

Additional Sketches

What was the last dream you remember? Use descriptive modifiers to depict the images and events, however bizarre or illogical, that surfaced from your unconscious.

Imagine that intergalactic tourists have asked you to tell them about life on Earth. Using colorful adjectives, describe to them what you think might be interesting for them to know.

Capitalization

PERSONAL NAMES AND TITLES, NATIONALITIES, AND RELIGIONS

Writing
—**TIP**—
Capitalizing correctly clarifies the distinction between specific persons, places, and things and general terms.

A **common noun** is the name of a general class or kind—woman, weaver, idea. Common nouns are not capitalized. A **proper noun** is the name of a particular person, place, thing, or idea. Proper nouns are capitalized. A **proper adjective** is an adjective that is formed from a proper noun and is also capitalized.

Common Noun	Proper Noun	Proper Adjective
country	Spain	Spanish olives
mountains	Alps	Alpine skiing

Proper nouns and adjectives sometimes occur in compound words. Capitalize only those parts of the words that would be capitalized when used alone. Prefixes such as *post-, anti-,* and *trans-* are not capitalized when they are connected with proper nouns and adjectives.

post-**W**orld **W**ar II   anti-**E**uropean   trans-**P**acific

The rules that follow indicate correct capitalization for proper nouns and adjectives.

Self-Portrait,
by Vincent van Gogh,
1853-1890

Personal Names and Titles

Capitalize the names and initials of persons.

Corazon **A**quino
W. E. B. Du **B**ois
John **F. K**ennedy

Many foreign names include particles such as *de, der, von, van,* and *O'.* The practice with regard to capitalizing the particles varies.

Simone de **B**eauvoir
Vincent van **G**ogh
Sandra Day **O'C**onnor
Cecil B. **D**e **M**ille

The abbreviations *Jr.* and *Sr.* after a person's name are part of the name and are capitalized. *Jr.* and *Sr.* are always preceded by a comma, and they are followed by a comma if they do not come at the end of a sentence.

> The book told about the efforts of Martin Luther King, **Jr.,** to bring about social justice.

Capitalize titles and the abbreviations of titles when they immediately precede a personal name, or part of the name, or when they are used in direct address.

> **M**ayor **E**dward **K**ingsley   **M**s. **Q**uinlan   **S**gt. **L**acey
> **R**everend **M**artha **P**ierce   **D**r. Larson   **P**rof. **L**eiferman
> **J**ustice **M**arshall   **L**t. **P**oe   **S**en. **S**imon

> What do you think the total cost will be, **M**ayor?
> Do you believe, **D**octor, that the flu epidemic is serious?

In general do not capitalize a title when it follows a person's name or when it is used alone.

> Diane Feinstein served as **m**ayor of San Francisco.
> Will someone please call a **d**octor?

Capitalize a title used alone when it refers to the head of a state or to a person in some other uniquely important position.

> the **P**resident and **V**ice-**P**resident of the United States
> the **S**ecretary of the **I**nterior (and other Cabinet officials)
> the **C**hief **J**ustice   the **P**ope   the **Q**ueen

Do not capitalize the prefix *ex-* or the suffix *-elect* when it is part of a title.

> ex-**M**ayor **F**rank **R**izzo   **G**overnor-elect Johnson

Kinship Names

Capitalize kinship names when they are used before a proper noun or when they are used alone in place of the name.

> When **A**unt Maura's book hit the best-seller list, **U**ncle Rob became a celebrity on the assembly line.

When preceded by articles or possessive words, kinship names are not capitalized.

> When my **m**om was in the hospital, she received a beautiful plant from an **u**ncle back home in Lumberton.

Writing
——TIP——
In formal writing use the word *former,* **not the prefix** *ex-.*

Names of Races, Languages, Nationalities, Tribes, and Religions

Capitalize the names of races, languages, nationalities, tribes, and religions. Capitalize any nouns or adjectives that are derived from these names. Capitalize both names when they are used in hyphenated compounds.

Spanish	**M**uslim	**N**orwegian handicrafts
Catholicism	**C**aucasian	**C**anadian flag
Indian	**L**utheran	**F**rench-**C**anadian
Asian	**A**pache	**E**nglish wool
African	**H**indu	**J**apanese yen

The Supreme Being, Other Deities, and Sacred Writings

Capitalize all words referring to God, the Holy Family, other deities, and religious scriptures.

God	**A**llah	the **G**ospel
the **H**oly **T**rinity	**K**rishna	the **T**almud

Personal pronouns referring to God are capitalized.

May the Lord give you **H**is blessing.

Usage Notes Do not capitalize relative pronouns that refer to the Deity.

Praise God from *whom* we receive all blessings.

The words *god* and *goddess* are not capitalized when they refer to the deities of ancient mythology.

The Greek poet paid homage to the goddess Athena.

The Pronoun *I* and the Interjections *O* and *Oh*

Always capitalize the pronoun *I*.

I strode into the mansion as if **I**'d lived there all my life.

Capitalize the interjection *O*, which often appears in poetry, the Bible, and prayers or petitions. Do not capitalize the interjection *oh* unless it is the first word of a sentence.

O Captain! My Captain!   **O** Lord, **O** King
Oh, how frightened we were, but oh so happy to be alive.

Practice Your Skills

A. CONCEPT CHECK

Capitalization   In each of the following sentences, find the words that need capital letters and write them correctly.

1. If american history were greek mythology, abigail adams would be a goddess of wit, wisdom, and determination.
2. The self-educated daughter of a protestant minister, she avidly read the bible and even taught herself to read french.
3. Abigail's husband was an important politician in the american movement to gain independence from british rule.
4. John adams admired james otis, jr., an early leader in the radical opposition to king george.
5. However, when it came to women's rights, abigail's ideas were much more radical than his.
6. As john and other men drafted laws for the new country, she wrote to him, "i desire you would remember the ladies and be more favorable . . . to them than your ancestors."
7. John adams was the first vice-president and the second president of the new nation.
8. The ex-president and the former first lady saw their son john quincy become secretary of state.
9. However, abigail adams died before her son, whom she teasingly called "mr. j. q. a.," became president.
10. History can thank charles francis adams for publishing grandma adams's letters in 1840.

B. REVISION SKILL

Capitalization   For each of the following sentences, rewrite each word that needs to be capitalized.

(1) As a young boy, edward h. thompson was fascinated by legends about the mayan ruins. (2) When he was appointed american consul to Mexico's Yucatan Peninsula, he hoped to learn whether the mayan indians of long ago had actually sacrificed young maidens to the rain god yum chac by flinging them into a sacred well. (3) When thompson climbed the Great Pyramid of Kukulcan, he saw below him the sacred well, home of yum chac. (4) He and his native helpers dredged the sunken lake and brought up the skull of a young girl, which appeared to confirm the ancient mayan legend. (5) thompson then donned diving equipment and found many other mayan treasures in the sacred well. (6) Today, thanks to the Carnegie Foundation, visitors can view the sacred well of yum chac.

Place Names

Capitalize the names of parts of the world, political divisions, topographical names, and the names of structures and public places. Do not capitalize articles or prepositions of fewer than five letters in such names.

Parts of the World	Africa, North America, Australia, Europe, the Southern Hemisphere, the Orient, Central America, the Middle East
Political Divisions	Scotland, North Korea, Montana, Kane County, the Province of Manitoba, Atlanta
Topographical Names	Lake Michigan, Grand Canyon, Swiss Alps, Caspian Sea, Gulf of Mexico, Siberia, Mount Vesuvius
Structures and Public Places	Zion National Park, Leaning Tower of Pisa, Mammoth Cave, Statue of Liberty, Empire State Building, Seventh Avenue, the Indiana Tollroad

Usage Notes Such words as *avenue, bridge, church, building, fountain, hotel, street, theater* are capitalized when they are part of an official or formal name but not when they stand alone or when they follow two or more proper names.

> London Bridge   the bridge   Peace and Royal bridges

In official documents such words as *city, state,* and *country* are capitalized when they are part of the name of a political unit.

> the City of Dallas (official document)
> the city of Dallas (regular usage)

Directions and Sections

Capitalize names of sections of the country but not of directions of the compass.

> The South is now heavily industrialized.
> Some people head south during the winter.
> Willa Cather wrote about the Midwest.
> In Columbus's time, Europeans did not know what lands lay to the west of the ocean.

Capitalize proper adjectives derived from names of sections of the country. Do not capitalize adjectives made from words telling direction.

a southerly wind   an **E**astern city
a westbound train   a **M**idwestern college

Astronomical Terms

Capitalize the names of stars, planets, galaxies, constellations, and other heavenly bodies. Do not capitalize *sun* and *moon.*

Pluto   **M**ilky **W**ay   **S**irius   the **L**ittle **D**ipper
Tuttle's **C**omet   **U**rsa **M**inor   **S**aturn   **J**upiter's moons

Usage Note   The word *earth* is capitalized only when it is used in context with other astronomical terms. *Earth* is never capitalized when it is preceded by the article *the.*

We studied the atmospheres of Venus, Mars, and **E**arth. Only the atmosphere of the earth can support life as we know it.

Vehicles

Capitalize the names of ships, trains, airplanes, and spacecraft.

U.S.S. *Constitution*   the *Orient Express*
Glamorous Glennis   the shuttle *Columbia*
Spirit of St. Louis   *Mariner IV*

Practice Your Skills

A. CONCEPT CHECK

Capitalizing Words   Rewrite the following sentences, capitalizing words as necessary.

1. Most of us have never climbed the matterhorn nor sailed the indian ocean nor gazed at alpha centauri from a spaceship.
2. Nevertheless, the whole universe, from main street to the andromeda spiral, is open to us through literature.
3. Readers can sail to tahiti on the *bounty* and ride across europe on the *orient express*.
4. Ray Bradbury transports readers to a colony on mars settled by former citizens of the earth.
5. Bradbury, very much a creature of earth, was born and raised in waukegan, an illinois city on lake michigan.

Writing
——**TIP**——
The names of ships, trains, airplanes, and spacecraft are italicized in print and underlined in handwriting.

Writing Theme
Travel

6. Another midwesterner, Mark Twain, pilots his readers down the mississippi and regales them with tales of california and the west.
7. Eudora Welty invites readers to the deep south and introduces them to small-town life.
8. The whole world is James Michener's domain; he transports readers to the exotic south pacific and the hawaiian islands.
9. Heading northeast, Michener's readers can also explore the states of colorado and alaska before they venture south to the caribbean.
10. Across the atlantic ocean, Doris Lessing offers readers a view of the sunrise on a veld in south africa.
11. Dorothy L. Sayers's readers solve crimes in london's west end or the halls of oxford university.
12. If one craves a view of mount kilimanjaro or longs for adventure on the battlefields of spain and italy, Ernest Hemingway obliges.
13. Through James Clavell's novels, armchair travelers to japan and the orient can explore the ancient city of edo.
14. Readers can soar in the space shuttle *discovery* or traverse north america on the amtrak's *zephyr* railroad.
15. A trip to the local library may transport a person to london bridge, the taj mahal, or broadway.

B. REVISION SKILL

Capitalization   After each sentence number, rewrite correctly the words that need capital letters. If no words need capital letters, write *Correct.*

(1) World travelers once had to spend months on seagoing vessels to circumnavigate the earth, with brief and infrequent stops. (2) Now travelers can make the trip on a *concorde* aircraft in twenty-three days, making seven stops of about three days each. (3) The first tour of this kind picked up passengers in new york, dallas, and oakland.
(4) The first destination was papeete, tahiti, with a side trip to the island of moorea, where american novelist James Michener and french painter Paul Gauguin had both been inspired by native beauty. (5) The second *concorde* stop was sydney, australia. (6) Entertainment in sydney included a cruise up the hawkesbury river and an australian barbecue. (7) Next, it was off to the far east, with stops in hong kong and beijing. (8) A meal at the aberdeen marina club highlighted the visit to hong kong. (9) In beijing the travelers toured mao's tomb and the summer palace. (10) Continuing westward, the flight made stops in india, africa, and france, before crossing the atlantic ocean to return to the united states.

Jousting tournament
during the Middle Ages

HISTORICAL EVENTS, ORGANIZATIONS, AND OTHER SUBJECTS

Here are some other groups of commonly used words and phrases that require capital letters.

Historical Events, Periods, and Documents

Capitalize the names of historical events, periods, and documents.

> **D**eclaration of **I**ndependence   **L**ouisiana **P**urchase
> **M**agna **C**arta   the **M**iddle **A**ges

Organizations and Institutions

Capitalize the names of organizations and institutions.

> **L**incoln **H**igh **S**chool   **F**ederal **B**ureau of **I**nvestigation **(FBI)**
> **R**epublican **P**arty   **N**ational **O**rganization for **W**omen **(NOW)**

Words such as *school, company, church, college,* and *hospital* are capitalized only when they are part of a proper name.

Months, Days, and Holidays

Capitalize the names of months, days, and holidays but not the names of seasons.

> **S**eptember   **W**ednesday   **L**abor Day   autumn

Time Abbreviations

Capitalize the abbreviations B.C., A.D., A.M., and P.M.

School began at 8:10 **A.M.** and ended at 3:20 **P.M.**
Ovid, a Roman poet, lived from 43 **B.C.** until **A.D.** 18.

Awards, Special Events, and Brand Names

Capitalize the names of awards and special events.

National **B**ook **A**ward   **O**lympics (*but* the Olympic games)

Capitalize the brand name of a product but not a common noun that follows a brand name.

Rice **K**rispies   **E**xquisite perfume

School Subjects and Names of School Years

Do not capitalize the general names of school subjects. Do capitalize the titles of specific courses and courses that are followed by a number. The name of a language course is always capitalized.

chemistry   **F**rench
Mathematics 120   **M**odern **B**ritish **L**iterature

Capitalize the words *freshman, sophomore, junior,* and *senior* only when they are used as adjectives referring to specific classes or when they are used as nouns in direct address.

The seniors encouraged everyone to attend the **S**enior **P**rom.
This year, **J**uniors, the **S**ophomore **C**lass won the trip!

Practice Your Skills

A. CONCEPT CHECK

Capitalizing Dates and Events Rewrite the following sentences capitalizing as necessary.

1. According to legend, just prior to the golden age the first marathon runner, a messenger, raced to athens to announce the victory of greece over persia in 490 b.c.
2. The modern foot race is named after the village on greece's northeastern coast where the battle of marathon was fought.
3. The marathon became an olympic event in a.d. 1896, nearly twenty-four centuries after the legendary messenger's run.
4. Today, throughout america, marathons are usually held in the fall, before thanksgiving, or in the spring, starting in april.

5. The chicago race starts in the shadows of the city's famous sky-scrapers and heads north on busy neighborhood streets.
6. Just past wrigley field, runners turn south onto lake shore drive and run along lake michigan to the finish in lincoln park.
7. Marathon races are usually scheduled on saturdays and sundays.
8. Some localities select holidays such as columbus day or the fourth of july for their races.
9. Runners gather early, usually before 7:00 a.m., to warm up for a race of 26 miles and 385 yards, the distance run by the legendary messenger.
10. The boston athletic association sponsors north america's most fa-mous marathon.
11. Many of those who participate in the boston marathon try to es-tablish a qualifying time for future olympic games.
12. Universities such as harvard, tufts, and northeastern enter their best distance runners, usually juniors or seniors.
13. Occasionally even students in freshman track 101 participate.
14. Winners of the race are sometimes asked to advertise products such as fleetfoot running shoes.
15. If he ran today, that early greek messenger would probably see him-self cross the finish line on an abc instant replay and then be asked to endorse lizardade!

B. REVISION SKILL

Capitalization The following sentences contain capitalization er-rors. Rewrite the sentences, capitalizing or lower-casing words as necessary.

1. The olympic games were held in a special stadium in olympia, greece, every four years from as early as 776 b.c. until Emperor Theodosius banned them in a.d. 394.
2. An earthquake later demolished the stadium, and from the dark ages until the late Nineteenth Century, the Games were forgotten.
3. Inspired by the discovery of the Stadium ruins in 1875, Baron Pierre de Coubertin of France convened the international olympic congress in july of 1894.
4. Two Summers later, nine Nations participated in the first modern olympic Games, held in athens, greece.
5. The Greek Spectators were especially delighted when a greek peas-ant, spirialon louis, won the marathon.
6. The london games of 1908 were well organized and produced the first thorough official Report, but there were some disputes.
7. The russians attempted to prevent the finns from displaying the finnish Flag, and the english did the same to the irish.

8. Because of world wars I and II, no games were held in 1916, 1940, or 1944.
9. The first Winter version of the olympics, which included skiing, figure skating, ice hockey, and bobsledding, was held on french soil in 1924.
10. Some olympic athletes have remained in the public eye, pursuing careers in broadcasting or endorsing products such as wheaties cereal or the american express card.

C. PROOFREADING SKILL

Correcting Errors in Capitalization Rewrite the following paragraphs, correcting all errors. Pay special attention to errors in capitalization.

On the streets of paris france, in 1808, a two-wheeled Machine called a two-wheeled draisienne appeared. This early forerunner of today's bicycle had no pedels, so riders moved it by pushing it along the Earth with there feet. Kirkpatrick macmillan a scottish Blacksmith built the first bicycle with pedals in the late 1830's. In the Decades that followed, bicycles became very popular, but their wooden wheels made riding on them very uncomfortable. People nicknamed the bicycles "boneshakers."

Early Bicycle modals had huge front wheels, and the seats were so high off the ground that falling off was really dangerous. The bicycle we know Today, with pedals that turn a chain and with two wheels of the same size, was manufactured by an english inventor j. k. starley during the 1880's.

A. Rewrite the following sentences, capitalizing correctly.

1. Little is known of the prehistoric people called mound builders, who lived before a.d. 1000 in what is now tennessee.
2. Did they worship the sun or tell legends about the north star and constellations such as ursa major?
3. By the time hernando de soto and a party of spanish explorers planted the flag of spain on the banks of the mississippi river in 1541, the area was populated by cherokees.
4. In 1673, two englishmen, james needham and gabriel arthur, explored the tennessee river valley.
5. By the early eighteenth century, france, spain, and england all claimed the region.
6. The english finally acquired the area by winning the french and indian war in 1763.
7. In 1775, the transylvania company bought a large area of land from the cherokees and hired daniel boone to blaze a trail through the cumberland gap.
8. Davy crockett, another famous frontiersman, became part of the folklore of tennessee in such stories as the one in which he caught halley's comet by the tail.
9. When the civil war broke out, tennessee was the last state to join the confederacy.
10. Senator andrew johnson of tennessee was abraham lincoln's vice-president in 1865 and became president when lincoln was assassinated on good friday, april 14, 1865.
11. The first school was opened in 1780, and today there are more than thirty institutions of higher learning, such as george peabody college for teachers and vanderbilt university.
12. The tennessee valley authority helped the state create new jobs during the years following the great depression.
13. Following world war II the state's economy shifted from agriculture toward industry and eventually tourism.
14. Tennessee is famous as the home of the grand ole opry and of entertainers such as porter wagoner and dolly parton.
15. Campers enjoy the great smokey mountains national park.
16. History buffs tour the hermitage, home of andrew jackson.
17. Most people in the state are american-born, and many are from british, scotch-irish, french huguenot, or german stock.
18. Many ways to worship god exist in tennessee, but the baptist church has the largest membership in the state.

B. APPLICATION IN LITERATURE

Capitalization   Rewrite the following paragraph, restoring capitalization as necessary.

> My grandma cynthia murray palmer lived in henning, tennessee (pop. 500), about 50 miles north of memphis. Each summer as i grew up there, we would be visited by several women relatives who were mostly around grandma's age, such as my great aunt liz murray who taught in oklahoma, and great aunt till merriwether from jackson, tennessee, or their considerably younger niece, cousin georgia anderson from kansas city, kansas, and some others. Always after the supper dishes had been washed, they would go out to take seats and talk in the rocking chairs on the front porch, and i would scrunch down, listening, behind grandma's squeaky chair, with the dusk deepening into night and the lightning bugs flickering on and off above the now shadowy honeysuckles. Most often they talked about our family—the story had been passed down for generations—until the whistling blur of lights of the southbound panama limited train *whooshing* through henning at 9:05 p.m. signaled our bedtime.
>
> **Alex Haley, *My Furtherest-Back Person—"The African"***

C. APPLICATION IN WRITING

A Report   What do you know about your state? Do some brief investigation about your state's history, geography, famous places, important institutions, politics, and/or well-known residents. Find out what movies or works of fiction have been set in your state. Write a brief report about the background of the state. You might wish to include an anecdote or two about your own or another family's history there. Be sure to follow the rules for capitalization given in this handbook.

FIRST WORDS AND TITLES

Capitalize the first words of sentences, lines of poetry, and direct quotations.

Sentences and Poetry

Capitalize the first word of every sentence.

In 1888, T. S. Eliot was born in St. Louis.

Capitalize the first word of every line of most poetry.

> **W**hen I was one-and-twenty
> **I** heard a wise man say,
> "**G**ive crowns and pounds and guineas
> **B**ut not your heart away;
> **G**ive pearls away and rubies
> **B**ut keep your fancy free."
> **B**ut I was one-and-twenty,
> **N**o use to talk to me.
> A. E. Housman, "When I Was One-and-Twenty"

Writing
—— **TIP**——
Sometimes the lines of a poem do not begin with capital letters. This is especially true for modern poetry.

Quotations

Capitalize the first word of a direct quotation.

Franklin Roosevelt said, "**P**eace, like charity, begins at home."

In a **divided quotation,** the first word of the second part of the quotation is capitalized only if it begins a new sentence.

"I agree," Maureen said, "that college can be expensive."
"I agree," Maureen said. "**C**ollege can be expensive."

Parts of a Letter

Capitalize the first word in the greeting of a letter. Capitalize the title and name of the person addressed or such words as *Sir* and *Madam*.

Dear **M**s. **M**iner,   **D**ear **S**ir or **M**adam:

Only the first word of a complimentary close is capitalized.

All my best,   **S**incerely yours,

Outlines and Titles

Capitalize the first word of each item in an outline and the letters that introduce major subsections.

I. **L**aws relating to children
  A. Family law
    1. **A**doption
    2. **C**hild abuse
  B. School law
  C. Child labor laws
II. **L**aws relating to business
  A. Laws regulating the stock market
  B. Laws governing employment practices

Writing

═ TIP ═

Titles are either italicized (under-lined) or enclosed in quotation marks. See Handbook 40, page 827 for punc-tuation rules.

Capitalize the first, last, and all other important words in ti-tles. Do not capitalize conjunctions, articles, or prepositions with fewer than five letters.

Book Title	**T**o **B**e **Y**oung, **G**ifted and **B**lack
Newspaper	**W**all **S**treet **J**ournal
Magazine	**P**ersonal **C**omputing
Play	**T**he **I**mportance of **B**eing **E**arnest
Movie	**T**he **A**frican **Q**ueen
TV Series	**N**ova
Work of Art	**M**ona **L**isa
Long Musical Composition	**W**est **S**ide **S**tory
Short Story	"**W**hy **I** **L**ive at the **P.O.**"
Poem	"**O**zymandias"
Song	"**S**end in the **C**lowns"
Magazine Article	"**A**re **P**ranks **A**lways a **L**aughing **M**atter?"
Chapter	"**C**hapter 2: **T**he **S**tudy of **D**rama"

The word *the* is capitalized when it is the first word of a title. The word *magazine* is capitalized only if it is part of the name.

The *New Yorker*   *Circus* **M**agazine   *Time* magazine

Usage Note   For hyphenated compounds in titles, always capitalize the first part. Capitalize the second part if it is a noun or a proper adjective or if it has equal force with the first element.

Nineteenth-**C**entury **L**iterature   **A**nti-**A**partheid **R**eader

Practice Your Skills

A. CONCEPT CHECK

First Words and Titles   Rewrite the following items, capitalizing words as necessary. Underline the words that you find italicized.

1. one of the great names among american composers and conductors of the twentieth century is leonard bernstein, who was born on august 23, 1918.

2. from the berkshire music center, bernstein wrote home, saying:

```
dearest folks:
   i have never seen such a beautiful setup in my
life. The inspiration of this center is terrific
enough to keep you going with no sleep at all. . . .
            all my love,
            lenny
```

Leonard Bernstein

3. he composed two early works, *music for two pianos* (1937) and *music for the dance* (1938), while attending harvard university.

4. bernstein not only conducted the new york philharmonic orchestra for many years, but also composed broadway musicals, including *candide, trouble in tahiti,* and *west side story.*

5. work on *west side story* began on january 6, 1949, when jerome robbins, a broadway director, called bernstein with an idea for a modern *romeo and juliet* set in the slums of new york city.

6. on march 17, bernstein wrote in his log: "chief problems: to tread the fine line between opera and broadway, between realism and poetry. . . ."

7. in 1974, with composer and lyricist stephen schwartz, who wrote *godspell,* he began work on a nontraditional theater piece.

8. *mass* combined opera and broadway music with church liturgy; it employed several choirs, a full orchestra, soloists, and dancers.

9. based on bernstein's own feelings during the tumultuous 1960's, one of the songs from *mass* begins:

   i don't know where to start
   there are scars i could show
   if i opened my heart
   but how far, lord, but how far can i go?
   i don't know.

10. "communication," bernstein once told the press, "is a way of . . . reaching out to people. love and art are ways of communicating. that is why art is so close to love."

B. REVISION SKILL

Capitalizing First Words and Titles   Rewrite the following items, using capitalization as necessary. Underline italicized words.

1. the *encyclopaedia britannica* might begin an outline article on the history and development of music like this:

   I. definition of music
   II. beginnings of western musical traditions
       a. church liturgy
       b. secular songs

2. in *rolling stone* you can read about the revolutionary music of today but not about musical innovations of earlier times.
3. in italy around 1600, for example, jacopo peri helped develop a new type of music drama that came to be known as opera.
4. three centuries later, the impressionistic harmonies of claude debussy's symphonies were controversial.
5. on may 13, 1913, igor stravinsky's *the rite of spring* so shocked the audience at its paris premiere that it caused a riot.
6. *porgy and bess* by george gershwin was a successful attempt at bridging the worlds of "serious" music and jazz.
7. The beatles sent teenagers—and their parents—into a frenzy in the 1960's.
8. "music hath charms," william congreve wrote, "to soothe"; but it certainly has the power to create controversy, too!

C. APPLICATION IN LITERATURE

Capitalization   In the following passage, some capital letters have been changed to lowercase letters and some lowercase letters have been capitalized. Rewrite the passage, correcting all errors.

> We must face the simple fact that the actual effect of art as such is intimate and personal. The Theater Critic Eric Bentley pointed out that beethoven's *ninth symphony* has done less to create Brotherhood among men than any performance by the salvation army. But He also insists that it would be ridiculous to reject Beethoven for that reason. What happens inside you when you see *lear* or read *crime and punishment* or look at *guernica* or listen to the *well-tempered clavichord* may be insignificant in comparison to the effects of a bomb, a speech by mao Tse-Tung, a new Law by Vorster or a riot in harlem . . . but that it *has* an effect which, in its own right, can be tremendous, cannot be denied. And it should never be underestimated.
>
> **André Brink, *Writing in a State of Siege***

CHECK POINT
PAGES 772–776

A. Find the words in the following items that are not capitalized but should be. Rewrite each item, capitalizing words correctly.

1. Yearly, the american academy of arts and sciences in hollywood awards an oscar to an outstanding motion picture.
2. Some films, such as *gone with the wind,* a romantic epic of the south, demonstrate both artistic merit and financial success.
3. But it's not always easy to please the public, as songwriter cole porter noted:

> today to get the public to attend a picture show
> it's not enough to advertise a famous star they know
> if you want to get the crowd to come around
> you've got to have
> glorious Technicolor, breathtaking cinemascope
> and stereophonic sound.

4. Audiences enjoy the musical *showboat* on stage, but moviegoers demand more realism; they want panoramic views of the rolling mississippi as well as songs.
5. Special effects have made space movies portraying colonies on jupiter's moons or beyond the milky way seem almost real.

B. Rewrite the following passage, capitalizing words correctly.

(1) steven spielberg, director of *e.t.* and *raiders of the lost ark,* is one of hollywood's renowned directors. (2) yet even spielberg could not make the movie *1941* a hit. (3) released in december of 1979, *1941* was a slapstick comedy about a suspected japanese invasion of california shortly after the attack on pearl harbor. (4) key scenes of the movie were shot on an elaborate re-creation of hollywood boulevard. (5) technicians copied or restored world war II planes, some miniaturized for flight scenes filmed over a model of the los angeles area. (6) "for me," spielberg said, "it was like making huge toys."

(7) despite its thirty-one-million-dollar budget, *1941* was a resounding dud. (8) john belushi, famous for his performance in *animal house,* did not live up to audience expectations. (9) an impressive debut by dan aykroyd from *saturday night live* was not enough to salvage the film. (10) *1941* illustrates how a movie can flop despite a celebrated director, popular comedians, and a huge budget.

GRAMMAR
HANDBOOK
37

Writing Theme
Journalism

A. Using Capital Letters Correctly Rewrite the following sentences, capitalizing words correctly.

1. originally, "magazine" meant a place where ammunition was stored—the storehouse for bullets at fort sumter, for example, or the cartridge chamber of a winchester rifle.
2. after johannes gutenberg developed the printing press, the word *magazine* also came to mean a storehouse of information.
3. the earliest magazine of this sort was a monthly publication started in 1663 by johann rist, a german poet and theologian.
4. soon numerous periodicals with a religious or philosophical bent, such as the royal society of london's *philosophical transactions,* appeared in other european countries.
5. *ladies' mercury,* the first women's magazine, was published in great britain in 1693.
6. in the american colonies, *poor richard's almanack,* published by ben franklin from 1732 to 1757, gained wide popularity.
7. for decades, three magazines—*time, life,* and *the saturday evening post*—dominated american magazine sales.
8. today, special interest magazines appeal to everyone from unitarian universalists to rhode island condominium owners.
9. in addition to english, periodicals are printed in numerous languages, such as hebrew, hopi, and lithuanian.
10. whether in tokyo, moscow, or cairo, people read magazines.

B. Capitalization Rewrite the following sentences, capitalizing words correctly.

1. dimitri kessel, a ukrainian, is one of the world's most respected photojournalists.
2. as a boy, he swapped his watercolor kit, a christmas gift, for a friend's kodak brownie camera.
3. in 1936, a *fortune* magazine editor gave kessel an assignment that resulted in his first publication in a magazine.
4. kessel was in czechoslovakia when Tomas masaryk, the first president of czechoslovakia and the "father of his country," died on september 14, 1937.
5. *life* magazine bought his pictures of masaryk's funeral, and thus began the photographer's long association with that publication.
6. kessel's assignments for *life* took him north, south, east, and west throughout the western hemisphere, europe, the middle east, africa, and even the arctic circle.
7. as kessel hid in a rome office building in 1948 to photograph a meeting of the italian communist party in duomo square, he was spotted, and a group stormed his location.

8. "here is the film," shouted an attacker who tossed kessel's film out a window. "next i will throw the photographer."

9. kessel returned to the soviet union in june of 1964 to do stories on siberia, the composer scriabin, and the olympic tryouts of 1979.

10. "if i had my life to live over again," kessel says in his book *on assignment: dimitri kessel,* "i would still choose to live it as a *life* photographer."

C. Using Capital Letters Correctly   For each sentence in the following paragraphs, write the correct form of all words with errors in capitalization, capitalizing or lower-casing as necessary.

(1) on may 2, 1986, two hundred photojournalists took the pictures that eventually appeared in the book *a day in the life of america*. (2) these award-winning photographers from thirty Countries, including korea, italy, and brazil, gathered in denver, colorado, to receive their assignments. (3) photojournalist rick smolan and editor david cohen directed the project.

(4) united airlines flew the photographers to their assigned locations. (5) one of the first photos in the book was taken by Aaron Chang at 6.30 a.m. in charleston, south carolina. (6) jay dickman, a pulitzer prize-winning photographer, was sent to the northeast, where his cameras iced over completely five minutes after he stepped out of the weather station at the summit of new hampshire's mount washington. (7) andy leven, who photographed the embattled Emergency Staff at Charity Hospital in new orleans, said, "i would not do this assignment again." (8) after running into security-clearance problems at the white house, brian lanker photographed america's top dog, rex, who was a gift to mrs. Reagan from the president.

(9) just inside the u.s. border, two young mexicans were photographed waiting for their chance to flee past Patrols from the immigration and naturalization service. (10) at the vietnam war memorial in washington, d.c., gary g. wright, jr., hoisted his son to kiss the name of his Grandfather. (11) sara leen turned into an alley off winston street in downtown los angeles as a mugging took place on the street. (12) mary ellen mark captured the prom at gibbs senior high school. (13) french photographer francoise huguier photographed the northbound evanston express waiting to cross lake street in chicago.

(14) from america's first sunrise over maine's mt. katahdin to the Sun setting over honolulu's ala moana park, the photographers took more than 235,000 Shots. (15) a glance through *a day in the life of america* will explain why the *minneapolis star and tribune* said, "they came, they saw, they caught it."

End Marks and Commas

END MARKS

The three types of end punctuation are the period, the question mark, and the exclamation point. The use of each is reviewed below.

The Period

Use a period at the end of all declarative sentences and most imperative sentences.

> The name *Hong Kong* means "fragrant harbor."
> Phone the florist and order fresh flowers for the table.

An imperative sentence may end with a period or an exclamation point. An imperative sentence usually ends with a period, but it may end with an exclamation point when strong emotion is expressed.

> Please pick up my clothes at the cleaners. Hurry, I'm late!

Use a period at the end of an indirect question.

An **indirect question** indicates that someone has asked a question, but it does not give the reader the exact words of the quotation.

> Cyd asked why I fixed my own car. Charles asked how.

Use a period at the end of an abbreviation or initial.

Ms.	Mmes.	Co.	250 B.C.
Mr.	Messrs.	Inc.	A.D. 1990
Mrs.	Dr. Indira L. Singh	Ltd.	C.P.D.
M.D.	12:00 P.M. (noon)	B.A.	R.F.D.

Periods are not usually used with abbreviations of metric measurements; acronyms; the initials of country, company, or organization names; or state names in postal usage. Check the dictionary to determine whether periods are used in a specific case.

cm	mg	NASA	US	USAF	MA
km	ml	WHO	USSR	NBC	ND

Use a period after numbers or letters in outlines or lists.

Outline	List
I. Water Sports	1. scalpel
A. Water Polo	2. sponge
B. Diving	3. sutures

Use a period with decimals.

$57.25   10.2%   0.32 second

The Question Mark

Use a question mark at the end of an interrogative sentence or a fragment.

> Did you know that the Hawaiian alphabet has only twelve letters?
> The *TV Guide*? Look under the couch.

Use a question mark after a declarative sentence that is pronounced with rising inflection and thus expressed as a question.

Declarative	Interrogative
The SAT is next Saturday.	The SAT is next Saturday?
That movie rated four stars.	That movie rated four stars?

The Exclamation Point

Use an exclamation point at the end of an exclamatory sentence or after a strong interjection or any other type of forceful expression.

An **interjection** is a word or words expressing sudden feeling. The sentence following an interjection may end with a period, a question mark, or an exclamation point.

> That's a fantastic sight!
> Thud! The body fell to the floor.
> Great! May I take as many as I want?
> Wow! She scored again!

Practice Your Skills

A. CONCEPT CHECK

End Marks Rewrite the following sentences, adding end marks and other punctuation as needed. If you are unsure about how to punctuate an abbreviation, consult the dictionary.

1. The United Nations charter, signed in 1945, states that membership in the UN is open to all "peace-loving states"
2. In 1946, John D Rockefeller, Jr, gave $85 (eight and one-half) million to buy land for UN headquarters in some part of the USA
3. Then the US Congress asked whether a loan would help with constructing the new buildings

Many exclamatory sentences begin with *what* or *how*. Check the punctuation at the ends of such sentences carefully.

Writing Theme
United Nations

4. In 1952, the following three main buildings were completed on land near the East River:
   a General Assembly Building
   b Secretariat Building
   c Conference Building
5. Within the UN, specialized agencies like UNICEF, the United Nations Children's Fund, operate to promote peace and human dignity
6. Distinguished Americans like Dr Ralph J Bunche have helped the UN in its peace-keeping efforts
7. A diplomat with the State Department in Washington, DC, Bunche became a UN negotiator
8. In 1949, he received the Nobel Peace Prize for negotiating a cease-fire in the Arab-Israeli wars
9. Have the member nations always been peaceful
10. Some conflicts at the UN have involved money
11. Member nations each must contribute not less than 01 (one one-hundredths) percent of the total UN budget
12. The UN charter says that a member who is two years behind in payments "shall have no vote"
13. The US made an effort to enforce this rule against the Soviet Union in 1964
14. No Do you mean that the US actually tried to stop the Soviets from voting
15. The USSR kept its vote because other nations worked out a compromise

B. APPLICATION IN WRITING

A Want Ad Want ads are frequently used by people who want to hire someone for a particular job. Think of the qualifications a person would need to work at the UN as a translator of one of the many languages spoken by member nations. Write a want ad for this position. Remember that in want ads, abbreviations are often used to save space. Make up an address in New York City to which a job applicant could write. Use the rules you have learned for end marks.

COMMAS: SERIES, INTRODUCTORY ELEMENTS, AND INTERRUPTERS

The comma is used to make the meaning of a sentence clearer or to enable the reader to understand the relation of its parts more quickly. The most important function of the comma is to prevent misreading.

Commas in a Series

Use a comma to separate the elements in a series.

A series may consist of three or more words, phrases, or clauses. When one or more of the elements contains a comma, semicolons are used to separate the elements. (See page 803.)

Words	I enjoy Olympic skiing, bobsledding, and skating.
Phrases	We searched for the keys in our pockets, under the books, and even behind the refrigerator.
Clauses	The coach felt that the players were in good physical condition, that they were highly motivated, and that they should win.

Do not use a comma when all the items in a series are joined by *and, or,* or *nor.*

Cassie didn't flinch or cry out or even blink.

Use commas after the words *first, second,* and so on when they introduce elements in a series.

Note also the use of semicolons as well as commas in this example:

Three animals stand out as a result of their intelligence: first, chimpanzees; second, orangutans; and third, gorillas.

Use commas between coordinate adjectives that modify the same noun.

The lush, green oasis looked like a mirage.

To determine whether adjectives are **coordinate**—that is, of equal rank—try placing *and* between them. If *and* sounds natural and if you can reverse the order of the adjectives without changing the meaning, then a comma is needed.

Mark always wore tight (and) faded jeans. (The *and* sounds natural, and the meaning is not changed by reversing the order of the adjectives. Therefore, a comma is needed.)
Mark always wore tight, faded jeans.

Ms. Rollins is a dedicated (and) committee member. (The *and* sounds awkward, and the adjectives cannot be reversed. No comma is necessary.)
Ms. Rollins is a dedicated committee member.

In general, no comma is needed after numbers and after adjectives of size, shape, and age.

four new wristwatches   a small oval mirror

Practice Your Skills

A. CONCEPT CHECK

Commas in a Series   Rewrite the following sentences, adding commas as needed. If a sentence does not need a comma, write *Correct*.

1. Today, with iron-on patches no-sew button fasteners and bonding tape, the need for hand sewing has almost disappeared.
2. One simple ingenious invention probably contributed greatly to this situation.
3. This invention is a small device that is easy to use is handy in an emergency and weighs almost nothing.
4. It is the convenient little safety pin.
5. The inventor of the safety pin, Walter Hunt, had three important qualifications: first a clever mind; second experience in designing gadgets; and third an urgent need for money.
6. Hunt owed a draftsman a large sum of money and had no other available resource than his quick mind.
7. Therefore, he made a quick drawing of the safety pin put together a working model and sold the rights for $400.
8. Walter Hunt thus discharged his debts ensured a place in history and put money in his pocket.

9. He should probably share his fame with the ancient Greeks Romans and northern Europeans.
10. Archaeologists have found crude examples of safety pins dating from the Bronze Age.

B. APPLICATION IN LITERATURE

Inserting Commas   Rewrite the following passage, restoring seven deleted commas.

> Mother reluctantly gave these implements to him. He marched off sat on the edge of his sofa in the middle of his bedroom and got ready to work. The gaslight was better by his bureau, but he couldn't sit on a chair when he sewed. It had no extra room on it. He laid his scissors the spool of thread and his waistcoat down on the sofa beside him wet his fingers held the needle high up and well out in front and began poking the thread at the eye.
> **Clarence Day, *Life with Father***

C. APPLICATION IN WRITING

Imaginative Writing   What will clothes be like in the future? Will seams be sewn, or somehow bonded together, perhaps by laser beams? Use your imagination to write a description of clothing of the future. Tell what it looks like, what features it has, and how it is made. Follow the comma rules to make your description clearer.

End Marks
and Commas

Commas with Introductory Elements

Use a comma after an introductory word, a mild interjection, or an adverb at the beginning of a sentence.

No, the floodlight is burned out.
Nevertheless, Juan—with a bandaged ankle—reported for work.

Use a comma after a series of prepositional phrases at the beginning of a sentence.

With the fall of Rome in A.D. 476, the empire crumbled.

A single prepositional phrase at the beginning of a sentence need not be followed by a comma unless the phrase is parenthetical or the comma adds clarity.

On Monday the stores are open late.
Without a formal introduction, Jenny felt out of place.

Use a comma after a participial or infinitive phrase at the beginning of a sentence.

Swimming strongly, Thuy won by two-tenths of a second.
To get a good job, first get a degree.

Use a comma after an introductory adverbial clause.

After Grant entered the room, everyone was uncomfortable.

For more information on verbals and adverbial clauses, see Grammar Handbook 32, pages 603–604 and 623–624.

Use a comma after words or phrases that have been moved to the beginning of a sentence from their normal position.

We'll be late as usual. (normal order)
As usual, we'll be late. (transposed order)

Commas with Interrupters

Use commas to set off nonessential appositives.

A **nonessential** (or **nonrestrictive**) **appositive** is a word or phrase that adds extra information to a sentence that is already clear and complete.

Hominy, a food made from hulled corn, has been a popular
    dish in the South since pioneer days.
A dish that is less well-known in the rest of the country is grits,
    a form of coarsely ground cornmeal used as breakfast cereal
    and as an ingredient in cornbread and muffins.

An **essential** (or **restrictive**) **appositive** qualifies or limits the word it modifies in such a way that it could not be omitted without affecting the meaning of the sentence. Do not set an essential appositive off with commas.

> The movie *Amadeus* is about the composer Mozart.
> My friend Cynthia is a talented harpist.

For more information about appositives, see Grammar Handbook 32, page 601.

Use commas to set off words of direct address.

> Trish, were you interviewed for the political opinion survey?
> I am sorry, José, that you misunderstood my suggestion.

Use commas to set off parenthetical expressions.

A **parenthetical expression** is a word or phrase inserted in a sentence as a comment or exclamation. The sentence is complete without it. It should always be set off with commas.

These expressions are often used parenthetically:

of course	I believe	for example
in fact	I suppose	on the other hand
by the way	in my opinion	in the first place

> This painting, I believe, is both interesting and fun.
> The school band, by the way, won first prize.

The same words and phrases are not set off by commas when they are used as basic parts of the sentence.

> I believe this painting is both interesting and fun.

When adverbs such as *however, therefore,* and *consequently* are used parenthetically in a sentence, they are set off with commas.

> The public library, however, is closed on Sundays.

When one of these same adverbs modifies a word in a sentence, it is an essential part of the sentence and is therefore not set off with commas.

> Rick cannot be punctual however hard he tries.

When these adverbs are used to join two independent clauses, they are called conjunctive adverbs. A conjunctive adverb is preceded by a semicolon and followed by a comma.

> The harvest was successfully completed; however, the drought
> had significantly decreased the expected yield per acre.

Practice Your Skills

A. CONCEPT CHECK

Introductory Elements and Interrupters   Rewrite the following sentences, adding commas where needed. If a sentence does not need additional commas, write *Correct.*

1. Without doubt suspense writer Stephen King is one of the ten most terrifying writers.
2. In *Murderess Ink* a book about mysteries King describes some sure-fire methods for making your writing scary.
3. Putting a child in danger for example will immediately upset most readers.
4. "Pretty dark out here, isn't it Maude?" is the name King gives to one technique.
5. This method in fact involves placing the victim in a deserted location in the middle of the night.
6. For another chill in King's repertoire claustrophobia is the key.
7. "My it's getting close in here," King names this technique.
8. A crowded elevator that is stalled between floors is an appropriate setting for this one.
9. Another spine-tingler the unidentified squirming blob under the bed also plays on people's phobias.
10. If you put your mind to it you may be able to guess how the next technique works.
11. In this method King asks, "What happened to the lights Jane?"
12. Making the darkness terrifying seems easy for King.
13. Continuing to explain his strategies King lists another effective technique.
14. To understand this one imagine that you have just come home as usual but you find the radio on a chair in the wrong place and water boiling on the stove.
15. No King doesn't recommend trying out his methods on your friends!

B. APPLICATION IN LITERATURE

Inserting Commas   In the following literary passages, taken from tales of terror, some commas have been omitted. Restore the sentences to their original form by adding the missing commas.

1. Later riding home in the empty elevated car he wondered how long he would be safe from the thing.   **Fritz Leiber**
2. Unconscious of his wife's shriek the old man smiled faintly put out his hands like a sightless man and dropped, in a senseless heap, to the floor.   **W. W. Jacobs**

3. "Should it prove to be an interesting case you would I am sure wish to follow it from the outset. I thought at any rate that I should give you the chance." **Sir Arthur Conan Doyle**

4. Oh Frankenstein generous and self-devoted being! **Mary Shelley**

5. Throwing [the bones] aside I soon uncovered a quantity of building stone and mortar. With these materials and with the aid of my trowel I began vigorously to wall up the entrance of the niche.
Edgar Allan Poe

6. He won't get in *here* again she thought and shivered.
Shirley Jackson

7. "Roscoe I am still a greenhorn. I dread the streets." **John Collier**

8. To start with he wasn't called Mackintosh Willy. I never knew who gave him that name. **Ramsey Campbell**

9. For that naturally was who I had beside me, there on that bench: Lucie Belmains who had died on the eighth of April, 1760.
Tanith Lee

10. When I saw it it had long been untenanted, and had the gloomy reputation beside of a haunted house. **J. Sheridan Le Fanu**

C. APPLICATION IN WRITING

A Rescue Report You have just saved a stranger from certain death. TV and newspaper reporters are hovering around you, asking you to describe what happened and what you did to effect the rescue. Write a chronological account of the accident. Explain how it happened, where the victim was, why you were on the scene, and how you made the rescue. Use clear, concise language. You may wish to use exclamations to make your account dramatic. Be sure to use commas and other punctuation correctly.

CHECK POINT
PAGES 780–789

Rewrite the following sentences, adding periods, question marks, exclamation points, and commas as needed.

1. Secret codes and ciphers the tools of espionage and war have been used since ancient times

2. The earliest known use however was around 500 BC

3. To send messages between military commanders the Spartans devised the scytale a wooden cylinder around which a narrow strip of paper was wrapped in a spiral

4. After the paper is wrapped a message is written across one side of the cylinder the cylinder is turned and the message is continued until it is finished

End Marks
and Commas

789

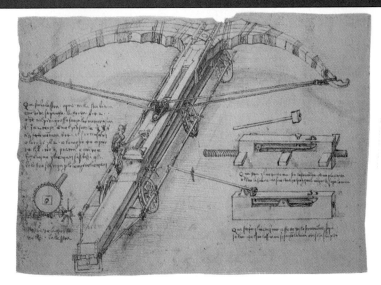

Sketch of a giant catapult by Leonardo da Vinci. The artist used his own code (writing backwards) to protect his inventions.

5. An enemy looking at the unrolled paper would see the markings on it as gibberish

6. The receiving Spartan commander simply took his scytale wrapped the paper around it and read the message

7. The ancient Egyptians Hebrews Babylonians and Assyrians also used secret code systems

8. The Roman emperor Julius Caesar created a cipher by shifting the letters of the alphabet by three characters

9. In this simple effective cipher the letter *A* would be written as the letter *D*

10. Remarkable How simple that cipher seems to us today

11. Wouldn't 99.9 (ninety-nine and nine-tenths) percent of all modern amateur cryptographers be able to crack that cipher

12. "Yes Watson As usual it's too elementary," a modern cryptographer might respond

13. Although it has been centuries since professional cryptographers have used such simple ciphers the need for secrecy was as great in AD 1945 as it was long ago.

14. In the Pacific battles of World War II coded radio communications were intercepted and broken by the Japanese

15. US intelligence officers needed a code that was unique did not resemble other codes and would be unbreakable

16. The Navaho language had the qualities they sought: first it was highly complex; second it resembled no other language; and third only the Navaho people of Arizona and New Mexico understood it

17. Eureka The perfect unbreakable code had been found

18. Before the war in the Pacific ended 420 Navahos had been called into service to transmit secret military messages

19. Likewise analysts intercepted and decoded Japanese messages that gave important information about the Japanese fleet's activities
20. Consequently because we successfully decoded secret Japanese messages the Battle of Midway a turning point in the war was won.

Commas: Quotations, Compound Sentences, and Clauses

Use commas to set off a direct quotation from the rest of the sentence.

The clause identifying the source of the quotation may appear at the beginning, in the middle, or at the end of the sentence. When it follows the quotation, the comma goes inside the quotation marks.

> Holly said, "I am learning to play chess."
> "I am learning to play chess," said Holly.
> "I am learning," said Holly, "to play chess."

Do not use commas with indirect quotations.

> Holly said that she was learning to play chess.

Commas in Compound Sentences

Use a comma before the conjunction that joins the two independent clauses of a compound sentence.

> Americans like coffee, but the British prefer tea.

Notice the difference between a compound sentence and a simple sentence with a compound predicate. Do not separate the elements in a compound predicate with commas.

> Willis cleaned his room, and Dad was shocked beyond belief. (compound sentence)
> The furnace broke down and could not be fixed. (simple sentence with compound predicate)

A comma is not necessary when the main clauses of a compound sentence are very short and are joined by the conjunctions *and, but, so, or,* or *nor.*

> Frogs are slimy but snakes are dry.

However, a comma should separate clauses joined by *yet* or *for.*

> Frogs are slimy, for moisture helps them survive.

Practice Your Skills

A. CONCEPT CHECK

Quotations and Compound Sentences   Rewrite the following sentences, adding commas where needed. If no commas are needed, write *Correct*.

1. "From the age of eight" remarked the lecturer "Jane Goodall was determined to live in Africa and study the animals there."
2. Goodall had no formal training in anthropology yet she became one of the world's leading experts in primate behavior.
3. Goodall's method combined close observation and careful record keeping.
4. The lecturer continued "Her subjects were the wild chimpanzees living on the Gombe Stream Reserve in East Africa."
5. Goodall went to Africa at age eighteen and met the anthropologists Louis and Mary Leakey.
6. The Leakeys were impressed by her determination and enthusiasm so they invited Jane Goodall to assist them in their research studies.
7. In 1960 Goodall went to the Gombe Stream Reserve and began her study of the wild chimpanzees.
8. "Chimpanzees had previously been studied only as components of a group" the lecturer added.
9. The lecturer explained that Goodall lived with the chimpanzees so that she could earn their trust.
10. She gradually began to recognize their distinct personalities and she was able to chart their individual development.

Jane Goodall uncovered many similarities between human beings and chimpanzees.

11. Goodall's methods were unusual but they resulted in some remarkable discoveries.
12. Goodall informed the scientific world that chimpanzees were not strict vegetarians.
13. They did eat plants but they also ate small game.
14. Toolmaking had been considered an exclusively human activity yet Goodall observed that chimps sometimes used simple tools such as sticks and stones.
15. "Because of her findings" finished the lecturer "she became only the eighth person in the history of Cambridge University to earn a Ph.D. without a previous bachelor's degree."

B. APPLICATION IN LITERATURE

Commas Restore the following passage to its original form by adding the missing commas. Write the words before and after each missing comma.

It came drifting through the tangled branches with all the gentle airy grace of a piece of thistledown. When it got nearer I discovered that it looked exactly like my idea of a leprechaun: it was clad in a little fur coat of greenish-grey and it had a long slender furry tail. Its hands which were pink were large for its size and its fingers, tremendously long and attenuated. Its ears were large and the skin so fine that it was semi-transparent; these ears seemed to have a life of their own for they twisted and turned independently sometimes crumpling and folding flat to the head as if they were a fan; at others standing up pricked and straight like anaemic arum lilies. The face of the little creature was dominated by a pair of tremendous dark eyes eyes that would have put any self-respecting owl to shame. Moreover the creature could twist its head round and look over its back. . . . It ran to the tip of a slender branch that scarcely dipped beneath its weight and there it sat clutching the bark with its long slender fingers peering about with its great eyes and chirruping dimly to itself. It was I knew a galago but it looked much more like something out of a fairy tale.

Gerald Durrell, "Shillings from the Fon"

Galago

C. APPLICATION IN WRITING

Writing Dialogue Write a conversation among several people about the advantages and disadvantages of different animals as pets. Imagine each of the people in your conversation defending a different animal. Use commas, periods, question marks, exclamation points, and quotation marks according to the rules you have learned. Vary the dialogue so that the clauses identifying the speakers fall at the beginning, in the middle, and at the end of sentences.

Commas with Nonessential Clauses and Phrases

Use commas to set off nonessential, or nonrestrictive, clauses.

A **nonessential,** *or* **nonrestrictive, clause** adds extra information to a sentence that would be complete without it. An **essential,** *or* **restrictive, clause** is necessary to complete the meaning of the sentence. Do not set off an essential clause with commas. See the examples on the next page.

Nonessential Clause	The English Channel, which is an arm of the Atlantic, separates England from France. (The clause can be dropped.)
Essential Clause	The channel that separates England from France is the English Channel. (The clause cannot be dropped.)

Use commas to set off nonessential participial phrases.

A **nonessential participial phrase** can be dropped without changing the meaning of a sentence. An **essential participial phrase** is necessary to complete the meaning of the sentence. Do not use commas with essential participial phrases.

Nonessential Participial Phrase	The Shakespearean actor, pacing back and forth, rehearsed his lines. (The participial phrase can be dropped.)
Essential Participial Phrase	The Shakespearean actor pacing back and forth is my favorite. (The participial phrase cannot be dropped.)

Practice Your Skills

CONCEPT CHECK

Nonessential Phrases or Clauses Rewrite the following sentences, adding commas where needed. If no commas are needed, write *Correct.*

1. One thing that sets Lope de Vega apart from other writers is the sheer volume of his work.
2. This Spanish writer reminiscing before his death in 1635 estimated that he had written more than 1,500 plays.
3. His *autos sacramentales* which are religious plays number about four hundred.
4. A person looking into Lope's life will find some stormy and violent incidents that included his expedition to the Azores and his service with the Armada.
5. For example, the young Lope seeking adventure with a friend was once returned to his home by the police.
6. His crimes which were minor included the sale of coins.
7. His desire to be noble or aristocratic haunted his life.
8. Lope living off his comedies always aspired to greater things.
9. The occupation that he held longest, however, was secretary to a duke.
10. His life which included turbulent adventures changed when he entered the priesthood.

Writing Theme
Lope de Vega

11. This playwright who was a priest never stopped writing.
12. Miguel de Cervantes who wrote *Don Quixote* called Lope a prodigy of nature.
13. Most of Felix Lope de Vega Carpio's three hundred or so surviving plays are action-filled epics resembling Shakespeare's historical dramas.
14. His best-known historical drama which has been produced often is *Fuenteovejuna*.
15. The story that makes this play timely is the revolt of a Spanish village against its oppressors.

COMMAS: OTHER USES

Following are some other situations in which commas are used.

Commas in Dates, Place Names, and Letters

In dates, use a comma between the day of the month and the year. When only the month and the year are given, no comma is needed.

> As the result of an earthquake, the San Francisco Giants and the Oakland A's did not play a World Series game on October 17, 1989.
> They played the series later in October 1989.

Use a comma after the year when the date falls in the middle of a sentence.

> November 22, 1963, was a sad day in American history.

Use a comma between the name of a city or town and that of the state or country.

> Milwaukee, Wisconsin   Rome, Italy

When an address or place name falls in the middle of a sentence, use a comma after the names of the street, city, and state or country. If the address includes a ZIP code, then put the comma after the ZIP code but not after the name of the state.

> Ten Soden Street, Boston, Massachusetts 02108, was my home.

Use a comma in the salutation of a friendly letter and after the closing of a friendly letter or a business letter.

> Dear Tom,   Your friend,   Sincerely yours,

Writing
—TIP—

Use a colon in the salutation of a business letter.

Commas to Avoid Confusion

Use a comma to separate words that might be misread.

The conjunctions *but* and *for* might be mistaken for prepositions.

Unclear	She had to run for the train was late.
Clear	She had to run, for the train was late.

Confusion can arise when a noun follows a verbal phrase.

Unclear	While playing Mick's stereo broke down.
Clear	While playing, Mick's stereo broke down.

An adverb at the beginning of a sentence may be mistaken for a preposition.

Unclear	Within the room was quite warm.
Clear	Within, the room was quite warm.

Commas with Titles and Numbers

A title following a personal name is set off with commas; the abbreviations *Inc.* and *Ltd.* are also set off with commas.

Willa Cox, Ph.D., joined Ambly, Ltd., last week.

In numbers of more than three digits, use commas between groups of three digits counting from the right, with the exception of ZIP codes, phone numbers, years, and house numbers.

California growers import more than 10,000 ladybugs annually for pest control.

Omitted Words

Use a comma to indicate the words left out of parallel word groups.

> Some people like baseball; others, soccer.
> One friend offered social companionship; another, intellectual stimulation.
> Sailboats are powered by wind; motorboats, gasoline.

Practice Your Skills

A. CONCEPT CHECK

Commas   Rewrite the following sentences, adding commas where needed.

Writing Theme
Working for Change

1. Charles R. Drew M.D. was a black physician who founded and directed the world's first blood bank.
2. Drew was born in Washington D.C. on June 3 1904.
3. He studied medicine at McGill University in Montreal Canada and later attended Columbia University in New York City.
4. At the Columbia Medical Center, Dr. John Scudder taught him blood chemistry; others surgical techniques.
5. While experimenting Drew discovered that blood plasma the fluid part of blood without the corpuscles could replace whole blood in transfusions.
6. Whole blood still contains red cells; plasma none.
7. Besides plasma could be stored for months or even frozen.
8. Whole blood storage was impractical for spoilage and contamination occurred quickly.
9. In 1940 at the start of World War II Drew set up a blood bank in New York City to collect blood that would be sent to injured British citizens.
10. The American Red Cross asked Drew to supervise a project to bank the blood of 100000 Americans.
11. At that time the blood of only white donors was acceptable to the U.S. military.
12. Drew argued against this discrimination and lost; to protest he tendered his resignation.
13. After resigning Drew went to Howard University to train new doctors.
14. On April 1 1950 Drew was seriously injured in an auto accident while driving to Tuskegee Alabama.
15. His death was ironic for the local hospital refused to give him the transfusion that might have been able to save his life just because he was black.

B. REVISION SKILL

Punctuating a Letter Rewrite this letter, adding commas where needed.

1627 8th Street
Berkeley California 94710
August 11 19 __

Robinson Kan Ph.D.
1435 Page Street Apt. A
San Francisco California 94114

Dear Rob

Just a quick note to let you know that while researching I found the information you needed for your article. The writer's name which you thought was Connor was James P. Comer M.D. He was born in East Chicago Indiana on September 25 1934. He studied at Indiana University Howard University College of Medicine and the University of Michigan.

After some digging the title of his book surfaced as well. It is called *Beyond Black and White.* Comer wrote it after he joined the Child Study Center which is attached to Yale University in New Haven Connecticut. Don't be put off by the title; inside the book is quite personal and engaging.

Dr. Comer's main emphasis seems to be school programs that balance students' social and psychological needs with their educational ones. I found a useful article in *The New York Times* of June 13 1990. It states that in 1990 the Rockefeller Foundation allocated $15000000 to set up educational programs designed by Comer.

I'll be relocating this week. After moving my address will be Biblio Inc. 1937 Carleton Street Berkeley California 94704.

All the best

C. APPLICATION IN WRITING

Organizational Plan Describe an organization for change you might start in your community. Give your organization a name. Tell what activities and services you would offer and what the members might do. Describe future plans. Use commas and other punctuation correctly.

CHECK POINT
PAGES 791–799

Rewrite the following sentences, adding commas where needed. If no additional commas are needed, write *Correct*.

Writing Theme
Ferdinand and
Isabella

1. Isabella I who became a powerful ruler was born on April 22 1451 in Castile Spain.
2. She was heir to the throne one of the mightiest in Spain.
3. At the time differences among the rulers governing separate kingdoms were critical for no one ruler united Spain.
4. Even within Castile, some people supported Isabella's brother King Henry IV; others her brother Alfonso; and still others Isabella.
5. Alfonso died on July 5 1468 and his supporters turned to Isabella.
6. Following Alfonso's death Isabella declared that while her brother King Henry lived "none other had a right to the crown."
7. Several suitors for Isabella's hand in marriage were disappointed for she chose to marry Ferdinand of Aragon.
8. Isabella's marriage to Ferdinand which eventually united two of Spain's largest states did not have the Castilian king's approval.
9. King Henry died in 1474 yet Isabella became queen of Castile only after four-and-a-half years of war.
10. Isabella knowing Ferdinand insisted that they rule Castile together.
11. Ferdinand who saw the wisdom of this arrangement made her joint ruler of Aragon in 1481.
12. They were rare monarchs for their relationship was based on mutual respect and shared authority.
13. Other rulers of the time were not as politically astute nor were they as militarily able as Ferdinand and Isabella.
14. The event that unified Spain was the conquest of Granada in 1491.
15. "Granada in 1492" wrote Américo Castro in a book published by Henry Holt and Co. Inc. "was the last stronghold of the Moslem sovereignty."
16. The victory depleted the treasury so an expedition to find a westward route to India seemed a possible source of new wealth.
17. Historical records indicate that contrary to popular belief Isabella did not sell her jewels to finance the expedition.
18. Therefore, when Isabella and Columbus met in Santa Fe Granada the queen could promise him only limited financial support.
19. April 17 1492 marks the date when the terms of the voyage which Columbus calculated to be about 3900 miles were drawn up.
20. The year before the monarchs had earned their place in history by uniting Spain; financing Columbus, they changed the world.

Writing Theme
Sports and
Hobbies

A. Using Punctuation Correctly Rewrite the following sentences, adding punctuation where needed.

1. The sixty-first annual All-Star Game was held on July 10 1990 in Chicago Illinois

2. The game took place in the home of the Chicago Cubs Wrigley Field which is located on the north side of town at 1060 West Addison Street

3. "My first All-Star Game was at Wrigley Field in 1962" said Hall of Fame star Billy Williams

4. He recalls that he achieved his first RBI by hitting the ball to third base which ordinarily would have been an out

5. Fortunately the infielders were playing back and not one of them caught the ball

6. As usual before this big event in baseball Williams and the fans anticipated the game with excitement

7. One highlight for the fans was the home run contest that was held on Monday July 9

8. Swarming on the sidewalk outside the park fans waited to catch baseballs that were hit over the walls

9. Predictably Ryne Sandberg representing the Chicago Cubs won the home run contest in his own park

10. Outside the hopeful fans shouted loud enough to be heard inside the ballpark, "Ryne hit a homer to us"

11. Under manager Tony LaRussa the American League All-Stars boasted many seasoned veterans yet the team could have been called the All-Star Juniors

12. That nickname would have been jokingly appropriate for the team included three juniors named Ken Griffey Jr Cal Ripken Jr and Sandy Alomar Jr

13. Coming from the National League manager Roger Craig's players were more familiar with Wrigley Field

14. The windy stormy day of the game was not ideal

15. Inside many of the 39071 excited happy fans hoped it wouldn't rain too hard

16. The start of the game which was scheduled for 7:35 PM was delayed for seventeen minutes by rain

17. Wouldn't it have been terrible if the game had been rained out

18. Baseball Commissioner Fay Vincent assured the media "Don't worry We'll get the game in"

19. The weather however was uncooperative for the rain caused another delay in the seventh inning.

20. Clearly the game was a low-hitting pitchers' duel: the American League scored two runs; the National League none

B. Finding Punctuation Errors Rewrite the following sentences, adding punctuation where needed.

1. In any discussion of hobbies one pastime that comes up frequently is reading and collecting comic books
2. Making its debut in 1896 the ancestor of American comics was "The Yellow Kid" which was created by Richard Outcault
3. In publishing the strip was innovative in two ways: first it had a continuing character; second the dialogue was printed inside the frame
4. The character as a matter of fact was a bald flap-eared boy in a yellow nightshirt
5. The early strips were small but their popularity was great
6. The first daily comic strip "Mr A Mutt" was printed in 1907
7. Reprints of this strip which was renamed "Mutt and Jeff" became one of the first comic books
8. In 1938 however a new American hero was born
9. Jerry Siegel and Joe Schuster created a man who was strong had super powers and fought for good and justice
10. Needless to say "Superman" was a sensation from the very first issue of *Action Comics*.
11. A person who found and sold a copy of that issue today could depending on its condition make about $50000
12. Other popular heroes followed in quick succession: Batman in 1939 Captain Marvel in 1940 and Wonder Woman in 1941
13. Created by psychologist W M Marston Wonder Woman became a symbol of independent female power
14. Following a slump in the 1950's the field was reenergized by *Marvel Comics*'s creation "The Amazing Spider-Man"
15. *Marvel*'s editor who signed his columns "Excelsior Stan" wanted readers to be part of "the Marvel Universe"

C. Proofreading Skill Rewrite the following passage, correcting errors in punctuation, spelling, and capitalization.

What do ceramics coins and comics have in common. They are all part of the phenomenon known as collecting Modern collectors find their treasures in attics at flea markets and under porches. For example one of the world's rarest stamps the Hawaiian "missionary" was found under the faded peeling wallpaper of an old house. Numismatists commonly called coin collectors look for mistakes, that often occur when coins are minted. The kinds of collections, and the reasons for collecting are as varied as the collectors themselves. The costs of collecting by the way vary greatly from $025 for a baseball card to $3000000 for a work of fine art

On the Lightside

THE POINT OF PUNCTUATION

"YOU WILL GO AND RETURN NOT DIE IN WAR." Clever fortune-tellers spoke this fail-safe message to Roman soldiers. If they lived through battle, the warriors visualized the prediction: YOU WILL GO AND RETURN, NOT DIE IN WAR. For the dead, it became: YOU WILL GO AND RETURN NOT. DIE IN WAR.

While punctuation is rarely a matter of life and death, it is essential to communication. Surprisingly, this has not always been the case. The creators of hieroglyphic and cuneiform writing and the scribes of ancient Greece and Rome used almost no punctuation, or even spaces, to separate words. Their wordsallran together. Later, dots or apostrophes separated 'one'word' from'the' next'like' this. Around

A.D. 600, word spacing became widespread.

The punctuation marks we use today developed slowly over the next several hundred years. They were used haphazardly without regard to clear meaning until printers standardized both punctuation and spelling in the 1500's.

The question mark and exclamation point were derived from the Latin words *quaestio,* meaning "question," and *io,* an exclamation of joy or surprise. The practice of writing *q* over *o* developed into *?.* *I* over *o* became *!.* Quotation marks are merely inverted double commas.

The word *punctuation* means "putting in points." People often disagree over the fine points of punctuation but not over its ultimate purpose—to make the meaning clear.

Semicolons, Colons, and Other Punctuation

THE SEMICOLON

A semicolon separates sentence elements. It indicates a more definite break than a comma does but not so decisive a break as a period.

Semicolons Used with Commas

Clauses in a sentence are usually separated by commas. If, however, the clauses themselves include commas, then separate the clauses with a semicolon.

A semicolon may be used between independent clauses joined by a conjunction if these clauses contain commas.

> Kristin, by dint of her talent, won the leading role in this year's school play; and, it is expected, she will give an electrifying performance.

> It was a long letter, with talk of Paris, of the book stalls along the Seine, of onion soup at the market, of Montmartre; but the highlight was the news of her forthcoming novel.

Use a semicolon to separate the items of a series if one or more of these items contain commas.

> The auctions will be held on Monday, September 10; Tuesday, September 11; and Friday, September 14.

> Twentieth-century Canadian prime ministers include Richard Bennett, Conservative; W. L. Mackenzie King, Liberal; and John Diefenbaker, Progressive Conservative.

Semicolons Between Independent Clauses

Use a semicolon to join the parts of a compound sentence if no coordinating conjunction is used.

A semicolon shows a more emphatic relationship between clauses than a conjunction such as *and, but,* or *for:*

> Our debating opponents were alert, but we were not.
> Our debating opponents were alert; we were not.

Writing
——**TIP**——
Using a semicolon to join clauses containing commas clearly marks the separation of units. It lessens the likelihood of confusing the reader.

Remember that a semicolon may be used only if the clauses are closely related. Do not use a semicolon to join unrelated clauses.

Incorrect	Carol I ruled Rumania; it was part of the Ottoman Empire.
Correct	Carol I ruled Rumania; his reign lasted from 1881 to 1914.

Semicolons and Conjunctive Adverbs

Use a semicolon before a conjunctive adverb or a transitional expression that joins the clauses of a compound sentence.

The test was long and difficult; however, everyone in the class managed to finish it on time.

The cosmopolitan high school has many advantages; for example, it brings together students of many different interests.

Note that the conjunctive adverb and the transitional phrase are followed by a comma. For a list of conjunctive adverbs see "Conjunctions" in Grammar Handbook 30, page 573.

Practice Your Skills

A. CONCEPT CHECK

Semicolons   Rewrite the following passages correctly, adding semicolons where needed.

1. Nothing worth doing is completed in our lifetime therefore, we must be saved by hope.   **Reinhold Niebuhr**
2. The largest and most awe-inspiring waves of the ocean are invincible they move on their mysterious courses far down in the hidden depths of the sea, rolling ponderously and unceasingly.   **Rachel Carson**
3. Art is not a handicraft it is the transmission of feeling the artist has experienced.   **Leo Tolstoy**
4. It is human, perhaps, to appreciate little of that which we have and to long for that which we have not but it is a great pity that, in the world of light, the gift of sight is used only as a mere convenience rather than as a means of adding fullness to life.   **Helen Keller**
5. The processes of nature are to be studied, not worshipped the laws of nature find best reverence in our intelligent understanding and observance, not in obsequious adoration.   **Charlotte Perkins Gilman**
6. Adversity is sometimes hard upon a man but for one man who can stand prosperity, there are a hundred that will stand adversity.   **Thomas Carlyle**

7. Victory at all costs, victory in spite of all terror, victory however long and hard the road may be for without victory there is no survival. **Winston Churchill**

8. The most vulnerable and at the same time the most unconquerable thing is human self-love indeed, it is through being wounded that its power grows and can, in the end, become tremendous. **Friedrich Nietzsche**

9. Youth is the time of getting, middle age of improving, and old age of spending a negligent youth is usually attended by an ignorant middle age, and both by an empty old age. **Anne Bradstreet**

10. My ward was divided into three rooms. . . . One I visited, armed with a dressing tray, full of rollers, plasters, and pins another, with books, flowers, games, and gossip a third, with teapots, lullabies, consolation, and, sometimes a shroud. **Louisa May Alcott**

B. REVISION SKILL

Semicolons Revise the following passage by inserting semicolons where needed and by changing some commas to semicolons. Not every sentence requires correction.

(1) William James, the American philosopher, offered a simple definition of philosophy, he said it is "an unusually stubborn attempt to think clearly." (2) The word *philosophy* comes from two Greek words, *philo* and *sophia,* and together they mean "the love of wisdom." (3) Early Greek philosophers varied in their view of the world, consequently, different ideas emerged. (4) Some said that things in the universe had come from and were made of a single element, such as water or air, but others believed in a living form of matter. (5) One argued that everything was in a state of change, another felt all was unchanging. (6) The Renaissance was characterized by a shift in concern indeed, philosophers questioned the way things happen on earth. (7) A few of these thinkers were Copernicus, who gave us the theory of a sun-centered solar system, Galileo, who demonstrated the truth of Copernicus's ideas, and Isaac Newton, who discovered three laws that explain the motion of physical objects. (8) By the 1600's, philosophers focused on reason rather than on experience thus, they believed knowledge could be gained through mathematics. (9) A century later, ideas changed observation and experience were thought to be the basis of knowledge. (10) Modern thinkers, such as John Dewey, from America, Jean-Paul Sartre, from France, and Bertrand Russell, from England, continued to question the world's nature.

Bertrand Russell, by Roger Fry, 1923

A colon marks an important division in a sentence. It is a signal that what follows is an explanation, an example, or a summation of what precedes it.

Use a colon to introduce a list of items.

A word or phrase such as *these, the following,* or *as follows* is often followed by a colon.

> Animals in danger of extinction include the following: the alligator, the bald eagle, and the mountain lion.

Note, however, that a colon should not be used before a series of modifiers or complements that immediately follows a verb.

> Egyptian tombs contain false doors, tunnels, and blocked passages to confuse grave robbers.

Do not use a colon within a prepositional phrase; and as a general rule, do not use a colon immediately after a verb. (One exception is after a verb that introduces a quotation.)

Incorrect	Gourmet cooking is practiced by: men and women.
Correct	Gourmet cooking is practiced by men and women.

Incorrect	During World War I the Allied powers included: France, Great Britain, and Serbia.
Correct	During World War I the Allied powers included France, Great Britain, and Serbia.
Correct	These countries were among the Allied powers during World War I: France, Great Britain, and Serbia.

Use a colon to introduce a quotation that is not preceded by an explanatory term, such as *he said* or *she asked*.

> Little Joey jumped and ran past the museum guard: "Can't catch me!"

Use a colon to introduce a long or formal quotation.

> John Milton, the great English poet and prose writer, wrote in 1644: "Where there is much desire to learn, there of necessity will be much arguing, much writing, many opinions; for opinion in good men is but knowledge in the making."

Use a colon between two independent clauses when the second clause explains the first.

> We soon learned the answer: someone had changed the report card.

> We now know what to expect from the new manager: Jean is going to be a strict disciplinarian.

Capitalize the first word of a formal statement following a colon. Also capitalize the start of a quotation or any proper noun. If a statement following a colon is informal in tone, do not capitalize the first word. Contrast the formality of the sentence below with the examples above.

> The investigating team promptly announced the reason for the discrepancies: Someone had changed the report card.

Punctuation Note A colon used in a sentence must be preceded by an independent clause and may be followed by an independent clause, a phrase, or a list.

Other Uses of the Colon

A colon is also used (1) after the salutation in a formal letter, (2) between hour and minute figures in clock time, (3) between chapter and verse in a Biblical reference, (4) between title and subtitle of a book, (5) after a label that signals an important idea.

Dear Dr. Fry: *The World: A Geography*
6:15 A.M.   Genesis 2:4–7
POISON: Not for internal use

Practice Your Skills

A. CONCEPT CHECK

Colons and Semicolons Rewrite each of the following sentences, adding colons and semicolons where necessary. If a sentence requires no change, write *Correct*.

1. Mural painting may include any of the following a work on an interior building wall, a painting on a free-standing or exterior wall, or a painting on the ceiling of a room.
2. Stone Age people painted scenes that told much about daily life, hunting, and family gatherings.
3. Renaissance muralists were in great demand there were a great many magnificent palaces and churches to decorate.

Detroit Industry
fresco by Diego Rivera,
(1932–1933)

4. Commonly, the Renaissance murals were frescoes, or watercolors painted directly on wet plaster, however, contemporary murals are often oils painted on materials such as these wood, metal, or canvas.

5. Michelangelo's *The Creation of Adam,* perhaps the most famous religious painting in the world, vividly illustrates Genesis 1 26 "And God said, Let us make man in our image, after our likeness."

6. Tintoretto, one of the last great Venetian muralists, was known especially for his rich colors and the fluid movement of his figures.

7. Murals by these contemporary artists have been exhibited throughout the United States and Mexico, Thomas Hart Benton, Diego Rivera, and José Orozco.

8. Diego Rivera studied the murals of the "old masters" in Italy, on his return to his homeland, he painted murals on the walls of the University of Mexico, the Ministry of Education, and the Agricultural College at Chapingo.

9. Perhaps inspired by Rivera's work, artist Judith Baca helped create the world's longest mural the one-mile-long piece made in 1980, called *The Great Wall of Los Angeles,* shows the contributions made by ethnic groups to the city.

10. Similarly, a group of women artists who were known as Las Mujeres Muralistas created murals with a message their goal was to present positive views of Latin American daily life.

B. REVISION SKILL

Colons and Semicolons Rewrite the following sentences, adding colons and semicolons where necessary.

(1) Dear Mrs. Flanagan

(2) The museum's exhibition committee meeting will take place on Tuesday at 9 00 A.M. (3) Items on the agenda are as follows exhibits for next season, improved hanging techniques, and better facilities. (4) Next, a review of the budget should clarify changes for the upcoming year, for example, it should make evident why we must cut back the number of new exhibits. (5) The committee must find ways to compensate for budget cuts one idea might be to have a longer run for exhibits.

(6) Following the formal meeting, lunch will be served at 12 00 noon. (7) After lunch, Martha Andrews, author of *Preserving Great Art A Practical Guide,* will address the committee. (8) Ms. Andrews is an expert in the following authenticating old paintings, restoring canvases, and reframing old works. (9) Ms. Andrews said after being invited "The committee will hear a great deal of information, certainly, it can be put to good use." (10) The meeting should adjourn a little before 5 00 P.M.

C. PROOFREADING SKILL

Colons and Semicolons Rewrite the following paragraphs, correcting errors in punctuation, capitalization, and spelling.

It is hard to believe that a young spainish girl named Maria could change the world's understanding of history however, that is what did indeed happen. Maria's father enjoyed exploring caves on the family's estate in northern Spain. Maria sometimes accompanied him. One day in 1879, Maria made a discovery cave art dating to the Ice Age. These pictures were important for one reason they had remaned hiden for all of recorded history. Maria's father was too tall to see the caves low cieling, fortunately, Maria was short enough to view lifelike animals painted their. The animals were: bison, antelope, and bulls painted in three colors red, brown, and black. An artist had used uneven surfaces to give them a three-dimminsional quality.

Marias discovery at the cave, now called altamira, led to much debate. Scientists believe that the paintings are about 15,000 years old, nonetheless, many questions remain. The most important question is the following What purpose did such beautiful art serve in the lives of prehistoric people.

A dash is most often used to indicate an abrupt change of thought or a pause within a sentence. The words, phrases, or clauses set off by dashes merely add extra information to an already complete thought. Sometimes a dash is used to mean *in other words* or *that is* before an explanation.

In informal writing using dashes occasionally can add interest, variety, and personality to your writing. However, since a dash usually marks a break in thought, too many dashes may confuse your reader or give the effect of vague, choppy writing. Dashes are seldom used in formal writing.

Use a dash to set off an explanatory statement that interrupts the thought. Also use a dash to set off a long parenthetical expression that requires special emphasis.

> Her dairy cattle—Jersey, Guernsey, and Holstein-Friesian—have brought her a good income.

> The moons of Jupiter—Io is perhaps the most spectacular—are being studied extensively by astronomers.

> Slavery—although an important issue—was not the only cause of the Civil War.

Use a dash to show an abrupt break in thought.

> If I don't go—and I don't see how I can—you'll have to take my place.

> The first time she wore the hat—wouldn't you know it—it rained.

A dash may indicate a break in thought caused by uncertainty. It adds a casual, conversational tone to written dialogue.

> "My favorite actress is Bette Davis, and my favorite Davis movie is *Dangerous*—no, I think it's *Jezebel*."

Use a dash to separate a series of elements from the subject pronoun in a summarizing statement.

> Writs of assistance, the quartering of soldiers in private homes, the insolent searches by royal officers—all of these the people of Boston had suffered with growing unease.

> Bottles, rags, old tin cans, discarded clothing, and papers—these were his stock in trade.

Practice Your Skills

A. CONCEPT CHECK

Dashes Rewrite the following sentences, adding dashes, semicolons, and colons where necessary.

1. The works of Ludwig von Beethoven constitute one of the greatest if not *the* greatest individual achievements in the history of the arts.
2. Beethoven's life a life that has inspired dozens of biographies is as interesting and remarkable as his music.
3. An epic struggle with deafness, chronic ill health, serious financial woes these were the adversities that formed Beethoven's life.
4. Beethoven's biographers depict a lonely man, a man whose life was ravaged by disorder and suffering, but he was also a man who found solace in the majesty of his music.
5. To investigate the details of Beethoven's life, biographers used the following factual accounts, written records, diary entries.
6. Beethoven's music is universally celebrated for its grandeur or is it the highly developed musical themes as well as its tremendous structural power.
7. Although his education was primarily musical, Beethoven had a great love of philosophy and literature, it is said that some of his music was directly inspired by Shakespeare.
8. He developed a lifelong habit of jotting down notes one might call them musical sketches that he often reworked for many years before the work was considered finished.
9. Among the composers who were influenced by Beethoven's genius were the following Schubert, Weber, and Brahms.
10. A recent biography, *Beethoven in Retrospect His Impact on Contemporary Music* I think that's the title details the composer's influence on modern classical music.

B. APPLICATION IN LITERATURE

Dashes Rewrite these passages, inserting dashes where needed.

1. Camouflage, mimicry, bluff, and flight all have failed.
   David Robinson
2. Sometimes the rows of flimsy buildings snow on their roofs, rootless white faces peering suspiciously out through their windows, kid's toys scattered like trash on the walks reminded him of old photographs he had seen of mining camps. **Margaret Atwood**
3. She moved with silent grace, and all her features voice, figure, gestures, her gray eyes and her fair hair formed a harmonious whole.
   Boris Pasternak

4. He thought of the jobs he had had since he quit school delivery boy, stock clerk, runner, lately working in a factory and he was dissatisfied with all of them. **Bernard Malamud**
5. I thought I overheard Miss Havisham answer only it seemed so unlikely "Well you can break his heart." **Charles Dickens**

C. APPLICATION IN WRITING

A Journal Entry Have you ever had a moment of great success or great failure? Think of a memorable experience of either adversity or triumph. Then write a brief journal entry describing the experience. Include semicolons, colons, and dashes in your journal entry. Check for the correct use of punctuation.

THE HYPHEN

A hyphen is a mark used to connect numbers, word elements, or the parts of a compound word.

Use a hyphen in compound numbers from twenty-one to ninety-nine.

forty-five minutes   fifty-eight miles

Use a hyphen in spelled-out fractions.

a one-fifth reduction   a two-thirds gain
one-half of the   three-fourths of a
  population   cup

Use a hyphen in certain compound words.

self-restraint   brother-in-law   vice-president

Use a hyphen between the words that make up a compound adjective when the modifier is used before a noun.

She was a well-informed candidate.

In general, do not hyphenate a compound adjective when it follows the noun it modifies.

In the debate the young candidate seemed well informed.

Use a hyphen in compounds in which the second element is a capitalized word or a date.

pre-Civil War   post-1945

Use hyphens to distinguish compounds from homonyms or to avoid confusion.

For example, use a hyphen to distinguish *re-cover* from *recover*.

Use a hyphen between syllables divided at the end of a line.

Many states have a requirement that students pass the "minimum competency" examinations.

Observe these rules when hyphenating at the end of a line:

1. A word may be divided only between syllables; only words with two or more syllables may be hyphenated.
2. At least two letters of the hyphenated word must fall on each line.

Practice Your Skills

CONCEPT CHECK

Hyphens   Rewrite the sentences below, adding hyphens and dashes where necessary or correcting the placement of hyphens.

1. If one didn't know that styles in fashion follow cycles, one might believe that today's clothing fads have been around no more than twenty five or thirty years.
2. However, the leotard and tights now popular garb for aerobics class are similar to the tight fitting costume worn by men in Europe throughout the Middle Ages and Renaissance.
3. Named for the lightly clad nineteenth century trapeze artist Jules Léotard the skin tight costume was his trademark today's leotard is made of new synthetic fibers.

Never hyphenate a compound modifier consisting of an adverb ending in -*ly* plus a participle or an adjective: *a highly priced hat.*

Writing Theme
Fashion

Semicolons and
Other Punctuation   **813**

4. In addition, the origin of today's popular blue jeans is traced to a self taught tailor named Levi Strauss.

5. Strauss was only seventeen years old when he arrived in pre Civil War San Francisco during the "gold rush" of the 1850's, but he was eager and he had ingenuity.

6. Tents, the cloth from covered wagons, and later miners' trousers these were some uses of the exceptionally sturdy canvas Strauss sold.

7. Genuine recreations of the blue "Levi's," as well as numerous look alikes, are now worn around the world; selling jeans is now a multimillion dollar industry.

8. The pump, a popular shoe style today, originated in the mid 1500's in Germany.

9. The pump a loose slipper that was originally plain or jeweled has a heel that is about one half the height of a high heeled shoe.

10. Indeed, fashion is constantly changing, although certain popular trends can be traced to the Greeks, Romans, and other early civilizations.

P A R E N T H E S E S

Parentheses are used in several ways. They are used to enclose the figures or letters that introduce the items of a list and are often used to enclose references to source materials. Like dashes, parentheses may also be used to enclose nonessential explanatory information or a phrase or clause that interrupts the even flow of a sentence.

Writing TIP

Parentheses signal the reader that the information contained is optional reading.

Use parentheses to enclose figures or letters that introduce the items of a list in a sentence.

In Chinese libraries, books are classified into the following four divisions: (a) Classics, (b) History, (c) Philosophy, and (d) Collected Works or Literature.

You may give in parentheses the source of the information you are using or credit for the ideas or quotations you are using in your writing.

"Life on the mountain-circled shore of Lake Chapala was, in many ways, quiet and idyllic for the Lawrences. Lorenzo . . . spent his days baking white loaves of bread, reading Mexican folklore—and, of course, writing" (Simpson 255).

Use parentheses to set off supplementary, explanatory, or digressive elements within a sentence.

The following example of this use of parentheses is from the work of a professional writer.

> The little snapping shrimps have been heard all over a broad band that extends around the world, between latitudes 35° N and 35° S (for example, from Cape Hatteras to Buenos Aires) in ocean waters less than 30 fathoms deep.
>
> **Rachel Carson**

Use punctuation within parentheses only when it belongs to the parenthetical material. Otherwise, place punctuation marks outside the closing parenthesis.

> The predominant species is sun bears (not, as was once thought, black bears).

> In a lecture given in 1870, Oliver Wendell Holmes, Sr., explored the subconscious mind (what he called "the underground workshop of thought").

BRACKETS AND ELLIPSES

Use brackets to enclose editorial corrections, explanations, or comments in quoted material.

> "The 18th Amendment, ratified in 1918 [1919], formally brought Prohibition to the country." (correction)

> The critic stated in his column: "I have always found her [Lina Wertmuller] to be a fascinating director." (explanatory information inserted by the writer)

Use ellipsis points, or dots, to indicate any omission of a word, phrase, line, or paragraph within a quoted passage.

Use three dots (. . .), with a space between each dot, to indicate an omission within a sentence; use four dots (. . . .) to indicate an omission between sentences.

> "In short, . . . to maintain one's self on this earth is not a hardship but a pastime, if we live simply and wisely."
>
> **Henry David Thoreau**

> In his most famous speech, Martin Luther King, Jr., said: "I have a dream. . . . And if America is to be a great nation, this must become true."

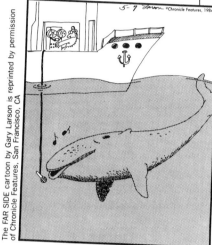

"A Louie, Louie . . .
wowooo . . .
We gotta go now . . ."

Writing Theme
Whales

Rewrite the following sentences, adding semicolons, colons, dashes, hyphens, parentheses, and ellipses where necessary.

1. Benjamin Franklin, who is not generally associated with whales, once wrote "The grand leap of the whale is esteemed, by all who have seen it, as one of the finest spectacles in nature" letter to editor of a London newspaper.

2. The blue whale is the largest animal that ever lived on the earth other types of whales are considerably smaller.

3. Some of these smaller whales include the following gray whale, humpback whale, and bottle nosed whale.

4. The Norwegians were the first whalers however, the Basque people of southern France and northern Spain created the first large whaling industry let's see, that was during the 900's, I believe.

5. The Soviet Union, which announced that it would stop whaling in mid 1988, will follow new laws, this country, among others, hopes to secure the safety of an endangered species.

6. Whale oil provides useful products cosmetics, soap, varnish, and margarine in addition, whale oil is used in manufacturing lubricants and automatic transmission fluid.

7. Harem schools, nursery groups, and bachelor schools these are all forms of whale social organization.

8. The terminology that describes whales includes the following words *cow,* the female whale, *bull,* the male whale, *calf,* the baby whale, and *herd,* a group of whales.

9. Whales communicate through phonations sounds of a wide variety that travel great distances.

10. The songs of humpback whales are eerie really quite beautiful! to listen to on recordings made by research scientists or well known folksingers.

11. The well developed whaling industry of nineteenth century America provided the backdrop for a great American novel.

12. The novel I'm sure you have already guessed is *Moby Dick* by Herman Melville.

13. When he was twenty two years old, Melville signed on as a sailor on a new whaling ship, the *Acushnet.*

14. Melville's first books, *Typee, Omoo, Mardi, Redburn,* and *White-Jacket* were well received, highly popular travel books, however *Moby Dick* established his reputation.

15. On the one hand, *Moby Dick* was a tale about a whale hunt on the other, it was a classic story of the symbolic struggle between human beings and nature.

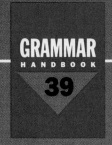

A. Semicolons and Other Punctuation   Rewrite the following sentences, adding semicolons, colons, dashes, hyphens, and parentheses when necessary. If a sentence requires no change, write *Correct*.

1. Fun loving Americans have long been enthralled with games of prowess however, today whimsical games are popular.
2. *The Browser's Book of Beginnings Origins of Everything Under (and Including) the Sun* explains the development of some of the following popular sports, games, and toys.
3. Kites, marbles, and yo-yos are generally thought of as children's games rather than adult sports.
4. The Chinese used kites around 1200 B.C. to send secret messages colors and flying patterns were codes between camps.
5. Kites have modern applications, too for example, they are used for atmospheric research.
6. The Chinese, who were kite flying experts, tried to build large paper hang gliders but, it seems, their success was limited.
7. Today, hang gliding a sport in which flyers glide on air currents is an increasingly popular pastime.
8. Another game with an interesting history is marbles it's among the oldest games dating back to ancient Egypt.
9. Marbles originally served to tell fortunes a number of ancient civilizations used them to predict the future.
10. Archaeologists believe that marbles had religious significance in Egypt and other countries they have found marbles in temple ruins and tombs.
11. The yo-yo was not always a toy instead, it was used by well trained hunters in the Philippines.
12. The yo-yo, the boomerang, and the bola these toys were once used as weapons for hunting animals.
13. Other toys that have faded in and out of popularity over the years include hula hoops, roller skates, and tops.
14. Three have become fads again hula hoops, which were first made in early Greece and Rome, roller skates, invented in the mid 1700's in Belgium, and tops, made in ancient Babylonia.
15. One can only wonder which of these much loved toys will still be popular in the twenty first century.

B. Punctuating Sentences Correctly   Rewrite the following sentences, adding semicolons, colons, dashes, hyphens, and parentheses where necessary.

1. To paraphrase 1 Corinthians 6 19, the body is a temple.
2. Some people assume they are fit because their bodies show no signs of disease this assumption is wrong.

3. Fitness testing and exercise physiology new fields in our fitness crazed culture provide guidelines for assessment of one's physical condition.
4. Many books for example, *Fit or Fat* by Covert Bailey and *Aerobics* by Kenneth Cooper describe self evaluation tests.
5. To measure cardiovascular fitness that is, how well the body uses oxygen Bailey suggests using the "stair step test".
6. During the test the following measurements are taken 1 resting pulse, the heart rate upon awakening 2 training pulse, the rate during intense activity and 3 recovery pulse, the rate as the heart recovers from activity.
7. Cooper's twelve minute walking test also assesses fitness.
8. It measures how far a person walks or jogs in twelve minutes however, guidelines vary according to age.
9. Dr. Bryant Stanford at the Louisville School of Medicine wrote "We're a compulsive society that believes . . . if a little is good, a lot is better an attitude which does not always create common sense fitness."
10. All tests need a label "Warning Consult your doctor."

C. Correcting Punctuation Errors Rewrite the following passage, correcting errors in capitalization and spelling and adding punctuation where necessary.

Are you one of the million Americans now active in one of these sports running, walking, cycling, climbing, backpacking, sking, swimming, wrestling, weight lifting? Vigorus exercise can make you feel your best, unfortunatly, it can also lead to the following aches and pains shin splints, hamstring pulls, sore muscles, charley horses to name but a few.

As more of us take an active interest in Participant sports, a new field of medicine has made its appearance yes, I mean sports medicine. Sports medicine is concerned not only with reparing injury it is also concerned with avoiding injury. Warm-up and cool down exercises are prescribed for various sports; fitness tests are administered; proper eccuipment, clothes, and gear are reccommended. Why don't you check out a book on the subject from your local library?

Apostrophes and Quotation Marks

APOSTROPHES

The apostrophe is used to show possession, to indicate omitted letters, and to form certain plurals, such as those of numbers.

Using Apostrophes to Show Possession

Use the apostrophe to form the possessive of singular and plural nouns.

To form the possessive of a singular noun, add an apostrophe and an *-s* even if the noun ends in *-s*.

Jason's	family's	parrot's
Bess's	princess's	Charles's

Punctuation Note The possessive of a name having more than one syllable and an unaccented ending pronounced *-eez* is formed by adding just an apostrophe: *Achilles', Euripides', Ramses', Xerxes'.* The possessive of *Jesus* and *Moses* is formed the same way: *Jesus', Moses'.*

To form the possessive of a plural noun that ends in *-s*, add an apostrophe only.

Joneses'	physicists'	mosquitoes'

To form the possessive of a plural noun that does not end in *-s*, add both an apostrophe and *-s*.

women's	alumni's	geese's

Mrs. Robert S. Cassatt, the Artist's Mother (Katherine Kelso Johnston Cassatt), by Mary Cassatt, c.1889

Only the last part of a compound noun shows possession. Add only an apostrophe or an apostrophe and -s, depending on the form of the word.

> sister-in-law's gifts (singular)
> sisters-in-laws' gifts (plural)

For nouns such as *Secretary of Transportation* and *Chairman of the Board,* add an apostrophe and an -s to the last word.

> the *Secretary of Transportation's* office
> the *Chairman of the Board's* decision

To avoid this awkward construction, it is often better to use a prepositional phrase instead.

> the office of the Secretary of Transportation

In a case of joint ownership, only the last name mentioned takes the possessive form.

> Caitlin and her sisters' Halloween party
> Rodgers and Hammerstein's musicals

The rule also applies to the names of organizations and firms that show joint ownership.

> Johnson and Johnson's products
> Hartwick and Forbes's annual report

If possession is not joint, each name takes the possessive form.

> Aaron's and Sonia's rooms
> Kimiko's, Rosa's, and Wanda's parents

If the possessive form is awkward, use a prepositional phrase.

> the parents of Kimiko, Rosa, and Wanda

To form the possessive of an indefinite pronoun, add an apostrophe and an -s.

> someone's   either's   anybody's   one's

To form the possessive of a compound indefinite pronoun, such as *someone else* and *no one else*, add an apostrophe and an -s to the last word.

> someone else's parka
> no one else's skis

Do *not* use an apostrophe with a personal pronoun to show possession.

> theirs   hers   ours   its   yours

Use the possessive form when nouns expressing time or amount are used as possessive adjectives.

> two weeks' vacation   a year's suspended sentence
> a dollar's worth   10 cents' worth

Using Apostrophes to Show Omissions

Use an apostrophe in contractions to show where letters have been omitted.

> wouldn't = would not   Eva's = Eva is

Use an apostrophe to indicate missing letters in dialect, archaic speech, or poetry.

> "*Where'er* you walk cool gales shall fan the glade."
> **Alexander Pope**
> "What did you hear *'bout 'em*?" (dialect)

Use an apostrophe to show the omission of figures.

> a reunion of the class of *'78*

Using Apostrophes to Form Certain Plurals

Use an apostrophe to show the plurals of letters, numerals, signs, and words referred to as words.

> *Disappear* has two *p*'s in it.
> I accidentally used <'s instead of >'s.
> My sister uses too many *like*'s in her conversation.

Note: The last two rules are sometimes considered optional.

Practice Your Skills

A. CONCEPT CHECK

Apostrophes   In the following sentences, correct each error in apostrophe usage. You may need to make spelling adjustments to possessives. If there are no errors, write *Correct*.

1. Its not known where or when the custom of gift-giving began.
2. However, many ancient and contemporary culture's new years celebrations involve the giving of messages and gifts.

Writing Theme
Holiday Traditions

Apostrophes and
Quotation Marks   **821**

Julian New Year
(January 13)
celebrated in
Appenzell, Switzerland

3. In ancient Egypt everyones' observance of the new year included sending a written message.
4. In fact, their's was the custom that later resulted in the introduction of greeting cards.
5. People's fondness for lucky pennies highlighted the Roman's new year's festivities.
6. Each lucky coin displayed the god Janus's two faces.
7. Todays' Italian children receive gifts of money called *strénna.*
8. New years day finds Portugals' young people in the streets singing *janerias,* or old songs, for which they get coins and treats.
9. Boys and girls' participation in water games along with gift-giving is the highlight of *Bassat,* the Hindu fire festival.
10. Ancient Japans' Boys' Festival has become modern Japans' Childrens' Day.
11. *Kodomo-no-hi's* festive kites and gifts remind Japanese children of the qualities of bravery and strength they should develop.
12. A bearer of gifts known worldwide is the subject of Clement Moore's poem that begins: "Twas the night before Christmas."
13. St. Nicholas' Russian equivalent, Grandfather Frost, brings gifts to children after a welcome two week's vacation from school.
14. Until the 1800s, wrapping someone elses' gift was unusual.
15. Thanks to the Victorians influence, wrapping gifts is today a common practice.

B. REVISION SKILL

Using Apostrophes Correctly   For the following sentences, rewrite each word that has an error in apostrophe usage.

1. A line in one of Shakespeares' plays states, "Sweet, sweet, sweet poison for the ages tooth."
2. The playwright's reference to everyones love of sugar sounds a little like the American Dental Associations' warning.
3. Apparently a love of sweets is an Achilles heel that is timeless.
4. Tutankamens and Ramses tombs contained recipes for candy.
5. Greeces' physicians coaxed bitter medicine down their patient's throats by coating the cup with honey.
6. Alexander the Greats' soldiers were fond of a confection called *kand,* perhaps the root of the word *candy.*
7. In the 1670s a choirmaster didnt know his' clever use of candy would lead to a Christmas tradition.
8. To help young singers mind their *p*s and *q*s, the choirmaster gave them candy.
9. It's shape, a shepherds crook, formed the first candy cane.
10. His canes of the 70's were plain; color came decades later.

C. PROOFREADING SKILL

Correcting Errors   Rewrite the following paragraphs, correcting all errors in spelling, capitalization, and punctuation. Pay special attention to the use of the apostrophe.

Just like decorations' in stores, one clear signal of the holiday season is the staging of Charles Dickens's novel *a Christmas Carol*. The play poses a particuler challenge to designers, who need to make the ghosts that lead to Scrooges spiritual awakaning seem supernatural.

At the renowned Guthrie theater in Minneapolis, several original effects meet the plays' design challenges. The Ghost's of Christmas Past costume is strung with Christmas lights on the end's of glass rods; in addition, lights seem to grow out of the actors fingertips while on his head is an illuminated candle hat. Even more striking is the Ghost of Christmas Present's cornucopia, which shoots flames out of its' horn. While the Ghost of Christmas Past and the Ghost of Christmas Present's costumes depend on the use of light. That of the Ghost of Christmas Future is a stark black robe. However, the actor wearing it is perched on stilts eight feet high, and a carved skeletal hand protrudes from the robes sleeve's to point ominously to Scrooge's future.

Quotation marks are used to set off direct quotations, titles, and words used in special ways.

Direct and Indirect Quotations

Use quotation marks to begin and end a direct quotation.

"I don't want to see that movie a third time," said Julia.

Do not use quotation marks to set off an indirect quotation.

Maria said that she didn't want to see the movie a third time.
Eric told us to send the schedule for the home games.

Note that an indirect quotation is the repetition without direct quotation of something said.

Punctuation of Direct Quotations

Enclose the exact words used by a speaker or writer in quotation marks. The first word of the quotation is capitalized.

"We'll be home at about six o'clock," said Heather.
Heather said, "We'll be home about six o'clock."

Note that commas and periods are always placed inside the quotation marks.

Put question marks and exclamation points inside the quotation marks if they are part of the quotation.

"Where did you find that foil wallpaper?" Fabiella asked.
"I had to walk all the way back to school!" Liz complained.

Put question marks and exclamation points outside the quotation marks if they are not part of the quotation.

Didn't you say, "Annie Dillard is an important American writer"?
I couldn't believe her telling me, "I'm sorry, but your grade on the essay is a D–"!

Put semicolons and colons outside quotation marks.

For pasta, Mr. Benigni listed three "criteria of excellence": a firm texture, a spicy sauce, and an abundant amount.
Kelly had just read "The Rime of the Ancient Mariner"; consequently, she knew the story well.

Enclose both parts of a divided quotation in quotation marks. Do not capitalize the first word of the second part unless it begins a new sentence.

"Boston's Old State House, built in the eighteenth century," the guide continued, "now has a subway stop underneath it."

"Boston's Old State House was built in the eighteenth century," the guide continued. "Now it has a subway stop underneath it."

Punctuation Note A person's thoughts are enclosed in quotation marks if they express the exact words of the thoughts.

John thought, "I can't believe I got the job."
Sheri kept saying to herself, "I know I can do it."

In dialogue, a new paragraph indicates a change in speaker.

"Why does your mother bother making bread herself?" asked Martha, starting on a second, warm slice. "It takes forever."

"Letting it rise does take time," replied Allison, "but the bread does that work on its own."

"Oh," said Martha, biting into a third slice. "In that case, I have an idea. Your mother can do the bread making, and I, the generous one, will help out with the bread eating!"

"Hey!" said Allison, "you'll never make the play rehearsal if you don't stop eating and get moving."

"Stardom, here I come," replied Martha.

Use single quotation marks for a quotation within a quotation.

"In Shakespeare's *Henry V*," said Mrs. Saxenian, "Henry rouses his soldiers with a famous speech that begins, 'Once more into the breach, dear friends.' "

"My sister Nora just told me that Dad said, 'Leave the car in the garage,' " replied Ruth. "I guess I can walk to your house."

In quoting passages of more than one paragraph, use a quotation mark at the beginning of each paragraph and at the end of the last paragraph only.

Note You may set off a long quoted passage from the text as an excerpt. For excerpts, double-space the quotation, indent all lines from the left, and do not use quotation marks.

Apostrophes and
Quotation Marks   **825**

If a prose quotation begins in the middle of a sentence, do not capitalize the first word.

When my mother says that "anytime is fine" to come home, she really means I had better be there by dinner.

Practice Your Skills

A. CONCEPT CHECK

Writing Theme
F. Scott Fitzgerald

Quotation Marks   Rewrite each of the following sentences, correcting all errors in punctuation and capitalization. If a sentence contains no errors, write *Correct*.

1. F. Scott Fitzgerald referred to his courtship with Zelda Sayre as "the most important year of my life;" moreover, he patterned many of his heroines after her.
2. When asked to describe herself as a child, Zelda said, I had great confidence in myself.
3. In fact, "she stated that she had never had a single feeling of inferiority."
4. "Zelda", Scott commented "Was a very popular and beautiful young lady . . . full of life and pep".
5. Zelda recalled that Scott wasn't her only suitor that first year.
6. "However", she noted "the competition inspired him".
7. After their marriage Zelda said of their life in New York, "We feel like small children in a bright, unexplored barn"!
8. Regarding the novel so like their courtship, Scott said, "I think the title should be *Gold Hatted Gatsby*. However, I will yield to Zelda. She told me "It should be *The Great Gatsby*."
9. Wasn't it T. S. Eliot who called *The Great Gatsby,* "the first step that American fiction has taken since Henry James?"
10. Hemingway commented, "If he could write a book as fine as *The Great Gatsby,* I was sure he could write an even better one."

B. APPLICATION IN LITERATURE

Quotation Marks In the following passage quotation marks and some paragraph indents have been omitted. Some punctuation has also been omitted. Rewrite the passage, restoring it to its original form.

> At a lull in the entertainment the man looked at me and smiled.
>
> Your face is familiar he said politely. Were'nt you in the Third Division during the war? Why yes, I was in the Ninth Machine-Gun Battalion.
>
> I was in the Seventh Infantry until June nineteen-eighteen. I knew Id seen you somewhere before.
>
> We talked for a moment about some wet, gray little villages in France. . . . It was on the tip of my tongue to ask his name. . . .
>
> This is an unusual party for me. I haven't even seen the host. I live over there—I waved my hand at the invisible hedge in the distance. And this man Gatsby sent over his chauffeur with an invitation.
>
> For a moment he looked at me as if he failed to understand.
>
> I'm Gatsby he said suddenly. What! I exclaimed. Oh, I beg your pardon.
>
> I thought you knew, old sport. Im afraid Im not a very good host.

> **F. Scott Fitzgerald,** *The Great Gatsby*

Setting Off Titles

Use quotation marks to enclose chapter titles, titles of short stories, poems, essays, articles, television episodes, songs, and short musical selections.

Chapter Title	Chapter 28: "Social Changes in the 1920's"
Short Story Title	Shirley Jackson's "The Lottery"
Poem	Edna St. Vincent Millay's "Afternoon on a Hill"
Essay	Lewis Thomas's "On Warts"
Magazine Article	"Your Body's Biological Clock"
Television Episode	"Birds of the Sun Gods" on *Nova*
Song	"You're the Top"

The titles of books, magazines, newspapers, movies, television series, plays, paintings, epic poems, and long musical compositions are underlined in writing and italicized in print.

Setting Off Words Used in Special Ways

Use quotation marks to give special expression to words.

You may use quotation marks to show emphasis or irony or to set off words classified as slang.

> With the "simple directions" for installing the VCR, I did the job in only three hours. (The term *simple directions* is set off in quotation marks to show that the writer is using it ironically.)
>
> If being "cool" means doing everything everybody else does, then I guess I'm just not cool. (The slang term *cool* is set off in quotation marks to show that it is unusual in the vocabulary of the writer.)

Punctuation Note Underline foreign words and words referred to as words. Also, underline letters or figures referred to as such. Use quotation marks, however, to enclose phrases.

> For her recital Kara sang a <u>lieder</u>, a song for solo voice and piano. (*Lieder* is underlined because it is a German word.)
>
> The word <u>perspicacious</u> is probably too difficult for a seventh-grade vocabulary list. (*Perspicacious* is underlined because it is referred to as a word.)
>
> Some words change the final <u>y</u> to <u>i</u> when forming the plural.
>
> Helen asked what the phrase "an Achilles' heel" meant. ("An Achilles' heel" is in quotation marks because it is a phrase.)

Practice Your Skills

A. CONCEPT CHECK

Special Uses for Quotation Marks Rewrite the following sentences, adding quotation marks where necessary. Indicate italics by underlining. If a sentence contains no error, write *Correct*.

1. For years, filmmakers have adapted novels such as Gone with the Wind and A Tale of Two Cities for the movie screen.
2. In the case of Mary Poppins, the popularity of the film added the the word supercalifragilisticexpialidocious to our vocabulary.
3. Plays such as The Glass Menagerie and Arsenic and Old Lace also became successful films.
4. The Greatest Gift, a short story, formed the basis for the movie It's a Wonderful Life so often shown on holidays.
5. Marlon Brando's stardom might be attributed to a nonfiction magazine article Crime on the Waterfront by Malcolm Johnson.

Writing
— **TIP** —

Used sparingly, slang can add realism to dialogue. Remember, however, that slang is inappropriate for formal writing.

Writing Theme
Filmmaking

6. Several movies have been made from the television series Star Trek; however, none of them included scenes from the popular episode The Trouble with Tribbles.
7. Occasionally, a movie such as The Odd Couple forms the basis for a television series.
8. The movie Alice's Restaurant took its plot from the lyrics of the song The Alice's Restaurant Massacre.
9. In some cases, movie phrases such as the way we were function both as a film title and a hit song.
10. Few people can hear the song As Time Goes By and not think of the movie Casablanca.

Vivien Leigh and Clark Gable in the epic movie *Gone with the Wind*

James Stewart and Donna Reed starring in the movie *It's a Wonderful Life*, 1946

B. REVISION SKILL

Using Quotation Marks Correctly Rewrite the paragraph below, correcting all errors, including errors in the use of quotation marks.

(1) Some time ago, an article in People magazine entitled Laurence Olivier Dies: The Rest Is Silence called Olivier the premier actor of the twentieth century.' (2) It pointed out that the word star was not good enough to describe him. (3) Olivier's own book, Confessions of an Actor, chronicles his life as actor, director, husband, and father. (4) For example, in Chapter 5, New Wife, New World, he tells how he left Britain for Hollywood. (5) He shares the awkward experience of having been fired by Greta Garbo from a film based on the short story Queen Christina. (6) Later success in the movie Wuthering Heights won him an Oscar. (7) Soon fan magazines were using the word "megastar" to describe him. (8) Chapter 13, The National Theater Launched, covers the founding of a company with worldwide acclaim. (9) His sixty-year career encompassed both great roles in "Hamlet" and "Henry V" and lesser parts in the films Marathon Man and The Jazz Singer. (10) The director Peter Hall said, He was perhaps the greatest man of the theater ever.

Apostrophes and Quotation Marks **829**

A. Rewrite the following sentences, adding necessary punctuation. Correct any errors in the use of apostrophes and quotation marks.

1. Webster's New World Dictionary defines the word *aquarist* as 'a person who keeps an aquarium as a hobby.'
2. Any aquarist who hasnt read Werner Weiss' book Aquarium Keeping: Easy as ABC should do so.
3. The chapter on diseases, When Fish Have the Measles, is especially interesting.
4. Weiss warns, Under no circumstances should an aquarium be at or parallel to the window.
5. He notes, The Asians' and American's common characteristics allow these fish to live together in what I call a *community tank*.

B. Rewrite the following paragraphs, correcting any errors in punctuation. Be sure to add apostrophes, quotation marks, capitalization, and paragraphing where needed.

Ecology research team members test the frigid waters of the Arctic.

(1) It wasn't by chance that I found myself on the shore of Lake Wapenaag on a bitter winters day. (2) I had read a newspaper article titled Diving for Pleasure. (3) The article described the procedure's for cutting through the ice and diving into freezing lake water. (4) Now here I was on the frozen shore, watching people in group's of twos and threes preparing for their dives. (5) I spoke to one man who introduced himself as Ed Collins. (6) Why do you do this I asked Ed. (7) For the sheer beauty of it he replied. (8) I'm a photographer, and the visibility is much better under the ice in the clear water of winter. (9) "But I asked doesn't it take a lot of equipment that may not be your's"? (10) "Yes, my groups' equipment includes underwater gear, tents, harnesses, a chainsaw, and emergency gear—all of which is my brother's-in-law.

(11) "Everythings done to ensure the divers' safety, I see. (12) Yes, we always dive in pairs, and our lines are not longer than 100 feet, Ed replied. (13) Do people dive for reasons other than just for the beauty of it, I asked. (14) "Yes. Today my buddys looking for a snowmobile that went down yesterday. (15) "Will he get paid for retrieving it?

(16) "Oh yes, but hed be out here anyway. (17) Its the thrill of being down there, you know. (18) Are you goin to try"? Ed asked.

(19) "Not today," I said as I smiled weakly. (20) "or tomorrow either, I whispered to myself.

A. Apostrophes and Quotation Marks   Rewrite the following sentences, correcting any errors, including errors in the use of apostrophes and quotation marks.

1. Why would someone, as the commentary on the book jacket of The Great Imposter states, 'spend his life pretending to be someone he isnt?'
2. One person, Sarah Wilson, did so to escape poverty and a chambermaids' social status.
3. In the 1700s she posed as the Queen's of England sister.
4. Ferdinand Demara, Jr., took a lieutenant's-of-the-guard post at a Texas prison and posed as a doctor in the Korean War.
5. He treated many soldiers minor ailments but referred the more serious problems to other military doctor's, asking, what do you think of this case?
6. He also took on a Trappist monks' role in a monastery.
7. When asked what his motivation was, he replied, "being an imposter is a hard habit to break"!
8. Chapter 5, The Counterfeit Count, tells the amusing tale of Victor Lustig.
9. Lustig *relieved* Chicagos' Al Capone of fifty thousand dollars.
10. Feigning a French counts title, he "sold" the Eiffel Tower.

Writing Theme
Imposters and
Deception

B. Using Apostrophes and Quotation Marks   Rewrite the following sentences, adding necessary punctuation and correcting any punctuation and capitalization errors.

1. Uncase the varlet! demanded Prince Prospero.
2. Poes character from the short story The Masque of the Red Death summarizes some peoples uneasiness about masks.
3. Yet, who hasnt thought, "I'd like to wear a disguise or take on someone elses personality?"
4. A psychologist might use the term "alter ego", the opposite side of someone's personality, in explaining a masks appeal.
5. Historian's record many societies ceremonial use of masks.
6. Supposedly, wearing a war mask enhanced a warriors courage.
7. The Sinhalese language uses the word rakasa, meaning disease devil masks.
8. The wearer would say, Disease, flee this ones body.
9. The term masque refers to dramatic entertainment of the Renaissance.
10. A theater-in-the-rounds placement of the audience allowed actors to wear masks on their front's and back's simultaneously.
11. In Elizabethan times, Ben Jonson and Indigo Jones collaboration produced masked dramas popular with royalty.

Apostrophes and
Quotation Marks   **831**

12. However, Jonson was a "quarrelsome and overbearing person;" thus, the collaboration ended in argument.
13. Sometimes, the construction of masks took months worth of work.
14. Since the 1800s masks have been collected as art.
15. "Indeed, interest in masks", said one expert, "Is tremendous"!

C. Application in Literature Apostrophes and quotation marks have been omitted from the following passage. Rewrite it, correcting punctuation. Add paragraphing where needed.

Often I just didnt go to something Id been invited to, more than once without bothering to RSVP. And when I did go, I refused to take it seriously. At one of the earliest parties I attended, when I was about thirteen, I inked sideburns' on my cheeks, imagining I looked like the hero of the moment, Elvis Presley. When Jacey saw me, he tried to get my mother not to let me go unless I washed my face.

Itll look worse if I wash it, I said maliciously. Its India ink. Itll turn gray. Itll look like dirt.

My mother had been reading when we came to ask her to adjudicate. . . . John, what I don't understand my mother said to Jacey—she was the only one who called him by his real name—is why it should bother you if Doug wants to wear sideburns. *Mother,* Jacey said. He was forever explaining life to her, and as far as he was concerned, she never got it.

This isnt a costume party. No one else is going to be *pretending* to be someone else. Hes supposed to just come in a jacket and tie and dance. And he isnt even wearing a tie. And that bothers you? she asked in her high-pitched voice. Of course, he said. She thought for a moment. Is it that your ashamed of him? This was hard for Jacey to answer. He knew by my mothers tone that he ought to be above such pettiness. Finally he said, Its *not* that Im ashamed. Im just trying to protect him. Hes going to be sorry. . . . He doesnt understand the *implications*.

Sue Miller, "The Lover of Women"

On the Lightside

HOW TO TALK TO YOUR MOTHER

Notice how the skillful use of punctuation and capitalization adds style and humor to dialogue between parent and teen.

You have just come home:

"Hi, Mom, did anyone call?"

"You did get one call, but I forgot to ask who it was."

"Male or female?"

"Male."

"And you didn't ask! Thanks, Mom, thanks a lot, I really appreciate it. For all I know it was the most important phone call of my life!"

You are upset about something that happened at school. Furthermore, you can't find the can opener. Your mother walks into the kitchen:

"What's wrong?"

"Nothing!" Slam the drawer closed.

"What do you mean, 'nothing'? Then why are you slamming drawers?"

"I am not slamming drawers!" Slam another.

"Sweetheart, what's the matter?"

"Will you get off my back! Just lay off, leave me alone, all right? Nothing is wrong! NOTHING IS WRONG! . . ."

Burst into tears, go to your room, slam the door, and turn on the stereo.

Your mother went out for dinner:

"Hi, Mom, how was the food?"

"Gross."

"Oh Mom, stop trying to act cool."

"Did you clean up your room?"

"Not yet—I will. . . ."

"Did you clean up your room?"

"Give me a break already, I said I'll clean it." . . .

"Did you clean up your room?"

"Cripes, can't you leave me alone for a change? I said I'll do it. I'll do it." . . .

"Did you clean up your room?"

"What?"

"Did you clean up your room?"

"What?"

"DID YOU CLEAN UP YOUR ROOM?"

"You don't have to yell. I'm not deaf. . . . Why don't you calm down. You know, Mom, you always tell me not to shout and then you practically burst a blood vessel. How can I clean up my room with you breathing down my neck? . . ."

"Did you clean up your room?"

"Almost."

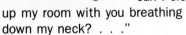

Delia Ephron

Skills

Directions One or more of the underlined sections in the following sentences may contain errors of grammar, usage, punctuation, spelling, or capitalization. Write the letter of each incorrect section; then rewrite the item correctly. If there is no error in an item, write *E*.

Example Since 1892, more than a dozen women have run
          A
for vice-president of the United States; however, in 1984 Geraldine
     B   **C**
Ferraro became the first from a major political party. No error
                                         D   **E**

Answer B—Vice-President

---

1. On October 3, 1966, Arthur Thompson of Victoria, british columbia, shot a round of
         A   **B**
   golf with a score lower than his age, which was ninety-seven at that time. No error
    C   **D**   **E**

2. The worlds record for the 100-yard dash is about nine seconds, however, tap dancer
       A   **B**   **C**
   Bill Robinson covered the distance in half again as much time, running backward.
    D
   No error
    E

3. The statue of liberty in New York City was entirely paid for by donations from
       A   **B**   **C**
   french citizens. No error
     D   **E**

4. In the early part of this century, Mrs. Frederica Cook left a will, that filled four
            A   **B**   **C**
   volumes and contained 95,940 words. No error
    D   **E**

5. Antonio Bin of Paris has painted the "Mona Lisa" at least three hundred times and each
    A   **B**   **C**
   copy sells for about $1,700. No error
           D   **E**

6. When professor Colin MacLaurin joined the faculty of Edinburgh University at the age
       A   **B**
   of twenty-seven, it surprised no one; he had become a full professor at nineteen and was
    C   **D**
   recommended for the job at Edinburgh by Sir Isaac Newton. No error
                                               E

7. "<u>Talking is</u> a hydrant in the yard and writing is a faucet upstairs in the <u>house.</u>" said
   A   B
   Robert Frost in *The Figure a Poem Makes.* "<u>Opening</u> the first takes all the pressure off
   C   D
   the second." <u>No error</u>
   E

8. <u>H.G.</u> <u>Wells the English novelist and historian</u> wrote in <u>1920;</u> "Human history becomes
   A   B   C
   more and more a race between education and <u>catastrophe.</u>" <u>No error</u>
   D   E

9. <u>Mrs. Marva Drew</u> <u>spent</u> six years typing the <u>numbers 1 to 1,000</u> in words on a manual
   A   B   C
   typewriter <u>because "she loves to type."</u> <u>No error</u>
   D   E

10. The <u>competative</u> events in the <u>Lumberjack World Championships</u> <u>include:</u> power saw,
    A   B   C
    one-man bucking, standing block chop, <u>underhand block chop,</u> and two-man bucking.
    D
    <u>No error</u>
    E

11. The hardest <u>substance that</u> <u>occurs</u> in nature <u>is of course</u> the <u>diamond which</u> is pure
    A   B   C   D
    carbon. <u>No error</u>
    E

12. The oldest major formal religion in the world is <u>hinduism,</u> which was brought to <u>India</u>
    A   B
    in an early form by the <u>Aryans</u> in about <u>1500 BC.</u> <u>No error</u>
    C   D   E

13. The flounder, halibut, and <u>sole</u> are all <u>flatfish—a kind</u> of <u>fish that</u> has both eyes on
    A   B   C
    the same side of <u>its head.</u> <u>No error</u>
    D   E

14. An orange tree known as the <u>"Constable Tree"</u> was taken to <u>europe</u> in <u>1421</u> and
    A   B   C
    produced its last fruit 473 years <u>later!</u> <u>No error</u>
    D   E

15. <u>In 1927</u> Charles Lindbergh <u>became</u> the eighty-first person to fly across the <u>atlantic</u>
    A   B   C
    <u>ocean; however,</u> he was the first to do it alone. <u>No error</u>
    D   E

16. "The <u>worst</u> tragedy for a <u>poet,</u>" said Jean Cocteau, "<u>is</u> to be admired through being
    A   B   C
    <u>misunderstood."</u> <u>No error</u>
    D   E

17. With a wingspan of only three <u>inches Helena's</u> hummingbird <u>weighs</u> only one-eighteenth
       _A   _B
    of an <u>ounce, which</u> is less than some <u>species</u> of moth weigh. <u>No error</u>
          _C   _D   _E

18. Marie and Pierre Curie won the <u>Nobel Prize</u> in physics in <u>1903 and</u> Marie alone won the
                                   _A   _B
    prize in chemistry in <u>1911,</u> making her one of three people <u>to win the prize twice.</u>
                          _C   _D
    <u>No error</u>
    _E

19. The <u>earliest</u> <u>amphitheaters that were used for the presentation of plays</u> date from the
        _A   _B
    <u>fifth century</u> <u>B.C.</u> <u>No error</u>
    _C   _D _E

20. Most of <u>us at some time</u> have <u>wondered how</u> long it is possible for a human being to
            _A   _B
    <u>live?</u> Delina Filkins of <u>Herkimer County, New York,</u> lived for almost 114 years. <u>No error</u>
    _C   _D   _E

21. To keep up with a <u>spine-tailed swift one</u> would need a <u>fast</u> car and a race <u>track, this</u> bird
                      _A   _B   _C
    <u>has been clocked</u> at 106.25 miles per hour. <u>No error</u>
    _D   _E

22. The <u>destrutcion</u> caused by the <u>Alaskan</u> earthquake of <u>64</u> was compounded by
        _A   _B   _C
    <u>below-freezing</u> temperatures and a snowstorm. <u>No error</u>
    _D   _E

23. <u>It's</u> true that dervishes are <u>dancers; however,</u> their prolonged dances are religious
    _A   _B
    <u>exercises through</u> which <u>they</u> seek a mystical experience. <u>No error</u>
    _C   _D   _E

24. People from a wide variety of backgrounds and occupations <u>have</u> served as intelligence
                                                              _A
    <u>agents. They include</u> the <u>following;</u> playwright Aphra Behn, novelist Daniel Defoe,
    _B   _C
    baseball player <u>Moe Berg,</u> and abolitionist Harriet Tubman. <u>No error</u>
                    _D   _E

25. Jonas <u>Salk, whose</u> <u>developement of a polio</u> vaccine saved innumerable <u>lives,</u> was never
          _A   _B   _C
    nominated for the <u>Nobel Prize.</u> <u>No error</u>
                      _D   _E

Directions   One or more of the underlined sections in the following sentences may contain errors of grammar, usage, punctuation, spelling, or capitalization. Write the letter of each incorrect section; then rewrite the item correctly. If there is no error in an item, write E.

> **Example**   The Solar <u>Systems</u> farthest, <u>strangest,</u> and <u>least-known</u>
> A   B   C
>
> planet was named Pluto because the mythical <u>Pluto's</u> brothers were
> D
>
> Jupiter and Neptune. <u>No error</u>
> E
>
> **Answer**   A—System's

1. <u>One</u> can only imagine <u>how many advances</u> in civil rights <u>might have occurred</u> if Martin
   A   B   C
   Luther King <u>would have escaped</u> his assassin's bullet. <u>No error</u>
          D   E

2. It <u>has been estimated</u> that, in the last <u>3,500 years</u> of the <u>worlds'</u> history, there <u>has been</u>
       A   B   C   D
   only 230 peaceful years. <u>No error</u>
          E

3. Franz Liszt was <u>such an energetic</u> piano player that <u>audience's</u> came to expect <u>him</u> playing
         A   B   C
   almost violently at <u>every performance.</u> <u>No error</u>
         D   E

4. Katharine Hepburn <u>has been</u> nominated for more Oscars <u>than any actress</u> in the <u>history</u>
         A   B   C
   of <u>those awards.</u> <u>No error</u>
     D   E

5. <u>Who began</u> as a bit player in *The Caine Mutiny Court-Martial* on <u>Broadway</u> in 1954
     A   B
   and later became one of television's most enduring <u>male stars?</u> A clue is that the
                                            C
   <u>young actor's</u> real name was James Bumgarner. <u>No error</u>
      D   E

6. A <u>person whose</u> job is to smell perfumes <u>must be able</u> to detect <u>no less than</u> 7,500
      A   B   C
   different <u>oders.</u> <u>No error</u>
        D   E

7. It might not be wise to try to cuddle the odd but <u>adorable</u> duck-billed <u>platypus, it</u> has a
   A   **B**
   hollow bone on each <u>foot that</u> shoots poison, like a <u>snake's</u> fang. <u>No error</u>
                        C   **D**   **E**

8. Harvey Bailey and his gang, who had <u>stole</u> two <u>milion</u> dollars in a 1930 bank robbery,
                                       A   **B**
   <u>were arrested</u> as they teed off at a <u>Kansas City</u> golf course. <u>No error</u>
   C   **D**   **E**

9. The common Norway <u>rat which actually originated in China</u> had <u>swam</u> and hitched <u>its</u>
                      A   **B**   **C**
   way to Europe by the <u>1550's and</u> to North America two hundred years later. <u>No error</u>
                        D   **E**

10. <u>It</u> took me fifteen years to discover that I had no talent for <u>writing,"</u> said Robert
    A   **B**
    Benchley, <u>"But</u> I couldn't give it up because by that time I was too <u>famous."</u> <u>No error</u>
              C   **D**   **E**

11. <u>To date,</u> more than four thousand people <u>have claimed</u> to <u>have seen</u> the hypothetical
    A   **B**   **C**
    creature known as the <u>Loch Ness monster.</u> <u>No error</u>
                          D   **E**

12. Each <u>foreign-born</u> man and woman who wants to become a citizen of <u>this here</u> country
         A   **B**
    <u>have</u> to take an oath to support and defend the <u>Constitution</u> and the laws of the United
    C   **D**
    States. <u>No error</u>
            E

13. The <u>Utah-Colorado-Arizona-New Mexico</u> junction of state <u>borders is</u> the only place in
        A   **B**
    the United <u>states where</u> a person can stand in four states <u>at one time!</u> <u>No error</u>
               C   **D**   **E**

14. <u>The word *Canada*</u> is thought to <u>derive</u> from an <u>iroquois Indian</u> word meaning <u>a group</u>
    A   **B**   **C**   **D**
    of nuts. <u>No error</u>
             E

15. On the <u>California Perfume Company's</u> fiftieth anniversary in <u>1936,</u> the <u>firm's</u> name was
           A   **B**   **C**
    changed to Avon because of the founder's admiration for Shakespeare and <u>Stratford-</u>
                                                                            D
    <u>upon-Avon.</u> <u>No error</u>
                    E

16. "When you let proud <u>words go,</u> it is not easy to call them <u>back,"</u> said Carl Sandburg in
                       A   **B**
    the poem <u>The Primer Lesson.</u> <u>"They</u> wear long boots, hard boots." <u>No error</u>
             C   **D**   **E**

17. There <u>is</u> 254 <u>counties</u> in the <u>State of Texas</u> and only three in <u>Delaware.</u> <u>No error</u>
        A   **B**   **C**   **D**   **E**

18. The <u>White House</u> is built of <u>sandstone, but</u> neither the Jefferson and Lincoln
        A   **B**
<u>memorials nor</u> the Washington Monument <u>are;</u> they are built of marble. <u>No error</u>
    C   **D**   **E**

19. After she had <u>spent</u> $720 on driving lessons and had <u>taken</u> the driving test forty
           A   **B**
times Mrs. Miriam Hargrave of <u>Wakefield, Yorkshire, England,</u> finally qualified
  C   **D**
for her license but could no longer afford a car. <u>No error</u>
                                    E

20. Isaac <u>Newton, who was a terrible student early in life,</u> might <u>easily</u> have said to future
                       A   **B**
generations, "Don't let <u>them</u> grades get you down." <u>No error</u>
     C   **D**   **E**

21. "Bugs" <u>Moran</u> must have <u>felt good</u> <u>when, having</u> arrived late for an appointment on
      A   **B**   **C**
<u>February 14, 1929,</u> he missed being shot in the St. Valentine's Day massacre by five
   D
minutes. <u>No error</u>
     E

22. What did <u>gunslinger Doc Holliday</u> have in common with <u>patriot Paul Revere.</u> Revere and
               A   **B**
<u>him</u> <u>were</u> both dentists. <u>No error</u>
 C **D**   **E**

23. Some <u>all-time</u> great song hits have had unlikely composers, including <u>these:</u> "Dixie," by
     A   **B**
Northern songwriter Dan D. <u>Emmett;</u> "The Battle Hymn of the Republic," music by
                  C
Southern composer William <u>Steffe;</u> "How Dry I Am," music by temperance workers
                  D
Edward Rimbault and Philip Dodridge. <u>No error</u>
                             E

24. <u>Some</u> scholars now believe that <u>pericles'</u> "Funeral Oration," Homer's *Odyssey,* and St.
  A   **B**
Paul's Epistle to the Hebrews <u>were</u> all written by women and <u>creditted</u> to men. <u>No error</u>
                  C   **D**   **E**

25. While she was certainly <u>best known</u> for her genius as an <u>actress Sarah</u> Bernhardt
                 A   **B**
also <u>loved:</u> <u>painting, sculpting, and writing.</u> <u>No error</u>
     C   **D**   **E**

AG
ACCESS GUIDE

Sometimes all you need is a starting point to find a writing idea. Read through the ideas on these two pages. Then use your own discovery techniques to narrow and develop a writing topic.

Narrative

an encounter between
  enemies
an experience that helped you
  gain confidence
a time when you faced danger
a misunderstanding between
  friends
a crucial error
a practical joke
an unexpected discovery
an incident with a pet
a mysterious stranger
an unusual dinner party
a nighttime adventure
a time when you were lost

Descriptive

a forest fire
a family reunion
a long, dark night
a summer festival
a scene from a trip
the huge crowd at the rock
  concert
the opening of a sports
  stadium
a park in your town
your favorite room
a stormy sky
a place you visit often
a person you admire
a favorite photograph
a street musician
an unusual painting
jewelry you admire
smells at a street fair
sounds at a beach

Literary

a poem about your
  neighborhood
a story about three friends
a science fiction fantasy
a poem about loneliness
a lost letter
a telephone call at midnight
a poem about time
a long-remembered experience
a dream
a song lyric
a trip you imagine taking
a remembrance of a friend
a holiday story

Informative Exposition

Compare two villains, either
  in history or in literature.
Compare two TV comedy
  shows.
Compare the lifestyles of
  two American Indian
  cultures.
Compare the work
  opportunities of men and
  women in our culture.
Compare a modern building
  with an ancient or classical
  one.
Compare the achievements of
  two U.S. presidents.
How has popular music
  changed in your lifetime?
What caused the rise and fall
  of the Mayan civilization?
Contrast two different
  lifestyles.

What causes rainbows?
Why did the dinosaurs
  become extinct?
How has your school changed
  over time?
How would you change
  political campaigns?
What would you do about
  violence on TV?
How should schools be run?

Persuasive

the decline in SAT scores
  among high school students
Should TV news ever invade
  people's personal lives?
Should athletes be required to
  maintain "C" averages?
an ad for a cause you believe in
controlling the rising costs of
  a college education
a public service ad
What is best about your
  community?
Should the government
  provide health insurance for
  all citizens?
Should day care programs be
  subsidized?
What can be done to improve
  life in big cities?
Should the school year extend
  over twelve months?
warning labels on records
Should driving privileges be
  withheld from dropouts?
banning advertising for
  alcohol and tobacco

The Arts

haiku

effective product designs

Compare/contrast Carson
  McCullers with Maya
  Angelou.

art made with scraps,
  discards, or junk

art therapy

the series paintings of Monet

why children draw

Compare electronic and
  acoustic instruments.

music and political
  movements

the Alvin Ailey dance
  company

The Arts

the plays of Tennessee
  Williams

protest themes in African-
  American folktales

cubism

special effects in modern
  films

the influence of Salvador Dali

the childhood genius of
  Mozart

the pop art movement

the importance of community
  theaters

giants of modern dance

the movie industry

photo journalism

the rise and fall of vaudeville

great Hollywood musicals of
  the 1930's and 1940's

the plays of Harold Pinter

Picasso's public sculpture

Science

why it is important to save
  endangered species

advances in computer
  technology

the limits of artificial
  intelligence

videodisc information
  technology

Do black holes really exist?

how smallpox was eradicated

the effects of rain forest
  depletion

genetic engineering

the effects of DDT on the
  food chain

What is geothermal energy?

Science

the development of the
  Hubble Telescope

medical truths known to the
  ancients

carbon dating

heart transplants

using science to solve crimes

predicting earthquakes

invention of cool electric
  lights

how new types of plants,
  flowers, and trees are bred

learning from dolphins

the story of the steppe bison

a mummy from Ice Age
  Alaska

How does the human
  immune system work?

Why is the Sahara Desert
  growing?

new kinds of fertilizers

Social Science

What is a developing country?

the future of Africa

migrant workers in the
  United States

history and society in the
  works of John Steinbeck

Moslem communities in the
  United States

description of an ancient
  trade route

the geography of the Middle
  East

early feminism

How does stock market
  trading work?

the voyageurs

Social Science

the origins of the factory
  system

early advertising

how the tobacco industry
  began in the United States

the first labor unions

Lindbergh's flight across the
  Atlantic

modern military weapons

the Boston Tea Party

the settlement at Jamestown,
  Virginia, in 1607

the first people of the
  Americas

the Green Revolution

the Reign of Terror

the American working class in
  the 19th century

psychology and nursery
  rhymes

how democracy works

An outline can help you organize your ideas for writing, and it can also be useful for taking notes. By helping you organize information in a concise and logical way, outlines can make both writing and notetaking easier.

A **formal outline** shows the main points of a topic, the order in which they are to be presented, and the relationships among them. Formal outlines are useful when writing formal compositions or speeches and when outlining chapters for study.

There are two types of formal outlines: sentence outlines and topic outlines. In a **sentence outline,** each main topic and subtopic is written in a complete sentence. Below is a portion of a sentence outline.

Beyond the Five Senses

Introduction—Animal sensory systems surpass human senses.
I. Humans are believed to have five senses: sight, hearing, touch, taste, and smell.
  A. Aristotle, a Greek philosopher, first categorized the senses.
  B. Modern physics and physiology reclassified the senses.
II. Photoreceptors are those sense organs in living organisms that react to light.
  A. The human eye is a photoreceptor.
  B. Animal photoreception can be superior to that of humans.
    1. Insects have specialized eyes.
    2. Nocturnal animals can see in the dark.
    3. Some animals see the world in false colors—that is, in colors that are different from those perceived by humans.

A topic outline is useful for the quick and efficient organization of ideas. The topic outline on the following page uses phrases instead of sentences.

The Development of Rocketry

Introduction — major developments in rocketry
I. Early history of rocketry
  A. Invention by Chinese in thirteenth century
  B. Development of early military rockets
    1. Congreve's explosive-carrying rocket
    2. Hale's finned rocket and the Mexican-American War
II. Development of modern rocketry
  A. Tsiolkovsky's theory of rocket power
  B. Goddard's invention of liquid-fueled rocket

Follow these guidelines for topic and sentence outlines.

1. Center the title at the top of the page. Below the title, write an introductory statement, a version of your thesis. Your outline may end with a concluding restatement of the main point.
2. Use standard outline form. The following is a sample arrangement of numerals and letters in outline form.

I. (Main point)
  A. (First subpoint)
  B. (Second subpoint)
    1.
    2.
      a.
      b.
        (1)
        (2)   } (Details and subdetails)
          (a)
          (b)

3. Indent subheadings below the first letter of the first word in the preceding heading.
4. Either use two or more subheadings or points under a heading or subheading, or use none at all.
5. In a topic outline, keep all items of the same rank parallel. (For instance, if A is a noun, then B and C should also be nouns.) Subtopics need not be parallel with main topics.
6. Begin each item with a capital letter. Do not use end punctuation in a topic outline.

A word processor can help you plan and write research papers and other long pieces efficiently. Here are some techniques to consider.

Goal	Technique	Comment
Brainstorm ideas for a research paper.	Create a file for each of the major sections of your topic. Then write down all the details and questions you can think of for each section.	Look for patterns in your ideas. Reorganize, reword, and delete ideas until a writing plan begins to emerge.
Organize and manage your work on long papers.	Keep different sections of the paper in different files. Finish each section as a whole. As you finish sections, print them out and plan transitions.	Keeping sections separate may help you concentrate better on what you want to achieve. In your draft, you might preface each section with a sentence beginning, "In this section, I will . . ."
Make notes to yourself as you write.	If you have a question or idea as you are writing, type a note to yourself in all capital letters wherever you are in your paper.	During revision you can insert new text to expand on a note and then delete the note.
Add, replace, or reorder text.	Use the insert, delete, replace, move, cut, and paste commands.	A word processor encourages revision and experimentation because changes are simple and easy to make.

Goal	Technique	Comment
Experiment with different ways of expressing ideas.	Write alternatives separated by slashes (/). At a later stage, use the search command to find the slashes— places where you will make choices.	As you write, include several alternatives but don't evaluate them. Later, delete or move the words or versions you don't wish to use.
Check your spelling.	Activate the "spelling" command if your program has one. In addition, always proofread carefully.	The program will highlight misspellings, many typing errors, and most proper nouns. Proofread for errors the program cannot catch, such as incorrect words.
Make your paper readable.	Set margins and line spacing. Insert headings and subheadings. Print a sample page and change the settings if necessary. Insert page breaks.	Your pages are most readable when page breaks come at natural divisions. Headings and subheadings divide the text into readable sections.
Create visually appealing pages.	Use boldface type and underlining to emphasize headings and subheadings. Use special fonts, to make an interesting title page.	Most word processors offer features such as type styles and sizes and centered text, to help set up an attractive page.
Keep a notebook of general writing ideas.	Create a file called "notebook." Record ideas, quotes, jokes, incidents— anything that may later serve as a writing topic.	An electronic notebook provides you with a way to find and retrieve ideas quickly and expand on them freely.

The following response techniques can help you give and receive useful responses as you share your writing with others. These techniques can also help you as the writer to be in charge of the feedback process and to find out what kinds of responses are most useful to you.

How to Use	When to Use
Sharing	
Read your words out loud to a peer. Your purpose is simply to share and to hear how your words sound. Your listeners may ask you to slow down or to read your piece again, but they offer no feedback or criticism of any kind.	Do this when you are just exploring and you don't want criticism. Reading to a peer is also useful when your writing is finished and you want to celebrate by sharing it with another person.
Saying Back or Restating	
Ask readers, "What do you hear me saying?" As readers say back what they hear, they are inviting you to figure out better what you really want to say.	Use this type of feedback when you are still exploring and when you want to find ways to change and develop your ideas.
Pointing	
Ask readers to tell you what they like best in your writing. Tell them to pick specific parts of the writing and to avoid simply saying, "I liked it."	Use this technique when you want to know what is getting through to readers or when you want some encouragement and support.

How to Use	When to Use
Summarizing	
Ask readers to tell you what they hear as the main meaning or message in your writing. Make clear that you don't want evaluation of the writing at this time.	Use this technique when you want to know what is getting through to readers.
Responding to Specific Features	
Ask for feedback on specific features of the writing such as the organization, or the persuasive power, or the spelling and punctuation. Ask readers to respond to specific questions, such as, "Are the ideas supported with enough examples?" "Did I persuade you?" "Is the organization clear enough so you could follow the ideas easily?"	Use when you want a quick overview of the strengths and weaknesses of your piece.
Replying	
Discuss the ideas in your writing with your readers. Ask readers to give you their ideas on the topic. Be sure to talk with your peer readers about *what* you have said, not *how* you have said it.	Use this strategy when you want to make your writing richer by using new ideas.
Playing Movies of the Reader's Mind	
Invite readers to tell you what happens inside their heads as they read your writing. Interrupt the reading and ask readers to tell you what they are thinking at the moment of interruption.	This technique is useful at any stage of the writing. Because it can lead to blunt criticism, use this peer response method only when you have a relationship of trust and support with your reader.

Adapted from *Sharing and Responding* by Peter Elbow and Pat Belanoff.

accept, except *Accept* means "to agree to or willingly receive something." *Except* usually means "not including."

> The Parks Department is *accepting* applications for summer jobs.
> No one *except* Cheryl understood the algebra lesson.

adapt, adopt *Adapt* means "to make apt or suitable; to adjust." *Adopt* means "to opt or choose as one's own; to accept."

> Mike, who had been playing forward, *adapted* well to playing guard.
> The artist *adopted* Navaho designs for use in her paintings.

advice, advise *Advice* is a noun; *advise* is a verb. You *advise* someone. What you give that person is *advice*.

affect, effect *Affect* means "to move or influence" or "to wear or to pretend to have." *Effect* as a verb means "to bring about." As a noun, *effect* means "the result of an action."

> That group's music doesn't *affect* me very much.
> Michelle *affected* indifference to the news that her story had been accepted by the literary magazine.
> We are trying to *effect* an increase in the size of the school paper.
> Diving into the cold lake had an invigorating *effect*.

all ready, already *All ready* means "completely prepared" or "all are ready." *Already* means "by the given time" or "even now."

> Are you *all ready* for the holidays?
> The Senate has *already* approved a compromise.

all right *All right* is the correct spelling. *Alright* is nonstandard English and should not be used.

all together, altogether The phrase *all together* means that the parts of the group referred to should be taken together or thought of as a whole. *Altogether* is an adverb that means "entirely" or "on the whole."

> *All together,* students have made up nine computer databases in science and geography.
> What the students discovered was *altogether* exciting.

a lot   is informal and should not be used in formal writing. *Alot* is always incorrect.

among, between   are prepositions. *Between* refers to two people or things. The object of *between* is never singular. *Among* refers to a group of three or more.

> After World War II, Germany was partitioned *among* four
> countries.
> There was a wall *between* East Berlin and West Berlin.

amount, number   *Amount* is used to indicate a quantity that is measured, not counted. *Number* refers to things that can be counted, including people.

> No *amount* of coaxing could convince her to join us.
> The *number* of people at our party was amazing.

angry at, with   A person may be angry *at* a thing or *with* a person.

> Josephine is angry *at* the schedule change.
> Mr. Lewis is angry *with* the people on the committee.

anywhere, nowhere, somewhere, and anyway   are correct. *Anywheres, nowheres, somewheres,* and *anyways* are incorrect.

> *Nowhere* does the author say anything about chess.

being   should not be used with *as* or *that* to form one of the awkward phrases "being as" or "being that." Use *since* or *because.*

> *Because* I am the leader, I will decide.

beside, besides   *Beside* means "at the side of." *Besides* means "in addition to."

> My best friend stood *beside* me at tryouts.
> *Besides* skill, the judges also looked for enthusiasm.

borrow, lend   *Borrow* means "to receive something on loan." *Lend* means "to give out temporarily" and is often used with an indirect object.

> He *borrowed* money to start a business.
> I'm not in the business of *lending* money.

bring, take   *Bring* refers to movement toward or with. *Take* refers to movement away from.

> Please *take* this hammer and give it to Janet.
> When you come, *bring* your guitar.

can, may *Can* means "to be able or to have the power to do something." *May* means "to have permission to do something" or "possibly will."

> You *may* not turn in your paper without revising it first.
> The apples *may* be ready for picking this week.
> She *can* find any word in the dictionary almost instantly.

continual, continuous *Continual* means "occurring repeatedly or at intervals over a long period." *Continuous* means "extending without interruption in space or time."

> The faulty alarm system *continually* caused problems.
> The din from the construction was *continuous,* night and day.

differ from, differ with One thing or person *differs from* another in characteristics. A person *differs with* another when the two disagree.

> Dad's method of fishing *differs from* Uncle Pete's.
> Cassandra *differs with* me about life in the city.

different from, different than In most situations *different from* is better usage than *different than.* In some situations *than* must be used to avoid awkwardness.

> Your translation of *The Miser* is *different from* mine.
> My school looks *different than* it did when I was a student.

disinterested, uninterested *Disinterested* means "neutral; unbiased by personal advantage." *Uninterested* means "having no interest."

> A good judge is fair and *disinterested.*
> Her friend was *uninterested* in attending the soccer games.

emigrate, immigrate To *emigrate* is to leave one's homeland. To *immigrate* is to enter a country in order to settle there.

> Thousands of people *emigrated* from Eastern Europe.
> My family *immigrated* to the United States from Jamaica.

farther, further *Farther* means "more distant." *Further* means "additional."

> *Farther* down the river are wild rapids.
> *Further* research may reveal a cure for cancer.

fewer, less *Fewer* refers to numbers of things that can be counted. *Less* refers to amount or quantity.

> We got *less* money because we had taken *fewer* cans to recycle.

hanged, hung   *Hanged* means "executed by hanging." *Hung* is the correct past tense and past participle form to apply to a thing.

> Nathan Hale was *hanged* as a spy.
> A frame enclosing a medal *hung* on the wall.

imply, infer   *Imply* means "to suggest something in an indirect way." *Infer* means "to come to a conclusion based on something that has been read or heard."

> The editor *implied* that he supported the teenagers.
> We can *infer* that trading enabled early people to eat a variety of different foods.

in, into   *In* means "inside something." *Into* tells of motion from the outside to the inside of something.

> My data disk is *in* the disk drive and nothing is happening!
> Try putting the program disk *into* the disk drive.

is where, is when   in definitions is nonstandard unless the definition refers to a time or place, as in the following.

> A river's source *is where* the river begins.
> July 14, 1789 *was when* the Bastille, a prison in Paris, France, was stormed and destroyed by revolutionaries.
> A slalom *is* a ski race over a zigzag course. (not "A slalom is where you ski . . . ")

it's, they're, who's, and you're   all are contractions, not possessives. The possessive forms are *its, their, whose,* and *your.*

> *They're* waiting for us in the terminal.
> *Your* spiral notebook was in our car.

kind of, sort of   Neither of these two expressions should be followed by the word *a.*

> What *kind of* pen is this?
> Mrs. Davis brought back from Algeria a *sort of* lute called an *ud.*

lay, lie   *Lay* is a transitive verb that means "to place." *Lay* is also the past tense of lie. *Lie* is an intransitive verb that means "to rest in a flat position" or "to be in a certain place."

> We could *lay* our blanket down here.
> Denver *lies* at the western edge of the Great Plains.

learn, teach *Learn* means to gain knowledge or acquire a skill. *Teach* means "to instruct."

> Sandy wants to *learn* Russian.
> After school she *teaches* small children to swim.
> After the counselors *learn* how to play the game, they will *teach* it to the campers.

leave, let *Leave* means "to go away from." Leave can be transitive or intransitive, but it is never used in a verb phrase. *Let* is usually used with another verb. It means "to allow to."

> We *leave* our garbage in cans in the alley.
> Shouldn't we *leave* now?
> Literature *lets* us see many aspects of life in other times and other places.

like, as, as if *Like* as a conjunction before a clause is incorrect. Use *as* or *as if.*

> I feel *as* you do about those electronic answering machines that are so popular today.
> Mr. Frederiksen answered my question *as if* he had read my mind.

majority means more than half of a group of things or people that can be counted. It is incorrect to use *majority* in referring to time or distance, as in "The majority of that book was useless."

> *Most* of the route goes along a steep mountainside.
> The *majority* of the workers voted for the contract.

most, almost *Most* can be a noun, an adjective, or an adverb, but it should never be used in place of *almost,* an adverb that means "nearly."

> *Most* of the river is navigable.   *Most* people want peace.
> *Most* often we walk there.   We *almost* always take the bus.

of is incorrectly used in a phrase such as *could of.* Examples of correct wordings are *could have, should have,* and *must have. Of* should not follow the verb *had* or the proposition *off,* as in "Take your coat *off of* the hanger."

> You *must have* left the other clothes in the washer.
> If I *had* remembered my book, I *could have* finished it on the train.
> I thought I would take these onions *off* my sandwich.

only The placement of this word can change, and sometimes confuse, the meaning of a sentence. For clarity, it should be positioned before the word(s) it qualifies. Notice the difference in meaning:

> Ten people are invited *only* to the ceremony.
> *Only* ten people are invited to the ceremony.

percent, percentage *Percent* is correct only if it is preceded by a number. Otherwise, use *percentage*.

> Only fifty *percent* of those registered voted.
> A *percentage* of everyone's income is paid to the government.

raise, rise *Raise* is a transitive verb that means "to lift" or "to make something go up." It takes a direct object. *Rise* is an intransitive verb that means "to go upward." It does not take a direct object.

> I tried to *raise* the curtain, but the cord wouldn't budge!
> In winter the sun doesn't *rise* until after seven o'clock.

real, really *Real* is an adjective meaning "actual; true." *Really* is an adverb meaning "in reality; in fact."

> *Real* artistry comes from patience and hard work.
> That store doesn't *really* offer much of a selection.

seldom should not be followed by *ever,* as in "Gina seldom ever goes surfing anymore." *Seldom, rarely, very seldom,* and *hardly ever* all are correct.

> We *seldom* notice the sound of the train.

their, they're, there *Their* is a possessive pronoun meaning "belonging to them." *They're* is a contraction for "they are." *There,* like *here,* refers to a place.

> *They're* painting *their* models over *there.*

unique *Unique* means "one of a kind." Therefore, it is illogical to qualify the word, as in "somewhat unique." Other absolute words that do not take comparatives or superlatives are *equal, fatal, final, absolute.*

> Vernon has a *unique* way of telling a story.

way refers to distance; *ways* is nonstandard and should not be used in writing.

> Our hotel was a long *way* from the beach.

IMPROVING YOUR SPELLING

Good spelling is important in all writing from personal messages and letters to school tests and essays. To improve your spelling review the following rules.

The Final Silent *e*

When a suffix beginning with a vowel is added to a word ending in a silent *e*, the *e* is usually dropped.

> approve + al = approval   desire + able = desirable
> write + er = writer   pore + ous = porous

When the final silent *e* is preceded by *c* or *g*, the *e* is usually retained before a suffix beginning with *a* or *o*.

> outrage + ous = outrageous
> change + able = changeable

When a suffix beginning with a consonant is added to a word ending in a silent *e*, the *e* is usually retained.

> blame + less = blameless   lone + ly = lonely

The following words are exceptions: *truly, argument, judgment, wholly, awful*.

Words Ending in *y*

When a suffix is added to a word ending in *y* preceded by a consonant, the *y* is usually changed to *i*.

Two exceptions are: (1) When *-ing* is added, the *y* does not change. (2) Some one-syllable words do not change the *y: dryness, shyness*.

> funny + er = funnier   luxury + ous = luxurious
> party + es = parties   fuzzy + ness = fuzziness

When a suffix is added to a word ending in *y* preceded by a vowel, the *y* usually does not change.

> pay + able = payable   play + ful = playful

Exceptions: day + ly = daily, gay + ly = gaily

The Suffixes *-ness* and *-ly*

When the suffix *-ly* is added to a word ending in *l*, both *l*'s are retained. When *-ness* is added to a word ending in *n*, both *n*'s are retained.

occasional + ly = occasionally
natural + ly = naturally
stubborn + ness = stubbornness
mean + ness = meanness

The Addition of Prefixes

When a prefix is added to a word, the spelling of the word remains the same.

dis + satisfied = dissatisfied
il + legible = illegible
im + movable = immovable
re + commend = recommend
mis + spell = misspell
trans + plant = transplant
co + author = coauthor

Words with the "Seed" Sound

Only one English word ends in *sede: supersede*
Three words end in *ceed: exceed, proceed, succeed*
All other words ending in the sound of "seed" are spelled *cede: secede, accede, recede, concede, precede*

Words with *ie* and *ei*

When the sound is long *e* (ē), the word is spelled *ie* except after *c*.

i before *e*
thief   grief   niece
chief   achieve   relieve
yield   brief   piece

except after *c*
ceiling   receive   deceit
conceive   perceive   receipt

Exceptions: *either, neither, financier, weird, species, seize, leisure.* You can remember these words by using a mnemonic device such as the following sentence: *Neither financier seized either weird species of leisure.*

Words of one syllable, ending in one consonant preceded by one vowel, double the final consonant before adding a suffix beginning with a vowel.

1. The words below are the kind to which the rule applies.

plan   sit   shun   red

These words double the final consonant if the suffix begins with a vowel.

plan + ing = planning   shun + ed = shunned
sit + er = sitter   red + est = reddest

2. The rule does not apply to the following one-syllable words because *two* vowels precede the final consonant.

clear   speak   coat   shoot

With these words, the final consonant is *not* doubled before the suffix is added.

clear + est = clearest   coat + ed = coated
speak + er = speaker   shoot + ing = shooting

3. The final consonant is doubled in words of *more* than one-syllable when these conditions are met:

1. When they end in one consonant preceded by one vowel.
2. When they are accented on the last syllable.

oc cur'   com pel'   sub mit'   pa trol'

The same syllable is accented in the new word formed by adding the suffix:

oc cur' + rence = oc cur' rence
com pel' + ing = com pel' ling
sub mit' + ed = sub mit' ted
pa trol' + er = pa trol' ler

If the newly formed word is accented on a different syllable, the final consonant is not doubled.

con fer' + ence = con' fer ence
de fer' + ence = def' er ence
re fer' + ence = ref' er ence
pre fer' + able = pref' er able

A sentence diagram is a drawing that helps you understand how the parts of a sentence are related. In addition, diagraming sharpens your critical thinking skills by requiring you to analyze sentences, classify their parts, and determine relationships among those parts.

Place the simple subject on the horizontal main line to the left of the vertical line. Place the simple predicate, or verb, to the right. Capitalize only those words that are capitalized in the sentence. Do not use punctuation except for abbreviations.

Coyotes howled.   Dusk had fallen.

In an interrogative sentence, the subject often comes after the verb or after part of the verb phrase. In diagraming, remember to place the subject before the verb to the left of the vertical line.

Was Dave sleeping?   Could I have helped?

In an imperative sentence, the subject is usually not stated. Since commands are given to the person spoken to, the subject is understood to be *you*. To diagram an imperative sentence, place the understood subject *you* to the left of the vertical line. Then enclose *you* in parentheses. Place the verb to the right of the vertical line.

Stop!   Help!

Diagram adjectives and adverbs on slanted lines below the words they modify. If an adverb modifies an adjective or another adverb, write the adverb on an L-shaped line connected to the adjective or adverb that it modifies. Keep in mind that words like *not* and *never* are adverbs.

The new stereo system did not perform very well.

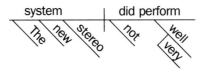

When two or more modifiers are connected by a conjunction, place the modifiers on slanted lines below the words they modify. Connect the slanted lines with a broken line and write the conjunction on it.

The tired but happy dancer waited quietly.

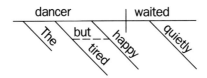

In a diagram, place the direct object on the main line after the verb. Separate the direct object from the verb with a vertical line that does not extend below the main line. Place indirect objects below the verb on lines parallel to the main lines and connected to the main line by slanted lines, as you see here.

Heidi brought Bill his assignments.

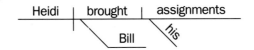

Place a predicate nominative or a predicate adjective on the main line after the verb. Separate the subject complement from the verb with a slanted line that extends in the direction of the subject.

My friend Bob is a skillful carpenter.
(Predicate nominative)

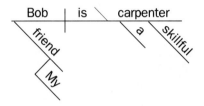

The young and enthusiastic golfer was lucky.
(Predicate adjective)

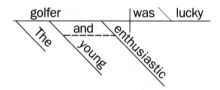

To diagram compound parts, place the parts on parallel horizontal lines as shown below. Then connect the parallel lines with a broken line. On the broken line, write the conjunction that connects the compound parts. Attach the compound parts to the main line with solid diagonal lines. The sentence below has a compound subject and a compound verb.

Dave, Jon, and Joe slept late and missed their scuba lesson.

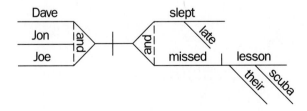

Compound Direct Objects and Indirect Objects To diagram compound direct objects or indirect objects, place the objects on parallel horizontal lines connected by a broken line. Write the conjunction on the line. Attach the compound parts to the main line as shown below.

The coach gave Marcia and her team the plays and signals.

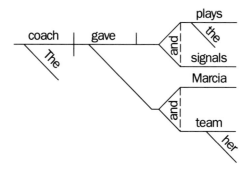

Draw a slanted line below the word the phrase modifies. From the slanted line, draw a line parallel to the main line. Place the preposition on the slanted line and the object of the preposition on the parallel line. Words that modify the object of the preposition are placed on slanted lines below the object.

Jerry took a picture of the fish.

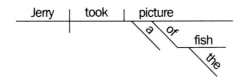

Between the skyscrapers stood an old diner.

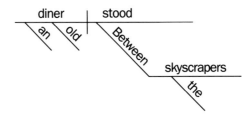

To diagram a gerund, place it on a line drawn as a step (⌐).
Put the step on a forked line (⅄) that stands on the main line.
The placement of the forked line is determined by how the gerund is
used.

Students dislike writing difficult papers hastily. (*gerund phrase used as direct object*)

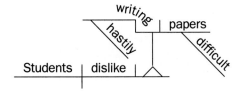

Before agreeing, we read the contract. (*gerund used as object of a preposition*)

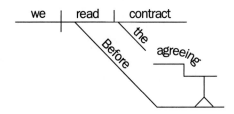

To diagram a participle, place the participle on an angled line
below the word it modifies. If the participial phrase includes a direct object and modifiers, separate the object and the participle with
a vertical line.

Bravely ignoring the bear's growl, Crockett moved closer.

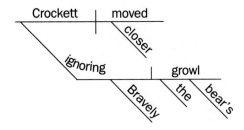

To diagram an infinitive, place the infinitive on an angled line. Write the word *to* on the slanted part and write the verb on the horizontal part of the angled line. Put the angled line on a forked line that stands on the main line. The placement shows how the infinitive or infinitive phrase is used in the sentence. In the sentences below, the infinitive phrase is used first as a direct object and then as a subject.

They hope to restore the old building.

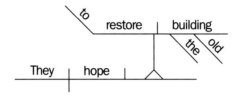

To work with the handicapped was her goal.

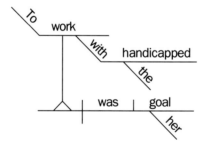

To diagram an appositive, place the appositive in parentheses after the word it identifies or explains. Place modifiers on slanted lines below the appositive.

Eudora Welty, a great American writer of short stories, was also a journalist.

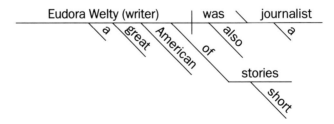

To diagram an adjective clause, place the clause on its own horizontal line below the main line and diagram it as if it were a sentence. Use a broken line to connect the relative pronoun in the adjective clause to the word that the clause modifies.

The purse that you found belongs to Ms. Weber.

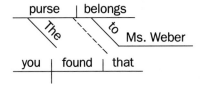

Diagram an adverb clause as you do an adjective clause. Use a broken line to connect the adverb clause to the word it modifies. Write the subordinating conjunction on the broken line.

When the boat arrived, we jumped aboard.

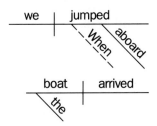

To diagram a noun clause, place the clause on a separate line that is attached to the main line with a forked line. The placement of the forked line in the diagram shows how the noun clause is used in the sentence. Diagram the word introducing the noun clause according to its function in the clause.

She saved a place for whoever was late. (*noun clause used as object of a preposition*)

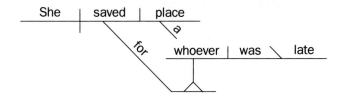

To diagram a compound sentence, place the independent clauses on parallel horizontal lines. Use a broken line with a step to connect the verb in one clause to the verb in the other clause. Write the conjunction on the step. If the clauses are joined by a semicolon, leave the step blank.

The car was nearly full, but we piled in.

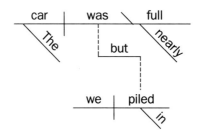

To diagram a complex sentence, decide whether the subordinate clause is an adjective clause, an adverb clause, or a noun clause. Then follow the rule for diagraming that kind of clause.

To diagram a compound-complex sentence, diagram the independent clauses first then attach the subordinate clause or clauses to the words they modify. Leave enough room to attach a subordinate clause where it belongs.

While the world listened, King Edward declared his love for Wallis Simpson, and he abdicated the throne.

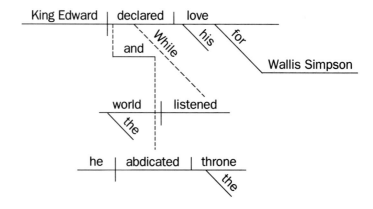

ALLITERATION   repetition of beginning sounds of words, in poetry or prose; for example, the "g" sound in "great grey wings."

ALLUSION   a reference to a historical or literary person, place, event, or aspect of culture.

ANALOGY   a comparison usually used to explain an idea or support an argument. For example, an analogy for a child's need for love might be created by comparing it to a plant's need for sunlight.

ANALYSIS   a way of thinking that involves taking apart, examining, and explaining a subject or an idea.

ANECDOTE   a brief story told as an example to illustrate a point.

ARGUMENT   speaking or writing that takes a position or states an opinion and provides the evidence or reasons to support it—often in a context of opposing points of view.

AUDIENCE   the readers or listeners to whom any discourse is directed.

AUTOBIOGRAPHY   a biography (life story) told by the person whose life it is.

BIAS   To have a bias or be biased is to lean toward one side in an argument or contest. To be *unbiased* is to be neutral.

BIBLIOGRAPHY   also called Works Cited. Lists all sources that contribute ideas or information to a research paper or report.

BRAINSTORMING   a way of gathering many ideas by quickly listing them as they occur, without judging their usefulness.

CAUSE AND EFFECT   a strategy for analyzing a subject by examining the reasons for specific actions or events or the consequences or results of certain causes.

CHARACTERIZATION   the way people (the *characters*) are portrayed in a narrative work.

CHRONOLOGICAL   organized according to time sequence.

CLARITY   the quality of being clear or easy to understand.

CLASSIFICATION   a type of writing that involves systematically grouping items by some system or principle; frequently involves defining or comparing and contrasting items or groups of items.

CLICHÉ a phrase, figure of speech, or idea used so often that it is predictable, showing little imagination or thought, as in "smooth as silk."

CLUSTERING a brainstorming technique that shows how ideas are connected to one another; gives a quick map of thoughts about a topic.

COHERENCE connectedness, a sense that parts hold together. An essay is coherent when its parts fit together logically and are linked by connecting words and phrases.

COLLABORATION working with other people; giving others support and advice; helping others solve problems.

COLLOQUIAL conversational, linguistically informal; the way people ordinarily speak in conversation.

COMPARISON AND CONTRAST a strategy for thinking or writing that involves explaining, defining, or evaluating subjects by showing how they resemble and differ from each other or from some standard for evaluation.

CONNOTATION the attitudes and feelings associated with a word or idea as opposed to its dictionary definition. The word "store" differs from "hoard" in its connotations.

CONTEXT the setting or situation in which something happens, particularly in which words or sentences are uttered or written.

CONTROVERSY a disagreement, often one that has attracted public interest.

COUNTERARGUMENT a refutation, an argument made to oppose (counter) another argument.

CRITICISM discourse (usually an essay) that analyzes something (usually a literary or artistic work) in order to evaluate how it does or does not succeed in communicating its meaning or achieving its purposes.

CUBING a method for discovering ideas about a topic by using six strategies (in any order) to investigate it: describe it, compare it, associate it, analyze it, apply it, argue for or against it.

DEDUCTIVE REASONING deriving a specific conclusion by reasoning from a general premise.

DENOTATION   the literal meaning of a word, without its *connotations*.

DESCRIPTION   an account, usually giving a dominant impression and emphasizing sensory detail, of what it is like to experience some object, scene, or person.

DIALECT   a form of language (usually regional) differing from the standard language in pronunciation, word choice, and syntax. Southern American English or New England English or Australian English are dialects of English.

DIALOGUE   the spoken conversation of fictional characters or actual persons as it is presented in a novel, story, poem, play, or essay.

DOCUMENTATION   naming the documents or other sources used to provide the information reported in an essay or other discourse: usually cited in footnotes or in parentheses.

ELABORATION   the development of an argument, description, narration, or explanation with details, evidence, and other support.

EXPOSITION   writing whose purpose is to explain an idea or teach a process rather than to tell a story, describe something, or argue for a point of view.

EXPRESSIVE   a kind of discourse full of meaning or feeling; often personal writing used by writers to explore ideas.

FICTION   made-up or imaginary happenings, as opposed to statements of fact or nonfiction. Short stories and novels are fiction, even though they may be based on real events. Essays, scientific articles, biographies, and news stories are nonfiction.

FIGURATIVE LANGUAGE   language that uses such figures of speech as similes, metaphors, and personification to show one thing as if it were something else.

FORMAL LANGUAGE   careful and somewhat rigid language often used in formal situations such as business communications or school reports.

FREEWRITING   a way of discovering what you know or think or feel by writing rapidly, without stopping, without editing, and without looking back (until you finish) at what you've written.

GENERALIZATION   a statement expressing a principle or drawing a conclusion based on examples or instances.

GLEANING a method of picking up ideas by observing events and by scanning through newspapers, magazines, and books and talking to others in order to find material to write about or to use in writing.

GRAPHIC ORGANIZER an illustration that visually organizes a complex body of information; includes charts, graphs, outlines, clusters, and tree diagrams.

IMAGERY figurative language and descriptions as the means of vividly rendering experience in language.

INDUCTIVE REASONING a method of thinking or organizing a discourse so that a series of instances or pieces of evidence lead to a conclusion or generalization.

INFERENCE a conclusion derived by reasoning from facts.

INTERPRETATION to explain the meaning of any text, set of facts, object, gesture, or event. To *interpret* something is to try to make sense of it.

INVISIBLE WRITING typing with a dimmed computer screen or writing with an empty ball point pen on a paper that covers a piece of carbon paper and a bottom clean sheet.

IRONY a figure of speech in which the intended meaning is the opposite of the stated meaning—saying one thing and meaning another.

JARGON the special language and terminology used by people in the same profession or who share specialized interests; for example, photographers, journalists, fishers.

JOURNAL a record of thoughts and impressions mainly for personal use.

KNOWLEDGE INVENTORY a list of statements or phrases representing what a writer knows about a topic, including questions to direct further research.

LEARNING LOG a journal or notebook used in connection with the study of a particular subject where a student records questions, problems, and states of understanding about the subject as it is studied and learned.

LOOPING a process for discovering ideas by freewriting on a topic, stopping to find promising ideas, then producing another freewrite on that subject, repeating the loop several times.

MAPPING   See clustering.

MEMOIR   an account of true events told by a narrator who witnessed or participated in the events, sometimes focusing on the personalities and actions of persons other than the writer.

METAPHOR   a figure of speech describing something by speaking of it as if it were something else, without using "like" or "as" to signal the relationship. To say "All the world's a stage" is to speak *metaphorically.*

MONOLOGUE   a speech by one person without interruption by other voices. A *dramatic monologue* reveals the personality and experience of a person through a long speech.

MOOD   feeling about a scene or subject created for a reader by a writer's selection of words and details. The mood of a piece of writing may be suspenseful, mysterious, peaceful, fearful, mirthful, and so on.

NARRATION   discourse that tells a story—either made up or true. Some common types of narrative are biographies, short stories, and novels.

NONSEXIST LANGUAGE   language free from gender bias, representing the equality of men and women and showing them in both traditional and nontraditional roles.

ONOMATOPOEIA   the use of words (usually in poetry) to suggest sounds: the *crackle* of a fire, the *hooting* of an owl, the *grumbling* of a complainer.

PARAPHRASING   rewording the meaning expressed in something spoken or written, using other words but retaining all of the original ideas.

PARENTHETICAL DOCUMENTATION   the placement of citations or other documentation within the text and in parentheses.

PEER RESPONSE   response to one's writing provided by other writers who are peers or classmates rather than teachers or other editors.

PERSONIFICATION   a figure of speech in which objects, events, abstract ideas, or animals are given human characteristics. "The jealous dog," "a chorus of crickets," and a "weeping brook" are examples of personification.

PERSUASION   discourse focused on influencing a listener or reader to support a point of view or take an action. Examples of persuasive discourse would include political speeches, advertisements, position papers, editorials, and courtroom speeches by lawyers.

PLAGIARISM   presenting the ideas or words of another as if they were one's own. Writers who use the ideas of others will avoid plagiarism by acknowledging their sources.

POINT OF VIEW   the viewpoint or perspective through which the reader views the events in a story; defines what a narrator can know and tell about.

PORTFOLIO   a place (usually a large folder) where writing is stored for future reference and review or to present for evaluation.

PRÉCIS   a short summary of an essay, story, or speech, capturing only the essential elements.

PROOFREADING   usually the last stage of the revising or editing process, when a writer checks work to discover typographical and other errors.

PROPAGANDA   discourse aimed entirely at persuading an audience, often containing distortions of the truth. Usually refers to manipulative political discourse.

PROSE   the usual language of speech and writing, lacking the special properties that define poetry; any language use that isn't poetry.

SATIRE   a literary form which ridicules or mocks the social practices or values of a society or group or important individual. To *satirize* something is to portray it in a way that shows it to be foolish.

SENSORY DETAIL   descriptive detail based on sensory experience— experiences associated with touch, smells, tastes, sights, and sounds.

SIMILE   a figure of speech comparing two things that are essentially unlike, signaling the comparison with "like" or "as."

SPATIAL ORDER   a pattern of organization based on space used in descriptive writing. For example, a scene may be described from foreground to background, from left to right, from top to bottom.

STYLE   refers to those features in a discourse or work of art that identify it as the work of a particular individual, type, period, or artistic philosophy.

SUMMARY   presents the theme or central idea in brief form.

SYMBOL   a word, object, or action that suggests something other than itself, as a heart can stand for affection or compassion, or in a story a river may suggest the passage of time.

SYNTHESIS   refers in writing or thinking to the putting together of ideas or information to reach a conclusion or achieve some insight or find a solution to a problem.

THEME   the underlying idea or central concern of a work of art or literature.

THESIS   the main point of an essay or other discourse.

TONE   the writer's attitude toward a subject—detached, ironic, serious, angry, and so on.

TOPIC SENTENCE   a statement expressing the main point of a paragraph; the idea (stated or unstated) around which a paragraph is organized.

TRANSITION   a smooth movement from one point to the next, usually marked in discourse with transitional words or phrases like "next," "furthermore," or "on the other hand."

TREE DIAGRAM   a visualized plan for an essay, also known as a "branching tree diagram" for the way it shows main and subordinate points as the trunk and main and minor branches of a tree.

TRITE PHRASE   a phrase used so commonly that it lacks precise meaning and suggests a lack of imagination, thought, or originality.

UNITY   oneness; the concept that in a written work all the parts must form a single whole, held together by a central theme or idea.

VENN DIAGRAM   a way of representing the relationship between two items that are distinct but have common or overlapping elements. The diagram consists of two circles drawn with an overlapping section to represent the common elements.

VOICE   the personality and distinct way of talking of a writer that allows a reader to "hear" a human personality in a piece of writing.

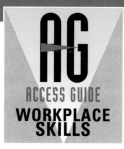

ACCESS GUIDE
WORKPLACE SKILLS

Workplace Know-how

What will the workplace of the future be like? What can you as a high school student do to prepare yourself to get a good job? A group of leaders in business, industry, and education, under the direction of the Secretary of the Department of Labor, explored these issues and published a report entitled *What Work Requires of Schools: A SCANS Report for America 2000.* (SCANS stands for the Secretary's Commission on Achieving Necessary Skills.) The SCANS study identified five competencies, or abilities, and a three-part foundation of skills and personal qualities that contribute to high-quality job performance.

Moreover, the study stressed that all students—not only those entering the workforce but the college-bound and those enlisting in the military—should acquire these competencies, skills, and personal qualities while in high school. Once you are in the workforce, you will continue to develop the know-how you have acquired in school.

The following guide summarizes the key points of the SCANS report. As you read, assess where you stand and what you need to do. Which competencies and skills are strong already? Which ones do you need to work on? What are the most effective ways to do so? Ask your teachers, counselors, and parents for suggestions. Think of your high school education as your passport to the world of work. Get yourself ready for the high-performance workplace of the 21st century.

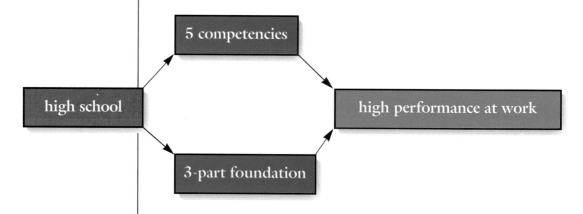

COMPETENCIES

Effective workers make use of competencies in five key areas for high achievement.

Resources They effectively manage resources like the following:

- **Time**—selecting activities relevant to a goal and prioritizing them, allocating time, preparing and following schedules
- **Money**—using or preparing budgets, making forecasts, keeping records, and making adjustments to meet goals
- **Material and facilities**—acquiring, storing, allocating, and using materials and space efficiently
- **Human resources**—assessing skills of others and distributing work accordingly, evaluating performance, and providing feedback

Interpersonal Skills They work well with others in these ways:

- **Participating as a member of a team**—contributing to group effort to complete a project successfully
- **Teaching others new skills**—sharing knowledge with others
- **Serving clients or customers**—working to satisfy clients' or customers' expectations
- **Exercising leadership**—communicating ideas clearly, persuading and motivating others, responsibly challenging existing procedures
- **Negotiating**—working toward agreement, resolving conflicts
- **Working with diversity**—working comfortably with men and women from different age groups and different racial or cultural backgrounds

Information They handle information efficiently using these skills:

- **Acquiring and evaluating information**—identifying the need for data, obtaining them, and evaluating their importance and accuracy
- **Organizing and maintaining information**—understanding, sorting, and classifying information
- **Interpreting and communicating information**—analyzing information and using oral, written, graphic, pictorial, or multimedia methods to convey it to others
- **Using computers to process information**—entering, modifying, retrieving, storing, and verifying information electronically

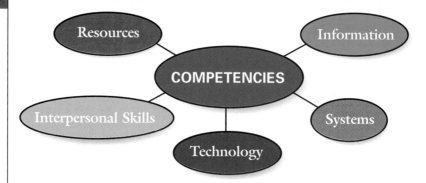

Systems They know how the parts of a system work together and are skilled at:

- **Understanding systems**—knowing how social, organizational, and technological systems work; for example, knowing the right people to ask for information
- **Monitoring and correcting performance**—looking for trends, predicting their impact, and making changes to improve a product or service
- **Improving or designing systems**—suggesting modifications to systems and developing new or alternative ways to improve performance

Technology They use appropriate technology to work more efficiently, including:

- **Selecting technology**—choosing the best procedures, tools, or equipment, including computers and related technology
- **Applying technology to a task**—understanding the overall goal of a project and the procedures for setting up and operating equipment
- **Maintaining and troubleshooting equipment**—preventing, identifying, or solving problems with equipment, including computers and other technologies

THE FOUNDATION

The five competencies just discussed are supported by basic skills and one's own personal qualities.

Basic Skills

- **Reading**—knowing how to locate, understand, and interpret written information, including manuals, graphs, and schedules

- **Writing**—communicating ideas, information, and messages in writing; creating documents such as memos, letters, directions, manuals, reports, graphs, and flow charts
- **Arithmetic/mathematics**—performing basic computations and using a variety of mathematical techniques to solve practical problems
- **Listening**—receiving, attending to, interpreting, and responding to verbal messages and other cues
- **Speaking**—organizing ideas and communicating orally

Thinking Skills

- **Creative thinking**—generating new ideas; finding new solutions to problems; viewing situations from different perspectives
- **Decision making**—identifying goals, generating alternatives, considering risks, and evaluating and choosing the best alternative
- **Problem solving**—recognizing problems and devising and implementing plans of action
- **Visualizing**—creating flow charts and processing symbols, pictures, graphs, objects, and other visuals
- **Knowing how to learn**—using efficient learning techniques to acquire and apply new knowledge and skills; knowing where and how to obtain the necessary information to solve problems
- **Reasoning**—discovering the principle underlying the relationship between objects and applying it when solving a problem

Personal Qualities

- **Responsibility**—exerting a high level of effort toward attaining a goal; setting high standards; paying attention to details
- **Self-esteem**—believing in yourself and maintaining a good self-image
- **Sociability**—demonstrating understanding, friendliness, adaptability, and empathy
- **Self-management**—being a "self-starter"; assessing your job performance accurately, setting realistic personal goals, monitoring your progress, and exhibiting self-control
- **Integrity/honesty**—choosing ethical courses of action

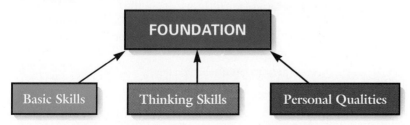

Writing Résumés

Your résumé is like an ad for yourself, highlighting your skills and accomplishments, your experience and responsibilities. A well-written résumé can help you obtain a part-time or full-time job, an internship, or admission to the college of your choice. The two sample résumés that follow are models you can use to write your own résumé. Of course, your résumé will look different depending on your purpose and where you choose to submit it.

Sample Résumé for a Part-time or Summer Job Applicant

Create a clear, logical, and attractive layout. Experiment with different formats to arrive at one that presents the information in the way that best highlights relevant areas.

In applying for a job, place your work experience early. Verb choice is especially important in a résumé. Use active, specific verbs, and be consistent in the form of the verb used.

Use a laser printer if possible, and print your résumé on good quality 8 1/2 by 11-inch stationery, preferably white or off-white.

Charles Flanigan
1404 Kendall Street
Drago, CA 41599
(215) 555-1212

OBJECTIVE Part-time position at a retail store

QUALIFICATIONS Interested in helping people solve problems
Ability to sell products effectively
Fluent in Spanish and German

WORK EXPERIENCE September 1994 through June 1995
Drago Daily Herald
Delivered weekly supplements every Wednesday after school.

June 1995 through June 1997.
Hamilton's Grocery
Stocked shelves, worked the register, and bagged groceries.

EDUCATION Drago High School, Class of 1998
Honor Roll

EXTRACURRICULAR ACTIVITIES Varsity Soccer
Debate team—treasurer, 1996;
vice-president, 1997

COMMUNITY ACTIVITIES August 1995—June 1997
Tutored senior citizens in computer skills three hours a week at Drago Public Library.

REFERENCES Available on request

Amy Li

1246 Acorn Lane
Whittier, Iowa 50142
(846) 555-1213

Education

Clemente High School, Whittier, Iowa, 1995–present; will
graduate in June 1998
4.8/5.0 average
Successfully completed pre-calculus and computer science
courses and advanced placement courses in history and math

Extracuricular Activities

Drama Club—secretary, 1997
Performed in *Guys and Dolls* (1995), *The Front Page* (1996), and *The
Music Man* (1997)

Awards

Received Division I rating in Iowa High School Computer
Olympics, April 1997

Awarded Principal's Certificate of Merit for success in organizing
fund-raising for school plays

Work Experience

June 1996 through September 1996. Counselor's Assistant. Tiny
Tykes Day Camp, Wooster Iowa. *Developed and supervised activities
(crafts, sports, nature hikes)*

September 1996 to June 1997. *Tutored in the computer lab at
Clemente High School*

Community Activities

Helped raise funds for Special Olympics, 1996

Hobbies

Singing, performing in community theater productions, dancing

References

Available on request

In a résumé to be included
with your college
application, mention any
academic achievements,
such as a high grade point
average or class rank.

Extracurricular activities,
awards, and the like
should be brief. List any
specific activities that
suggest your talents
and skills.

Be sure to include
volunteer work as part of
your work experience.
The skills you developed
are valuable even if you
were not paid.

Small details can make a positive impression on the person who reads
your résumé. That's why it's important to check your résumé carefully
for accuracy and for correct grammar, usage, and spelling. You might
include a draft of your résumé in your writing portfolio and update it
as your skills, education, and experiences increase through high school.
Save a copy of your résumé on your computer or on a disk for
easy updating.

ACCESS GUIDE

TECHNOLOGY

Using Electronic Resources

Electronic resources provide you with a convenient and efficient way to gather information. Many libraries offer computerized catalogs and a variety of other electronic resources.

Computerized Catalogs

You can search for a book in a library by typing the title, author, or subject into a computer. Most libraries also have software programs that allow you to search by typing in "keywords," that is, any word or combination of words found in the title, the subject, or the author's or publisher's name. When a book is not available, a librarian usually can search the catalogs of other libraries to locate another copy.

Other Electronic Resources

Many libraries offer a variety of electronic indexes. A newspaper index allows you to search the files of a particular newspaper, such as the *Chicago Tribune*, for recent articles on a chosen topic. *InfoTrac* provides a magazine index that lets you type in the subject you are interested in. The screen then displays a list of articles from several magazines that deal with that subject, with the most recent articles listed first. For each article, the index provides either an abstract (a kind of summary) or an extended citation that you can print directly from the screen. Another useful index, called *SIRS*, lists magazine and newspaper articles that concern social issues.

CD-ROM

A CD-ROM (compact disc–read-only memory) stores data that may include text, sound, photographs, and video. Almost any kind of information can be found on CD-ROMs, including

- encyclopedias, other reference books, and indexes
- news reports from newspapers, magazines, television, or radio
- literature and art collections
- back issues of magazines

ON-LINE RESOURCES

When you use your computer to communicate with another computer, you are working "on-line." On-line resources include commercial information services and Internet resources.

Commercial Information Services

Computer users can subscribe to various services that offer access to the following:

- up-to-date news, weather, and sports reports
- encyclopedias, magazines, newspapers, dictionaries, almanacs, and databases (collections of information)
- electronic mail (e-mail) to and from other users
- forums, or ongoing electronic conversations among users interested in particular topics
- the Internet

Internet

The **Internet**, a vast network of computers, allows computer users to exchange information with millions of other computer users throughout the world. News services, libraries, universities, researchers, organizations, government agencies, schools, and individuals use the Internet to communicate with people worldwide.

Finding and Exploring Sites The **World Wide Web**, one of the most popular resources on the Internet, connects pages of text and graphics stored on computers throughout the world. Each Web site has a specific location—somewhat like a postal address—known as its **URL**, short for Universal Resource Locator. When you type in a URL address in the Location field of a browser, your computer displays the corresponding site on your computer screen.

Following Links A Web site contains icons, pictures, or underlined and colored words and phrases called **links**. By clicking on a link, you immediately go to another site that contains related information. These links provide options, allowing you to explore subjects in more detail and to visit Web sites in the order you choose.

Using a Search Engine To find Web sites of interest to you, try using a **search engine**, or a navigational tool. Somewhat like an electronic card catalog, a search engine lets you search for sites by typing in a topic or key words.

> ### What You'll Need
>
> - To access on-line resources, you can use a computer with a modem linked to a telephone line or a television set with an Internet-ready box. Your school computer lab or resource center may be linked to the Internet or to a commercial information service.
> - To use CD-ROMs, you need a computer system with a CD-ROM drive.

COMPUSERVE

Yahoo, a popular search engine, offers an excellent menu of topic headings. Each time you click on a link, *Yahoo* scans thousands of databases to display the results on your computer screen.

Finding Newsgroups On the Internet you can visit thousands of "newsgroups" that contain articles about common areas of interest as well as postings from other computer users. You might even choose to add a posting of your own and chat electronically with others. Since computer users worldwide can access newsgroups, do not provide personal information if you decide to post something.

Exploring Other Areas of the Internet Tools such as Gopher and FTP (File Transfer Protocol) let you access other kinds of Internet documents. Available before the World Wide Web was created, Gopher and FTP contain pages of text without graphics or links. Gopher pages, which are run by colleges and universities, provide menus to conduct your searches. FTP servers store files such as transcripts of White House speeches. Even if your computer is connected to the Web, you might want to use Gopher and FTP to find information currently not available on the Web.

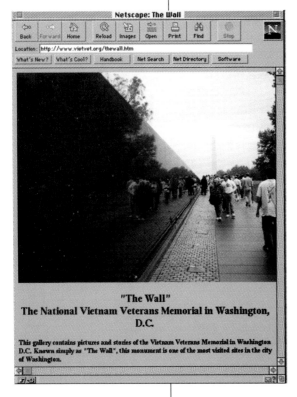

"The Wall"
The National Vietnam Veterans Memorial in Washington, D.C.

This gallery contains pictures and stories of the Vietnam Veterans Memorial in Washington D.C. Known simply as "The Wall", this monument is one of the most visited sites in the city of Washington.

Using Information from the Internet

As you explore the Internet, you can print files or **download** them, that is, make an electronic copy to store on a computer. Be very careful when evaluating electronic information. Since computer users worldwide can put information on the Internet, the quality of the information varies greatly. Some information is excellent; other information, however, may be misleading, out of context, or even inaccurate. Consider the source of a piece of information carefully. National research centers such as the Library of Congress are highly reputable. Home pages created by individuals, however, usually are less reliable. Of course, it is important to check and then double check all information from electronic sources.

As when working with information from printed sources, avoid plagiarism, or appropriating someone else's words or ideas. Get into the habit of paraphrasing ideas—that is, stating them in your own words—and then crediting the source and listing the access date.

Follow these models to credit electronic sources in a list of works cited:

- **CD ROM**
  The CIA World Factbook. CD-ROM. Minneapolis: Quanta, 1992.
- **On-line Service**
  "Middle Ages." Academic American Encyclopedia. Online. Prodigy. 30 Mar. 1992.
- **An Electronic Text On-line**
  Shakespeare, William. Hamlet. The Works of William Shakespeare. Ed. Arthur H. Bullen. Stratford Town ED. Stratford-on-Avon: Shakespeare Head, 1911. Online. Dartmouth Coll. Lib. Internet. 26 Dec. 1992.

Publishing on the Internet

Why not consider publishing your own work on the Internet? If your school has a home page on the Web, you might publish your writing or a multimedia presentation on this site. You may also choose to send completed pieces electronically to an Internet site that showcases student writing, such as the McDougal Littell home page, at the following address.

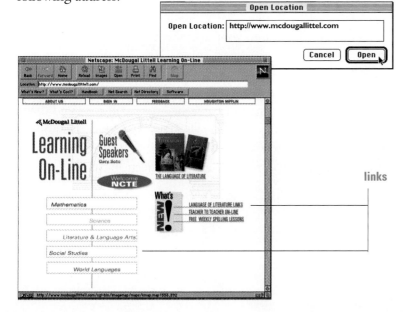

TECHNOLOGY
——— TIP ———

The Modern Language Association has not standardized the format for citing Internet sources. Generally, however, try to provide as much of the following information as you can.

- the author's name
- the title of the material, in quotation marks
- the title of the complete work (if applicable)
- the date of the material
- the database title (if applicable)
- the publication medium (online)
- the name of the computer service (if applicable)
- the date of access

What You'll Need

- computer
- word-processing program
- printer
- a graphics program to create visuals
- access to clip-art files from a CD-ROM, a computer disk, or an on-line service

Writing with Computers

Word-processing programs provide tools for drafting, revising, and editing your writing. The techniques on pages 846–847 will help you incorporate technology into your writing process. This section will give you tips for creating visuals and for peer editing. Computers can help clarify and enhance your writing and also make it easy to share your writing with others.

USING VISUALS

Many computer programs include tools for creating graphics. Charts, graphs, diagrams, and pictures can enhance your writing by illustrating complex concepts, clarifying the steps in a process, or graphically summarizing statistical information. They can also make a page look more appealing. The visuals you choose will depend on the type of information you want to convey.

Kinds of Visuals

Combining words with pictures or graphics can increase a reader's understanding and enjoyment of your writing. Many computer programs enable you to create and insert graphs, tables, time lines, diagrams, and flow charts into your document. Some also allow you to import graphics and clip art into your document.

Tables Tables allow you to arrange facts or numbers into rows and columns so that your reader can compare information more easily. In many word-processing programs, you can create a table by choosing the number of vertical columns and horizontal rows you need and then entering information in each cell, as the illustration shows. A spreadsheet program provides you with a preset table that you can adapt to fit your data. Spreadsheet programs also perform mathematical functions for you.

Overview of Dance Budget

	A	B	C	D	E	F	G
1		1997	1997	1998	1998	1999	1999
2		Estimate	Actual	Estimate	Actual	Estimate	Actual
3	Decorations	$75.00	$98.00	$100.00	$112.28	$115.00	
4	Advertisements	$50.00	$45.50	$52.00	$56.72	$65.00	
5	Refreshments	$75.00	$100.00	$85.00	$92.50	$110.00	
6	Music	$200.00	$200.00	$150.00	$175.00	$175.00	
7	Souvenirs	$25.00	$25.00	$35.00	$35.00	$50.00	
8	TOTALS	$425.00	$468.50	$422.00	$471.50	$515.00	

Graphs and Charts A graph or chart allows you to present complex information in a single image. For example, you could use a line graph to show how a trend changes over time, a bar graph to compare statistics, or a pie chart to compare percentages. You might want to explore ways of displaying data in more than one visual format before deciding which will work best for you.

Other Visuals Art and design programs enable you to create visuals for your writing. Many programs include the following features:

- drawing tools that allow you to draw, color, and shade pictures you create and to import them into your text
- clip art that you can copy or change with drawing tools
- page borders that you can use to decorate title pages, invitations, or brochures
- text options that allow you to combine words with your illustrations
- tools for making geometric shapes in flow charts, time lines, and process diagrams
- tools that allow you to import your own photographic images to create slide shows or other multimedia presentations
- tools that allow you to animate your visuals

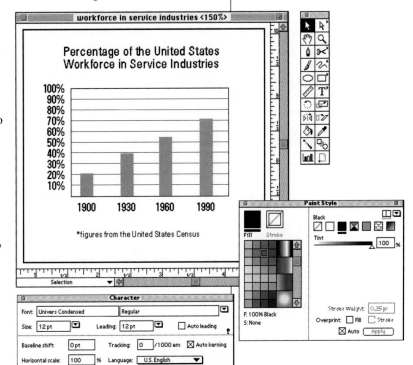

PEER EDITING YOUR WRITING

Improving your writing becomes easier when you use a word-processing program to elicit responses from your peers.

Peer Editing on a Computer The writer and the reader can both benefit from the convenience of peer editing "on screen." To use this method, be sure to first save your current draft and then make a copy of it for each of your peer readers. If your word-processing program has a

COMPUTER
TIP

To help your readers easily understand the different parts of a pie chart or bar graph, use a different color or shade of gray for each section.

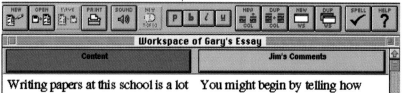

Workspace of Gary's Essay

Content	Jim's Comments
Writing papers at this school is a lot different than writing at the school I came from. Most papers are usually essays, with clear cut questions to be answered. This year we wrote a persuasive, an explanation, and an imaginative paper.	You might begin by telling how you feel about writing in general and using that as a way to compare the two schools. I can't tell if you like our school better or if you like the one you came from. Are you praising your old school or complaining? I'm also not sure if you like to write or you don't. It might be more interesting if I knew that.
I came from Johnson High where writing was one of the most important classes at the school. Once a week we had what was	

split-screen function, like Writing Coach, be sure to allow space in the side column so that your peer reader can write comments or questions. As an alternative, have your readers enter their comments within your text. In this case, have them use a different color, typeface, or type style from the one you used for your document.

Send a copy of your work to someone via e-mail or put it in someone's drop box if your computer is linked to others on a network. Ask each reader to include his or her initials in the file name. Then use the feedback of your peers to help you revise your writing. If your peer readers prefer to respond to a draft on paper rather than on the computer, remember to double-space or triple-space your document and leave wide margins so that your peer editors have space to ask questions, note their reactions, and make suggestions.

COMPUTER
— TIP —

Some programs include templates and stylesheet functions that make it easy to format your documnents.

EDITING AND FORMATTING

Once your readers have commented on your writing, you can use electronic editing tools to recheck your spelling and grammar and to address your readers' comments. Consider each suggestion carefully before making a change. With spell-checking and grammar-checking software, in particular, you may often decide against a suggested change. And even with spell-checking software, you must be sure to proofread your work. The computer will not recognize that you may have used *lead* when you meant to use *led*. You can also use an electronic thesaurus to find synonyms for words you want to replace.

When you are satisfied with the content and the style of your writing, consider the format—the layout and appearance— of your work. Options such as type size and position of the text can help you distinguish the levels of headings or call attention to important information. The guidelines of your assignment or your plans for publishing your writing may affect the formats you choose. Keep your format simple. Your goal is to create an attractive, easy-to-read document.

Creating a Multimedia Presentation

A multimedia presentation is a combination of text, sound, and visuals such as photographs, videos, and animation. You can combine these elements in an interactive presentation—one in which the user chooses a path to follow in exploring the information.

LEARNING ABOUT MULTIMEDIA

To start planning a multimedia presentation, you need to know the options available to you. Ask your school's technology adviser which of the following elements you could include.

Sound

Including sound in your presentation can help your audience understand information in your written text. For example, the user may be able to listen to and learn from

- the pronunciation of an unfamiliar or foreign word
- a speech
- a recorded news interview
- a musical selection
- a dramatic reading of a work of literature

Photos and Videos

Photographs and live-action video clips can make your subject come alive. Here are some examples of visuals that can be downloaded or scanned in:

- video of news coverage of a historical event
- video of music, dance, or theater performances
- photos of an artist's work
- photos or video of a setting that is important to the text

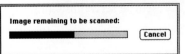

Animation

Many graphics programs allow you to add animation, or movement, to the visuals in your presentation. Animated figures add to the user's enjoyment and understanding of what you present. You can use animation to illustrate

- the steps in a process
- changes in a chart, graph, or diagram
- ways your user can explore information in your presentation

PLANNING YOUR PRESENTATION

To plan a multimedia presentation, first choose your topic and decide what you want to include. For example, instead of writing a research report (see pages 272–305), Craig might want to create a multimedia presentation about Stephen Crane's portrayal of Henry Fleming in *The Red Badge of Courage*. He could include the following items:

- introductory text about the novel
- time line and maps of the Civil War
- video footage of Civil War reenactment
- audiotaped readings of excerpts from the novel (each one focusing on a specific aspect)
- memoirs of Civil War soldiers with accompanying Civil War photos
- text drawing conclusions about the realism of the novel

Next plan how you want your user to move through your presentation. You can choose one of the following ways to organize your presentation:

- step by step with only one path, or order, in which the user can see and hear the information
- a branching path that allows users to make some choices about what they will see and hear, and in what order

If you choose the second way—an interactive presentation—you need to map out your presentation in a flow chart, or navigation map. This will help you figure out the paths a user can take through your presentation. Each box in the navigation map on the following page represents a screen in Craig's presentation.

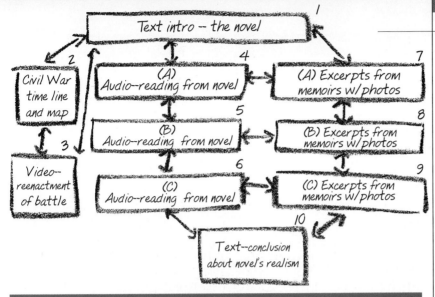

In a written compare-and-contrast essay, you must organize your information either by feature or by subject. In this presentation, however, the user can choose between either option.

CREATING YOUR PRESENTATION

As you create your multimedia presentation, use the navigation map as a guide.

When you have decided on the content of a screen, it is helpful to sketch the screen out. Remember to include in your sketch the links you will create to other screens in the presentation. Refer to the navigation map to see what links you need to add to each screen.

The example below shows screen 4 from the navigation map above.

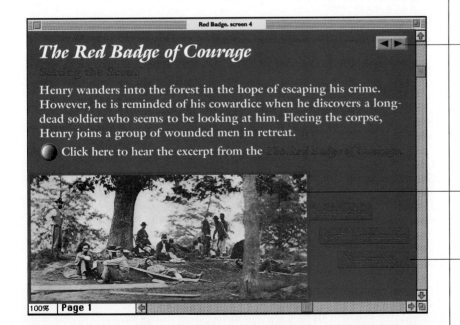

Navigational buttons can take the user back and forth, one screen at a time.

This screen includes an audio file and a photograph that has been scanned in.

The user clicks on these links to move to a different screen.

A

a, an, 566
  capitalization rules for, 774
ACT. *See* Standardized tests
A.D., 768
A.M., 768
Abbreviations, 575
  capitalization of, 761
  commas with, 761, 796
  periods with, 780
Absolute modifiers, 740
Absolute phrases, 614
Abstract nouns, 557
accept, except, 850
Acronyms, 575, 780
Action pentad, 392
Action questions, 392
Action verbs, 194, 562, 563
Active voice, 674–75
adapt, adopt, 850
Addresses
  in business letter, 525
  commas in, 795
Adequate detail, 405–6
Adjective clauses, 620–21
  diagraming, 865
  essential/nonessential, 621, 793–94
  words that introduce, 620–21
Adjective phrases, 599–600
Adjectives, 565–66, 736–37, 739–41
  or adverbs, determining, 737
  articles, 566
  commas between, 784
  comparative forms of, 739–41
  coordinate, 784
  diagraming, 860
  infinitive phrases as, 605
  infinitives as, 604
  irregular forms of, 741
  nouns as, 566
  participles as, 566, 607
  position of, 565
  positive forms of, 739
  predicate, 566
  pronouns as, 566
  proper, 566

  superlative forms of, 740–41
Adjective suffixes, 481
Admission to college, applying for, 523–24
adopt, adapt, 850
Adverb clauses, 155, 623–25
  commas after, 624, 786
  diagraming, 865
  elliptical clauses, 625
  words that introduce, 155, 624
Adverb phrases, 600
Adverbs, 568, 736–37
  or adjectives, determining, 737
  commas with, 786, 787, 796
  comparative forms of, 739–42
  conjunctive, 185, 573, 629, 633
  diagraming, 860
  directive, 568
  as idioms, 568
  infinitive phrases as, 605
  infinitives as, 604
  as intensifiers, 568
  irregular forms of, 741
  positive forms of, 739
  or prepositions, determining, 796
  relative, 620–21
  superlative forms of, 740–42
Advertisement copy, 230–34
  creating, 233
  planning, 232–33
  reviewing and publishing, 234
Advertising techniques.
  See Persuasion, listening to and evaluating
advice, advise, 850
affect, effect, 31, 850
Agreement, pronoun-antecedent, 725–26
  ambiguous reference, 729
  in gender, 726
  indefinite reference, 728
  in number, 725–26
  in person, 726
  unidentified reference, 727–28
Agreement, subject-verb, 685–702
  and collective nouns, 694
  and compound subjects, 687
  and *don't, doesn't,* 693
  and indefinite pronouns, 690–91

in inverted sentences, 692
in number, 685
with numerical terms in subjects, 695
with phrases and clauses as subjects, 695
and predicate nominatives, 692
with relative pronouns as subjects, 561
and singular nouns ending in -*s,* 694
with titles as subjects, 695
and words between subject and verb, 686
and words of amount or time, 695
Airplanes, capitalizing names of, 765
Alliteration, 456, 867
all ready, already, 850
all right, 850
all together, altogether, 850
Allusion, 867
Almanacs, 509–10
almost, most, 854
a lot, 851
Ambiguous reference, 729
among, between, 851
amount, number, 851
Analogy, 380, 867
Analogy questions, 533
Analysis, 867
    of sentences, 47–49
    of word parts, 478–86
    of the writing activity, 333
    of writing assignments, 334–35
    of writing community, 335–38
    see also Informative exposition: analysis
Analysis frames, 356
Anecdotes, 867
    in conclusions, 385
    in introductions, 379
angry at, with, 851
Antecedents
    agreement with pronouns, 559, 725–26
    and pronoun reference, 727–29
    of relative pronouns, 698
Antonym questions, 532
anywhere, 851
Apostrophes, 819–21
    in contractions, 821
    to form plurals, 821
    to show omissions, 821
    to show possession, 819–21
Appeals, persuasive, 544–46
    by association, 546
    to authority, 546

to emotion, 546
to reason or common sense, 546
Application and Review, 576–77, 596–97,
    640–41, 683–84, 701–2, 732–33, 754–55,
    778–79, 800–1, 817–18, 831–32
Appositive phrases, 601–2
    commas with, 601, 786–87
    diagraming, 864
    essential/nonessential, 601–2
    as fragments, 636
Appositives, 601–2
    commas with, 786–87
    diagraming, 864
    essential/nonessential, 601–2
    position of, 601
    with pronouns, 720
    pronouns as, 720
Argument, 867
Argumentation, 490–91
    deductive reasoning, 492
    inductive reasoning, 491
Art
    capitalization of titles, 774
    ideas for writing about, 843
    italics for titles, 827
    personal response to, 256–60
Articles (*a, an, the*), 566
    definite, 566, 774
    indefinite, 566
as, as if, like, 854
Assessment. *See* Evaluation standards;
    Peer response; Skills assessment
Assessment, writing for, 314–25, 530–40
    essay tests, 530–31
    questions on standardized tests, 532–40
    standardized tests, 531–32
    written exams, 316–25
Associations, as sources, 513
Assonance, 456–57
Astronomical terms, capitalization of, 765
Atlases, 509–10
Audience, 11, 333, 350, 867
    for ad copy, 232
    for analysis of change, 150
    for classification, 122
    for college application essay, 39
    for dramatic scene, 104
    focusing a topic, 350
    identifying, 11
    for interview profile, 59

for opinion poll, 199
for persuasive essay, 215
for satire, 228
for short story, 91
Author, evaluating, 279
Author's expansions, 327–29
Authors, reference works, 510–11
Autobiography, 867
Auxiliary verbs, 563
  with infinitives, 604
  with participles, 607
Awards, capitalization of, 768

B

B.C., 768
bad, badly, 749
Bandwagon appeal, 233, 546
barely, hardly, scarcely, 750
Base words, 478
be, singular and plural forms of, 685
being, 851
beside, besides, 851
between, among, 851
Bias, 867
  misquoting, 547
  quoting out of context, 547
  recognizing, 547
  stacking the evidence, 547
Bibliography, 278, 867
  see also Works Cited list
Bibliography cards. *See* Source cards
Biographical reference works, 510
Bodies of the universe, capitalization of, 764
Body, of business letter, 525–26
Book Review Digest, 511
Books
  about authors, 510–11
  capitalization of titles, 774
  colons in titles, 807
  italics for titles of, 827
  in Works Cited list, 291–92
borrow, lend, 851
Brackets, 815
  in a transcript, 77
Brainstorming, 148–49, 212, 244, 867
  to find a topic, 347
  to focus a topic, 351–52
  on word processor, 846
Brand names, capitalization of, 768

Bridge-building, 376
Bridges, capitalization of, 764
bring, take, 851
Browsing, 343
Buildings, capitalization of, 764
Business letters, 521, 525–29
  colons in, 795, 807
  commas in, 795

C

Call for action in conclusions, 384
can, may, 852
Capitalization, 760–79
  abbreviations, 761
  astronomical terms, 765
  awards, special events, 768
  bodies of the universe, 764
  brand names, 768
  deities, 762
  directions, 764
  in divided quotations, 773
  events, documents, periods of time, 767
  family relationships, 761
  first words, 772–74
  geographical names, 764
  and hyphenated compounds, 762, 813
  I, 762
  initials, 760
  kinship names, 761
  languages, 762
  in letters, 773
  months, days, holidays, 767
  nationalities, races, 762
  O, Oh, 762
  organizations, institutions, 767
  in outlines, 773, 845
  parts of the world, 764
  personal names and titles, 760–61
  place names, 764
  poetry, 773
  political divisions, 764
  and prefixes, 760, 761
  proper adjectives, 760
  proper nouns, 760
  quotations, 773
  religions, 762
  school subjects and class names, 768
  sections of a country, 764–65
  structures and public places, 764

Narration, 871
in drawing conclusions, 182
in memoir, 28
to present characters, 470
to present setting, 472
Narrative conclusions, 388–89
climactic event in, 389
resolution of conflict in, 389
using the last event in, 388
Narrative introductions, 386–88
describing the main character in, 387
introduction of conflict in, 387
introduction of major symbol in, 387–88
setting the scene in, 386
Narrative and literary writing, 83–112
dramatic scene, 102–6
narrative poem, 108–12
short story, 84–101
Narrative poem, 108–12
drafting, 111
planning, 110
publishing, 112
reviewing, 112
Narrative writing, ideas for, 842
Nationalities, capitalization of, 762
-ness, 857
Neuter gender, 559
Newsgroups, 882
News reporting, 541–48
Newspapers and newspaper articles
capitalization of titles, 774
italics for titles, 827
source cards for, 280–81
in Works Cited list, 292–93
New York Times Index, 278, 507
Nominative case, pronouns, 559, 708, 710
Nonessential appositives, 601–2
commas with, 786
Nonessential adjective clauses, 621
commas with, 793–94
Nonessential participial phrases, 608
commas with, 794
Nonfiction
classification of, in libraries, 503–4
conclusions, 382–85
introductions, 378–82
point of view in, 458–60
Nonprint materials in libraries, 505
Nonrestrictive appositives, 786
Nonrestrictive clauses, 793
Nonsexist language, 871

Note taking
note card, 283
organizing, 284
for research report, 281–83
Noun clauses, 626–27
diagraming, 865
words that introduce, 627
Nouns, 557–58
abstract, 557
as adjectives, 566
collective, 558, 694
common, 557
compound, 558
concrete, 557
gerunds and gerund phrases as, 609–10
infinitive phrases as, 605
infinitives as, 603
proper, 557
Noun suffixes, 480
nowhere, 851
Number
of personal pronouns, 559, 708
pronoun-antecedent agreement in, 725–26
and subject-verb agreement, 685
number, amount, 851
Numbers
apostrophes with, 821
colons with, 807
commas in, 796
hyphens in, 812
parentheses with, 814
plurals of, 821

O

Objective case, pronouns, 559, 708
711–712
Objective complements, 585
Object of the prepostion, 569
pronouns as, 712
Observation charts, 354–55
Observation and description, 51–78
eyewitness report, 68–73
interview profile, 52–67
oral history, 74–78
Observation techniques, 70–72
Observing, 340
Occasional speech, 514
Occupation Outlook Handbook, 520
of, 854

adjective, 599–600
adverb, 600
appositive, 601–2
  commas with, 783, 786, 794, 796
dangling modifiers, 613–17
diagraming, 862–64
essential/nonessential, 601–2, 608
as fragments, 635–36
gerund, 609–10
infinitive, 603–5
misplaced modifiers, 612–13
participial, 607–8
prepositional, 599–600
to subordinate ideas, 441
verbal, 603–10
Pictorial essay, 166–70
  creating, 169–70
  planning, 168–69
  publishing, 170
  reviewing, 170
Place names
  capitalization of, 764
  commas in, 795
Plagiarism, 285, 495–97, 872, 883
Plain-folks appeal, 546
Planets, capitalization of, 765
Planner's blackboard, 370–71, 372
Planning for writing
  analyzing the writing process, 333–38
  in collaboration, 370–73
  finding a topic, 339–47
  focusing (refining) a topic, 349–52
  organizing, 361–69
  using graphic devices (organizers), 347, 352, 353–60
Playing movies of the reader's mind, 849
Playwriting, 104–6
  see also Dramatic scene
Plot
  in critical analysis, 243
  in short story, 88–90
Plural pronouns, 559, 708
Plurals
  apostrophes to form, 821
  and subject-verb agreement, 685
Poem, writing. See Narrative poem
Poems
  capitalization in, 773
  capitalization of title of, 774
  titles of, in quotation marks, 827

Poetry, writing. See Figurative language; Narrative poem; Sound devices
Pointing, 848
Point of view, 458–63
  experimenting with, 462
  in fiction, 460–61
  first-person, 458–59, 460
  judging, 547
  limited, 460–61
  in nonfiction, 458–60
  omniscient, 461
  in poem, 111
  second-person, 458, 459–60
  in short story, 90
  third-person, 458, 459, 460–61
  vantage point, 462–63
Political divisions, capitalization of, 764
Polling results, 546
Portfolio, writing, 19, 872
Possession, apostrophes to show, 819–21
Possessive case, pronouns, 559, 708, 715–16
Possessive pronouns, 559, 715–16
  modifying gerunds, 715–16
Précis, 500, 872
Predicate adjectives, 566
  diagraming, 861
Predicate nominatives, 585
  diagraming, 861
  predicate nouns, 585
  predicate pronouns, 585
  pronouns as, 710
  and subject-verb agreement, 692
Predicate nouns, 585
Predicate pronouns, 585
  and infinitives, 712
Prediction
  in conclusion, 384
  as reading strategy, 494
Prefixes, 478–79
  ex-, 761
  and spelling problems, 857
Prepositional phrases, 569, 599–600
  as adjective phrases, 599–600
  as adverb phrases, 600
  commas after, 786
  and compound objects, 599
  diagraming, 862
  introductory, and commas, 786
  objects of, 599
Prepositions, 569–70

punctuation of, 791
in research report, 281
use of *sic,* 251
see also Dialogue; Direct quotations;
Divided quotations
Quoting out of context, 547

R

raise, rise, 678–79, 855
Reader's circles, 18
Readers' Guide to Periodical Literature,
278, 506
Reading-comprehension questions, 535
Reading log, 243
Reading strategies, 494–95
identifying main ideas, 494
identifying relationships, 494
inferring, 495
note taking, 494
predicting, 494
previewing, 494
questioning, 494
responding, 495
reviewing, 495
summarizing and paraphrasing, 495
real, really, 855
Reasoning, faulty, 547
Recalling, 339–40
Reducing sentences, 438–39
Redundancy, correcting, 437–38
Reference, of pronouns, 730–31
Reference works, 507–12
almanacs, yearbooks, and atlases, 509–10
bibliographies, 278
biographical references, 510
dictionaries, 508
encyclopedias, 278, 508–9
literary, 510–12
Peterson's guide books, 520
specialized dictionaries, 508
Reflecting, 339–40
Reflexive pronouns, 560, 722
Regular comparisons, 740–41
Regular verbs, 646–47
Related assignments, 5
ad copy (for advertisement), 230–34
college application (essay), 36–41
comparison and contrast (essay), 130–34
dramatic scene, 102–6

eyewitness report, 68–73
genealogical research, 306–8
lab report, 190–95
narrative poem, 108–12
opinion poll, 196–201
oral history, 74–78
organizational chart, 136–40
parody, 262–66
personal response, 256–60
pictorial essay, 166–70
satire, 224–28
science fiction (story), 160–65
song lyric, 42–46
Relationships, identifying, 494
Relative adverbs, 620–21
Relative clauses, 620
See also Adjective clauses
Relative pronouns, 561, 620, 621
to introduce adjective clauses, 620, 621
as subject of subordinate clauses, 561
and subject-verb agreement, 698
Religions, capitalization of, 762
Repetition, 408
eliminating, 579
in song lyrics, 45–46
Replying, 849
Reports
analysis of change, 146–58
family history, 306–8
lab (science), 190–95
research, 272–305
Research papers, 272–305
choosing and limiting a topic for,
274–77
documentation, 285–86
drafting, 285–87
evaluating sources, 279
model paper, 295–304
Modern Language Association
guidelines, 294
organization for, 284, 286
outline for, 284
planning, 274–77
prewriting for, 274–77
purpose and, 276–77
research for, 277–84
revising, 288–94
source cards, 280–81
source materials for, 278–80
taking notes for, 281–83

in compound-complex sentences, 633
in compound sentences, 629, 803–4
with conjunctive adverbs, 185, 804
quotation marks with, 824
in series, 803
Sensory details, 397, 435, 872
elaborating with, 397
imagery and, 453–54
for revision, 435
Sentence-completion questions, 534
Sentence composing
analyzing sentences, 47–49
author's expansions, 327–29
elaborating on complex sentences, 235–37
elaborating on compound
sentences, 203–5
elaborating on compound-complex
sentences, 267–69
elaborating on sentences, 79–81
elaborating on simple sentences, 141–43
inverting and compounding subjects
and verbs, 113–15
reviewing sentence composing skills, 309–13
varying sentence types, 171–73
Sentence-correction questions, 538
Sentence outline, 844
Sentences, 578–93, 629–34
analyzing, 47–49
awkward beginnings, 439–40
capitalization in, 772
classification, 579, 629
complements, 582–86
complete predicates, 578
complete subjects, 578
complex, 235–37 632–33
compound, 629–30
compound-complex, 267–69, 633–34
compound verb, 579
correcting modifiers, 440
correcting redundancy, 437–38
declarative, 580
diagraming, 859–66
direct objects, 582–83
with *don't* and *doesn't,* 693
elaborating on, 79–81
empty, 429–30
exclamatory, 581
fragments, 587–90, 635–37
imperative, 580–81
indirect objects, 584

interrogative, 580
making parts parallel, 443
objective complements, 585
overloaded, 431–33
patterns, 580
precise word usage in, 434–39
predicate nominatives, 585
predicates of, 578
reducing, 438–39
relating parts, 442
run-on, 592–93
simple, 629
simple predicates, 578
simple subjects, 578
structure and style, 444–45
subject complements, 585
subjects of, 578
subject-verb agreement in, 685–702
subordinating ideas, 440–41
see also Sentence composing
Sequence, transitions that show, 405
Series
commas in, 783, 786
dashes with, 810
semicolons in, 803
set, sit, 679
Setting, 470–72
in critical analysis, 243
in dramatic scene, 105
Sharing, 18–19, 423–25, 427–28, 848
collected works, 19
formal publishing, 428
informal publishing, 427
with peers, 423–25
performances for, 19
portfolios, 19
preparing materials for, 428
print media, 19
readers' circles, 18
self-publishing, 427
techniques for finding ideas, 848
videos or multimedia presentations, 19
writing exchange groups, 19
see also Publishing; Writing process
Ships
capitalization of names of, 765
italics for names of, 765
Short stories
capitalization in titles of, 774
quotation marks with titles of, 827
Signature, on business letters, 525–26

Statistics, elaborating with, 397
Story, 658
  titles in quotation marks, 827
Story writing, 84–101, 160–65
  characters, 88, 89, 164
  conflict, 88, 90
  drafting, 92–94, 164–65
  organization, 93
  plot, 88, 90
  point of view, 90, 164
  prewriting, 88–92, 163–64
  publishing, 96, 165
  reviewing and revising, 94–96, 165
  setting, 88, 89–90, 164
Story poem, 108–12
  see also Narrative poem
Strategies
  for answering essay questions, 530–31
  for drafting, 28, 60, 92, 124, 151,
    181–82, 217, 247–48
  for planning test responses, 319
  for prewriting. See Exploratory
  activities
Structure, 361–69
  revising for, 418
  see also Organization of writing
Style, 444–46, 872
Subject areas, ideas for writing about, 843
Subject complements, 585–86
  diagraming, 861
  after linking verbs, 585–86
  predicate adjectives, 586
  predicate nominatives, 585
Subjects, of sentences
  agreement, with verbs, 685–702
  collective nouns as, 694
  compound, 114, 687
  diagraming, 859
  in imperative, 580–81, 676
  indefinite pronouns as, 690–91
  inverting, 113
  numerical terms in, 695
  pronouns as, 710
  relative pronouns as, 698
  titles as, 695
Subjunctive mood, 676–77
Subordinate clauses, 618
  adjective, 620–21
  adverb, 623–25
  commas with, 633
  in complex sentences, 235–37, 632–33

  in compound-complex sentences, 633–34
  as fragments, 636–37
  noun, 626–27
Subordinating conjunctions, 572, 624
  combining sentences with, 235, 571
  with adverb clauses, 624
  with noun clauses, 627
Subordinating ideas, 440–41
  upside-down subordination, 441
  using clauses, 440
  using phrases, 441
Suffixes, 478, 480–81
  adjective, 481
  noun, 480
  and spelling problems, 857
Summarizing, 40, 495, 500–1, 849, 873
Superlative degree, 740–41
Supporting details, 362–63, 401
  for paraphrasing, 498
Surveying, 121
Suspense, creating, 92
Syllables, hyphens between, 813
Symbolism, 455
Symbols, 873
  introducing, 387–88
Synonyms and near synonyms, 409
Synthesis, 873
  see also Informative exposition:
    synthesis

T

take, bring, 851
Tall tale, 612
Tape-recording, for interview
  asking permission, 77
  editing transcription, 77–78
  of eyewitness report, 71
  and notes, 77
  transcribing, 77
teach, learn, 854
Technology, 880–89
Television programs
  capitalization in titles, 774
  italics for series titles, 827
  quotation marks for episode titles, 827
Temporal relationships, transitions
  that show, 155, 194, 405
Tenses, 658–63
  future, 658, 659, 661
  future perfect, 658, 659, 662

U

Unbiased, 873
Underlining. *See* Italics
Unfinished claims, 545
Unidentified reference, 727–28
uninterested, disinterested, 852
unique, 855
United States government, as information
  source, 512–13
Unity, 401–3, 873
  in compositions, 410–11
  in description, 403
  in paragraphs, 401–3
  see also Coherence; Transitional devices
Unsupported opinions, correcting, 429–30
Upside-down subordination, 441

V

Vantage point, 462–63
Vehicles, capitalization of, 765
Venn diagram, 358, 873
Verbal phrases, 603–10
  commas after, 786, 794, 796
  as fragments, 636
Verbals, 603–10
  gerunds, 609–10
  infinitives, 603–5
  participles, 607–8
Verb phrases, 563, 646
Verbs, 562–64, 646–84
  action, 194, 562, 563, 646
  agreement with subjects, 685–702
  auxiliary, 563, 646
  commonly confused, 678–79
  compound, 114, 579
  conjugation, 658–59
  diagraming, 859
  emphatic forms, 666
  future perfect tense, 658, 659, 662
  future tense, 658, 659, 661
  helping (auxiliary), 563, 646
  improper shifts in tense and form, 667
  infinitives, 646, 663
  intransitive, 563–64
  inverting, 113
  irregular, principal parts of, 648–57
  linking, 563, 646
  main, 563
  mood of, 676–77
  past, 646, 648–49, 654
  past participle, 646–47, 648–49, 652,
    654, 656–57
  past perfect tense, 658, 659, 661
  past tense, 658, 659, 660
  perfect tenses of, 658, 659, 661, 662
  present, 646
  present infinitive, 646
  present participle, 646–47
  present perfect tense, 658, 659, 661
  present tense, 658, 659, 660
  principal parts of, 646
  progressive forms, 665–66
  regular, principal parts of, 646–47
  as simple predicate, 578
  simple tenses of, 658, 659, 660–61
  specific, choosing, 435–37
  tenses of, 658–63
  transitive, 563–64
  voice of, 673–75
Vertical file, 505
Videos
  for sharing writing, 19
  with multimedia presentation, 887
Vocabulary
  analyzing word parts, 478–86
  clichés, 450
  context clues, 474
  euphemisms, 450
  gobbledygook, 451
  idioms, 450
  inferring meaning from context,
    473–75
  jargon, 451
  slang, 450
  word parts, 478–86
  see also Word families; Word parts,
    analyzing; Word roots; Word usage
Voice, 333, 444–46, 873
  of character, 446
  of verbs, 674–75

W

way, 855
Webster's Biographical Dictionary, 510
*Webster's New World Dictionary of the
  American Language,* 508
*Webster's Third New International
  Dictionary,* 508

A CKNOWLEDGMENTS

Sources of Quoted Materials

22: Brandt & Brandt Literary Agency: For excerpts from "The Town Dump," from *Wolf Willow* by Wallace Stegner. **36:** Seana Gamel: "I Used to Live For Glory" by Seana Gamel. By permission of the author. **42:** EMI Music Publishing: "All That You Have Is Your Soul" by Tracy Chapman. Copyright © 1989 EMI April Music Inc./Purple Rabbit Music. All rights controlled and administered by EMI April Music, Inc. All rights reserved. International Copyright © secured. Used by permission. **52:** The New Yorker Magazine, Inc.: "Artist," from "The Talk of the Town," from *The New Yorker,* July 23, 1990. Copyright © 1990 The New Yorker Magazine, Inc. By permission of The New Yorker Magazine, Inc. **68:** Sandy Lord for Bette Bao Lord: For an excerpt from "These People Have No Fear" by Bette Bao Lord, from *Newsweek,* May 29, 1989. Reprinted by permission. **74:** Doubleday & Company, Inc.: "ANNA TUTT," as told to Lynn Butler, from *Foxfire 8,* edited by Eliot Wigginton. Copyright © 1984 by The Foxfire Fund, Inc. Used by permission of Doubleday, a division of Bantam Doubleday Dell Publishing Group, Inc. **84:** José Armas: "A Delicate Balance" by José Armas, from *Nuestro,* May 1978. By permission of the author. **108:** University of Pittsburgh Press: "Oranges," from *Black Hair* by Gary Soto. Copyright © 1985 Gary Soto. By permission of the University of Pittsburgh Press. **116:** HarperCollins Publishers: "Mirror," from *The Collected Poems of Sylvia Plath,* edited by Ted Hughes. Copyright © 1963 by Ted Hughes, originally appeared in *The New Yorker.* By permission of HarperCollins Publishers. **118:** W. W. Norton & Company, Inc.: For an excerpt from *Once More Around the Block,* Familiar Essays by Joseph Epstein. Copyright © 1987 by Joseph Epstein. By permission of W. W. Norton & Company, Inc. **160:** Roberta Pryor, Inc. Literary Agent: For an excerpt from "Earthmen Bearing Gifts," from *The Best of Fredric Brown.* Copyright © 1977 by Elizabeth C. Brown, Executrix of the Estate of Fredric Brown. Reprinted by permission of The Estate of Fredric Brown and Roberta Pryor, Inc. **176:** Sports Illustrated: For excerpts from "Dark Forces" by Sarah Boxer, from *Sports Illustrated,* April 17, 1989 issue. Copyright © 1989, The Time Inc. Magazine Company. By permission of Sports Illustrated, the Time Inc. Magazine Company. All rights reserved. **190:** Doubleday & Company, Ind.: For an excerpt from "Calls in the Night." from *Dolphins* by Jacques-Yves Cousteau and Philippe Diole **196:** Fortune, The Time Inc. Magazine Company: For excerpts from "The U. S. Mood: Ever Optimistic" by Louis Kraar, from *Fortune,* Copyright © 1990 The Time Inc. Magazine Company. **208:** Douglas George, ed. Akwesasne Notes: For excerpts from the proclamation "We Hold the Rock," from *Alcatraz Is Not an Island* by Indians of All Tribes, Inc., edited by Peter blue cloud, Copyright © 1972 by Peter blue cloud. **224:** Time, The Time Inc. Magazine Company: For an excerpt from "These Foolish Things Remind Me of Diet Coke" by Michael Kinsley, from Time, June 11, 1990 issue. Copyright © 1990 The Time Inc. Magazine Company. Reprinted by permission. **240:** Doubleday & Company, Inc.: "Harrison Bergeron," from *Welcome to the Monkey House* by Kurt Vonnegut, Jr. Copyright © 1961 by Kurt Vonnegut, Jr. Used by permission of Delacorte Press/Seymour Lawrence, a division of Bantam, Doubleday, Dell Publishing Group, Inc. **272:** National Geographic Society: For an excerpt from "The Underground Railroad" by Charles L. Blockson, from *National Geographic,* July 1984 issue. **549:** Franklin Watts, Inc.: For excerpts from "The Interrogative Putdown," from *How to Win a Pullet Surprise* by Jack Smith. Copyright © 1982 by Jack Smith. **735:** Dave Barry: For an excerpt from "What Is and Ain't Grammatical" by Dave Barry. Copyright © 1980 Dave Barry. **833:** Penguin Books USA, Inc.: For excerpts from *Teenage Romance* by Delia Ephron. Copyright © 1981 by Delia Ephron. Reprinted by permission of Viking Penguin, a division of Penguin Books USA, Inc. The authors and editors have made every effort to trace the ownership of all copyrighted material found in this book and to make full acknowledgment for their use.

Illustration and Photography Credits

Commissioned Illustrations: Mark DaGrossa: **121,** *chart* **174,** *map* **750;** Christopher Herrfurth: **50, 144, 174, 190/191, 734;** James Higgins: **575;** Gary Sanders: **1,** *background* **750;** Leslie Staub Shattuck: **64, 182, 186, 238, 245, 266, 270, 314, 321, 334, 335, 343, 350, 356, 372, 374, 499, 589, 637, 647, 660, 684, 709, 724, 743, 775, 785;** Sharon Stolzenberger: **74/75;** Christopher Vallo: **20, 82, 262/263, 332;** Rachel L. Witt: **625. Assignment Photography:** France Photography: **xvi,** *l & tr* **21, 22/23, 36/37, 52/53,** *br* **83, 108/109,** *l* **117, 118/119,** *l & br* **175, 177,** *l & br* **207, 210/211, 230/231,** *tr* **239, 240/241, 256/257, 315, 316/317;** Patterson Graphics: **xiii,** *b* **46, 215, 277,** *t* **332, 503, 509,** *all* **524, 713. Photos and Illustrations: vi:** Jeffrey L. Rotman; **vii:** Pete Turner, The Image Bank; **viii:** Howard Sokol Photography; **ix:** Courtesy SmithKline Beecham; **xi:** Superstock; **xii:** Rafal Olbinski; **xiv:** © Joe Viesti, Viesti Associates, Inc.; **xv:** Lee Brazeal; **1:** John S. Dykes; **3:** Martha Swope Photography; **7:** Albright-Knox Gallery Buffalo, N.Y. Gift of Seymour H. Knox in memory of Helen Northrup Knox, 1971 (oil on canvas 23 3/8" × 28 1/2"); **12:** Superstock; **14:** Jeffrey L. Rotman; **20:** *t* Comstock; *b* Frank Cezus, TSW-Click; **21:** *br* Globe Photos, Inc.; **25:** Pete Turner, The Image Bank; **26:** Jim Whitmer Photography; **35:** Bradford Veley; **40:**

918   Acknowledgments

Jim Whitmer Photography; **43:** Globe Photos, Inc.; **45:** Jim Salvati, The Image Bank; **46:** t Globe Photos, Inc.; **50:** The Granger Collection; **51:** l © Nancy Dantonio, April Sandmeyer; tr © J. Langeuin, SYGMA; **53:** © Nancy Dantonio, April Sandmeyer; **56:** © Gary Bumgarner, TSW-Click; **58:** Howard Sokol Photography; **67:** Martha Swope; **68:** © J. Langeuin, SYGMA; **69:** AP/Wide World Photos; **71:** l Reuters, Bettmann; r © J. Langeuin, SYGMA; **73:** Courtesy of J. Barrett Galleries, Toledo, Ohio; **83:** l Courtesy SmithKline Beecham; tr Superstock; **85:** all Courtesy SmithKline Beecham; **86/87:** Courtesy SmithKline Beecham; **89:** Superstock; **93:** Comstock; **95:** © Dan Miller, The Stock Solution; **98:** Comstock; **102/103:** Superstock; **105:** © Jozef Sumichrast; **106:** Don Weller, The Weller Institute Design Firm; **107:** Ed Lindlof; **111:** James Schnepf Photography; **112:** Shooting Star; **116:** © Rollie McKenna; **117:** tr Superstock; br John P. Kelly, The Image Bank; **119:** l Peter Karas, FPG; cl Jim Whitmer Photography; cr Tony Freeman, FPG; r Robert J. Bennett, FPG; **127:** Comstock; **129:** © 1990 by Jill Krementz; **130/131:** Superstock; **130:** Superstock; **131:** Superstock; **132:** Shooting Star; **133:** l Gene Trindl, Shooting Star; tc Shooting Star; bc Shooting Star; r Eaton, Shooting Star; **134:** Collection of Whitney Museum of American Art. Purchase, with funds from the Howard & Jean Lipman Foundation, Inc. 70.1572; **135:** Culver Pictures, Inc.; **136:** Superstock; **137:** t John P. Kelly, The Image Bank; b Alan Becker, The Image Bank; **144:** Kobal Collection, Superstock; **145:** l Superstock; tr © Don Dixon; br AP/ Wide World Photos; **146/147:** W.D. Murphy, Superstock; **146:** Superstock; **149:** David Northcott, Superstock; **153:** Superstock; **154:** Charles Moore, Black Star; **156:** Dan McCoy, Black Star; **159:** © 1989, OGPI. Distributed by Los Angeles Times Syndicate. Reprinted by permission; **160/161:** © Don Dixon; **162:** © Don Dixon; **165:** Art Ringger, The Image Bank; **166:** Superstock; **167:** AP/Wide World Photos; **167:** all Ralph Perry, Black Star; **169:** all Jim Whitmer Photography; **175:** br Reprinted with permission of Fortune magazine; **179:** © 1990 Tim Doty Photography; **183:** Rafal Olbinski; **188:** Willard Clay, TSW-Click; **189:** © 1960, Reprinted with special permission of King Features Syndicate; **192:** © Kurt Vargo; **193:** Laurence Gould, Earth Scenes; **193:** Mickey Gibson, Animals Animals; **195:** © Washington Post Writers Group; **196/197:** Reprinted with permission of Fortune Magazine; **201:** Courtesy Springfield (Va.) Journal; **202:** © J.W. Stewart; **208/209:** Superstock; **216:** Carin Krasner Photography; **218:** Min Jae Hong; **228:** H. Clay Bennitt, St. Petersburg Times; **229:** © Universal Press Syndicate; **234:** Bruce Hurwit, Art Director; Thomas D. Morse, Writer; Stavros Cosmopulos, Creative Director; Martha Crowley, Producer; Bob Brown, Director; Vizwiz, Inc., Production Company; Cosmopulos, Crowley & Daly, Inc. (Boston), Advertising Agency: Massachusetts Society for the Prevention of Cruelty to Animals, Client; **238:** © 1990 by Nicole Hollander; **245:** © 1990 Barbara Karant, Karant & Associates, Inc.; **248:** © Joe Viesti, Viesti Associates, Inc.; **251:** FPG; **252:** Bradford Veley; **257:** Amherst College Library; **259:** © 1991 ARS N.Y./SPADEM, Sipa Press, Art Resource; **261:** © Mort Walker; **265:** Steven Guarnaccia; **266:** Henry Gris, FPG; **271:** l The Granger Collection; r Ulli Steltzer, from The New Americans Newsage Press, C.A.; **273:** The Granger Collection; **275:** Lee Brazeal; **279:** all The Bettmann Archive; **283:** Larry Ross, The Image Bank; **288:** Painting by Thomas Lovell, © National Geographic Society; **298:** H. Armstrong Roberts; **300:** H. Armstrong Roberts; **303:** Bettmann; **304:** Art Resource; **306:** The Newberry Library; **307:** Ulli Steltzer, from The New Americans Newsage Press, C.A.; **308:** Courtesy of Jay Johnson America's Folk Heritage Gallery, New York, N.Y.; **321:** Yves Lefevre, The Image Bank; **326:** © Clint Clemens; **330:** Linda Montgomery; **332:** b Comstock; **334:** c The Nelson-Atkins Museum of Art; **339:** © Universal Press Syndicate; **344:** Bradford Veley; **345:** M.C. Escher Heirs/Cordon Art-Baarn-Holland; **347:** Ian Pollock, The Image Bank; **348:** all Harold Edgerton, Palm Press; **361:** TSW-Click; **363:** TSW-Click; **372:** Mark English, Bill Erlacher Artists Associates; **374:** Philippe Weisbecker; **376:** Whitney Museum of American Art, N. Y.; **378:** © United Syndicate Feature; **383:** Superstock; **386:** Judy Pedersen; **391:** © Joe Viesti, Viesti Associates, Inc.; **393:** Denis Parkhust; **395:** Superstock; **400:** Photograph by Ben Blackwell; **402:** Grandma Moses Properties Co.; **406:** Lisa Pomerantz, The Image Bank; **411:** Vandystadt, Photo Researchers, Inc.; **412:** Francis Livingston, The Image Bank; **415:** © 1990 TFC, Inc.; **416:** The Bettmann Archive; **421:** Scala, Art Resource; **422:** © Chronicle Features; **429:** Mercedes McDonald; **430:** FPG; **432:** Doug Taub; **436:** Weldon King, FPG; **442:** D. Hallinan, FPG; **447:** Larry Ross, The Image Bank; **451:** Robert Kopecky; **453:** © 1991 ARS N.Y./SPADEM, Superstock; **456:** © 1989 by Mick Stevens. Reprinted by permission of Simon & Schuster, Inc.; **458:** William Gelling, Superstock; **459:** Julian Allen; **462:** Tom Levy, San Francisco Chronicle; **464:** David Lesh; **467:** Dallas Museum of Fine Arts; **469:** Jack E. Davis, Richard Solomon Representative; **471:** Michael de Camp, The Image Bank; **477:** all © Dan McCoy, R. Langride, Rainbow; **478:** FPG; **482:** Kobal Collection, Superstock; **484:** Jerry N. Uelsmann; **485:** FPG; **487:** © Kurt Vargo; **489:** Brad Holland; **493:** Bill Vuksanovich; **494:** YoungSook Cho; **499:** Graphic produced by The Courier-Journal Promotion Department, Louisville, K.Y.; **500:** Collection of Westmoreland Museum of Art, Gift of Friends of the Museum, Greensburg, P.A.; **514:** © 1967 by James Wyeth; **516:** © 1990 by NEA, Inc.; **518:** UPI, Bettmann Newsphotos; **522:** Superstock; **523:** all Courtesy Wright State University; **529:** Philadelphia Museum of Art: The Louis E. Stern Collection; **531:** Jean-Francois Podevin, The Image Bank; **535:** Dave Archer, The Image Bank; **537:** Giraudon, Art Resource; **541:** © 1990 Cartoonists & Writers Syndicate; **543:** H. Armstrong Roberts; **544:** l Jim Whitmer Photography; r Runk, Schoenberger, Grant Heilman Photography; **547:** Kobal Collection, Superstock; **549:** © Cindy Rymer, TSW-Click; **550:** Dallas

Museum of Art; **555:** Jim Whitmer Photography; **557:** Linda Gist, Siddall, Matus & Coughter, Inc.; **560:** Courtesy National Museum of the American Indian; **562:** Dan Nardi, FPG; **567:** © Andy Selters, Viesti Associates, Inc.; **570:** Scala, Art Resource; **571:** Scala, Art Resource; **579:** Peter C. Borsari, FPG; **583:** Steve Shapiro, Black Star; **585:** FPG; **589:** © Kraft, Explore, Photo Researchers, Inc.; **593:** The Granger Collection; **594:** Kobal Collection, Superstock; **598:** © 1980 Sandy Skoglund; **602:** Kobal Collection, Superstock; **606:** Linda Bohm; **608:** © 1980 by The Metropolitan Museum of Art, Wolfe Fund, 1922. Catharine Lorillard Wolfe Collection (22.181); **612:** Carlos Castellanos; **619:** Bettmann, Hulton; **623:** Jerzy Kolacz, The Image Bank; **630:** Kobal Collection, Superstock; **632:** © 1991 ARS N.Y./SPADEM, Art Resource; **634:** Fred Lynch; **637:** Sanso Collection, NSA; **639:** © Chronicle Features; **645:** Lawrence Manning, TSW-Click; **647:** c UPI, Bettmann; **651:** t Culver Pictures; **655:** Giraudon, Art Resource; **657:** Superstock; **660:** The Granger Collection; **664:** FPG; **669:** The Metropolitan Museum of Art; **672:** Painting by Robert E. Hynes, © National Geographic Society; **675:** © Susan Stillman, Electric Images; **677:** Scala, Art Resource; **678:** A. Jenik, The Image Bank; **680:** Collection Walker Art Center, Minneapolis; **688:** all The Granger Collection; **691:** Courtesy Drum Corps International; **693:** Courtesy Ad Council; **697:** Courtesy American Red Cross; **700:** © Myron 1990; **703:** Mr. & Mrs. Potter Palmer Collection, 1922.440. Photo © 1990, The Art Institute of Chicago. All Rights Reserved; **707:** Thomas Zimmermann, FPG; **709:** UPI, Bettmann; **714:** Etienne Delessert; **719:** Giraudon, Art Resource; **721:** © Greg Nikas, Viesti Associates, Inc.; **724:** Linda Gist; **729:** T. Zimmermann, FPG; **730:** DF, Outline; **734:** UPI, Bettmann Newsphotos; **738:** Collection of the Brandywine River Museum. Purchased through a gift from the Mabel Pew Myrin Trust; **743:** The Old Print Shop, Inc.; **745:** © 1989 Tim Olive, SharpShooters; **746:** © Universal Press Syndicate; **751:** The Library of Congress; **759:** © 1989 OGPI; **760:** Bridgeman, Art Resource; **767:** Historical Pictures, FPG; **775:** Vytas Valaitis, FPG; **782:** Superstock; **785:** all Kobal Collection; **788:** © Universal Press Syndicate; **790:** Superstock; **792:** Penelope Breese, Gamma Liaison; **793:** © Tom McHugh, Photo Researchers; **796:** Jerzy Kolacz, Reactor Art & Design Limited; **799:** Art Resource; **802:** Superstock; **805:** The Granger Collection; **808:** © The Detroit Institute of Arts; **811:** Mansell Collection; **812:** Jim Whitmer Photography; **816:** © Chronicle Features; **819:** The Fine Arts Museums of San Francisco, Museum purchase, William H. Noble Bequest Fund; **822:** © Joe Viesti, Viesti Associates, Inc.; **826:** Amanda Wilson; **829:** all Kobal Collection, Superstock; **830:** TSW-Click; **833:** Dave Jordano; **841:** Eugene Mihaesco; **881:** top Prodigy Internet and the Prodigy Internet logo are trademarks of Prodigy Services Corporation. For subscription information, call 1-800-PRODIGY or visit our Web Site at www.prodigy.com; center Copyright © 1997 America On Line. Used by permission; bottom CompuServe logo courtesy of CompuServe, Incorporated; **882, 883:** Copyright © 1996 Netscape Communications Corp. All rights reserved. This page may not be reprinted or copied without the express written permission of Netscape. Netscape Communication Corporation has not authorized, sponsored, or endorsed, or approved this publication and is not responsible for its content. Netscape and the Netscape Corporate logos are trademarks of their respective owners; **885:** Adobe and Adobe Illustrator are trademarks of Adobe Systems Incorporated; **887, 889:** computer screen Used with permission of Hewlett Packard; photo inset Corbis-Bettmann.

Cover Photography: Ryan Roessler